The Encyclopaedia of
FLAT RACING

Also by Howard Wright

Bloodstock Breeding (revised edition)

The Encyclopaedia of
FLAT RACING

Second Edition

Revised and Enlarged by
HOWARD WRIGHT

ROBERT HALE · LONDON

*First edition written and
compiled by Roger Mortimer © 1971
© Revised and enlarged edition
Howard Wright and Robert Hale Ltd, 1986*

ISBN 0 7090 2639 0

Robert Hale Limited
Clerkenwell House
Clerkenwell Green
London EC1R 0HT

British Library Cataloguing in Publication Data

Wright, Howard
    Encyclopaedia of flat racing.—2nd ed.
    1. Horse-racing—Dictionaries
    I. Title   II. Mortimer, Roger
    798.4'3'0321   SF321.5

ISBN 0-7090-2639-0

Photoset in North Wales by
Derek Doyle & Associates, Mold, Clwyd
Printed in Great Britain by
St. Edmundsbury Press, Bury St. Edmunds, Suffolk
WBC Bookbinders Limited

Author's Note

The major criterion for including subjects, whether horses, personalities, organizations or definitions, has been their importance to Flat Racing in Britain not only in the past but also today. Horses which have won the major races – the Classics, the Eclipse Stakes, the King George VI and Queen Elizabeth Stakes, the Ascot Gold Cup and the Champion Stakes – qualified for automatic inclusion; so did the major personalities of the past. Others had to earn their entry by outstanding contribution, or be worthy of a place because they play a part at the moment.

Not everyone will agree with the choice, and some readers may be critical of certain omissions. To them I offer my apologies but hope they can appreciate some restriction had to be placed on the number of entries, due to the limitation of space.

To render the book more suitable as a source of reference, a number of items have been gathered in the form of appendices at the back. These include the lists of amateur riders, top breeders, jockeys, owners, sires and trainers, as well as the results of major races, mostly since 1930, and racecourse details.

Individual entries for horses include the following details after the name: year of birth; coat colour and sex; name of sire; name of dam; name of dam's sire. Coat colours are: b – bay; ch – chestnut; br – brown; bl – black; gr – grey. Sex is denoted by: c – colt; f – filly; g – gelding.

In compiling this encyclopaedia every care has been taken to ensure accuracy, but the publishers cannot accept responsibility for any errors or omissions.

HW
April 1986

Contents

Acknowledgements

For permission to reproduce particulars about racecourses I am indebted to two eminent Turf publishers. The racecourse maps have been prepared by the Timeform Organization of Halifax, West Yorkshire. Best Times are reproduced from Raceform, the Official Form Book, by kind permission of the Proprietors, Raceform Ltd, 2 York Road, London SW11 3PZ.

I am also grateful for Geoffrey Hamlyn's contribution in the section covering Bookmakers and Bookmaking, and the painstaking assistance of John Randall in reading the proofs.

HW

List of Illustrations

Races: *Between pages 294 and 295*

Acknowledgements

BBC Hulton Picture Library: 1, 2, 8, 20-23, 28, 30; S & G Press Agency: 5-7, 9, 11, 13, 24-7, 32-3; Vidocq Photo Library/Bernard Parkin: 12; Alec Russell: 15, 29, 34; Alan Johnson: 16; George Selwyn: 17; and Bob Thomas Sports Photography: 18.

A

ABERNANT
(1946, gr c Owen Tudor – Rustom Mahal, by Rustom Pasha)

Bred by the Aga Khan and owned by Lady Macdonald-Buchanan, Abernant was one of the fastest horses of this century, displaying the speed associated with his grandam Mumtaz Mahal. Trained by Noel Murless, Abernant was beaten first time out at Lingfield but then won successively the Chesham Stakes, National Breeders' Produce Stakes, Champagne Stakes and Middle Park Stakes. As a three-year-old he was beaten only by inches by Nimbus in the 2,000 Guineas but won the Somerset Stakes at Bath, King's Stand Stakes, July Cup, King George Stakes and Nunthorpe Stakes.

In his third and final season he failed by half a length to concede 23lb to Tangle in the King's Stand Stakes, but won the Lubbock Stakes at Sandown, July Cup and Nunthorpe Stakes. His fourteen wins from seventeen races earned over £26,000.

Until his retirement in 1970 he stood at the Egerton Stud, Newmarket. His offspring included Abermaid (1,000 Guineas), Abwah (Duke of York Stakes, York), the useful handicapper Aberdeen, Gwen (second in 1,000 Guineas) and Abelia (Queen Mary Stakes).

ABDULLAH, Khalid (b. 1942)

Khalid Abdullah, a Saudi prince whose interests are in banking, became the first Arab to own a British Classic winner when Known Fact was awarded the 2,000 Guineas on the disqualification of Nureyev in 1980. He first came into racing two years previously and has since expanded his interests to France and America as well as with his principal trainers in Britain – Jeremy Tree, Guy Harwood and Barry Hills. Apart from Known Fact, his best horses have been Bel Bolide (Gimcrack), Abeer (Queen Mary), Alphabatim (William Hill Futurity), Rousillon (Waterford Crystal Mile, Sussex Stakes), Band (Yorkshire Cup), Ballinderry (Ribblesdale) and Rainbow Quest (Arc de Triomphe, Great Voltigeur and Coronation Cup). He has studs in Britain and America.

Racing colours: green, pink sash and cap, white sleeves.

ABERGAVENNY, Marquess of (b. 1914)

Best known in Flat racing as Her Majesty's Representative at Ascot, to which post he succeeded the Duke of Norfolk in 1972 and which he held for nine years. His major preoccupation has been with National Hunt racing, under which rules he rode from 1935 to 1939. Elected to the NH Committee in 1942, he served three terms as Steward and, as a director of Massey-Ferguson and Lloyds Bank, was heavily involved in sponsorship arrangements at Cheltenham, where he was appointed a director. He was elected to the Jockey Club in 1950.

Racing colours: scarlet, white cross-belts.

ABERMAID
(1959, gr f Abernant – Dairymaid, by Denturius)

Owned by Mr R. More O'Ferrall and trained by Harry Wragg, Abermaid won the 1962 1,000 Guineas, her only success as a three-year-old after winning her three races at two years. Her Newmarket success gave Australian jockey Bill Williamson the first of his two British Classic wins, both in the 1,000 Guineas. At stud Abermaid's best produce was her first foal, Great Host (by Sicambre), winner of the Chester Vase.

1

ABOYEUR
(1910, b c Desmond – Pawky, by Morion)

The 1913 Epsom Derby was perhaps the most sensational in the race's history, and Aboyeur, who started at 100-1, was promoted the winner after the stewards had instigated an objection, on the grounds of jostling, against the 6-4 favourite Craganour, who came in first by a head. During the race King George V's colt Anmer was brought down at Tattenham Corner by the Suffragette Miss Emily Davison, who sustained fatal injuries.

As a three-year-old Aboyeur ran in the colours of Mr A.P. Cunliffe, and in the Derby was ridden by an unfashionable jockey, E. Piper. He was trained at Druid's Lodge, near Salisbury, by Tom Lewis, in whose colours he ran as a two-year-old. He never won again after the Derby and, having been sold for £13,000 to the Imperial Racing Club in Russia, was lost without trace in the Revolution.

ABSURDITY
(1903, b f Melton – Paradoxical, by Timothy)

Absurdity, owned by Mr J.B. Joel, is one of the few mares to have bred Classic winners in consecutive years. She was responsible for Jest (1913 1,000 Guineas and Oaks) and Black Jester (1914 St Leger). Others to have accomplished this feat are: Galicia, dam of Bayardo (1909 St Leger) and Lemberg (1910 Derby); Devotion, dam of Thebais (1881 1,000 Guineas) and St Marguerite (1882 1,000 Guineas); and Set Free, dam of Julio Mariner (1978 St Leger) and Scintillate (1979 Oaks).

ACCEPTOR

Horses which remain in a race after the stipulated time of a forfeit stage are known as acceptors. The term arises from the practice in major handicaps where an owner is deemed to signify his acceptance of the handicapper's assessment of his horse's chances by staying in the race for a further stage.

ACCUMULATOR

An accumulator is a multiple bet involving four or more horses, all of which must win to be successful, or must be placed if the bet is an each-way accumulator. All the money won from the first horse, plus the stake, goes onto the next horse, and so on.

ADAM'S APPLE
(1924, b c Pommern – Mount Whistle, by William the Third)

Owned by Mr C.W.S. Whitburn, Adam's Apple won the 1927 2,000 Guineas at 20-1 by a short head from Call Boy, who turned the tables in the Derby. Adam's Apple went wrong in his wind after his Classic success and was exported to Argentina, where he proved a moderate sire.

ADDED MONEY

Money contributed towards the stakes by the race fund, or from other sources such as the Horserace Betting Levy Board or sponsors, is known as added money. It is distinct from money contributed by the owners of horses engaged in the race.

ADMINISTRATION

The days when the Jockey Club was omnipotent are gone. Nowadays racing functions under a much-changed, and much-changing, set of controls.

The Jockey Club maintains authority for the day-to-day running of racing. It licenses courses, officials and many participants; it allocates fixtures and imposes conditions under which certain races are run; and it deals with the maintenance of law and order under its rules. It does not control the purse-strings; this is essentially the job of the Horserace Betting Levy Board, which since its inception in 1961 has emerged as the single biggest influence in racing.

Since neither Jockey Club nor Levy Board can exist alone, matters of mutual interest were dealt with through the Joint Racing Board, on which the chairman of the Levy Board and the Senior Steward of the Jockey Club sat as co-chairmen.

The Joint Racing Board, completed by two members of the Jockey Club, two members of the Levy Board, and a secretary from each to act jointly, was wound up in October 1982 and replaced by informal contact.

The several other organizations involved in racing can make their feelings known to the Joint Racing Board by way of the Horseracing Advisory Council, which since January 1980 has taken over many functions previously performed by the Jockey Club's Racing Industry Liaison Committee.

(See also: HORSERACE BETTING LEVY BOARD; HORSERACING ADVISORY COUNCIL; JOCKEY CLUB; JOINT RACING BOARD).

ADMIRATION
(1892, ch f Saraband – Gaze, by Thuringian Prince)

From modest beginnings – her dam was sold for 7gns and 15gns, and she herself was a moderate performer on the racecourse – Admiration became a great influence on bloodstock breeding. Mated with Gallinule, who broke blood vessels and was unsound in his wind, she produced the famous Pretty Polly, one of the greatest fillies of all time and ancestress of Brigadier Gerard. Admiration bred eight other winners and started one of the most prolific families of the twentieth century.

AGE

No matter when a thoroughbred foal is born in the Northern Hemisphere, each subsequent birthday will always be on 1 January. Even if a foal were born in December, it would automatically become a yearling on the first of the following month. Southern Hemisphere ages are taken from 1 August.

A horse is described as a foal from birth to the age of one; a yearling from the first birthday to the second. A horse described as 'aged' is one over the age of six, though the distinction is little used nowadays.

AGGRESSOR
(1955, b c Combat – Phaetonia, by Nearco)

Bred by the Someries Stud and retired there as a stallion when his racing career ended as a five-year-old, Aggressor had his finest hour in his final race, when he defeated the brilliant Petite Etoile in the King George VI and Queen Elizabeth Stakes. Winner in all of eleven races for over £36,200, he was at his best as a five-year-old, when he also took the John Porter Stakes and Hardwicke Stakes. Well suited by soft ground, he got several offspring who showed similar tendencies, before his export to Italy in 1971. His best produce was the filly Dibidale, winner of the Cheshire Oaks, Irish Guinness Oaks and Yorkshire Oaks but unlucky in the Epsom Oaks, when her saddle slipped and her jockey was forced to ride bareback for much of the way.

AIRBORNE
(1943, gr c Precipitation – Bouquet, by Buchan)

Airborne, bought by his owner Mr J. Ferguson for 3,300gns as a yearling, won the first Derby on its return to Epsom after the Second World War. Trained by Dick Perryman at Newmarket, he started at 50-1 for the Derby but was favourite when he won the St Leger. He was a failure at stud, where his best produce was Silken Glider, a narrowly beaten second in the Oaks.

AGA KHAN, HH (1877-1957)

The Aga Khan, the outstanding figure in European racing for 25 years from 1922, the first year he raced in Britain, declined to take up the sport until he reckoned he had both the time and the money to operate on a big scale. Although he had been inspired with a love of the Turf by Lord Wavertree as far back as 1904, it was not until 1921 that he asked George Lambton to advise in the purchase of yearlings with the object of forming a stud.

Lambton's stable being full, the Aga Khan's horses were trained by Richard Dawson until owner and trainer fell out in

1931, when Frank Butters took over. On Butters' retirement in 1949, he was succeeded by Marcus Marsh and then Noel Murless. In 1954, owing to the lower costs and higher level of prize money in France, the Aga Khan transferred his racing interests there, and from then on most of his horses were trained by Alec Head.

Of the earliest purchases for the Aga Khan, Diophon and Salmon-Trout both won Classics, while the fillies Mumtaz Mahal, Cos and Teresina were not only successful on the racecourse but proved admirable foundation mares for the stud. Eventually the Aga Khan established a chain of studs in Ireland and France which enabled him to breed bloodstock on a scale unapproached by any other British owner-breeder and only by M. Marcel Boussac in France.

The Aga Khan shares with Lord Egremont the distinction of having won the Derby five times. His winners were: Blenheim (1930), Bahram (1935), Mahmoud (1936), My Love (1948) and Tulyar (1952). Blenheim he bought as a yearling; Bahram, Mahmoud and Tulyar he bred himself; and My Love he owned in partnership with the colt's breeder, M. Leon Volterra.

His other British Classic winners were: *2,000 Guineas:* Diophon (1924), Bahram (1935); *1,000 Guineas:* Rose Royale II (1957); *Oaks:* Udaipur (1932), Masaka (1948); *St Leger:* Salmon-Trout (1924), Firdaussi (1932), Bahram (1935), Turkhan (1940), Tehran (1944), Tulyar (1952).

When Firdaussi won the St Leger, the Aga Khan owned four of the first five finishers. He also won twelve Classics in Ireland.

He was acutely conscious of the commercial aspect of racing and, as the shrewdest of dealers, he never permitted sentiment to interfere with business. He sold all his Derby winners, and the export of Blenheim, Bahram and Mahmoud proved a hard blow to the British bloodstock industry, surpassed only by his sale of Nasrullah, who on export to America became one of the world's most successful and sought-after stallions. By and large the Aga Khan's princely patronage conferred considerable benefits on British racing, but those benefits would have been greater, and he himself would have been regarded with more respect had he been a little less commercially minded.

AGA KHAN, HH (b. 1936)

When the Aga Khan died in 1957, he was succeeded as the Imam (spiritual leader) of the Ismaili sect of the Shia Muslims by his grandson Karim and not by the latter's father, the Aga Khan's elder son, Aly Khan.

Aly Khan had maintained his father's colours of green and chocolate hoops, but on his death in a car accident in 1960, the new Aga Khan allowed the family's interests to wane. It was not until the 1970s that he resumed on anything like the old scale in France, where in 1973 he built a new stud in Normandy. In September 1977 he paid nearly £1.3m for 82 mares, yearlings and foals owned by the late Mme Dupré; the following year he opened a new training complex near Chantilly, and in July 1978 he paid £4.7m for more than a hundred head of bloodstock owned by the late M. Marcel Boussac, in a deal which did not go through without dispute.

Some of the old style had been brought back to the Aga Khan's colours in France, and in 1979, after an absence of fifteen years, they were seen again in Britain, where he sent a number of horses to be trained by Michael Stoute and Fulke Johnson Houghton. The one distinction was that in 1974 the Aga Khan had changed his racing colours to those used in France, green with red epaulettes. He emulated his grandfather by winning the Derby with Shergar in 1981, and the French Derby with Top Ville (1979), Darshaan (1984) and Mouktar (1985). In 1981 he won the Champion Stakes with Vayrann, and in 1982 the Prix de l'Arc de Triomphe with Akiyda.

AKEHURST, Reg (b. 1929)

A former National Hunt jockey, Reg Akehurst began training in 1962. He moved from Epsom to Lambourn in 1972 and gained his biggest successes with Gold Rod (Greenham Stakes, Prix du Moulin), whose dam cost 100gns as a two-year-old and whose sire, Songedor, stood at a fee of £98 when he sired Gold Rod. He gave up training at the end of 1981, returned at Upper Lambourn a year later and in 1985 moved back to Epsom.

ALBINA, Michael Hanna (b. 1941)

After a successful riding and training career in Jordan, Michael Albina became private trainer to Mahmoud Fustok at Newmarket in 1981. Winners were hard to come by, and though he trained two useful horses in Famous Star (Ayr Gold Cup) and Silver Hawk (Craven Stakes, second in Irish Sweeps Derby and third in Derby), he lost his job to Olivier Douieb at the end of 1983. Albina returned to training at Newmarket on a much smaller scale in 1985.

ALCIDE
(1955, b c Alycidon – Chenille, by King Salmon)

Alcide will be remembered as a Derby favourite who had to miss the Classic because of foul play. Winner of the Chester Vase and Lingfield Derby Trial (by twelve lengths), he met with an injury a week before Epsom which led to his withdrawal. The cause was, at first, a mystery, but connections gradually realized that the large lump or swelling on his near-side back ribs was the result of a blow in his box that had broken a rib.

He recovered to win the St Leger by eight lengths at 9-4 on but was dogged by misfortune again as a four-year-old, when his preparation for the Ascot Gold Cup was held up. Nor was his regular jockey, Harry Carr, who had recently undergone a kidney operation, at his best, and Alcide went down by inches to Wallaby II. However, a month later Alcide ended his racing career in a blaze of glory by winning the King George VI and Queen Elizabeth Stakes, a particularly fine effort in this mile-and-a-half race after being trained for the mile-longer Ascot Gold Cup.

For a horse of fine racing ability and good conformation – he was a strongly-made, medium-sized bay – Alcide was not an outstanding success at stud. His best offspring were Oncidium (Coronation Cup, Jockey Club Cup), Approval (Observer Gold Cup), Atilla (Grosser Preis von Baden, Vaux Gold Tankard), Alignment (Ebor Handicap), Remand (Royal Lodge Stakes), Sea Anchor (Doncaster Cup) and Grey Baron (Goodwood Cup, Jockey Club Cup). Alcide died in 1973.

ALEXANDRA PARK

As a racecourse, Alexandra Park below Alexandra Palace, commonly known as Ally Pally, survived determined assaults on its existence by property developers, as well as the late Frederick Temple, Archbishop of Canterbury, when he was holding sway as Bishop of London, but it could not hold off the Levy Board. After a non-profit-making company took over the course at the end of 1968, the Levy Board met annual losses of around £5,000, until in September 1970 they said they were no longer able to assist, and the race company gave in. The final meeting was held on Tuesday 8 September 1970, and the course then passed into the hands of the Greater London Council.

Amenities on the course failed to keep pace with the general rise in the standard of living, and the track itself was cramped, but it had a unique atmosphere, was regarded with affection by its regular racegoers and was the only course within the boundaries of London, being six miles from Charing Cross. Its unrivalled shape gave it the nickname 'The Frying Pan.' Races of 1m 160yd and 1m 5f started in front of the stands; the horses raced down the straight away from the stands and completed one or two circuits of the round course before coming back up the straight to the finish. The only other starting gate was for 5f races and was out of sight of the stands. Not surprisingly, the Ally Pally specialist was a horse to follow!

ALICE HAWTHORN
(1838, b f Muley Moloch – Rebecca, by Lottery)

A racing record which stretched over seven seasons and resulted in 52 victories from 71 races ensured Alice Hawthorn's becoming one of the most celebrated of British mares. Her wins included the Goodwood and Doncaster Cups. At stud her winners included Thormanby, successful in the Derby and Ascot Gold Cup.

ALLENDALE, Lord (b. 1922)

The third Viscount Allendale is a staunch supporter of racing in the North, where he is a director of Newcastle racecourse and a steward at several other tracks, including York and Thirsk. He has served three terms as a Steward of the Jockey Club, the latest from 1980, and has been Senior Steward. Stayers have brought him his biggest successes as an owner, most notably Tenterhooks (Queen's Vase and Goodwood Cup) and Alignment (Ebor Handicap), trained by Captain Charles Elsey and his son Bill respectively.

Racing colours: pink, purple sleeves and cap.

ALLEGED
(1974, b c Hoist the Flag – Princess Pout, by Prince John)

Bought in the United States as a two-year-old for $175,000, Alleged twice won the Prix de l'Arc de Triomphe in the colours of Robert Sangster, the first to do so since Ribot (1955-6). Trained by Vincent O'Brien, Alleged won the Great Voltigeur but was beaten at odds-on in the St Leger before winning his first Arc from Balmerino in 1977. The following year he beat the fillies Trillion and Dancing Maid, both times ridden by Lester Piggott. His first-prize earnings were £327,315, and on retiring to stud in Kentucky he was valued at $16m. He is the sire of the Irish Sweeps Derby winner Law Society and the Irish St Leger winner Leading Counsel, both trained by Vincent O'Brien, and Midway Lady (Prix Marcel Boussac).

ALLEZ FRANCE
(1970, b f Sea-Bird II-Priceless Gem, by Hail To Reason)

Daniel Wildenstein bought Allez France privately in the United States, where she retired to stud after winning thirteen of her 21 races, for the equivalent of £493,100, and remaining in training until a five-year-old. She was one of the best racemares of the post-war period, and her victories included the Prix de l'Arc de Triomphe (in which she was also second) and French 1,000 Guineas and Oaks. A magnificent-looking filly with a flawless pedigree, Allez France did not give British racegoers a true indication of her prowess and was twice second in the Champion Stakes.

ALLOWANCES

The concept that a horse ridden by an apprentice should, in certain races, carry less weight than if he were ridden by a senior jockey, to compensate for his jockey's lack of experience, has been expanded enormously since the turn of this century, when the sole allowance an apprentice could claim was 5lb 'in all selling races which are not handicaps, provided no horse carry less than 6st.' The allowance applied for one year from the time of the apprentice's first success, and there was no restriction on the number of winners he could ride in that time.

In the first decade of the twentieth century a separate rule relating to apprentice allowances was introduced, and lads under the age of 21 were allowed to claim 5lb in all selling races, handicap stakes to which not more than £200 was added and handicap plates of the advertised value of not more than £200, except in races confined to apprentices. The lad lost the right to claim the allowance – from which the term 'claimer' derives – after 40 winners, or three years after his first winner.

The financial limitation was gradually raised to £500, until a system of graduated allowances was introduced when full-scale racing resumed after the Second World War. Apprentices were allowed to claim 7lb until they had ridden six winners, then 5lb until they had ridden 25 winners, and then 3lb until they had ridden 40 winners, at which stage they were deemed to be capable of competing against senior jockeys on level terms. The conditions applied to all handicaps and certain stakes races and plates, but apprentice races were excluded.

With modifications to allow for a rise in the value of races, these conditions stayed until 1966, when the scale was altered to allow a 7lb claim up to ten winners, then 5lb up to 50 winners, and then 3lb up to 75 winners. The only subsequent changes have been to the conditions under which a claim cannot be exercised.

ALOE
(1926, b f Son-in-Law – Alope, by Gallinule)

Aloe, a sister to Foxlaw, never won a race but, after being sold when her breeder Sir Abe Bailey dispersed his bloodstock, she proved extremely influential at stud. From her daughter Feola are descended many of the best performers bred by the Royal Stud, such as Hypericum, Angelola, Kingstone, Above Board, Doutelle, Above Suspicion, and more recently Highclere. Another descendant is the important American winner Round Table. From another daughter of Aloe, Sweet Aloe, are descended the St Leger winner Alcide and the Derby winner Parthia.

ALSO RAN

Any horse in a race which is not placed first, second or third by the judge is generally described as 'an also ran.'

ALTESSE ROYALE
(1968, ch f Saint Crespin III – Bleu Azur, by Crepello)

Bred and owned by the Hue-Williams family, Altesse Royale was the Noel Murless stable's second choice when she won the 1,000 Guineas at 25-1. She went on to win the Epsom and Irish Oaks. She has not bred anything approaching her own calibre at stud.

ALYCIDON
(1945, ch c Donatello II – Aurora, by Hyperion)

Alycidon was the last of the many great horses to carry the colours of the 17th Earl of Derby, who died in 1948. Trained at Newmarket by Walter Earl, Alycidon was backward and made no show on the two occasions he ran as a two-year-old, but the following year he made immense improvement. He might have done even better than he did, but Earl was in failing health (he died in 1950), and Doug Smith had been ill and was not available to ride in the early part of the season.

On his first outing at three years Alycidon failed to start, and thereafter he always wore blinkers. He won the 1m Classic Trial Stakes at Thirsk, thereby showing he was not devoid of speed; the Royal Standard Stakes at Manchester; Princess of Wales's Stakes at Newmarket; St George Stakes at Liverpool; Jockey Club Stakes at Newmarket; and 2m King George VI Stakes at Ascot. He was second to Black Tarquin in the St Leger.

As a four-year-old Alycidon stamped himself as a stayer of the highest class, winning the Ormonde Stakes, Corporation Stakes at Doncaster, Ascot Gold Cup, Goodwood Cup and Doncaster Cup. He was not beaten again after the St Leger, and in all won eleven races worth £37,201.

Alycidon was syndicated for £140,000 and stood at the 18th Earl of Derby's Woodpark Stud. Like his sire, Donatello II, he was inclined to be a shy breeder. By 1962 his fertility was below 30 per cent, and the following year he was withdrawn from stud duties and painlessly destroyed in the autumn. In contrast to his fertility, his stock showed no lack of quality: he was champion sire in 1955, second in 1958 and 1959, third in 1957 and fourth in 1964. The best of his colts was Alcide, and the pick of his fillies were Meld (1,000 Guineas, Oaks and St Leger) and Homeward Bound (Oaks).

ALY KHAN, Prince (1911-60)

In 1959 the racing career of Prince Aly Khan was on the crest of a wave. That year he was the first owner to win over £100,000 in stakes in Britain, and as all his winners were bred by himself, in conjunction with his late father, the Aga Khan, he reached a six-figure total as a breeder too. In France he also set a record for an owner, winning 212,314,631 francs.

Horses carrying his colours in 1959 won the 2,000 Guineas (Taboun), 1,000 Guineas (Petite Etoile), Oaks (Petite Etoile), Eclipse Stakes (Saint Crespin III), Middle Park Stakes (Venture VII) and Champion Stakes (Petite Etoile) in Britain; the Prix de l'Arc de Triomphe (Saint Crespin III) and 1,000 Guineas (Ginetta) in France; and 1,000 Guineas (Florentina) in Ireland.

On 8 May 1960 two horses owned by Prince Aly Khan were short-headed in successive races at Longchamp. Surveying the two photo-finish prints, he observed with a rueful smile that his luck was beginning to run out. Four days later he was killed in a car crash near Paris. The break in the good fortune enjoyed by his horses was brief, for later that year Charlottesville won the French Derby and Grand Prix de Paris, Sheshoon the Ascot Gold Cup and Grand Prix de Saint-Cloud, Petite Etoile the Coronation Cup, and Venture VII the St James's Palace Stakes and Sussex Stakes.

Prince Aly Khan was possessed of immense charm and unquenchable zest for the good things of life, the pursuit of which brought him headlines in the popular Press, especially after his second marriage, to the film star Rita Hayworth. He was sometimes harshly criticized about certain aspects of his life by people who had never met him, but those who actually knew him were almost invariably captivated by his perfect manners, his gaiety and his sense of fun. He was extremely popular with the racing public too, because of his lack of pomposity and the fact that his horses were invariably doing their best to win.

The only surviving son of the Aga Khan and his second wife, Teresa Magliano, Prince Aly Khan took a keen interest in racing and bloodstock breeding from an early age, and in addition became an extremely competent amateur rider on the Flat. After the Second World War, in which he served in the Wiltshire Yeomanry, he bought a half-share in his father's racing interests and thus benefitted from the efforts of such as Masaka, Migoli, Palestine and Tulyar. On his father's death he bought out the inherited interests of the Begum Aga Khan and of his half-brother Sadruddin, assuming sole responsibility for an immense racing empire.

When Prince Aly Khan died, he owned six studs in Ireland, four in France and approximately a hundred broodmares. He was also part-owner of a dozen mares in America. During the time of his partnership with his father, he bought the entire bloodstock interests of Mr Wilfrid Harvey and most of the thoroughbreds owned by the American Mr 'Laudie' Lawrence. Like his father, the Prince was a shrewd dealer and a sound judge of a horse and a pedigree.

AMATEUR RIDER

The widest definition of the term 'amateur rider' is a jockey who receives no fee for his (or her) efforts and who has been granted a permit to ride by the Jockey Club, which does not sanction Flat races between amateur and professional jockeys. More specifically under the Jockey Club Rules, an amateur rider must not have held a professional rider's licence in any country, other than as an apprentice or conditional jockey; he (or she) must not have been paid directly or indirectly for riding in a race; his principal paid occupation for the previous twelve months must not have been to ride or groom for a licensed or permitted trainer; and in the previous twelve months he must not have worked as a paid groom in private, livery or horse-dealer's stables or as a hunt servant.

The popularity of races for amateur riders has fluctuated this century. It reached its peak in the years between the two wars, with almost 50 races, dwindled through the 1950s, picked up slightly in the 1960s and then received a massive boost when the Jockey Club sanctioned twelve Flat races restricted to women amateur riders in 1972. This figure was increased to twenty in 1973, and when women were allowed to ride against men for the first time in 1974, provision was made for each course to stage at least one such race. Only Catterick and Windsor declined. In 1985 59 races were staged for amateur riders including a handful restricted to women.

AMATEUR RIDERS, LEADING (MALE): see Appendix II

AMATEUR RIDERS, LEADING (FEMALE): see Appendix II

AMATO (1835, br c Velocipede – Jane Shore, by Woful)

Amato, the first Derby winner to be trained at Epsom, was also noteworthy because he had not run before the Classic and did not run again. Bred and owned by Sir Gilbert Heathcote, who lived at The Durdans, adjoining Epsom racecourse, Amato was trained on the Downs by Ralph Sherwood. Amato's feat as an Epsom-trained Derby winner was not repeated until April the Fifth won in 1932, since when none has occurred at the Surrey track, though Straight Deal won a substitute race at Newmarket in 1943.

AMBIGUITY (1950, b f Big Game – Amber Flash, by Precipitation)

Bred by the Astor Studs, Ambiguity was backward as a two-year-old but showed great improvement at three years and won the valuable White Rose Stakes at Hurst Park before beating Kerkeb by a length in the Oaks to give jockey Joe Mercer his first Classic success at the age of eighteen. Ambiguity went on to win the Jockey Club Cup but proved a disappointment at stud.

AMERICUS GIRL (1905, ch f Americus – Palotta, by Gallinule)

Winner of the Fern Hill Stakes at Royal Ascot and the Portland Handicap at Doncaster, Americus Girl founded a family whose outstanding characteristic is speed. She bred six winners, the most important being Lady Josephine, and the family produced such brilliantly fast performers as Mumtaz Mahal, Tudor Minstrel, Royal Charger, Fair Trial and Abernant, while among its most notable middle-distance horses are Mahmoud, Migoli, Nasrullah, Court Martial and Petite Etoile.

AMISS

A filly or mare is described as being 'amiss,' or 'in season,' during the period of sexual activity known as oestrus, when she will accept a stallion. During spring and summer, when the sexual cycle is more regular, the period of oestrus is usually five days, and that of dioestrus (when the filly or mare rejects the stallion) fifteen days. The racing performance of a filly or mare may be affected during the period of oestrus, which is often the reason for an otherwise unaccountable loss of form.

ANGUS, Nigel (b. 1944)

After two years as assistant trainer to Harry Whiteman at Cree Lodge, Ayr, Old-Etonian Nigel Angus took over the licence in 1969. His first winner was on his local course – Dual Wonder on 19 April 1969 – and appropriately his biggest successes were gained in the Ayr Gold Cup, with Swinging Junior in 1972 and Roman Warrior in 1975. He handed in his licence at the end of the 1977 season and was succeeded by his former head lad, 'Charlie' Williams.

ANIMAL HEALTH TRUST

The Animal Health Trust was founded in 1942 by Dr W.R. Wooldridge and is a charitable organization supported entirely by voluntary contributions. It carries out scientific research into the causes, prevention and treatment of disease in all types of domesticated animals. Its relevance to racing is through the establishment at Newmarket of its own Equine Research Station, where research is directed entirely to the problems of the horse. The Equine Research Station, at

Balaton Lodge, has the co-operation of a special committee designated the Bloodstock Industry Committee and presided over by Major M.G. Wyatt.

Animal Health Trust: Lanwades Hall, Kennett, nr Newmarket, Suffolk CB8 7PN (Phone 0638-751030)

Equine Research Station: Balaton Lodge, Snailwell Road, Newmarket, Suffolk (Phone 0638-661111)

APOLOGY
(1871, ch f Adventurer – Mandragora, by Rataplan)

Apology was bred and owned by a parson, the Reverend John King, who raced under the name 'Mr Launde.' She won the 1,000 Guineas, Oaks and St Leger in 1874 and subsequently the Ascot Gold Cup.

APPRENTICE

The age-old system of apprenticeship, whereby a stable employee became indentured to a trainer for a minimum period of time and was granted a licence to ride on application to the Jockey Club, was radically altered in the 1970s. In 1975 girls were allowed to become apprenticed for the first time and could ride against fellow male apprentices on the Flat; and in 1977 a new-style Standard Apprentice Riding Agreement was introduced after recommendations by a committee under the chairmanship of Lt.-Col. Piers Bengough.

Prior to 1977, apprenticeships lasted for a minimum of three years and usually ended after five years, though a period of eight years was not unknown. The minimum age for an apprentice was school-leaving age, and indentures terminated at the age of 23 or before. The terms of the apprenticeship were a matter between the employee and his master, but an apprentice usually rode for half fee, which was saved until he had ended his term, and the other half was taken by his master.

In 1975 the Bengough Committee was set up as a result of recommendations by the Joint Racing Board's inquiry into the Manpower of the Racing Industry, which found there was no standard form of indentures and suggested that the apprentice system was in urgent need of modernization. When the Bengough Committee's findings were put into practice for the 1977 Flat season, the minimum period of apprenticeship was abolished and the new Standard Apprentice Riding Agreement introduced, to be signed by the trainer and apprentice jockey, renewable annually and to include strict control of the fees earned by the apprentice and details of how those fees were accounted for and paid. Only on production of the riding agreement will the Jockey Club now grant an apprentice riding licence, so that the contract between trainer and apprentice entered Jockey Club jurisdiction for the first time.

The majority of apprentices never progress to become jockeys, and many never ride in public. For this, increasing weight in some cases and lack of natural ability in many more are the most significant reasons. The prime responsibility for educating apprentices in race-riding skills still rests with their masters, but in recent years few have shown themselves able, or willing, to devote their energies to individual training of apprentices. Among the notable exceptions have been Sam Armstrong, 'Frenchie' Nicholson, Reg Hollinshead and Ian Balding.

Since 1968 the Betting Levy Board has recognized the need for assistance for apprentice training by providing two forms of financial assistance. A series of evening lectures was introduced at the five main training centres in the winter of 1968-9, and they continued with various changes of venue until lack of support brought them to an end after the 1978-9 sessions. In the meantime, riding courses introduced in 1969 provided practical training.

The riding course took place originally at Great Bookham in Surrey under the direction of Major George Boon and then Gerry Scott; in July 1973 they were moved to the National Equestrian Centre at Stoneleigh and came under the guidance of former hurdles jockey Johnny Gilbert, and in December 1975 they were sited at Goodwood. The number of courses was gradually increased to six; girls became eligible in 1974, and the first mixed courses were introduced during the 1979-80 sessions. When the Betting Levy Board first became involved in apprentice training, their contribution amounted to £5,849; in 1979-80 the total cost was £71,916, of which £33,848 came from a deduction from owners' prize money. Owners contributed directly to apprentice training for the first time from 1 January 1972, when a deduction of 0.25 per cent was authorized from the winner's prize. From 1976 this became a deduction of 0.20 per cent from the prize fund. The scheme, renamed the British Racing School, moved to purpose-built facilities at Newmarket in 1984. The popularity of the riding courses was quickly established, and most were over-subscribed. Their value was given credence when Jimmy Bleasdale, a graduate of Stoneleigh, became champion apprentice in 1977.

APPRENTICES, Leading: see Appendix II

APRIL THE FIFTH
(1929, br c Craig an Eran – Sold Again, by Call o' the Wild)

April the Fifth took his name from the date he was foaled, which also happened to be the birthday of his breeder, Mr Sidney McGregor, who owned him in partnership with Mr G.S.L. Whitelaw. When the colt came up for sale at Newmarket to dissolve the partnership, Mr McGregor retained April the Fifth with a bid of 200gns. He then formed a new partnership, this time with the actor and trainer Mr Tom Walls, who looked after the horse at his Epsom stables in lieu of payment.

April the Fifth failed to win as a two-year-old but, after taking the Lingfield Derby Trial by two lengths, won the Derby. His preparation for the St Leger was twice interrupted by mishaps and he was unplaced. He never ran again and before his death in 1954 was a failure as a sire, his most successful produce being the steeplechaser Red April. Bright Lady,

a daughter of April the Fifth, bred the fine staying mare Gladness.

AQUINO II
(1948, b c Tornado – Apulia, by Apelle)

Raced in France for his first two seasons, Aquino II joined Sam Armstrong's stable at Newmarket as a four-year-old and won the Ascot Gold Cup and Doncaster Cup, while in between he showed the bad-tempered side of his nature by ducking out of the course in the Goodwood Cup. He was exported to stud in Poland.

ARBAR
(1944, b c Djebel – Astronomie, by Astérus)

M.Marcel Boussac's French-bred stayer Arbar, narrowly beaten by Sayajirao in the St Leger and winner of the King George VI Stakes at Ascot as a three-year-old, achieved the rare distinction the following year of winning the Ascot Gold Cup and its French equivalent, the Prix du Cadran at Longchamp. He broke down in the Goodwood Cup and was retired to stud, where he produced the similarly named fillies Altana (second in the 1954 Epsom Oaks) and Astana (dam of the 1969 French Oaks winner Crepellana), as well as Arcor, runner-up in the 1962 Epsom Derby. Since Arbar, the Anglo-French Gold Cup double has been completed by Levmoss (1969), Lassalle (1973) and Sagaro (1976). Rock Roi was first past the post in both races in 1972 but lost the Ascot Gold Cup on a disqualification.

ARBUTHNOT, David William Patrick (b. 1953)

Son of a noted Master of Foxhounds, David Arbuthnot worked for Bryan Marshall, Toby Balding and George Fairbairn before becoming assistant to Fulke Johnson Houghton for six years. He began training at Lambourn in 1982 and had his first winner with Warri at Epsom on 22 April 1982. In 1985 he moved to bigger stables at Compton.

ARCHER, Fred (1857-86)

Fred Archer was born in Cheltenham, the son of a steeplechase jockey, and became the greatest jockey of the nineteenth century, possibly the greatest of all time. In 1868 he was apprenticed to Mat Dawson at Newmarket, and he was closely associated with that stable for the rest of his all-too-short life.

He rode his first winner in 1870 and two years later won the Cesarewitch. The turning-point of his career came in 1874, when Lord Falmouth chose him as stable jockey on Tom French's death. In his first season for Lord Falmouth, Archer won the 1,000 and 2,000 Guineas and the Oaks. From then on his career was one of unbroken success. His Classic winners were: *2,000 Guineas:* Atlantic (1874), Charibert (1879), Galliard (1883), Paradox (1885). *1,000 Guineas:* Spinaway (1875), Wheel of Fortune (1879). *Derby:* Silvio (1877), Bend Or (1880), Iroquois (1881), Melton (1885), Ormonde (1886). *Oaks:* Spinaway (1875), Jannette (1878), Wheel of Fortune (1879), Lonely (1885). *St Leger:* Silvio (1877), Jannette (1878), Iroquois (1881), Dutch Oven (1882), Melton (1885), Ormonde (1886).

He rode in 8,084 races and won 2,748 of them. Gordon Richards, the first jockey to pass that total, retired with 4,870 winners to his name, but they were amassed from 21,843 mounts over a period of 33 years.

Archer was 5ft 10in, tall for a jockey, good looking but with a hint of melancholy in his expression, quiet in dress and manner, and possessing much charm. He weighed well over 10st in winter, and only the most drastic methods that were undoubtedly detrimental to his health kept his weight down during the season.

He had a wonderful nerve and was at his best at Epsom. He had immense determination, coupled with an uncanny appreciation of the ability of the horses he rode. In a race he was wonderfully cool, and very observant too. He rode a strong finish, though his style of sitting forward with a loose rein was rated more effective than elegant. There was no draw in his day, and he used to leave the paddock early to get the best position. He was sometimes unduly hard on a horse he had backed – jockeys were allowed to bet in his day – and sometimes his tactics against a fancied rival were the reverse of scrupulous.

Archer, who could have married a duchess had he wanted to, enjoyed tremendous popularity and prestige, but success and adulation never turned his head. He owed a lot to the influence of Mat Dawson, who kept him well clear of the riff-raff inseparable from the Turf.

In 1883 Archer married a daughter of Mat Dawson's brother John, but she died a year later, after giving birth to a daughter. It was a blow from which Archer never really recovered. In 1886 his health was deteriorating fast from the fearful demands he made on it, and a chill caught after the Cambridgeshire was followed by typhoid. In the course of the illness, and in a moment of dire depression, he took a revolver and shot himself. The whole of sporting Britain went into mourning.

ARCTIC PRINCE
(1948, br c Prince Chevalier – Arctic Sun, by Nearco)

Bred and owned by Mr Joseph McGrath, Arctic Prince was trained by Willie Stephenson at Royston and ridden by Charlie Spares, better known as a rider over hurdles, when he won the Derby by six lengths. He gave Stephenson the first leg of a rare double, which when Oxo won at Aintree in 1959 meant he was one of the few trainers responsible for a Derby winner and a Grand National winner.

Arctic Prince broke down badly in his only race after the Derby, the King George VI and Queen Elizabeth Stakes, and retired to stud. Before his export to America in 1956, he sired a number of useful middle-distance horses and stayers, the best being Arctic Explorer (Eclipse Stakes), Exar (Goodwood and Doncaster Cups), Avon's Pride (Cesarewitch) and Shatter (Ascot Stakes). Arctic Prince was destroyed in 1969 after breaking a leg.

ARD PATRICK
(1899, br c St Florian – Morganette, by Springfield)

Owned and bred by Mr John Gubbins and trained at Beckhampton by Sam Darling, Ard Patrick won the 1902 Derby, the only Classic that year which did not fall to the filly Sceptre. The following season Ard Patrick won a famous race for the Eclipse Stakes, in which he beat Sceptre and Rock Sand, winner of the Triple Crown in 1903. Ard Patrick was exported to Germany at the end of his racing career but was not a great success as a sire, though one of his sons, Ariel, won the German Derby.

ARDROSS
(1976, b c Run the Gantlet – Le Melody, by Levmoss)

Ardross retired to stud in Newmarket in 1983 with a valuation of £2m and a reputation as an outstanding stayer who possessed a useful turn of foot. His fourteen wins from 24 races included the Ascot Gold Cup twice, French St Leger, Goodwood Cup, Yorkshire Cup (twice) and Doncaster Cup. He was second in the Ascot Gold Cup as a four-year-old behind Le Moss, whose trainer, Henry Cecil, took him over the following year when he was bought by Charles St George from the executors of his breeder, Paddy Prendergast.

ARMSTRONG, Frederick Lakin (1904-83)

Christened Frederick after an uncle but known by his nickname throughout his career, Sam Armstrong achieved the feat of training at least one winner on every Flat-race course in Britain before his retirement in December 1972. The son of North Country trainer Bob (R.W.) Armstrong, he left school in 1920 to become a pupil of Lambourn trainer Harry Cottrill, and spent a year as a private trainer in Ireland before taking out his first public licence in 1924, to train at Ashgill stables in Middleham, Yorkshire.

Having ridden under National Hunt Rules between 1921 and 1924, with some 50 successes to his credit, it was not surprising he began training with a mixed stable, but he quickly established himself as a Flat-race trainer, especially in handicaps, winning the 1937 Northumberland Plate (Nectar II) and 1938 Wokingham Stakes (Bold Ben).

His ambition to move to the south was fulfilled in 1946, when he accepted an invitation from the Maharajah of Baroda to train at Warren Place at Newmarket. The year before, he had paid a record price for a yearling on behalf of the Maharajah, when he bid 28,000gns at the Doncaster Sales for a colt that was to be named Sayajirao. Third in the Epsom Derby after having his spring preparation held up, Sayajirao won the Irish Derby and Doncaster St Leger.

Within a few years of moving to Newmarket, Armstrong left Warren Place to train at St Gatien, where he remained until his retirement.

Apart from Sayajirao, the best non-handicap horses he trained included My Babu (2,000 Guineas), Aquino II (Ascot Gold Cup), Bebe Grande (Gimcrack Stakes, Champagne Stakes) and Petingo (Gimcrack Stakes, St James's Palace Stakes). He gave Bebe Grande the unorthodox programme of competing in both Guineas races – she was second in the 2,000, beaten four lengths by Nearula, and two days later third in the 1,000, beaten seven lengths by Happy Laughter. Armstrong won the Nunthorpe Stakes three times, with Royal Palm (1955), Matatina (1963) and Caterina (1966). His major handicap successes were achieved in the Stewards' Cup and Northumberland Plate, which he won three times each; the Lincoln Handicap, Great Metropolitan, Chester Cup, Portland Handicap and Cesarewitch, which he won twice each; and Ebor Handicap, Ayr Gold Cup and Royal Hunt Cup.

One of the first trainers in the post-war period to encourage foreign-based owners and exploit cheaply-bought American-bred horses, Armstrong further pointed the way to his colleagues by winning the 1939 Irish 2,000 Guineas with Cornfield, and was noted for his education of apprentices. He tutored three champions

– Willie Snaith (top apprentice in 1949), Willie Carson (a future leading jockey on the Flat) and Josh Gifford (a subsequent National Hunt champion rider).

ARNULL, John (1753-1815)

John Arnull was the first jockey to ride five Derby winners. His successes were on Serjeant (1784), Rhadamanthus (1790), Didelot (1796), Archduke (1799) and Election (1807). This was a period of remarkable success in the Derby for the Arnull family. John's younger brother, Sam Arnull (1760-1800), won the first running of the Epsom Classic, on Diomed, and was also successful on Assassin (1782), Sir Peter Teazle (1787) and Sir Harry (1798). John's son, William Arnull (1785-1835), won the race on Hannibal (1804), Octavius (1812) and Blücher (1814), so that the name Arnull figures on the list of winning riders twelve times in the first 35 years of its history.

ARREARS

'Arrears' are any sums unpaid under the Jockey Club Rules in respect of fines, compensation, fees, entrance money, stakes, subscriptions, forfeits and purchase money in respect of races with selling conditions.

ASCOT

Ascot racecourse was founded at the request of Queen Anne, and the first race was run there on 11 August 1711. By tradition the first race on the opening day of the Royal Ascot meeting in mid-June is the Queen Anne Stakes. Ascot is the only racecourse in Britain which belongs to the Crown, the Queen's Representative at Ascot being responsible for the general management of the course and for the planning and organization of the meetings there.

Easily accessible from London, via the M4, Ascot stands in pleasant surroundings on the edge of Windsor Forest. A lot of money has been spent on improvements in recent years and two big, up-to-date stands have been erected, including the Queen Elizabeth II Stand in Tattersalls, built at a cost of £1m and opened in May 1961. Viewing from the lower reaches of this enclosure can be difficult at the royal meeting.

At all meetings the standard of racing is good, and it is unsurpassed during the royal meeting, when a touch of pageantry in the form of the royal procession up the straight mile is added to sport of the highest class. Until 1939 there were only four days' racing a year on the course, but now better use is made of it, and there are 14 days' Flat racing. A new National Hunt course was used for the first time in April 1965, and eight days' jumping are now staged.

Despite the decline in the popularity of staying races, the Ascot Gold Cup, over $2\frac{1}{2}$ miles, remains the principal race at the royal meeting, and in 1985 it had £55,000 added to its stakes, including £11,000 from the Horserace Betting Levy Board. The Gold Cup was first run in 1807. In 1844 Tsar Nicholas I of Russia visited Britain and went to Ascot on Gold Cup day. The race was won by Lord Albemarle's Defence, and to please the Tsar the winning owner renamed his colt Emperor. The Tsar in return asked to be allowed to present each year a piece of plate worth £500, to be called the Emperor's Plate and to take the place of the Gold Cup. Accordingly, the Gold Cup became the Emperor's Plate until the Crimean War in 1854, when the race reverted to its original title.

The most valuable race at Ascot is the King George VI and Queen Elizabeth Diamond Stakes, sponsored by De Beers and run over a mile and a half in July. It was largely the creation of Sir John Crocker Bulteel, the Clerk of the Course. Designed to test three-year-olds against their elders, and to attract top-class horses from overseas to tackle the best from Britain and Ireland, it was staged originally to mark the 1951 Festival of Britain and for the first year was called the King George VI and Queen Elizabeth Festival of Britain Stakes. Sponsorship of the race was approved by the Queen in 1972, and the following year it became the first race worth £100,000 to be staged under Jockey Club Rules. The word 'Diamond' was added to the title in 1975. Through the added support of De Beers, Ascot put on its first race for women riders in 1973, the second year such events were sanctioned.

The Ascot course was reconstructed after the last war, and the present one dates from 1955. It is a right-handed, triangular track of just over 14f round. The first 3f are downhill, and the last half (including the Old Mile which starts on a chute) is uphill, with a straight run-in of $2\frac{1}{2}$f. The relatively short run-in means horses rarely come from far back to win, and more than one race has been lost by a jockey giving his mount too much ground to make up from the final turn. All races under a mile are run on the straight course, which forms part of the one-mile Royal Hunt Cup course. The ground rarely gets heavy, but, as on other courses equipped with an artificial watering system, the effect of the draw on the straight course can tend to be unpredictable after rain. Rain has occasionally played havoc with the royal meeting. In 1930 a tremendous thunderstorm caused racing to be abandoned for the afternoon after the Royal Hunt Cup, the second of seven scheduled races. In 1964 the last two days of the meeting had to be abandoned because of torrential rain.

ASHWORTH, Peter (b. 1924)

Peter Ashworth, who trained at Treadwell Stables, Epsom married a daughter of the former jockey Herbert Packham. He was apprenticed to Stanley Wootton and Harold Wallington and rode on the Flat from 1936 to 1955, when he took out a trainer's licence. The best winners he had were Lady Senator (Irish 1,000 Guineas, 1961) and Rory's Rocket (Queen Mary Stakes, 1975). He gave up his licence in 1984.

ASMENA
(1947, ch f Goya – Astron-
omie, by Astérus)

Asmena was the middle leg of a marvellous Classic treble for M. Marcel Boussac in 1950, when she won the Oaks. Two days previously her owner had won the Derby with Galcador, and that year he won the St Leger with Scratch II. Asmena was a half-sister to Marsyas II, Caracalla II and Arbar.

ASMUSSEN, Cash (b. 1962)

The American jockey Cash Asmussen came to Europe in 1982 to ride for French trainer François Boutin and in his second season won the French 2,000 Guineas (L'Emigrant). In 1984 he won the Prix de Diane and Prix Vermeille on Northern Trick. He has been an occasional visitor to Britain and achieved the distinction of becoming the first American to ride a winner for the Queen, when Reflection was successful at Chepstow in September 1983. Christened Brian Keith, he had his name legally changed to Cash in 1977.

ASSUMED NAME

It was fashionable early in the twentieth century for owners to race under an assumed name, but this is no longer permitted, and the Rules of Racing specifically state that any horse entered under an assumed name is liable to disqualification. The last horse to win the Derby under an owner's assumed name was Gay Crusader, who in 1917 was assigned to Mr 'Fairie,' the name adopted for racing purposes by Mr A.W. Cox, an Australian who also won the Derby in 1910 with Lemberg.

ASTERUS
(1923, b c Teddy – Astrella, by
Verdun)

Bred in France by Baron M. de Rothschild, Astérus raced in the colours of M. Marcel Boussac and won five races, including the French 2,000 Guineas. In Britain he won the Royal Hunt Cup and Champion Stakes. He proved a most successful sire, having great influence on bloodstock breeding throughout the world, especially through his daughters, who included Adargatis, the French Oaks winner.

ASTOR, Waldorf, 2nd Viscount
(1879-1952)

Lord Astor, who died at the age of 73, had been a breeder of thoroughbreds for exactly 50 years when in 1950 he divided his famous stud between two of his sons,

Mr William Waldorf Astor, who eventually succeeded to the title, and Mr John Jacob Astor.

Lord Astor never won the Derby but was second in that race with Blink, Buchan, Craig an Eran, Tamar and St Germans. He won the 2,000 Guineas with Craig an Eran (1921), Pay Up (1936) and Court Martial (1945); the 1,000 Guineas with Winkipop (1910) and Saucy Sue (1925); the Oaks with Sunny Jane (1917), Pogrom (1922), Saucy Sue (1925), Short Story (1926) and Pennycomequick (1929); and the St Leger with Book Law (1927). He also won the Eclipse Stakes five times, Champion Stakes twice and Coronation Cup. From 1913, all his horses were trained at Manton, first by Alec Taylor and later by Joe Lawson.

The foundation mare of his stud was Conjure, whom he bought for £100 when still at Oxford. Two other famous mares he owned were Popinjay and Maid of the Mist. He bred all his great winners himself. He never went racing unless he had a runner and never had a bet. For many years he was a member of the Jockey Club.

ASTOR, William Waldorf, 3rd Viscount (1908-1966)

The third Viscount Astor succeeded his father in 1952 but did not enjoy his father's success on the Turf, though he won the 1953 Oaks with Ambiguity trained by R.J. Colling. Other good horses to carry his colours were Hornbeam, Counsel and that fine stayer Grey of Falloden whose most memorable feat was to win the 1964 Cesarewitch carrying 9st 6lb.

He gained his second Classic success with another stayer, Craighouse, in the 1965 Irish St Leger. Craighouse was descended from Conjure.

When Lord Astor died, aged 58, his bloodstock was offered for sale by sealed bid and went to the American Mr William Hackman, who sold the mares, foals and yearlings in America and allowed Lord Rotherwick to buy the horses in training. Lord Astor's Cliveden Stud, which he had inherited from his father, was bought by Mr Louis Freedman.

ASTOR, Sir John Jacob MBE (b. 1919)

Fourth son of the second Viscount Astor, Sir John Astor served during the war in the Household Cavalry and the SAS. In his younger days he rode under both Rules.

He had the reputation of being one of the most progressive members of the Jockey Club, but when in 1974, after having trained jumpers under permit, he took out a public licence to train, he resigned the position. In 1975 he cut down his racing interests drastically and returned to the Jockey Club, while Major Dick Hern trained his horses. Sir John's British Classic winners have been in the St Leger, with Provoke (1965) and Cut Above (1981), while he won the 1973 Irish 2,000 Guineas with Sharp Edge. One of the country's largest owner-breeders, he is a steward at several meetings and served on the Horserace Totalisator Board from October 1962 until December 1968.

Racing colours: light blue, pink sash.

ATHASI (1917, b f Farasi – Athgreany, by Galloping Simon)

Bred by Mr Peter Murphy in Co. Wicklow, Athasi was by Farasi, who was sold for 35gns as a yearling. Athasi herself was sold as a yearling for 270gns and at one time was competing over hurdles without success. Bought by Mr D.W. Barnett and on his death acquired by his brother, Mr W. Barnett, Athasi proved a wonderfully successful broodmare, being the dam of ten winners of 29 races worth over £50,000. Her offspring included Trigo, winner of the Derby, St Leger and Irish St Leger, Athford, winner of the Coronation Cup, Harinero, winner of the Irish Derby and Irish St Leger, Primero, who dead-heated for the Irish Derby and won the Irish St Leger, and Harina, who won £4,128 in stakes and was the grandam both of the Derby winner Tulyar and of Saint Crespin III, winner of the Prix de l'Arc de Triomphe. More recently she has appeared as the fourth dam of both Young Emperor (Coventry Stakes and

Gimcrack Stakes) and Monteverdi (William Hill Dewhurst Stakes), who were out of daughters of Athasi's grand-daughter Jennifer. Athasi died in 1944.

ATHENS WOOD
(1968, b c Celtic Ash – Belle of Athens, by Acropolis)

Athens Wood cost 3,100gns as a yearling and was bought principally as a prospective jumper. He never got the chance to show his prowess in that field since his eight wins on the Flat included the St Leger and Great Voltigeur Stakes, when trained by Tom Jones. Nor, unfortunately, did he get a proper opportunity to prove his worth at stud in Britain, for he suffered from the modern stigma of being a stayer and after a short spell was sold to Russia, where he became a leading stallion.

AUNT EDITH
(1962, ch f Primera – Fair Edith, by Hyperion)

Aunt Edith was bred by the West Grinstead Stud, owned by Lt.-Col. John Hornung and trained by Noel Murless. She won the Nassau Stakes, Prix Vermeille, Yorkshire Cup and King George VI and Queen Elizabeth Stakes for a total of £66,167. When her racing career was over, she was sold for export to America.

AURELIUS
(1958, b c Aureole – Niobe II, by Sir Gallahad III)

Aurelius belonged to Mrs Vera Lilley (later Mrs Hue-Williams) and was trained by Noel Murless. He won seven races including the St Leger, King Edward VII Stakes and Hardwicke Stakes for a total of £43,818, but proved useless as a stallion and was eventually brought back into training, running with enough credit over hurdles and fences to win five races for £4,057. He finished second in the 1967 Champion Hurdle but was disqualified for interference.

AUREOLE
(1950, ch c Hyperion – Angelola, by Donatello II)

Aureole, bred by King George VI, is the best colt to have carried the Queen's colours. A high-mettled chestnut, he needed the great trainer Sir Cecil Boyd-Rochfort to get the best out of him. After winning the Lingfield Derby Trial in 1953, the year of the Queen's coronation, he was second to Pinza both in the Derby and in the King George VI and Queen Elizabeth Stakes. In the St Leger he failed to stay the distance. As a four-year-old he was a very good horse indeed, winning the Coronation Cup, Hardwicke Stakes and King George VI and Queen Elizabeth Stakes. He did extremely well as a sire, being champion in 1960 and 1961. He sired one Derby winner in St Paddy, and three St Leger winners: St Paddy, Aurelius and Provoke. His other important winners were Saint Crespin III (awarded Prix de l'Arc de Triomphe after dead-heating, and won Eclipse Stakes), Hopeful Venture (Hardwicke Stakes, Grand Prix de Saint-Cloud), Aurabella (Irish Oaks), Vienna (sire of Vaguely Noble) and Miralgo (Hardwicke Stakes, Timeform Gold Cup). Aureole died in 1975.

AUTHORITY TO ACT

Nearly all owners give someone of trust, usually their trainer, the right to act on their behalf. This 'Authority to Act' is a form drawn up by Messrs Weatherby which permits the trainers to make entries, forfeits, declarations and so forth in the name of the owner. An Authority to Act is valid only for a single season.

AUTUMN DOUBLE

The two big handicaps run at Newmarket in October, the Cambridgeshire and the Cesarewitch, comprise the Autumn Double, in which punters try to couple in bets the winners of the two races to bring off a spectacular win.

AYR

Ayr is Scotland's premier racecourse and one of the best in Britain, with spectator facilities progressively improved since 1965, when the Craigie Stand was opened in the cheapest enclosure, and 1966, when the Carrick Stand was opened in the Silver Ring. Modernization was completed before 1971 with new stands in the main enclosure and Club area. A favourable climate ensures racing when other venues are hit by the weather, and improved prize money has led to a better standard of racing, with the four-day Western meeting in September being of a very high order indeed. That famous 6f sprint, the Ayr Gold Cup, remains the highlight of the season, following sponsorship for the first time in 1972 by Burmah-Castrol, until Ladbroke's took over in 1979.

The course is left-handed, just over $1\frac{1}{2}$m round and with a straight run-in of 4f. It has easy bends, is almost flat throughout and confers no advantage on a particular type of horse.

B

BACHELOR'S DOUBLE
(1906, ch c Tredennis – Lady Bawn, by Le Noir)

Bachelor's Double, a good racehorse and a most influential sire, was an extremely rare type: he was by a non-winning sire, out of a non-winning dam, by a non-winning maternal grandsire, out of a non-winning grandam. What's more, his dam was a twin.

BAHRAM
(1932, b c Blandford – Friar's Daughter, by Friar Marcus)

Bahram, the Triple Crown winner bred and owned by the Aga Khan, was out of Friar's Daughter, a mare the Aga Khan had bought for less than £300. Trained by Frank Butters, Bahram proved himself an outstanding horse by winning all his nine races and over £43,000 in stakes. His five successes as a two-year-old included the National Breeders' Produce Stakes, Gimcrack Stakes and Middle Park Stakes. The following year (1935) he won the 2,000 Guineas, Derby, St James's Palace Stakes and St Leger.

Placid and indolent by nature, Bahram seldom gained his victories spectacularly but was never really in danger of defeat, and certainly no opponent ever succeeded in getting to the bottom of him. He might well have made a superb four-year-old, but his owner hustled him off to stud with almost indecent haste after the St Leger. The Aga Khan once declared he would never part with Bahram but, to the undisguised resentment of many British breeders, he sold him in 1940 for £40,000 to an American syndicate. Bahram was not in the best of health when he landed in America, and breeders there never really took to him. In 1946 he was exported to Argentina. For so great a horse his stud record was rather disappointing, but his career as a sire was hardly helped by the changes in climate and environment. The best horses he sired in Britain were Big Game (2,000 Guineas), Turkhan (St Leger) and Persian Gulf (Coronation Cup).

BAILEY, Sir Abe (1864–1940)

For more than 50 years one of the leading personalities in public life in South Africa, Sir Abe Bailey bred and raced on a lavish scale in Britain, among his trainers being H.L. Cottrill, R. Day, Hon. G. Lambton, H.S. Persse and J. Lawson. He made many attempts to win the Derby but the nearest he came to success was when Robin Goodfellow finished second to Bahram in 1935. The following year Sir Abe gained his only Classic success when his 33-1 outsider Lovely Rosa won the Oaks. He owned that fine stayer and very successful sire Son-in-Law and he won the Ascot Gold Cup with Foxlaw and Tiberius. He was made a member of the Jockey Club in 1929. Towards the end of his life he had to have both his legs amputated but this misfortune was not permitted to interfere with his many interests or his pleasure in the society of his friends.

BAILEY, Alan

Born in Lancashire, Alan Bailey served his time as an apprentice with Robert Colling at Newmarket and was then called up for National Service. He had a number of jobs in and out of racing before joining Bill Wightman in Hampshire and then spending fourteen years with Peter Walwyn. He began training on his own account for owner John Murrell at Newmarket in 1980 and quickly took on more owners. His first winner was El Presidente at Newmarket on 3 May 1980.

BAILLIE, John Ursel (b. 1905)

Before becoming a member of the London Stock Exchange, John U. Baillie

19

was a regular soldier in the Coldstream Guards. Before the war he was a well-known point-to-point rider and also rode winners under Jockey Club and National Hunt Rules. His trainers have included the late Dawson Waugh, Ryan Price, Sir Mark Prescott and John Dunlop. He is the owner of the successful Crimbourne Stud, where the two fine sprinters Lucasland and So Blessed were bred. A member of the Jockey Club, he was President of the Racehorse Owners' Association from 1969 to 1970.

Racing colours: black, straw sleeves, pale blue cap.

BAIRD, Brig. E.W.D. (1864-1956)

Brigadier 'Ned' Baird had the distinction of being a member of the Jockey Club for no fewer than 62 years. He won the Grand National in 1887 with his half-bred hunter Playfair and the St Leger in 1907 with Wool Winder.

BALDING, Arthur (b. 1906)

Arthur Balding served his apprenticeship with Bert Lines and Peter Gilpin. He won the 1,000 Guineas in 1927 on Cresta Run, and several other important races, including the Chester Cup, Kempton Jubilee, City and Suburban and Queen's Prize. He began training in 1930 and with the help of his large family maintained a string of horses at Bawtry, near Doncaster, until his retirement at the end of 1985.

BALDING, Gerald Barnard (b. 1936)

Christened Gerald Barnard but known by his nickname of Toby, he is the elder brother of Ian Balding. Toby first took out a licence in 1957, and his stable is at Fyfield House, Weyhill, near Andover. The emphasis is on jumpers rather than Flat-race horses, and his biggest triumph was to win the 1969 Grand National with Highland Wedding. On the Flat he has won the Portland Handicap (New World) and John Porter Stakes (Decent Fellow).

BALDING, Ian Anthony (b.1938)

Ian Balding is a son of the late Gerald Balding, an outstanding polo-player and also a successful trainer. A good all-round athlete who played rugby for Cambridge, he was a successful amateur rider and assisted the late Captain Peter Hastings-Bass (whose daughter Emma he married in 1969) at Kingsclere after a period with Herbert Blagrave. On the sudden death of Hastings-Bass in 1964 he took over the Kingsclere stable.

The best horses he has trained have belonged to Mr Paul Mellon, whose Mill Reef won the 1971 Derby, as well as the Eclipse Stakes, King George VI and Queen Elizabeth Stakes and Prix de l'Arc de Triomphe. The same colours were carried by Silly Season (Dewhurst Stakes and Champion Stakes, and second in 2,000 Guineas), Berkeley Springs (Cheveley Park Stakes, and second in 1,000 Guineas and Oaks), Glint of Gold (Grand Prix de Paris, and second in Derby and St Leger) and Diamond Shoal (Grand Prix de Saint-Cloud, second in King George VI and Queen Elizabeth Stakes, and third in St Leger).

The Queen's best horses at Kingsclere have been Example (Park Hill Stakes), Escorial (Musidora Stakes) and Magna Carta (Doncaster Cup). Ian Balding's other important winners have included Mrs Penny (Cheveley Park Stakes, Prix de Diane and Prix Vermeille), Siliciana (Cambridgeshire), Centurion (Cesarewitch) and Fair Season (Lincoln Handicap).

Always keen to promote the interests of apprentices, he was responsible for the early careers of Ernie Johnson, Philip Waldron and John Matthias.

BALLYMOSS (1954, ch c Mossborough – Indian Call, by Singapore)

One of the best Irish-trained horses, Ballymoss was bred by Mr Richard Ball and bought as a yearling by the American owner Mr J. McShain for 4,500gns. Trained by Vincent O'Brien, he was second to Crepello in the 1957 Derby and then won the Irish Derby and the

Doncaster St Leger. As a four-year-old he was the best horse in Europe, his victories including the Coronation Cup, Eclipse Stakes, King George VI and Queen Elizabeth Stakes and Prix de l'Arc de Triomphe. Altogether he won £107,165 in stakes, a record at that time. He sired only one really top-class horse, Royal Palace, winner of the 2,000 Guineas, Derby, Coronation Cup, Eclipse Stakes and King George VI and Queen Elizabeth Stakes. He sired two winners of the Irish Guinness Oaks in Merry Mate and Ancasta. He died after a heart attack in July 1979.

BALTO
(1958, b c Wild Risk – Bouclette, by Victrix II)

The French stayer Balto won the Ascot Gold Cup in 1962, having won the previous year's Grand Prix de Paris.

BARCALDINE
(1878, b c Solon – Ballyroe, by Belladrum)

Barcaldine was a great racehorse, never meeting with defeat, and a very successful sire. The interesting point about him is that he was almost incestuously bred, his sire, Solon, being out of Darling's Dam, while his grandam was out of Darling's Dam too. He himself was largely responsible for the continuation of the Matchem male line.

BARCLAY, Alexander (b. 1948)

'Sandy' Barclay, son of the Scottish trainer John Barclay, joined Harry Whiteman's stable at Ayr in 1964, rode his first winner in 1965 and was champion apprentice the following year. In 1967 he became second jockey to George Moore with Noel Murless, and in 1968 was appointed No.1 at the stable, the most powerful in the country. In that season he rode 116 winners, and only Lester Piggott rode more. He won the 1,000 Guineas on Caergwrle; the Coronation Cup, Eclipse Stakes and King George VI and Queen Elizabeth Stakes on Royal Palace; the Oaks in 1970 on

Lupe, the Coronation Cup in 1970 on Caliban and the Grand Prix de Saint-Cloud on Hopeful Venture.

The Murless connection was severed at the end of 1970 when Barclay accepted a job in France with François Boutin. He stayed there for three years but could not repeat his outstanding success achieved in Britain, and when he returned in the summer of 1973, his career spluttered and virtually came to a stop after one successful spell in the north of England. His fall was as meteoric as his rise, and though he did well in India later, his return to Britain was unrewarding. 1968 remains his most successful season.

BARLING, Frank (1869-1935)

Originally a veterinary surgeon in Wales, Frank Barling became trainer to Lord Glanely at the end of World War I but his health was poor and he did not retain the appointment for long. His big year was 1919 when he won the Derby with Lord Glanely's Grand Parade and trained seven winners for the same owner at Royal Ascot. He handed over his stable to his son Geoffrey in 1932.

BARLING, Geoffrey (1902-84)

Geoffrey Barling held a trainer's licence from 1932 until his retirement in 1974, but his career was interrupted during World War II by service overseas with the Royal Artillery. His Newmarket stable was especially successful with middle-distance horses and stayers, and his best winners included Pandora Bay (Ribblesdale Stakes and third in the Oaks), Frawn (Ascot Stakes twice), Le Tellier (Chester Cup), Piaco (Doncaster Cup and Northumberland Plate), Outcrop (Yorkshire Oaks and Park Hill Stakes) and Erimo Hawk (Doncaster Cup, and Ascot Gold Cup on a disqualification). He also trained Tower Walk, a fine sprinter who won the Nunthorpe Stakes, Flying Childers Stakes and Prix de l'Abbaye. Tower Walk finished second in the 2,000 Guineas, and Barling trained Pentland Firth to be third in the Derby. He died in October 1984.

BATH

Bath provides opportunities in congenial surroundings for horses that for the most part are of modest ability. Situated at more than 500 ft above sea-level, the course has an oval track that is mainly flat but has a sharp final bend along a run-in of 4f. The nature of the run-in means that not all horses act well on the course, and the presence of course specialists – especially among jockeys – is not a coincidence.

The course is laid on old downland turf, and the going is usually good. Viewing is also excellent, and opening of the Severn Bridge in 1966 brought fresh impetus.

BATTHYANY, Countess Margit (b. 1911)

Countess Margit Batthyany, who lives in Switzerland, had horses trained in Britain, Ireland, France and Germany before she decided to concentrate on breeding in 1974. She won the 1967 Oaks with Pia, whom she had bred herself. Pia had been sent up for sale as a yearling but failed to reach a modest reserve and went into training with Bill Elsey. Countess Batthyany gained her biggest success in France with a filly, San San, who won the Prix de l'Arc de Triomphe, and she won the German Derby with Orsini.

Racing colours: blue, orange sleeves, check cap.

BATTHYANY, Prince (1803-83)

A Hungarian who loved the British way of life, or at any rate the way of life of the British aristocracy, Prince Batthyany won the 1875 Derby with Galopin and was the breeder of the great St Simon. Elected a member of the Jockey Club in 1859, the Prince died on 2,000 Guineas day 1883 on the steps of the Jockey Club Luncheon Room at Newmarket.

BAXTER, Geoffrey Edward (b. 1946)

Geoff Baxter served five years of his apprenticeship with Arthur Budgett and two years with Ifor Lewis until he went freelance in June 1974. He rode his first winner on the eleven-year-old, 25-1 chance Jules in a selling handicap at Wolverhampton on 15 October 1963. For much of his senior career he has been associated with Bruce Hobbs' stable but he also rode regularly for Paul Cole, for whom he won the Wokingham Stakes and Stewards' Cup on Calibina in 1977. His most important successes for Hobbs have been with Shebeen (Jockey Club Stakes), Grey Baron (Jockey Club Cup), Vielle (Nassau Stakes), Count Pahlen (William Hill Futurity) and Gay Lemur (Jockey Club Stakes). He has also won the Lincoln (King's Ride), Chester Cup (Contester) and Dewhurst Stakes (Kala Dancer), and his best season was 1975 with 65 winners.

BAYARDO (1906, b c Bay Ronald – Galicia, by Galopin)

Bayardo, owned and bred by Mr A.W. Cox, who raced under the name of 'Mr Fairie,' was probably the best of the many great horses trained by Alec Taylor at Manton. His sire, Bay Ronald, was no more than a fair sort of handicapper, but his dam, Galicia, also bred the Derby winner Lemberg and Kwang-Su who was second in the Derby. In appearance Bayardo was a long, lop-eared bay who stood noticeably over at the knee. His weak point was his sensitive, fleshy feet that gave him trouble throughout his career.

He came to hand early and was a brilliant two-year-old, winning in succession the New Stakes, National Breeders' Produce Stakes, Richmond Stakes, Buckenham Stakes, Rous Memorial Stakes, Middle Park Plate and Dewhurst Plate.

It was a very cold, dry spring in 1909. Even the best Manton gallops were hard, and Bayardo had to be treated with care on account of his feet. He was nothing like at his best when he finished unplaced in the 2,000 Guineas, and he was still backward when he was down the course behind Minoru in the Derby. Soon afterwards, though, Taylor had him to his liking and Bayardo won in succession the Prince of Wales's Stakes at Ascot,

Sandringham Foal Stakes at Sandown, Eclipse Stakes, Duchess of York Plate at Hurst Park, St Leger, Doncaster Stakes, Champion Stakes, Lowther Stakes, Sandown Foal Stakes, Limekiln Stakes and Liverpool St Leger.

As a four-year-old he was better than ever and started by winning the Newmarket Biennial Stakes, Chester Vase, Ascot Gold Cup and Dullingham Plate. In the Goodwood Cup he started at 20-1 on and the race was regarded as a mere formality. Unfortunately Danny Maher rode a foolish, over-confident race on him, and the great horse, in what was his final appearance on a racecourse, was beaten a neck by a three-year-old, Magic. In all Bayardo won 22 races worth over £44,000.

He was a great success as a sire, and it was a severe loss to breeders when he died of a thrombosis aged eleven. He sired two 'Triple Crown' winners, Gay Crusader and Gainsborough.

BAYUDA
(1916, b f Bayardo – Jessica, by Eager)

Bayuda won the Oaks in 1919 for Lady James Douglas. At stud she bred one moderate winner before her death in 1929.

BEAM
(1924, b f Galloper Light – Mistrella, by Cyllene)

Lord Durham's Beam won the Oaks in 1927. She was not a success as a broodmare, producing only two minor winners before her death in 1941.

BEARY, Michael (1896-1956)

Michael Beary was a voluble and engaging Irishman from Tipperary. He spent part of his apprenticeship in H.S. Persse's stable, and it was on Steve Donoghue's recommendation that he obtained his first ride in public. At his best – consistency was hardly one of his virtues – he was a top-class jockey, a stylist and often brilliant with difficult horses. He won the 1937 Derby on Mid-day Sun, the St Leger on Trigo and

Ridge Wood, and the Oaks on Udaipur. He started training in 1951 and won the 2,000 Guineas that year with Ki Ming, but he never had any head for business and was soon in financial difficulties. He was a poor man when he died. His great trouble throughout his life was his own unequable temperament and an over-abundant self-confidence that at times could be extremely irritating.

BEASLEY, Harry (1889-1959)

Harry Beasley was the brother of Pat Beasley and the son of Harry Beasley senior who won the 1891 Grand National on Come Away. His uncle, Tom Beasley, rode three Grand National winners, while his own son Bobby won the National, Cheltenham Gold Cup and Champion Hurdle.

Soon after the conclusion of World War I Harry Beasley came to Britain and rapidly established himself as a highly competent rider. For several seasons he rode for 'Atty' Persse's stable and in 1929 he won the 2,000 Guineas on Mr Jinks. His best season was in 1930 when he rode 56 winners.

BEASLEY, Patrick Thomas (1906-82)

A member of a famous Irish racing family, 'Rufus' Beasley had a long and successful career as a jockey and for many years was associated with Sir Cecil Boyd-Rochfort's stable. He won the St Leger on Boswell and Ascot Gold Cup on Precipitation. He trained at Malton in Yorkshire from 1946 until his retirement in 1974. His biggest successes were in the Cambridgeshire (which he won three times, twice with Sterope), Royal Hunt Cup, Wokingham Stakes, Middle Park Stakes, July Cup, Dewhurst Stakes and Manchester November Handicap. His Bounteous was second in the St Leger.

BEATTY, Hon. Peter (1910-49)

Younger son of Admiral of the Fleet Lord Beatty, Mr Peter Beatty was 28 years of age when he bought the French colt Bois Roussel for 8,000gns in April 1938. Two months later Bois Roussel, trained by Fred Darling, won him the Derby by four lengths. Mr Beatty, who bred the 1948 2,000 Guineas winner My Babu, suffered throughout his life from defective eyesight. He knew he was faced with total blindness when he fell to his death from a window of the Ritz Hotel in 1949.

BEAVERBROOK, Marcia, Lady (b. 1911)

Lady Beaverbrook took up racing following the death of her husband, the newspaper proprietor, on the advice, it is said, of Lord Rosebery. She became one of the boldest bidders at the sale ring and spent over £1½m between 1966 and 1976, including a British record of 202,000gns for a Mill Reef colt in 1975. Named Million, the colt raced for three seasons, won two staying races worth a total of £4,376 and was exported to Australia. His example was fairly typical of the rewards Lady Beaverbrook received for her outlay.

She had a policy of giving her horses names with seven letters, the best being Bustino (1974 St Leger, second to Grundy in an epic race for the King George VI and Queen Elizabeth Stakes), Relkino (Benson & Hedges Gold Cup), Niniski (Irish St Leger and French St Leger), Hametus (Dewhurst Stakes), the sprinter Boldboy, who established a record for prize money won by a gelding, and Petoski (King George VI and Queen Elizabeth Diamond Stakes). Major Dick Hern and Michael Jarvis are the trainers who have been most successful with her horses.

Racing colours: beaver brown, maple-leaf green cross-belts and cap.

BEBE GRANDE (1950, ch f Niccolo dell'Arca – Grande Corniche, by Panorama)

Owned and bred by Mr J.S. Gerber and trained by 'Sam' Armstrong, Bebe Grande won eight races and over £18,000 in stakes. As a two-year-old her victories included the National Breeders' Produce Stakes and Champagne Stakes. The following season she was second in the 2,000 Guineas and third two days later in the 1,000 Guineas. She bred five minor

winners including Baby Doll, whose produce included Pieces of Eight (Eclipse Stakes and Champion Stakes) and Chappaquiddick (dam of the American racer Tiller, whose sixteen wins were worth $867,988).

BECKWITH-SMITH, Major Peter (1919-84)

Major Peter Beckwith-Smith was educated at Eton and the RMC and served in the Welsh Guards 1938-46. He was Clerk of the Course at Lingfield Park from 1947 until 1974, when his family sold the course to the bookmakers Ladbroke's. He held the same post at Hurst Park from 1956 until its closure in 1962, having been at Aintree from 1950 to 1956. He was Clerk of the Course at Epsom from 1964, and at Sandown Park from 1966. Ill health forced him to retire from Epsom in 1984, having given up Sandown shortly before, and he died in September 1984.

BEDFORD, 5th Duke of (1765-1802)

The Duke of Bedford was only 25 years of age when he won the 1789 Derby with Skyscraper. He also won the Derby in 1791 and 1797. He was 37 years old when he died as the result of an old injury received when playing cricket as a boy at Westminster.

BEEBY, George (1904-77)

The son of a well-known horse-dealer in the Midlands, George Beeby took out a trainer's licence in 1924. At first he was associated with jumpers and trained many good chasers for the first Lord Bicester, including Silver Fame, Roimond and Finnure. In due course his stable became a 'mixed' one but in later years, before his retirement in 1971, he confined his attention to the Flat. He trained that good but temperamental sprinter Grey Sovereign, subsequently a highly successful sire, and among the races Beeby won were the Stewards' Cup, Cambridgeshire, Wokingham Stakes and City and Suburban Handicap. His stables were at Compton in Berkshire and his last runner, Grey Gaston at Newmarket on 28

October 1971, was a winner. His son, Harry Beeby, has been a prime mover behind the resurrection of bloodstock sales at Doncaster.

BEESWING

Foaled in 1833, Beeswing, by Doctor Syntax, was a very tough mare who raced for eight seasons. She won 51 races including the Ascot Gold Cup and the Doncaster Cup (four times). She was then used as a park hack for a year before starting her stud career. She was the dam of Newminster, who won the St Leger and became champion sire, and of Nunnykirk, winner of the 2,000 Guineas.

BELL, Christopher Adam (b. 1960)

Having worked for Ian Balding, two studs in Kentucky and as assistant to David Elsworth, Chris Bell had a disastrous start to his training career when the company for which he began at Malton in October 1983 went into liquidation within a month. He remained at Malton until moving to Sparsholt near Wantage towards the end of 1984. His first winner was over hurdles at Huntingdon in February 1984, and his first on the Flat with Rotherfield Greys at Redcar on 29 May that year. He moved to Newmarket early in 1986.

BELL, Charles Henry

Harry Bell trained a mixed string, concentrating mainly on jumpers, at Hawick, and won the Scottish Grand National twice. He had his licence withdrawn for seven months by the Jockey Club disciplinary committee in January 1985, following his conviction for failing to provide proper veterinary care for a mare. The ban lasted only until 1 September but Bell said he would not reapply for a licence, and his stable was taken over by his daughter Margaret.

BELL, Captain O.M.D. (1871-1949)

Captain 'Ossie' Bell was a charming, modest Australian who, after service in World War I, started training at Lambourn. He met with considerable success, winning the Derby in 1928 with Felstead and the 1,000 Guineas and Oaks in 1938 with that very fine filly Rockfel.

BELLA PAOLA
(1955, br f Ticino – Rhea II, by Gundomar)

Bella Paola, owned and bred by M. François Dupré and trained in France by François Mathet, was essentially German in pedigree. A filly of quite outstanding ability, she won the 1,000 Guineas, Oaks and Champion Stakes in Britain and the Grand Critérium and Prix Vermeille in France. Her daughter Pola Bella (by Darius) won six races, including the French 1,000 Guineas, finished second in the French Oaks and bred several winners, including the dam of Vayrann (Champion Stakes).

BELLE OF ALL
(1948, b f Nasrullah – Village Beauty, by Winalot)

Bred by the Earl of Dunraven, Belle of All won four races and over £25,000 for Henry Tufton, including the 1,000 Guineas, Coronation Stakes and Cheveley Park Stakes. The best of her offspring was Principal Boy, winner of the News of the World Stakes and Peter Hastings Stakes, but she is also responsible for the maiden Pendragon, whose sons included the fine steeplechaser Pendil, and the one-race winner Love-in-the-Mist, dam of Perdu (Coventry Stakes and July Stakes).

BENSTEAD, Christopher John (b. 1928)

From being assistant at his father's pony stables and to Peter Thrale, John Benstead began training under NH Rules in 1955 and in 1959 took out a licence for the Flat at Epsom. He has an interesting association with the Autumn Double, having trained Orchardist, who was first past the post in the 1962 Cesarewitch but was relegated to second for boring into Golden Fire, and Baronet, whose Cambridgeshire record from 1977 to 1981 was second, won, sixth, won, second. His other notable performer has been Operatic Society, who won 30 races and well over £30,000 in stakes from 1959.

BENTINCK, Lord George (1802-48)

The outstanding personality in British racing from 1836 to 1846 was unquestionably Lord George Bentinck, son of the fifth Duke of Portland. 'He feared no one,' wrote the diarist Charles Greville, who knew him as well as any man, 'and did nothing by halves.'

Lord George was an owner on a big scale and a fearless gambler. In 1846 he quite suddenly sold his horses and decided to devote himself to politics as assiduously as he had devoted himself to the Turf. In the House of Commons he became the leader of the newly formed Protectionist Party with Disraeli as his lieutenant. Two years later he died of a heart attack.

He was the dominating member of the Jockey Club and introduced order and regularity into race-meetings, previously very rough-and-ready affairs, with a view to improving the sport from the spectators' point of view. He declared unrelenting war on the crooks and defaulters who infested the Turf, and it was largely through his efforts that the Running Rein fraud was unmasked – Running Rein, first past the post in the 1844 Derby, being in reality a four-year-old called Maccabaeus. In appreciation, grateful followers of racing presented him with a sum of money which at his suggestion was used to start a fund (Bentinck Benevolent Fund) to help trainers, jockeys and their dependants who had fallen on hard times.

Lord George devised the system of different-priced enclosures and insisted on punctuality, fining clerks of the course 10 shillings for every minute that a race was started late. He also insisted on a comprehensive number-board and every horse being numbered on the racecard. He ordered that horses be saddled in one special place and paraded in front of the stands. He banned the pernicious custom of winning owners giving a present to the judge after a big race. He greatly improved the system of starting and was largely responsible for the development of Goodwood.

To sum up, he did much to banish the corruption that was bringing the Turf into utter disrepute, while his administrative reforms were a stepping-stone between the haphazard, rough-and-ready race-meetings of the early nineteenth century and the organized, disciplined sport that exists today.

Lord George was not a wholly likeable character although by and large he served racing so well. Aloof to the point of arrogance, he himself sometimes did things in the sphere of racing that in a more enlightened and less privileged age might well have got him 'warned off.' Those who knew him intimately could detect a strain of hypocrisy, or at the very least of remarkable self-deception, that enabled him to pursue unblushingly a course of conduct that he would have been the first to condemn in others.

BENTLEY, Walter (b. 1936)

Walter Bentley, who was apprenticed to Avril Vasey and rode his first winner in 1953, spent most of his career as a lightweight jockey in the North of England, where his biggest successes were in the Manchester November Handicap (Tearaway 1955) and Chester Cup (Altogether 1970, Crisalgo 1973). He turned trainer at Middleham at the start of 1979 and in his first season won the Ayr Gold Cup with Primula Boy.

BERRY, Jack (b. 1937)

Jack Berry was forced to give up his riding career as a jump jockey in the North because of injury, and started training at Doncaster in 1968. In August 1972 he moved his small mixed string to Cockerham, near Lancaster, and had his first winner on the Flat with Fiona's Pet, at Wolverhampton on 6 April 1974, ridden by his wife Jo. He enlarged his stables, switched the emphasis to Flat racing early in the 1980s and had his best season in 1983 with 43 winners. His most important success has been with Touch Boy in the Portland Handicap.

BERTIE, Norman (1893-1971)

Norman Bertie was for many years employed in Fred Darling's stable and rose to the position of head lad there. After Darling's retirement, he trained for some years at Newmarket, but although the licence was in his name, much of the control of the stable was in the hands of Jack Clayton, at that time Sir Victor Sassoon's racing manager. The stable's main triumphs were to win the Derby and King George VI and Queen Elizabeth Stakes with Pinza and the National Breeders' Produce Stakes, Cheveley Park Stakes, 1,000 Guineas and Coronation Stakes with Belle of All. Bertie retired in 1961, when Clayton took over the licence.

BETHELL, Hon. James David William (b. 1952)

Educated at Harrow, James Bethell assisted Arthur Budgett for five years before taking over his Whatcombe stables in 1975, and had his first winner with Baffin Bay at Bath on 28 April 1975. In December 1977 he moved to the Whitsbury stables and in 1982 to Didcot. His best horse has been the sprinter Daring March, and his best season numerically was 1977 with 25 winners.

BETTING SHOPS

Betting shops opened under the new Betting and Gaming Act on 1 May 1961.

BEVERLEY

Without the resources of some other northern racecourses, Beverley has fought hard in recent years to compete with its neighbours and has done well to encourage sponsors and to bring a level of racing that attracts important trainers from the South. The new Tattersalls' stand, opened in 1967, helped to improve the somewhat spartan surroundings of the only course in what was once the East Riding of Yorkshire. The land is rented from the local pasture-masters, and relations between landlord and tenant have not always been cordial.

The right-handed track is wide and oval, flat for the most part but with a stiff, uphill finish of almost 4f that demands resolution. The nature of the straight 5f means it is particularly testing for early-season two-year-olds. The fairly tight turns also make it a difficult course for the awkward galloper.

BIG GAME
(1939, b c Bahram – Myrobella, by Tetratema)

Bred at the National Stud, Big Game was a massive, heavy-topped colt. Leased to King George VI for racing and trained by Fred Darling, he was a really good horse up to $1\frac{1}{4}$m; in fact his only defeat was in the Derby, in which his stamina gave out. His eight victories included the 2,000 Guineas, Champion Stakes, Coventry Stakes and Champagne Stakes.

He never fulfilled expectations as a sire, and his fillies were noticeably more successful than his colts. He got two Classic winners, Queenpot (1,000 Guineas) and Ambiguity (Oaks). The best of his colts was Combat, the unbeaten winner of nine races worth over £7,000. Big Game died in 1963, and is best remembered as a sire of successful broodmares.

BIGGEST FIELD

The biggest field for a race under Jockey Club Rules was 58 in the Lincolnshire Handicap in 1948, when, despite the enormity of the opposition, Commissar at 33-1 landed a gamble for the Budgett brothers. The advent of starting-stalls and safety limits means such numbers will never again turn out for a race, though Newmarket can accommodate 50 over 7f to $1\frac{1}{4}$m on the straight Rowley Mile course.

BIRCH, Mark (b. 1949)

Oldham-born Mark Birch was apprenticed to Geoffrey Barling at Newmarket before having his indentures transferred to Peter Easterby at Malton. Easterby trained his first winner, Bollin Charlotte (at Chester on 26 July 1968), and he has remained with the stable. He lost his claim without riding out his allowance but has developed into one of the best riders in the North, attracting attention from southern trainers to the extent of winning the Northumberland Plate (Dawn Johnny) for Michael Stoute and Ebor (Protection Racket) for Jeremy Hindley in 1981. However, his chief successes have been for Easterby, on Sea Pigeon (Chester Cup twice), Bronze Hill (Lincoln), Sonnen Gold (Gimcrack) and Able Albert (Ayr Gold Cup). His best season was 1979 with 77 winners.

BIREME
(1977, ch f Grundy – Ripeck, by Ribot)

Bred by her owner Dick Hollingsworth and trained by Dick Hern, Bireme ran only four times, but won three races, including the Oaks and Musidora Stakes on her two outings at three years. She was retired to stud as a result of injuries sustained when she got loose on the road soon after her Classic triumph.

BLACK CHERRY FAMILY

Foaled in 1892, Black Cherry is the ancestress of Classic winners such as Sun Chariot, Carrozza, Santa Claus, Night Hawk and Cherry Lass. Perhaps the most important of her descendants, though, is the great stallion Blandford, who sired four Derby winners.

BLACK JESTER
(1911, br c Polymelus – Absurdity, by Melton)

Black Jester won the St Leger in 1914 for Mr J.B. Joel. He also won the City and Suburban among his nine successes for £15,680. He was not a success as a sire, though his daughter Black Ray was influential as the dam of two good American colts, Jacopo and Foray, and two important mares, Eclair (dam of Khaled) and Infra Red (ancestress of Mill Reef).

BLACKSHAW, Harry Fawcus
(b. 1919)

Harry Blackshaw was apprenticed to the late Dawson Waugh at Newmarket. He rode with considerable success and had lost his right to claim the allowance before he was seventeen. During the last

war he served for six years in the Royal Army Veterinary Corps, after which he resumed his riding career under both codes. His last winner was on Pappatea in the 1948 Northumberland Plate, and having taken out a licence to train at Middleham, where he had a small string of mainly modest, cheap horses, his last runner before he retired, in May 1980, was also a winner. His son Martin rode under NH Rules with success before moving to France, where he started training at Chantilly in 1980. Harry came out of retirement in 1983 at his Middleham yard and the following year spent part of the year with a team of horses in Italy but relinquished his licence in 1985, sold the yard and returned to Italy.

BLACK TARQUIN
(1945, br c Rhodes Scholar – Vagrancy, by Sir Gallahad III)

Bred in America, Mr W. Woodward's Black Tarquin was trained by Sir Cecil Boyd-Rochfort. He won eight races including the Gimcrack Stakes, St James's Palace Stakes and St Leger. In a famous race for the Ascot Gold Cup he was vanquished by Alycidon. He was not a very successful sire but got that very game stayer Trelawny and the Cambridgeshire winner Tarqogan.

BLACKWELL, George
(1861-1942)

George Blackwell is one of the few trainers to have won both the Derby and the Grand National. He won the Derby in 1903 with Rock Sand and the Grand National in 1923 with Sergeant Murphy. Rock Sand also won the 2,000 Guineas and St Leger, while Blackwell won the 1,000 Guineas with Aïda in 1901.

BLACKWELL, Thomas Francis
(1912-83)

During World War II Tom Blackwell served in the Coldstream Guards and was Brigade Major to the 5th Guards Armoured Brigade. He had many business interests. Chairman of Turf

Newspapers Ltd and a director of Tote Investors Ltd, he was also well known as an administrator in the golfing world and was captain of the Royal and Ancient Golf Club, St Andrews.

Mr Blackwell had been an owner since he was an undergraduate at Cambridge. The best horses to carry his colours included Rich and Rare (Windsor Castle Stakes and Cheveley Park Stakes), Silver Cloud (Chester Vase and Princess of Wales's Stakes) and Potier (Stewards' Cup) which were trained by Sir Jack Jarvis. Both Silver Cloud and Potier were bred at Mr Blackwell's Langham Hall Stud, Bury St Edmunds. On the death of Jarvis in 1968, his horses were transferred to Bruce Hobbs and later included Catherine Wheel (Musidora Stakes and Nassau Stakes) and Vielle (Nassau Stakes).

His energy, drive and business experience made Mr Blackwell an invaluable member of the Jockey Club, and his term of office as Senior Steward in 1966 was rated an eminently successful one. He was largely responsible for the introduction of starting-stalls. When the Jockey Club and the National Hunt Committee were amalgamated, he was appointed a Deputy Senior Steward, which post he also held in 1973. He died in December 1983.

BLAGRAVE, Herbert Henry Gratwicke (1899-1981)

Herbert Blagrave took out a licence to train in 1928 and conducted an extremely successful private stable at Beckhampton, Wiltshire, the horses belonging either to himself or to his wife. Ascot was always his lucky course and his victories there included the Royal Hunt Cup (three times), Gold Vase, King Edward VII Stakes, Coronation Stakes, Ribblesdale Stakes, Ascot Stakes and Granville Stakes. He also won the Manchester Cup and Kempton Jubilee (three times). He was Governing Director of the Harwood Stud, Newbury, until its sale to Mr James McCaughey in December 1979, and also owned the Mount Prospect Stud, Co Kildare. He died on 4 July 1981, a few days before the running of the Welsh

Derby at Chepstow, a race which he had seen resurrected under his sponsorship.

BLAIR ATHOL

Blair Athol was bred, owned and trained by Mr William I'Anson at Malton, Yorkshire. He was a superbly bred colt being by the great sire Stockwell out of Blink Bonny, winner of the Derby and the Oaks. He had never run before the 1864 Derby but he won that race comfortably despite attempts to prevent his running, and he won the St Leger as well. He was four times champion sire, his son Silvio winning the 1877 Derby and St Leger, before his death in 1882.

BLAKENEY
(1966, b c Hethersett – Windmill Girl, by Hornbeam)

Blakeney was bred by Arthur Budgett and as a yearling he went up for sale at Newmarket but failed to reach a reserve of 5,000gns. Budgett therefore retained him to train himself, disposing of shares to Mrs H.H. Renshaw and Mrs J.M. Carnegie.

He won once from two races as a two-year-old, and once as a three-year-old, in the 26-runner Derby, where he got a smooth run on the inside and won by a length from Shoemaker. Second in the Ascot Gold Cup as a four-year-old, he occupied the same place, two lengths behind Nijinsky, in the King George VI and Queen Elizabeth Stakes.

Retired to the National Stud after a half-share in him had changed hands for £250,000, he sired Juliette Marny (Oaks and Irish Oaks) in his first crop, and three years later came Juliette Marny's brother Julio Mariner (St Leger). Blakeney's more recent Classic winners have been Tyrnavos (Irish Derby), Welnor (Italian Derby) and Mountain Lodge (Irish St Leger). In the meantime, Blakeney's half-brother Morston (by Ragusa) won the Derby in 1973.

BLANDFORD
(1919, br c Swynford – Blanche, by White Eagle)

Blandford was one of the greatest sires of this century. Bred at the National Stud, he was a delicate foal and as a yearling was bought by Mr R.C. Dawson, the Whatcombe trainer, and his brother, Mr S.C. Dawson, for 730gns. He was by no means easy to train, being heavy topped and not possessing the best of joints. In fact he ran only four times, winning on three occasions. When he died at the comparatively early age of sixteen in 1935, his stock had won over 300 races worth over £327,000. He sired four Derby winners – Trigo (1929), Blenheim (1930), Windsor Lad (1934) and Bahram (1935). He was champion sire three times and in the year of his death was champion in both Britain and France. In France he sired Brantôme, one of the most brilliant horses in France in the inter-war era.

BLANSHARD, Michael Thomas William (b. 1954)

Michael Blanshard had no family connections with training, but after four years as assistant to Henry Candy he began on his own account at Upper Lambourn in late 1979. His first Flat-race winner was Muppet at Windsor on 24 May 1980. Numerically his best season was 1985, with fifteen winners.

BLEASDALE, James (b. 1957)

Jimmy Bleasdale rode a winner on his first ride, Croisette at Redcar on 24 April 1975, and two years later he was the country's leading apprentice with 67 winners. Attached to Sam Hall's stable from 1973, he stayed on when Chris Thornton took over on Hall's death in 1977, and despite offers to move South, he has remained there. Ironically, his biggest success came for an outside stable, on Move Off in the Ebor Handicap. He followed his apprentice championship year with his best season, 90 winners, but a bad fall in 1981 cost him half a season, and with the Thornton stable occasionally out of sorts he has not found it easy to get back to the top, though his confidence and loyalty remain undiminished.

BLENHEIM (1927, br c Blandford – Malva, by Charles O'Malley)

Bred by Lord Carnarvon and bought as a yearling on behalf of the Aga Khan for 4,100gns, Blenheim won the 1930 Derby, trained by R.C. Dawson and ridden by Harry Wragg. Owing to a strained tendon he never ran again. As a sire he was an outstanding success. In his first crop of runners he got Mumtaz Begum, dam of Nasrullah; in his second crop came the Derby winner Mahmoud. He also sired Donatello II, who was bred in Italy and after a distinguished racing career became an influential sire in Britain. Exported to America in his prime, Blenheim did equally well over there, his best winners being Whirlaway and Jet Pilot.

BLINK BONNY (1854, b f Melbourne – Queen Mary, by Gladiator)

Blink Bonny was owned by Mr William I'Anson and trained by him at Malton in Yorkshire. She won eight of her 11 races as a two-year-old in 1856, and the following season won both the Derby and the Oaks. Charlton, the jockey in her Epsom triumphs, pulled her in the St Leger at the instigation of John Jackson, a bookmaker who specialized in the corruption of jockeys. Blink Bonny was the dam of the 1864 Derby winner Blair Athol.

BLOWER, THE

'The Blower' is a special office-to-course telephone service for the benefit of bookmakers. It is operated by the Exchange Telegraph Co. ('Extel') which has direct telephonic communication with racecourses, paying rental for special telephones.

BLUE PETER (1936, ch c Fairway – Fancy Free, by Stefan the Great)

Bred and owned by Lord Rosebery, Blue Peter was an exceptionally handsome colt who as a two-year-old did not appear until the autumn, when he was fifth in the Imperial Produce Stakes at Kempton and second in the Middle Park Stakes at Newmarket.

Blue Peter was a magnificent three-year-old and was undefeated, winning the Blue Riband Trial Stakes at Epsom, 2,000 Guineas, Derby and Eclipse Stakes, in all of which he was ridden by Eph Smith. He did a marvellous trial before the St Leger, in which he would have met the unbeaten French colt Pharis, but the outbreak of war prevented the Classic from being run. As such uncertainty existed over the future of racing, Lord Rosebery retired Blue Peter to stud forthwith. Blue Peter, who died in 1957, was hardly the success anticipated as a sire. The best horses he got were Ocean Swell (Derby and Gold Cup), Botticelli (Ascot Gold Cup) and Peter Flower (Hardwicke Stakes and Kempton Jubilee).

BLUE WIND
(1978, ch f Lord Gayle-
Azurine, by Chamossaire)

Blue Wind was bought for 5,600gns as a yearling and after winning two of her five races in Ireland as a two-year-old was sold for 180,000gns, and moved from the stable of Paddy Prendergast jnr to that of Dermot Weld. She proved a bargain for both sets of connections, for as a three-year-old she won three races, including the Epsom Oaks. She was also beaten by a short head in the Irish 1,000 Guineas.

BLUM, George (b. 1924)

'Gerry' Blum worked for several trainers including Harry Wragg and Captain Charles Elsey before he began training with a small yard at Newmarket in 1968. He usually turns out a winner or two every season with mainly cheaply bought horses.

BOIS ROUSSEL
(1935, br c Vatout – Plucky
Liège, by Spearmint)

Bois Roussel was bred in France by M. Léon Volterra, out of a mare, Plucky Liège, who was 23 years old when she foaled him. He never ran as a two-year-old and after winning the Prix Juigné the following April, Mr Peter Beatty bought him to be trained in Britain by Fred Darling. Starting at 20-1 and ridden by Charles Elliott, Bois Roussel won the 1938 Derby by four lengths after being at the tail end of the field at Tattenham Corner. In his only other race, the Grand Prix de Paris, he was third. Although a good many of his stock were unreliable, he was almost champion sire in 1949. He sired two St Leger winners, Tehran and Ridge Wood, Migoli, winner of the Eclipse Stakes and Prix de l'Arc de Triomphe, and two Irish Derby winners, Fraise du Bois II and Hindostan (who did well at stud in Japan).

BOLKONSKI
(1972, ch c Balidar –
Perennial, by Dante)

Bought as a foal for 7,000gns by the Italian owner Carlo d'Alessio, Bolkonski raced in Italy as a two-year-old, winning two of his three races and finishing second in the other. He was sent to Newmarket as a three-year-old to be trained by Henry Cecil but his regular rider, Gianfranco Dettori, retained the ride and he won a further three races – the 2,000 Guineas (from Grundy), St James's Palace Stakes (very easily) and Sussex Stakes (from the fillies Rose Bowl and Lianga). He ran badly on his last outing in the Queen Elizabeth II Stakes and was retired to stud in Normandy, where he has made a slow start as a stallion.

BOND, Alan Maurice (b. 1953)

Alan Bond, who was apprenticed to Ted Smyth at Epsom, had an unpromising start to his riding career – his first mount was left at the start. But after riding his first winner on Swagman at Brighton on 24 August 1972, he was twice champion apprentice, with 40 winners in 1974 and 66 in 1975, which remains his best season. In 1976 he had a season as stable jockey to Henry Cecil, winning the Ribblesdale Stakes on Catalpa, but the momentum was not maintained. He continues to be based in Newmarket.

BOOK LAW
(1924, b f Buchan – Popingaol, by Dark Ronald)

Probably the best filly ever bred at Lord Astor's Cliveden Stud, Book Law won the Coronation Stakes at Ascot and the St Leger and was second in both the 1,000 Guineas and the Oaks. She bred five winners including Rhodes Scholar, who won the Eclipse Stakes. She was also the dam of Archive, sire of the great steeplechaser Arkle.

BOOKMAKERS and BOOKMAKING
By GEOFFREY HAMLYN

Although there has been more or less organized racing in Britain since the days of Charles II, the bookmaker is a comparatively recent phenomenon.

In his book *Come Racing With Me,* the late Major Eric Rickman, a leading authority on betting throughout his lifetime, states that it was about 1790 that a man named Ogden began laying bets against more than one runner in a race, after the style of the present-day bookmaker. Prior to then, owners and their stable connections betted only against each other.

In the late eighteenth century two famous names appear, both of whom made a considerable impact on racing and betting. They were Richard Tattersall and William Crockford.

Richard Tattersall, born in 1724, came from West Yorkshire to London, where he was much engaged in the sale of horses. He was a constant visitor to Beevor's Horse Repository in St Martin's Lane and eventually obtained an interest in this concern. Later he was put in charge of the Duke of Kingston's stud. There was at this time no place where sales could be held at fixed periods, so he offered his services as auctioneer, and the project was taken up by Lord Grosvenor, and the first Tattersalls premises were built on his estate at Hyde Park Corner.

The present-day reference to the main racecourse ring as Tattersalls stems from the days when it was an enclosure used principally by bookmakers and backers who were members of Tattersalls Subscription Rooms, set aside for them in the London premises of Richard Tattersall's firm of auctioneers. The Subscription Rooms as such ceased many years ago, but Tattersalls Committee, authorized by and responsible to the Jockey Club, was formed in 1886 to settle betting disputes and to report or have 'posted' all defaulters, whether backers or layers. This committee still gets through an immense amount of work in the course of a year, meeting once every two or three weeks in the Café Royal, Regent Street.

William Crockford (1775-1844), the founder of Crockford's gambling saloon in Newmarket, had originally been a fishmonger. At this trade he had prospered exceedingly, and in 1827 he bought a gaming table in King Street, St James's, London. A lucky wager on a Derby outsider caused his table to thrive, and in company with a man called Gye he proceeded to fleece various members of the nobility to the tune of £100,000. Following this success he acquired his famous premises on the site of 50-53 St James's Street, and to this gaming club went all the leading personalities of the day, including Disraeli, Bulwer-Lytton and the Duke of Wellington. The cuisine, which was free to all members, had a nationwide reputation. By 1829 Crockford had become a bookmaker and bought a house in Newmarket High Street and also a farm in the district. Subsequently he bought a large house in New Station Road, with gaming premises just across the street on the site of which is now Railway House.

By 1859, the *Sporting Life* had been founded, and shortly afterwards the present starting-price system began to evolve. What happened was this. On race days, bookmakers used to congregate in Hyde Park, on the site of what is now Speakers' Corner, and chalk up their own lists of runners and prices, usually on blackboards or lists affixed to trees. This was obviously illegal, and the police moved them on, until eventually they came to congregate in clubs and dens, mainly in the Fleet Street area. Most of their clients were gentry, who preferred to settle their accounts weekly, so the bookmakers stated in their rules that they would settle weekly on the prices published in the sporting Press. The first national newspaper to publish the starting prices was the *Evening News* in 1883, whose editor at that time was the notorious Frank Harris. It is significant that the circulation of the paper trebled within three months. For the next forty years or so, until after World War I, each sporting paper published its own set of starting prices, until the *Sporting Life* (in modern parlance) 'took over' *Bell's Life in London, The Sportsman* and the *Sporting Telegraph.* Then, in 1926, the *Sporting Chronicle,* by then the only other sporting paper interested, agreed with the *Sporting Life* to publish a combined return of prices compiled by a representative of each paper. This obtained until 31 December 1984, when the Press Association took the place of the defunct *Sporting Chronicle.* The starting-price return is sent out to all bookmakers, newspapers, radio and television by the Exchange Telegraph who have their own representative in the ring on every racecourse. Although very much more streamlined than previously, the system has stood the test of time, surviving two world wars and the introduction of more than 10,000 betting shops.

Prior to 1939, the volume of starting-price business was not enormous. The bookmakers who advertised in the sporting Press could be numbered on two hands, though it included such well-known names as Duggie Stuart, David Cope, James Maclean, McLaughlans and Scotland & Co.

William Hill was a meteor who had not yet appeared in the sky, and Corals and Ladbroke's were relatively small family concerns. Hill made a book at Northolt Park pony racing track in the early 1930s, and he also bet in the cheaper rings at Harringay and White City. When the war broke out, he was 36 but medically unfit for military service. At that time, somewhat naturally, the advertising bookmakers began to draw in their horns, and in any case, the sporting papers were only coming out once or twice a week. Hill, always a dissenter,

took exactly the opposite course. He embarked on a programme of expansion, sinking every penny of his capital into his Park Lane premises, advertised widely and made a book on the rails at every principal meeting throughout the war. This policy paid off handsomely, and by the time the boom period of betting began in 1945, he was well on the way to being the biggest bookmaker in the land. Within five years he had achieved that object and moved his offices to Piccadilly Circus. About that time he began to concentrate on fixed odds football betting, and within a year or so his firm was taking £500,000 a week. The death knell of this remarkable enterprise was sounded in 1964 by the then Chancellor of the Exchequer, Mr Reginald Maudling. He slapped on a 25 per cent tax on this type of betting and within eighteen months killed it virtually stone dead. In 1965, by reason of this tax, William Hill showed a loss for the first time.

Hill ploughed an enormous amount of money back into racing and was the owner of two of the leading studs in the country, Whitsbury and Sezincote. He bred the winners of the Derby and 2,000 Guineas (Nimbus), St Leger (Cantelo), and Gimcrack and Champagne Stakes (Be Careful). He also bred Grey Sovereign, one of the most prolific sires of sprinters since the war. William Hill died of a heart attack in the Rutland Hotel, Manchester, in October 1971. He was 68.

The other big names in bookmaking are Corals, Ladbroke's, Mecca and now the Tote. Joe Coral, the presiding genius of the firm that bears his name, has been making a book since 1926. The firm has expanded enormously in the last fifteen years and now has the best part of 1,000 betting shops.

Corals sponsor a number of races, the most important of which is the Coral-Eclipse Stakes run at Sandown Park in early July. Corals were represented on the course by Neville Berry and John Hudson during the 1970s but have now given it up. They took over the long-established firm of Heathorns Ltd in the winter of 1984, with their 60-odd shops, and a pitch on the rails at all the important meetings.

Ladbroke's is now run by Cyril Stein, nephew of Max Stein, better known to racegoers as Maxie Parker, who died twenty years ago. The four Stein brothers, Harry, Jack, Max and Isaac, were the sons of European immigrants who came to Britain before World War I. Harry, alternatively known as Dick or 'Snouty,' was the biggest rails bookmaker when war broke out in 1939. He died in 1945 and his business was taken over by Max, who also traded as Max Parker Ltd. In 1957 he bought the old-fashioned firm of Ladbroke's from its founder, Arthur Bendir, and installed his nephew Cyril as Managing Director. An immediate policy of expansion was embarked upon. Various firms have been taken over, and more than 1,000 betting shops purchased over a wide area. The empire controlled by Cyril Stein surpasses all other bookmaking firms, comprising, as it does, hotels, betting shops and many other aspects of the leisure industry, not only in Britain but in Europe and America as well. All this is a very far cry from the illegal bookmakers in Hyde Park.

Mecca are part of the Grand Metropolitan Hotels set-up and were masterminded by the late Maxwell Joseph. Mecca ran cafés, dance halls etc under the chairmanship of Eric Morley, who was also the first chairman of BOLA for a number of years prior to Joe Ward Hill. They have about 600 betting shops and sponsor the valuable Mecca-Dante Stakes at York in May.

It is not generally known that Tote Bookmakers are now an active offshoot of the Tote, and have been in operation for more than ten years. Their first Managing Director was William Balshaw, who was Chairman of William Hill (Holders Investment Trust) Ltd, following William Hill's death in 1971. Balshaw remained chairman until it was taken over by Sears Holdings. The Tote own more than 100 shops and were represented on the rails for a couple of years in the 1970s. They have now given this up.

The bookmaking organizations, which, like the trades unions, have such difficulty in controlling their members, date back no further than 1921. In that year the late 'Hoppy' Beresford, a lame bookmaker who used to bet sitting on a stool, together with a few South Country colleagues, formed what was then called the Bookmakers and Backers Protection Association, and a year later a northern branch was formed by George Picken and George Yates. The latter, a highly respected member of his profession, became the first chairman of the famous Victoria Club, then in Wellington Street, Strand but now in the Edgware Road.

The regional associations have now become the National Association of Bookmakers, whose chairman is the Scotsman Alfie Bruce. There is also the Betting Offices Licensees' Association, or BOLA, whose chairman Don Bruce took over in February 1986 after a five-year tenure by Joe Ward Hill, youngest brother of the late William Hill.

The future of the bookmaking profession looks more assured than it did twenty years ago, when there was strong pressure from interested parties to force a Tote monopoly on the racing public. If only the Government did not take more than £2m a year out of the betting industry, it would be brighter still.

BOOTH, Charles Benjamin Brodie (b. 1946)

Charlie Booth was a pupil assistant with Bill Elsey before training point-to-pointers and taking out a permit. He was granted his first licence in 1976 to train near Malton, and his best season was 1983, with thirteen winners.

BOOTS

Materials such as felt, leather or elastic, or a combination of those, are made into a cover for part of a limb, especially the hock and ankle, to provide protection or support. They are close fitting and kept in position by straps. They protect a horse that is liable to strike into itself with its own feet, or alternatively provide support in the case of some leg weakness.

BOSS, Ronald (b. 1938)

Welshman Ron Boss began in racing as a stable lad with Noel Murless and rode winners over jumps when head lad and

stable jockey for Ifor Lewis. He took out
his first training licence in 1972 at
Newmarket and had his first winner on
the Flat with Sidewalk at Nottingham on
2 April 1972. He won the Queen Mary
Stakes in 1976 with Cramond, the
following year had his first Classic
success with Olwyn in the Irish Oaks, and
in 1978 won the Lincoln with Captain's
Wings. Numerically his best season was
1980, with 21 winners.

BOSWELL
(1933, b c Bosworth – Flying
Gal II, by Sir Gallahad III)

Mr W. Woodward's Boswell was not
entirely predictable and started at 20-1
when he gained his two most important
successes, in the St Leger and Eclipse
Stakes. He failed as a sire in America and
Canada.

BOSWORTH
(1926, b or br c Son-in-Law –
Serenissima, by Minoru)

Bred and owned by Lord Derby,
Bosworth won four races for £7,909, the
most important being the Ascot Gold
Cup as a four-year-old. He was second,
beaten a short head by Trigo, in the St
Leger. He was not a great success as a
sire but got Boswell and Plassy, winner of
the Coronation Cup and Jockey Club
Stakes.

BOTTICELLI
(1951, b c Blue Peter –
Buonamica, by Niccolo
dell'Arca)

Bred and raced by the Razza Dormello-
Olgiata, Botticelli won fourteen of his
eighteen races in three seasons' racing. In
his native Italy he won the Derby, St
Leger and Gran Premio d'Italia, and in
Britain he won the Ascot Gold Cup as a
four-year-old. A smart stayer who did not
relish soft ground, he was at stud in
Britain and later in Germany. His best
offspring was his son Antelami (Italian
Derby), while in Britain Aegean Blue won
the Chester Cup.

BOTTOMLEY, Horatio
(1860-1933)

Born in the East End of London, the son
of a tailor's cutter, Horatio Bottomley
was a journalist, promoter of scores of
dubious financial schemes, a formidable
lawyer and a Member of Parliament. He
was also perhaps the greatest 'con' man
of his time, who managed to escape gaol
until 1922, when he received a seven-year
sentence.

On the Turf he was a heavy but rash
and unskilled gambler. Most of the horses
he owned were very bad, but he won a lot
of money when Wargrave won the
Cesarewitch for him and Northern
Farmer the Stewards' Cup. He also
cleared £15,000 when his sprinter, Le
Blizon, beat Mr Jack Joel's Sundridge in
a match at Hurst Park.

It is interesting to recall that in
Parliament over 70 years ago Bottomley
was demanding the annual licensing of
bookmakers and the introduction of a
betting tax. During World War I he was
Chairman of the Racing Emergency
Committee, designed to ensure the
continuance of the sport.

He died penniless in the public ward of
a London hospital.

BOUCHER
(1969, ch c Ribot – Glamour,
by Nasrullah)

Boucher was bred in the United States by
his owner Ogden Phipps, was trained in
Ireland by Vincent O'Brien, gained his
biggest success in Britain in the St Leger
and took up stallion duties in Australia.
He was a good-class two-year-old winner
of the Beresford Stakes but suffered from
a virus after winning his first race at three
years before recovering his form in the
autumn. In all he won six races.

BOUSSAC, Marcel
(1889-1980)

Marcel Boussac built his considerable
racing empire on the foundation of a
fortune made in the textile industry of
France in the First World War. The
eventual fall of his business and racing
interests was as spectacular as their rise.

He had his first Classic success with Ramus in the 1922 French Derby, and within ten years his stud was the best in France, later developing on the influence of the sires Tourbillon, Astérus and Pharis II. A number of his horses were trained in Britain by Basil Jarvis and George Lambton, and he won his first British Classic in 1940 with Djebel. It was immediately after the Second World War that the powerful Boussac stable reached its peak. His main successes in Britain at this time were the Derby with Galcador (1950), Oaks with Asmena (1950), St Leger with Scratch II (1950) and Talma II (1951), Gold Cup with Caracalla II (1946), Arbar (1948), Elpenor (1954) and Macip (1956), Eclipse Stakes with Djeddah (1949) and Argur (1953), and Champion Stakes with Djeddah (1949) and Dynamiter (1951-52).

In 1956 he completed the French Derby and Oaks double with Philius and Apollonia but did not have another Classic success until 1969, when Crepellana won the French Oaks. The influence of the Boussac stallions had been played out, and though his stud maintained its numbers, the quality disappeared. When his Acamas won the French Derby in 1978, it was in the manner of a death rattle from a once-great empire. That summer the textile business was bankrupt and the Boussac bloodstock was being sold by the liquidators to the Aga Khan, while Stavros Niarchos bought the stud. M. Boussac died in March 1980.

BOWES, John (1814-85)

John Bowes of Streatlam Castle, Co Durham, won the Derby four times – with Mündig (1835), Cotherstone (1843), Daniel O'Rourke (1852) and West Australian (1853). He also won the 2,000 Guineas with Meteor (1842), Cotherstone and West Australian, while the last-named became the first horse ever to complete the Triple Crown series when he won the St Leger. A member of the Jockey Club, Bowes owned horses for more than 50 years and was a patron of John Scott's powerful Malton stable.

Bowes was a son of Lord Strathmore and would have succeeded to the title but for the fact that he was born nine years before his parents married. Shy and reserved, he lived for the most part quietly in Paris, and in later life tended to become a complete recluse. For 30 years before his death he never set foot on a racecourse. He was only 21 and still at Cambridge when he won the Derby with Mündig (*Mündig* is the German for 'of age').

BOYD, George Henderson (b. 1907)

George Boyd, one of the most consistently successful Scottish trainers since the Second World War, learnt the art from his father, J.N. Boyd. George Boyd rode under both Rules as an amateur from 1929 to 1939 and, apart from a spell of service in the RAF, assisted his brother Alec from 1936 till he set up on his own at Dunbar ten years later. He retired in 1969.

His main triumph was with Rockavon, who won the 1961 2,000 Guineas at 66-1. His imposing list of successes in handicaps included the Northumberland Plate three times, Lincoln, Cambridgeshire, Zetland Gold Cup and Ayr Gold Cup. On his retirement, the stables were taken over by his nephew, Tommy Craig.

BOYD-ROCHFORT, Captain Sir Cecil Charles CVO (1887-1983)

Sir Cecil Boyd-Rochfort was a success from the moment he took out a trainer's licence in 1923, the year he won the July Cup with Golden Corn, and remained so until he handed over to his stepson Henry Cecil in 1968, the year he was awarded a knighthood. Educated at Eton, he served in the Scots Guards in World War I, when he was awarded the Croix de Guerre. He learned the art of training from 'Atty' Persse and was for a time assistant to Captain R.H. Dewhurst, as well as managing the horses owned by Sir Ernest Cassels and Mr Marshall Field. It was with help from the American Field that he started training.

He won almost every important race in the calendar and was particularly successful with stayers. He certainly did not scorn handicaps, and his stable landed some notable gambles in the Cesarewitch, Cambridgeshire and Royal Hunt Cup.

A perfectionist, he demanded the highest standards and had as little use for clock-watching employees as for indifferent horses. No doubt he was fortunate in that he trained for wealthy patrons, many of them American, who sent him high-class horses and could afford to be patient. However they would not have remained his patrons for long had they not been justifiably confident of his high professional ability.

In 1943 he was appointed trainer to King George VI on the death of W.R. Jarvis, and continued to hold this appointment after the accession of Queen Elizabeth until his own retirement. During the early years of the Queen's reign, the Sandringham stud was enjoying a phase of brilliant success and among the good horses who carried the royal colours in that period were Aureole, Doutelle, Almeria, Pall Mall and Above Suspicion.

Probably the two best horses he trained were the triple Classic winner Meld and the St Leger and King George VI and Queen Elizabeth Stakes winner Alcide.

His chief successes were: *2,000 Guineas:* Pall Mall (1958), *1,000 Guineas:* Brown Betty (1933), Hypericum (1946) and Meld (1955), *Derby:* Parthia (1959), *Oaks:* Hycilla (1944) and Meld (1955), *St Leger:* Boswell (1936), Sun Castle (1941), Black Tarquin (1948), Premonition (1953), Meld (1955) and Alcide (1958), *Coronation Cup:* Persian Gulf (1944) and Aureole (1954), *Ascot Gold Cup:* Precipitation (1937), Flares (1938) and Zarathustra (1957), *Eclipse Stakes:* Royal Minstrel (1929), Loaningdale (1933), Boswell (1937) and Canisbay (1965), *King George VI and Queen Elizabeth Stakes:* Aureole (1954) and Alcide (1959), *Goodwood Cup:* Zarathustra (1956), Dickens (1959), Sagacity (1962), Raise You Ten (1964), Apprentice (1965) and Gaulois (1966), *Champion Stakes:* Flares (1937) and Hycilla (1944).

He also won the Kempton Jubilee four times, Lingfield Derby Trial ten times, St James's Palace Stakes three times, Coronation Stakes three times, Royal Hunt Cup four times, Champagne Stakes five times, Park Hill Stakes five times, Middle Park Stakes three times, Cesarewitch three times and Cambridgeshire twice.

Tall, erect and impeccably dressed, a figure of considerable dignity, Sir Cecil had clear-cut likes and dislikes in the racing world and was inclined to express himself freely. He spent his retirement in Ireland and died there in March 1983, aged 95.

BRASSEY, Kim Maurice (b. 1955)

Kim Brassey began training at Upper Lambourn in 1981 and, having won his first race with a selling hurdler at Devon & Exeter, he was successful with his first runner on the Flat, Seven Hearts at Newcastle on 12 April 1982. He had previously worked for Tim Forster, Toby Balding and Charlie Millbank in France, as well as gaining experience in the United States before joining Nick Vigors as assistant. His biggest success came in 1985 in the Henry II Stakes with Destroyer, who also finished second in the Ascot Gold Cup.

BREASLEY, Arthur Edward (b. 1914)

'Scobie' Breasley ranks with the best Australian jockeys who have ridden in Britain such as Frank Wootton, Frank Bullock and Bernard Carslake. Born in Australia, he was apprenticed there to P.B. Quinlian and rode his first winner in August 1928. In 1950 he came to Britain to ride for Noel Cannon's stable and swiftly established his reputation. His first Classic success came in 1951 when he rode Ki Ming to victory in the 2,000 Guineas. He subsequently won the 1,000 Guineas on Festoon, and the Derby for the first time at the age of 50 on Santa Claus and again two years later on Charlottown. He also won the King George VI and Queen Elizabeth Stakes, Prix de l'Arc de Triomphe, Grand Prix de Saint-Cloud and Irish 1,000 Guineas.

Five times runner-up in the jockeys' list, the last occasion a year before he retired in 1967, he was champion jockey four times, his best season being in 1962, when he had 179 winners. He retained the title in 1963 with 176 winners, one more than Lester Piggott.

Level-headed, businesslike, unemotional, a dedicated professional, Breasley emulated the best Australian riders as a superb judge of pace and excelled in split-second timing. He was a master, too, at winning on two-year-olds and highly strung fillies without subjecting them to a hard race. If he had a weakness, it was perhaps a tendency to stick to the rails at all costs, a habit that sometimes resulted in his getting boxed in, while his marked preference for waiting tactics made him seem at times inflexible in his methods compared with the best British riders. He lacked nothing in toughness and courage.

His training career took him from a six-year spell at Epsom – where his biggest success was with Steel Pulse in the Irish Sweeps Derby – to France and America, where he trained privately for Mr Ravi Tikkoo. Breasley returned to Britain in September 1978 to resume as a public trainer until his retirement at the end of 1980, when he left for the West Indies.

BREEDER

By definition in the Rules of Racing, the breeder is 'the person or entity who owns the dam when the foal is dropped.'

BREEDERS, Leading: (see Appendix II)

BRIGADIER GERARD (1968, b c Queen's Hussar – La Paiva, by Prince Chevalier)

There have been few better post-war racers than Brigadier Gerard, who won his first fifteen races, was beaten by Roberto in the Benson & Hedges Gold Cup and came back to win his last two outings. Bred and owned by the Hislop family, Brigadier Gerard was trained by Dick Hern and ridden by Joe Mercer. He was rated slightly inferior to Mill Reef

and My Swallow as a two-year-old, when his four wins included the Middle Park Stakes, but as a three-year-old he beat both in a stirring race for the 2,000 Guineas and went on to establish himself as Europe's top miler with six victories, the last being a hard-fought battle against Rarity over 10f in the Champion Stakes.

As a four-year-old, Brigadier Gerard won his first five races, from a mile in the Lockinge Stakes, to 10f in the Eclipse, to 12f in the King George VI and Queen Elizabeth Stakes. Attempting to match Ribot's record of sixteen straight wins, Brigadier Gerard came across the Derby winner Roberto in scintillating form on firm ground at York and went down by three lengths. It was a disappointment equalled only by the fact that he did not meet Mill Reef again after the Guineas, but Brigadier Gerard redeemed himself by winning the Queen Elizabeth II Stakes and Champion Stakes (for the second time). Having gained first-prize earnings of £243,924, he was retired to stud in Newmarket at a valuation of £1m, a great deal less than had he been sold to the United States but a reflection of the desire by his breeders to keep him in Britain.

It would have been remarkable if Brigadier Gerard had bred a racer close to his own calibre, but his stud career has been slightly disappointing, especially in comparison with his great rival Mill Reef. Brigadier Gerard's first Classic winner was Light Cavalry (St Leger), and his other major winner is Vayrann (Champion Stakes).

BRIGHTON

Brighton racecourse occupies a breezy position high on a hill above the town with a view of the English Channel. Modern stands in Tattersalls have improved the standard of comfort, and the course is equally popular with regular racegoers and with south-coast holidaymakers. Increased prize money has helped to attract better horses than in the past, though because of its unique nature – a U-shaped track which follows the rim of a housing estate in the basin below – it is not surprising that some horses become course specialists. The track is left-handed, and no race is run over further than

1½ miles, of which the first 3f are slightly uphill. Then there is a slight descent, followed by a rise to about 4f from home. The ground then falls quite steeply until 2f from the finish when there is a rise with the final 100 yd level.

It is a sharp course, and a horse needs good conformation and a good action as well to cope with the various gradients. A low draw is an advantage in races up to a mile, though the relatively modern habit of jockeys tacking over to the stands rails when the going is on the soft side negates that advice. In olden times they used to have hurdle races here with one hurdle sited halfway down that steep hill.

BRITT, Edgar (b. 1913)

Edgar Britt came to Britain in 1945 from his native Australia, where he rode his first winner in 1930, and was retained by the Maharajah of Baroda, for whom he had ridden in India. He gained his first Classic successes in the 1947 Irish Derby and Doncaster St Leger on Sayajirao, owned by the Maharajah, but lost his job that year to Charlie Smirke. Britt rode for Captain Boyd-Rochfort when his stable jockey Harry Carr was injured, and so won the St Leger on Black Tarquin. His other Classic wins came for Captain Charles Elsey, by whom he became retained, in the 2,000 Guineas on Nearula, 1,000 Guineas on Musidora and Oaks on Musidora and Frieze. After his retirement in 1959, he returned to Australia, where he took up a career in broadcasting.

BRITTAIN, Clive Edward (b. 1933)

Clive Brittain came late to training, having worked for Noel Murless for 21 years. Putting his gambling earnings to good use, he started training at Newmarket in 1972 and had his first winner with Vedvyas at Doncaster on 1 April 1972. Two years later he moved to Carlburg Stables in Newmarket when they were purchased by his main patron, Captain Marcos Lemos. Though gaining a reputation for flying high with his horses, Brittain has had his own faith justified several times, winning the St Leger with Julio Mariner, 1,000 Guineas with Pebbles, Hardwicke Stakes with Jupiter Island, and St James's Palace Stakes with Averof and Radetzky, as well as major handicaps such as the Victoria Cup (Private Line), Cambridgeshire (Braughing), Ebor (Jupiter Island) and Royal Hunt Cup (Come on the Blues).

Numerically his best season in Britain was 1981, with 54 winners, but 1985 stands out because of the achievements of Pebbles in winning the Eclipse Stakes and Champion Stakes in this country and the Breeders' Cup Turf race in the United States. Despite his late start, Brittain has been in the forefront of technical innovation at his stables, which contain some of the most up-to-date equipment.

BRITTAIN, Melvyn Anthony (b. 1943)

Managing Director of a firm of steel stockholders, Mel Brittain had horses with several trainers in the North and then employed a series of private trainers before he was granted his own licence to train near York in 1985. In his first season he won 22 races, the best being Grey Desire's Abernant Stakes, and was granted a public licence for 1986.

BROADCASTING

The first successful broadcast of a horse race was for the Grand National of 1927, the year that the Derby was broadcast for the first time, following an unsuccessful attempt the previous year.

BROODMARE

A broodmare is a filly of any age being kept at a stud for breeding purposes.

BROOKE, Major Geoffrey Thomas (b. 1896)

For twenty years Geoffrey Brooke assisted his brother-in-law 'Atty' Persse before taking out a licence himself in 1949. For a brief spell he acted as private trainer to Major Lionel Holliday, and when that arrangement came to an end in 1952, he set up as a public trainer at Newmarket and enjoyed consistent success until his retirement in 1967, when he went to live in Ireland.

Like Persse, he preferred speed to stamina, and most of his successes were with fast two-year-olds, sprinters and milers rather than with stayers. However, he won the 1951 Oaks with Neasham Belle for Major Holliday. He won the 2,000 Guineas for Mr David Robinson with Our Babu, and among other good horses he trained were Durante, Masham, Rustam, Crocket and Sammy Davis.

BROWN, Lionel Gerald (b. 1933)

Lionel Brown, who served his apprenticeship with George Colling and Ernie Davey, rode his first winner in 1950 and enjoyed a successful career in the North, where the best horses he rode were the sprinters Goldhill, Fleece and Lochnager. His best season was in 1965, with 58 winners. He retired in 1976 but stayed in racing to assist his brother-in-law Jimmy Etherington and to run a horsebox business at Malton.

BROWN BETTY
(1930, b or br f Friar Marcus – Garpal, by Phalaris)

An exceptionally good-looking filly, Brown Betty won six races including the 1,000 Guineas for a total of £11,637. She had been bought for 1,600gns as a yearling on behalf of the American Mr William Woodward, and retired to stud in the United States.

BROWNHYLDA
(1920, b f Stedfast – Valkyrie, by Eager)

Brownhylda won five races, including the Oaks, to return £12,080 for the 310gns she cost as a yearling. Her one winner at stud was Firdaussi, who won the St Leger and Jockey Club Stakes.

BROWN JACK
(1924, br g Jackdaw – Querquidella, by Kroonstad)

Brown Jack, a stayer famous for his courage and toughness, was one of the most popular horses to run on the British Turf. He was bred in Ireland and after a brief and unsuccessful racing career

there, was bought as a three-year-old for 750gns by Aubrey Hastings, who was acting for Sir Harold Wernher, at that time a jumping enthusiast and particularly keen to win the Champion Hurdle.

Brown Jack's first outing in Britain was at Bournemouth in the autumn of 1927 when he finished third in a novices' hurdle. He soon proved himself a formidable hurdler and won seven times that season, his big triumph being in the Champion Hurdle, a fine achievement for a four-year-old. Among those who saw him win at Cheltenham was Steve Donoghue, who advised that Brown Jack's attention should be turned to the Flat. Brown Jack never ran again under National Hunt Rules.

As a four-year-old Brown Jack won the Ascot Stakes, and the following six years he won the Queen Alexandra Stakes, thereby achieving the unequalled feat of winning a race at Royal Ascot seven years running. His final Ascot victory was the occasion of a memorable scene of enthusiasm and affection, the old gelding and his rider, Donoghue, being given a reception that a Derby winner in the royal colours might have been afforded.

Brown Jack's other wins included the Goodwood Cup, Ebor Handicap and Rosebery Memorial Plate. In all he ran 65 times, winning 25 races worth over £23,000. He lived in happy retirement till his death in 1948.

It only remains to add that Aubrey Hastings died suddenly in 1929 and that his successor at Wroughton was Ivor Anthony, who trained Brown Jack for the rest of his career.

BRULETTE
(1928, b f Brûleur – Seaweed, by Spearmint)

Bred in France by Lt.-Col. C.W. Birkin, Brulette was a fine stayer who won the Oaks, Goodwood Cup and Prix du Cadran while trained in France. Sold into Fred Darling's stable, she won the Goodwood Cup and walked over for the Jockey Club Cup. The best of her seven fairly modest winners was probably Tropical Sun, third in the Oaks and third dam of both the smart German horse Lombard and the Arc de Triomphe winner Vaguely Noble.

BRUNI
(1972, gr c Sea Hawk II – Bombazine, by Shantung)

Bruni, who cost 7,800gns as a yearling, reached the high spot of a career in which he won five races and was placed nine times when he won the St Leger by ten lengths. Not every decision taken on his behalf after that did his reputation much good. He ran in the Prix de l'Arc de Triomphe as a three-year-old and finished seventh, and he was never the same again after being sent to race in the United States at the end of his four-year-old season. The result was that his standing had greatly diminished by the time he was retired to stud in Ireland in 1978. He remained there for four years until he was exported to Kuwait.

BUCHAN
(1916, b c Sunstar – Hamoaze, by Torpoint)

Buchan was a good but unlucky horse belonging to the second Lord Astor. He was narrowly beaten in the Derby, a race he ought to have won, and was disqualified after winning the 1920 Gold Cup. He did, however, win eleven races, including the Eclipse Stakes twice. He did well at stud and was champion sire in 1927, the year his daughter Book Law won the St Leger.

BUCKLE, Dennis (b. 1929)

Dennis Buckle was one of several apprentices brought on by Ernie Davey, and after riding his first winner in August 1946 – beating a 7-4-on chance and surviving an objection into the bargain – he was leading apprentice in 1947 and 1948. Based in the North, he had his best season in 1964, with 27 winners. When opportunities grew scarcer early in the 1970s, he left for a career on the Continent.

BUCKLE, Frank (1766-1832)

Frank Buckle was a great jockey and in his heyday enjoyed a popularity equal to that of Fred Archer, Steve Donoghue and Gordon Richards.

Son of a Newmarket saddler, he had a long career as a jockey, his final ride in 1831 being 50 years after joining Mr Vernon's stable as a small boy. For much of his life he lived at Peterborough, where he farmed successfully, being famous for his butter. He also bred greyhounds, bulldogs and fighting cocks and at one period was a Master of Hounds. He was a tough little man who thought nothing of hacking over to Newmarket to ride to work and then riding home to Peterborough in time for tea, a total distance of , 90 miles. His whip, covered in silver and bearing the record of his Classic successes, was for many years a coveted racing trophy in Germany.

Between 1792 and 1827, he won the 2,000 Guineas five times, 1,000 Guineas six times, Derby five times, Oaks nine times and St Leger twice to create a record of 27 Classic wins that stood until passed by Lester Piggott in 1984.

BUDGETT, Arthur Maitland (b. 1916)

Only two men have bred, owned and trained two Derby winners. The first was the Scot William I'Anson, with Blink Bonny (1857) and her son Blair Athol (1864); the second was Arthur Budgett, who retained a half-share in the 1969 winner Blakeney and owned the whole of the 1973 winner Morston, both being out of his Ribblesdale Stakes winner and Oaks runner-up Windmill Girl.

Budgett comes from a family well-known in hunting and polo circles. He was educated at Eton and Oxford and took out a licence to train in 1939. Army service interrupted his career, and Commissar, whom he owned in partnership with his elder brother Alan, was trained by Eric Stedall when he won the 1946 Stewards' Cup. However, Budgett trained Commissar when he won the 1948 Lincoln as an eight-year-old.

In 1969 he also won the Middle Park Stakes with Huntercombe. He trained Huntercombe's sire Derring-Do to win over £20,000 in stakes, his victories including the Imperial Stakes, Cornwallis

Stakes and Queen Elizabeth II Stakes. He ended 1969 as leading trainer with 35 wins worth £105,349.

His stables at Whatcombe, Berkshire, were taken over by his former assistant, James Bethell, at the end of 1974, and a year later Budgett relinquished his licence. He was elected to the Jockey Club in December 1977 and acts as a steward at Newbury and Salisbury.

Racing colours: Salmon pink, grey sleeves, quartered caps.

BULL, Philip (b. 1910)

Phil Bull has been an easily recognizable figure in the racing world since he began his publications aimed at helping the punter in the 1930s, and with no hesitation in expressing his strong views about the running of racing, he is among the most notable non-establishment personalities. When he did gain high office, as the first chairman of the Horseracing Advisory Council in March 1980, he retained the position for only four months before resigning. Without evidence to the contrary, it was suggested that his individual style did not flourish in an atmosphere of committee. Through his Halifax publishing company, Portway Press, Bull has conferred services of great value by the publication of *Timeform* and the annual 'Racehorses' series, and his views on mile races for two-year-olds led him to sponsor, through his company, the Timeform Gold Cup, which later became the Observer Gold Cup and William Hill Futurity Stakes, at Doncaster.

Bull has also had many successes as breeder and owner. Among the good winners to carry his colours are Orgoglio (Champagne Stakes and Victoria Cup); Orinthia (Kempton Jubilee and Manchester Cup); Pheidippides (Gimcrack Stakes); and Sostenuto (Ebor Handicap). He also bred Eudaemon (Gimcrack Stakes and Champagne Stakes), and Romulus (Sussex Stakes and Queen Elizabeth II Stakes).

Most of his biggest successes as an owner were shared with trainer Captain Charles Elsey, but since the latter's death Bull has had several trainers, including Staff Ingham, Vincent O'Brien, Teddy Lambton, Peter Robinson, Barry Hills,

and Peter Easterby. Both his stud and stable declined in terms of success in the 1970s, and since 1980 he has rarely had more than one horse in training.

Racing colours: cerise, white circle.

BULTEEL, Sir John Crocker KCVO, DSO, MC (1890-1956)

Sir John Crocker Bulteel was Clerk of the Course at Ascot and at Hurst Park when he died. By common consent he was the outstanding racing official of his time, bringing to racecourse management and programme planning an imaginative and enlightened appreciation of modern needs in an era when the general standard was out-dated and deplorably unprogressive. One of his more important contributions was to institute the King George VI and Queen Elizabeth Stakes at Ascot. Invariably courteous and with a charming personality, he was extremely well liked in the racing world.

BUMPER

'Bumper' is a slang term for an amateur rider on the Flat.

BUNBURY, Sir Charles (1740-1821)

Sir Charles Bunbury, whose name is commemorated at Newmarket in the Bunbury Mile course and the Bunbury Cup run on the July course, played a very important part not only in the development of British racing but in the extension of the authority of the Jockey Club, of which he was regarded as 'the Perpetual President.' On the Turf his word was law, and it was his action after the inconsistent running of the Prince of Wales's horse Escape that led to the Prince (afterwards George IV) shaking the dust of Newmarket off his heels for good.

Sir Charles won the first Derby in 1780 with Diomed. He also won that race with Eleanor and Smolensko, but the best horse he bred was Highflyer, whom he sold to Lord Bolingbroke.

BURNS, Thomas P. (b. 1924)

Apprenticed in Britain to Steve Donoghue, he returned to Ireland, the land of his birth, on the outbreak of war. He rode his first winner at the age of thirteen and for many years was one of the leading Irish riders, equally good on the Flat or over hurdles. His main triumph in Britain was to win the St Leger on Ballymoss, on whom he also won the Irish Derby. On retiring from race-riding in November 1975 he stayed to assist Vincent O'Brien, trainer of Ballymoss.

BUSTINO
(1971, b c Busted – Ship Yard, by Doutelle)

Bustino cost Lady Beaverbrook 21,000 gns as a yearling. He was trained by Dick Hern and won five races, including the St Leger and Coronation Cup, but he will be best remembered for his exciting but narrowly unsuccessful battle with Grundy for the 1975 King George VI and Queen Elizabeth Diamond Stakes in one of the best races since the last war. Bustino never ran again and was syndicated for stud at a valuation of £600,000. His most important winners have been Easter Sun (Coronation Cup) and Alma Ata and Borushka (both Park Hill Stakes), along with the smart gelding Bedtime, Classic-placed Bustomi and Supreme Leader, and the useful Italian filly Stufida.

BUTLER, Francis (1818-56)

Frank Butler was a nephew of Sam Chifney junior and inherited a touch of his genius. He got his big chance when appointed stable jockey to John Scott at Malton, and rode two winners of the Derby, Daniel O'Rourke and West Australian, and six winners of the Oaks, four of them in succession. He was only 38 when he died, having had problems with his weight that were not helped by his liking for drink.

BUTTERS, Joseph Arthur Frank (1878-1957)

Frank Butters was one of the most successful and most respected trainers of his time. He was born in Vienna, the eldest son of Joseph Butters who was training there at the time. After being educated in Britain he returned to Austria, where he helped his father for some years before becoming private trainer to Mautrer de Markham. During World War I he was interned in Austria, and after the Armistice he trained with success for a number of years in Italy.

In 1926 he succeeded George Lambton as Lord Derby's trainer, being given a four-year contract. He won the St Leger and Eclipse Stakes with Fairway, Eclipse Stakes with Colorado, 1,000 Guineas with Fair Isle, Oaks with Toboggan and Gold Cup with Bosworth. All these belonged to Lord Derby and he won the Oaks for Lord Durham with Beam. However, in August 1930 Lord Derby informed him, that owing to the world economic crisis, he was reducing his racing commitments and that their contract would not be renewed. Thus at the age of 52 and at a time of acute financial depression, Butters found himself out of a job.

He was not unemployed for long, for after the Aga Khan's break with Dick Dawson, Butters was asked to take the Aga Khan's horses. He agreed to do so and trained them with immense success until he retired in 1949, that retirement being caused by a serious accident when riding his bicycle. He trained the following Classic winners for the Aga Khan; *2,000 Guineas:* Bahram, *Derby:* Bahram and Mahmoud, *Oaks:* Udaipur and Masaka, *St Leger:* Firdaussi, Bahram, Turkhan and Tehran.

In the 1932 St Leger he saddled four horses for the Aga Khan – Firdaussi (first), Dastur (second, beaten a neck), Udaipur (fourth) and Taj Kasra (fifth). He also won the Oaks for Sir Alfred Butt with Steady Aim. Altogether he won in Britain 1,019 races worth over £930,000. At Royal Ascot in 1934 he trained the winners of nine of the 28 races.

Butters combined a high degree of professional skill with intense devotion to the interests of his patrons. He seldom betted, and his one big bet was on Fairway in the Derby, in which the horse ran unplaced. He believed in giving his horses plenty of work, and those who stood up to his methods came onto the racecourse fit to run for their lives. The tragedy of his life was when his son Victor, his valued assistant, died suddenly during a holiday in Switzerland.

BUTTERS, Frederick Stanley (1888-1967)

Fred Butters' racing career was overshadowed by that of his brother Frank. Before World War I Fred trained in Austria. After four years' internment in Austria, he returned to Britain, where for some years he assisted his father before setting up on his own, training at Newmarket from the early 1930s until his retirement in 1950, with the exception of a five-year spell at Kingsclere before the outbreak of war in 1939. His biggest success was in the 1937 Derby with Mid-day Sun.

C

CADWALADR, George (b. 1945)

George Cadwaladr, who served his apprenticeship with Eric Cousins, had his best season in 1966, when his 31 winners included the Royal Ascot double of King's Stand Stakes (Roughlyn) and Wokingham Stakes (My Audrey). He rode mainly abroad after 1976.

CAERGWRLE
(1965, ch f Crepello – Caerphilly, by Abernant)

Caergwrle was a fast filly up to a mile and won the 1,000 Guineas for her owner-breeder Mrs Gwen Murless, whose husband, Noel, trained the filly. She bred three minor winners at stud.

CAIRN ROUGE
(1977, b f Pitcairn – Little Hills, by Candy Cane)

Cairn Rouge, an unprepossessing Irish-trained filly who was retained for 3,000 gns as a yearling, ran her best races in the Champion Stakes, winning as a three-year-old from Master Willie and going down by two lengths into second place the following year. In between, she was sold privately to an American breeder, and after two runs in the States at the end of 1981 she retired to stud there. In all she won six races, including the Irish 1,000 Guineas and Royal Ascot's Coronation Stakes.

CALIGULA
(1917, gr c The Tetrarch – Snoot, by Perigord)

Owned by Mr M. Goculdas and trained by Harvey Leader, Caligula won the St Leger in 1920. He was the first of three sons of The Tetrarch to win that race. He was exported to Germany but proved very infertile as a sire.

CALLAGHAN, Neville Anthony (b. 1946)

Irish-born Neville Callaghan was a pupil with Ken Cundell before becoming assistant to Bruce Hobbs and then taking out a training licence for the first time at Newmarket in 1971. His first winner was Blessed Beauty at Wolverhampton on 9 March 1971, for the Stafford-Smith family for whom he was private trainer for a short time. He moved into a new yard in Newmarket in 1975, and in 1978 gained his first major success with Stanford in the Gimcrack Stakes. His best season numerically was 1978, with 40 winners.

CALL BOY
(1924, ch c Hurry On – Comedienne, by Bachelor's Double)

Call Boy, owned by Mr Frank Curzon and trained by Jack Watts, won the Derby in 1927. Mr Curzon was dying and knew it but he bravely mustered his last reserves of strength and led his colt in at Epsom. A few weeks later he was dead. Call Boy, whose four wins were worth £19,062, died in 1940, having proved almost sterile at stud.

CALVERT, John Boyd (b. 1917)

Jack Calvert began training under National Hunt Rules in 1948 and saddled his first winner on the Flat the following September, at Edinburgh. He trained first near Middlesbrough and moved to Hambleton in Yorkshire in 1955. His most notable winners were the sprinters Dondeen and Highland Melody, and the more stoutly constituted handicapper

Move Off. He retired before the start of the 1983 season and was succeeded at the leased Hambleton House stables near Thirsk by William Pearce.

CAMACHO, Maurice James Christopher (b. 1944)

Maurice Camacho worked for five years for *Timeform* before in 1966 he joined his stepfather Charlie Hall as assistant at their stables at Towton near Tadcaster. Camacho gradually took over more responsibility, and in 1975 he took over the licence, winning the Mackeson Gold Cup with Clear Cut in his first week. His first Flat winner was Burcom Buoy at Ripon on 2 June 1976. In 1982 he moved to Star Cottage at Malton in order to improve his facilities and in his first season equalled his best total of sixteen winners.

CAMAREE (1947, br f Maurepas – Couleur, by Biribi)

Camarée won the 1,000 Guineas in 1950 to give her French owner Jean Ternynck his first Classic success. She also won three races in France but failed in the Oaks, for which she started favourite. She was a half-sister to Marmelade, grandam of the Derby winner Sea-Bird II.

CAMBREMER (1953, ch c Chamossaire – Tomorrow, by Easton)

Bred in France by his owner, Mr R.B. Strassburger, Cambremer won the St Leger in 1956. The following season he won the Prix du Cadran and was second in the Ascot Gold Cup. He had no lasting effect as a sire.

CAMERA PATROL

The camera patrol, which began its first full year of operation in 1961 with 120 days' racing and seventeen courses covered by the Race Finish Recording Company, films a race to provide a lateral and head-on view of it. The film is available to the stewards within minutes of the race being over and is an invaluable witness in cases of alleged rough-riding, crossing, swerving, excessive use of the whip and so forth. It also exposes the cruder examples of lack of effort on the part of a jockey. The cost of the operation, now run by Racecourse Technical Services, was taken over by the Levy Board, and with rapid advances in technology, including the use of video recording, its scope has been considerably widened, so that in the Levy Board's financial year 1984-5, 726 days' racing was covered by a combination of film patrol and video patrol. To cut down the number of days without camera patrol, coverage by a single head-on camera was introduced in 1981.

CAMERONIAN (1928, b c Pharos – Una Cameron, by Gainsborough)

Cameronian was bred by Lord Dewar and on his death in 1930 passed into the possession of Mr J.A. Dewar, his nephew. Cameronian was trained by Fred Darling and in 1931 won the 2,000 Guineas and Derby. He started a hot favourite for the St Leger. Normally placid, he behaved like a mad horse before the race, when he kicked Orpen savagely, and also during it, when he fought for his head, ran himself out and was stone cold over half a mile from home.

Darling calmly refuted any suggestion that Cameronian had been 'got at' and, incredible as it may now seem, the stewards took no action. Cameronian had a temperature after the race and ran a slight put persistent temperature for a year afterwards. It was not until October 1932 that he really recovered his form and won the Champion Stakes in splendid style. As a sire he enjoyed only modest success both in Britain and in Argentina, where he was exported at the age of thirteen and died in 1955.

CAMPANULA (1931, b f Blandford – Vesper Bell, by Pommern)

Bred by her owner, Sir George Bullough, Campanula was a beautiful little filly who won the 1,000 Guineas and three other races for a total of £10,228. She bred six modest winners including Calluna, third dam of the St Leger winner Athens Wood, the Champion Stakes winner Vitigès and the 2,000 Guineas winner Bolkonski.

CANDY, Derrick Warner John (1908-83)

Derrick Candy, a regular soldier in the Sherwood Foresters before he served three years as assistant trainer to Miss Norah Wilmot, set up on his own in 1937. Apart from a brief return to military service in the Second World War, he continued to train in Berkshire until handing over to his son Henry in 1973. Though he won races at Royal Ascot in 1953 and 1954, his biggest successes came towards the end of his career, the most important being in the 1967 Ascot Gold Cup with Parbury. Candy went on to win several good races, including the King's Stand Stakes with the sprinter Song, the Jockey Club Cup three times with High Line, and the Cambridgeshire twice, with King Midas and Negus.

CANDY, Henry David Nicholas Bourne (b. 1944)

Having learnt about training in Australia and France, Henry Candy assisted his father, Derrick, before taking over the licence at Kingstone Warren at the end of the 1973 season. He won with his first runner, Kambalda, at Nottingham on 2 April 1974. He won the Cesarewitch with Assured in 1977 and two years later had big-race successes with Pipedreamer (Royal Hunt Cup), Quay Line (Park Hill Stakes) and Nicholas Bill (Jockey Club Cup). His next smart horse was Master Willie, winner of the Benson & Hedges Gold Cup, Jockey Club Stakes and Eclipse, and in 1982 he had his first Classic success, with Time Charter in the Oaks; she went on to win the Sun Chariot Stakes and Champion Stakes, and the following year took the King George VI and Queen Elizabeth Diamond Stakes. In 1984 she won the Coronation Cup, one of the few successes in a season when the stable was badly hit by a virus. Candy

has also become noted for his apprentices, including Billy Newnes and Tyrone Williams. His best season numerically was 1979 with 39 winners.

CANNON, Herbert Mornington (1873-1962)

Mornington Cannon was the son of Tom Cannon, a great rider in his day, and was named after a horse that won at Bath for his father the day he was born. 'Morny' himself was a beautiful horseman and excelled in waiting-tactics. He was at his best before the 'American Invasion' at the end of the nineteenth century, which caused races to be run at a faster pace and jockeys to pull up their leathers. He won the Triple Crown in 1899 on Flying Fox and was champion jockey on six occasions.

CANNON, Noel Victor Sharp (1897-1959)

Born near Newmarket, Noel Cannon was the son of Joe Cannon, who had won the Grand National on Regal and had a distinguished record as a trainer. Noel Cannon, who had been wounded in World War I when serving in the 3rd Hussars, trained in India and at Newmarket before running the famous Druid's Lodge establishment for its successive owners, Mr J.V. Rank, Mr J.A. Dewar and Mr Jack Olding. He won the St Leger with Scottish Union, Oaks with Why Hurry and 1,000 Guineas with Festoon. He was runner-up in the Derby with Scottish Union and Gay Time. He was responsible for bringing the Australian jockeys Scobie Breasley and Jack Purtell to ride in Britain. A forthright, friendly man, he was genuinely devoted to his horses, particularly to some of the old geldings that served him well season after season. He gave up training in 1958 and died the following year after a long illness.

CANNON, Thomas (1846-1917)

Born at Eton, Tom Cannon was one of the best riders of his day and won the Derby in 1882 on Shotover, as well as the 2,000 Guineas four times, 1,000 Guineas three times, Oaks four times and St Leger once. Imperturbable, a shrewd tactician and a wonderful judge of pace, he was gifted with the lightest of hands and was a brilliant rider of two-year-olds. Delicate in appearance, he was tougher than he looked, both on and off a horse, and seldom came off second best in a matter of business. When he gave up riding he trained a lot of winners at Danebury, and he was a very good trainer of jockeys too. His sons Mornington and Kempton both won the Derby in their day, and as a boy Jack Watts, who rode four Derby winners, was under his care.

CANNON, Walter Kempton (1879-1951)

Kempton Cannon was the brother of Mornington Cannon. Kempton rode his first winner at the age of fourteen and continued riding till shortly before World War I, in which he served in the RFC. He had a long association with Mr Leopold de Rothschild, for whom he won the St Leger on Doricles in 1901 and the 2,000 Guineas and Derby on St Amant in 1904. He married the widow of the famous jockey Jack Watts and for some years ran a garage at Newmarket, finally retiring to Hove where he lived in placid retirement till his death.

CANTELO (1956, b f Chanteur II – Rustic Bridge, by Bois Roussel)

Cantelo, owned and bred by the bookmaker Mr William Hill and trained by Captain Charles Elsey, won the St Leger in 1959. As she had been beaten by a 33-1 chance in the Park Hill Stakes two days previously, her victory was not well received by certain sections of the crowd. Cantelo also won the Royal Lodge Stakes, Cheshire Oaks and Ribblesdale Stakes and was second in the Oaks. She was not an outstanding success at stud, her best offspring being the Blue Riband Trial Stakes winner Cambridge.

CANTERBURY PILGRIM (1893, ch f Tristan – Pilgrimage, by The Earl or The Palmer)

Canterbury Pilgrim, foaled in 1893, was one of the many famous mares owned by the 17th Earl of Derby. She was by Tristan, a bad-tempered but game horse whose 25 victories included the Ascot Gold Cup, out of Pilgrimage, who won both the 1,000 and 2,000 Guineas and who bred the 100-1 Derby winner Jeddah, and also Loved One, sire of the dams of the Derby winners Sunstar and Sansovino. Canterbury Pilgrim herself won the Oaks and Jockey Club Cup and bred Swynford, who won the St Leger and Eclipse Stakes. She also bred Chaucer, who was outstandingly successful as a sire of broodmares.

CANYON (1913, b f Chaucer – Glasalt, by Isinglass)

canyon was one of the many good mares owned by the 17th Earl of Derby. She won the 1916 1,000 Guineas, and bred seven winners including Colorado (£30,358) and Caerleon (£11,210, including the Eclipse Stakes).

CAPTAIN CUTTLE (1919, ch c Hurry On – Bellavista, by Cyllene)

Bred by Lord Woolavington, Captain Cuttle was a fine, big chestnut. Trained by Fred Darling, he won four races, including the Derby (after being replated before the start) and St James's Palace Stakes. Owing to leg trouble he could not compete in the St Leger. As a four-year-old he ran only once and failed to stand further training. Retired to stud, he got Scuttle, who won the 1,000 Guineas for King George V, in his first crop. Captain Cuttle was sold for £50,000 and was exported to Italy in 1927. He did well there but died following an accident in 1932.

CARACALLA II
(1942, br c Tourbillon – Astronomie, by Astérus)

M. Boussac's Caracalla II won the Ascot Gold Cup in 1946 and was one of the best winners of that race this century. In an unbeaten career he also won the Grand Prix de Paris, French St Leger and Prix de l'Arc de Triomphe. He was not a success as a sire.

CARBINE
(1885, b c Musket – Mersey, by Knowsley)

Bred in New Zealand in 1885, Carbine had a fine racing record there and also in Australia, winning 33 races in four seasons. After four years at stud in Australia, he was bought by the Duke of Portland and brought to Britain. He was not an unqualified success in Britain but sired Spearmint, winner of the Derby and Grand Prix de Paris in 1906.

CAREY, Thomas Henry
(1905-71)

Tommy Carey was born in London and apprenticed to William Nightingall at Epsom at the age of fourteen. He rode a winner over hurdles when he was only sixteen, but he established his reputation before the war as the outstanding rider under Pony Turf Club rules. He won the Northolt Derby on several occasions. One of his principal Northolt patrons was Miss Dorothy Paget and, having been granted a licence to ride under the Rules of Racing in 1941, he won the 1943 Derby for her on Straight Deal. In 1946 he set up as a trainer at Epsom and for a time was very successful, Castleton winning the Blue Riband Trial Stakes and King Edward VII Stakes in 1952, but heavy gambling brought about his eventual downfall, and he handed in his licence in 1963. He died in America in April 1971.

CARLISLE

Carlisle provides unpretentious racing in a most attractive setting, the Lakeland hills forming the background. It is a right-handed, pear-shaped course just over 1½m round. The run-in of 3½f is uphill to the distance post from which point it is level, placing a premium on stamina in two-year-old races of 6f especially. The 6f course bears right for the first 1½f and there is a further bend just before the run-in. In races up to a mile, high numbers have the advantage. The main meeting is at the beginning of July when the Cumberland Plate (1½m) and the Carlisle Bell (1m) are run. Both events are now sponsored.

A matter of fifteen minutes prevented Carlisle from making history on 2 July 1929, when the earlier-starting Newmarket meeting claimed the first Tote dividend returned in British racing. Most significant recent improvements to Carlisle's facilities include a new Silver Ring and weighing-room block, while accessibility has been improved by means of the nearby M6 motorway.

CARNARVON, sixth Earl of (b. 1898)

Lord Carnarvon served in the 7th Hussars from 1915 to 1923. He rode on the Flat as an amateur for fourteen years and won seven races on Patmos. He bred many good horses at his Highclere Stud, including Blenheim, winner of the Derby, and King Salmon, second in the Derby and winner of the Eclipse Stakes. The best horse to carry his colours in recent years was Queen's Hussar, who, trained by Major Peter Nelson, won seven races, including the Sussex Stakes, and on retirement to his owner's stud produced a better racer than himself in Brigadier Gerard, as well as the Queen's filly Highclere. On Major Nelson's retirement, Lord Carnarvon had his horses trained by Captain Ryan Price, but his racing interests waned considerably while his son, Lord Porchester, took over Highclere.

Racing colours: scarlet, blue collar, white cap.

CARR, Ernest Joseph (b. 1915)

Joe Carr was apprenticed from 1930 to 1935 to Captain Cecil Boyd-Rochfort. He rode with some success under National Hunt Rules from 1936 to 1940 until his career was terminated by a bad fall which resulted in the loss of his right leg. He was serving in the Green Howards at the time. He began training in 1941 at Hambleton in Yorkshire and retired in June 1985.

CARR, Frank (b. 1927)

Frank Carr served his apprenticeship in Ireland with Joe Davis, before he travelled three horses to Britain in December 1947 and stayed. Carr worked for various trainers, mainly around Malton, and began his training career there in 1961 with a National Hunt licence. Two years later he moved into the famous Whitewall Stables and did well during a short, stormy but fruitful spell training for bookmaker John Banks, for whom he won the 1969 Royal Hunt Cup with Kamundu. When he relinquished his licence in January 1977 to start training in Hong Kong, he handed over the running of his stables to his former head man, Ted Carter. He returned to Britain to train again in 1984 but he found races harder to win with modest material, and had two winners in his first season and more in 1985.

CARR, William Henry (1916-85)

Harry Carr was born in Cumberland and as a boy was apprenticed to R.W. Armstrong, to whom his father acted as head lad. He rode his first winner in 1930. He was a sound, reliable, sensible rider and an extremely loyal servant, for many years associated with Sir Cecil Boyd-Rochfort's stable and retained as royal jockey from 1947. He retired in 1964 and ran the Genesis Green Stud near Newmarket, until selling to the Swinburn family in 1984.

His big winners were: *1,000 Guineas:* Meld (1955), *Derby:* Parthia (1959), *Oaks:* Meld (1955), *St Leger:* Meld (1955), Alcide (1958) and Hethersett (1962), *King George VI and Queen Elizabeth Stakes:* Alcide (1959).

He also won the Lingfield Derby Trial five times, Lingfield Oaks Trial five times, Doncaster Cup three times, Goodwood Stakes three times, Coventry Stakes three times and Yorkshire Cup three times. In India, where he used to ride in the winter, he won the Indian Derby and the King Emperor's Cup.

CARROZZA (1954, br f Dante – Calash, by Hyperion)

Bred by the National Stud and leased to the Queen for racing, Carrozza became Her Majesty's first Classic winner when she won the Oaks in 1957. Before her sale to America for 20,000gns at the 1964 Newmarket December Sales, she bred three moderate winners, including Battle-Waggon, who became a leading sire on export to New Zealand. Carrozza is the grandam of the 1975 Grand Prix de Paris winner Matahawk.

CARSLAKE, Bernard (1886-1941)

Dark and somewhat saturnine, Bernard Carslake was popularly known as 'Brownie' and was one of the best and most stylish of the many good Australian jockeys who have ridden in Britain. He made a brief visit to Britain in 1906, but before World War I he rode with success in Austria-Hungary, moving on at the outbreak of war to Rumania and from there to Russia, whence he escaped with difficulty during the Revolution, arriving in Britain penniless in 1917. A particularly powerful finisher, he soon established himself and, though he never won the Derby, he had six victories in the Classics – one each in the 2,000 Guineas and Oaks, two in the 1,000 Guineas, and three in the St Leger. His win in the 1924 St Leger on Salmon-Trout was a truly remarkable one and gave rise to some sinister rumours. One leading bookmaker, who had laid Salmon-Trout as if he knew that the horse could not possibly win, was placed in grave financial difficulties.

Throughout his career Carslake had trouble in keeping his weight down, and constant wasting ultimately undermined his health. He was only 55 when he died. His ashes were scattered over Newmarket Heath.

CARSON, Alexander (1926-81)

Jock Carson was a well-known northern lightweight jockey for many years. He had his best season of 38 winners in 1946, while still apprenticed to Matt Peacock, when his total was only two short of the leading apprentice and included twenty trained by Noel Murless. His most important victory was in the 1949 Chester Cup on the 25-1 chance John Moore. He retired in 1972, having ridden his last winner in 1968.

CARSON, William Hunter (b. 1942)

Willie Carson's career as a jockey provides a perfect advertisement for the virtue of patience. Born in Stirling, he was three years into his apprenticeship with Gerald Armstrong at Middleham before he rode his first winner, at Catterick Bridge in July 1962. The following year, when Gerald Armstrong retired, Carson's indentures were transferred to his brother Sam at Newmarket, and when he ended his apprenticeship in 1965, he had ridden 58 winners. Six years later he rode 100 winners in a season for the first time, his total of 145 putting him second in the jockeys' table to Lester Piggott, and in 1972 he rode his first Classic winner, High Top in the 2,000 Guineas, and was champion jockey for the first time, with 132 winners.

Champion jockey again in 1973 with 164 winners, Carson was principally employed by Bernard van Cutsem, but in 1975 he rode for Barry Hills and in 1976 for Clive Brittain. In the summer of 1976 it was announced that Carson was taking over from Joe Mercer the following year as stable jockey for Major Dick Hern, and in his first season, the year of the Queen's Silver Jubilee, he won the Oaks and St Leger on Her Majesty's Dunfermline. He won the Derby for the stable on Troy (1979) and Henbit (1980) and completed the Epsom Classic double in 1980 on Bireme in the Oaks, which he might have won six years earlier but for Dibidale's saddle slipping under her belly. He also won the 2,000 Guineas (on Known Fact), French Derby (on Policeman), and Irish Oaks (on Shoot A Line) in 1980, and his subsequent Classic winners, all for Hern, have been Swiftfoot (Irish Oaks), Sun Princess (Oaks and St Leger) and Helen Street (Irish Oaks).

Carson was champion jockey again in 1978 (his best season with 182 winners), 1980 (166) and 1983 (159) and managed to retain second place with 114 winners in 1981 despite having to miss the rest of the season after a horrific fall at York on 18 August. Determination to win and a pleasing personality have made Carson as popular with the racing public as any jockey in recent years.

CARTER, Gary (b. 1965)

Born in West Ham, Gary Carter followed his year-older brother Roy into racing stables at Newmarket, having spells with Gerry Blum, Paul Kelleway and 'Chuck' Spares before he joined Geoff Huffer in 1983. Carter's career blossomed in 1985, and having set himself a target of 20 winners, a sustained late run of success, including on Shellman in the £15,000 *Mail on Sunday* Autumn Handicap, took him to 37 winners from 379 rides and a share of the apprentice championship with the more-experienced Willie Ryan.

CARTER, Thomas (b. 1930)

Tommy Carter served his apprenticeship with George Todd and for many years retained a reputation as one of the best lightweight jockeys. Though he won several rich handicaps, including the Newbury Spring, Summer and Autumn Cups, the City and Suburban, William Hill Gold Cup and Cesarewitch, he also won the Nunthorpe Stakes (on My Beau) and Queen's Vase (Yellow River) when weight was at a premium. He was forced to retire in January 1976 as a result of an injury sustained the previous July.

CAST IN HIS BOX

A horse is said to be cast in his box when he has got down in a stable or vehicle and has difficulty in getting up without assistance.

CATHERINA

Catherina, who was foaled in 1830 and raced from 1832 to 1841, established a record for success that has never been broken nor is ever likely to be broken. She raced 176 times – on the first two occasions without a name – and won 79 times for total earnings of just over £5,000. She had her first foal in 1846 but, after proving barren to her 1857 mating, was put down the following year at the age of 28.

CATTERICK BRIDGE

Catterick Bridge will never rival some other Yorkshire courses for its beauty, but the enterprising direction of Major Leslie Petch on appointment as Clerk of the Course in 1947 and managing director four years later brought many improvements to the track and its facilities. It is a sharp, undulating, left-handed course that is only just over a mile round with a run-in of 3f. It is an ideal track for quick starters and front-runners, the reverse for big, long-striding horses that take time to settle down. A low draw is essential in sprint races, but a fast start is as important.

CAUTHEN, Stephen Mark (b. 1960)

Steve Cauthen came to Britain from the United States in 1979 in a blaze of publicity, following his breaking of several US records, and he got away to a flying start by winning on his first ride, Marquee Universal at Salisbury on 7 April 1979.

Cauthen rode his first winner shortly after his sixteenth birthday; in 1977 he won more than $1m dollars in the first six weeks and ended with 487 winners for $6m from 2,075 rides; in 1978 he won the US Triple Crown on Affirmed but then had a lean spell and accepted Robert Sangster's offer to come to Britain. In his first year he won the 2,000 Guineas on Tap On Wood and rode 52 winners. Each year has been one of successive progress, with one small exception, and in 1984 he became the first American to be British champion jockey, with 130 winners, since Danny Maher in 1908 (when Maher won the title in 1913 he was a naturalized Briton).

In this period his big winners for Barry Hills, with whose stable he was most

associated, included Tap On Wood, Arapahos (Chester Cup), Last Feather (Musidora Stakes), Desirable (Cheveley Park), Cormorant Wood (Champion, Benson & Hedges Gold Cup) and Gildoran (Ascot Gold Cup, Goodwood Cup), but he soon attracted support from other major stables, winning important handicaps, such as the Cambridgeshire (Braughing) and Lincoln and Royal Hunt Cup (Mighty Fly), and conditions events such as the Goodwood Cup (Heighlin), William Hill Sprint (Sharpo) and St James's Palace Stakes (Horage).

In 1984 he won the Mecca-Dante Stakes on Claude Monet for Henry Cecil. This was to preface his move to Warren Place, to replace Lester Piggott as stable jockey, in 1985, and the association was an instant success, winning four of the five Classics with Oh So Sharp (1,000 Guineas, Oaks and St Leger) and Slip Anchor, whose success in the Derby made Cauthen the first to complete the double of Kentucky and Epsom Derbys. Cauthen retained his title in 1985 with 195 winners, the highest total since Gordon Richards in 1952.

CECIL, Henry Richard Amherst (b. 1943)

Stepson of Sir Cecil Boyd-Rochfort, Henry Cecil is married to Sir Noel Murless's daughter Julie. He began training at Newmarket after Sir Cecil's retirement in 1968 and was instantly successful, winning the Eclipse Stakes in 1969 with Wolver Hollow in his first season, when he also won the Observer Gold Cup with Approval. He won his first Classic with Cloonagh, owned by his half-brother Arthur Boyd-Rochfort, in the 1973 Irish 1,000 Guineas, and his first British Classic two years later with Bolkonski in the 2,000 Guineas. He won the 2,000 Guineas again in 1976, with Wollow, and that year was leading trainer for the first time.

Leading trainer in 1978 and 1979, he had record earnings (£683,971) and a twentieth-century record number of winners (128) on the latter occasion, when he won the 1,000 Guineas with One In A Million and completed the Cup treble at

Ascot, Goodwood and Doncaster with Le Moss, a feat he repeated with the same horse in 1980, when he also won the St Leger with Light Cavalry. He might have made it a hat-trick of Cup hat-tricks had he not withdrawn Ardross on the day of the 1981 Doncaster Cup after winning at Ascot and Goodwood.

A meticulous planner who would prefer to be at home with his horses rather than travelling the country unnecessarily, Cecil rarely runs his horses where they do not have a chance (especially abroad) and has shown himself adept with all types, from sprinters to stayers, and two-year-olds to seniors. He achieved one of the few feats left open to him when winning the Derby with Slip Anchor in 1985, the year he also won the 1,000 Guineas, Oaks and St Leger with Oh So Sharp, and became leading trainer for the sixth time with record win-money earnings of £1,148,189, from a twentieth-century record total of 132 winners.

CHALK JOCKEY

At most courses there are boards with the names of established jockeys on them ready for use in the number boards. Little-known riders have their names inscribed on blank boards in white chalk. The term is steadily going out of fashion, since most courses realize the value of sophisticated presentation of information for their customers.

CHALONER, Thomas (1839-86)

Tom Chaloner rode Macaroni to victory in the 1863 Derby. He also rode five winners of the St Leger and three of the 2,000 Guineas. He had the reputation of being an honest, reliable and unassuming man.

CHAMOSSAIRE (1942, Precipitation – Snowberry, by Cameronian)

Bred by the National Stud, Chamossaire was bought for 2,700gns as a yearling to be owned by Mr Stanhope Joel and trained by Dick Perryman. He won four races worth over £11,000 including the St Leger which in 1945 was run at York. His record as a sire was inconsistent, but he was champion in 1964 when his son Santa Claus won the Derby and Irish Derby. He also sired the St Leger winner Cambremer and two other Irish Derby winners in Chamier and Your Highness. He died in 1964.

CHAMPION

Champion, who won the Derby in 1800, was the first such winner to win the St Leger as well. He was owned by Mr Christopher Wilson of Tadcaster, Yorkshire.

CHANTEUR II (1942, br c Château Bouscaut – La Diva, by Blue Skies)

Bred in France, Chanteur II was brought to Britain as a five-year-old after being bought by the bookmaker Mr William Hill. He won seven races in France and three in Britain, including the Coronation Cup. He was twice second in the Gold Cup. He did well as a sire and was champion in 1953, the year his son Pinza won the Derby. He also sired the St Leger winner Cantelo and Only For Life, winner of the 2,000 Guineas. His daughters, apart from Cantelo, included Bracey Bridge (Ribblesdale Stakes and Park Hill Stakes), Patti (second in St Leger) and Chorus Beauty (dam of Windmill Girl). Chanteur II died in 1962.

CHAPMAN, David William (b. 1933)

One horse can make the difference to a trainer, and Soba did it for David Chapman when she won eleven races in 1982, including the Stewards' Cup. For eighteen years he got by with little publicity and winners in single figures, having taken out a permit to train at his family's York farm in 1964, a jump licence in 1967 and a Flat licence in 1971. Then came Soba, and Chapman's string increased and so did his number of winners, with 1984 bringing his best season with 34.

CHARLEBELLE
(1917, bl f Charles O'Malley – Bushey Belle, by Bushey Park)

Owned and bred by Mr A.P. Cunliffe, Charlebelle won five races for £6,733, including the Oaks in 1920. She bred one moderate winner before being exported to America as an eight-year-old.

CHARLOTTESVILLE
(1957, b c Prince Chevalier – Noorani, by Nearco)

Connections did well with Charlottesville who was not easy to train yet won five races in a row as a three-year-old, including the French Derby and Grand Prix de Paris. In all he won six races for the equivalent of £75,507, and his syndication gave him a record European stallion valuation of £336,000. Owned and bred by the late Aga Khan and Prince Aly Khan, he retired to their stud in Ireland, and his best offspring were Charlottown (Derby), Carlemont (Sussex Stakes), Canterbury (second in St Leger, won Doncaster Cup), Bonconte di Montefeltro (Italian 2,000 Guineas and Derby), Meadowville (second in Irish Sweeps Derby and British and Irish St Legers) and Biskrah (Doncaster Cup). Charlottesville died suddenly after a heart attack in 1972.

CHARLOTTOWN
(1963, b c Charlottesville – Meld, by Alycidon)

Charlottown, bred and owned by Lady Zia Wernher and trained by Jack Gosden at Lewes, was unbeaten as a two-year-old in 1965. The following year, when trained by Gordon Smyth following Gosden's retirement through ill health, he won the Derby and was runner-up in the Irish Derby and the St Leger. As a four-year-old he won the Coronation Cup, but he did not run again after his only bad race, when he finished down the course in the Grand Prix de Saint-Cloud. His seven victories were worth £101,210. He did not fulfil expectations at stud and in 1976 became the first Derby winner to be exported to Australia, where he was put down three years laters after an accident.

CHARNOCK, Lindsay (b. 1955)

Born at Wigan, Lindsay Charnock began his apprenticeship near home, with Ron Barnes in Cheshire, ending it with Denys Smith at Bishop Auckland. His first winner came on his thirteenth ride in public, on Sally's Choice at Lanark on 1 May 1972. His first major success came on Last Tango in the 1976 Ayr Gold Cup, a ride he picked up on the day when the horse's intended jockey failed to arrive because of fog. Charnock left the Smith stable in 1979 and has been a freelance in the North ever since. He won the Portland Handicap in 1984 with Dawn's Delight and the following year had his first Royal Ascot win on Clanrallier in the Bessborough Stakes. His best season was 1985 with 32 winners.

CHATELAINE
(1930, b f Phalaris – Herself, by Neil Gow)

Bred at the Sledmere Stud in Yorkshire, Châtelaine won 3½ races for a total of £8,332, including the Oaks at 25-1 in 1933 for Mr E. Thornton-Smith. Her first foal had to be put down, and she died after producing a dead foal to her second service.

CHELANDRY
(1894, br f Goldfinch – Illuminata, by Rosicrucian)

Lord Rosebery's Chelandry, a half-sister to the Derby winner Ladas, won the 1897 1,000 Guineas, and over £13,000 in stakes. At stud she bred six winners of over £42,000 in stakes including Neil Gow, winner of the 2,000 Guineas. Chelandry is one of the great tap roots of modern bloodstock and her descendants include further British Classic winners in Pogrom, Saucy Sue, Pay Up, Book Law, Galatea II, Ocean Swell and Never Say Die, the Italian Derby winners Traghetto and Barba Toni, and the Kentucky Derby winner Tomy Lee.

CHEPSTOW

Chepstow is the newest course to operate Flat racing under Jockey Club Rules, having first come into operation in 1926. The setting is most attractive, and the combination of go-ahead management, new grandstands built in 1965 and the improvement of access brought about by the opening of the Severn Bridge in 1966 has increased its popularity, though the quality of the racing remains competitive rather than high class.

It was at Chepstow in 1933 that Gordon Richards rode all six winners on the first day of a meeting and the first five winners on the second day.

It is a left-handed track about 2m round with a run-in of 5f. The mile course is straight and undulating. The various gradients call for an adaptable, well-balanced horse. High numbers are reckoned to hold a slight advantage on the straight course.

CHERIMOYA
(1908, b or br f Cherry Tree – Svelte, by St Simon)

Ridden by Fred Winter, father of the famous National Hunt rider, Cherimoya won the Oaks in 1911 at 25-1. That was her only race. She bred three winners of no particular merit on the racecourse, but her maiden daughter Una Cameron bred Cameronian.

CHERRY LASS
(1902, b f Isinglass – Black Cherry, by Bendigo)

Colonel W. Hall Walker's Cherry Lass won ten races and prize money of over £15,000, including the 1,000 Guineas and Oaks in 1905. She died in 1914 after producing two winners from her four foals.

CHESTER

Chester's Roodee is one of the most famous and unusual courses in the country. It is also one of the most ancient, and records of racing there exist from 1540. The course is shaped like a plate, just over a mile in circumference, and the run-in is only 230 yds, the shortest on any British track. Low numbers are favoured in the draw, more so in sprints, where it is equally important to get a fast break to make the most of the advantage. Horses are racing on the bend the whole way and not surprisingly a number fail to adapt themselves to the conditions. Nevertheless the Chester Vase is regarded as a significant Derby trial and numbers among its winners Derby victors such as Papyrus, Hyperion, Windsor Lad, Henbit and Shergar.

The big meeting at Chester is early in May, and the most famous race, the Chester Cup, is a 2¼m 97yd handicap in which the runners pass the stands three times. Particularly on Cup day, spectators throng the city walls in thousands to watch the sport. In the last century the Cup was second only to the Derby in the volume of ante-post betting it inspired.

CHIFNEY, Samuel
(1753-1807)

Sam Chifney senior, who won the 1789 Derby on Skyscraper, was the best jockey of his day. A native of Norfolk, he was a man whose personality was a mixture of genius, low cunning and unbelievable conceit. However, his reiterated claim – 'I could ride horses in a better manner in a race than any other person known in my time' – was doubtless justified. Moreover, he was responsible for the training of his son, also Sam Chifney, who became an even better rider than his father.

The Escape affair was Chifney senior's downfall. On 20 October 1791 he rode the Prince of Wales's Escape at Newmarket and finished last of four. Escape was favourite and there was a widely held suspicion that Chifney had not done his best to win. Chifney, however, said the horse was short of a gallop. Escape ran again the following day and won. There was an inquiry by the stewards, and Sir Charles Bunbury, the leading figure on the Turf at that period, told the Prince that no gentleman would run his horse against him if he continued to employ Chifney. The Prince stood up for his servant, shook the dust of Newmarket off his heels, and never raced there again.

The Prince promised to continue paying Chifney his retaining fee of 200gns but the promise was not fulfilled and Chifney died in the Fleet Prison, to which he had been committed for debt.

Today, Chifney's explanation might well have been accepted. Escape had never been a consistent horse and in any case he may well have needed a race. Furthermore the two races were over different distances. Probably the stewards were determined to drop on Chifney, who had for long been under suspicion, but they selected an unsuitable occasion for so doing.

Chifney completed the Epsom Classic double in 1789, on Skyscraper (Derby) and Tag (Oaks), and won the Oaks on a further three occasions.

CHIFNEY, Samuel (1786-1854)

Sam Chifney junior was, like his father, a brilliant rider and like his father too, he was rated unscrupulous. He was 32 when he won the Derby in 1818 on Sam, and he won the race again two years later on Sailor, both trained by his brother Will. Sam was 57 when he won his last Classic race, the 1,000 Guineas, on Extempore in 1843. Phlegmatic and indolent by nature, he became downright slothful as he grew older and in consequence missed many winning rides, a deprivation that did not perturb him in the least.

CHIFNEY, William (1784-1862)

Son of Sam Chifney senior, Will Chifney became a very successful trainer, noted for the regularity with which he brought off betting coups. His three Derby winners were Sam (1818), Sailor (1820) and Priam (1830). Priam, generally rated an outstanding Derby winner, was owned by Chifney, who bought him as a two-year-old for 1,000gns, but was the only one of the three not ridden by his brother Sam, who was claimed for another runner. Towards the end of his career, Will Chifney suffered serious losses, and he died in poverty at the age of 77.

CHILDS, Joe (1885-1958)

Joe Childs, a great jockey, rode fifteen British Classic winners and two winners of the Grand Prix de Paris. For the last ten years of his career he was jockey to King George V.

He was born in France, at Chantilly, one of five brothers who became jockeys. He came to Britain to be apprenticed to Tom Jennings junior and rode his first winner in 1900. Receiving scant patronage once he had lost his allowance, he returned to France in 1903. At that stage of his life he could never control his explosive temper in face of criticism, and jobs with M. Caillault, the Duc de Gramont and an Italian stable were held briefly.

His luck turned in 1908 when he won the Grand Prix on North East, and the following year he rode with success for Prince Murat. Constant wasting, though, was affecting his health and he agreed to ride for two years for the Weinberg brothers in Germany, the contract containing no stipulation with regard to a minimum weight. Fred Darling was then training for the Weinberg brothers, and with two such peppery individuals in one stable, the sparks flew with no little frequency.

In 1912 Childs returned to France and that year won the Oaks on Mirska. In 1914 he got out of Chantilly by the last train before the Germans arrived, leaving all his possessions behind him. He joined the RFC but even the fairly liberal concept of discipline in that organization was too much for him and he transferred to the 4th Hussars, a friendly regiment that gave him plenty of riding leave. In 1918, when he won the Triple Crown on Gainsborough, he gave all his riding fees to regimental funds. In 1916 he had ridden his first Derby winner on Fifinella.

In 1919 he was beaten in the St Leger on the odds-on favourite, Lord Astor's Buchan. Major Gerald Deane, Lord Astor's racing manager, made some sarcastic comments; Childs never rode for Lord Astor again.

He had his third Derby winner in 1926 on Coronach, who also won the St Leger. In 1928 he won the 1,000 Guineas for the

King on Scuttle. Probably the best race he ever rode was the Hardwicke Stakes, which he won for the King on Limelight.

Strong and exceptionally patient, Childs excelled at the waiting game. Tall for a jockey, lithe and beetle-browed, he could be formidable, and young jockeys stood in fearful awe of him, but he mellowed considerably with age. On retirement he controlled a greyhound racing track at Portsmouth and occasionally owned a horse in partnership with his friend George Digby.

Childs' Classic winners were:

2,000 Guineas: Gainsborough (1918), Cameronian (1931).

1,000 Guineas: Scuttle (1928), Brown Betty (1933).

Derby: Fifinella (1916), Gainsborough (1918), Coronach (1926).

Oaks: Mirska (1912), Fifinella (1916), Bayuda (1919), Love In Idleness (1921).

St Leger: Gainsborough (1918), Polemarch (1921), Solario (1925), Coronach (1926).

CHULMLEIGH
(1934, b c Singapore – Rose of England, by Teddy)

Bred and owned by Lord Glanely, Chulmleigh won two races – a three-runner event at Chepstow and the St Leger, both in 1937. He did not run again after the Leger and, after limited opportunities in seven seasons at stud in Britain, was exported to Argentina.

CHURCHILL, Sir Winston Leonard Spencer (1874-1965)

Lord Randolph Churchill, Winston's father, had been a keen racing man and won the Oaks with L'Abbesse de Jouarre. Sir Winston himself liked horses and hunting and was an enthusiastic polo-player during his service in India with the 4th Hussars, but he was 75 years of age when he first registered his racing colours (of pink, chocolate sleeves and cap) and appointed Walter Nightingall his trainer. His first horse was the stout-hearted French-bred grey Colonist II, who won 13 races, including the Jockey Club Cup

and the Winston Churchill Stakes, and became a great favourite with the public. High Hat won for Sir Winston over £15,000 in stakes and became a successful sire, while Vienna won £14,900 in stakes in Britain, 103,350 NF in France, and sired Vaguely Noble. Sir Winston also owned Welsh Abbot, who won the Portland Handicap at Doncaster as a three-year-old with 9st 2lb, and Tudor Monarch, who won the Stewards' Cup at Goodwood. Sir Winston was a member of the Jockey Club.

CICERO
(1902, ch c Cyllene – Gas, by Ayrshire)

Cicero won the 1905 Derby for Lord Rosebery, his third and last Derby winner. He had won four races as a two-year-old, when he did not race after July. At stud the best horse he got was the speedy Friar Marcus.

CIECHANOWSKI, John Mary Stanislas (b. 1921)

A Pole who fled to France in the Second World War, John Ciechanowski rode as an amateur immediately after the war and then pursued a varied career with horses all over the world. He was with Tom Masson at Lewes, went to Brazil and assisted Maurice Zilber in France, Tom Jones in Britain and Vincent O'Brien in Ireland, as well as advising a number of studs in France at various times. He then became private trainer to Sheikh Mohammed in Dubai, where he had a stable of 120 horses; that led to his taking up a similar position at Lambourn in 1983. He had his first winner with Non-Wet at Lingfield on 8 July 1983, his only success that season. He retired in 1985.

CINNA
(1917, b or br f Polymelus – Baroness La Flèche, by Ladas)

Cinna won three races for £8,811, including the 1,000 Guineas in 1920. She was also second, beaten a neck, in the Oaks. She bred eight winners, including Beau Père, a moderate racehorse who became an outstanding sire in New Zealand, Australia and finally America.

CIRCUS PLUME
(1981, b f High Top – Golden Fez, by Aureole)

Having sold Golden Fez for 15,000gns in 1977, Sir Robin McAlpine bought her 1981 produce as a foal for 98,000gns. Named Circus Plume, she won once as a two-year-old and three times the following year, including the Epsom Oaks and Yorkshire Oaks. She got a bad run when second in the Irish Oaks but did really well when runner-up in the Prix Vermeille. She was not so effective as a four-year-old and retired to stud without further success.

CLAIMER, Claiming race

The term 'claimer' is used loosely to describe an apprentice who is claiming an allowance for not having ridden a certain number of winners. A claiming race is one in which the runners can be subject to sealed bids up to ten minutes after the weighed-in signal is given. If there are two or more equal claims for the same horse, the successful bid is drawn by lot. No-one may claim more than one horse in a race; no horse may be claimed by its owner or part-owner or their spouses, and the successful claimant is not allowed to send the horse to the person who trained it for the claiming race.

CLARISSIMUS
(1913, b c Radium – Quintessence, by St Frusquin)

Clarissimus won the 2,000 Guineas and Champion Stakes. He was exported to France and did well at stud there, especially as a producer of mares, who included the dams of Donatello II, Pharis II and Brantôme.

CLARK, Anthony Stephen (b. 1962)

Welshman Tony Clark served his apprenticeship with Guy Harwood, winning his first race in 1979, and has remained with the Pulborough stable as understudy to Greville Starkey. When given the chance in major events, he has not let anyone down, winning the Stewards' Cup on Repetitious, the Wokingham on Battle Hymn and the Laurent Perrier Champagne Stakes on Lear Fan. His best season was 1984, with 29 winners.

CLARK, Robert Sterling
(1877-1956)

Mr Robert Sterling Clark, a great American sportsman with no interest in the betting side of racing, became a patron of the British Turf in 1930. After a dispute with the New York Jockey Club in 1946 he transferred all his racing interests, bar his stud, to Britain. At one time he owned a stud in France, but all the buildings there were destroyed in the Normandy battle in 1944. He won the 1,000 Guineas and Oaks in 1939 with Galatea II, and the Derby and St Leger in 1954 with Never Say Die. Both were trained for him by Joe Lawson, though Arthur Budgett, who trained the speedy Hook Money, and Harry Peacock also trained for him.

CLASSIC RACE

Though the term 'Classic race' has not been officially defined by the major racing powers, it has become generally accepted that there are five such events run in Britain. In chronological order of inception they are: the St Leger (first run in 1776), the Oaks (1779), the Derby (1780), the 2,000 Guineas (1809) and the 1,000 Guineas (1814). In chronological order through the season they are the 1,000 and 2,000 Guineas, both run over 1m at Newmarket; the Derby and the Oaks, both run over 1½m at Epsom; and the St Leger, run over 1m 6f 127yd at Doncaster. No horse has won all five Classics, but Sceptre won all bar the Derby, in which she was fourth in 1902. As a filly, Sceptre was eligible for all five Classics. Colts are not eligible for the 1,000 Guineas and Oaks, and geldings are no longer eligible for any.

CLAYTON, John Maurice (1902-75)

Jack Clayton, a well-liked member of the racing community and a familiar figure on the Turf for almost 50 years, had the reputation of being a bold punter in his younger days. Later he was racing manager to Mr and Mrs J.V. Rank and subsequently to Sir Victor Sassoon. He was a powerful influence in the Newmarket stable for which Norman Bertie held the licence and which won the Derby with Pinza and the 1,000 Guineas with Belle of All. When Bertie retired in 1961, Clayton took out a licence himself at Bedford House Stables in Newmarket. He won the 1962 Doncaster Cup with the ex-Italian colt Bonnard in his first season but could not recapture the glory of former years, and his biggest wins came in handicaps, the 1968 News of the World Stakes with Principal Boy and the 1974 Portland Handicap with Matinée.

CLAYTON, Stanley Thomas (1926-85)

Stan Clayton was apprenticed from 1940 to 1949 to Billy Smallwood, in his native South Yorkshire, and rode his first winner in 1943 at Pontefract. His two most important successes as a rider were to win the Oaks for Major Holliday on Neasham Belle and the Eclipse for the Queen on Canisbay. He also won the Portland Handicap on Sir Winston Churchill's Welsh Abbot on the owner's golden wedding anniversary. Clayton's other notable successes included the Goodwood Cup (twice), City and Suburban (three times), Ribblesdale Stakes, Yorkshire Oaks and Yorkshire Cup. He retired from riding in 1969 and enjoyed success as a trainer in Scandinavia until returning to Britain as assistant trainer to Jack Clayton (who was no relation). Stan Clayton was at Newmarket from 1972 until 1975, when he joined Major Dick Hern, but ill health forced him to retire from racing in 1979. He returned to his home town of Doncaster and died there in September 1985.

CLIFT, William (1762-1840)

William Clift rode the first of his five Derby winners in 1793, the last in 1819. A hardy South Yorkshireman who began life as a shepherd, he was notoriously uncouth and a contemporary described him as a 'rough, uncultivated Indian'. His manners towards his employers were brusque in the extreme, no matter how exalted their status. He was honest but unpolished in his methods and inclined to be hard on his horses. When he was nearly 80 years old, he used to walk to Newmarket from Bury St Edmunds and back again 'just to give my legs a stretch'. His Derby successes were on Waxy (1793), Champion (1800), Ditto (1803), Whalebone (1810) and Tiresias (1819). He also won the 2,000 Guineas, 1,000 Guineas, Oaks and St Leger twice each.

COATES, David (b. 1950)

Apprenticed to the County Durham trainer 'Taffy' Williams, David Coates dead-heated with Richard Dicey for the position of leading apprentice in 1968. Both rode 40 winners. Increasing weight soon restricted Coates's chances, and from 1971 he rode with success in Scandinavia.

COCHRANE, Raymond (b. 1957)

Ray Cochrane owed his initial success to the filly Nagwa, whom he rode while apprenticed to Barry Hills to win nine races in 1975, and his emergence as a senior jockey to Chief Singer, on whom he won the St James's Palace Stakes, July Cup and Sussex Stakes in 1984 for Ron Sheather. He also won the Lincoln Handicap on Saher for Sheather, whom he joined as a work rider in 1978. His best season was 1985, with 51 winners, including, Lochtillum in the Portland Handicap.

COLE, Paul Frederick Irvine (b. 1941)

Paul Cole was assistant to Richmond Sturdy and George Todd and had spells with the Cheveley Park Stud and Les Kennard before he began training in 1968 at Lambourn. His first major wins were in handicaps, with Calibina (Wokingham Stakes and Stewards' Cup) and Crimson Beau (Extel Stakes), and he was also responsible for two leading apprentices in Robert Edmondson and David Dineley in the 1970s, and they were followed by Richard Quinn in 1984. Quinn became the exception by remaining with Cole when he came out of his time for the 1985 season, when the trainer moved to Whatcombe with the backing of his principal owner, Fahd Salman. Numerically his best seasons were 1979 and 1984, with 61 winners.

COLLING, George Scott (1904-59)

George Colling came of sound racing stock. His father was the Newmarket trainer R.W. Colling, who had married a daughter of the steeplechase jockey Robert I'Anson and was 81 when he retired from training in 1953.

George Colling was a fine rider in his youth and as an apprentice rode over 70 winners in 1919. Increasing weight caused him to relinquish his licence in 1922. For many years he assisted his brother, Robert John Colling, and it was not until 1935 that he set up as a trainer on his own. He was just beginning to establish himself when war broke out. He at once joined the Royal Artillery, in which he served till invalided out in 1942.

After the war his stable at Hurworth House, Newmarket, rapidly filled. In 1949 he won the 2,000 Guineas and Derby with Nimbus but was ill on Derby Day and never saw the race.

In 1950 he was asked by Lord Derby to train for him at Stanley House and agreed to do so, but he never settled down happily there and in 1956 he was back at Hurworth House. Among the notable horses he trained were Wilwyn, winner of the inaugural Washington D.C. International at Laurel Park in 1952, when he won eleven consecutive races; Ark Royal, whose misfortune it was to be born in the same year as Meld; Acropolis, third in the Derby, and Mossborough.

Quiet, courteous and extremely shrewd, Colling possessed a high degree of professional ability. For much of his life, though, he was dogged by indifferent health which was doubtless the cause of his somewhat pessimistic views on many aspects of life.

COLLING, Robert John (1900-81)

Jack Colling was born in Yorkshire, the son of Bob Colling and elder brother of George. He spent about six years as a jockey, finishing second in the 1918 Derby, but increasing weight forced him to take up training soon after World War I. He spent 30 years at Newmarket, where his best horses included Cat O'Nine Tails (Ebor Handicap), the smart sprinters Bellacose and Portobello, and the highly successful gelding High Stakes. Lord Astor owned High Stakes and Colling continued to train for the family when he moved to West Ilsley in 1949.

Colling won his only Classic, the Oaks, with the 3rd Lord Astor's Ambiguity in 1953, but Hornbeam finished second in the St Leger, Rosalba second in the 1,000 Guineas and Escort fourth in the Derby, all winning good races besides. He retired from training in 1962 but for several years advised Mr David Robinson on the purchase of bloodstock.

COLOMBO (1931, b c Manna – Lady Nairne, by Chaucer)

Bred by Sir Alec Black and owned by Lord Glanely, who bought him as a yearling in 1932 for 510gns, Colombo swept aside all opposition as a two-year-old and was prematurely hailed as 'the horse of the century'. The following season he maintained his unbeaten record in the spring by winning the Craven Stakes and 2,000 Guineas. He was favourite for the Derby at 11-8 but in a sensational race finished only third to Windsor Lad and Easton. Possibly he was not a true stayer, but the fact remains that his rider, W.R. Johnstone, rode a very indifferent race. After the Derby Colombo, still feeling the effects of his Epsom exertions, was beaten by Flamenco in the St James's Palace Stakes at Ascot. He never ran again. As a sire he was not altogether a success, although he got the 2,000 Guineas winner Happy Knight and Dancing Time, winner of the 1,000 Guineas.

COLORADO
(1923, b c Phalaris – Canyon, by Chaucer)

Bred and owned by the 17th Earl of Derby, Colorado was trained by George Lambton and won nine races worth £30,358, including the 2,000 Guineas and Eclipse Stakes. He made a wonderful start as a sire, and his death after only two years at stud represented an extremely serious loss to British breeders. He sired Felicitation (Ascot Gold Cup), Loaningdale (Eclipse Stakes) and Colorado Kid (Royal Hunt Cup and Doncaster Cup), and several of his sons became important sires in South America.

COLOURS, Coat

Identification of horses by coat colouring follows the description used when the foal is registered. It is not always an exact statement since the colouring occasionally changes with age, especially in grey horses, who get progressively whiter as they change coat each year. The common descriptions are: black (in which black pigment is general in the coat and on the limbs, mane and tail); brown (a mixture of black and brown pigment in the coat, with black limbs, mane and tail); bay or brown (brown predominates in the coat, with a bay muzzle and black limbs, mane and tail); bay (the considerable mix which fits the range between bay or brown to chestnut, distinguished from the latter by the bay's black mane and tail); chestnut (yellow hair in different degrees of intensity, ranging from the 'true' chestnut which has a chestnut mane and tail that may be of different intensity to the body colour, to the lighter-coloured chestnut which may have a flaxen mane and tail); grey (a body coat of black and white hairs with a black skin); and roan (a combination of white hair and the permanent body colour gives a lightening effect to the latter). A few foals have been registered as white – as opposed to

albino, which is white hair on a pink skin – but this is very rare.

COLOURS, Racing

Racing colours have to be registered annually at a fee of £9.50 (plus VAT). Colours thus registered cannot be taken by any other person. Disputes as to the right to particular colours must be settled by the stewards of the Jockey Club. Anyone running a horse in colours other than those registered in his own name without special declaration at the racecourse is liable to a fine of £50.

The first mention of racing colours was made in 1762. The earliest silks comprised a single colour, which in a few instances can still be seen – as in Lord Howard de Walden's 'apricot' and the Duke of Devonshire's 'straw'. Various combinations of colours were introduced, and various unusual motifs were used, for example the large 'B' back and front which Mr John McShain, owner of Ballymoss, adopted. More recently colours have become standardized, and the authorities have set out eighteen basic colours, twenty basic jacket markings, eight basic sleeve markings and seven basic cap markings. The list leaves plenty of room for manoeuvre but no room for individuality.

COLT

An ungelded male racehorse under five years of age is a colt, after which he is referred to as a horse.

COMMANCHE RUN
(1981, b c Run the Gantlet – Volley, by Ratification)

Bought for 9,000gns as a yearling, Commanche Run won three races as a three-year-old, including the St Leger, in which he gave Lester Piggott a record 28th British Classic success. He enhanced his reputation over middle distances as a four-year-old, his wins including the Benson & Hedges Gold Cup and Phoenix Park Champion Stakes, before it was announced in September 1985 that he would be syndicated to stand at Coolmore Stud in Ireland from the following year.

COMMON

Owned in partnership by Lord Alington and Sir Frederick Johnstone and bred at Crichel by the former, Common, a son of Isonomy, won the 'Triple Crown' in 1891. He was trained by John Porter at Kingsclere. As a sire he was a failure with the exception of producing the 1,000 Guineas winner Nun Nicer.

COMMOTION
(1938, b f Mieuxcé – Riot, by Colorado)

Owned and bred by Mr J.A. Dewar, Commotion won three races for £2,514, including the 1941, Oaks at 20-1. She bred eight winners, among them Combat, the unbeaten winner of nine races and a successful sire; Faux Tirage, winner of over £8,000 and a successful sire in New Zealand; and Aristophanes, who won over £4,000 and did well as a sire in Argentina, where he produced the international stallion Forli.

COMRADE
(1917, bl c Bachelor's Double – Sourabaya, by Spearmint)

Comrade, bred in Ireland by Mr L. Neumann, was sold for only 25gns as a yearling. He won some £25,000 in stakes, including the 1920 Grand Prix de Paris and a new race called the Prix de l'Arc de Triomphe. He was trained at Newmarket by Peter Gilpin. He retired to stud in France but died after only four seasons.

CONJURE

Conjure was a foundation mare of the second Lord Astor's stud, having been bought for £100 as a five-year-old. A daughter of Juggler, she was foaled in 1895, and her descendants include Winkipop (1,000 Guineas), Blink (second in the Derby), Short Story (Oaks), Pennycomequick (Oaks), Pensive (Kentucky Derby), Court Martial (2,000 Guineas) and Ambiguity (Oaks).

CONNORTON, Brian (b. 1935)

Brian Connorton was successively apprenticed to Norman Bertie in his home town of Newmarket, Peter Ward and 'Snowy' Gray, and rode his first winner in 1953 at Yarmouth. He chiefly rode in the North, where he had a fruitful association with the Gray stable at Beverley, for which he won the Dante Stakes (Lucky Brief) and Champagne Stakes (Chebs Lad). He was forced to retire in August 1976 as a result of a leg injury sustained almost a year previously, but continued to be involved in racing with promotional work at York racecourse. His son Nicky (born 1962) rode his first winner as an apprentice in May 1979 and was apprenticed to Bill Watts at Richmond, Yorkshire. Connorton senior spent three years in charge of Singapore's apprentice school before returning to Britain in April 1985 to succeed Johnny Gilbert as chief instructor at the British Racing School at Newmarket.

COOK, Paul Allan (b. 1946)

Under the guidance of 'Frenchie' Nicholson, Paul Cook was one of the outstanding apprentices since the Second World War. In 1963 he rode his first winner; in 1964 and 1965 he was champion apprentice with 46 and 62 winners; in 1966 he was riding for Jack Jarvis's stable and very nearly won the Derby on Prétendre. That season he rode 93 winners and won the 1,000 Guineas on Glad Rags. Perhaps he had gone to the top rather more swiftly than was really good for him, and he was not the first apprentice whose star waned rapidly. His total of winners in a season plummeted from 83 in 1966 to a mere nine in 1970, but two years later he began his comeback, winning the Stewards' Cup in 1972 and 1973 on Touch Paper and Alphadamus. Gradually he regained the respect of notable trainers, winning the July Cup in 1977 on Gentilhombre, the Ebor Handicap in 1978 on Totowah, and the Champagne Stakes in 1979 on Final Straw, and recording his best seasons with 90 winners in 1978 and 1980. He had a brief spell as first jockey to Tom Jones, for whom he won the St Leger on Touching Wood in 1982 – 16 years after his first Classic success.

CORBETT, Hon Thomas Anthony (1921-76)

A son of Lord Rowallan, at one time the Chief Scout, 'Atty' Corbett was educated at Eton and served with distinction in the Grenadier Guards. For a time he was attached to Fred Rimell's stable and rode with success under National Hunt Rules, as an amateur and professional, winning the National Hunt Chase on Ellesmere and the Mildmay Memorial Chase on Domata.

He started his training career in 1958 with a few jumpers but gradually switched to the Flat on his move from Compton in Berkshire to Newmarket in 1968. His best winners were Talahasse (Gimcrack and Champagne Stakes), Queen's Hussar (Lockinge and Sussex Stakes), Sweet Revenge (King's Stand Stakes) and the Free Handicap winners Kibenka and Shiny Tenth. A bachelor with a considerable sense of humour, he died in November 1976 as a result of injuries received in a road accident while walking his horses at Newmarket.

CORONACH
(1923, ch c Hurry On – Wet Kiss, by Tredennis)

Coronach was bred and owned by Lord Woolavington and trained by Fred Darling. A big, light-coloured chestnut with a flaxen mane and tail, he was high-mettled and wilful and hated restraint. As a three-year-old he was trounced by Colorado in the 2,000 Guineas but went on to win the Derby by five lengths, the St James's Palace Stakes by twenty lengths, the Eclipse Stakes by six lengths and the St Leger in record time.

There had always been rumours that he was not quite sound in his wind, and as a four-year-old he was undoubtedly hampered by respiratory trouble. He won the Coronation Cup and the Hardwicke Stakes, but Colorado slammed him in the Princess of Wales's Stakes and the Eclipse Stakes. Retiring with a record of ten wins for £48,224, Coronach was not a stud success in Britain but sired a top-class filly in M. Boussac's Corrida. In 1940 Mrs Macdonald-Buchanan, Lord Woolavington's daughter, made a gift of Coronach to New Zealand, and it was there that he spent the last nine years of his life. His stud record there was good.

CORMORANT WOOD
(1980, br f Home Guard – Quarry Wood, by Super Sam)

A mile and a quarter was Cormorant Wood's optimum distance, though her dam stayed much further, and she rounded off three straight wins as a three-year-old by touching off Tolomeo and Flame of Tara in the Champion Stakes. She stayed in training at four and won twice more, dead-heating for the Lockinge Stakes and winning the Benson & Hedges Gold Cup, where she again beat Tolomeo. She injured a tendon in the big York race and was retired to stud with six wins to her credit from her thirteen races.

CORRIDA
(1932, ch f Coronach – Zariba, by Sardanapale)

Corrida was bred and owned by Marcel Boussac and was one of the best fillies to race in Europe between the wars, despite disappointing in Britain in the 1,000 Guineas and Oaks. She twice won the Prix de l'Arc de Triomphe and won good races in Britain, Belgium and Germany as well. She was stolen by the Germans during the war and was never recovered. Her son Coaraze won the French Derby.

COTTRILL, Harry Lawson (1882-1955)

Harry Cottrill had a happy, sanguine disposition and never lacked friends. Before World War I he was well known in hunting and point-to-pointing circles in Cheshire. He paid for his fun by making hunters and selling them. He began his training career with a few jumpers at Tarporley, but he was granted a licence to train on the Flat in 1915. At the end of the war he went to Seven Barrows, Lambourn, to train for the uncouth, ill-fated Lancashire financier Mr James White, a vain, self-opinioned man, difficult to get on with, but fortunately the debonair Cottrill had a buoyant temperament. Perhaps the best horse he trained for White, who eventually committed suicide, was Irish Elegance, who put up a memorable performance to win the Royal Hunt Cup with 9st 11lb.

Cottrill was very successful in big handicaps. He won the Cesarewitch with Ivanhoe; the Portland Handicap with Irish Elegance, who carried 10st 2lb; the Royal Hunt Cup, apart from Irish Elegance, with Guinea Gap and Caerloptic; the Stewards' Cup with Western Wave and Solerina; the Chester Cup with Chivalrous (twice) and Faites vos Jeux; the Cambridgeshire with Dan Bulger; the Lincolnshire with Granely; and the Ascot Stakes with Miss Sport and Doreen Jane. His two Classic successes were the 2,000 Guineas in 1927 with Col. S. Whitburn's Adam's Apple and the Oaks in 1936 with Sir Abe Bailey's Lovely Rosa.

Harry Cottrill, who retired in 1943, had two sons, Alec, a fine amateur rider who was assistant to George Lambton at Stanley House when he died in 1933 as the result of a fall at Lewes, and Humphrey.

COTTRILL, Humphrey Lawson (b. 1906)

Humphrey Cottrill, a son of Harry Cottrill, assisted his father from 1928 to 1937. He served in India and Burma during the war, and for four years after it was a stipendiary steward in South Africa. Returning to Britain in 1950, he assisted Willie Pratt and then Marcus Marsh. He took out a licence in 1952 and had a spell as private trainer for Major Lionel Holliday, for whom he trained such good horses as Narrator, Chatsworth, Pirate King and Gratitude. With the termination of that arrangement, he became a public trainer at Beverley House, Newmarket, where the big races he won included the Irish Derby, Champion Stakes, Manchester Cup (twice), Kempton Jubilee, Coventry Stakes, St James's Palace Stakes, Queen Mary Stakes, National Breeders' Produce Stakes, Coronation Cup and Nunthorpe Stakes.

He retired at the end of the 1974 season, and in his role as bloodstock agent managed the racing affairs of Mr Khaled Abdulla, for whom he bought the 2,000 Guineas winner Known Fact.

COURT MARTIAL
(1942, ch c Fair Trial – Instantaneous, by Hurry On)

Court Martial was bred and raced by the second Viscount Astor. He won six races for £11,666, including the 2,000 Guineas and Champion Stakes, and was third in the Derby. He was an outstanding success as a sire, being twice champion before being exported to America in 1958. His only Classic winner was Timandra (French 1,000 Guineas) but he also sired Major Portion (top of the 1957 Free Handicap), Rosalba (second in 1,000 Guineas), the Coventry Stakes winners King's Bench and Ratification, and Crimea II (Cheveley Park Stakes). His son Wilkes was leading sire in Australia.

COUSINS, Eric (b. 1921)

Eric Cousins became noted as a trainer for his skill at placing horses to win major handicaps in the 1960s. He served as a pilot in the RAF. Keen on hunting, he rode with some success as an amateur under National Hunt Rules and took out a licence to train in 1954. He won the Jubilee at Kempton four years in a row, with Chalk Stream (1961), Water Skier (1962-3) and Commander in Chief (1964). He also won the Lincoln Handicap (1961, 1962), Ayr Gold Cup (1960, 1965, 1969), Victoria Cup, Cambridgeshire, Wokingham Stakes and Portland Handicap. He retired from training in 1977 to concentrate on his farming interests and work as a bloodstock agent, and handed over his stables at Tarporley, Cheshire, to his son Martin, who had his first Flat-race winner at Edinburgh on 3 July 1978, with Small Mercy, after the original first-past-the-post had been disqualified.

CRAGANOUR
(1910, b c Desmond – Veneration II, by Laveno)

Mr C. Bower Ismay's Craganour, ridden by Johnny Reiff, was first past the post in the 1913 Derby but was disqualified by the stewards for not keeping a straight course, interfering with other horses, and boring Aboyeur, who was awarded the race. Craganour, whose six undisputed victories were worth £10,990, was subsequently sold to Señor Martinez de Hoz for £30,000 and proved a great success as a sire in Argentina. W.T. (Jack) Robinson, who trained Craganour, was never the same man after Craganour's disqualification and died two years later.

CRAIG AN ERAN
(1918, b c Sunstar – Maid of the Mist, by Cyllene)

Bred and owned by Lord Astor, Craig an Eran won three races for a total of £15,345 in 1921: the 2,000 Guineas, St James's Palace Stakes and Eclipse Stakes. In the Derby he was beaten by a neck, perhaps a shade unluckily, by Humorist. He sired April the Fifth, winner of the Derby; Admiral Drake, winner of the Grand Prix de Paris; and Mon Talisman, winner of the Prix du Jockey-Club and Prix de l'Arc de Triomphe.

CRATHORNE, Lord
(1897-1977)

Lord Crathorne was, as Sir Thomas Dugdale, for 30 years Conservative MP for the North Riding of Yorkshire (Richmond). From 1951 to 1954 he was Minister of Agriculture. A member of the Jockey Club, he was Senior Steward in 1962 and was a member of the Horserace Betting Levy Board from 1963 to 1973. His horses were trained by Dick Peacock.

CREMORNE

Mr H. Savile's Cremorne won the Derby and Grand Prix de Paris in 1872 and the following year the Ascot Gold Cup. His Grand Prix victory was ill-received in France as the British were thought to have been unhelpful in the recent Franco-Prussian War. His most notable offspring was the brilliant filly Kermesse.

CREPELLO
(1954, ch c Donatello II – Crepuscule, by Mieuxcé)

Crepello, owned and bred by Sir Victor Sassoon and trained by Noel Murless, was a very good horse if not an entirely sound one. He won the 2,000 Guineas and Derby in 1957 but never ran again after Epsom, breaking down in a gallop three weeks after being pulled out of the King George VI and Queen Elizabeth Stakes on the morning of the race. His three wins from five races were worth £34,201. His stud career was chequered, with Busted (Eclipse Stakes and King George VI and Queen Elizabeth Stakes) his best colt, and Cacrgwrle (1,000 Guineas), Celina (Irish Oaks), Crepellana (French Oaks) and Mysterious (1,000 Guineas and Oaks) among his fillies. His daughter Bleu Azur bred four useful winners including Altesse Royale (1,000 Guineas, Oaks and Irish Oaks). Crepello was put down in 1974, a month after his grandson Bustino won the St Leger.

CREPUSCULE
(1948, ch f Mieuxcé – Red Sunset, by Solario)

Crepuscule, a pillar of the Sassoon stud, is one of the most successful modern broodmares, her offspring including Crepello (2,000 Guineas and Derby), Honeylight (Free Handicap and 1,000 Guineas) and Twilight Alley (Ascot Gold Cup). She herself won one maiden race. She died in 1970 but her name has been carried down mainly by Honeylight, grandam of Attica Meli (Yorkshire Oaks, Park Hill Stakes, Doncaster Cup) and Royal Hive (Park Hill Stakes).

CRESTA RUN
(1924, b f Hurry On – Bridgemount, by Bridge of Earn)

Bred by Lt.-Col. Giles Loder, Cresta Run won three races for £14,540, including the 1,000 Guineas. She made no mark as a broodmare.

CROSS, Vernon Bertram (1908-79)

Vernon Cross was employed for twenty years by the late Lord and Lady Stalbridge, for the last five (1947-52) as private trainer. He was associated with such notable jumpers as the 1940 Grand National winner Bogskar and Red April. He became a public trainer at Chattis Hill, Stockbridge, where the late 'Atty' Persse used to train, and gained his biggest success with Eric in the 1972 Chester Cup. He died in December 1979, having collapsed three weeks previously at the races.

CROW (1973, ch c Exbury – Carmosina, by Right of Way)

Bred by his owner Daniel Wildenstein, Crow was trained originally in France and as a three-year-old won three races, from the mile of the Prix Eugène Adam to the extended distance of the 200th running of the St Leger. He was below form as a four-year-old, including in two races in the United States, but returned to his best at five years, when trained in Britain by Peter Walwyn, and won the Ormonde Stakes and Coronation Cup. A setback kept him out of the King George VI and Queen Elizabeth Diamond Stakes, and in the autumn of 1978 he was sold to stand at stud in Kentucky.

CULLEN, Desmond (b. 1940)

A very useful, Irish-born lightweight jockey, Des Cullen won several major handicaps after completing his apprenticeship with Willie Stephenson. He won the Extel Stakes (twice), Stewards' Cup, Royal Hunt Cup, Ayr Gold Cup and Cambridgeshire but was forced to retire in 1977 on medical grounds after being injured in a fall while exercising a two-year-old. His best season was 1971, with 45 winners. He was for a time a jockeys' valet.

CUMANI, Luca Matteo (b. 1949)

Son of leading Italian trainer Sergio Cumani, Luca was the top amateur rider in his native country before joining Henry Cecil as assistant for two years until he began training at Bedford House, Newmarket, in 1976. His first winner was Three Legs in the Duke of York Stakes at York on 13 May 1976. He never overraces his horses but has developed a high ratio of good-class winners to runners, though he had five Classic places, with Freeze the Secret (two), Vaguely Deb, Konafa and Tolomeo, before his first such victory, with Commanche Run in the 1984 St Leger. His other major winners have been Alma Ata (Park Hill Stakes), Century City (Cambridgeshire), Old Country (Italian and French St Legers and Jockey Club Cup) and Free Guest (Extel and Sun Chariot Stakes). Tolomeo won the rich Arlington Million in Chicago in 1983. His best season numerically was 1985, with 60 winners, from runners in 237 races.

CUNDELL, Francis Lawrence (1909-83)

Frank Cundell, a qualified veterinary surgeon, as was his father, joined the Royal Army Veterinary Corps in 1931 and became a highly competent amateur rider under National Hunt Rules. On leaving the Army, he was for three years veterinary officer and stipendiary steward to the Royal West India Turf Club before returning to Britain to assist his uncle, L.A. Cundell, who was training at Chilton. He took out a licence to train in 1939, but shortly after was called up for military service.

After the war he gradually built up a 'mixed' stable at Aston Tirrold near Didcot. The majority of his most important successes were gained with jumpers, including Crudwell, winner of 50 races, and his best Flat-racer was Celtic Cone (Yorkshire Cup and Queen Alexandra Stakes). He retired from training in 1976 and acted as a steward at a number of southern courses until the time of his death in January 1983.

CUNDELL, Kenneth Stratton (b. 1914)

Ken Cundell began training in 1947, having assisted L.A. Cundell, his second cousin Frank's uncle, for some years before the war. The most notable Flat races won from his 'mixed' stable at Compton, Berkshire, were the Wokingham Stakes, Cork and Orrery Stakes, Queen Anne Stakes, Blue Riband Trial Stakes and Victoria Cup. He did especially well with sprinters, handling March Past as well as King George VI and Queen Elizabeth Stakes runner-up Zucchero, and ended his career by winning the 1974 Vernons Sprint Cup with Princely Son, four years after his success with Golden Orange in the same race. On his retirement he handed over his stable to his son Peter (born 1948). Peter's best Flat-racers have been King of Spain and the Chester Cup winner Contester.

CUP

A 'cup' is officially defined in the Jockey Club Rules as any prize not given in money.

CURANT, Robert Dennis (b. 1949)

Fulham-born Bob Curant was apprenticed to Dermot Whelan at Epsom but left to ride abroad after coming out of his time, travelling to Australia and Jamaica before returning to Britain for the 1973 season. Based at Lambourn, he had his best season in 1979, with 31 winners.

CUSTANCE, Henry (1842-1908)

A native of Peterborough, Henry Custance was better educated than most jockeys of his era, better-mannered and more reliable. He kept the money he made and on retirement for some time acted as a starter. He is the only man to have ridden in the Derby and to have started it as well; he despatched the 1885 Derby field in faultless fashion. He rode three Derby winners – Thormanby (1860), Lord Lyon (1866) and George Frederick (1874). He also won the 1,000 Guineas and St Leger once each.

CUT ABOVE (1978, b c High Top – Cutle, by Saint Crespin III)

Cut Above raced only seven times before he was retired to stud in Ireland at the end of his three-year-old days. He was placed in both outings as a two-year-old and won two out of five at three years, including the St Leger, in which he started at 28-1. His trainer Dick Hern saddled two others in the Doncaster Classic, including the better-fancied Bustomi, against the odds-on Derby winner Shergar, but while Bustomi finished third and Shergar fourth, Cut Above won decisively by $2\frac{1}{2}$ lengths. Cut Above never showed in the Prix de l'Arc de Triomphe, his next race, and did not run again.

van CUTSEM, Bernard Henry Harcourt (1916-75)

Bernard van Cutsem was prominent in sporting circles at Cambridge, and shortly after leaving the university he took out a licence to train at Newmarket. His career, though, was interrupted by the war during which he served in the Life Guards. He resumed training in 1955, moving to Lord Derby's Stanley House Stables in 1964, and gradually established a reputation as one of the shrewdest and most competent men in the game. He held strong views on the structure of racing in Britain, and on more than one occasion his comments irked the bookmaking profession considerably, since he greatly favoured a Tote monopoly.

He succeeded Jack Watts as Lord Derby's trainer and at his peak had nearly 70 horses under his care. The best winner he trained was that gallant mare Park Top, whose victories included the Ribblesdale Stakes, Coronation Cup, Hardwicke Stakes and King George VI and Queen Elizabeth Stakes. He trained two Classic winners: High Top (2,000 Guineas) and Decies (Irish 2,000 Guineas), and a number of high-class two-year-olds including Crowned Prince (Dewhurst and Champagne Stakes), Sharpen Up (Middle Park Stakes) and Noble Decree (Observer Gold Cup). His other good winners included Park Top's sire Kalydon, Mandamus, winner of eight races and over £24,000, that fine sprinter Mountain Call, and Karabas, winner of the City and Suburban, and Washington D.C. International at Laurel Park.

He died in December 1975 after a long illness, during which his stable was supervised by Mick Ryan, now training on his own account.

CYLLENE

Cyllene, foaled in 1895, was so small as a yearling that he was not entered for the Classics. A chestnut by Bona Vista, he grew to full size and won the Ascot Gold Cup. He sired four Derby winners (Cicero, Minoru, Lemberg and Tagalie) as well as the five-times champion sire Polymelus, being exported to Argentina for £25,000 at the age of thirteen. He did well there, too, until his death at the age of 30.

D

D'ABERNON, Viscount (1857-1941)

A noted diplomat, Lord D'Abernon served as British Ambassador in Berlin. He bred a number of good horses including Diadem, who won the 1,000 Guineas and 23 other races in his colours, and Diophon, whom he sold to the Aga Khan and who won the 2,000 Guineas. He was the first President of the Thoroughbred Breeders Association. A man of wide interests, he was a subaltern in the Coldstream Guards when in 1879 he published a grammar of modern Greek that became the standard work in Greece.

DAHLIA
(1970, ch f Vaguely Noble – Charming Alibi, by Honeys Alibi)

Bred and owned by Nelson Bunker Hunt, Dahlia was an outstanding filly who won fifteen of her 48 races and campaigned in France, Britain, Ireland, and the United States and Canada. She is the only dual winner of the King George VI and Queen Elizabeth Stakes (1973 and 1974) and Benson & Hedges Gold Cup (1974-75), and the only horse to be voted Racehorse of the Year in Britain twice (1973 and 1974). Her other wins included the Irish Oaks, Grand Prix de Saint-Cloud, Washington D.C. International and Canadian International Championship. At stud her best offspring has been the Prix Lupin winner Dahar.

DALE, Leonard Sydney (b. 1915)

Syd Dale was head lad to his father David for five years and to Ryan Price for eleven years before he took out a licence to train in 1956. The most important Flat race winner from his Epsom stable was Hoy (Chester Cup). He retired from training in January 1974.

DANCING TIME
(1938, b f Colombo – Show Girl, by Son-in-Law)

Dancing Time was bred and owned by Lord Glanely and won the 1,000 Guineas and was third in the Oaks and St Leger. She bred six winners, the best being the smart Irish-trained middle-distance colt Arctic Time (fourth in King George VI and Queen Elizabeth Stakes and sire of the Irish St Leger winner Arctic Vale). Her unraced daughter Star Dancer bred the Irish 1,000 Guineas winner Royal Danseuse.

DANTE
(1942, br c Nearco – Rosy Legend, by Dark Legend)

Dante was bred by Sir Eric Ohlson and remained in his ownership after failing to reach his reserve when offered for sale as a yearling. Trained in Middleham by Matt Peacock, he ran six times as a two-year-old and was undefeated. The following season he was beaten a neck by Court Martial in the 2,000 Guineas, but was handicapped by an eye affliction that had become apparent only a few days earlier. He won the Derby in great style by two lengths. It was the last war-time Derby to be run at Newmarket.

Before the St Leger there were persistent rumours about Dante's well-being. On 22 August there was an encouraging statement from Middleham, but only three days later he was scratched from the final Classic on the grounds that 'he could not be got ready in time'. He never ran again and was retired to stud where in due course he became totally blind. As a sire he was a qualified success. He got a fair number of winners, but a good many of his offspring were distinctly temperamental. His best off-spring were Darius (2,000 Guineas), Carrozza (Oaks), Toulouse Lautrec (third in Italian Derby) and Diableretta (best two-year-old filly of her generation).

DARIUS
(1951, b c Dante – Yasna, by Dastur)

Bred and owned by Sir Percy Loraine and trained by Harry Wragg, Darius won nine races for £38,105, including the 2,000 Guineas, Eclipse Stakes and St James's Palace Stakes. His most notable winners at stud were Pola Bella (French 1,000 Guineas), Varano (Italian Derby), Pia (Oaks), Dart Board (third in Derby, Dewhurst Stakes), Derring-Do, Darling Boy and Cyrus. Darius died of cancer in 1968.

DARLEY ARABIAN

The Darley Arabian is a significant name in tracing the origins and development of the Thoroughbred. Foaled in 1700, he was a bay with a white blaze and three white feet and was stated to belong 'to the most esteemed race among the Arabs both by sire and dam'. He was sent to Britain as a four-year-old by Thomas Darley, the British Consul in Aleppo. He lived to the age of 30, and standing in Yorkshire he founded a dynasty that has persisted to the present day.

Of modern, important male lines, those tracing from Blandford, Phalaris, Teddy, Son-in-Law, Gainsborough and St Simon are all derived from the Darley Arabian.

DARLEY, Kevin Paul (b. 1960)

One of several talented apprentices raised by Reg Hollinshead, Kevin Darley rode his first winner on Dust Up at Haydock Park on 5 August 1977. He was leading apprentice the following year, with 70 winners, as well as Crown Apprentice champion. He lost his riding allowance on a working holiday in Kenya early in 1979, and later that year rode his hundredth winner. Since 1980 he has been associated mainly with Jack Berry's stable but in 1986 he is to be retained by Mel Brittain. An occasional partnership with Fulke Johnson Houghton's runners

in the North provided him with a big race success on Borushka in the Park Hill Stakes.

DARLING, Frederick (1884-1953)

Son of Sam Darling, who trained two Derby winners, Fred Darling has claims to be regarded as among the top three British trainers of this century.

Darling served as an apprentice for a brief period but never held a jockey's licence. He began his training career at Kentford near Newmarket with a few jumpers, owned by Lady de Bathe (the famous Lily Langtry). He next trained for the Weinberg brothers in Germany, returning to Britain just before the start of World War I to take over the famous Beckhampton stable from his father.

Though often handicapped by ill-health, his record was one of remarkable success up to his retirement in 1947. Taciturn, secretive and quick-tempered, he had no time for fools, bores or importunate members of the racing Press. A perfectionist, he was a ruthless martinet in the stable, insisting at all times on the highest standards and the closest attention to detail. In a clash of wills with a difficult horse he rarely came off second best. His training methods were based on the conservation of vital energy for the racecourse rather than expending it on the gallops and his horses could be relied on to be at their peak on the day that really mattered. Moreover, they invariably carried an air of well-being and distinction that set them apart from their rivals in the paddock. To an unusual degree Darling possessed the art of getting a horse fit and building up its constitution simultaneously.

He had nineteen successes in Classic races. He won the Derby with Captain Cuttle (1922), Manna (1925), Coronach (1926), Cameronian (1931), Bois Roussel (1938), Pont l'Evêque (1940) and Owen Tudor (1941). Only Robert Robson and John Porter have trained as many Derby winners. The best horse he trained was Hurry On, who was never beaten, the best filly, the brilliant but temperamental Sun Chariot, who won the 1,000

Guineas, Oaks and St Leger in 1942.

Darling died in 1953, three days after Pinza, whom he bred, had won the Derby.

DARLING, Samuel Henry (1881-1967)

Sam Darling's racing career was overshadowed by that of his brother Fred. His main achievement was to land the Autumn Double in 1925, Forseti winning the Cesarewitch and Masked Marvel the Cambridgeshire. Both horses were owned by Mr A.K. Macomber. The feat, accomplished only once previously with different horses, has never been repeated. Darling trained for Marcel Boussac and won the 1930 Lincolnshire Handicap for him with Leonidas II at 66-1. He trained at Newmarket from 1907 until his retirement in 1946.

DASTUR (1929, b c Solario – Friar's Daughter, by Friar Marcus)

The Aga Khan's Dastur won $6\frac{1}{2}$ races for £11,626 but is best remembered for finishing second in the 2,000 Guineas, Derby and St Leger in 1932. He won the Irish Derby and the following year the Coronation Cup. His stud career, though lasting nineteen years, was not marked by outstanding success.

DAVEY, Robert Ernest (1890-1977)

Ernie Davey, who served his apprenticeship with Bert Gordon at Wroughton, rode in Ireland from 1910 to 1919. He took out his first trainer's licence in 1922 and trained at Star Cottage, Malton, from 1935 until his retirement in 1974, at the age of 84. He usually had some sharp two-year-olds for the start of the season and won the Brocklesby Plate four times. He rarely paid high prices for his horses, and sprinters did him proud, especially Fair Seller, who cost £50 and won the Ayr Gold Cup in 1951, and Granville Greta, winner of seventeen races after he bought her out of a seller for 530gns. Davey was also noted for the number of apprentices he brought along.

DAVEY, Robert Paul (b. 1925)

Paul Davey assisted his trainer-father Ernie Davey until in 1968 he became one of Mr David Robinson's private trainers at Newmarket. He twice trained the Gimcrack Stakes winner, with Yellow God (1969) and Wishing Star (1971), and followed his father's example by winning the 1971 Brocklesby Stakes with Deep Diver, that season's leading two-year-old and successful in the following year's Nunthorpe Stakes. When Mr Robinson began to wind down his racing interests, Davey left Newmarket at the end of the 1974 season, returned to the North and was lost to the training profession.

DAWSON, Daniel

Daniel Dawson was hanged before 15,000 spectators at Cambridge in 1811 for poisoning a number of horses at Newmarket. A tout by trade, he was hired to do the dirty work by two unscrupulous bookmakers called Bland, who went unpunished.

DAWSON, Mathew (1820-98)

Mathew Dawson can be rightly termed one of the greatest trainers, having won the Derby with Thormanby (1860), Kingcraft (1870), Silvio (1877), Melton (1885), Ladas (1894) and Sir Visto (1895). He also trained St Simon, who was never beaten.

A Scotsman, Dawson cared nothing for petty economies and ran his stable in a lavish manner. He was a strong, fearless character who was never reluctant to speak his mind but was invariably courteous not only to his owners but to those whom he employed. He had no patience with weak men and bad horses and he loathed heavy betting. In fact, he fundamentally despised money, unlike Fred Archer with whom he was closely associated and whom he once summarized as 'that damned, long-legged, tin-scraping young devil'. He was as good a gardener as he was a trainer and liked to appear on the gallops in a top hat and varnished boots with a wonderful flower in his buttonhole.

During a career which took him to Newmarket in 1866 after twenty years in

Berkshire, he won the 2,000 Guineas and Oaks five times each, and the 1,000 Guineas and St Leger six times each. He was still training when he died in 1898 at the age of 78.

DAWSON, Richard Cecil (1866-1955)

Richard Dawson, one of the most successful trainers in the first 30 years or so of this century, was born in Ireland and trained there for some years after leaving Dublin University. In 1897 he moved to Whatcombe in Berkshire and the following year won the Grand National with Drogheda, a horse he had bought at the Dublin Show. During World War I he moved to Newmarket and trained Fifinella to win the Derby for Mr E. Hulton. He returned to Whatcombe in 1919, and in 1921 was appointed trainer to the Aga Khan, George Lambton having previously declined that position. The association lasted ten years, and among the notable winners were Diophon (2,000 Guineas), Blenheim (Derby), Salmon-Trout (St Leger) and Mumtaz Mahal, a brilliant filly with phenomenal speed. During the same period Dawson won the Derby and St Leger for Mr William Barnett with Trigo, and the Oaks for the Vicomte de Fontarce with Brownhylda. In 1931 there was a serious disagreement between the Aga Khan and Dawson and the Aga Khan's horses left the stable, which Dawson continued to run in a smaller way until his retirement in 1945.

In appearance Dawson was hardly the typical trainer, and in manner he was not the Englishman's notion of an Irishman. With his drooping moustache, pince-nez and sombre style of dress, he looked more like an old-fashioned schoolmaster. He had little sense of humour to help him through the ups and downs of fortune that are inevitable in racing.

DAWSON, Stephen (b. 1963)

Apprenticed to Nicky Vigors, Southport-born Steve Dawson rode his first winner on Queen Kate at Windsor on 23 August 1980 and had his first big-race success on Out of Hand (Portland Handicap). His

career slumped slightly in 1983, and the following summer he badly broke his leg in a fall at Brighton. He returned in time for the end of the season and won the Cesarewitch on Tom Sharp.

DAY, John (1819-83)

John Day trained at Danebury and won the Derby with Cossack (1847) and Andover (1854). He had been a successful jockey and won the 2,000 Guineas in 1844 on The Ugly Buck, owned and trained by his father, John Barham Day, at Danebury.

DAY, Nigel (b. 1960)

Nigel Day completed a five-year apprenticeship with Henry Cecil in 1983, having had his first success in 1978 and his best season in 1981, with 32 winners. He remained with the stable, but in 1984 he was suspended for three months for accepting a gift from a professional gambler. Day continued to work for Cecil, and in 1985 he gained a retainer to ride horses owned by the Matthews family in training with Mrs Jocelyn Reavey.

DAY, Reginald (1883-1972)

Reg Day, the middle generation of three highly esteemed Newmarket veterinary surgeons, had an exceptionally long career as a trainer, starting in 1900 and retiring in 1968. At one period he trained in Germany and won the German Derby three times. He also won the Grand Prix d'Ostende. In his younger days he rode under National Hunt Rules.

He was particularly renowned as a trainer of stayers; he won the Ascot Gold Cup twice, Goodwood Cup twice, Doncaster Cup twice, Jockey Club Cup four times, Yorkshire Cup, Gold Vase, Jockey Club Stakes and Goodwood Stakes. He also did well with fast two-year-olds, winning the Middle Park Stakes twice, Gimcrack Stakes twice, Queen Mary Stakes and Imperial Produce Stakes. For Sir Abe Bailey he trained two fine stayers in Son-in-Law (Goodwood Cup, Jockey Club Cup and Cesarewitch), and Foxlaw (Northumberland Plate, Jockey Club Stakes and

Ascot Gold Cup). The best horse to pass through his hands was Solario (St Leger and Gold Cup). Solario won the St Leger in 1925, and his trainer had to wait 36 years for his next Classic winner, Sweet Solera (1,000 Guineas and Oaks).

DAY, Samuel (1802-66)

Sam Day was cheerful, hardy and a good deal more honest than certain members of the Day family of that era. He was a fine rider and won the Derby on Gustavus (1821), Priam (1830) and Pyrrhus the First (1846). He also won the 1,000 Guineas and Oaks in 1846 on Mendicant.

DEAD-HEAT, Run-off

Until the Jockey Club Rules were altered in 1930 the owner of a horse which had dead-heated could challenge the other to a run-off, and if the challenge was turned down, the other was deemed to be the winner. The last dead-heat to be run off was at Newbury on 25 June 1930, when Ruby's Love won the decider after dead-heating with the favourite Walloon in a 7f selling handicap.

DEAD-HEAT, Triple

Multiple dead-heats rarely occur since the advent of the photo-finish camera. Quadruple dead-heats were recorded in 1808, 1851 and 1855; the last officially recorded triple dead-heat was at Newmarket on 23 April 1924, between Hope Deferred, Vaddy and Buddha. There was a triple dead-heat between Breezy Heather, Golden Book and Rocos at Folkestone on 5 September 1925, but Rocos was disqualified and placed last.

DEAN SWIFT
(1901, ch g Childwick –
Pasquil, by Plebeian))

Mr J.B. Joel's popular handicapper Dean Swift is worthy of note because he ran eight times in the City and Suburban. He won in 1906 and 1908, was second twice, third twice and twice unplaced. He also won the Coronation Cup at the age of eight in 1909.

DERBY, The – see EPSOM

DERBY, 12th Earl of
(1752-1834)

The Derby at Epsom was named in honour of the Earl of Derby, a popular, easy-going, hospitable and self-indulgent man. He himself won the Derby in 1787 with Sir Peter Teazle, by Highflyer. Despite long and liberal support of the Turf, the Stanley family failed to win the Derby again till Sansovino triumphed in 1924. The Oaks was named after the twelfth Earl's house near Epsom.

DERBY, 17th Earl of
(1865-1948)

A great Englishman, whose long life was devoted to the service of his country, the seventeenth Earl of Derby inherited from his father a love of racing and bloodstock breeding. As an owner he proved wonderfully successful, and there were no more popular colours in his day than the familiar black jacket, white cap. As a breeder, his stock exerted immense influence on the breeding of thoroughbreds all over the world.

His Classic successes were as follows:

2,000 Guineas: Colorado (1926); Garden Path (1944)

1,000 Guineas: Canyon (1916); Ferry (1918); Tranquil (1923); Fair Isle (1930); Tide-way (1936); Herringbone (1943); Sun Stream (1945)

Derby: Sansovino (1924); Hyperion (1933); Watling Street (1942)

Oaks: Toboggan (1928); Sun Stream (1945)

St Leger: Swynford (1910); Keysoe (1919); Tranquil (1923); Fairway (1928); Hyperion (1933); Herringbone (1943)

Among the great stallions he owned were Chaucer, Swynford, Phalaris, Pharos, Colorado, Fairway and Hyperion, while there are few more famous mares in the Stud Book than Canterbury Pilgrim, Gondolette, Serenissima, Selene, Scapa Flow and Aurora.

Lord Derby's eldest son, Lord Stanley, died in 1938, and the famous Stanley House Stud passed to Lord Stanley's eldest son, Edward John Stanley.

DERBY, 18th Earl of (b. 1918)

The eighteenth Earl of Derby, who served with distinction throughout the war in the Grenadier Guards, inherited the racing interests of his grandfather but not the same involvement nor the same level of success. Until Teleprompter won the valuable Arlington Million in Chicago in 1985, the last major winners for the black jacket and white cap were in the early 1960s, with Alcove (Cesarewitch) and Tudor Treasure (St James's Palace Stakes). In 1976 Lord Derby sold the Stanley House Stable, built by the sixteenth Earl, and with only a few horses in training and his broodmare strength down to single figures, the great days seem to be over.

Racing colours: black, white cap.

DERBY AND OAKS, Winners of

Eleanor (1801), Blink Bonny (1857), Signorinetta (1908) and Fifinella (1916) are the only fillies to have won both the Derby and the Oaks. Fifinella's victories were in war-substitute races at Newmarket. Under modern conditions it is unthinkable that any horse would be asked to run in both races.

de TRAFFORD, Sir Humphrey (1891-1971)

Sir Humphrey de Trafford served with the Coldstream Guards and rode with some success under National Hunt Rules. He was a noted racing administrator and served three terms of office as steward of the Jockey Club. As an owner his two great years were 1958, when he won the St Leger with Alcide, and 1959, when he won the Derby with Parthia and the King George VI and Queen Elizabeth Stakes with Alcide. Both were trained by Cecil Boyd-Rochfort. His last major winner was Approval (Observer Gold Cup), trained by Henry Cecil.

DEVONSHIRE, 11th Duke of (b. 1920)

The Duke of Devonshire served with distinction throughout World War II in the Coldstream Guards. He was Minister of State, Commonwealth Relations Office 1962-64. He has been a member of the Jockey Club since 1956 and was a steward from 1966 to 1969. He has served on the Horserace Totalisator Board from 1977 and was president of the Thoroughbred Breeders' Association. By far the best performer to carry his colours so far is Park Top whom he bought for 500gns. Her thirteen successes included the Ribblesdale Stakes, Coronation Cup, Hardwicke Stakes and King George VI and Queen Elizabeth Stakes.

Racing colours: straw.

DEWAR, John Arthur (1891-1954)

When not yet 40 years of age, John Dewar inherited from his uncle, Lord Dewar, a vast fortune, a stud and a string of racehorses that included Cameronian, destined to win the 2,000 Guineas and Derby in 1931. Dewar had had little interest in the Turf before this stroke of good fortune, but he soon developed one and maintained it until his death. His other Classic winners were Tudor Minstrel, a superb miler who won the 2,000 Guineas by eight lengths in 1947; Commotion, winner of the Oaks in 1941; and Festoon, who won the 1,000 Guineas in 1954. He also owned Fair Trial, a good racehorse and a highly successful sire. He bought the Beckhampton gallops and establishment on Fred Darling's retirement for £60,000 but sold the property in 1952 when Noel Murless, Darling's successor there, announced his intention of moving to Newmarket. Dewar's last trainer was Noel Cannon, who trained at Druid's Lodge. Dewar left an estate valued at over £3,000,000, and when his horses in training, mares, yearlings and foals were sold, they realized the gigantic total of 398,595gns.

DIADEM (1914, ch f Orby – Donnetta, by Donovan)

Bred and owned by Lord D'Abernon and trained by George Lambton, Diadem was noted for her speed, toughness and courage, and racing up to the age of seven, she won 24 races for a total of £16,058, including the 1,000 Guineas. She was a half-sister to Diophon (2,000 Guineas) and a sister to Diadumenos (Kempton Jubilee and Liverpool Autumn Cup). She herself bred three winners, including Dian, who won over £4,000 in stakes, but she had no live produce after being sold for 10,000gns in 1928.

DIAMOND JUBILEE

Bred and owned by the Prince of Wales, later King Edward VII, and trained by Richard Marsh, Diamond Jubilee was foaled in 1897 and was a full brother of the 1896 Derby winner Persimmon. His ability was of the highest but he was temperamental and at times savage. Marsh found it no easy task to train him without taking measures that might have broken the colt's spirit.

Diamond Jubilee and the stable jockey Jack Watts regarded each other with mutual dislike so Mornington Cannon was engaged to ride in the 2,000 Guineas. However, after a gallop not long before the race, Diamond Jubilee tried to kill Cannon and the ride was then given to Herbert Jones, a lad of Marsh's who rode Diamond Jubilee in most of his work. Jones not only won the Guineas on the royal colt but the Derby, St Leger and Eclipse Stakes as well.

Diamond Jubilee never found his form as a four-year-old. He was sold for 32,500gns to a South American breeder and did well at stud in Argentina, where he died aged 26.

DICEY, Richard (b. 1950)

Richard Dicey was attached to Ted Smyth's Epsom stable when he rode 40 winners in 1968 and shared the position of top apprentice with David Coates. Very surprisingly, he announced his retirement from racing in the spring of 1970, though he reappeared later riding abroad.

DILLON, Bernard (1887-1941)

Bernard Dillon was born in Ireland and brought to Britain as a boy by Captain W.B. Purefoy. He was apprenticed to Jack Fallon at Druid's Lodge and later rode as first jockey for Peter Gilpin's powerful Clarehaven stable. His career as a rider began in 1901 and ended in 1911. Brilliant at his best, he became notorious for his addiction to drink, and towards the close of his career he was liable to be alarmingly erratic. He died penniless.

Dillon won the Derby in 1910 on Lemberg and rode a brilliant race on Spearmint to win the Grand Prix de Paris in 1906. He was also associated with Pretty Polly in some of her victories. He was the third husband of the famous music hall artiste Marie Lloyd, but the marriage proved anything but a success.

DINGWALL, Mrs Louie E. (1889-1982)

Formerly assistant to Cecil Ray, Mrs Louie Dingwall trained her first winner, unofficially, in 1932 and continued to handle a small string at Poole, Dorset, until failing eyesight forced her to retire after the 1980 season. She gained her richest successes when taking Treason Trial to the south of France in 1969, when at the age of 80 she was still driving her own box.

DIOLITE (1927, b c Diophon – Needle Rock, by Rock Sand)

Diolite, owned by Sir H. Hirst and trained by F. Templeman, won six races worth £17,066, including the 2,000 Guineas and Coventry Stakes. He started favourite for the Derby but finished third to Blenheim. He was not a success as a sire and was exported to Japan.

DIOMED

Diomed, owned by Sir Charles Bunbury, won the first Derby on 4 May 1780. As a sire in Britain he was not a success, and his fee sank to 2gns. At the advanced age of 21 he was exported to America. He survived the voyage, lived for another ten years and founded a dynasty. From him are descended many of the greatest horses, such as Lexington, in American racing history. When he died, there was as much grief among horse-loving Virginians as there had been at the passing of George Washington, and his death was regarded as a national catastrophe.

DIOMEDES
(1922, b c Argos – Capdane, by Captivation)

Diomedes proved himself one of the best sprinters of this century, winning $16\frac{1}{2}$ races worth £11,820. He proved a disappointing sire, his best produce being Shalfleet, dual winner of the Portland Handicap.

DISTANCE

The distance is a point 240yd from the winning post. One or two courses have 'distance posts' to mark the point. If a judge rules that a horse has 'won by a distance', he means by a margin greater than thirty lengths.

DJEBEL
(1937, b c Tourbillon – Loïka, by Gay Crusader)

Bred and owned by Marcel Boussac, Djebel was a smallish horse of great quality, very tough and game. In Britain he won the Middle Park Stakes and 2,000 Guineas. He would very likely have won the Derby, too, but owing to the war situation his owner sent him to the south of France out of harm's way. Djebel resumed racing in the autumn and won the long-postponed French 2,000 Guineas. The older he got, the better he got, and as a five-year-old he ran seven times and was undefeated, so that he retired having won fifteen races.

Djebel proved a highly successful sire. Among his offspring were Galcador (Derby), My Babu (2,000 Guineas), Hugh Lupus (Irish 2,000 Guineas and Champion Stakes), Djelfa (French 1,000 Guineas), Coronation V (French 1,000 Guineas and Prix de l'Arc de Triomphe), Arbar (Ascot Gold Cup and second in the St Leger) and Djeddah (Eclipse Stakes, Champion Stakes and six races in France). Djebel died in 1958.

DOG

Dog is a derisory, slang term given to a horse that dislikes racing and does not put as much effort as he might into his race.

DONATELLO II
(1934, ch c Blenheim – Delleana, by Clarissimus)

Donatello II was bred in Italy by Signor Federico Tesio. His dam, Delleana, won both Italian Guineas races and the Gran Premio d'Italia. Donatello II was unbeaten in Italy; his one defeat came most unluckily in the Grand Prix de Paris. Shortly afterwards Mr E. Esmond bought him for £47,500 and sent him to stud in Britain.

Donatello II was not a prolific sire of winners, but he got some very good horses and exerted immense influence on bloodstock breeding in Britain. His most notable winners were Alycidon, who won the Ascot Gold Cup and over £37,000 in stakes, and Crepello, winner of the 2,000 Guineas and Derby. Donatello II also sired the 1,000 Guineas winner Picture Play, from whom the 1967 2,000 Guineas and Derby winner Royal Palace is descended.

Donatello mares did well at stud. The 1953 Derby winner, Pinza, was out of a Donatello mare, and so were Aureole, winner of the King George VI and Queen Elizabeth Stakes and twice champion sire, and Wilwyn, who won the Washington D.C. International at Laurel Park. Donatello II died in 1955, two years before Crepello's great wins.

DONCASTER

The opening of new grandstands, at a cost of £1 million, in 1969 brought Doncaster's amenities up to the same high standard as the course itself, and with an indoor betting hall and improved catering facilities allowed the building to be used for non-racing activities.

The course, which has a sandy subsoil and becomes heavy only after very prolonged rain, stands on the historic Town Moor, one of the old commons of Britain, now vested in the Doncaster Corporation by virtue of a charter granted by Henry VIII.

The St Leger, the last of the five Classic races, run over 1m 6f 127yd in

September, is the oldest of the Classics, having been founded in 1776, four years before the Derby. It is named after a highly esteemed Yorkshire sportsman of that period, Lt.-Gen. Anthony St Leger, who lived at Park Hill, near Doncaster. The Park Hill Stakes is also run in September and is for three-year-old fillies competing over the full St Leger course. The Doncaster Cup, over $2\frac{1}{4}$ miles, was first run in 1766 and is the oldest race still run under the Rules of Racing.

The track is left-handed and pear-shaped. It is nearly 2m round with a sweeping turn into the straight about $4\frac{1}{2}$f from the winning-post. The straight mile is wide and flat. Mile races are also run on the round course. High numbers are usually favoured in the draw on the straight course.

Doncaster took over the Manchester November Handicap when the Lancashire course closed in 1963, and the Lincoln Handicap under similar circumstances from 1965, so that Doncaster now starts and ends the Flat season. The William Hill Futurity Stakes – run as the Timeform Gold Cup from 1961 to 1964 and the Observer Gold Cup from 1965 to 1975 – is the season's richest race for two-year-olds.

DONOGHUE, Stephen (1884-1945)

Steve Donoghue, destined to become the most famous and popular jockey of his day, was the son of an iron-worker and was born in that very unattractive town Warrington. His early life was hard, even by the standards of those days, and fame and fortune did not come to him swiftly or easily. He ran away from home more than once and had experience of a number of well-known British stables, among them those of Dobson Peacock and Alfred Sadler, before, at the age of eighteen, he accepted a post in France with the American trainer Edward Johnson. It was in France that he rode his first winner in 1905. He gained useful experience, if not much else, in riding second-rate horses at trappy little French courses in the provinces. After some of those tracks, Epsom seemed easy. In

1907 he left France and rode in Ireland. His first British retainer was with 'Atty' Persse's stable in 1911. Thus he was associated in 1913 with The Tetrarch, probably the fastest horse ever seen on the British Turf.

Once established in Britain, Donoghue made rapid headway, and he won war-substitute Derbys on Pommern (1915) and Gay Crusader (1917). The heyday of his career was the 1920s, particularly the first six years of that decade, and it was then that the famous cry of 'Come on, Steve!' became a part of the English language. He won the Derby on Humorist (1921), Captain Cuttle (1922), Papyrus (1923) and Manna (1925). Altogether he had fourteen victories in British Classic races. He also won the Irish Derby four times and the Grand Prix de Paris twice. He was champion jockey ten years running, from 1914 to 1923, on the last occasion sharing the title with Charlie Elliott, and his best season was 1920, with 143 winners.

He partnered the great stayer Brown Jack, who won the Queen Alexandra Stakes at Royal Ascot six years running. His last important success was to win the 1937 Oaks on Exhibitionnist. He was then 52 years of age. His last mount was in the Final Plate at Manchester that year. Not once in his 33 years as a jockey was he up before the stewards for an infringement of the rules.

Donoghue was above all a superb horseman with beautiful hands, and it was a pleasure to see him cantering down to the start on a highly-strung two-year-old. He genuinely loved horses, and they went kindly for him. His iron nerve remained unimpaired to the end. He had some dreadful falls and after a shattering crash in the 1920 Derby on very hard ground, when he lay prone in the path of the oncoming field, he walked back to the weighing room and rode two more winners that afternoon. He was at his brilliant best at Epsom, and that downhill gallop to Tattenham Corner never gave him a second's anxiety.

A little, short-legged man with a husky voice and a charming smile, he had a most attractive personality. He was kind and generous – too generous for his own good, in fact – and even at the zenith of his popularity he never became swollen-headed or over-bearing. Sometimes he was deplorably casual towards those who employed him, but his charm usually extricated him from unpromising situations. Both as a breeder of bloodstock and as a trainer he was notably less successful than he had been as a rider. All who followed racing felt they had lost a friend when he died quite suddenly in 1945.

DOPING

Doping falls into two categories: doping to win and doping to stop a horse from winning.

Doping to win was introduced into Britain by the American trainers who came to the country at the turn of the century. In general it is reasonable to assume that doping to win is done by the trainer or by someone closely connected with the horse who knows its physical condition, disposition and plans made for it. Horses do not all react in the same manner to a stimulant; a dose that may produce highly satisfactory results in one horse may send another almost mad.

Several years ago there was probably a fair amount of doping to win taking place but this evil was firmly tackled by the authorities, and figures suggest it is now a thing of the past, thanks to greater awareness and international co-operation among the various racing authorities. In Britain the Levy Board spends a lot of money yearly on anti-doping precautions. The danger, of course, is that chemists, for ever discovering new drugs, may always be a step or two in front of the analysts.

Doping to stop a horse from winning is certainly never done by the trainer, who has simpler methods at his disposal if he does not wish a horse of his to win. If the object is to prevent a horse from running, crude methods can be used once access has been obtained, and it does not matter to the perpetrators if the horse is seriously injured. In ante-post betting, punters lose their money if a horse does not run.

A higher degree of skill is needed if a horse is to be well enough to go to the post but at the same time sure to run badly. The ideal situation is a small field with only two horses fancied. Those in the know, not necessarily only the perpetrators, can then lay the doped horse and back the other.

Racecourse Security Services Ltd, set up in 1972, is responsible for the integrity of racing in Britain, a part of which involves post-race testing of horses. In the year 1980-81 5,414 samples were taken, of which twelve contained 'prohibited' substances, these being substances on a list of proscribed drugs which are not permitted to be present in a horse's system since they may unnaturally affect a horse's performance in a race. Five years later 5,503 samples were taken. Sixteen contained positive substances, usually the result of contaminated foodstuffs, and for the first time the 1984 Flat season produced no positive samples.

DOUBLE LIFE
(1926, ch f Bachelor's Double – Saint Joan, by Willbrook)

Double Life was the foundation mare of the Someries Stud at Newmarket. She was bought as a yearling by Captain Cecil Boyd-Rochfort for 600gns on behalf of Lady Zia Wernher, and proved a wonderful bargain. She won six races for £5,647, including the Cambridgeshire, Duke of York Handicap and Chesterfield Cup. Among her offspring were Precipitation, who won seven races worth over £17,000, including the Ascot Gold Cup, and who sired the Derby winner Airborne; and Persian Gulf, who won the Coronation Cup and sired the Derby winner Parthia. Double Life's other two winners were Casanova, who won the Dewhurst Stakes, and Fairly, dam of the Irish St Leger winner Judicate. Among Double Life's most distinguished descendants are Meld (1,000 Guineas, Oaks and St Leger), Charlottown (Derby), Sagacity (Goodwood Cup) and Double Eclipse (third in Derby).

DOUBLES

A common form of betting is a double, in which a bet is made involving two horses in separate races, and the total return from the first horse is invested on the second. To be successful in a win double, both horses must win; in an each-way double both must be placed. The winnings from a horse successful at 5-1 (i.e. £5 plus £1 stake = £6) provide £6 to be invested on the second winner at 3-1 (£18 winnings plus £6 stake = £24) to earn £24 (less any betting tax) for an outlay of £1, odds of 23-1.

In 'mixed doubles' a punter selects a number of horses, and each horse is doubled with all the others in turn.

DOUGLAS-HOME, James A.T. (b. 1952)

Jamie Douglas-Home worked for Bill Wightman and Peter Walwyn for seven years before setting up as a trainer in 1980 at Wantage. He moved to nearby Chilton early in 1985, which was his best season numerically with six winners, including Lochtillum in the Portland Handicap.

DOUGLAS, Lady James (1854-1941)

Lady James Douglas was born in France, the daughter of Mr F. Hennessy, a member of the famous Anglo-French brandy-distilling family. She first married a relation, Mr R. Hennessy, and after his death in 1888, married Lord James Douglas, who died in 1891. She bought the Harwood property near Newbury in 1910, and there she bred Gainsborough, winner of the 'Triple Crown' in 1918. Lady James Douglas therefore became the first woman to win a Classic race in her own colours and the first woman to own a winner of the Derby. She also won the Oaks in 1919 with Bayuda.

DOUIEB, Olivier (b. 1946)

Olivier Douieb came to Britain in 1984 to be private trainer at Newmarket to Mahmoud Fustok, and extended to other owners the following year. He had made his name in his native France with such good horses as Northjet (Prix du Moulin), Detroit (Arc de Triomphe) and L'Attrayante (French and Irish 1,000 Guineas). In his first season in Britain he won fifteen of the 60 races his horses contested, the best

being Meis El-Reem, who was his first runner and winner in the Salisbury 1,000 Guineas Trial on 7 April 1984. Meis El-Reem also won the Child Stakes and was second in the 1,000 Guineas. He trained fifteen winners from 75 runners in Britain in 1985.

DRUID'S LODGE CONFEDERACY

In the early years of this century, the Druid's Lodge stable near Salisbury was famous, even notorious, for bringing off successful coups in big handicaps. 'The Confederacy' consisted of Captain W.B. Purefoy, Mr J.H. Peard, Captain F. Forester, Mr A.P. Cunliffe and Mr E.A. Wigan. They knew the racing game from A to Z, and their skill in weighing up form and a horse's capabilities was remarkable. They betted heavily and won very large sums, especially on Hacklers Pride (Cambridgeshire, 1903 and 1904), Ypsilanti (Jubilee, 1903 and 1904) and Christmas Daisy (Cambridgeshire, 1909 and 1910).

Jack Fallon was the trainer at Druid's Lodge during its heyday, but his job there was merely to carry out the instructions he was given by 'The Confederacy', the shrewdest of whom was Captain Purefoy. Jack Fallon died 'broke'; most members of 'The Confederacy' left big fortunes.

DUFFIELD, George Peter (b. 1946)

George Duffield has been one of Britain's most consistently successful jockeys in the last ten years, but he had to wait some time to get his chance. Born in Wakefield, he was apprenticed to Jack Waugh at Newmarket from 1962 but did not have his first ride in public until 1967. That year he had his first winner, Syllable at Yarmouth on 15 June, and his first major wins came three years later with Fluke (Jersey Stakes) and Calpurnius (Royal Hunt Cup). Though based at Newmarket, Duffield is as likely to be found riding in the North, because of his association with Sir Mark Prescott's much-travelled stable, and it was for Prescott that in 1980 he rode Spindrifter to win ten races in succession. Duffield also rides regularly for Gavin Pritchard-Gordon, for whom he won the 1983 Sussex Stakes on Noalcoholic. His best season was 1983, with 98 winners.

DUNFERMLINE
(1974, b f Royal Palace – Strathcona, by St Paddy)

The Queen bought Stroma on her own judgement as a yearling, and in 1977, the year of her Silver Jubilee, that mare's grand-daughter Dunfermline won the Oaks and St Leger in the royal colours. Dunfermline stayed in training as a four-year-old but, though second in the Hardwicke Stakes, she failed to enhance her reputation and retired to stud the winner of three races and placed eight times.

DUNLOP, John Leeper (b. 1939)

John Dunlop was an assistant for two years with Neville Dent and for a further two years with Gordon Smyth. He succeeded the latter as trainer at the Duke of Norfolk's Arundel stable in 1966. He achieved a notable success for the Duke only a year before the latter died when Ragstone won the Ascot Gold Cup in 1974. Other good horses Dunlop trained in his earlier years were Black Satin (1970 Irish 1,000 Guineas), John Splendid (Ayr Gold Cup), Mount Athos (third in Derby), Scottish Rifle (ten races including Eclipse Stakes) and Pitcairn (Goodwood Mile). In 1978 he won the Derby with Shirley Heights, who went wrong before his Yorkshire owner Lord Halifax could run him in the St Leger. Dunlop won his second British Classic in 1980 with Quick As Lightning (1,000 Guineas), the year he trained the smart miler Posse and the Coronation Cup winner Sea Chimes, and in 1984 he won the Oaks with Circus Plume. In 1985 he became the first trainer in Britain to have a string of 200 horses, and took possession of Ryan Price's former Findon stables to accommodate the extra ones. That year also brought the retirement from his stable of Snaafi Dancer, at $10.2m the world's most expensive

yearling but who never raced in two years in training.

DURBAR II
(1911, b c Rabelais – Armenia, by Meddler)

Bred and trained in France and owned by Mr H. B. Duryea, an American, Durbar II won the Derby in 1914. He was the first French horse to win since Gladiateur in 1865. In fact he had no French blood in his veins, being by the British-bred Rabelais, who had won the Goodwood Cup for Mrs Arthur James, out of Armenia, who was by the British-bred Meddler out the American-bred Urania. Under the rules then existing, Durbar II was not classified as a thoroughbred since Urania's family, one of the best-known in America at that time, was ineligible for inclusion in the British Stud Book. It was not until changes were made in 1949 that Durbar II and his descendants were allowed into the Stud Book. As a sire, Durbar II is best remembered through Durban, a very fast two-year-old and the dam of Tourbillon, winner of the French Derby and four times champion sire in France. Durbar II was eventually exported to America, where he died aged 21.

DURHAM, 3rd Earl of (1855-1928)

Lord Durham, brother of the famous trainer George Lambton, was a member of the Jockey Club from 1882 till his death. Sagacious, fearless, impulsive at times but never vindictive, he served five terms of office as steward, and his energy as a Turf administrator stood out in contrast to the complacent inertia of most of his contemporaries.

In 1887 he made a hard-hitting speech at the annual dinner of the Gimcrack Club, making biting allusions to the in-and-out running of horses in Sherrard's stable, which in fact was controlled by Sir George Chetwynd, a former Senior Steward of the Jockey Club who was in reality little more than a professional backer, and by the stable jockey Charles Wood. Sir George at once sued Lord Durham for libel, having been dissuaded from challenging him to a duel. A protracted case ended with the downfall of Sir George, who was compelled to retire from the Turf, and also of Wood, who forfeited his licence for a number of years.

Lord Durham was a powerful advocate of the introduction of the starting-gate to supplant starting by flag. Careless of unpopularity, he banned smoking in the weighing-room and the jockeys' room. During World War I he never set foot on a racecourse but did all he could to see that the sport continued in a much reduced form. As an owner he was never very lucky, but he won the Oaks with Beam in 1927 and won the Northumberland Plate three times.

DURR, Francis (b. 1926)

Frankie Durr was born in Liverpool and apprenticed to Jack Payne and then to Willie Pratt. He had his first ride in 1942 and three years later rode ten winners to share the position of top apprentice with Tommy Gosling. After completing his apprenticeship, it took him some little time to establish his reputation, but in the early 1950s he began a six-year association with the Duke and Duchess of Norfolk. Subsequently he had several retainers, the most fruitful being for Mr David Robinson, in whose colours he won the Gimcrack Stakes three times (Tudor Music, Yellow God, Wishing Star), July Cup twice (So Blessed, Tudor Music), Jockey Club Stakes (Meadowville), Ebor (Knotty Pine) and Champagne Stakes (Breeders Dream). Durr's most important wins were in the Irish Sweeps Derby and Doncaster St Leger on Sodium. He won the St Leger again on Peleid, and the 2,000 Guineas on two outsiders, Mon Fils and Roland Gardens, the last-named in 1978, the year he retired from riding to start training at Newmarket, where he had bought a substantial farm in 1958. His biggest early wins as a trainer have been with the sprinters Ahonoora (William Hill Sprint), Swelter (Portland Handicap), Crews Hill (Stewards' Cup) and Camps Heath (Ayr Gold Cup), and the miler Sagamore (Cambridgeshire). His best season as a jockey was 1969, with 87 winners, and as a trainer 1980, with 51 winners.

DWYER, Christopher Ambrose (b. 1948)

Chris Dwyer served a seven-year apprenticeship with Staff Ingham and rode his first winner on the stable's 20-1 chance Nahum at Lingfield on 15 April 1967. In 1971 he renewed his apprentice indentures with Jimmy Etherington at Malton and has remained there as a senior jockey. His best season was 1980, with 23 winners.

E

EARL, Walter (1890-1950)

Walter Earl, an extremely good trainer and a very popular personality, was born in Bohemia of British parents, his father being a trainer for over 40 years in Austria-Hungary. At the age of fourteen Walter Earl came to Britain and was apprenticed to Willie Waugh, riding his first winner in 1906. He soon became too heavy for the Flat and rode quite successfully for a time under National Hunt Rules.

In 1920 he took out a licence to train, and in 1924 became private trainer to Mr 'Solly' Joel, for whom he won the Eclipse Stakes, Goodwood Cup, Manchester Cup, Doncaster Cup, Ebor Handicap, Irish Derby and many other good races. When Mr Joel died, in 1931, he became a public trainer, but in 1939, following Colledge Leader's death, he was appointed private trainer to Lord Derby at Stanley House. For Lord Derby he won six Classic races within four seasons, including the 1942 Derby with Watling Street. He also had active charge of the great stayer Alycidon from his arrival at Stanley House till his triumph in the Gold Cup at Ascot. Earl had a serious illness in 1949 and died the following year.

EASTERBY, Michael William (b. 1931)

Mick Easterby is the younger of the Easterby brothers, and having assisted their uncle Walter he started training on his own account at Flaxton, Yorkshire, in 1961. Though he won the Cesarewitch with Boismoss in 1967, the peak of his career came in 1976, when he was the first northern trainer to win more than £100,000 in stakes, his chief earner being the tip-top sprinter Lochnager (King's Stand Stakes, July Cup, William Hill Sprint). The following year he won the 1,000 Guineas with Mrs McArdy, as well as the Portland Handicap–Ayr Gold Cup double with Jon George. His best season numerically was 1975, with 65 winners.

EASTERBY, Miles Henry (b. 1929)

Christened Miles Henry but always known as Peter, Easterby runs one of the biggest and most successful mixed stables in the North, evidenced by the fact that he was the first trainer to win £100,000 in stakes in each of successive National Hunt and Flat-racing seasons, which he did in the winter of 1978-79 and the summer of 1979.

After working for Frank Hartigan and Walter Easterby, he took out a trainer's licence in 1950 and gained his first big wins in 1965, winning the Lincoln Handicap with Old Tom and the King's Stand Stakes with Goldhill. In the 1970s he won the Lincoln again, with Bronze Hill, and the Gimcrack Stakes, with Sonnen Gold, but that period is best remembered as the heyday of the brilliant, dual-purpose gelding Sea Pigeon, who twice won the Champion Hurdle, as well as the Chester Cup twice and Ebor. A man of few words but a shrewd and highly skilful trainer, Easterby also farms extensively at Habton Grange, near Malton, and runs the Easthorpe Hall Stud, established in 1965. His best season numerically was 1979, with 74 winners.

EASTON (1931, Dark Legend – Phaona, by Phalaris)

Easton was bred in France by Mr R.B. Strassburger and was bought by Lord Woolavington and trained by Fred Darling. He ran second in the 2,000 Guineas and Derby in 1934, and in the following year was second in the Coronation Cup. He won the Select Stakes and March Stakes in Britain, while in Belgium he won the Grand International at Ostend. He failed as a sire and died in America.

ECCLESTON, Clive (b. 1947)

Originally apprenticed to Eric Cousins, Clive Eccleston became top apprentice with 41 winners in 1969, the year he joined Frank Carr at Malton. That proved to be his best season, and after riding only four winners in 1979 he left to try his luck abroad, principally in India.

ECLIPSE

Eclipse, a chestnut foaled in 1764, was one of the greatest horses in British racing history. Bred by William, Duke of Cumberland, he was sold after his breeder's death for 75gns to Mr Wildman, a meat salesman at Smithfield. In 1770 Major O'Kelly bought a half-share in him for 650gns and later paid an extra 1,100gns to buy him outright. O'Kelly was an Irish adventurer who had been a billiards marker; it was said that the nearest he ever got to religion was to own a parrot that could whistle one of the psalms.

Eclipse was never beaten; furthermore he was never even extended. In the famous words of O'Kelly, it was always a case of 'Eclipse first, the rest nowhere'. At stud he sired the winners of over 860 races for almost £160,000. When he died, aged 25, he was still covering 50 mares a season. He sired three winners of the Derby: Young Eclipse, Saltram and Serjeant.

The element of pure chance is inseparable from racing. Squirt, grandsire of Eclipse, was being led off to a dog-kennel for execution when a groom persuaded his owner, Sir Harry Harpur, to spare his life, and he was reprieved at the very last moment.

EDDERY, Patrick James John (b. 1952)

Son of Jimmy Eddery, who rode with much success in Ireland and was second in the 1955 Derby and 1957 Oaks, Pat Eddery gave notice of his prowess when,

as an apprentice to 'Frenchie' Nicholson, he rode five winners from seven mounts at Haydock in August 1970, sixteen months after riding his first winner and a few weeks before losing his allowance. He was leading apprentice in 1971 with 71 winners; he succeeded Duncan Keith as stable jockey to Peter Walwyn after ending his apprenticeship in September 1972, and he was champion jockey for the first of four successive occasions in 1974, when his 148 winners included his first Classic success, on Polygamy (Oaks).

The partnership with Walwyn reached a peak in 1975 when Grundy won the Derby and King George VI and Queen Elizabeth Stakes, but it was ironic that his other big wins that season included the Waterford Crystal Mile on Gay Fandango, trained by Vincent O'Brien. In 1980 Eddery ended his association with Walwyn – whose defence of his stable jockey once led to Mr Daniel Wildenstein removing his horses – and signed for Vincent O'Brien and his major owner Mr Robert Sangster.

Eddery's main successes outside the Walwyn stable were in the Oaks (Scintillate), Ascot Gold Cup (Erimo Hawk on a disqualification) and Gimcrack Stakes (Stanford, Bel Bolide). In his first season after the break he won the Irish 2,000 Guineas and Sussex Stakes (Kings Lake), Champagne Stakes (Achieved) and Cheveley Park Stakes (Woodstream) for his new connections, as well as the Dante Stakes and Benson & Hedges Gold Cup on Beldale Flutter.

Though 1977 remains his best season, with 176 winners, his strike-rate in big races has continued to grow. In 1982 he won the Derby on Golden Fleece and Benson & Hedges Gold Cup on Assert; in 1983 the 2,000 Guineas on Lomond, Benson & Hedges Gold Cup on Caerleon and Eclipse Stakes on Solford; in 1984 the 2,000 Guineas and Irish Sweeps Derby on El Gran Senor (beaten a whisker in the Derby), and Eclipse Stakes on Sadler's Wells; and in 1985 the Irish Sweeps Derby on Law Society, Champion Stakes and Breeders' Cup Turf race on Pebbles, and Coronation Cup and Arc de Triomphe on Rainbow Quest.

EDDERY, Paul (b. 1963)

Eleven years younger than his brother Pat, Paul Eddery was apprenticed to Reg Hollinshead from 1979 until his indentures were transferred to Henry Cecil in 1983. Eddery remained with Cecil as second jockey to Lester Piggott and then Steve Cauthen before becoming first jockey to Peter Walwyn in 1986. His first two important successes came in handicaps, in the 1982 Ayr Gold Cup on Famous Star and 1983 Northumberland Plate on Weavers Pin. His best season was 1985, with 50 winners.

EDINBURGH

Threats of closure, when the Levy Board announced its withdrawal of financial support from Edinburgh in 1963, were held off, mainly through the efforts of Lord Rosebery, and were again thwarted after his death in 1974, when the Levy Board again refused direct help towards improvements. So Edinburgh lives on, to provide bright entertainment and opportunities for moderate horses trained in Scotland and the North of England. The course is a seaside one, being situated at Musselburgh, about five miles outside Edinburgh, and consists of an oval track about $1\frac{1}{4}$m round and with a run-in of approximately 4f. The straight 5f course is generally reckoned a fast one and to favour the quick starter. The turns at the top end of the course and into the straight are rather sharp and need a handy horse to negotiate them to the best advantage. High numbers are usually favoured in races of 7f and 1m. Plans to build a National Hunt track were announced in 1985.

EDWARD VII, King (1841-1910)

King Edward VII, as Prince of Wales, registered his colours in 1875. At first he contented himself with a few jumpers trained by John Jones at Epsom, but in 1885 he went to the Newmarket Sales to buy some fillies with a view to founding a stud at Sandringham. His first trainer was John Porter at Kingsclere but in 1893 his horses were transferred to Richard Marsh at Newmarket. There had been a frequent clash of wills between honest, stubborn John Porter and the Prince's racing manager, that witty and sometimes impetuous Irishman Lord Marcus Beresford.

Porter had scant success with the Prince's horses but he supplied the Sandringham Stud with a great foundation mare when he bought Perdita II for the Prince for £900. She bred two Derby winners, Persimmon and Diamond Jubilee, the winners of over £72,000 in stakes.

In 1896 Persimmon won the Derby amid scenes of unforgettable enthusiasm; he also won the St Leger and as a four-year-old the Eclipse Stakes and Gold Cup at Ascot. He is the last Epsom Derby winner to have carried off the Cup. Diamond Jubilee, also by St Simon, won the 'Triple Crown' in 1900, the year the Prince won the Grand National with Ambush II. The King's third and final Derby winner was in 1909 when he won with Minoru, leased from Colonel W. Hall Walker, later Lord Wavertree.

The King was keener on racing and the smart racing set than was his son, King George V, but he was not so good a judge of horses.

EGREMONT, 3rd Earl of (1751-1837)

The third Earl of Egremont was a man of immense wealth and remarkable generosity. He gave away £20,000 every year, and it was said that he delighted in giving as other rich men delighted in accumulating. He never married, and on his death his estates passed to his illegitimate son Colonel George Wyndham, later Lord Leconfield.

For many years Lord Egremont ran a great race meeting in his park at Petworth, and it was the discontinuance of this fixture that led to the Duke of Richmond establishing the Goodwood meeting in 1801. Lord Egremont won the Oaks five times and the Derby five times, with Assassin (1782), Hannibal (1804), Cardinal Beaufort (1805), Election (1807) and Lap-dog (1826). Some of these Derby winners were probably four-year-olds. Bird, who trained for Lord Egremont, admitted on his deathbed that he had twice won the Derby with four-year-olds by the simple expedient of slipping two-year-olds into the yearling paddock. There were usually 300 horses at Petworth, and, as the management was casual to a degree, discovery was highly unlikely. Lord Egremont himself knew nothing of the deception practised.

ELA-MANA-MOU
(1976, b or br c Pitcairn – Rose Bertin, by High Hat)

Ela-Mana-Mou, a first foal whose dam, grandam and great-grandam were also first foals, proved a bargain for two sets of owners. Bought for 4,500gns as a yearling, he raced in the colours of Mrs Andry Muinos for two seasons, winning the Royal Lodge Stakes at two years and King Edward VII Stakes at three, before being sold to a partnership of Tim Rogers and the Weinstock family for £500,000. At four years he moved from Guy Harwood's stable to that of Dick Hern and won four straight races, including the Eclipse Stakes and King George VI and Queen Elizabeth Diamond Stakes. On his only other outing he finished about half a length third in the Prix de l'Arc de Triomphe, and was retired to stud in Ireland with a valuation of £3.2m. His first crop, born in 1982, included the Grand Prix de Paris winner Sumayr.

EL GRAN SEÑOR
(1981, b c Northern Dancer – Sex Appeal, by Buckpasser)

El Gran Señor beat an exceptionally strong field for the 2,000 Guineas with ease, rounding off a run of six races without defeat, including the Dewhurst Stakes and three others as a two-year-old which put him at the top of the Free Handicap. He ran only twice more, going down by a short head to Secreto in the Derby, after looking sure to win until the last furlong, and winning the Irish Sweeps Derby. A foot problem kept him out of autumn objectives, and in November 1984 it was announced that he would be retired to stud in Maryland, where he was bred by Edward Taylor and sold to Robert Sangster. His valuation on retirement was around $32m.

ELDIN, Eric (b. 1932)

Eric Eldin was apprenticed to Ryan Jarvis, and among the good horses with which he was associated were Lomond, whose many victories included the Ebor Handicap, Lucasland, winner of the Diadem Stakes and July Cup, and Front Row, who gave him his one European Classic success in the Irish 1,000 Guineas. He rode more than 400 winners abroad, mainly in India, as well as 600 in Britain, before taking up training at Newmarket for the start of the 1980 season. His best season as a trainer was 1982, with 27 winners.

ELEANOR

Sir Charles Bunbury's filly Eleanor won the Derby and the Oaks in 1801. She was the first of the four fillies who have accomplished that feat, the others being Blink Bonny (in 1857), Signorinetta (1908) and Fifinella (1916). Eleanor continued to race till she was seven and is probably the only Derby winner to have won a race at Huntingdon as well.

ELIZABETH II, HM Queen (b. 1926)

The Queen is as great a racing enthusiast as was her great-grandfather, King Edward VII, and on all Turf matters she is very knowledgeable. In the years immediately following her accession to the throne, she was extremely successful as both owner and breeder, and the combination of Captain Charles Moore as racing manager and Captain Cecil Boyd-Rochfort and Noel Murless as trainers was an extremely powerful one.

Indifferent results in the 1960s were improved in the 1970s, when Lord Porchester became her racing manager, and her horses were trained by Dick Hern, Ian Balding and William Hastings-Bass. The development of the Royal Stud produced two very good Classic-winning fillies in Highclere (1,000 Guineas and French Oaks) and Dunfermline (Oaks and St Leger).

Previously, superbly bred fillies and colts were leased to the Queen for their racing career by the National Stud. It was these, among whom were Hopeful

Venture and Carrozza, who were trained by Noel Murless.

Good winners to have carried the Queen's colours include Aureole (King George VI and Queen Elizabeth Stakes, Coronation Cup, Hardwicke Stakes), Pall Mall (2,000 Guineas, Lockinge Stakes twice), Canisbay (Eclipse Stakes), Carrozza (Oaks), Doutelle (John Porter Stakes, Ormonde Stakes), Above Suspicion (St James's Palace Stakes, Gordon Stakes), Miner's Lamp (Blue Riband Trial Stakes, Princess of Wales's Stakes), Mulberry Harbour (Cheshire Oaks), Hopeful Venture (Grand Prix de Saint-Cloud, Princess of Wales's Stakes, Hardwicke Stakes), Aiming High (Coronation Stakes), Almeria (Ribblesdale Stakes, Yorkshire Oaks, Park Hill Stakes), Restoration (King Edward VII Stakes), Pindari (King Edward VII Stakes, Great Voltigeur Stakes), Landau (Sussex Stakes), Gaulois (Goodwood Cup), Apprentice (Goodwood Cup, Yorkshire Cup) and Agreement (Doncaster Cup twice, Chester Cup).

Racing colours: purple, gold braid, scarlet sleeves, black velvet cap, gold fringe.

ELLANGOWAN
(1920, b c Lemberg – Lammermuir, by Sunstar)

Ellangowan was owned and bred by Lord Rosebery, for whom he won the 1923 2,000 Guineas ridden by Charlie Elliott. He also won the St James's Palace Stakes and Champion Stakes for a total of £14,885. He was not a success as a sire.

ELLIOTT, Edward Charles (1904-79)

Charlie Elliott was for more than 25 years a leading jockey. He was still apprenticed to Jack Jarvis when in 1924 he ended a ten-year run by Steve Donoghue as champion jockey. In 1923 he had shared the title with Donoghue, both of them riding 89 winners. A very polished and resourceful horseman, strong, self-confident and intelligent, Elliott had fourteen successes in British Classic races. They were:

2,000 Guineas: Ellangowan (1923); Flamingo (1928); Djebel (1940); Lambert Simnel (1941); Nimbus (1949)
1,000 Guineas: Plack (1924); Four Course (1931); Kandy (1932); Picture Play (1944)
Derby: Call Boy (1927); Bois Roussel (1938); Nimbus (1949)
Oaks: Brulette (1931); Why Hurry (1943).

Elliott rode many big winners in France, the best horse he was associated with there being Marcel Boussac's unbeaten Pharis, winner of the French Derby and Grand Prix in 1939. When Elliott gave up riding at the end of 1953, he became trainer to M. Boussac in France but unfortunately he assumed that post just as the Boussac fortunes were beginning to decline. In 1958 Elliott returned to Newmarket and trained a few horses there, but he had little success before handing in his licence at the end of 1962.

ELLIOTT, Robert Peter (b. 1941)

Bobby Elliott was apprenticed to Tom Masson and rode his first winner, Dante's Inferno, at Lewes on 18 August 1958. He was champion apprentice the following year with 27 winners, and again in 1960 with 30 winners, his best season. In those years he did remarkably well at Royal Ascot, winning the Wokingham (Golden Leg), Ascot Stakes (Shatter) and Royal Hunt Cup (Small Slam). His fortunes dipped in the mid-1970s and he went to ride and train in the United States. He returned in 1982 to ride for Tommy Fairhurst, and his win on Ben Jarrow at Hamilton, on 22 July 1982, was his first in Britain since 1977.

ELPENOR
(1950, br c Owen Tudor – Liberation, by Bahram)

Elpenor is one of the few horses to have won the Ascot Gold Cup and also its French equivalent, the Prix du Cadran. He won at Ascot in 1954, after having run second in the Cadran as pacemaker for the beaten Talma II, and won the Cadran the following year before finishing third at Ascot. He was bred and owned by Marcel Boussac.

ELSEY, Captain Charles Frederick (1882-1966)

One of the most respected and best-liked personalities in the racing world, Captain Charles Elsey year after year sent out more winners from his stable at Malton in Yorkshire than any other northern trainer, and altogether he won 1,148 races worth nearly £800,000. He was leading trainer in 1956.

He won the 2,000 Guineas with Nearula; 1,000 Guineas with Musidora and Honeylight; Oaks with Musidora and Frieze, and St Leger with Cantelo. Notable handicap victories included the Lincolnshire with Double Harness and Babur (twice), City and Suburban with Light Sussex, Chester Cup with Peperium, Jubilee with Commander III and Orinthia, Victoria Cup with Orgoglio and Dionisio, Northumberland Plate with Leonard, Union Jack and Gusty, Ebor Handicap with Yorkshire Hussar, Procne and Bob, Cesarewitch with Woodburn, and Cambridgeshire with Disarmament.

Charles Elsey was a dedicated trainer, intensely loyal to his friends, and devoted to every form of sport. His elder brother took holy orders and became a bishop.

ELSEY, William Edward (1855-1922)

W.E. Elsey trained 124 winners in 1905, the highest number of winners this century until Henry Cecil trained 128 in 1979. His feat was all the more remarkable since his horses had to travel long distances from his stable at Baumber in Lincolnshire, and for a month in August and September he did not have one winner. His winning stakes of £17,207 put him in fifth place in the trainers' list. Elsey was assisted by his son Charles.

ELSEY, Charles William Carlton (b. 1921)

Bill Elsey assisted his father, Captain Charles Elsey, from 1951 to 1960 and on the latter's retirement took out a licence

himself in 1961 and assumed control of the stables at Highfield House, Malton. He has been unable to emulate his father's numbers of winners in a season and gradually has had fewer horses in the stable, but among the good horses he has trained are Pia (Oaks), Peleid (St Leger), Henry the Seventh (Eclipse Stakes, dead-heat in Cambridgeshire), the Ebor winners Sostenuto and Alignment, Double Cream (Lincoln Handicap) and Don (St James's Palace Stakes).

ELSWORTH, David Raymond Cecil (b. 1939)

A West Country jump jockey until he became assistant trainer to Ricky Vallance, David Elsworth took out his own licence to train near Salisbury late in 1978. He began with a mixed yard and had his first winner on the Flat with Raffia Set at Salisbury on 7 April 1979. A few days later he won the Great Metropolitan Handicap at Epsom with Skyline Drive, and he won the race the following year with Heighlin, also successful over hurdles and in both the Goodwood Cup and the Goodwood Stakes. He moved stables to Wiltshire briefly but in 1982 went to Whitsbury and in his first year won the Great Met for the third time, with Right Regent. In 1983 he won the Lincoln and Royal Hunt Cup with Mighty Fly, as well as the Wokingham with Melindra, and in 1984 he had Mighty Flutter run third in the Derby. His best seasons on the Flat were 1983 and 1984, with 24 winners.

EMPERY (1973, b c Vaguely Noble – Pamplona II, by Postin)

Empery exemplifies the internationalism of modern racing. He is by a British sire out of a mare who raced in Peru, ran in the colours of Texan Nelson Bunker Hunt, was trained by Egyptian Maurice Zilber in France and retired to stud in the United States. He won twice, a new-comers' race and the Epsom Derby, in which he beat Relkino by three lengths. He was second in the Irish Sweeps Derby and did not race again. Injury kept him out of one objective in Britain, and loss of condition prevented his running on his arrival in the United States. He was syndicated for stud at a valuation of $6m. His early achievements at stud have not been outstanding, with Bay Empress (Brownstown Stakes) his best winner in Europe.

ENCLOSED MEETING

The first enclosed meeting was Sandown Park, where racing began in 1875.

ENGELHARD, Charles William (1917-71)

American Charles Engelhard brightened the British racing scene all too briefly, for his colours were carried for little more than ten years, in which time his horses – trained by Fulke Johnson Houghton, Jeremy Tree and Jack and Bill Watts in Britain, and Vincent O'Brien in Ireland – won more than £532,000 in stakes. His finest hour came in the Triple Crown success of Nijinsky in 1970. Other important winners were: Indiana (St Leger), Ribocco (Irish Derby and St Leger), Ribero (Irish Derby and St Leger), Ribofilio (Champagne Stakes, Dewhurst Stakes, second in Irish Derby and St Leger), Romulus (Sussex Stakes and Queen Elizabeth II Stakes) and Habitat (Lockinge Stakes, Wills Mile and Prix du Moulin).

His racing affairs in Britain and Ireland were managed by Mr David McCall, and together they had high regard for the stock of Ribot. When Mr Engelhard died, his widow Jane gradually dispersed the bloodstock, and by 1979 the racing empire had broken up, with Rose Bowl (Champion Stakes) the last big winner to carry the Engelhard colours of green, yellow sleeves, scarlet cap.

ENSTONE SPARK (1975, b f Sparkler – Laxmi, by Palestine)

Though Enstone Spark won five times, her most important victories both came as a surprise. She started at 33-1 when winning the Lowther Stakes on her eighth start as a two-year-old, and at 35-1 when taking the 1,000 Guineas on her first

outing as a three-year-old. Between seasons she moved from Richard Hannon to Barry Hills on changing ownership for considerably more than the 3,400gns she cost as a yearling. She showed nothing like her Guineas form in four subsequent outings, in one of which she fell.

ENTRIES, FORFEITS AND DECLARATIONS

The process by which horses are raced revolves round a system of entries, forfeits and declarations. All are processed by Weatherbys, the Jockey Club secretariat, at their Wellingborough offices, and the timing of events usually varies according to the importance of the race. Entries for some prestige races, including the Classics, are made months in advance; entries for other races, including handicaps which attract ante-post betting, are made weeks in advance; entries for the majority of races are made no earlier than 25 days before the event.

Entries are made by persons holding an authority to act for the owner to the Racing Calendar Office and are subject to withdrawal or alteration up to the time of closing. Entries may also close at the Irish Turf Club or to any recognized Turf Authority if special mention is made of this in the advertisement of the race in the *Racing Calendar*.

Races which close early have provision for one or more stages when declaration of forfeit can be made, and the Rules of Racing contain a detailed time schedule for these stages. Horses which stand their ground at a forfeit stage do so at a progressively increased cost.

In all races there is a declaration of runners four days before the race (known as the four-day stage), and another at 11 a.m. on the day before the race (known as the overnight stage), unless unusual circumstances force the Jockey Club stewards to modify these arrangements. The result is that, instead of printing a list of probable runners, as happened in the past, newspapers for the evening before or the morning of the meeting are able to provide an accurate list of runners for their readers.

EPSOM

Epsom is perhaps the most celebrated of all British racecourses because the Derby, the most famous race in the world, is run there.

Epsom is not by any means an easy meeting to run because the course is on a ·Metropolitan Common and is therefore subject to all the regulations applicable to London Commons. In the old days no racing could take place there before the consent of the lord of the manor had been obtained. The stewards of the meeting had a small stand almost opposite the present grandstand, while on the other side of the course there was the Prince's Stand, which was originally built for the Prince Regent.

There was no permanent stand for racegoers until in 1828 a rather shady Doncaster speculator called Charles Bluck applied to the manor court for permission to erect one. It was completed in 1830. Bluck had obtained from the lord of the manor a 90-year lease for an acre of land at £30 a year. Not long afterwards, though, some local notables bought out Bluck for £750, formed the Epsom Grandstand Association and raised £20,000 for building the stand and running it. At first the Association was merely concerned with running the stand but eventually they took over the control and management of the racing as well.

In 1890 the Association obtained a lease of the whole Downs, including the course, from the lord of the manor, and in 1903 Henry Dorling, on behalf of the Association, arranged with the lord of the manor to surrender the existing lease and to pay him a premium of £25,000 and a yearly rental of £3,354 for a new lease covering 106 years. In 1888 the Association had purchased from the lord of the manor of Walton over 200 acres of Walton Downs so they now appeared to be comfortably in control of the situation. That appearance was subsequently to prove deceptive.

After World War I it was somewhat tardily admitted that the old 1830 grandstand and the other stands were totally inadequate for Derby Day. The Association, therefore, decided to face the big expenditure involved and to construct a new stand. As the Association only leased the site of the stands, it was decided to purchase the freehold of the Downs and the lord of the manor's rights attached to it. This was done in 1925 for £57,000. At the same time, the greater part of Walton Downs was sold to the Epsom trainer Mr Stanley Wootton, for £35,000. Mr Wootton in 1969 assigned his part of Walton Downs to the Levy Board, then chaired by Lord Wigg, thus ensuring their continuance as grounds for working horses. The new grandstand was completed in 1927 at a cost of nearly £250,000, a trifling sum compared with what it would cost today.

The Association was faced with a new worry in 1925 by the passing of the Law of Property Act which gave members of the public the right of air and exercise over any part of the Metropolitan Common and prohibited the erection of any building, enclosure or fence which might impede the public from enjoying full use of the common. By this Act the Association was deprived of the right to stop people walking on the course even while a race was in progress, while the erection of temporary stands, rails and car-park enclosures became illegal. Luckily for the continuance of Epsom as a racecourse, the Act gave the Association the right to petition the Minister of Agriculture to impose conditions on the public's rights that would enable the Association to continue in business without injury.

As a result of many meetings with the Epsom and Ewell Urban District Council, a scheme was devised by the Association for the running of Epsom Downs and the adjacent Walton Downs. The outcome was the Epsom and Walton Downs Regulation Act of 1936. This empowered the formation of a body to conserve the Downs, and set down in detail the powers of the conservators, the rights of the public and also the rights of the Association and of Mr Wootton.

The Act made Epsom racing safe for the future, but it was not until legislation was passed in time for the 1985 Derby meeting that parts of the Downs were fenced off and admission could be charged. Until then only those in the stands had to pay, and admission to all the Downs was free.

It is impossible to say when racing first took place at Epsom but in 1648, during the Civil War, the Earl of Clarendon recorded that a party of Royalists met at Epsom Downs 'under pretence of a horse-race, intending to cause a diversion on the King's behalf'. After the Restoration, the first recorded race meeting on the Downs took place on 7 March 1661, and the King himself was present.

At the end of the seventeenth century Epsom enjoyed wide popularity as a spa, and regular race meetings took place there. When in the following century the spa became less fashionable, racing was little affected as the Downs were so handily situated for sportsmen from London. Regular spring and summer meetings were established as far back as 1730.

The turning-point in Epsom's fortunes can be said to have come in 1773 when the twelfth Earl of Derby, then aged 21, took over the lease of The Oaks, a country house on the outskirts of Epsom, from his uncle by marriage, General Burgoyne. The Earl used to act as a steward at Epsom and invariably entertained a large party of friends for the races. The May meeting of 1778 was of the customary type, comprising races run in heats over 2m or 4m, but Lord Derby and his friends founded a race for three-year-old fillies, to be called the Oaks and to be run over a mile and a half the following year.

The first race for the Oaks, which attracted a field of twelve, was rated a success and another three-year-old race, this time for colts and fillies and to be run over a mile, was proposed for 1780. A toss of the coin is said to have decided whether the new race was named the Derby Stakes, or the Bunbury Stakes, in honour of Sir Charles Bunbury, the foremost racing man of the day. As Lord Rosebery said a century later: 'A roystering party at a country house founded two races, and named them gratefully after their host and his house, the Derby and the Oaks. Seldom has a carouse had a more permanent effect.'

The first race for the Derby was won by Sir Charles Bunbury's Diomed. In 1784 the distance of the race was increased to 1½m, and it has remained so ever since.

By 1830 the Derby had gradually established itself as the prime event of the racing year. By then racing had ceased to be the pastime of the privileged few; it was becoming the business and pleasure of many, while betting, together with bookmakers, was playing an ever-increasing part. Newspapers, in particular *Bell's Life*, were starting to exploit the growing public interest, and the introduction of the railway system not only abolished the long and tedious journeys on foot for horses but enabled enthusiasts for the sport to travel from meeting to meeting with comparative speed and in modest comfort. Amenities for the racing public were still primitive, but Lord George Bentinck was to instil some badly needed order and discipline into a sport which was apt to reflect, unpleasantly so at times, the hard, rough standards of the age.

In the mid-Victorian era, Derby Day was essentially a great public holiday. Parliament did not sit on Derby Day, and it was Disraeli himself who first described the Derby as 'the Blue Riband of the Turf'. People went in thousands to Epsom, not really to see the race but to enjoy themselves at the gigantic fairground on the Downs. For years Barnum's Show occupied a site on the rails between Tattenham Corner and the winning-post. Whatever aesthetic shortcomings it possesses, Frith's famous picture of Derby Day accurately reflects the carnival atmosphere of Epsom Downs in the heyday of Queen Victoria. By the end of the century something of the festival spirit had disappeared, while the race itself assumed a greater significance. The crowd began to be composed of a higher proportion of racing enthusiasts and fewer people just out for a 'beano'. There is still a fairground on the Downs today but it has been removed from the centre of the course and is an anaemic affair compared with the acres of brash, colourful, hilarious entertainment provided for a less sophisticated public a hundred years ago.

For many years there were intermittent hostilities between those who paid to use the stands at Epsom and the 'Dictator of Epsom', Henry M. Dorling, Clerk of the Course from 1883 to 1919. This official possessed abundant energy but neither tact nor manners. 'Everyone hates me,' he declared, 'and I like it.' He was frequently in trouble with the stewards and was several times fined for derelictions of duty, on the last occasion when he was over 80 years of age. In his days scant attention was paid to the subject of public relations, but Dorling's truculent intransigence certainly did Epsom no good.

The Derby is a great test of a thoroughbred, and it is a race rarely won by a horse of poor conformation or of indifferent pedigree. In order to win, a horse must possess a combination of speed and stamina. The ability to gallop downhill is essential, and this is usually something beyond the powers of horses that are back at the knee or straight in the shoulder. Sometimes, of course, luck plays an important part in the Derby but usually the race is won by the best horse on the day. With the passing of the years the Derby has retained its prestige, and it is not too much to say that the moment the winner passes the post, his value is at least £5 million and possibly a great deal more.

When jockeys adopted the forward seat at the beginning of this century and race-riding became a much more streamlined affair, the pace of the Derby became hotter. In 1856 Ellington took 3min 4sec when he won: 80 years later the record time of Mahmoud was 2min 33.8sec. As well as the pace, the value of the race has increased. Diamond Jubilee won £5,450 by his victory in 1900; Slip Anchor won £204,160 by his in 1985. This latter sum owed much to the arrival of Ever Ready Ltd as sponsors of the Derby and Oaks in 1984, and their massive commitment will also allow for refurbishment of the grandstand.

The Oaks has never aroused interest comparable with the Derby. The Coronation Cup, first run in 1902, is a prestige race for four-year-olds and upwards over the Derby course. At the spring meeting the old-established handicap, the Great Metropolitan lost its old attraction as a $2\frac{1}{4}$m race which wound its way over the Downs when in 1985 it was reduced to $1\frac{1}{2}$m because of course restrictions, but the City and Suburban remains, as well as the Classic trials, the Blue Riband Trial Stakes and the Princess Elizabeth Stakes.

The $1\frac{1}{2}$m Derby course is left-handed and shaped something like a horseshoe. There is a rise of roughly 150 feet over the first half-mile. The next quarter-mile is virtually level. Then, however, there is a sharp descent to Tattenham Corner, $3\frac{1}{2}$f from the winning post. There is a gradual descent in the straight until the final 50yd which are uphill. The 5f course, a very fast one, joins the Derby course at Tattenham Corner. The 6f and 7f courses are on short spurs leading from the Derby course. Low numbers are favoured in the draw in races from 5f to 1m inclusive. In races of $1\frac{1}{4}$m and $1\frac{1}{2}$m middle numbers are thought advantageous when there is a big field.

DERBY RECORDS

Most Successful Owners

Lord Egremont (5):
    Assassin 1782
    Hannibal 1804
    Cardinal Beaufort 1805
    Election 1807
    Lap-dog 1826

Aga Khan (5):
    Blenheim 1930
    Bahram 1935
    Mahmoud 1936
    My Love 1948
    Tulyar 1952

Mr J. Bowes (4):
    Mündig 1835
    Cotherstone 1843
    Daniel O'Rourke 1852
    West Australian 1853

Sir J. Hawley (4):
    Teddington 1851
    Beadsman 1858
    Musjid 1859
    Blue Gown 1868

Duke of Westminster (4):
    Bend Or 1880
    Shotover 1882

Ormonde 1886
Flying Fox 1899
Sir V. Sassoon (4):
Pinza 1953
Crepello 1957
Hard Ridden 1958
St Paddy 1960

The first woman to own a Derby winner was Lady James Douglas, who won a war-substitute race with Gainsborough in 1918.

The first woman to own an Epsom Derby winner was Mrs G. B. Miller, whose Mid-day Sun, whom she owned in partnership with her mother, Mrs Talbot, won in 1937.

Most Successful Jockeys
L. Piggott (9):
Never Say Die 1954
Crepello 1957
St Paddy 1960
Sir Ivor 1968
Nijinsky 1970
Roberto 1972
Empery 1976
The Minstrel 1977
Teenoso 1983
J. Robinson (6):
Azor 1817
Cedric 1824
Middleton 1825
Mameluke 1827
Cadland 1828
Bay Middleton 1836
S. Donoghue (6):
Pommern 1915
Gay Crusader 1917
Humorist 1921
Captain Cuttle 1922
Papyrus 1923
Manna 1925
J. Arnull (5):
Serjeant 1784
Rhadamanthus 1790
Didelot 1796
Archduke 1799
Election 1807
W. Clift (5):
Waxy 1793
Champion 1800
Ditto 1803
Whalebone 1810
Tiresias 1819

F. Buckle (5):
John Bull 1792
Daedalus 1794
Tyrant 1802
Phantom 1811
Emilius 1823
F. Archer (5):
Silvio 1877
Bend Or 1880
Iroquois 1881
Melton 1885
Ormonde 1886

Four winners were ridden by S. Arnull, T. Goodisson, W. Scott, J. Watts and C. Smirke; three by C. Hindley, W. Arnull, S. Day, S. Templeman, J. Wells, H. Custance, C. Wood, D. Maher, J. Childs, E.C. Elliott, H. Wragg, W. Nevett and W. Johnstone.

The oldest winning rider is J. Forth, who was over 60 when he won on Frederick in 1829. The youngest this century is Lester Piggott, who was eighteen when he won on Never Say Die in 1954; Walter Swinburn was nineteen when he won on Shergar in 1981, and Ernie Johnson was 21 when he won on Blakeney in 1969. The age of the boy Parsons, who won on Caractacus in 1862, is unknown.

Most Successful Trainers
R. Robson (7):
Waxy 1793
Tyrant 1802
Pope 1809
Whalebone 1810
Whisker 1815
Azor 1817
Emilius 1823
J. Porter (7):
Blue Gown 1868
Shotover 1882
St Blaise 1883
Ormonde 1886
Sainfoin 1890
Common 1891
Flying Fox 1899
F. Darling (7):
Captain Cuttle 1922
Manna 1925
Coronach 1926
Cameronian 1931
Bois Roussel 1938
Pont l'Evêque 1940

Owen Tudor 1941
F. Neale (6):
    Assassin 1782
    Saltram 1783
    Noble 1786
    Sir Thomas 1788
    Sir Harry 1798
    Hannibal 1804
M. Dawson (6):
    Thormanby 1860
    Kingcraft 1870
    Silvio 1877
    Melton 1885
    Ladas 1894
    Sir Visto 1895
V. O'Brien (6):
    Larkspur 1962
    Sir Ivor 1968
    Nijinsky 1970
    Roberto 1972
    The Minstrel 1977
    Golden Fleece 1982
R. Prince, D. Boyce, J. Edwards and J. Scott trained five winners, and J. Pratt and R. Marsh trained four.

Most Successful Sires
Sir Peter Teazle, Waxy, Cyllene and Blandford all sired four winners.

Sir Peter Teazle sired the first three to finish in 1803; Stockwell accomplished the same feat in 1866.

The following owners won the Derby and the Oaks in the same year: Lord Clermont (1785), Duke of Bedford (1791), Sir F. Standish (1796), Mr J. Gully (1846), Mr J. Merry (1873) and M. M. Boussac (1950).

The following fillies have won the Derby and the Oaks: Eleanor (1801), Blink Bonny (1857), Signorinetta (1908) and Fifinella (1916). Other fillies to have won the Derby are Shotover (1882) and Tagalie (1912).

The only horse to have won the 2,000 Guineas, Derby, St Leger, Grand Prix de Paris and Ascot Gold Cup is the French-bred colt Gladiateur (1865-6).

Thirty-seven Derby winners have been sired by Derby winners.

Horses bred in North America won ten times in the seventeen years 1968 to 1984.

The longest-priced winners: Jeddah, Signorinetta and Aboyeur (all 100-1).

Fastest time: Mahmoud 2min 33.8sec in 1936. Fastest electrical timing: Golden Fleece, 2min 34.27sec in 1982.

Dead-heats: Cadland and The Colonel, 1828. Cadland won the run-off. St Gatien and Harvester, 1884. Stakes divided.

The Prince of Wales won the Derby and the Grand National in 1900.

G. Blackwell, R.C. Dawson, J. Jewitt, V. O'Brien and W. Stephenson have trained winners of the Derby and the Grand National.

In 1893 H. Barker rode the second in both the Derby and the Grand National.

The smallest field was four in 1794; the largest 34 in 1862.

ERIMO HAWK
(1968, gr c Sea Hawk II – Nick of Time, by Nicolaus)

Erimo Hawk cost 10,000gns as a yearling and came into his own at extreme distances. He completed the Ascot Gold Cup-Goodwood Cup double in 1972 for the first time since Gladness in 1958, but only on the disqualification of Rock Roi after he had hampered Erimo Hawk close home at Ascot. Erimo Hawk was sold to stand at stud in Japan at the end of his four-year-old career, and left as the winner of seven races.

ETHERINGTON, James (b. 1934)

Jimmy Etherington was apprenticed to the Malton trainer Ernie Davey and rode his first winner in 1951. In a lengthy career in the North his most important winners were the stayer Sweet Story (Yorkshire Cup and Northumberland Plate) and the sprinter Goldhill (King's Stand Stakes). He retired from riding in 1970 to begin training at Malton and won the Royal Hunt Cup with Fear Naught in 1978. His best season numerically was 1977, when his horses won 29 races.

EUROPEAN BREEDERS' FUND

The European Breeders' Fund (EBF) was launched in June 1983, when representatives of breeders in Britain, Ireland and

France signed an agreement to create a fund into which stallion owners would pay an annual contribution equal to the average covering fee for each sire being nominated to the scheme, and from which only the progeny of those participating stallions would be eligible to benefit.

The proceeds of the fund in the British part of the scheme are channelled into prize money, breeders' prizes for horses sired by British-based stallions, owners' premiums for selected Pattern and Listed races on the Flat, and veterinary research.

The EBF, which was introduced in the wake of Levy Board prize-money cuts, was modelled on the similarly-funded American Breeders Cup Scheme, to which a cross-registration agreement was negotiated. Each of the three countries involved in the EBF agreed that from 1984 half their two-year-old maiden races would be restricted to the progeny of EBF-nominated stallions, and in Britain this amounted to approximately 220 races. The great majority of stallions were entered, the most notable absentee being Brigadier Gerard, whose owners disagreed with the fund's concept.

EXBURY
(1959, ch c Le Haar –
Greensward, by
Mossborough)

Exbury was bred and owned by Baron Guy de Rothschild. A beautifully made little horse from the first crop of Le Haar, he was a late developer but proved himself a top-class performer on the racecourse, winning seven races in France including the Prix Daru, Prix Ganay, Grand Prix de Saint-Cloud and Prix de l'Arc de Triomphe. In Britain he won the Coronation Cup. He retired to stud in France in 1964, having won the equivalent of £167,000. He was syndicated for £420,000 and at the time of his death from a twisted gut in April 1979 had sired the winners of more than £1.25m. His best winners were Crow (St Leger), Example (Park Hill Stakes), Smuggler (Yorkshire Cup) and Zamazaan (Prix Jean Prat). In the year of Exbury's death, his son Soleil Noir won the Grand Prix de Paris and was second in the St Leger.

EXHIBITIONNIST
(1934, b f Solario – Lady
Wembley, by Tredennis)

Bred and owned by Sir Victor Sassoon and trained by Joe Lawson, Exhibitionnist won the 1,000 Guineas and Oaks, as well as one other race for a total of £15,185. At stud she bred half a dozen winners, the best being Sweet One (Ribblesdale Stakes), who herself bred six winners. Exhibitionnist was the last Classic winner ridden by Steve Donoghue.

F

FAIRHAVEN, Lord (b. 1936)

A steward of the Jockey Club from 1981, having been elected in 1977, Lord Fairhaven succeeded Lord Manton as Senior Steward in the summer of 1985. His horses have been trained by Sir Mark Prescott and Bruce Hobbs since Jack Waugh retired, and the best have been the sprinters Quy and Questa Notte and the middle-distance filly Calaba.

Racing colours: silver, copper hoop, armlets and cap.

FAIRHURST, Thomas (b. 1928)

Better known by his nickname 'Squeak', Tommy Fairhurst has spent all his racing career at Middleham, where he was apprenticed to Matt Peacock and later head lad to Jack Fawcus and Ernie Weymes, for whom he also rode with success. He began training at Middleham in 1969, and his best season was 1978, with 34 winners.

FAIR ISLE
(1927, b or br f Phalaris – Scapa Flow, by Chaucer)

Owned and bred by Lord Derby, Fair Isle was a sister of the St Leger winner Fairway. She won the 1,000 Guineas and four other races for a total of £13,219. She bred one winner, St Magnus, who won over £3,000 in stakes and became a leading sire in Australia. She is the fourth dam of the champion sprinter Sandford Lad.

FAIR SALINIA
(1975, b f Petingo – Fair Arabella, by Chateaugay)

Fair Salinia, Michael Stoute's first Classic winner, was also the first filly to win the Epsom, Irish and Yorkshire Oaks, though she had fortune on her side in being awarded the Irish race on the disqualification of Sorbus. Fair Salinia, a 13,000gns yearling, won on her two-year-old debut and finished second in the 1,000 Guineas before her three successes at a mile and a half.

FAIR TRIAL
(1932, ch c Fairway – Lady Juror, by Son-in-Law)

Fair Trial, owned and bred by Mr J.A. Dewar and trained by Fred Darling, was by the St Leger winner Fairway out of Lady Juror, from whom can be traced the most potent influence in his pedigree, that of the speedy Americus Girl. He himself proved a good horse up to a mile, winning seven races worth £5,100 and being beaten only on the two occasions he ran at $1\frac{1}{4}$m.

As a sire he was an outstanding success and when he died aged 26 in 1958, his stock had won $529\frac{1}{2}$ races worth £302,389. He was leading sire in 1950 and on nine other occasions finished in the top six. His best winners were Palestine (2,000 Guineas), Court Martial (2,000 Guineas and Champion Stakes), Festoon (1,000 Guineas) and Petition (Eclipse Stakes). The triple Classic winner Meld was out of a Fair Trial mare, and so was the St Leger winner Premonition.

FAIRWAY
(1925, b c Phalaris – Scapa Flow, by Chaucer)

Fairway was one of the best of the many great horses owned by the seventeenth Earl of Derby. He was bred by his owner and was a brother to Pharos, second in the Derby, and to Fair Isle, winner of the 1,000 Guineas.

Fairway won twelve races worth £42,722, including the St Leger and Eclipse Stakes. He was favourite for the 1928 Derby but the crowd got out of control and mobbed him on his way to the post, pulling hair out of his tail by the handful. By the time he reached the starting-gate he looked as if he had been dragged through a pond. Not surprisingly, as he was a highly strung colt, he failed utterly in the race. He was undoubtedly, though, the best three-year-old of that season.

At stud he did extremely well and was four times leading sire. The best horse he got was Blue Peter, winner of the 2,000 Guineas and Derby in 1939. His other Derby winner was Watling Street, who won in 1942. Altogether Fairway sired the winners of seven Classic races. He died in 1948.

FAIRY FOOTSTEPS
(1978, b f Mill Reef – Glass Slipper, by Relko)

Bred and owned by Jim Joel, Fairy Footsteps had an all-too-short career of six races, winning three. By claiming the 1,000 Guineas with an all-the-way success over Tolmi, she became her dam's second Classic winner in as many years, following Light Cavalry (St Leger). After the Guineas she was surprisingly beaten in the Musidora Stakes, and having galloped badly in preparation for the Oaks she was retired to stud.

FALMOUTH, 6th Viscount
(1819-89)

The son of a parson, the sixth Viscount Falmouth began to own horses in 1857 and won the 1,000 Guineas with Hurricane in 1862 and the Oaks with Queen Bertha in 1863. Those fillies were trained for him by John Scott, and after Scott's death his horses were sent to Mathew Dawson at Newmarket. Between 1870 and his retirement from racing in 1883, Viscount Falmouth enjoyed an era of outstanding success with animals bred by himself at Mereworth in Kent. In that period he won the 2,000 Guineas with Atlantic, Charibert and Galliard, the 1,000 Guineas with Cecilia, Spinaway and Wheel of Fortune, the Derby with Kingcraft and Silvio, the Oaks with Spinaway, Jannette and Wheel of Fortune, and the St Leger with Silvio, Jannette and Dutch Oven.

FEILDEN, Major-General Sir Randle Guy (1904-81)

Major-General Sir Randle Feilden served in the Coldstream Guards. He made his military reputation as a highly efficient administrator and on retirement in 1949 was Vice-Quartermaster General at the War Office. That year he was elected to the Jockey Club, and so began a period of service that made him one of the most notable members this century. He was Senior Steward on three occasions, including from 1965 to 1973, when he was also the first chairman of the Turf Board. These periods were an especially eventful time for racing and coincided with several clashes with Lord Wigg, the Levy Board chairman. Sir Randle brought greater efficiency and less aloofness to the Jockey Club's treatment of the racing public.

When he retired as Senior Steward in 1973, his duties were divided among three men. He became chairman of Cheltenham Racecourse until 1979, and chairman of the Stable Lads' Welfare Trust until 1980.

FELICITATION
(1930, b c Colorado – Felicita, by Cantilever)

Bred and owned by the Aga Khan, Felicitation was a fine stayer who won eight races worth £14,675, including the Ascot Gold Cup, in which he trounced Hyperion. He also won the Jockey Club Cup, Yorkshire Cup and Churchill Stakes. After a brief period at stud in Britain, he was exported to Brazil. His most notable produce was Morogoro, second in a wartime 2,000 Guineas and Derby.

FELSTEAD
(1925, b c Spion Kop – Felkington, by Lemberg)

Bred and owned by Sir Hugo Cunliffe-Owen and trained by Captain O.M. Bell, Felstead was ridden by Harry Wragg and started at 33-1 when he won the 1928

Derby. He never ran again. At stud he sired Rockfel, a great filly who won the 1,000 Guineas and Oaks, and Steady Aim, who won the Oaks in 1946, the year that Felstead died.

FERRY
(1915, b f Swynford – Gondolette, by Loved One)

Owned and bred by Lord Derby, Ferry won one race, the 1,000 Guineas, in 1918. A sister to the Derby winner Sansovino, she was not a success at stud and ended her life in Poland.

FESTOON
(1951, ch f Fair Trial – Monsoon, by Umidwar)

Festoon was bred and owned by Mr J.A. Dewar and was trained by Noel Cannon. She won the 1,000 Guineas, Coronation Stakes and over £15,000 in stakes. After Mr Dewar's death in 1954, she went up for sale at Newmarket and was bought for a world-record price for a broodmare at public auction, 36,000gns, by Mr A.B. Askew. She bred seven winners, easily the best being Atilla, who amassed over £41,000 in stakes from six victories as far apart as the Vaux Gold Tankard at Redcar, the Gran Premio del Jockey Club in Italy and the Grosser Preis von Baden in Germany.

FIFINELLA
(1913, ch f Polymelus – Silver Fowl, by Wildfowler)

Owned by Mr (later Sir) Edward Hulton and trained at Newmarket by R.C. Dawson, Fifinella was ridden by Joe Childs when she won a war-substitute Derby and Oaks at Newmarket in 1916. She was a highly strung, rather wayward filly and at stud was inclined to transmit similar characteristics to her stock, the best of whom was Press Gang, winner of the Middle Park Stakes. She died in 1931.

FIGHTING CHARLIE
(1961, b c Tenerani – Flight of the Heron, by Cameronian)

Owned and bred by Lady Mairi Bury,

Fighting Charlie was a good game stayer who won eight races and was placed in a further nine. He won the Ascot Gold Cup in both 1965 and 1966. He was put down in 1971, after four years at stud, and his only winner of note was Tom Cribb (Northumberland Plate).

FINANCE OF RACING

There are many aspects to the finance of racing, and the importance and order of suggested priorities usually depend on the observer's own position. Owners breed, buy or lease their horses and pay their training fees directly to the trainer. Training fees vary according to the trainer and to his location; trainers in the North generally charge less than those in the big centres at Newmarket and Lambourn. Most trainers own or lease the establishment at which they train, but some stables belong to an owner or syndicate of owners who pay the trainer a salary. It is up to the trainer to pay his stable staff.

Owners maintain an account at Weatherbys through which entrance fees, forfeits, jockeys' fees, registrations fees etc are paid. Into this account prize money won is paid.

As for racecourses, some are run as companies to make profits for shareholders; others operate on a non-profit-making basis – that is to say, the profits, if any, are used for improving amenities or augmenting the prize money. Others are under the control of borough corporations, and all are eligible for grants or loans from the Horserace Betting Levy Board, the establishment of which has totally transformed the financing of horse racing in Britain.

Bookmakers and the Horserace Totalisator Board pay an annual contribution to the Levy Board, the money received being spent by the board for the general benefit of the sport.

In their annual report the Levy Board detail major expenditure under the heading 'Improvement of Horseracing', and the following details show where this, from income of £20.8m, was distributed in the financial year 1984-85.

	£
Modernisation of racecourses	2,513,358
Prize money	10,392,830
Fixture fees	1,097,150
Racing industry benefit scheme	37,830
Overnight declarations	156,000
Apprentice School Charitable Trust	111,180
Aid of farriery	25,000
Integrity (RTS, RSS)	4,180,321
Point-to-points	126,368

FIRDAUSSI
(1929, ch c Pharos – Brownhylda, by Stedfast)

Firdaussi was bred and owned by the Aga Khan and won eight races worth £21,550, including the St Leger and Jockey Club Stakes. He spent one year at stud in Britain, four years in France, and was then sent to Rumania. He sired the French 2,000 Guineas winner Panipat.

FIRING

Firing, as cauterization is generally known, is a veterinary treatment in which heat is applied to weakened tendons, usually by a metal instrument known as an iron and used with a local anaesthetic on the skin over the part of the leg to be treated. This toughens the structures beneath and acts as a support.

In bar or line firing the hot iron is drawn across the skin in lines about an inch apart. In pin firing the point of the iron enters the thickness of the skin to the tissue or tendon, or even bone, below. In acid firing, one of the oldest-known methods now enjoying a revival, concentrated sulphuric acid is applied to the skin.

FISHERMAN

Bred in 1853, Fisherman won 69 of his 119 races, including 23 in 1856, a record for one season in Britain. He won the Ascot Gold Cup twice and was sent to stud in Australia.

FITZGERALD, James Gerard (b. 1935)

Jimmy FitzGerald turned to training when a bad fall in a hurdle race ended his career as a jump jockey in November 1966. Born in Tipperary, he arrived in England at the age of 16 and his most important riding win was in the Scottish Grand National on Brasher. He began training at Malton in 1969 with a string of mainly jumpers, and had his first winner on the Flat with his first runner, Dale, a six-year-old mare at Hamilton Park in May 1970. His biggest triumph was with Kayudee in the 1985 Cesarewitch, a few months after he had won the Cheltenham Gold Cup with Forgive 'N' Forget. Numerically his best Flat season was 1983, with 24 winners.

FLAGS

Communications with racecourse spectators are still carried out by means of flags, and the significance of those displayed on the number boards on the authority of the Clerk of the Scales is as follows:

Blue flag: Riders weighed in.
Red flag: Objection to winner.
Red and white flag: Objection to any other placed horse.
Red flag with white E: Enquiry called for by the stewards.
White flag: Enquiry completed, objection overruled, placings unaltered.
Green flag: Enquiry completed, objection sustained, placings altered.
Black and white flag: Number withdrawn.

FLAMINGO
(1925, b c Flamboyant – Lady Peregrine, by White Eagle)

Flamingo was owned by Sir Laurence Philipps (later Lord Milford). Trained by Jack Jarvis, he won the 2,000 Guineas and five other races for a total of £20,925. He was a somewhat unlucky second in the Derby, in which he was not ridden with the best judgement. He sired the Gold Cup winner Flyon, and Flamenco, winner of the St James's Palace Stakes and Lincolnshire Handicap.

FLARES
(1933, b c Gallant Fox – Flambino, by Wrack)

An American-bred horse trained by Capt Cecil Boyd-Rochfort, Flares won eight races worth £17,828, including the Ascot Gold Cup, Champion Stakes, Newmarket Stakes and Princess of Wales's Stakes. He failed as a sire in both the United States and Canada.

FLATMAN, Elnathan (1810-60)

Nat Flatman was a leading jockey during the mid-Victorian era. He rode for 30 years, and his services were in great demand as not only was his skill of a high order but he was honest and could keep his mouth shut. He was champion jockey seven years running when the records were first compiled from 1846, and was first past the post in the 2,000 Guineas, 1,000 Guineas and St Leger three times each. He was credited with winning the Derby when Orlando was awarded the race on the disqualification of the four-year-old Running Rein in 1844. His career ended with a fall in 1859 and he died the following year.

FLAT-RACING SEASON

No Flat race can be run earlier than the week that includes 25 March (unless that be the one next before Easter Sunday, in which case races may be run in the week preceding) or later than the week that includes 22 November.

FLEET (1964, b f Immortality – Review, by Panorama)

Bred in Ireland by Commander Peter FitzGerald, Fleet was bought for 11,000gns as a yearling by Mr R. C. Boucher, who sent her to Noel Murless to be trained. Fleet won five races worth a total of £47,284, including the 1,000 Guineas, Cheveley Park Stakes and Coronation Stakes. After a year at her owner's stud she was exported to America.

FLYING CHILDERS

The Duke of Devonshire's Flying Childers, foaled in 1715 and sired by the Darley Arabian, has been described as 'the first great racehorse'. Few of his performances were recorded but it is known that he ran against the best horses of his time at Newmarket and was never beaten. He achieved such a reputation for invincibility that eventually he received forfeit in most of his matches.

FLYING FOX

The first Duke of Westminster is the only man who has bred and owned two Triple Crown winners – Ormonde in 1886 and Flying Fox in 1899. Both were trained by John Porter at Kingsclere.

Flying Fox, who was by Orme out of Vampire, won just over £40,000 in stakes for the Duke. Because of his owner's death, Flying Fox came up for sale in 1900 and was bought by M. Edmond Blanc for 37,500gns, a huge price at that time. Flying Fox proved a stud success and his name is among sire lines of powerful influence in France, Italy and America, chiefly since his son Ajax sired Teddy.

FLYING WATER (1973, ch f Habitat – Formentera, by Ribot)

Bred and owned by Daniel Wildenstein, Flying Water was an outstanding racemare who overcame serious injury as a three-year-old and campaigned until she was five. Winner of her only race as a two-year-old, she was successful in her first two outings at three years, including a spectacular victory in the 1,000 Guineas, but missed the rest of the season after sustaining a leg injury following her next race. She was operated on in the United States and returned to win three races at four years, including the Champion Stakes, and was successful in America in 1978, but she died there the same year.

FLYON (1935, ch c Flamingo – Acquit, by Hurry On)

Flyon was bred and owned by Lord Milford. Trained by Jack Jarvis, he won seven races worth £12,165, including the Ascot Gold Cup, Newmarket St Leger and Liverpool St Leger. He was a failure as a sire.

FOLKESTONE

Kent's sole racecourse is situated about eight miles from the town of Folkestone and is served by its own railway station, Westenhanger. It escaped the Levy Board's 1963 axe to continue providing races for mainly modest horses in surroundings that assume greater attractiveness in the summer. It is a right-handed track, about 1m 3f round, with a run-in of $3\frac{1}{2}$f. Both the round course and the straight 6f are undulating but the final 2f are flat. It is generally reckoned a fairly easy course that demands adaptability more than stamina.

FORDHAM, George (1837-87)

George Fordham, one of the greatest of nineteenth century riders, was born at Cambridge. He was very small indeed when he won his first race in 1851 at Brighton, and the following year he won the Cambridgeshire at the astonishing weight of 3st 12lb. As he grew older and stronger his skill increased, and in his prime he was inferior only to Fred Archer, and very little inferior at that. Though in his career he won the 2,000 Guineas three times, the 1,000 Guineas seven times and the Oaks five times, for years the Derby eluded him and he retired without winning that race. However, unsuccessful business ventures compelled him to return to the saddle and at long last he achieved his great ambition and won the 'Blue Riband' on Sir Bevys in 1879.

His style was unique and by no means graceful but it was undoubtedly effective. His sense of timing was superb, and again and again he got up in the last few strides to win by inches. He used the whip far less than most contemporaries and had the knack of getting the utmost from a horse while riding it out with his hands. Much respected for his integrity, he loathed gambling and did all he could to stop his own son from coming into contact with the racing world. He died at Slough.

FOREIGN HORSES

A horse foaled elsewhere than in Great Britain, Ireland or the Channel Islands, or which has been outside Great Britain, cannot be declared a runner for any race until a passport has been lodged with the clerk of the course and verified by a vet. For horses from countries without a passport system, a certificate of pedigree and identification must be lodged at the racecourse, checked by a vet and sent on to the Racing Calendar Office so that declaration can be made.

FORFEIT LIST

The 'forfeit list' is defined in the Rules of Racing as a record of arrears published under the sanction of the Turf Authorities of Great Britain, Ireland and the Channel Islands. Arrears are built up by owners who fail to pay declaration and forfeit fees, or fines imposed under the Rules of Racing. A list of arrears, known as the Unpaid Forfeit List, is kept at the Racing Calendar Office, and the appearance of an owner's name carries the ultimate sanction of being declared a disqualified person. The list is published in the *Racing Calendar* six times a year, and arrears cannot be removed from the list until they are paid direct to the Racing Calendar Office.

A horse which is sold but is in the forfeit list cannot be entered to run until the arrears have been paid. It is up to the buyer to determine whether his purchase is in the list, otherwise he could be landed with another bill, not to mention the possibility of inconvenience and embarrassment.

A corrected alphabetical index of the horses and owners in the last forfeit list and the Irish forfeit list is published in the first *Racing Calendar* of every month during the racing season.

If a horse or its owner in the forfeit list is entered for any race in contravention of the Rules, the nominator of the horse is liable to a fine of up to £130.

FORTH, John (1769-1848)

John Forth is generally accepted as the oldest man to ride a Derby winner as he was over 60 years of age when he trained Frederick and rode him to victory in the Derby of 1829. That year the second horse was The Exquisite, owned by

Forth, who won the Derby again as a trainer in 1845 with The Merry Monarch.

FOSTER, Christopher N. (b. 1946)

Christopher Foster's appointment as secretary to the Jockey Club, announced in January 1983 following the death of Simon Weatherby, broke the tradition of more than 200 years in which the position had gone to a member of the Weatherby family. Foster joined the firm in 1973, working in the racing division at Wellingborough, before transferring to London two years later, where he worked closely with Simon Weatherby. A qualified chartered accountant, he was made a Weatherbys' director in 1975, became assistant secretary to the Jockey Club in 1980 and deputy secretary two years later.

FOUR COURSE
(1928, b f Tetratema – Dinner, by Dinneford)

Four Course was bred by Mr J.P. Arkwright and was sold as a foal for 910gns to Fred Darling, who sold her to Lord Ellesmere for 3,000gns the following year. She won four races for a total of £14,074, namely the 1,000 Guineas, Gimcrack Stakes, Richmond Stakes and July Stakes. She was second in the Oaks. She died early in her stud career.

FOUR-FURLONG RACE

The last 4f race to be run under Jockey Club Rules was on 27 May 1912. The following year the Rule regarding distance was amended to read, 'There shall be no race of less distance than 5f.'

FOX, Frederick Sydney (1888-1945)

Fred Fox was born in Wiltshire. Apprenticed to Fred Pratt at Lambourn, he rode his first winner in 1907 and the following season won the Cesarewitch on Yentoi. For two years before World War I he rode in Germany and Austria for the Weinberg stable but he had numerous pre-war successes in Britain including the 1,000 Guineas on Atmah and the Ascot Gold Cup on Bomba and Aleppo.

From 1914 till he retired in 1936 he rode with much success in Britain. He won the 2,000 Guineas on Diolite in 1930, Derby on Cameronian in 1931, 2,000 Guineas and Derby on Bahram in 1935, and St Leger on Firdaussi in 1932. A fall prevented his riding Bahram in the St Leger. He rode five winners in a day at Sandown in 1929 and was champion jockey in 1930. A sound horseman who rode regularly to hounds in the winter, he was never bothered by weight troubles and to the end of his career could go to scale without difficulty at 7st 7lb.

Affectionately known as 'the Mayor of Wantage', he became a Justice of the Peace. A thoroughly kindhearted and generous man, his closing years were saddened by the death of his son Michael who was killed while serving in the RAF. He himself was killed in a car accident.

FOX, Richard Daniel Stuart (b. 1954)

Richard Fox began his apprenticeship with Seamus McGrath in his native Ireland and rode his first winner on Cusheen Loo at The Curragh on 3 November 1972. He completed his time with Frenchie Nicholson at Cheltenham and rode his first winner in Britain on Quite Sweet at Nottingham on 2 October 1973. His best season came while he was still apprenticed, with 53 winners in 1975, the season he won the Lincoln on Southwark Star. In 1976 he won the Extel Stakes on Il Padrone. He had a brief spell as stable jockey to Clive Brittain in 1977 but has been freelance since.

FOXHUNTER
(1929, ch c Foxlaw – Trimestral, by William the Third)

Foxhunter was by an Ascot Gold Cup winner and half-brother to the dual Ascot Gold Cup winner Trimdon. Trained by Jack Jarvis for Mr E. Esmond, he won the Ascot Gold Cup, Doncaster Cup and two other races for a total of £7,755. He was at stud in France, Britain and finally

Argentina, and did well in all three locations.

FOXLAW
(1922, br c Son-in-Law – Alope, by Gallinule)

Owned by Sir Abe Bailey and trained by Reg Day, Foxlaw won five races for a total of £13,536, including the Ascot Gold Cup, Prince of Wales's Stakes, Northumberland Plate and Jockey Club Stakes. He died at the age of thirteen but had done well in his comparatively brief spell at stud. As well as Foxhunter, he sired another Ascot Gold Cup winner in Tiberius, and the eleven-times New Zealand champion sire Foxbridge.

FRAMPTON, Tregonwell
(1641-1727)

At his death, Tregonwell Frampton was described as 'Father of the Turf'. He trained for William III and held the post of Keeper of the Running Horses at Newmarket to Queen Anne, George I and George II. Born in Oxfordshire, the son of a country gentleman, he was equally devoted to field sports and to money. His appearance was unattractive as he habitually wore an expression in which meanness and guile seemed to battle for supremacy. He was eccentric in his dress and found women detestable.

He was very shrewd in matching his horses, betted heavily and was rarely hampered by the exercise of moral scruples. He could be very cruel, and it was sometimes said that, 'Sin came upon the Turf with the advent of Frampton.' However, he had an unrivalled knowledge of horses and did much to improve the art of training. Bit by bit he succeeded in introducing rules and methodical procedure into racing. Respect for him, if not affection, increased with the years, and despite his many faults he unquestionably played a valuable part in the development of British racing.

FRANCIS, Merrick Ewen Douglas (b. 1950)

Son of the former royal jump jockey and now crime-writer Dick Francis, Merrick took out his first licence to train at Dorking in December 1974 and moved to Lambourn in February 1979. His first Flat win was with Cunning Trick at Yarmouth on 26 May 1976, and his biggest success has been with Weavers Pin in the Northumberland Plate in 1983. He has yet to reach double figures in a Flat season.

FREEDMAN, Louis (b. 1917)

Louis Freedman, whose business was in property, had his colours first carried prominently by I Say, third in the Derby and winner of the Coronation Cup. Since the death of I Say's trainer, Walter Nightingall, his principal trainers have been Peter Walwyn and Henry Cecil, while his best horses have mainly been fillies – Lucyrowe (Sun Chariot Stakes), Attica Meli (Yorkshire Oaks, Park Hill Stakes), Polygamy (Oaks) and Royal Hive (Park Hill Stakes). Elected to the Jockey Club in 1975, he was a steward from 1979 to 1980 and deputy senior steward from 1981 to 1983. He bought the Cliveden Stud from the Astor family in 1966, and the Beech House Stud from the Sassoons in 1971 but this was sold four years later.

Racing colours: yellow, black spots, yellow sleeves and cap.

FREE HANDICAP

A Free Handicap is defined in the Rules of Racing as one in which no liability for stakes or forfeit is incurred until acceptance. At the end of each season the Jockey Club Handicappers and their counterparts from Ireland, France, Italy and West Germany compile handicaps of the leading older horses, three-year-olds and two-year-olds, thereby providing an official estimate of the best performers, of both sexes, of those groups. The ratings for horses of three years and upwards are published only for information, but the two-year-old Free Handicap provides the basis for the race which is run over 7f at the Newmarket Craven Meeting the following April and is frequently a useful guide to the Classics. The race was first run in 1929, with Sir Cosmo the winner, and the handicap was opened to horses

The Derby, Epsom

Two notable Derby firsts as, above, the Prince of Wales, later Edward VII, leads in his 1896 winner Persimmon, the first of three victories he and the public enjoyed at Epsom; and, below, Lady James Douglas is seen with Gainsborough, the 1918 winner and the first to carry the colours of a woman owner to success in the Derby.

Above: Hyperion, ridden by Tommy Weston, is led in after his 1933 Derby success by his owner-breeder Lord Derby. Below: 1949 and the first photo-finish in the Derby. Nimbus and Charlie Elliott win by a head from Amour Drake, with Swallow Tail (No. 9) another head away third.

History begins, as Lester Piggott enters the winner's circle on Never Say Die after the 1954 Derby. It was the first of Piggott's record-breaking nine victories in the race.

Two brilliant Derby winners: above, Nijinsky (Lester Piggott) claims the second part of his Triple Crown by beating Gyr and Stintino in 1970; and below, Shergar (Walter Swinburn) races home ten lengths clear of Glint of Gold (noseband) in 1981.

which had not run in Britain for the first time in 1980, though no foreign-trained horse has taken advantage of the new conditions.

Leading Weights in Free Handicap (2-y-o): see Appendix II.

FREER, Geoffrey Hubert (1887-1968)

Geoffrey Freer was an outstanding racing official. From 1945 till 1962 he was the Jockey Club Handicapper and was rated even superior to his uncle Mr T.F. Dawkins who had held that position from 1912 till 1931. Mr Freer was also at various times Clerk of the Course at Newmarket, Newbury, Manchester, Salisbury and Warwick. Immensely popular and with a wonderful dry sense of humour, he was rightly regarded as one of the wisest men in racing. It was largely due to his energies that Newbury made such progress after the Second World War, and he is commemorated there by a Pattern race in the summer.

FRIAR MARCUS (1912, b c Cicero – Prim Nun, by Persimmon)

Friar Marcus was bred at the Sandringham Stud and was probably the best colt owned by King George V. He had great speed and won nine races worth £9,435 including the Middle Park Plate. He did well as a sire and among his offspring were the 1,000 Guineas winner Brown Betty and Friar's Daughter, dam of the 'Triple Crown' winner Bahram.

FRIAR'S DAUGHTER (1921, br f Friar Marcus – Garron Lass, by Roseland)

Friar's Daughter was one of the Aga Khan's cheaper purchases as she cost only 250gns as a yearling. Though of small account on the racecourse, she proved a wonderful bargain as she bred the 'Triple Crown' winner Bahram as well as Dastur, second in the 2,000 Guineas, Derby and St Leger. She also bred Fille

de Salut, grandam of Sunny Boy III, a leading sire in France, and Fille d'Amour, grandam of The Phoenix, winner of the 2,000 Guineas and Derby in Ireland.

FRIEZE (1949, b f Phideas – Cornice, by Epigram)

Frieze, bred and owned by Captain A.M. Keith, was trained by Captain Charles Elsey. She won seven races worth a total of £19,969, including the Oaks and Yorkshire Oaks. Her record at stud was disappointing, with one winner to her credit.

FRIZETTE FAMILY

Frizette was foaled in 1905 in America and was sent to France in 1908. Her descendants have achieved success in Britain, the United States and France, notably Baldric II (2,000 Guineas and Champion Stakes), Black Tarquin (St Leger), Kentucky Derby winner Jet Pilot, Tourbillon, Cillas, Djeddah, Auriban, Macip, Apollonia, Dahlia and Acamas.

FRY, Martin James (b. 1960)

Though born in Somerset, Martin Fry was apprenticed to Denys Smith in Bishop Auckland from 1981, when he rode his first winner, and he remained with the stable until going freelance in the North in the middle of 1985. His best season was 1983, with 31 winners.

FULL DRESS II (1966, b f Shantung – Fusil, by Fidalgo)

Bred at the White Lodge Stud, owned by Mr R.B. Moller and trained by Harry Wragg, Full Dress II won three races worth a total of £24,446, including the 1,000 Guineas, surviving an objection for boring and crossing. The best of her four winning produce is Fairly Hot, who was placed in the Nell Gwyn Stakes and Musidora Stakes, and bred Hot Touch, the Mecca-Dante Stakes winner.

G

GAINSBOROUGH
(1915, b c Bayardo –
Rosedrop, by St Frusquin)

Gainsborough, bred and owned by Lady James Douglas, became the first Derby winner owned by a woman. Trained by Alec Taylor and ridden by Joe Childs, he won a war-substitute 'Triple Crown' among his five successes for a total of £14,080. As a sire he was a great success, being champion in 1932 and 1933, second in 1931, third in 1930 and 1935, and fourth in 1925, 1926 and 1927. His best winners were Hyperion (Derby and St Leger), Solario (St Leger and Gold Cup), Orwell (2,000 Guineas) and Singapore (St Leger). His fillies were markedly inferior to his colts, but his daughters bred the Derby winners Cameronian and Mahmoud.

GALATEA II
(1936, br f Dark Legend –
Galaday II, by Sir Gallahad III)

Owned and bred by Mr R.S. Clark and trained by Joe Lawson, Galatea II was a filly of the highest class. She won three races worth a total of £16,131, including the 1,000 Guineas and Oaks. She bred three winners at stud, including Sugar Bun, the dam of Darling Boy (smart handicapper), grandam of Transworld (Irish St Leger) and third dam of the useful Italian-trained miler Brook, who had the good fortune to be awarded the Queen Anne Stakes at Royal Ascot after the three horses who finished in front of him were disqualified.

GALCADOR
(1947, ch c Djebel – Pharyva, by Pharos)

Galcador won the Derby for his owner-breeder Marcel Boussac, beating the favourite Prince Simon by a head. In France he won twice and was second in the French 2,000 Guineas. A failure as a sire in Europe, he was exported to Japan.

GALICIA

Mr A.W. Cox's Galicia is one of the most famous mares in the Stud Book. Foaled in 1898, she was by Galopin, who was 26 years old when she was born, out of Isoletta, by Isonomy. Galicia bred Lemberg, who won six good races as a two-year-old, and then the Derby, St James's Palace Stakes, Eclipse Stakes (dead-heat), Jockey Club Stakes, Champion Stakes and Coronation Cup. She bred an even better horse in Bayardo, whose 22 victories included the National Breeders' Produce Stakes, Middle Park Plate, Dewhurst Plate, Prince of Wales's Stakes, Eclipse Stakes, St Leger, Champion Stakes, Chester Vase and Ascot Gold Cup. Another of Galicia's sons, Kwang-Su, was second in the 2,000 Guineas and Derby. Her daughter Silesia bred the Oaks winner My Dear and was grandam of the brilliant Picaroon, who won over £13,000 in stakes and died when in training.

GALLINULE

Foaled in 1884, Gallinule was by Isonomy out of Moorhen, a very tough mare who won on the Flat, including selling plates and hunters' flat-races, over hurdles and over fences. Gallinule was a good two-year-old but he went wrong in his wind and developed a tendency to break blood-vessels, so it is hardly surprising he failed to win during the next three seasons. However, Captain Greer, later Sir Henry Greer, Director of the National Stud, thought he had possibilities as a sire and bought him for £1,000. Gallinule proved a wonderful investment as he sired four Classic winners, including

Pretty Polly, one of the greatest fillies of all time. He was on two occasions champion sire.

GALLOPER LIGHT
(1916, br c Sunstar – Golden Hair, by Golden Sun)

Galloper Light is one of the few British-trained horses to have won the Grand Prix de Paris at Longchamp this century, a feat he accomplished in 1919 when French racing had not recovered from the war. (Comrade, in 1920, and Lemonora, in 1921, were the only other winners from Britain between Galloper Light and Glint of Gold in 1981.) Galloper Light was not on the whole a successful sire, but among his offspring was the Oaks winner Beam.

GALOPIN

Prince Batthyany's Galopin, by Vedette out of Flying Duchess, won the 1875 Derby trained by J. Dawson and ridden by Morris. After a slow start he became a highly successful sire and was champion on three occasions. He exercised a profound influence on bloodstock breeding, since he was the sire of St Simon.

GALTEE MORE

Bred in Ireland by his owner John Gubbins and trained at Beckhampton by Sam Darling, Galtee More won the Triple Crown in 1897. At the end of his three-year-old season he was sold to the Russian Government for £21,000. He did well as a sire in Russia but was exported to Germany for £14,000. He died in 1917.

GARDEN PATH
(1941, br f Fairway – Ranai, by Rabelais)

Bred by Lord Derby, Garden Path was a sister of the Derby winner Watling Street. Trained by Walter Earl, Garden Path won the 2,000 Guineas, the only filly to do so since Sceptre in 1902. She bred five winners, of whom Leading Light won over £4,000 in stakes.

GASELEE, Nicholas Auriol (b. 1939)

Nick Gaselee, who served for six years in the Life Guards and was a leading amateur rider under National Hunt Rules, had a varied career as journalist, assistant Clerk of the Course at Ascot and assistant trainer to Fulke Walwyn before he started training on his own account at Upper Lambourn in 1976, with a predominantly jumping stable.

GAY CRUSADER
(1914, b c Bayardo – Gay Laura, by Beppo)

Gay Crusader, bred and owned by 'Mr Fairie' (the *nom de course* of Mr A.W. Cox) and trained by Alec Taylor at Manton, won a total of eight races worth £11,246, including the Triple Crown of 1917. Steve Donoghue reckoned him the best horse he rode. Gay Crusader sired a number of horses placed in Classics but is best remembered as the broodmare sire of Djebel and Prince Rose.

GELDING

A gelding is a male horse of any age that has been castrated. In Britain it is illegal to carry out the operation without an anaesthetic. A gelding rarely develops the physique or temperament of a stallion and thus tends to retain his zest for racing longer than an entire horse. Though geldings in America are allowed to tackle almost all races open to entire horses, they were barred from Group One Pattern races in Europe until relaxation of the Rules in 1986 was brought about by pressure from Britain. Geldings were excluded from the Derby for the first time in 1904.

GEORGE IV, King (1762-1830)

The first success gained by the royal colours in the Derby was that of the Prince of Wales's Sir Thomas in 1788. The Prince began racing in 1784 at the age of 21. His ownership was conducted in absurdly extravagant fashion, and two years later he was heavily in debt. However, he was rescued by Parliament and restored to solvency. In 1790 he ran no fewer than 39 horses. The following year came the scandal over the in-and-out running of his horse Escape at Newmarket. This separated him temporarily from the Turf, although it must be emphasized that his own integrity was never called in question. The Prince of Wales later became Prince Regent and subsequently King George IV.

GEORGE V, King (1865-1936)

George V was keener on racing than many people imagined although, unlike his father, he was unattracted by the smart racing set. He was fond of horses, a good judge of them, and he possessed a fair knowledge of the Stud Book. In particular he liked Newmarket and staying informally at the Jockey Club Rooms. Best of all he enjoyed going round stables quietly in the evening. He never had much luck as an owner, and his best horses were Friar Marcus, who was unbeaten as a two-year-old and was later a successful sire, Scuttle, who won the 1,000 Guineas, Weathervane, winner of the Royal Hunt Cup, and Limelight, winner of the Jersey Stakes, Hardwicke Stakes and Newbury Spring Cup. His trainers were Richard Marsh and William Jarvis.

On his coronation, the lads at Newmarket subscribed 6d each and gave him a pair of raceglasses. He was greatly touched by this, and of all the thousands of presents he received, this was the one he insisted on giving thanks for in person.

GEORGE VI, King (1895-1952)

King George VI won four of the five Classic races in 1942. Big Game won the 2,000 Guineas, and Sun Chariot the 1,000 Guineas, Oaks and St Leger. Both were leased from the National Stud and trained by Fred Darling. King George VI also won the 1,000 Guineas with Hypericum, whom he bred from his fine mare Feola and who was trained by Capt Cecil Boyd-Rochfort.

GIACOMETTI
(1971, ch c Fabergé II – Naujwan, by Ommeyad)

Giacometti was bought as a yearling for 5,000gns by Charles St George and

trained by Ryan Price. He won his three races as a two-year-old, including the Gimcrack Stakes and Champagne Stakes, and was placed in all three Classics open to him – second in the 2,000 Guineas and St Leger and third in the Derby – before winning the Champion Stakes on his last outing at three years. He disappointed when placed in his only two races as a four-year-old and was sold to stand at stud in the United States from 1976. He returned to Britain six years later.

GILDORAN
(1980, b c Rheingold – Durtal, by Lyphard)

Bred by Robert Sangster's Swettenham Stud, Gildoran was trained by Barry Hills, who also trained his sire and dam, and won the Ascot Gold Cup in 1984 and 1985, the fifth horse to do so in successive years since the Second World War. He also won the Goodwood Cup at four years. In the autumn of 1985 he was exported to Australia.

GILLES DE RETZ
(1953, b c Royal Charger – Ma Soeur Anne, by Majano)

Gilles de Retz was bred at the Eveton Stud of his owner, Mr A.G. Samuel. Trained unofficially by Mrs Helen Johnson Houghton (who was not allowed by the Jockey Club to hold a licence) and ridden by Frank Barlow, he won the 2,000 Guineas at 50-1. He showed nothing like that form again, failed to make much mark as a sire and in 1965 was exported to Japan, where he died in 1969.

GILPIN, Peter Valentine Purcell (1858-1928)

Peter Gilpin served for some time in the 5th Lancers and was a successful amateur rider. After marriage, he left the army and began training at The Curragh where he soon established his reputation. On moving to Newmarket he was equally successful; he won the Derby with Spearmint (1906), who also won the Grand Prix de Paris, and with Spion Kop

(1920). He trained the immortal Pretty Polly, one of the outstanding fillies of this century and winner of the 1,000 Guineas, Oaks and St Leger. Gilpin had a second Grand Prix success with Comrade, bought for 25gns as a yearling. Comrade also won the Prix de l'Arc de Triomphe. On his retirement in the 1920s, Gilpin's stable, Clarehaven, at Newmarket, was taken over by his son Victor, who gave up training during World War II.

GIMCRACK

Gimcrack, who stood only just over fourteen hands, was a famous racehorse of the eighteenth century, who won 26 of his 36 races between his first appearance as a four-year-old in 1764 and his last in 1771. He was beaten in the only two races he had at York, but there his fame is commemorated in the Gimcrack Stakes. At the annual dinner of the Gimcrack Club in December, it is a tradition that the main speech of the evening is made by the guest of honour, the owner of the winner of that year's Gimcrack Stakes.

GINEVRA
(1969, b f Shantung – Zest, by Crepello)

Bred by Lord Suffolk, Ginevra failed to make a small reserve at the yearling sales and was bought privately by Charles St George for 2,000gns. She amply repaid him in training with Ryan Price by winning four races, including the Oaks, and then made the highest price for a mare at public auction in Britain when sold to Japanese interests for 106,000gns at the 1972 Newmarket December Sales. She also finished third in the St Leger.

GINISTRELLI, Cavaliere Odoardo (1833-1920)

The Cavaliere Ginistrelli came to Britain from Italy in the 1880s and trained a few horses for himself at Newmarket. He was not taken very seriously by the racing world but undoubtedly knew his job and had a wonderful triumph in 1908, when he won the Derby and Oaks with Signorinetta, whom he had bred himself. In both races Signorinetta was ridden by William Bullock, who certainly did not profit financially, the Cavaliere evidently considering that presents for jockeys were unnecessary.

GLADIATEUR

Owned and bred by Comte Frédéric de Lagrange, Gladiateur was foaled in 1862 and was the first French-bred horse to win the Derby, an event that aroused immense enthusiasm in France and inflicted a painful blow to British self-esteem, though he was trained at Newmarket by Tom Jennings. Gladiateur was a remarkable horse as he suffered from chronic lameness yet, as well as the Derby, he won the 2,000 Guineas, St Leger, Grand Prix and Ascot Gold Cup, a record that remains unequalled. Not for nothing was he called 'The Avenger of Waterloo', and his statue occupies a prominent place at Longchamp racecourse. Rumour that he was a four-year-old when he won the Derby had no foundation in fact and stemmed from the chagrin of defeat by a foreigner. He was not a success at stud and died of navicular disease in 1876.

GLADNESS
(1953, b or br f Sayajirao – Bright Lady, by April the Fifth)

Gladness, bred in Britain by Mr S. McGregor and Mr T. Venn and trained in Ireland by Vincent O'Brien, was a late-maturing filly who won eight races worth over £27,000, including the Ascot Gold Cup, Goodwood Cup and Ebor Handicap. She was also second in the Prix du Cadran and in the King George VI and Queen Elizabeth Stakes. She bred four winners, including Merry Mate (1966 Irish Oaks) and Glad One (second in 1968 Irish 1,000 Guineas and Epsom Oaks).

GLANELY, Lord (1868-1942)

Lord Glanely, who was killed in an air-raid in 1942, was born William Tatem. A Cardiff ship-owner, he was a vigorous, forceful personality and was raised to the peerage in 1918. After

World War I he was an owner and breeder on a very lavish scale and spent a fortune on bloodstock. On the racecourse he was irreverently but affectionately known as 'Guts and Gaiters'. He won the 1919 Derby with Grand Parade and the following year bought Lagrange Stable at Newmarket, which he maintained until it was requisitioned by the Army in 1939. His other notable winners were Rose of England (Oaks), Colombo (2,000 Guineas), Singapore (St Leger), Chulmleigh (St Leger) and Dancing Time (1,000 Guineas).

GLOVER, Major Sir Gerald Alfred (b. 1908)

Major Gerald Glover, a lawyer and landowner, won the 2,000 Guineas in 1962 with Privy Councillor, who was bred at his Pytchley House Stud.

Racing colours: white, maroon hoops on body, white cap.

GODIVA
(1937, b f Hyperion – Carpet Slipper, by Phalaris)

Godiva, owned by Lord Rothermere and trained by W. Jarvis, won six races for £7,804, including the 1,000 Guineas and Oaks in 1940. She was a high-mettled, temperamental filly with a strong will of her own, and in both her Classic successes she was ridden by Doug Marks, then a little-known apprentice and later a successful trainer. Godiva died before she could be put to stud.

GOLD BRIDGE
(1929, ch c Swynford or Golden Boss – Flying Diadem, by Diadumenos)

An exceptionally handsome chestnut, Gold Bridge was a top-class sprinter who won $7\frac{1}{2}$ races for £6,895, including the King's Stand Stakes twice, and became a highly successful sire, with his sons Golden Cloud and Vilmorin going on to make successful stallions. Golden Boss, the likely sire of Gold Bridge, once stood at a fee of 9gns, and met with such scant success that he was sold as a remount sire to the American Government.

GOLDEN FLEECE
(1979, b c Nijinsky – Exotic Treat, by Vaguely Noble)

Golden Fleece's careers on the racecourse and at stud were cut short prematurely. Bred in Kentucky, he was bought by Robert Sangster for $775,000 as a yearling. He raced a mere four times, was unbeaten and unextended and won the Derby in a fast time by three lengths on his last outing and sole appearance outside Ireland, where he was trained by Vincent O'Brien. Lameness in a hind leg caused his early retirement to stud, where his nomination fee was fixed at 100,000 Irish guineas. He completed one season as a stallion. In November 1983 he suffered a bout of colic; the following January he was operated on for a malignant cyst, and in March 1984 he died of a perforated bowel.

GONDOLETTE
(1902, b f Loved One – Dongola, by Doncaster)

Gondolette is one of the most famous mares in the Stud Book. She was bought for 75gns as a yearling by Mr George Edwards of Gaiety Theatre fame and resold for 360gns to Colonel W. Hall Walker (later Lord Wavertree) for whom she bred Great Sport and Let Fly, both placed in the Derby, and Dolabella, dam of the very fast Myrobella who bred the 2,000 Guineas winner Big Game.

In 1912 Lord Derby purchased Gondolette, who was then ten years old. She bred six winners for him including Serenissima Ferry (1,000 Guineas) and the 1924 Derby winner Sansovino. Serenissima bred eight winners of 40 races worth over £47,000 including Bosworth (Gold Cup), Tranquil (1,000 Guineas and St Leger) and Selene, who won £14,000 in stakes and bred Hyperion, winner of the Derby and St Leger, to say nothing of Sickle and Pharamond, both successful sires in the United States, and Hunters Moon, a leading sire in Argentina. Gondolette's name continues to crop up in big-race pedigrees, the latest being as ancestress of the Derby winner Snow Knight.

GOODISSON, Thomas (1782-1840)

Tom Goodisson was the son of Dick Goodisson, a blunt, rough-tongued Yorkshireman who for years was trainer and jockey to the Duke of Queensberry, commonly known as 'Old Q'. Tom, a sound rider, was retained for many years by the Duke of York and also rode frequently for the Duke of Grafton and Sir Charles Bunbury. He rode four Derby winners – Pope (1809), Smolensko (1813), Whisker (1815) and Moses (1822) – as well as winners of the Oaks (twice) and St Leger.

GOODWILL, Arthur William (b. 1911)

Arthur Goodwill is one of those racing characters better known by their nickname, in this case 'Fiddler', which he is said to have earned when he arrived as an apprentice at Harvey Leader's stable with a violin in his luggage. For a short time he rode on the Flat and for a much longer period under National Hunt Rules. From 1933-9 and from 1945-6 he rode jumpers for T. Leader. He took out a licence to train at Newmarket in 1945 and earned a reputation for his skill in placing moderate horses to the best possible advantage. On 1 August 1966 he trained four winners with four runners at Wolverhampton. He was persuaded to postpone his retirement in 1980 to become private trainer to Mr Michael Mouskos, but the arrangement ended after one season and Goodwill handed in his licence.

GOODWOOD

Admittedly Goodwood is not the most easily accessible of courses, but it is beyond question the loveliest in Britain. Laid out on the Duke of Richmond's estate some five miles from Chichester, it overlooks a superb stretch of the Sussex countryside with hardly a house to be seen, while behind the stands in the valley lies Chichester Cathedral and beyond it the Solent. Amenities were improved when the Richmond Stand was demolished and a new structure erected, with help from a Levy Board loan of £2.75m, in 1980.

The course was laid out by the third Duke of Richmond, and the first meeting, organized by members of the Goodwood Hunt and officers of the Sussex Militia, took place in 1801. Goodwood has come a long way since then, and its successful development was due largely to the energy and organizing ability of Lord George Bentinck. The five-day meeting at the end of July is the highlight, though it is no longer fair to say that its sport is not far short of Royal Ascot standard. At the same time there is a pleasing air of holiday informality. The other meetings are of less significance, but a much-sponsored mile race, at present backed by Waterford Crystal, has given a boost to the second August fixture.

At the big meeting the 6f Stewards' Cup is a handicap that always secures a big field and inspires some lively betting. The Goodwood Cup, still started by flag, is a prestige race for stayers, though the Sussex Stakes has outstripped it for prize money as the most valuable race of the week, especially since it became sponsored by the Swettenham Stud in 1984 and had £160,000 added to the stakes in 1985. The major two-year-old races are the 6f Richmond Stakes, 7f Lanson Champagne Stakes and 5f Molecomb Stakes, the latter once restricted to fillies but opened to colts in 1981.

The Cup Course is about 2m 5f. It starts below the winning post and runs the reverse way of the course, turning left after about 4f and returning to the straight 5f run-in by the top bend. The Stakes Course is the last 2m 3f, the Bentinck Course the last 1m 6f, and the Gratwicke Course the last 1m 4f of the Cup Course. The Craven Course is 1¼m, starting in almost the same place as the Gratwicke Course but running in the reverse direction and returning to the straight 5f run-in by the top bend. The Old Mile starts on the Cup Course and joins the 5f course on the lower bend. The 5f and 6f (Stewards' Cup) courses are dead straight, the first furlong of the latter being uphill, followed by a descent for 4f. High numbers are favoured in sprints, and a fast start is a big advantage.

GORTON, John (b. 1946)

Born in South Africa, John Gorton had his first full season's riding in Britain in 1969, after a visit in the autumn of 1966. Sir Jack Jarvis persuaded him to ride in Britain, and on Sir Jack's death in December 1968 it was arranged that Gorton should be first jockey to Lord Rosebery, for whom he won the 1969 Oaks and Ribblesdale Stakes on Sleeping Partner. He returned to South Africa to take up training at the end of the 1974 season in Britain, where he rode a total of 326 winners and had his best season with 67 in 1972.

GOSDEN, John Montague (1904-67)

'Towser' Gosden, as he was always known on the racecourse, made a name for himself in the 1920s as an amateur rider under National Hunt Rules and from 1924 to 1927 assisted the Lewes trainer G.C. Poole. He himself began training at Lewes in 1928 and up till World War II conducted an extremely successful jumping stable. After the war his stable became a 'mixed' one but in the end he dropped the jumpers and concentrated on the Flat. A dedicated professional, he was an extremely skilful trainer, equally at home with a high-class horse or placing moderate performers to the best advantage in small handicaps. Among the good horses he trained were Aggressor (King George VI and Queen Elizabeth Stakes and Hardwicke Stakes), Impatient (Hardwicke Stakes), Tintinnabulum (Manchester Cup twice), the Ayr Gold Cup winners Orthopaedic and Precious Heather, Damredub (Manchester November Handicap), Concealdem (Manchester Handicap) and Tahiri (City and Suburban). He trained Charlottown as a two-year-old, but ill-health compelled him to retire at the end of the 1965 season, so it was his successor, Gordon Smyth, who trained the following year's Derby winner.

GOSLING, Captain Henry Miles (b. 1927)

Captain Miles Gosling served for five years in the 11th Hussars and was a competent amateur rider under National Hunt Rules. He was elected a member of the National Hunt Committee in 1965 and became a steward of that body in 1966. On the amalgamation of the Jockey Club with the National Hunt Committee in 1968, he became a steward of the Jockey Club and was deputy senior steward from 1975 to 1978.

Racing colours: crimson, gold striped sleeves, quartered cap.

GOSLING, Tommy (b. 1926)

Tommy Gosling began his career as a successful apprentice, with Captain O. Bell at Lambourn, and was joint leading apprentice in 1945, with ten winners. For several years he was associated with Walter Nightingall's stable, scoring many wins on Sir Winston Churchill's stout-hearted stayer Colonist II. In 1964 he set up as a trainer at Epsom, and among the good races he won were the Irish 1,000 Guineas with Ardent Dancer, Vaux Gold Tankard and Yorkshire Cup with Quartette and Extel Stakes with Sol' Argent. He did not renew his licence in 1983.

GRAND PARADE (1916, bl c Orby – Grand Geraldine, by Desmond)

Grand Parade was bred by Mr R. Croker and bought by Lord Glanely as a foal for 470gns. He won five of his six races as a two-year-old and two more the following year for a total of £10,982. Trained by Frank Barling at Newmarket, he won the first post-war Derby, ridden by Fred Templeman and starting at 33-1. He also won the St James's Palace Stakes at Ascot. He is the only black to win the Derby since Smolensko in 1813. At stud he sired a large number of moderate winners, his solitary Classic winner being Diophon (2,000 Guineas).

GRAY, Clifford William (b. 1923)

Cliff Gray took over the Beverley stables from his father 'Snowy' in 1980 and had his first Flat win with Loch Boyle at Ayr on 12 May 1980. At the end of six seasons he had trained seventeen winners from a small string.

GRAY, William Harrison (b. 1902)

Before becoming a successful North-Country trainer, 'Snowy' Gray served his apprenticeship with Sir John Renwick and from 1925 to 1949 assisted Captain J. Storie at Beverley. In 1950 he succeeded Storie, and among his best horses were the Dante Stakes winners Ballymarais and Lucky Brief, and Cheb's Lad (Champagne Stakes). He retired early in 1980 and handed over to his son Cliff.

GREAT NEPHEW
(1963, b c Honeyway – Sybil's Niece, by Admiral's Walk)

Winner of five races for £65,861 and placed eleven times, including second, beaten a short head, in the 2,000 Guineas, Great Nephew was a useful racehorse who proved capable of siring horses better than himself. His position as champion sire in 1975 and 1981 owed itself largely to his Derby winners Grundy and Shergar. His other Classic winners were Mrs Penny (French Oaks), Nikoli (Irish 2,000 Guineas) and Good Times (Italian 2,000 Guineas), while Full of Hope, Tolmi, Vaigly Great and Centurius were in the highest bracket. It took five seasons for Great Nephew to break six figures for his winning progeny, but after a slowish start he blossomed into one of the most effective stallions of the 1970s. His best distance was around a mile but he got horses able to stay further than he did. He was retired from stud duties after the 1985 season.

GREENING, Derrick

'Mickey' Greening was one of the busiest lightweight jockeys of the post-war era, having been apprenticed to Harold Bazley at Malton and Harvey Leader at Newmarket. He rode his first winner in 1940 and, before retiring in 1974 to become assistant to Gavin Pritchard-Gordon, his major successes were in important handicaps such as the Wokingham Stakes, Royal Hunt Cup and Manchester November Handicap.

GREY SOVEREIGN
(1948, gr c Nasrullah – Kong, by Baytown)

Bred by Mr William Hill, Grey Sovereign was a three-parts brother to the Derby winner Nimbus. A good but somewhat temperamental sprinter, Grey Sovereign won eight races worth over £8,000. As a sire he proved an outstanding success, and his offspring included the French 2,000 Guineas winners Don II and Zeddaan, while his grandsons Caro (by Fortino II) and Kalamoun (by Zeddaan) also won that race. Grey Sovereign's other important winners included Sovereign Lord (Richmond and Gimcrack Stakes), Sovereign Path (Queen Elizabeth II Stakes and a leading sire), Silver King (£14,372), La Tendresse (£10,412), Queensberry (£10,221), Matatina, Young Emperor, Cynara and Gustav. He was retired from stud in 1972 and died four years later.

GROSVENOR, Richard Grosvenor, 1st Earl (1731-1802)

The first Earl Grosvenor raced on a gigantic scale which cost him a quarter of a million pounds during his lifetime. Founder of the Eaton Stud in Cheshire, he won the Derby in 1790, 1792 and 1794, and the Oaks five times between 1781 and 1799.

GRUNDY
(1972, ch c Great Nephew – Word From Lundy, by Worden II)

Grundy was bought as a yearling for Carlo Vittadini for 11,000gns and, in training with Peter Walwyn, won eight of his eleven races. He topped the Free Handicap after four undefeated outings at two years, including the Champagne Stakes and Dewhurst Stakes. His early three-year-old career was hampered by being kicked in the face by a stablemate, but after finishing second in the 2,000 Guineas he won the Irish equivalent. He went on to beat the filly Nobiliary for the Derby and came out on top in a magnificent race with Bustino for the

King George VI and Queen Elizabeth Diamond Stakes. He failed to show his form in the Benson & Hedges Gold Cup and was retired to stand at the National Stud with a total valuation of £1m. He got the Oaks winner Bireme in his first crop, and the Ascot Gold Cup and Goodwood Cup winner Little Wolf in his second, but his popularity waned and an offer from Japanese interests was accepted for him in 1983.

GUBBY, Brian (b. 1934)

Garage-owner and hotel-proprietor Brian Gubby began training his own horses at Bagshot in 1976 and has done particularly well with the sprinter Gabitat, three times a winner in Germany, where Gubby first ventured as a motor-racing driver around 1970.

GUEST, Rae (b. 1950)

Rae Guest rode almost 300 winners in Scandinavia before he scored his first in Britain though he spent two years of his apprenticeship with Sir Gordon Richards. He has also ridden eleven Classic winners in India. He joined Luca Cumani's stable at Newmarket in 1980 and has developed a reputation for handling awkward horses, one of the earliest being World Leader, on whom he finished third in the 1980 St Leger. His best season in Britain was 1985 with 42 winners, three times his previous top score the year before.

GUEST, Raymond (b. 1907)

Mr Guest, for several years American Ambassador in Ireland, can be regarded as one of the more fortunate owners, since from few horses to represent him he won the Derby twice (with Larkspur in 1962 and Sir Ivor in 1968), not to mention the Grand National and Cheltenham Gold Cup with L'Escargot. Vincent O'Brien trained his two Derby winners. The best horse to carry his colours in America was Tom Rolfe (Preakness Stakes).

Racing colours: chocolate, pale blue hoops and cap.

GUEST, Walter Nelson (b. 1942)

Nelson Guest was a work rider for Sir Gordon Richards for ten years before he took up a training position in Denmark in 1967. He returned to Britain in 1976 to begin training at Newmarket and had his first winner with Mahadeo at Windsor on 16 August 1976. His best season numerically was 1979 with fourteen winners. He gave up training in 1985.

GULLY, John (1783-1863)

John Gully, a former prize-fighter who became Member of Parliament for Pontefract, won the 1846 Derby with Pyrrhus the First, and the 1854 Derby with Andover. He was hard hit when, after buying the 1827 Derby winner Mameluke and backing him to win £40,000 in the St Leger, the starter was bribed to get the horse left and he was narrowly beaten. It was not long before he had better fortune, and he went on to win every other Classic once.

GUSTAVUS

Mr J. Hunter's Gustavus, foaled in 1818, was the first grey horse to win the Derby. He was eventually exported to Prussia.

H

HABITAT
(1966, b c Sir Gaylord – Little Hut, by Occupy)

An American-bred colt, Habitat cost Mr Charles Engelhard the equivalent of almost £38,200 as a yearling, but though he proved difficult to train and as a two-year-old never ran, his trainer Fulke Johnson Houghton's patience paid off to the extent of five wins for £40,840. As a three-year-old he proved himself the best miler in Europe, at any rate provided the ground was not too firm. Retired to stud in Ireland, he became a magnificent success. His two-year-old winners include four in the Middle Park Stakes (Steel Heart, Habat, Hittite Glory and Bassenthwaite). Flying Water (1,000 Guineas), Rose Bowl (Champion Stakes) and the leading sprinters Double Form, Marwell and Habibti proved his stock are capable of training on, and such as Strigida (Ribblesdale Stakes) and Acclimatise (second in Oaks), showed he could sire stayers. More recently he has quickly proved himself as a significant broodmare sire, with Never So Bold the most important example.

HAIGH, William Wilson (b. 1931)

Bill Haigh, who was apprenticed to Captain Elsey and later rode over jumps, trained at Catterick and Middleham for a time before working for Freddy Maxwell at Lambourn and Bill O'Gorman at Newmarket. He resumed training at Penrith in 1970 and moved to Malton six years later. Numerically his best season was 1980, with thirteen winners.

HALF-BRED

A horse is said to be half-bred if one of its parents is ineligible for the General Stud Book.

HALIFAX, Ruth, Countess of (b. 1916)

Ruth, Lady Halifax formerly owned the Swynford Paddocks Stud, Newmarket, where many good horses, including Acropolis, have been bred. The best horse to carry her colours is Frankincense (Lincoln Handicap), whom she bred. A past chairman of the Thoroughbred Breeders' Association, she was appointed a steward at York in 1975 and became one of the first three women elected to the Jockey Club in December 1977.

Racing colours: light blue, chocolate striped sleeves, hooped cap.

HALIFAX, Charles Ingram Courtenay Wood, 2nd Earl of (1912-80)

Lord Halifax served in the Royal Horse Guards. A member of the Jockey Club, he was Senior Steward in 1950-51 and in 1958-59. He acted as steward at several courses, including Beverley, Doncaster, Epsom and Thirsk, and on his death was chairman of the York Race Committee, on which he had served for 35 years. His proudest moment as an owner came when Shirley Heights, whom he bred at his Garrowby Stud in Yorkshire and owned in partnership with his son Lord Irwin, won the Derby in 1978.

HALL, Leslie Alexander (b. 1907)

Les Hall was apprenticed to Captain Percy Whitaker and Walter Earl. He trained for a time under Pony Turf Club Rules before taking out a licence under Jockey Club Rules in 1952. Until his retirement in 1979, he trained at Winchester, and won the 1954 Stewards' Cup with Ashurst Wonder and the 1964 Middle Park Stakes with Spanish Express.

HALL, Sarah Elizabeth (b. 1939)

Miss Sally Hall became the first licensed woman trainer in the North when in 1968 she succeeded her uncle, Sam Hall, at Brecongill, Middleham. She had made a name as a horsewoman in the Newmarket Town Plate and in Jersey in days before women were allowed to ride under Jockey Club Rules. She had her best season numerically in 1982, with 22 winners, and won her first Pattern race in 1985 with Hallgate in the Cornwallis Stakes.

HALL, Samuel (1916-77)

A genial Yorkshireman whose stout figure was familiar until illness came late in his life, Sam Hall spent several years as assistant to his brothers 'Charlie' and Tom, broken by a spell in the Royal Navy from 1940 to 1946, before taking out a licence himself in 1949. He was notably successful in big handicaps, winning the Cesarewitch, Ebor Handicap (three times), Manchester November Handicap (four times), Lincolnshire Handicap (twice), Zetland Gold Cup (three times), Vaux Gold Tankard, Wokingham Stakes (twice), Royal Hunt Cup, Ayr Gold Cup and William Hill Gold Cup. He used to train at Brecongill, Middleham, but in 1967 he moved to Spigot Lodge, near Leyburn. Second to Noel Murless in the list of winning trainers in 1960, he sent out his thousandth winner at Ayr in July 1974. On his sudden death in July 1977, he was succeeded by his assistant, Chris Thornton.

HALSEY, William (1867-1961)

William Halsey was a fine all-round rider. In 1900 he was second in the Grand National on Barsac and in 1901 he won the 2,000 Guineas on Handicapper. On giving up riding, he trained with success at Newmarket, his chief patron being Sir Ernest Cassell. In 1907 he won the St Leger with Wool Winder, and he won the Ascot Gold Cup in 1907 and 1908 with that fine stayer The White Knight. He retired in 1924 and died at the age of 94. His son Claude Halsey trained with

success in France between the wars and subsequently in Britain.

HAMILTON OF DALZELL, Gavin George Hamilton, 2nd Earl (1872-1952)

A member of the Jockey Club for 44 years and a steward for seven, Lord Hamilton of Dalzell was largely responsible for the introduction of the totalisator to British racecourses in 1929. From 1934 to 1945 he was His Majesty's representative at Ascot (succeeded by the Duke of Norfolk).

HAMILTON PARK

The Lanarkshire course, 9m from Glasgow and the first in the country to stage evening racing (in 1947), has set two more recent patterns, being the first to race on a Saturday morning (1971) and dispensing with the silver ring and cheap enclosure to become a 'one-ring' course (1976).

The course is a straight 6f track with a pear-shaped, right-handed loop. The 1m 5f start is in front of the stands; the horses then run down the straight, round the loop and back up the straight to the winning post. The turns are not sharp, and the track is mainly undulating. It is laid out at the head of a valley, the hollow of which is responsible for a pronounced dip about $2\frac{1}{2}$f out, from which point there is a stiff climb to the winning-post. Middle numbers are favoured in the draw on the straight course.

HAMPTON

Foaled in 1872, Hampton, by Lord Clifden, was a small horse standing only 15.2 hands and began his racing career in selling plates. He made immense improvement and became a top-class stayer, winning the Goodwood and Doncaster Cups and Northumberland Plate. He proved a highly successful sire, and sired three Derby winners, Merry Hampton, Ayrshire and Ladas. He also established a prominent sire line, to which Hyperion belongs.

HANBURY, Benjamin (b. 1946)

An amateur rider and professional over jumps, Ben Hanbury spent three years as assistant to Bernard van Cutsem before starting to train at Newmarket in 1973. His first winner was Double Sensation at Thirsk on 13 April 1973. He suffered a severe blow at the end of 1975, his best season, with 52 winners, when one of his main patrons, Ravi Tikkoo, took his horses to France, and it was almost ten years before the stable picked up again. Ironically in 1984 he had his biggest success in the Dewhurst Stakes with Kala Dancer, owned by Mr Tikkoo. In 1983 his New Coins was third in the Oaks. The following year he trained a good two-year-old filly, Kashi Lagoon, for Mr Tikkoo.

HANDICAP

By Jockey Club definition, a handicap is a race in which the weights carried by the horses are adjusted by the Handicapper for the purpose of equalizing their chances of winning.

Not more than four handicaps are allowed on any day's programme, and only with Jockey Club permission can a handicap have more than £15,000 in added money.

A horse is not eligible to run in a handicap until it has either run three times or won a weight-for-age or selling race; and before mid-September no two-year-old can run in a nursery until it has finished in the first four in a weight-for-age or selling race.

The term 'long handicap' describes the way the Handicapper frames the weights below the permitted minimum weight to be carried in the race itself, so that weights can be raised at certain stipulated stages of declaration.

See also Free Handicap.

HANDICAPPER

The job of the Handicapper is to provide a framework of weights so that each horse entered in a handicap has an equal chance of winning. Licensed annually by the Jockey Club, he was originally appointed to work on individual meetings, which he would then attend in person. This led to the possibility of different regard for a horse's ability being held by different Handicappers, and trainers were

able to choose where they thought their horse was best treated. But in 1973, with the aid of computers to cut out some of the tedious clerical work involved in keeping a handicap of all horses in training, a centralized handicapping system was introduced, and members of the team of Handicappers were assigned to certain horses determined by age and distance. One man looks after the two-year-olds, while three-year-olds and upwards are split into those racing over 5f to 7f, 1m to $1\frac{1}{4}$m, and 11f and further. The senior member of the team is known as the Jockey Club Handicapper, a position currently held by Geoffrey Gibbs, who succeeded Major David Swannell.

HANDS

The unit of horse measurement is the hand, which equals four inches. Measurements are taken from the ground to a horse's withers. Officially, the measure was outlawed as a result of Common Market legislation which came into force on 1 January 1980, but so far custom and practice have defeated bureaucracy.

HANLEY, David Louis (b. 1928)

David Hanley rode as an apprentice on the Flat from 1943 to 1946 and held a licence to ride under National Hunt Rules from 1944 to 1958. He was assistant trainer to his father, S.D. Hanley, from 1956 to 1960 before he took out a licence to train at Epsom, moving to Lambourn in 1966. Among the important races he has won are the Portland Handicap, Wokingham Stakes, Ebor Handicap and Cambridgeshire.

HANNON, Richard Michael (b. 1945)

Richard Hannon took over the licence at East Everleigh, near Marlborough, when his father, Harry, retired in 1970, and within three years he had won the 2,000 Guineas with Mon Fils. The stable strength soon grew to about 70 as a result, though it was not until 1982 that he won another major event, the Ebor, with Another Sam. His first winner was with Ampney Prince at Newbury on 17 April 1970, and numerically his best season was 1983, with 49 winners.

HAPPY KNIGHT
(1943, b c Colombo – Happy Morn, by D'Orsay)

Happy Knight, bred and owned by Sir William Cooke and trained by Henri Jelliss, won one race before the age of five, the 1946 2,000 Guineas at 28-1. He changed stables at the end of that season and won twice over 6f in 1948.

HAPPY LAUGHTER
(1950, ch f Royal Charger – Bray Melody, by Coup de Lyon)

Happy Laughter was bred by the Ballykisteen Stud. Sold as a yearling for 3,500gns, she was owned by Mr David Wills and trained by Jack Jarvis. Although dogged by ill-health throughout her life, she won nine races worth £26,908, including the 1,000 Guineas, Coronation Stakes and Falmouth Stakes. She was a failure at stud.

HARD RIDDEN
(1955, b c Hard Sauce – Toute Belle II, by Admiral Drake)

Hard Ridden, trained by Mick Rogers at The Curragh, was Ireland's second Derby winner, after Orby in 1907. By the sprinter Hard Sauce, he was bought at the 1956 Dublin Sales as a yearling for 270gns by Sir Victor Sassoon. Besides winning the Derby, he also won the Irish 2,000 Guineas. He failed in the King George VI and Queen Elizabeth Stakes and never ran again. Possibly he was a lucky Derby winner as Alcide, indisputably the best three-year-old that season, met with a mishap just before Epsom and could not run. Hard Ridden was partnered in the Derby by Charlie Smirke, who was then in his 52nd year. As a stallion Hard Ridden's only produce of note were Hardicanute (Timeform Gold Cup), Giolla Mear (Irish St Leger) and Hardatit (French Champion Hurdle), but he became a leading sire in Japan on export in 1967.

HARDY, Jack (b. 1920)

A former bookmaker who took out his first training licence in 1968, Jack Hardy runs a small mixed stable at Staunton, Nottinghamshire. In 1968 he won the Ascot Stakes with King of Peace.

HARICOT

Foaled in 1847, Haricot was by Mango or Lanercost out of Blink Bonny's dam, Queen Mary. She was famous for toughness and vitality. After racing till she was six, she retired to stud, producing her first foal at eight and her last at 25. She was dam of Caller Ou, winner of the St Leger. When 21, Haricot produced Lady Longden, dam of the Derby winner Sir Bevys and of Hampton, a great racehorse and influential sire.

HARTIGAN, Frank (1880-1952)

The son of an army veterinary officer, Frank Hartigan was a big, tall Irishman who rode with success under National Hunt Rules as an amateur and professional. He subsequently trained with success both jumping and on the Flat. He won the 1,000 Guineas with Vaucluse and Roseway, and the Grand National with Shaun Goilin. He was trainer for some years for Lord Rosebery before the horses were transferred to Jack Jarvis. His son Joe Hartigan (b. 1919) assisted him, with a break for war service, from 1936 to 1952, and trained at Middleham from 1954 to 1970.

HARTIGAN, Martin (1888-1942)

Martin Hartigan trained between the wars at Ogbourne in Wiltshire. He was a highly competent member of his profession whose chief wins were in the Cambridgeshire and Manchester November Handicap, but he is chiefly remembered because it was to him that Gordon Richards was apprenticed.

HARWOOD, Guy (b. 1939)

Guy Harwood rode a number of winners as an amateur under National Hunt Rules and for a time assisted Bryan

Marshall before taking out a licence in 1966 to train at Pulborough in Sussex. His gradual emergence to the top of the tree has resulted in his stable being one of the most modern in the country, and the results have grown with it. His first major success came in 1967 with the Jockey Club Stakes winner Acrania, but it was not until thirteen years later that he began a consistent assault on top prizes and in 1981 he won his first British Classic, the 2,000 Guineas, with To-Agori-Mou. This remains his sole Classic winner, but having reached 97 winners in 1981, he went on to compile scores of 120, 104, 93 and 84, including such smart horses as Kalaglow (King George VI and Queen Elizabeth Diamond Stakes and Eclipse), Sandhurst Prince (Waterford Crystal Mile), Lear Fan (Champagne), Alphabatim (William Hill Futurity), Rousillon (Waterford Crystal Mile and Sussex), Crazy (Ebor), Young Runaway (Champagne) and Bakharoff (William Hill Futurity). He has been admirably served by his assistant (and brother-in-law) Geoff Lawson and the bloodstock adviser James Delahooke.

HASLAM, Patrick Charles (b. 1948)

Patrick Haslam was assistant to George Todd, Gordon Smyth and Alec Kerr before he began training at Lambourn early in 1972. His first Flat-race win was with Melody Way at Pontefract on 27 June 1972. He moved to Newmarket in the autumn of 1978 and has done well in competitive handicaps, especially in 1984, when he won the Victoria Cup with Mummy's Pleasure and the Royal Hunt Cup with Hawkley. Numerically his best season was 1980, with 38 winners.

HASTINGS-BASS, Captain Peter Robin Hood (1920-64)

Captain Peter Hastings-Bass was only 43 and seemed to have a great future ahead of him when he was stricken with a grave illness and died in 1964. He was in his first season as one of the Queen's trainers.

A notable athlete, he won the quarter-mile for Oxford and played rugby for Oxford and the Army. During the war he served with the Welsh Guards and was wounded. Racing was in his blood, though, as his father, Aubrey Hastings, had trained three Grand National winners, riding one of them to victory himself. Aubrey Hastings died suddenly in 1929, and the Wroughton stable, then primarily concerned with jumping, was taken over by Ivor Anthony. Peter Hastings, who assumed the additional name of Bass by deed poll in 1954, assisted Anthony at Wroughton from 1946 to 1952. In the meantime he , purchased the famous Kingsclere training establishment from Evan Williams, at one time the Wroughton stable jockey, and in 1953 set out to train Flat-racers there. He was immediately successful, and among the 340 winners he had sent out before his death were Kings Troop (Royal Hunt Cup), King Bruce (Stewards' Cup) and Midsummer Night II (Cambridgeshire). He was succeeded at Kingsclere by Ian Balding, who in 1969 married his daughter Emma. His widow, Mrs Priscilla Hastings, was among the first three women elected to the Jockey Club in December 1977.

HASTINGS-BASS, William (b. 1948)

Son of Peter Hastings-Bass, who trained at Kingsclere, William worked as assistant to Noel Murless and gained experience in Australia and the United States before he set up training at Newmarket in 1977. His first runner, Better Blessed, was a winner, at Nottingham on 11 April 1977. The following year he trained horses for the Queen and also gained his biggest success, with Greenland Park in the Queen Mary Stakes. He handed in his licence at the end of 1982 to go to Australia, and trained near Sydney for a year, but returned to Newmarket to start again in 1984. He leased a stable from Lester Piggott for one season and for the start of 1985 moved into Coronation House Stables. His best season was 1981 with 44 winners.

HAWLEY, Sir Joseph Henry (1814-75)

An outstanding figure in mid-Victorian racing, Sir Joseph Hawley, after serving for a short time in the 9th Lancers, settled in Italy, and it was there that he developed a taste for the sport.

His connection with British racing began in 1844. Alec Taylor trained for him at Fyfield in Wiltshire, and his Teddington won the 1851 Derby. Subsequently, after a brief and unsatisfactory period with the Days at Danebury, Sir Joseph's horses were trained by George Manning at Cannons Heath, and after Manning's death by John Porter at Kingsclere. Sir Joseph won the Derby on three more occasions, with Beadsman (1858), Musjid (1859) and Blue Gown (1868), and won the other four Classics once.

Sir Joseph, as a member of the Jockey Club, interested himself in Turf reform, and there was much to be said for his plans to restrict two-year-old racing and to extend the privilege of Jockey Club membership to a wider circle. He was, though, neither liked nor entirely trusted, and his speeches on the iniquities of gambling, in view of his own record in that respect, laid him open to the charge of hypocrisy. He was never able to enlist the all-important support of Admiral Rous, and his proposals for reform were defeated.

HAYDOCK PARK

Though Manchester has vanished from the fixture list and the fate of Liverpool has been uncertain, Haydock Park remains deservedly popular as the sole track offering Flat racing in what was once the county of Lancashire. Within handy reach of big industrial areas, it is nevertheless attractively set out in parkland surroundings, and has been enhanced by improved amenities with the building of a new grandstand opened in 1982. Significant increases in prize money have also recently improved the standard of racing.

The track is a left-handed, undulating circuit about 1m 5f round, with one right-handed bend just over a mile from home. The straight 6f (opened in 1986) and the 1½m course start on spurs projecting from the round course. The 4f run-in is slightly uphill the whole way. It is a fair track in all essentials but short-runners do not care for the stiff finish. Low numbers are thought to possess a slight advantage in races of 6f, 7f and 1m but in soft ground fields tend to make for the stands side in the straight, and the advantage may be nullified.

HAYNES, Michael John (b. 1931)

The last apprentice signed by Stanley Wootton, Fulham-born Michael Haynes rode more than 100 winners on the Flat and over jumps before he left racing. He remained in the Epsom area and began training there in 1974, his first Flat winner coming with Some Jewel at Windsor on 21 July 1975. His two best horses have been at either end of the distance scale – the sprinter Vorvados (Portland Handicap) and the stayer Popsi's Joy (Cesarewitch), though both have been kept in great heart for several years.

HEAD, Alec (b. 1924)

Alec Head comes from a famous Anglo-French racing family. He rode on the Flat and over hurdles, including finishing second in the Champion Hurdle, before beginning training at Chantilly in 1947. In 1952 he took over the Aga Khan's horses previously trained in England, and that year won for him the Prix de l'Arc de Triomphe with Nuccio. Two years later he had his first notable success in Britain, when Nahar won the Lincolnshire Handicap. Since then his most important wins in this country have been:

1,000 Guineas – Rose Royale (1957)
2,000 Guineas – Taboun (1959)
Derby – Lavandin (1956)
Ascot Gold Cup – Sheshoon (1960)
Eclipse – Saint Crespin III (1959)
King George VI and Queen Elizabeth Stakes – Vimy (1955)
Champion – Hafiz II (1955), Rose Royale II (1957).

His runners in Britain dwindled in numbers from the mid-1960s, and his last big-race winners were Mige (Cheveley Park Stakes) in 1968, and Green Dancer (William Hill Futurity) in 1974, both belonging to his major patron, the Wertheimer family. Head continued to do well in France where he won the 1,000 Guineas five times, 2,000 Guineas four times, Derby three times and Oaks twice. He also won the Arc de Triomphe again with Saint Crespin III (1959), Ivanjica (1976) and Gold River (1981). In 1984 he retired from training to concentrate on his considerable stud interests.

HEAD, Christiane (b. 1948)

'Criquette' Head emulated her father Alec by training a winner of the Prix de l'Arc de Triomphe early in her career, when Three Troikas won in 1979, having earlier been successful in the French 1,000 Guineas. Her other French Classic winners have been Harbour (1982 Oaks) and Silvermine (1985 1,000 Guineas). She has had few runners in Britain but won the Cheveley Park Stakes in 1982 and 1,000 Guineas the following year with Ma Biche.

HEAD, Frederic (b. 1947)

Freddie Head, son of the trainer Alec Head, is the only jockey who has consistently kept in touch with Yves Saint-Martin's record among the top French jockeys, but his visits to Britain have not always brought out the best in him. After several fancied attempts he rode his first British Classic winner in 1982, on Zino (2,000 Guineas), and the following year won the 1,000 Guineas on Ma Biche. One of his first big wins in France, on Goodly in the 1969 Derby, was for his grandfather Willie. In all he has won the French Derby four times, 2,000 Guineas twice, 1,000 Guineas four times, Oaks three times, and Prix de l'Arc de Triomphe three times, on San San (1972), Ivanjica (1976) and Three Troikas (1979).

HENBIT
(1977, b c Hawaii –
Chateaucreek, by
Chateaugay)

Henbit became the seventh American-bred winner of the Derby in twelve years, but he was an exception in that his breeding was not out of the top drawer and he cost only $24,000 as a yearling. Bought for Mrs Arpad Plesch (owner of the Derby winner Psidium) and trained by Dick Hern, he won once as a two-year-old, was unbeaten in three outings at three years but cracked his off-fore cannon bone about a furlong out in the Derby and did not race again that season. He was brought back for two modest runs as a four-year-old and was retired to stud in Ireland to stand his first season in 1982.

HERMIT

Mr Henry Chaplin's Hermit, despite a tendency to break blood-vessels, won the 1867 Derby on a day when snow fell. He was narrowly beaten by Achievement in both the St Leger and the Doncaster Cup that year. Despite his original modest stud fee of 20gns, he proved an outstanding sire and was champion seven years running, siring two Derby winners in Shotover and St Blaise.

HERN, Major William Richard (b. 1921)

Dick Hern controls one of the most powerful stables in the country at West Ilsley, Berkshire, with the Queen as one of his patrons. His first appointment was from 1952 to 1957 when he assisted Major M.B. Pope. He became private trainer to Major L.B. Holliday, for whom he won the 1962 St Leger with Hethersett, but at the end of that season, when he was leading trainer for the first time, he gave up the appointment to succeed R.J. Colling at West Ilsley.

He won the St Leger again with Provoke in 1965. Then the stable was struck by virus infections in the late 1960s before emerging to great effect in the 1970s with Classic success through Brigadier Gerard (2,000 Guineas), High-clere (1,000 Guineas and French Oaks) and the St Leger winners Bustino and Dunfermline, the last-named also winning the Oaks for the Queen in her Silver Jubilee year, 1977. Brigadier Gerard was one of the best horses of the age, winning seventeen out of eighteen races.

Most of Hern's major successes were shared with Joe Mercer, who served his apprenticeship at the stable and was Hern's stable jockey for fourteen years, until in 1976 Sir Michael Sobell and his son-in-law Sir Arnold Weinstock, owners of the stable, ended the association and brought in Willie Carson, who thus took the ride on the Derby winners Troy (1979) and Henbit (1980), and the Oaks winners Bireme (1980) and Sun Princess (1983), the latter also winning the St Leger. Hern also won the St Leger in 1981 with Cut Above, but Carson was injured and Mercer was called on for a most popular success.

Brigadier Gerard and Troy both won the King George VI and Queen Elizabeth Stakes, which Hern also won in 1980 with Ela-Mana-Mou after he had won the Eclipse Stakes. Leading trainer in 1972, Hern achieved the position for the third time in 1980, with British record earnings of £831,964 and again in 1983.

Having trained his first winner at Lincoln in 1958, Hern saddled his thousandth in Britain with More Light at Kempton Park in 1978.

He was badly injured in a hunting accident in December 1984, and it was six months before he was able to walk unaided because of his paralysis. He enjoyed an enormous tonic when Petoski won him a record fourth King George in July 1985, a fortnight after he had won the Irish Oaks with Helen Street.

HERRINGBONE
(1940, b f King Salmon – Schiaparelli, by Schiavoni)

Bred and owned by Lord Derby, Herringbone won four races worth £5,327, including the wartime 1,000 Guineas and St Leger. At stud she bred eight winners, including Entente Cordiale, whose twelve victories included the Doncaster Cup. Herringbone has appeared more recently as fourth dam of

the Ascot Gold Cup winner Ragstone.

HETHERSETT
(1959, b c Hugh Lupus – Bride Elect, by Big Game)

Owned and bred by Major L.B. Holliday and trained by Dick Hern, Hethersett started favourite for the 1962 Derby but was one of seven horses brought down in a pile-up on the descent to Tattenham Corner. In the autumn he won the St Leger, having little difficulty in defeating the Derby winner Larkspur. He retired to stud as the winner of four races worth £44,240 and soon began to make his mark as a sire. It was a severe loss to British breeders when he died in 1966, emphasized by the victory of his son Blakeney in the 1969 Derby.

HIDE, Edward William George (b. 1937)

Edward Hide, son of the trainer Bill Hide, was following hounds on his pony at the tender age of six. Apprenticed to his father, he rode his first winner in 1951 at Chepstow and had his first major success for him when he won the 1956 Cesarewitch on Prelone. The following season he rode 131 winners, his best effort until he notched 137 in 1974. He was associated with the stable of the Elsey family at Malton from the age of fifteen until the end of 1968 and, except for brief spells with Sir Gordon Richards and Clive Brittain, remained based in the North.

For the Elseys he rode his first Classic winners, Cantelo (St Leger) and Pia (Oaks), and he has since won the 1,000 Guineas (Waterloo and Mrs McArdy) and Derby (Morston). A dedicated professional with a keen tactical brain, he rode a winner on every course in Britain. With rides in Britain diminishing, he went to Hong Kong in the autumn of 1984 but returned the following summer to ride the few winners he needed to pass George Fordham and become the sixth most successful jockey in British history.

HIGGINS, John James (b. 1948)

Apprenticed to Ron Mason from 1964 to 1971, John Higgins had his best season in 1968, with 28 wins. His most important wins have been in the Ayr Gold Cup (Petite Path), Northumberland Plate (Tartar Prince) and Newbury Autumn Cup (Greatham House). His brother Willie (b. 1956) emulated his success in the Ayr Gold Cup on Primula Boy in 1979.

HIGGS, William Arnold (1879-1958)

Billy Higgs rode 1,002 winners and was champion jockey in 1906 and 1907. On Willonyx he won the Chester Cup, Ascot Stakes, Ascot Gold Cup, Cesarewitch (with 9st 5lb) and Jockey Club Cup. He trained with moderate success at Blewbury from 1923 to 1940.

HIGHCLERE (1971, b f Queen's Hussar – Highlight, by Borealis)

Highclere, bred by the Queen, improved greatly on her two-year-old form to become the first filly to win the 1,000 Guineas and French Oaks (Prix de Diane). The British Classic was her first race of the season, and she went on to distinguish herself further by finishing second to Dahlia in the King George VI and Queen Elizabeth Stakes. She was retired to stud after two further unplaced outings. Her first foal, Milford, won the Princess of Wales's Stakes, and her daughter Height of Fashion won five straight races, including the Hoover Fillies' Mile and Princess of Wales's Stakes, before being bought by the Maktoum family for a sum reported to be not far short of £1.5m.

HIGHEST STAKES WON IN A SEASON

Horse: Shergar – five races worth £388,571, 1981.
Trainer: Henry Cecil – 67 winners of 132 races worth £1,148,189, 1985.
Owner: Sheikh Mohammed – 69 winners of 115 races worth £1,082,668, 1985.

Breeder: Aga Khan – thirteen winners of 23 races worth £445,368, 1981.
Sire: Northern Dancer – 27 wins, 44 places worth £1,041,346, 1984.

HIGHFLYER

Highflyer, who sired the Derby winners Noble, Sir Peter Teazle and Skyscraper, was bred in 1774 by Sir Charles Bunbury and then sold to Lord Bolingbroke, who gave him his name through being foaled in a field where some highflyer walnut trees were growing. In 1779 Lord Bolingbroke re-sold him to Mr Richard Tattersall of the famous firm of auctioneers. Highflyer, by Herod, was never beaten and was the outstanding horse of his day. His pedigree contained the blood of the Byerley Turk, the Godolphin Arabian and the Darley Arabian in almost equal proportions, and at stud he proved the ideal sire for mares by Eclipse. Tattersall always tried to purchase an Eclipse mare if one happened to come on the market, and he made a handsome fortune in selling his young stock. When Highflyer died, aged twenty, his owner had the following words engraved on the memorial stone: 'Here lieth the perfect and beautiful symmetry of the much lamented Highflyer, by whom and his wonderful offspring the celebrated Tattersall acquired a noble fortune, but was not ashamed to acknowledge it.'

HIGH STAKES (1942, ch g Hyperion – Pennycomequick, by Hurry On)

High Stakes, a tough and consistent gelding, won 34 races (including two dead-heats) for his breeder Lord Astor, though at Goodwood in 1949 he won first prize in the Bentinck Stakes only because the Judge misinterpreted the photo-finish print. His prize-money earnings of £21,602 stood as a record for a gelding for many years.

HIGH TOP (1969, b c Derring-Do – Camenae, by Vimy)

High Top was bred by Bob McCreery, raced in the colours of Sir Jules Thorn and was trained by Bernard van Cutsem. Having won the Observer Gold Cup at two years, he became his sire's first Classic winner when beating Roberto by half a length in the 2,000 Guineas. He did not win again but was second in the Sussex Stakes. Retired to stud in 1973 at a valuation of £320,000, he has proved a great success, endowing his produce with more stamina than might have been expected from a miler. His best offspring are the Classic winners Circus Plume (Oaks), Top Ville (French Derby), Cut Above (St Leger) and My Top (Italian Derby), and the smart fillies Circus Ring and Triple First.

HILLS, Barrington William (b. 1937)

Son of a head lad to Tom Rimell, Barry Hills learned his trade as apprentice, travelling head lad and head lad before he was able to set up on his own, thanks to the proceeds of astute betting while with the stable of John Oxley at Newmarket. He began at Lambourn in 1969 and within four years had won the Arc de Triomphe with Rheingold, who in 1973 was among more than 100 horses trained by Hills.

Rheingold also won the Grand Prix de Saint-Cloud twice, to mark Hills' emergence among international trainers, and in 1974 he was unfortunate not to win the Oaks with Dibidale, whose saddle slipped under her. Dibidale did win the Irish Oaks and Yorkshire Oaks, while Hills' other important winners include Our Mirage (Jockey Club Stakes), Proverb (Goodwood Cup twice and Doncaster Cup), Hawaiian Sound (Benson & Hedges Gold Cup and beaten a head in the Derby), Durtal (Cheveley Park Stakes), Sexton Blake (Champagne Stakes), Cormorant Wood (Champion Stakes, Benson & Hedges Gold Cup) and Gildoran (Ascot Gold Cup twice, Goodwood Cup). His two British Classic wins have been in the Guineas, with Enstone Spark (1,000) and Tap On Wood (2,000), and numerically his best season was 1978 with 86 winners.

HILLS, Michael Patrick (b. 1962)

Twin brother of Richard and son of trainer Barry, Michael Hills was apprenticed to his father and rode his first winner on his first ride, Sky Thief at Nottingham on 13 August 1979. His indentures were later transferred to Jeremy Hindley, and his career was interrupted in 1982 when he was suspended for six months after striking jockey Susan Gilbert across the face after a race. He resumed with the Hindley stable and in 1983 was leading apprentice with 39 winners. He had his best season in 1985, with 45 winners, including his most important, Huntingdale in the Dewhurst Stakes.

HILLS, Richard James (b. 1962)

Richard Hills rode his first winner a couple of months after his twin brother Michael, on Border Dawn at Doncaster on 26 October 1979. He too was apprenticed to his father Barry but had his indentures transferred to Tom Jones, for whom he has ridden Ilium to win the Yorkshire Cup and At Talaq to finish fourth in the Derby. His best seasons were 1984 and 1985 with 39 winners each time.

HINCHLIFFE, Michael John (b. 1937)

A former chauffeur to Lester Piggott, Michael Hinchliffe began training in 1980 with a small mixed string near Newbury but in 1984 moved to stables owned by Piggott at Newmarket with a team of 70 horses, many bought for large amounts as yearlings and principally owned by a Swiss-based company called Swinton Holdings. The stable made a good start by winning the Free Handicap with Cutting Wind but only six more winners followed, and before the end of the season Hinchliffe had moved out to take up training in Leicestershire.

HINDLEY, Charles

Very little is known of this jockey bar the fact that he rode three Derby winners –

Young Eclipse (1781), Saltram (1783) and Aimwell (1785).

HINDLEY, Sir Clement Daniel Maggs (1874-1944)

Formerly Chief Commissioner of Railways with the Government of India, he was selected in 1928 to be the first Chairman of the Racecourse Betting Control Board on the introduction of the totalisator into British racing.

HINDLEY, John Jeremy (b. 1943)

The Hindley family owned extensive property at Gisburn in Lancashire. Jeremy Hindley rode as an amateur and was assistant to Tim Forster, Tom Jones and Noel Murless before he bought Kremlin House at Newmarket from Teddy Lambton in 1969. Two years later he started training, and his first Flat-race win was with Fivepenny Piece at Yarmouth on 9 June 1971. He bought and moved to Clarehaven Stable at Newmarket in 1978. He has had big-race success across the spectrum, with the sprinters Some Hand, The Go-Between, He Loves Me and Orojoya, the good two-year-old Huntingdale, the milers Sin Timon, Star Pastures and Muscatite, and the stayers Coed Cochion, Nearly A Hand, Crash Course and Protection Racket, who gave him his one Classic success, in the Irish St Leger.

HISLOP, John Leslie (b. 1911)

John Hislop was educated at Wellington and the RMC, but ill-health prevented him from becoming a regular soldier. Before the war he assisted Victor Gilpin, who trained first at Newmarket and later at Findon. He became a highly proficient amateur rider under both codes but especially on the Flat, where he was leading amateur from 1946 to 1956. For many years racing correspondent of *The Observer* and *News of the World*, he is the author of numerous books, most notably on breeding. With his wife he established a small stud near Newbury and saw theory put into marvellous practice by breeding Brigadier Gerard. He was elected to the Jockey Club in December 1971.

HISTORY OF BRITISH HORSE-RACING

The development of horse-racing in Britain can be said to date from the seventeenth century, although it is known to have taken place in many parts of the country for a great many years before then. There are records of it during the Roman occupation. During the reign of Henry II there were races on public holidays at Smithfield, the great London horse-market, while at Chester there are old records of Shrove Tuesday races for a wooden ball embellished with flowers.

It was during the reign of James VI and I that racing first began to be organized. James took a great liking to Newmarket, then an obscure, wooden-hutted village, and had a royal palace constructed there. He was keener on hawking and hunting than on racing, but racing at this period was very popular in Scotland and members of the Court from north of the border lost little time in establishing the sport at Newmarket. James himself realized the importance of testing and improving the breed of horses in England and established public races in many parts of the country. The prize was usually a silver bell, and courses where these races were held were known as 'Bell Courses'. An ancient silver bell long remained a trophy at Lanark. James also saw that native blood was judiciously reinforced by the import of suitable horses from abroad.

Charles I maintained the royal association with Newmarket, and Charles II was a racing enthusiast. He rode in races himself and founded races known as Royal Plates, while the Rowley Mile course at Newmarket is named after him, as 'Old Rowley' was his nickname, derived from his favourite hack which bore that name.

As the popularity of racing increased under royal patronage, the breeding of racehorses developed with remarkable swiftness, thanks largely to the import of Arabian horses. At the same time the control of the sport gradually fell into the hands of the Jockey Club, which was founded – the precise date is unknown – somewhere around the middle of the eighteenth century. Up to this time racing had comprised for the most part matches run over long distances, racing men of that era placing much emphasis on stamina. Gradually, however, more attention was given to speed; horses began to compete at a younger age and over shorter distances. The first Classic race, the St Leger, was instituted in 1776, followed by the Oaks in 1779 and Derby in 1780.

Racing continued to prosper in the nineteenth century. Improved transport facilities were of great assistance to the sport, which began to receive more attention in the leading newspapers. There was a marked increase, too, in the volume of betting. Originally betting on horse-racing had been largely confined to owners wagering on the result of matches in which one of their own horses was engaged. With the advent of professional betting men and of bookmakers (then known as 'legs', short for 'blacklegs'), a new and often undesirable element crept into the sport. Villainy abounded and, but for the unrelenting war waged by Lord George Bentinck on crooks and welshers, racing might have become too disreputable to survive. Lord George also established order, discipline and punctuality in the conduct of race-meetings and improved the quality of officials which till then had been low.

As leading figure of the Jockey Club, Lord George was followed by the forthright, honourable and occasionally impulsive Admiral Rous, who brought the Rules of Racing up to date and set a new high standard in handicapping. The level of integrity throughout racing, and particularly among jockeys, gradually improved, and in the 1890s the patronage of the Prince of Wales afforded fresh prestige to the sport.

This century, racing has survived two major wars, but only just. The fact that racing was permitted to continue on a greatly reduced scale in both world wars was largely due to the tact and negotiating skill of the stewards of the Jockey Club, who had to contend with some bitter, and occasionally prejudiced, opposition.

After the Second World War the status of the British thoroughbred suffered a temporary decline through the many successes of horses from overseas in the main races. The demand for British bloodstock, though, remains high. On the racecourses, many technical innovations have been introduced, and the Betting and Gaming Act, which legalized betting shops, means that betting now makes a substantial contribution towards the general good of the sport through the Horserace Betting Levy Board which, with the Jockey Club, is one of the twin forces propelling the sport towards the 21st century.
(See also JOCKEY CLUB.)

HOBBS, Bruce Robertson (b. 1920)

Bruce Hobbs, son of the National Hunt trainer Reg Hobbs, was a brilliant horseman as a boy and had his first ride over fences as an amateur at the age of fourteen. He turned professional and was only seventeen when he won the Grand National on the American horse Battleship, trained by his father.

In the war he served as a captain in the Queen's Own Yorkshire Dragoons and was awarded the MC. He took out a licence to train under National Hunt Rules in 1945 and had jumpers belonging to Mr and Mrs John Rogerson, but in 1951 he gave up his licence to become assistant to George Beeby. Subsequently he was assistant to Capt Cecil Boyd-Rochfort, 1953-60, and to Jack Clayton, 1961-3. There followed a brief but successful spell as private trainer to David Robinson before he set up as public trainer at Palace House, Newmarket in 1966. His important wins included the Goodwood Cup twice, Stewards' Cup (Touch Paper), Northumberland Plate (Tom Cribb) and Extel Stakes (Take A Reef), and he trained smart two-year-olds in Jacinth (Cheveley Park Stakes), Tumbledownwind (Gimcrack Stakes), Cry of Truth (Cheveley Park Stakes), Tachypous (Middle Park Stakes) and Tromos (Dewhurst Stakes), but he had to wait until 1980 for his only Classic win, when Tyrnavos took the Irish Sweeps Derby at 25-1. He retired from training at the end of 1985 to run a stud near Newmarket, and that winter was elected a member of the Jockey Club.

HOBDAYING

Hobdaying is an operation on the larynx to relieve a horse's respiratory trouble which shows itself in roaring or whistling. It was originated by the late Sir Frederick Hobday, principal of the Royal College of Veterinary Surgeons.

HODGSON, Kevin (b. 1961)

Kevin Hodgson quickly established himself as an apprentice with Peter Easterby, for whom he had his biggest success with Polly's Brother in the 1983 Ayr Gold Cup, and with whom he stayed associated when he ended his apprenticeship in 1984. He had his best season in 1985, with 33 winners, including his first Pattern-race success, on Hallgate in the Cornwallis Stakes.

HOLDEN, William (b. 1930)

William Holden was apprenticed to Jack Reardon. He rode on the Flat as an apprentice and after a spell in the Merchant Navy, when his weight increased, he returned to ride under National Hunt Rules. He took out a licence to train under National Hunt Rules in 1958 and on the Flat the following year and maintains a small stable at Newmarket.

HOLLIDAY, Major Lionel Brook (1881-1965)

Major Lionel Holliday was one of racing's 'characters', and no-one could ever accuse him of courting popularity; quite the reverse. Self-opinionated and self-assertive, he was never an easy or pleasant man to work for and changed his trainers and jockeys with considerable frequency. He was liked and admired by the racing public, as his horses were always out to win.

He founded a powerful racing empire and could have justly claimed to be the foremost British owner-breeder of his day. Lost Soul, by Solario, was the famous foundation mare of his stud, and she and her daughter Phase were the cornerstones of his racing successes. He never won the Derby – though he bred both sire and dam of the 1969 winner Blakeney – but he won the 1951 Oaks

with Neasham Belle, trained by Geoffrey Brooke, the 1962 St Leger with Hethersett, trained by Dick Hern, and the 1965 1,000 Guineas with Night Off, trained by Walter Wharton. He was leading owner in 1956, 1961 and 1962, and leading breeder in 1954, 1956 and 1962. He bred Vaguely Noble, who was sold as a two-year-old in 1967 for the record price for a horse in training in Britain of 136,000gns and later won the Prix de l'Arc de Triomphe. At the 1966 dispersal of his bloodstock, 28 horses in training, twenty mares and four foals fetched a total of 158,425gns.

A good judge of a horse and a better one of a foxhound, Major Holliday was the head of a dye-manufacturing firm in Huddersfield. A few years before his death he was elected to the Jockey Club, an honour that would have come sooner had he been less dictatorial and more willing to compromise. He died, aged 85, in December 1965, a few days after his wife died.

HOLLIDAY, Lionel Brook (b. 1928)

Mr L. Brook Holliday, son of Major Lionel Holliday, sold Cleaboy Stud in Ireland for £710,000 in 1978 and maintained the family interest on a much-reduced scale after death duties forced him to sell much bloodstock, including Vaguely Noble. He was elected to the Jockey Club in 1964 and started his first term as steward in 1979. He has been a steward at Newcastle, Newmarket, Stockton and Thirsk.

Racing colours: white, maroon hoops, armlets and cap.

HOLLINGSWORTH, Richard Dunbavin (b. 1918)

Dick Hollingsworth, a stockbroker, served in World War II in the Royal Berkshire Regiment. A member of the Jockey Club, he owns the Arches Hall Stud, Hertfordshire, which he inherited from his father, and his success as an owner-breeder can be traced to the mare Felucca and her descendants. Felucca was the dam of three Park Hill Stakes winners, Ark Royal, Kyak and Cutter, grandam of Buoy (Coronation Cup), Hermes (Great Voltigeur Stakes), Mariner (King Edward VII Stakes) and Cut Above (St Leger), great-grandam of Bireme (Oaks) and Sharp Edge (Irish 2,000 Guineas), and fourth dam of Sea Anchor (King Edward VII Stakes). Sharp Edge and Cut Above were owned and bred by Sir John Astor after he and Dick Hollingsworth, who both have horses with Dick Hern, exchanged a mare.

Racing colours: crimson, silver braid.

HOLLINSHEAD, Reginald (b. 1924)

Reg Hollinshead rode under National Hunt Rules first as an amateur and then as a professional. He continued to ride for several years after taking out his first licence to train in 1954, when he started his mixed stable at Upper Longdon, near Rugeley, Staffordshire. Progress has been achieved steadily, and he had his best season in 1981, with the winners of 57 races worth £131,238. His best horse has been Remainder Man, second in the 2,000 Guineas and third in the Derby in 1978, and winner of the Ormonde Stakes the following year. He has also been responsible for two champion apprentices in Steve Perks and Kevin Darley, and a joint-champion in Willie Ryan.

HOMEWARD BOUND (1961, ch f Alycidon – Sabie River, by Signal Light)

Bred and owned by Sir Foster Robinson and trained by John Oxley, Homeward Bound won the Princess Elizabeth Stakes, Oaks and Yorkshire Oaks in 1964 for a total of £42,243. After Sir Foster Robinson's death in 1967 she was sold for export to America. Her daughter Prime Abord won three races in France and bred the Grand Critérium winner Super Concorde.

HONEYLIGHT (1953, b f Honeyway – Crepuscule, by Mieuxcé)

A half-sister to Crepello and Twilight Alley, Honeylight was bred by Sir Victor Sassoon and trained by Captain Charles Elsey. She won five races worth £14,899, including the Free Handicap and 1,000 Guineas. In view of her pedigree and racing record, she was disappointing at stud, though her daughter Come On Honey bred the Park Hill Stakes winners Attica Meli and Royal Hive.

HORNET'S BEAUTY (1908, b g Tredennis – Hornet, by Hackler)

Hornet's Beauty won 31 races worth £12,483. As a three-year-old in 1911, he won fifteen of his sixteen races including three at Royal Ascot, his only defeat coming at Ostend.

HORGAN, Cornelius Augustus (b. 1945)

Con Horgan, for two years assistant to Angel Penna in America, was for several years assistant to Ryan Price and took over the Findon stables in February 1983 when the latter retired. The arrangement did not work out, and after two years Horgan moved to new stables near Wokingham. He had his best season in 1985, with 21 winners, including Western Dancer in the Ebor Handicap.

HORSERACE BETTING LEVY BOARD

Racing underwent a fundamental change in 1961 when the Betting Levy Act introduced the Horserace Betting Levy Board to assess and collect monetary contributions from the bookmakers and totalisator. It enabled money wagered on horse racing to be channelled into the sport for the statutory purposes of:
1. the improvement of breeds of horses;
2. the advancement and encouragement of veterinary science or veterinary education;
3. the improvement of horse racing.

Passage of the Betting and Gaming Act, which legalized betting shops, made a levy possible, but it was not until the chairmanship of Lord Wigg, when collection of the levy was changed from a proportion of profits to a charge on turnover, that significant amounts were made available to the Board. The latter consists of a chairman and two members appointed by the Home Secretary, two members appointed by the Jockey Club, the chairman of the Horseracing Advisory Council (who took a seat previously held by a Jockey Club nominee) and two ex-officio members, the chairman of the Bookmakers Committee and the chairman of the Horserace Totalisator Board.

The Home Secretary's nominees must be persons who have no interests connected with horseracing which might hinder them from discharging their functions as members of the Board in an impartial manner. This proviso is evident in the choice of the various chairmen: Field-Marshal Lord Harding (1961-7), Lord Wigg (1967-72), Sir Stanley Raymond (1972-4), Lord Plummer (1974-82) and Sir Ian Trethowan (1982-).

Failure to agree with the Board's assessment of levy requirements, by either bookmakers or totalisator, is dealt with by the Home Secretary.

Under its obligation towards the improvement of breeds of horses, the Levy Board took over control of the National Stud in 1963 and, having supervised the change of policy from boarding mares to standing stallions, has acted on the advice of its Stallion Advisory Committee to purchase horses who might otherwise have gone abroad.

By far the largest amount of Levy Board support has gone on the improvement of racing, especially through the Prize Money Scheme and on loans and grants for racecourse improvement schemes. In the calendar year 1984, the Levy Board contributed over £10 million, or 40.5 per cent, to Flat and jumping prize money. Its wholly owned subsidiary Racecourse Technical Services Ltd provides equipment necessary to maintain the integrity of racing, such as photo-finish cameras, starting stalls and camera patrol, while it contributes almost all the finance required by the independent Racecourse Security Services Ltd, which provides facilities for the security of racing. Another wholly owned subsidiary, Metropolitan and Country Racecourse Management and Holdings Ltd, was formed in 1969-70 as a holding company

for United Racecourses (Holdings) Ltd, which controls Epsom, Sandown Park and Kempton Park. The Board also wholly finances the Horseracing Advisory Council, and makes an annual grant to the Racecourse Association towards the expenses of the Racing Information Bureau.

The income of the Levy Board between its institution on 1 September 1961 and 31 March 1985 amounted to £209,379,000, made up of £192,955,000 (or 92 per cent) from the bookmakers; £13,358,000 (7 per cent) from the totalisator; and £3,066,000 (1 per cent) from net interest, taxation recovered and the National Stud.

Allocation of funds during the same period included the following:

Prize money and racehorse transport (50%)	£105,243,000
Assistance to racecourses (20%)	£41,240,000
Assistance for maintaining the integrity of racing (9%)	£20,186,000
Administrative expenditure (4%)	£7,952,000
Assistance for veterinary science and education (3%)	£6,137,000
Assistance for breeding (1%)	£2,018,000
Assistance to racing industry labour force (1%)	£2,682,000

HORSERACE TOTALISATOR BOARD

The Racecourse Betting Act, which became law in August 1928 and provided for the creation of a statutory body, the Racecourse Betting Control Board, brought Britain into line with France, where *pari-mutuel* betting had operated since 1872, and the United States, where bookmakers had been outlawed by 1913. The Act, brought before Parliament in a Bill presented by Major Ralph Glyn, Conservative MP for Abingdon, introduced pool betting through the totalisator ('tote') on racecourses. It also contained provisions to protect racecourse bookmakers and set out that all surplus earnings should be devoted to the benefit of racing and other statutory objectives. The idea that money might be diverted from betting into racing was crystallized by Lord Hamilton of Dalzell, a Jockey Club member, and support for it grew when Winston Churchill's 1926 Betting Tax soon proved to be costing more to collect than was being raised.

Major Glyn's Bill narrowly obtained a second reading and at the committee stage had to face stern opposition from the moralists and the bookmakers. But the objections were overcome, and the twelve-man Racecourse Betting Control Board came into being, comprising a chairman and one member appointed by the Home Secretary, three members from the Jockey Club, three from the National Hunt Committee, and one each appointed by the Chancellor of the Exchequer, the Secretary for Scotland, the Minister of Agriculture, the Racecourse Association and Tattersalls Committee. Only the chairman was salaried.

Today, the Horserace Totalisator Board, into which the RBCB was reconstituted in 1961 when new betting legislation formulated the Horserace Betting Levy Board, comprises eight members, including a salaried chairman, all appointed by the Home Secretary, and has the services of a chief executive.

One item which the Racecourse Betting Act 1928 did not mention was money, and though the new RBCB were quickly accommodated when they approached the banks, the early years were strewn with financial difficulties. By 1937 it had become possible to fund £1.2m of the Board's debt to the banks by a public issue of stock on a four per cent basis. The bank debt was fully liquidated in 1945, and all the Debenture Stock was redeemed by 1950, 30 years after the Tote had begun operating.

From the start the RBCB decided to erect buildings on all racecourses, in most cases built of brick, and to provide full mechanization to handle on-course bets as a first priority. One was costly, the other was both costly and fraught with operational difficulties, and at the end of World War II it was decided to confine mechanization to Ascot, Newbury and Newmarket.

Mechanization and its possible implementation has occupied the thoughts of Tote executives more than any other subject, and it is only with the more general introduction of computerized machinery in the early 1980s that the problems have begun to be ironed out so as to provide quick and efficient service in sale of tickets and a correspondingly speedy pay-out.

When the RBCB began operating, there were 48 courses servicing 330 days' racing on the Flat, and 79 providing 269 days' NH racing, as well as several point-to-points. By the summer of 1934 all courses were equipped for totalisator betting. Newmarket returned the first Tote dividend, on 2 July 1929, when their 2p.m. start ensured a fifteen-minute historical advantage over Carlisle. Betting consisted of win and place, and dividends were declared to a 2s (10p) unit.

First Tote on tracks still operating:
2 July 1929 – Newmarket, Carlisle
12 July 1929 – Chepstow
2 August 1929 – Catterick
9 August 1929 – Thirsk
12 August 1929 – Folkestone
21 August 1929 – Bath
18 September 1929 – Ayr
25 September 1929 – Perth Hunt
30 September 1929 – Hamilton
5 October 1929 – Stratford
8 October 1929 – Kelso
9 October 1929 – Fontwell
11 October 1929 – Haydock
16 October 1929 – Hexham
23 October 1929 – Wetherby
26 October 1929 – Towcester
30 October 1929 – Sedgefield
1 February 1930 – Plumpton
27 February 1930 – Taunton
3 March 1930 – Uttoxeter
11 March 1930 – Cheltenham
20 March 1930 – Sandown
4 April 1930 – Lingfield
7 April 1930 – Leicester
9 April 1930 – Pontefract
11 April 1930 – Newbury
19 April 1930 – Southwell
21 April 1930 – Kempton, Wincanton, Hereford
25 April 1930 – Bangor
28 April 1930 – Epsom
16 May 1930 – Newton Abbot, Ripon
19 May 1930 – Windsor
21 May 1930 – Beverley

27 May 1930 – York
9 June 1930 – Redcar, Wolverhampton
24 June 1930 – Newcastle
7 July 1930 – Nottingham
23 July 1930 – Liverpool
27 August 1930 – Devon and Exeter
17 September 1930 – Yarmouth
23 September 1930 – Brighton
16 October 1930 – Ludlow
20 October 1930 – Market Rasen
5 November 1930 – Worcester
17 November 1930 – Warwick
5 May 1931 – Chester
16 June 1931 – Ascot
11 July 1931 – Edinburgh
28 March 1932 – Huntingdon
25 July 1933 – Goodwood
11 April 1934 – Doncaster
31 May 1934 – Salisbury

Not all racecourses welcomed the Tote. Doncaster, Liverpool and Manchester demanded permission to run their own totalisators under licence. This was turned down, but Doncaster hung on longer than the others and was the penultimate course to provide the service. The subject of racecourses running their own totes is one which resurfaces every so often.

The Ascot executive took the view that only they had the legal right, or could be permitted to erect buildings on their course. They also insisted there should be no tote operation until it became possible to give a fully mechanized and efficient service. Shortly before the 1931 royal meeting, the Ascot Authority demanded rental of £12,500 per annum for the Tote buildings, to which the RBCB offered £7,500. Despite the dispute, the service was provided for the first time that year, but in 1933 the Authority repeated their rental demand and threatened to bar the Tote. It was only on the intervention of King George V that arbitration took place and terms were agreed.

Tote Investors Ltd

Apart from failing to mention finance, the Racecourse Betting Act 1928 also ignored the question of off-course betting. It was left to private enterprise to plug the gap when during 1931 the RBCB did a deal with Guardian Pari-Mutuel Ltd, a venture organized principally by Lord Milford, then Sir Laurence Philipps. Later known as Tote Investors Ltd and now as Tote Credit Ltd, the company undertook a credit business which channelled bets into the Tote pools from a nationwide chain of branches, linked by telephone to the main London office, and also set up credit facilities on every racecourse. In return they were given a commission.

Today, Tote Credit have approximately 30 branches and facilities on all racecourses. Limitations of the machinery for transmitting details of bets placed off-course mean it is possible to include only a proportion of them in the on-course pools.

Shareholders in Tote Investors rarely saw much benefit from their investment, a quarter of which was lost in the first year, and in a number of years they received no dividend. On at least two occasions the directors considered winding up the company and were saved only when the staff voluntarily agreed to a reduction of one-third of their fees, salaries or wages. In 1962 the Tote Board acquired the entire share capital of Tote Investors Ltd.

Deductions and donations

At the outset the deduction from tote bets was six per cent (ten at point-to-points) but that soon became ten per cent all round. An amendment to the Betting and Lotteries Act in 1934 allowed the RBCB to make their deduction from all or part of the money in their pools, and the deduction was altered to fifteen per cent of losing stakes only.

The sums given over to racing generally represented about twenty per cent of the working capital from which each year the Tote had to pay running-costs. The money went to a variety of causes, and when in 1961 the Betting Levy Board assumed responsibility for schemes previously supplied by the Tote, it took over the Racecourse Fund, the Racecourse Totalisator Charity Trust, travelling allowances, the overnight declaration scheme, and grants to point-to-point meetings.

Today, deductions made by the Tote on on-course bets are twenty per cent for win bets, 28 per cent for place bets, 30 per cent for Jackpot and Placepot bets and 33 per cent for dual forecast bets. All these include four per cent on-course betting tax. Bets placed off course pay an additional six per cent to bring the deductions up to the usual ten per cent for betting tax and Levy Board payments.

The Tote's first annual donation to racing was in 1933, when £9,841 was handed over from a turnover of £4.4m (0.2 per cent). In the last year before the Levy Board took over the responsibility, the Tote Board contributed £613,000 from turnover of £30.25m (2.03 per cent).

Changes in presentation of the Tote's financial reports from the mid-1970s make it less easy to compare performances, but the latest figures, for 1984-5, say that by way of the levy (£676,311), sponsorship (£210,826) and payments to racecourses (£881,192), the Tote contributed £1.768m to racing from a turnover of £105m (1.68 per cent).

Sponsorship in 1985 amounted to £245,525 and included many small races at minor tracks, as well as the Cheltenham Gold Cup (from 1980), Ebor Handicap (from 1976) and Cesarewitch (from 1978).

Legislation of 1960, 1961 and 1972
The return of a Conservative government in 1959 led to two-fold legislation which had far-reaching effects on racing in general and the Tote in particular.

First, the Betting and Gaming Act 1960 legitimized off-course cash bookmakers and granted the RBCB the exclusive right to carry on pool betting on horse-racing, to receive or negotiate bets at tote prices and to authorize others to conduct such business on their behalf.

The response from bookmakers to trade at Tote odds was poor; by 1968 there were 15,000 off-course licensed betting shops but only 1,853 bookmakers held the authority to accept bets at Tote prices. Nor did it greatly help the Tote that for a year after the 1960 Act came into force licensing authorities were empowered to give preference to the Tote and existing bookmakers in granting betting-office licences. The Tote had never had betting offices before (since they were illegal) and shortage of capital meant they could not buy the nationwide chain of premises they desired.

The Betting Levy Act 1961, which reconstituted the RBCB into the Horserace Totalisator Board with effect from 1 September 1961, deliberately set the Tote's contribution to the new Betting Levy Board at a high level in the early years in order to establish the operation of the scheme. In the first five years the Tote contributed 32 per cent of the levy, though their share of betting turnover was barely five per cent.

The combination of the two Acts, and the introduction of Rateable Value Tax, which involved payment of three times the rateable value of each premise used for betting purposes, brought the Tote to the point of financial crisis whereby in September 1969 they were owing £693,072 to the Levy Board. For two years they were excused payment to the Levy Board, then the Home Secretary, Mr Reginald Maudling, stepped in to secure the Tote's future.

The Horserace Totalisator and Betting Levy Boards Bill arrived on the statute books in September 1972, though not in the form envisaged when the original bill was introduced to the House of Commons.

At first it contained seven major clauses, the most significant seeking to extend the Tote's betting powers beyond horse racing; to allow licensing authorities to sanction Tote betting-shop facilities regardless of demand, and to enable the Tote to draw on financial support from the Levy Board. By the time the major bookmakers had marshalled their opposition in Parliament, only the clause extending Tote betting powers remained.

The 1972 legislation did save the Tote's skin, but the Board's hopes that it might provide short-term privileges to enable them to catch up on the years when they were unable to compete with bookmakers in off-course betting were dashed. The 1978 Royal Commission on Gambling had this pithy observation to make: 'The 1972 incursion into general bookmaking, including the acceptance of bets on greyhound racing and other sporting events, had very little logic to commend it. The object was only to enable the Tote to make a profit; power to run a chain of hamburger restaurants might have served equally well.'

The Tote as bookmaker

The Royal Commission may have treated the 1972 legislation lightly but it proved the turning-point for the Tote, since it opened up the SP market. But financial progress was not achieved without some setbacks.

Lord Mancroft was appointed chairman of the Tote in 1972 and the Board pressed ahead in their acquisition of betting shops. From the four they owned when the 1972 Act was passed, they grew to almost 250 in 1980. In the summer of 1985 the number of betting shops run by the Tote was 118, with similar facilities on eighteen racecourses. It is largely as a result of being able to act as a bookmaker that the Tote have been able to increase total turnover from a low point of £26.8m in 1971-72 to the latest audited figure of £105.4m for 1984-5. Whereas the proportion of on-course to off-course turnover was approximately equal in 1970-71, the off-course figure subsequently surged ahead to account for threequarters of turnover, and in 1984-85 had slipped back only slightly to figures of 30 per cent (£32m) on-course and 70 per cent (£74m) off-course. In the first year of Tote Bookmakers, off-course turnover was £17m; six years later it had grown by almost 400 per cent.

Inexperience of the bookmaking industry, delays to computerization and the naturally labour-intensive Tote system meant that in the year immediately after 1972 the Tote's trading loss on the betting operation was heavy. Nor were a series of blunders guaranteed to instil confidence.

In June 1976 the *Sporting Chronicle* revealed that Tote officials had changed the method of calculating dividends on winning bets without making public their intention. The Tote defended the move as an experiment designed to provide increased competition with SP odds, but they backed down within five weeks.

In July 1979 John McCririck's painstaking research for the *Sporting Life* revealed that an unusually low dual-forecast dividend at Carlisle was one of 21 dividends doctored by bets which entered the pool after the result was known. An inquiry by Crown Court judge Francis Aglionby found that they 'arose out of misplaced enthusiasm'. Woodrow Wyatt, by then Tote chairman, described the Carlisle affair as a 'one-off cock-up' and later labelled the miscreants as 'clowns'.

In October 1980 a Tote credit client betting at Newmarket won £199,039.46, less tax, on a successful Yankee bet, but £178,000 of it went to clear the punter's outstanding debts.

Each episode was followed by the departure of at least one Tote employee, the last claiming Bill Balshaw, a former managing director of William Hill, the bookmakers, who joined the Tote in 1973 to guide their off-course cash division. But the chairman, Woodrow Wyatt, survived them all, and with chief executive Brian McDonnell he has gone on to see the Tote into calmer waters and greater financial stability.

Pruning the Tote operation, including its betting shops, moving the headquarters from central London to Putney, improving computerization, encouraging the growth of on-course betting by use of mini-booths and giving the racecourses a percentage of turnover from them, steering clear of advocating a Tote monopoly as he did in his early days and generally putting the emphasis on the bookmaking aspect have enabled Wyatt to preside over the Tote's new-found prosperity.

The future for the Tote as a viable pool-betting operation remains less certain. It has been so since the Tote's annual report for 1976-77 which, in pointing out that the purpose of the 1928 legislation was to raise money for racing, made this declaration of intent: 'Pool betting is an important but certainly not the only means to that end. Since the overwhelming part of the betting market nowadays is off-course and SP, the Tote has to secure a significant part of this market and to do so it must engage in whole-hearted competition with the other bookmakers. In the opinion of the present Board this means that the Tote must become as competitive and as profit conscious as the most efficient of private enterprises.'

Tote pools:

Win and place pools were the first to be introduced, followed by the daily double (naming the winners of two stipulated races) in 1930. Forecast betting (naming the first and second in a race) appeared briefly before the Second World War and was strengthened after it. The daily treble (naming the winners of three stipulated races) was introduced at Ascot and extended to all courses from September 1959.

A quadpool (naming the winners of four stipulated races) led to the introduction of the jackpot (naming the winners of six races at a meeting, and pools not won to be carried forward to another day or another meeting) in June 1966. The jackpot became a five-race pool, operating almost every day of the week, in 1977, but returned to a six-race pool in March 1981.

The roll-up failed to survive in the summer of 1973. Marketed in the manner of an alternative to football pools, the roll-up required punters to forecast the first six in correct order in a nominated Saturday race whose runners and riders were published four days in advance. The races were televized handicaps additional to the existing programme, carried minor prize money and often attracted poor fields below the expected maximum of sixteen runners. The third week of the 31-week season brought a record dividend of £70,759 for a 5p stake, but interest waned and the final dividend was £13,226.

Latest casualties have been the double and treble pools, scrapped in March 1985 because of dwindling support, which has gone instead to dual forecasts (nominating first and second in either order in a race), which were extended to include all races with at least three runners in 1977, and the placepot (nominating a horse to be placed in each of the first six races), which was introduced in November 1977 and extended to all meetings except Bank Holidays and evenings from March 1981.

Pools, as from 30 September 1985 are:
Win – minimum stake £1 (£2 in Members' and Tattersalls' enclosures).
Place – 1-2: five, six and seven runners; 1-2-3: all races eight runners or more; 1-2-3-4: handicaps of sixteen runners or more; minimum stake £1.
Dual forecast – first or second in either order, three runners or more; minimum stake £1 (£2 in Members' and Tattersalls' enclosures).

Jackpot – first six winners at nominated meeting, percentage of pool carried forward if not won; minimum stake £1 (in units of 50p).
Placepot – one placed horse in each of first six races, pool carried forward if not won; minimum stake £1 (in units of 50p).
Tote dividends for win, place and dual forecast are declared to £1 stake.

Record Tote pools (to 14 March 1985)
Turnover: (one day) £721,547.16, 14 March 1985, (Cheltenham and Hexham)
(one meeting) £717,287.71, Cheltenham, 14 March 1985
(one meeting, all days) £2,379,341.22, Ascot, 18-22 June 1985
(one meeting, course cash only) £673,828.41, Cheltenham, 14 March 1985
(one day, cash only) £676,866.11, 14 March 1985, (Cheltenham and Hexham)
One race (win, place and forecast) £155,779.50, Epsom, 5 June 1985, Derby
Win and place: £135,654, Epsom, 5 June 1985, Derby
Win: £87,493, Epsom, 5 June 1985, Derby
Place: £65,315.80, Epsom, 7 June 1967, Derby
Straight Forecast: £15,683.60, Royal Ascot, 17 June 1964, Coronation Stakes
Dual Forecast: £20,125.50, Epsom, 5 June 1985, Derby
Daily Double: £36,770.50, Royal Ascot, 14 June 1961
Daily Treble: £15,930.25, Royal Ascot, 19 June 1963
Quadpool: £10,572.50, Royal Ascot, 17 June 1965
Jackpot: (one day) £253,741.00, Total £380,898.40, Goodwood, 28 July 1967
Placepot: £26,275.70, Cheltenham, 14 March 1985
Special pool: £47,503.00, Epsom 1936 (Derby Forecast)
All figures (except where stated) are combined on- and off-course pool takings.

Record Tote dividends (to 31 March 1985)
Win: £341 2s 6d, (2s stake), Haydock, 30
  November 1929, Coolie
Place: £67.32 (10p stake), Nottingham, 31
  October 1978, Strip Fast
Straight Forecast: £97 19s 9d (2s stake),
  Towcester, 23 October 1954, Hislet
  and Another Rake
Dual Forecast: £329.98 (10p stake), Ayr,
  21 September 1979, Primula Boy and
  Valeriga
Daily Double: £5,062 13s (10s stake),
  Liverpool, 25 March 1938, Races 3
  and 5
Daily Treble: £4,307 17s (5s stake),
  Ascot, 19 June 1952, Races 2, 4 and 6
Jackpot: £63,114 3s (5s stake), Ascot, 18
  June 1966
Placepot: £3,881.75 (50p stake), Doncas-
  ter, 22 March 1985
Quadpool: £2,510 8s (5s stake), Ascot, 18
  June 1965
Special Event: £8,899 10s, Lincoln-
  National Spring Double, 1947

*Chairmen of Racecourse Betting Control
Board and Horserace Totalisator Board*
Sir Reginald Blair (acting chairman), 25
  August to 31 October 1928
Sir Clement Hindley, 1928-44
Sir Reginald Blair, 1944-47
Gen. Sir Miles Dempsey, 1947-51
Sir Dingwall Bateson, 1951-60
Sir Alexander Sim, 1960-70
Mr A.W. Taylor, 1970-72
Lord Mancroft, 1972-76
Sir Woodrow Wyatt from 1976 (current
  term ends 30 April 1988)

HORSERACE WRITERS AND REPORTERS ASSOCIATION

Formed in 1969 to succeed the
Racecourse Press Committee, the
Horserace Writers and Reporters
Association exists to obtain fair and
proper treatment for its members and to
help sustain and extend the appeal of the
sport. Membership is drawn from those
who hold an annual Press badge from the
Jockey Club or whose business involves
access to racecourse Press facilities.

HORSERACING ADVISORY COUNCIL

The Horseracing Advisory Council was
established in 1980 in the wake of the
1978 Royal Commission on Gambling,
which had given as its major recommendation the establishment of a British
Horseracing Authority. The Commission
envisaged this taking over most of the
Levy Board's functions and some of the
Jockey Club's. The chances of the idea
taking off were diminished by the
apparent lack of responsibility to Parliament of a body which would spend public
money (the levy), and instead a working
party led by Air-Commodore Brookie
Brooks of the Racecourse Association set
about forming a consultative organization.

The HAC grew as an extension of two
existing bodies, the Bloodstock and
Racehorse Industries Confederation
(BRIC) and the Racing Industry Liaison
Council (RILC), which drew members
from the various sections of racing but
lacked direct access to the Levy Board
and Jockey Club. HAC had that access
since its chairman was given one of the
Jockey Club's seats on the Levy Board.

There are two tiers to the HAC: the
general council, to which all the sectional
interests belong and to which such as the
bookmakers and Tote, Levy Board and
Jockey Club send observers, and the
executive committee. The general council
provides a forum for ideas; the executive
committee distils the view, co-ordinates
them into policies and pursues them with
the Jockey Club, Levy Board and
Government.

First representatives of the general
council and executive committee were
elected in December 1979. A four-man
panel was chosen to find a chairman, and
one of those, Phil Bull, took on the job
himself on a part-time basis. Mr Bull
stepped down in 1980, saying that
travelling from his Halifax home was too
exhausting but leaving behind the impression that he had not been able to come to
terms with the slow progress which the
HAC made in relation to his own views.
He was succeeded in August 1980 by
Maj.-Gen. Bernard Penfold, the HAC's

first full-time chairman, with Stanley Jackson as secretary. Maj.-Gen. Penfold retires in September 1986 and will be succeeded by Sir Nevil Macready.

Critics of the HAC will always point to its advisory nature as a weakness; its lack of a strident public image may be regarded as another disadvantage. However, it has made steady if silent strides in its early history and has been particularly successful in such areas as taxation and race-planning.

HOUGHTON, Richard Fulke Johnson (b. 1940)

Fulke Johnson Houghton is bred to be a trainer. His father, Gordon Johnson Houghton, was a successful trainer till killed in the prime of life in 1952 in an accident out hunting, while his mother is Fulke Walwyn's sister. After her husband's death Mrs Johnson Houghton kept the stable at Blewbury going, assisted successively by Colonel Dick Poole, Charles Jerdein and Peter Walwyn.

After leaving Eton, Fulke Johnson Houghton was a pupil with Major John Goldsmith and later with Jack Cunnington in France. He also travelled horses abroad for the Epsom bloodstock agent George Forbes. In 1961 he took over the stable from his mother, backed by her guidance and experience. He brought off a notable achievement by winning the St Leger and Irish Sweeps Derby with the full brothers Ribocco and Ribero. Both were owned by Mr Charles Engelhard, for whom he also won important races with Romulus (Sussex Stakes), Ribofilio (Dewhurst Stakes), Habitat and the two-year-olds Tin King and Falcon. Rose Bowl (Champion Stakes) was owned by Mrs Engelhard, and Ile de Bourbon (King George VI and Queen Elizabeth Stakes) was bred from an Engelhard stallion and mare.

For other owners his important winners include Aegean Blue (Chester Cup), Parsimony (July Cup), Double Form (King's Stand Stakes), Smartset (Cambridgeshire), Borushka (Park Hill Stakes) and Kirmann (Jockey Club Stakes).

HOWARD de WALDEN, John Osmael, 9th Baron (b. 1912)

Lord Howard de Walden, an industrious and go-ahead racing administrator, was elected to the Jockey Club in 1952 and was Senior Steward in 1957, 1964 and 1976-9. He was at one time a member of the Racecourse Betting Control Board. He owns the Plantation Stud, Newmarket, and Thornton Stud, Yorkshire, and achieved his lifetime ambition when Slip Anchor, whom he bred and owns, won the 1985 Derby. The same year his wife won the Scottish Derby with Eagling. Among the other good horses he has bred and raced are Amerigo, who won the Coventry Stakes at Ascot and twelve races worth $419,000 in America; Oncidium (Jockey Club Cup, Coronation Cup), Almiranta (Park Hill Stakes), Falkland (Queen's Vase), Magic Flute (Cheveley Park Stakes), Kris (champion miler), Diesis (top two-year-old of 1982) and Lanzarote (Champion Hurdle).

Racing colours: apricot.

HUE-WILLIAMS, Mrs Vera

Mrs Hue-Williams, formerly Mrs T. Lilley, has enjoyed many successes as breeder and owner. In conjunction with her husband, Colonel F.R. Hue-Williams (b. 1909), she owns the Woolton House Stud, Newbury, and previously owned the Rathasker Stud, Co Kildare. The best horses she has owned include Supreme Court (King George VI and Queen Elizabeth Festival of Britain Stakes), Aurelius (St Leger), I Titan (Vaux Gold Tankard), Yaroslav (Royal Lodge Stakes) and English Prince (Irish Sweeps Derby).

Racing colours: scarlet, white V and cap.

Colonel Hue-Williams' best horses have included Altesse Royale (1,000 Guineas, Oaks and Irish Oaks), Rock Roi (twice disqualified after passing the post first in the Ascot Gold Cup) and Imperial Prince (second in the Derby and Irish Sweeps Derby).

Racing colours: white, scarlet V, scarlet cap with white button.

HUFFER, Geoffrey Allen (b. 1947)

Geoff Huffer had a number of jobs in racing in and around Newmarket before he went north to assist John Bingham training at Haxey, near Doncaster. He took out his own licence in 1978 as private trainer at the Cheveley Park Stud, Newmarket, but two years later he moved across town to La Grange. His first Flat winner came with his first runner, Irish Poet at Doncaster on 23 March 1979, and he has won two major handicaps in the Cesarewitch (Sir Michael) and Ayr Gold Cup (First Movement, who beat his stablemate Tina's Pet). Numerically his best season was 1985, with 30 winners.

HUGHES, John Philip Victor (b. 1926)

One of the more inventive Clerks of the Course since the Second World War, John Hughes began as assistant at Epsom in 1954 and has variously been involved as Clerk at Haydock Park, Nottingham, Leicester, Chepstow and Liverpool. Publicity-conscious, he was quick to see the value of sponsored races, especially those involving a series of qualifiers leading to a heavily-financed final.

HULA DANCER
(1960, gr f Native Dancer – Flash On, by Ambrose Light)

Bred in the United States by her owner Mrs P.A. Widener, Hula Dancer was trained in France by Etienne Pollet. Her eight victories worth the equivalent of £105,160 included the Grand Critérium and Prix du Moulin de Longchamp in France, and the 1,000 Guineas and Champion Stakes in Britain. At the dispersal of Mrs Widener's bloodstock in 1968, Hula Dancer was bought by Mr Raymond Guest, to be mated with Sir Ivor, for the equivalent of approximately £86,150. Her son Dancing Lad, who raced only once and was unplaced, sired the French St Leger winner Brave Johnny.

HULTON, Sir Edward (1869-1925)

Sir Edward Hulton is the only leading newspaper-owner to have gone in for racing in a big way. Lord Beaverbrook admittedly launched out in great style in the 1920s, but he soon got bored and gave up. Hulton was trained for the priesthood but when his elder brother died he entered the newspaper business to help his father. At first he went in for coursing and twice won the Waterloo Cup, but eventually racing became his hobby and relaxation. When he died, his horses were sold and realized 288,000gns. He won the Derby with Fifinella, the 1,000 Guineas with Roseway and the Oaks with Fifinella and Straitlace.

HUMBLE DUTY
(1967, gr f Sovereign Path – Flattering, by Abernant)

Bred in Ireland by Frank Tuthill, Humble Duty cost her owner, Jean, Lady Ashcombe, 17,000gns as a yearling. She headed the fillies in the Free Handicap by winning three of her four races at two years, including the Cheveley Park Stakes, and the following year set a twentieth-century record for the greatest winning margin, seven lengths, in the 1,000 Guineas, where she was Lester Piggott's first winner in the race. Humble Duty also won the Coronation Stakes and Sussex Stakes as a three-year-old and retired to stud having won eight of her eleven races. She died in 1975.

HUMORIST
(1918, ch c Polymelus – Jest, by Sundridge)

Mr J.B. Joel's Humorist, trained by Charles Morton, won four races worth £9,571, including the Derby in 1921. He must have been a very game horse as he was suffering from a tubercular lung condition and within a fortnight of his Epsom triumph he was dead.

HUNTER, Gavin Howard (b. 1941)

A pupil with Tom Jones and then assistant to Atty Corbett, Gavin Hunter had spells as private trainer to Mr T. Venn and Captain T. Langton from 1965 until taking out a public licence to train at

East Ilsley in 1970. He won important
two-year-old races such as the National
Stakes and July Stakes but his biggest
success was in the Doncaster Cup with
Shangamuzo. In July 1985 he revealed
he would give up training at the end of the
season because of rising costs and bad
debts.

HURRY HARRIET
(1970, b f Yrrah Jr –
Somnambula, by Chanteur)

Irish-trained Hurry Harriet, the only
significant produce of her American-bred,
briefly Irish-based sire, kept her form in
the highest company until the age of five
and won seven races and was placed in
thirteen others. Her chief claim to fame
was her 33-1 success over Allez France in
the Champion Stakes as a three-year-old.
She is the dam of a useful French racer,
Load the Cannons.

HURRY ON
(1913, ch c Marcovil – Tout
Suite, by Sainfoin)

It is probable that the best horse to run in
Britain during World War I was Hurry
On, described by his trainer Fred Darling
as 'the best horse I have ever seen, the
best I am ever likely to see'. By Marcovil,
who was not an outstanding racehorse
and had very bad legs, out of Tout Suite,
a little pony too small to be put into
training, Hurry On was a magnificent
great chestnut standing 17 hands with a
girth of $82\frac{1}{2}$ in and $9\frac{1}{4}$ in of bone below
the knee. Bought as a yearling for 500gns
by Mr James Buchanan, later Lord
Woolavington, he ran only as a three-
year-old, winning all his six races
including the war-substitute St Leger and
the Jockey Club Cup. He was never
extended. At stud he was champion sire
in 1926 and got three Derby winners:
Captain Cuttle, Coronach and Call Boy.
At the age of twenty he sired his most
influential son, Precipitation. Above all he
revived the Matchem male line which was
nearly extinct when he retired to stud.

HYCILLA
(1941, Hyperion – Priscilla
Carter, by Omar Khayyam)

Owned and bred by Mr W. Woodward
and trained by Cecil Boyd-Rochfort,
Hycilla won two races for £4,538, the
Oaks and Champion Stakes. She was
beaten favourite for the St Leger and,
after being kept in training as a
four-year-old, was retired to stud in
America.

HYPERICUM
(1943, b f Hyperion – Feola,
Friar Marcus)

Hypericum was bred and owned by King
George VI and trained by Cecil
Boyd-Rochfort. She won three races for
£8,372, including the Dewhurst Stakes in
1945 and the following season the 1,000
Guineas. She bred five winners, notably
Restoration, who won £5,177, including
the King Edward VII Stakes, and is the
grandam of Ben Marshall (Italian St
Leger) and Highclere (1,000 Guineas and
French Oaks).

HYPERION
(1930, ch c Gainsborough –
Selene, by Chaucer)

Bred and owned by the 17th Earl of
Derby, Hyperion won the Derby and St
Leger in 1933 and was the greatest 'little'
horse of this century. He also proved an
outstanding success as a sire.

He was out of the Chaucer mare
Selene, who won over £14,000 in stakes.
Selene also bred Sickle, from whom are
descended Native Dancer and Dan
Cupid. A chestnut with four white
stockings, Hyperion was so small and
weedy as a foal that there was talk of
putting him down. He gradually
improved but was not sent into training
with Lord Derby's other yearlings and
would probably have been sold but for
the intervention of Lord Derby's trainer
George Lambton, who was impressed by
the colt's beautiful action and by his
head, so full of character and courage.
When fully grown Hyperion stood only
$15.1\frac{1}{2}$ hands high. His lack of inches,

though, was deceptive as his length and depth were those of a taller horse; it was the shortness of his cannon bones that brought him so near to the ground.

Hyperion never showed much at home, and in his first race, a maiden event at Doncaster worth £162 to the winner, he started at 25-1. He displayed encouraging promise, though, to finish fourth and on his next appearance won the New Stakes at Royal Ascot. At Goodwood he was a hot favourite for the 6f Prince of Wales's Stakes but in heavy ground only dead-heated with the Stairway, who could certainly go when in the mood. He was rested till the autumn, when over 5f at Newmarket he was outpaced by the brilliant but erratic Manitoba. However, he finished the season well by winning the 7f Dewhurst Stakes at Newmarket very smoothly. In the Free Handicap he was given 9st, 7lb less than the speedy filly Myrobella.

As a three-year-old Hyperion was never beaten. He won the Chester Vase, the Derby by four lengths, the Prince of Wales's Stakes at Ascot, and the St Leger in a canter by three lengths. The following year his career was an anti-climax. Lambton had ceased to train for Lord Derby and was succeeded by Colledge Leader, who did not understand Hyperion as well as Lambton had done. The chestnut was not an easy horse to get fit as he was habitually indolent at home; moreover, he was a distinct individualist with a number of odd habits, including an inclination to play to the gallery. Lambton understood him thoroughly, realized he was a 'character' and was never disturbed or put out by his moods and quirks. Leader probably failed to realize the amount of work required to get such a lazy horse fit for the Gold Cup and perhaps was a bit too tender and respectful to a dual Classic winner. In the Gold Cup Hyperion finished a very weary third behind Felicitation, who made all the running and, as had been planned, kept Hyperion at full stretch from the start. In his final outing Hyperion failed to concede 29lb to his solitary opponent Caithness, who beat him by a short head. He had won nine races worth £29,509.

As a sire Hyperion was a great success. Not only did he get many winners himself but his sons made good sires and his daughters admirable mares. When he died, in 1960, he had sired the winners in Great Britain of 748 races worth £557,009. It must be remembered, too, that many of the best of his offspring ran during World War II, when opportunities were scarce and prize money low. He was leading sire in 1940, 1941, 1942, 1945, 1946 and 1954. He was second four times and third once. He was leading sire of broodmares in 1948 and 1957 and was five times second. His Classic winners were Godiva (1,000 Guineas and Oaks), Owen Tudor (Derby), Sun Castle (St Leger), Sun Chariot (1,000 Guineas, Oaks and St Leger), Hycilla (Oaks), Sun Stream (1,000 Guineas and Oaks) and Hypericum (1,000 Guineas).

His skeleton is preserved in the Natural History Museum, South Kensington.

I

IDENTIFICATION OF HORSES

Passports are issued annually for named two-year-old horses in the care of licensed trainers and other horses as authorized by the stewards of the Jockey Club. They are returnable on demand, and it is up to the horse's trainer to make sure that the passport is available for inspection any time the horse enters racecourse property. Whenever a horse which has been out of Britain is declared to run there again, the passport must be lodged with the Clerk of the Course and verified by a veterinary officer.

ILE DE BOURBON
(1975, br c Nijinsky – Roselière, by Misti IV)

By a Triple Crown winner out of the best European three-year-old filly of 1968, Ile de Bourbon lived up to his breeding by winning five races, though his career did not always go smoothly. In the middle of three straight wins as a three-year-old he beat the French Derby winner Acamas in the King George VI and Queen Elizabeth Diamond Stakes, but then he flopped in the St Leger. He won his first two races at four years, including the Coronation Cup, but was off the course all summer and was below his best on his return. He was retired to stud at Newmarket in 1980 at a valuation of £4m, and in his first crop got the German Derby winner Lagunas and in his second the German Oaks winner Padang and useful colt Iroko.

IMPRUDENCE
(1944, br f Canot – Indiscretion, by Hurry On)

Madame P. Corbière's Imprudence won two races in Britain for £15,271, the 1,000 Guineas and Oaks, and four races in France, including the 1,000 Guineas. She was trained in France by J. Lieux and ridden by W.R. Johnstone.

INBREEDING

Inbreeding has been defined as the mating of closely related individuals, as opposed to outbreeding, which means the mating of less related or unrelated individuals. All thoroughbreds are inbred in comparison with the members of most human societies since the average sire is expected to cover at least 40 mares each year.

INDIANA
(1961, b c Sayajirao – Willow Ann, by Solario)

Indiana won four races for £72,059, including the St Leger, and was placed six times, including second in the Derby, for Mr Charles Engelhard. In the Derby he was beaten a length. After a brief period at stud in Britain he was exported to Japan in 1966.

INGHAM, Stafford Walter Henry (1908-77)

'Staff' Ingham was apprenticed to Stanley Wootton. Before he became too big and tall, he rode with success on the Flat, winning the Irish 2,000 Guineas and also the 1923 Royal Hunt Cup on Weathervane, who belonged to King George V. With the swift increase in his weight, he turned his attention to jumping and became a stylish and most accomplished rider over hurdles. He chose not to ride over fences.

He took out a licence to train in 1939, but then came the war in which he rose to be squadron leader in the RAF. From 1945 to his death in February 1977 he trained with consistent success at Epsom. He was particularly adept with early two-year-olds, and in 1967 Porto Bello won six straight races, but he was equally successful with other types, and his important winners included Richer (Cambridgeshire), Chantry (Cesarewitch), Just Great (Great Voltigeur Stakes), Le Cordonnier (News of the World Stakes), Soderini (Hardwicke Stakes), Philoctetes (Northumberland Plate), Crazy Rhythm (Ebor Handicap) and Cider With Rosie (Cesarewitch). He was succeeded by his son Tony (b. 1947), who trained his first winner at Sandown in April 1977, but he moved across Epsom in 1979 when the stable at Headley was sold to Geoff Lewis.

INTERMEZZO
(1966, b c Hornbeam – Plaza, by Persian Gulf)

Bred by his owner Mr G.A. Oldham and trained by Harry Wragg, Intermezzo won three races for £49,647, including the St Leger, but, though first past the post in the Great Voltigeur Stakes, was disqualified in that race. He stayed in training as a four-year-old but failed to win and that year was exported to Japan.

INTERNATIONAL CLASSIFICATIONS

In order to make an accurate assessment of racing merit between the major countries of Europe, the Handicappers of Britain, Ireland and France got together for the first time in 1977 to publish a common handicap of the best three-year-olds and older horses from the three countries. The following year the first list of two-year-olds was published. The classifications were linked to a norm of 100, representing a horse capable of dominating his or her contemporaries, but this notation was discarded in 1985. However, the ratings can still be used to judge the relative merit of succeeding generations. In 1985 form shown in Germany and Italy was introduced to the annual lists, which are broken down into age and distance categories, and in the near future it is expected that North American form will also be linked. (For tables of leading horses since 1977 see Page 424.)

INVERSHIN
(1922, b c Invincible – Ajantia, by Ajax)

Invershin, bred and owned by Mr J. Reid Walker, won nine races for £12,074, including the Ascot Gold Cup in 1928 and 1929. He proved a stud failure.

IRONS

This is an abbreviation for stirrup irons. If a jockey is said to have 'lost his irons', his feet have come out of the stirrups.

IROQUOIS

Iroquois, owned by Pierre Lorillard, won the Derby and St Leger in 1881. He was the first American-bred horse to win the Derby.

ISINGLASS

Isinglass, who gained the 'Triple Crown' in 1893, was one of the greatest Derby winners. Only once was he beaten during four seasons in training, and all told he won £57,455 in stakes, a sum that stood as a record in Britain till surpassed by Tulyar in 1952.

Isinglass was a big, strong bay by Isonomy and was owned by Mr (later Colonel) Harry McCalmont. Throughout his career he was trained by James Jewitt, whose stable was managed by the shrewd Captain Machell.

Isinglass resented hard ground but had to content with firm going for much of his career. In consequence his victories were rarely impressive, and usually at some stage of the contest the cry went up 'The favourite's beat'. In addition he was always ridden by the short-legged Tommy Loates, who could not get the best out of such a big horse. When he ran in the Eclipse Stakes as a four-year-old, Isinglass at last got the going he needed and showed the critics what he could do. As a five-year-old he won the Gold Cup at Ascot, his only race that season. As a sire he was not a failure, but hardly fulfilled expectations considering his racing record and the high quality of the mares sent to him.

ISONOMY

Isonomy, foaled in 1875, stood barely 15.2 hands but was a really good horse, winning the Ascot Gold Cup twice, Goodwood Cup, Doncaster Cup and Cambridgeshire. He did not run in the Classics as his owner, Mr Gretton, preferred to keep him dark and go for a big win in the Cambridgeshire, in which he won over £40,000 in bets, whereas the Derby in those days was seldom worth more than £6,000 to the winner. Isonomy proved a stud success and sired Isinglass and Common, who both won the 'Triple Crown'.

IVES, Tony Alexander (b. 1952)

Born in North Yorkshire, Tony Ives served his apprenticeship with Willie Stephenson and Snowy Wainwright, winning his first race on Moor Court at Hamilton on 18 July 1970. He struggled to get rides after losing his claim until becoming stable jockey to Reg Hollinshead for whom he rode Remainder Man to finish second in the 2,000 Guineas and third in the Derby of 1978. After five years in the Midlands, Ives joined Bill O'Gorman as stable jockey at Newmarket, and he has gradually established himself in the top flight. As well as riding the record-breaking Provideo to his sixteen wins in 1984, his major successes in Britain have been on Alma Ata (Park Hill Stakes), Touch Boy (Portland Handicap), Superlative (Flying Childers Stakes) and Tale Quale (Jockey Club Cup), though he easily surpassed those in prize money when winning the 1985 Arlington Million in Chicago on Teleprompter. Numerically his best season was 1984, with 90 winners.

IVORY, Kenneth Thomas (b. 1935)

Ken Ivory served as an apprentice and rode on the Flat before being called up for National Service, and on his return he went into the family haulage business. In 1968 he took out a permit under National Hunt Rules and was granted a licence in the 1973-4 season, training at Radlett, Hertfordshire. He has a good record with mainly cheap horses and gained his biggest success on the Flat with Dawn's Delight in the Portland Handicap.

J

JAGO, Brian (b. 1938)

Brian Jago was apprenticed for eight years to Victor Smyth. Six years spent in Nairobi and breaking the same leg twice in twelve months hindered his success in Britain but among his biggest wins have been the Zetland Gold Cup, Liverpool Spring Cup, Newbury Summer Cup and, most important, the Northumberland Plate on Tom Cribb. His best season was 1980, with 30 winners.

JARVIS, Alan Peter (b. 1938)

Alan Jarvis, who was born at Wimbledon, went into racing from school as a stable lad and rode over jumps, but without success. He took out a licence to train mainly jumpers for the first time in 1969, moved from a yard at Oakham to Coventry in 1972 and settled at his present yard at Royston in 1980. Numerically his best season on the Flat was 1982, with 34 winners.

JARVIS, Basil Ernest (1887-1957)

Basil Jarvis was born at Newmarket and was the son of William A. Jarvis, who trained there. He rode for a time on the Flat but soon became too heavy and rode a few winners under National Hunt Rules, including one at Newmarket's last jumping meeting in 1905, before taking out a licence to train in 1909.

In 1921 he trained four winners at Royal Ascot, one being Mr Ben Irish's Periosteum, who won the Gold Cup. Mr Irish had paid 260gns for Periosteum; with part of his Gold Cup winnings he

paid 3,500gns for a yearling by Tracery out of Miss Matty. He named this colt Papyrus and in 1923, trained by Basil Jarvis and ridden by Steve Donoghue, Papyrus won the Derby. On the same afternoon at Epsom, Basil's brothers Jack and William both won races.

Basil Jarvis trained a few horses for Marcel Boussac, for whom he won the Hardwicke Stakes and Champion Stakes in 1932. He retired in 1948.

JARVIS, Sir John Layton (1887-1968)

One of the most capable and distinguished trainers of the twentieth century, Jack Jarvis was deservedly knighted for his services to racing in 1967. He was the son of the Newmarket trainer William A. Jarvis, while his brothers William and Basil were successful trainers. Apprenticed to his father, he was a good lightweight jockey, and among his victories were the 1903 Cambridgeshire on Hacklers Pride, the Ayr Gold Cup and the Derby Cup. When he became too heavy for the Flat, he rode for a time under National Hunt Rules, his chief win being in the Liverpool Hurdle.

He began training in 1914 and enjoyed consistent success throughout his long career. His principal patrons were the fifth Earl of Rosebery, the sixth Earl of Rosebery, Sir George Bullough, Mr E. Esmond, Mr A. Gordon-Smith, Sir John Jarvis, Lord Milford, Mr J.P. Philipps, Mr T.F. Blackwell, Mr D.H. Wills and Mr J.A.C. Lilley. His successes in Classic races were as follows:

2,000 Guineas: Ellangowan (1923); Flamingo (1928); Blue Peter (1939);
1,000 Guineas: Plack (1924); Campanula (1934); Happy Laughter (1953)
Derby: Blue Peter (1939); Ocean Swell (1944)
St Leger: Sandwich (1931).

He had four Gold Cup winners: Golden Myth, Foxhunter, Flyon and Ocean Swell; and three Eclipse Stakes winners: Golden Myth, Miracle and Blue Peter. He also won the Victoria Cup four times, Ayr Gold Cup three times and Stewards' Cup twice. He excelled in the preparation of stayers but trained two outstanding sprinters in Honeyway and Royal Charger.

He had the reputation of possessing a somewhat explosive temper, but he never harboured resentment and was well known to be one of the most generous and hospitable characters in the racing world. He was a coursing enthusiast – he won the Waterloo Cup – and a supporter in one way or another of nearly every form of sport. He died suddenly in December 1968.

JARVIS, Michael Andrew (b. 1938)

Michael Jarvis, a son of the steeplechase jockey Andrew Jarvis, rode three jumping winners, and was for many years associated with J.M. Gosden's stable. In 1968 he became one of Mr and Mrs David Robinson's private trainers at Newmarket, and in eight seasons in that capacity won 337 races worth £351,986, including the July Cup (So Blessed and Tudor Music), Gimcrack Stakes (Tudor Music), Nunthorpe Stakes (So Blessed), Vernons Sprint Cup (Tudor Music and Green God), Great Voltigeur Stakes (Meadowville) and Ebor Handicap (Knotty Pine). As Mr Robinson reduced his interests, Jarvis started a public stable in 1976, and his important winners since have included the Ebor Handicap (Totowah), William Hill Futurity, Dante Stakes and Benson & Hedges Gold Cup (Beldale Flutter), Coronation Cup (Easter Sun) and Stewards' Cup and Vernons Sprint Cup (Petong). His best season was 1975 with 58 winners, and since training publicly 1982, with 40.

JARVIS, William (b. 1960)

The fourth generation in the Jarvis family to train at Newmarket, William Jarvis, who began training in 1985, is the son of Ryan, to whom he was assistant before joining Henry Cecil in a similar capacity in 1979, after a short spell in Australia. He took over at his father's yard and had his first win with Dorset Cottage (owned by Sheikh Mohammed) at Beverley on 4 June 1985 with 12 winners.

JARVIS, William Joseph Ryan (b. 1913)

Ryan Jarvis is a member of a famous family, his father being William Jarvis who trained for King George V and King George VI. He himself assisted Fred Butters and then took out a licence to train in 1936, his career being interrupted by service in the Grenadier Guards from 1939 to 1945. Among the good horses he trained before retiring at the end of 1979 were Lomond (Princess of Wales's Stakes, Ebor Handicap), Front Row (Irish 1,000 Guineas), Smokey Eyes (Stewards' Cup), Even Say (Northumberland Plate), Gold Pollen (Portland Handicap), Quizair (Lincoln Handicap) and Absalom (Vernons Sprint Cup). When he retired, the family had no training representative for the first time in over 100 years, until his son William started on his own account in 1985.

JARVIS, William Rose (1885-1943)

The eldest son of William Arthur Jarvis, a respected Newmarket trainer, William, like his brothers Sir Jack Jarvis and Basil Jarvis, became a trainer. In 1924 he succeeded Richard Marsh as trainer to King George V and in due course trained for King Edward VIII and King George VI. He won the 1,000 Guineas in 1928 for King George V with Scuttle. In 1940 he won the 1,000 Guineas and Oaks with the brilliant but temperamental Godiva, owned by Mr E. Harmsworth.

JEDDAH

Owned by Mr J.W. Larnach and trained by Richard Marsh, Jeddah won the Derby in 1898 and was the first 100-1 winner of that race. He made no mark as a sire.

JEFFERSON, Joseph Malcolm

Malcolm Jefferson began training at Malton in 1981, after thirteen years spent as travelling head lad and head lad with Gordon Richards at Greystoke. He struck out on his own with a small mixed string and had a good winner at Newmarket in 1983 with High Debate, who was later sent to a bigger stable at Newmarket and failed to live up to his promise.

JERSEY ACT

At the beginning of the twentieth century the importation of horses from America, many of them extremely moderate, was causing concern to those intent on preserving the purity of the British Thoroughbred, as in many cases the pedigrees of these imported horses could not be traced back beyond a certain point.

The problem was referred to the stewards of the Jockey Club who, after consulting most of the leading breeders, concluded that any animal claiming admission to the Stud Book should be able to prove satisfactorily some eight or nine crosses of pure blood, to trace back for at least a century and to show such performances of its immediate family on the Turf as to warrant belief in the purity of its blood. Therefore all the imported horses and mares included in Volume XIX of the Stud Book, published in 1901, had been submitted to the test.

Among the famous animals who thus secured admission were Rhoda B, Americus Girl and Sibola. Rhoda B was dam of the 1907 Derby winner, Orby. Americus Girl, by the imported American sire Americus, left an army of high-class descendants, including Mumtaz Mahal, Mahmoud, Nasrullah, Never Say Die, Tudor Minstrel, My Babu and Palestine. Sibola was great-grandam of Nearco, one of the greatest stallions of recent times. But for the relaxation afforded by the ruling of 1901, not one of the descendants of Rhoda B, Americus Girl and Sibola would have been eligible for the Stud Book.

In 1909 racing in America faced a dangerous crisis, and legislation was introduced that almost brought the sport to a close for a number of years. In Britain the Turf authorities visualized with horror the prospect of the country being overrun by a horde of American horses of doubtful pedigree. The result was the following notice in Volume XXI of the Stud Book published in September 1909:

The Editors beg to inform Subscribers that, since the last volume of the Stud Book was published, they have had cause to consider the advisability of admitting into the Stud Book horses and mares which cannot be traced to a thorough-bred root, but which have fulfilled the requirements given in the preface to Vol. XIX. They have decided that, in the interests of the English Stud Book, no horse or mare can be admitted unless it can be traced to a strain already accepted in the earlier volumes of the Book. The Editors must, therefore, rescind the Notice published in Vol. XIX. The Stewards of the Jockey Club, who kindly consented to consider the question, fully endorse the decision arrived at by the Editors.

The barrier erected in 1909 proved only partially successful in checking the flow of American horses into Britain and at a Jockey Club meeting in 1913 Lord Jersey, who had held office as Senior Steward the year before, put the following question before the stewards:

Whether, in view of the fact that a new volume of the Stud Book will be published this year, they will consider the advisability of suggesting to Messrs Weatherby, the Editors, that the last sentence of the first paragraph of the preface be added to, so as to read as follows: 'They have decided that, in the interests of the English Stud Book, no horse or mare can, after this date, be considered as eligible for admission, unless it can be traced, without flaw on both sire's and dam's side of its pedigree, to horses and mares already accepted in the earlier volumes of the Book'?

The members of the Jockey Club gave full approval to Lord Jersey's suggestion, and thus was born what came to be known as the 'Jersey Act'. The Americans were naturally furious. The British had placed the stamp of 'half-breds' on American horses with dire results to the American export market. Moreover, the Americans declined to accept that the British were really motivated by a burning desire to keep the Stud Book 'pure'; they reckoned the Jersey Act was framed to protect the export trade of British thoroughbreds and that the Jockey Club's action was typical of British selfishness and hypocrisy. Forced into the half-bred category was the 1914 Derby winner Durbar II, who has had great influence on bloodstock breeding in France through his daughter Durban, dam of Tourbillon. Descendants of Tourbillon such as Djebel (2,000 Guineas), Caracalla II (Gold Cup) and Arbar (Gold Cup) were all ineligible for the Stud Book at the time of their victories.

The post-war successes of the descendants of Durbar II gave rise to a feeling that the rules for Stud Book inclusion were too rigid. That sentiment was reinforced in 1947 and 1948 when My Babu and Black Tarquin were not only top-class two-year-olds but the following season won the 2,000 Guineas and St Leger respectively. Neither was eligible for the Stud Book but it was thought that, if they retired to stud in Britain, breeders would not hesitate to patronize them and a situation might eventually arise in which the Stud Book could be thrown into chaos and ridicule.

A committee was therefore appointed by the Jockey Club to look into the matter, and its members, the Duke of Norfolk, Lord Rosebery, Lord Allendale, Mr Peter Burrell and Mr Francis Weatherby, reported that some modification was desirable. In Volume XXXI of the Stud Book published in 1949, the Jersey Act was repealed and it was stated that any animal claiming admission from then onwards had to be able to prove satisfactorily some eight or nine crosses of pure blood, to trace back for at least a century and to show such performance of its immediate family on the Turf as to warrant belief in the purity of its blood.

The Americans were delighted but regarded the repeal of the Jersey Act not as a belated act of justice and fair play to American breeders but as recognition by the British Turf authorities that the high quality of French and American half-breds was in process of making the Stud Book, in its battle for purity, look absurd.

JERSEY, George Child Villiers, 5th Earl of (1773-1859)

A tall, handsome man who was Lord Chamberlain to William IV and Master of the Horse to Queen Victoria, the fifth Earl of Jersey won the Derby with Middleton (1825), Mameluke (1827) and Bay Middleton (1836). Despite success in ten Classics, his racing is said to have cost him over £400,000.

JEST
(1910, b f Sundridge – Absurdity, by Melton)

Jest was bred and owned by Mr J.B. Joel. She won four races for £12,550, including the 1,000 Guineas and Oaks. The only winner she bred was Humorist, her first foal, winner of the Derby in 1921, the year Jest died.

JOCKEY

By definition a jockey is a person who holds a licence from the stewards of the Jockey Club to ride for hire.

No-one is allowed to ride in a race before the age of sixteen and until he (or she) has obtained a licence from the stewards of the Jockey Club. A jockey must apply for his licence annually, giving his full name and address to the Registry Office. (There are different regulations for apprentices and amateur riders.)

Licences are granted on the condition that the jockey is not the owner or part-owner of any racehorse and does not bet on horses racing or receive presents in connection with a race from persons other than the owner of the horse he rides in that race. Any jockey who the stewards of the Jockey Club prove has contravened any of the conditions may have his licence withdrawn.

Every jockey has to pay £24 (plus VAT) for his licence, and a trainer £12 (plus VAT) for every apprentice, in each case £1 being his subscription to the Bentinck Benevolent Fund.

A jockey whose licence has been withdrawn for misconduct is a disqualified person. If a jockey becomes a disqualified person, his licence is revoked.

Once a jockey has ceased to be an apprentice, he is free to form engagements for himself irrespective of any made for him during his apprenticeship. Employers retaining the same jockey have precedence according to the priority of their retainers. The terms of all agreements have to be registered at the Racing Calendar Office, and half the fee paid in advance, the rest at the termination of the retainer.

In Flat races the fee to a jockey is £36.50 (from 1 August 1985). At the start of the twentieth century a winning jockey received 5gns and a losing jockey 3gns.

JOCKEY CLUB

There is no precise knowledge of how, when and why the Jockey Club was founded. The first intimation of its existence came in 1752. There is no evidence to suggest that the club was founded with any high-minded notion of governing or reforming the Turf. No doubt it was originally a social club aiming to promote good fellowship among racing and horse-breeding gentlemen from all over the country. As the members included some of the most influential men of the day, the club naturally acquired authority and prestige.

Originally the club met at the Star and Garter in Pall Mall, but meetings also took place at the Thatched House in St James's Street, the Clarendon in Bond Street and the Corner, Hyde Park, where Mr Tattersall was good enough to provide a room and a cook. When Tattersall's premises moved to Knightsbridge, the club's London headquarters became established with those of their agents, Messrs Weatherby, in Bond Street.

Naturally the club wanted a place to foregather at Newmarket. In 1752 the lease of a plot of land there was obtained and a building, known as the Coffee Room, was constructed. There is reason to believe that the original Coffee Room stood upon the site of the room of that name in the present Jockey Club premises. Before half the lease had expired, it was transferred to Mr R. Vernon, a member of the club, and the other members became Mr Vernon's tenants. When in due course Mr Vernon's lease of the Coffee Room expired, the freehold of the lots comprising the Coffee Room, the New Rooms and adjuncts thereof was bought with money advanced

by the Duke of Portland. In 1831 the estate was conveyed in trust to Lord Lowther, the Duke of Richmond and the Earl of Verulam, presumably stewards of the club at that time. It was not until 1835 that an official list of members was published.

Once the Jockey Club was established and began to exercise authority, its most important member was Sir Charles Bunbury, born in 1740. When he was only 28 he was Steward of the Jockey Club, there being a single steward at that time. As from 1770, though, it became the custom to have three stewards. That practice held good for nearly 200 years, a steward holding office for three years, becoming Senior Steward the final year, at the termination of which he nominated his successor. Bunbury is best remembered as having owned Diomed, first winner of the Derby, and for the part he played in the sensational case involving Escape, a horse belonging to the Prince of Wales (later George IV) and the Prince's jockey Sam Chifney.

In 1757 a dispute over a race at The Curragh was referred to the Jockey Club, proof of the club's growing influence beyond its own immediate jurisdiction, while the following year, in respect of overweight, it issued for the first time an authoritative order. In 1784, when the Government proposed to increase the tax that already existed on racehorses, a deputation from the Jockey Club went to see Mr Pitt in London, and the proposed increase was cancelled. In 1807 the Calendar for the first time published the details of certain cases dealt with by the Jockey Club, this being done to provide a guide for the stewards at other meetings. Nine years later the club, which still possessed no power of jurisdiction outside Newmarket, expressed a willingness to help settle racing disputes if called upon to do so.

The first 'Warning Off' notice appeared in 1821, when William Taylor, a tout commonly known as 'Snipe', was warned by notice from Mr Weatherby to keep off that part of the Heath occupied by tenants of the Jockey Club. 'Snipe' was not in a position to fight back, but Mr S. Hawkins, whose chief offence was to swear horribly at Lord Wharncliffe, was made of sterner material and declined to accept a 'warning off' notice. However, in an action for trespass against him in 1827, the Jockey Club established a legal right to warn an individual off Newmarket Heath.

In 1832 the Jockey Club issued a notice in the Calendar to the effect that, as much uncertainty prevailed with regard to the Rules and Orders of the club, they thought it proper to declare that these applied solely to races run at Newmarket. They themselves had no authority whatsoever to extend their rules and orders to any other place, but for the sake of uniformity and certainty, they recommended the adoption of those rules to stewards at other courses. It was furthermore made clear that the Jockey Club was unwilling to settle disputes that arose at meetings at which the Rules and Regulations of Newmarket were not in force.

This announcement clearly had for its object the uniting of all meetings under the single control of the Jockey Club and placing all others outside the pale of recognized authority. This small start towards uniting the various race-meetings in Britain under a single authority finally culminated in reciprocal agreements with the Jockey Club and Turf authorities of practically every country in the world where racing takes place today.

From 1836 to 1846 the outstanding member of the club was Lord George Bentinck, second son of the fifth Duke of Portland. Aloof, arrogant, dictatorial and at times impulsive, there were undoubtedly aspects of his racing career that were open to criticism and made him seem on occasions hypocritical, but on balance he unquestionably conferred great benefits on the Turf. Before he took matters in hand, racing was carried on in a haphazard, disorganized fashion, no attention being paid to the comfort or well-being of spectators. Lord George decreed different-priced enclosures, with amenities varying according to the price paid. He insisted on punctuality and ensured it by fining clerks of the course 10s. for every minute a race started late. He installed comprehensive number

boards and insisted on proper race cards with the horses numbered. He ordered that horses be saddled in one special place and parade in front of the stands before a race. He abolished the pernicious practice of the winning owner giving a present to the judge, and he raised both the standard of officials, which was lamentably low, and the standard of starting. Above all he waged unrelenting war on the crooks and parasites who had started to infest the Turf when the scale of betting began to increase. But for his efforts, which included the exposure of the Running Rein scandal in the 1844 Derby, racing might, like the prize-ring, have sunk into utter disrepute. He gave up racing quite suddenly to devote himself to politics. He was still in the prime of life when he died from a heart attack.

In 1836 the Jockey Club tried to tackle the ever-present problem of non-triers and published a notice expressing extreme disapprobation of horses that were started with no intention of winning. An important step was taken in 1842 when the club decided to take no further cognisance of matters connected with betting. Up till then much of the stewards' time had been consumed by betting problems and disputes. Such matters are now handled by Tattersall's Committee.

In 1858, in order to cope with the ever-changing conditions of the Turf, the existing rules having been found totally inadequate, the stewards appointed a committee to revise and recast the rules concerning horse-racing in general and also the rules and orders of the Jockey Club. The rules concerning horse-racing governed all meetings subject to the established Rules of Racing, but the orders of the Jockey Club applied to Newmarket only. The old rules, which with slight alteration and addition had sufficed for over 100 years, were superseded by a new code of 66 rules which were thought to be sufficiently comprehensive to deal with any eventuality. So rapid was the Turf's expansion, though, that they lasted only ten years. Furthermore, there was another thorough revision that came into force in 1871.

Admiral Rous, who died in 1877, dominated racing in the mid-Victorian era. A man of complete integrity, greatly liked and immensely respected, he guided the Jockey Club along the paths of progress and commonsense, his one weakness being a tendency to write letters for publication in *The Times* without first having ascertained all the facts of the case. By shrewd management, he greatly strengthened the Jockey Club's financial position, while he was largely instrumental in ensuring that the Rules of Racing were in line with the requirements of those times. A tireless worker, he laboured unceasingly for the good of the sport and set new standards by the excellence of his handicapping. Of the three so-called 'Dictators of the Turf', Bunbury, Bentinck and himself, he was the greatest benefactor to racing and he never permitted his determination to achieve his objectives to degenerate into conduct that could have been condemned as arrogant. He formed a link between the haphazard sport characteristic of the early days of the Jockey Club and the beginnings of highly organized racing that we know today.

In 1879 the club decided that jockeys should be licensed, and issued a warning that if any jockey was found to be an owner, or part-owner, of racehorses, or in the habit of betting, his licence could be withdrawn at the discretion of the stewards. Four years later it was found necessary to put some check on the great increase in race-meetings throughout the country, there being serious difficulty in allotting days for racing at meetings already in existence.

A major Jockey Club scandal occurred in 1887. At the annual dinner of the Gimcrack Club, Lord Durham, a member of the Jockey Club, in the course of his speech, cast reflections on the conduct of Sir George Chetwynd, another member, who not long before had held office as Senior Steward. The matter became a subject of litigation, and eventually it was decided, in view of the technical nature of the matters involved, to submit it to arbitration. Owing to legal delays the case was not heard till 1889, when the stewards, acting as arbitrators, awarded purely nominal damages to Sir George

Chetwynd, who at once resigned from the Jockey Club and severed his connection with the Turf.

The starting-gate was introduced at the turn of the century, and in 1903, in consequence of certain notorious incidents, the stewards found it necessary to introduce the following rule: 'If any person shall administer, or cause to be administered, for the purpose of affecting the speed of a horse, drugs or stimulants internally or by hypodermic or other method, he shall be warned off the Turf.'

During World War I there was a strong movement in certain quarters to curtail racing completely for the duration of hostilities. That racing was permitted to continue on a greatly reduced scale was largely due to the tact and commonsense of Lord Jersey, Senior Steward at the time, supported by Lord Rosebery, Lord Derby, Lord Durham and Lord Crewe. Powerful support for these influential noblemen came from that famous demagogue and notorious con-man, Horatio Bottomley MP.

After the war serious gang warfare broke out on British racecourses, and the Jockey Club wisely appointed their own officials under Major Wymer to protect the public and to supervise security arrangements on individual racecourses.

In 1919 the Jockey Club set up a committee under Lord Hamilton of Dalzell to inquire into the policy to be adopted for racing in the future. The committee suggested that certain courses could with advantage be amalgamated with others, and that steps should be taken to improve transport, lower costs and bring amenities up to date.

The war had to some extent lowered the rigid social barriers existing up to 1914, and the Jockey Club, thanks to the example of Lord Jersey and Lord Hamilton of Dalzell, managed to shed a little of its traditional aloofness. There was a marked improvement, too, in relations between the Jockey Club and members of the racing Press. Lord Hamilton was largely responsible for the introduction of the totalisator into British racing.

For many years the Jockey Club had been worried by the question of nominations rendered void by the death of an owner. The club, on legal advice, had always acted on the assumption that fees and forfeits incurred for horses entered under Jockey Club rules could not be recovered under process of law, because if they were contracts, they were contracts by way of gaming and wagering and therefore without legal sanction.

The matter was under discussion in 1927 when Edgar Wallace, the well-known journalist and author, suggested a 'friendly' action between the Jockey Club and himself. The final verdict went to the Jockey Club (for details, see NOMINATIONS, Void).

The change in the rule made possible by this action came just in time for Cameronian to win the 1931 Derby. Lord Dewar, owner-breeder of Cameronian, died in 1930 and left the colt to his nephew, whose colours Cameronian carried to victory at Epsom.

An incident occurred in 1930 which ultimately involved the Jockey Club in an important law suit. Don Pat, trained by Charles Chapman at Lavant, won a race at Kempton Park. Don Pat was tested for dope, and it was found that a fairly large dose of caffeine had been administered.

The matter was the subject of a thorough investigation by the stewards of the Jockey Club, who, at the conclusion of the case, addressed Chapman in these words: 'We have given most careful thought to this case. We have come to the conclusion that Don Pat was doped and he is disqualified for life. We consider you, as trainer, were directly responsible for the care of the horse. Your licence to train is revoked and you are warned off Newmarket Heath.'

The findings and decision were fully within the powers conferred on the stewards by the Rules of Racing. Chapman, bound by those rules as a licensed trainer, had no redress. Furthermore the wording seemed to make it clear that the stewards found nothing against him bar the fact that he had failed in his duty as a trainer in so far as a horse under his care had been doped. There was no imputation against his integrity. Unfortunately when the stewards published their decision the wording was altered. The words 'you, as trainer, were

directly responsible for the care of the horse' were omitted. The statement in the *Racing Calendar* was repeated in *The Times* under a heading: 'Racing. Another trainer warned off. The doping of Don Pat.'

The Press naturally seized with relish on what was considered a first-class racing scandal and from the articles that appeared, it was clear that most people thought that Chapman himself had been guilty of fraud. Thus, besides losing his licence, Chapman found himself branded as a crook. He thereupon brought an action for libel against the stewards for their publication in the *Racing Calendar*, and against *The Times* as well for having repeated the statement.

The case was heard by Mr Justice Horridge. Sir Patrick Hastings, representing Chapman, made a great point of the fact that the stewards had done nothing to remove the false impression created, though it would have been perfectly easy for them to have done so. The jury found for Chapman and awarded him £13,000 against the *Racing Calendar*, and £3,000 against *The Times*.

An appeal was at once lodged. It was argued for four days, and eventually the court decided that the stewards and Messrs Weatherby were protected and the verdict against them could not be maintained. On the other hand there was no privilege in the case of *The Times*, but the view was taken that the damages awarded were too high, and a new trial was ordered in respect of *The Times*. The new trial, however, never came to court, Mr Chapman deciding, quite rightly, that his character had been publicly vindicated.

In 1948 another trainer, James Russell, whose licence had been withdrawn following a case of doping, sued the stewards, alleging that his licence had been wrongfully withdrawn and claiming damages for alleged breach of contract. He also claimed damages for libel from Messrs Weatherby, publishers of the *Racing Calendar*. Both actions were unsuccessful, and that verdict was upheld by the Court of Appeal.

In 1936 the Jockey Club decided to appoint officials designated stewards' secretaries, who were to hold no executive powers, their duty being to bring to the notice of local stewards any matter in connection with the running or riding of any horse at the meeting that might, on investigation, be found to be irregular. Some of the local stewards, a fair number of whom were notoriously incompetent – at one course the stewards were known as the 'Three Blind Mice', at another as 'unburied dead' – at first resented this innovation, which on the whole has proved highly successful.

During phases of World War II there was bitter hostility to racing from certain quarters, and it required considerable tact on the part of the Jockey Club to keep the sport going at all, even on a greatly reduced scale. Lord Ilchester, who had just retired from being Senior Steward, made an admirable reply to a leading article in *The Times* which had stated that the resumption of racing in the autumn of 1940 – there had been no racing at all from June till mid-September – was deeply resented. Lord Sefton was Senior Steward for much of the war period and carried out his duties at a very difficult time with marked success.

In the dark days of 1941 the Jockey Club formed a committee, with Lord Ilchester as chairman, to consider the whole future of racing. In 1943 an excellent report was produced, progressive and far-reaching. Unfortunately many of the reforms suggested never came into force, possibly for financial reasons. 'It is like the Beveridge Report,' said one influential Jockey Club member. 'It is a very good plan when they have the money.' Looking back, it is hard to avoid the impression that a great opportunity was missed, particularly as the spirit of reform, which had temporarily infected the Jockey Club, soon seemed to fade quietly away.

However, there were certain changes. At last the Jockey Club recognized the significance of public relations and appointed Mr J.H. Freeman, late of the *Daily Mail*, as Public Relations Officer. The photo-finish was introduced, and so was the racecourse commentary. The programmes at Newmarket were revised, strengthened and in certain cases cur-

tailed, while a number of Saturday programmes were introduced. None too soon, an attempt was made to shed the Newmarket meetings of their old-fashioned exclusiveness and to attract the general public. Gradually admission to the members' enclosure was made far more accessible. To alleviate the possible tedium of race after race on the straight course, a round course, named after Lord Sefton, was constructed but it did not prove a notable success. In 1967 a re-building scheme was begun on the Rowley Mile course, and when completed a year later it met with general approval, it being considered that the standard of comfort had been greatly increased and the bleak, rather unfriendly atmosphere substantially reduced.

A long-standing and ridiculous attitude by the Jockey Club was to permit horses to run unnamed. It was not until 1946 that a rule was brought in demanding that all horses be named before they ran.

A disquieting episode took place in 1951 when a private test showed that Lord Rosebery's filly Snap had been doped, Lord Rosebery having initiated the test because Snap had run far below her usual form. At that time a trainer lost his licence when a horse of his was found to have been doped, regardless of whether the animal in question had been doped to win or to lose, although, as Lord Rosebery pointed out, no trainer in his right mind would dope one of his own horses to lose when so many simpler and equally effective methods were available. The racing public was naturally disturbed at the thought that, if the test had been official, Lord Rosebery's much-respected trainer, Jack Jarvis, would have lost his licence. The Jockey Club set up a committee under Major (later Sir) Reginald Macdonald-Buchanan to inquire into the whole problem of doping, but they apparently saw no reason to alter the rules after the presentation of the committee's report.

In 1954 the Jockey Club decided that its own stewards should not function at Newmarket meetings, a pool being created from within the membership of the club from which 'local' stewards would from then on be drawn. This year, too, the stewards let it be known that they were prepared to grant licences to Newmarket trainers whose patrons included bookmakers.

By the mid-fifties it had become apparent that some big changes in the laws affecting betting and gaming in Britain were due in the not far distant future. It had also become distressingly obvious that British racing was resting on a dangerously insecure financial basis, largely because such a tiny proportion of the vast profits from betting was ploughed into the sport. In 1956, therefore, the Jockey Club set up a joint committee, which included various interested organizations, to work out a plan that would embody certain fundamental principles which would be of benefit to the sport as a whole and could be presented at the opportune moment to the Home Secretary.

In 1960 public confidence in the conduct of racing was shaken by a series of doping scandals. The Jockey Club felt compelled to set up a three-man committee to review the rules and procedures dealing with the administration of dope to racehorses, and to look into the efficiency of the existing rules on that subject.

There was fortunately a much brighter side to racing that year. The government-appointed committee under Sir Leslie Peppiatt reported that it was both desirable and practicable that persons engaged in betting on horses should make a contribution for purposes conducive to the improvement of the breed and of the sport in general. The committee outlined suggestions for raising £1-£1¼ million annually, although the Jockey Club had requested a sum of £3 million. Despite some disappointment that the Jockey Club's request had been turned down, it was generally recognized that the Peppiatt Committee's report represented a milestone of great significance in British racing history and that financial assistance would be forthcoming in time to save the racing industry from possible collapse.

The provisions of the report were incorporated into the Betting Levy Bill which set up a board, under the Home Office, empowered to collect contributions from the bookmakers and the Tote and to apply those contributions to the general good of racing.

The new situation meant that all punters, on-course and off-course, were contributing to racing and that the Jockey Club had to give far more attention to the demands of the betting public than it had done in the past. Accordingly the existing system of declaring runners was scrapped and a form of overnight declarations instituted in its place.

In 1961 the Duke of Norfolk's committee on doping, which included Sir Laurence Byrne, lately a High Court Judge, and Dr Wooldridge, chairman and scientific director of the Animal Health Trust, published a comprehensive report. Not the least of its recommendations was to remove 'the sword of Damocles' from over the heads of trainers, through which, under the old rule, they had immediately and irrevocably been disqualified if any of their horses was found to have been doped, whether the doping was done to improve a horse's chance of success or to prevent it from winning.

In 1963 a committee, comprising members of both the Jockey Club and the National Hunt Committee, was set up under the chairmanship of Lord Howard de Walden to analyse the various categories of stewards' work, to recommend a method which would enable that work to be more easily handled, and to suggest any necessary reorganization.

The committee's report was received the following year and was accepted in principle. The main feature was the formation of a new supreme authority, the Turf Board, to operate as from January 1965. The Turf Board was to be formed from the Jockey Club and National Hunt Committee, and there was to be continuous representation as well of the policy and views of the Levy Board.

It was stated that the main function of the Turf Board was to deal with matters of general policy, the board's decisions being implemented by the Jockey Club and the National Hunt Committee. The chairman of the Turf Board was to be *ex officio* the Senior Steward of the Jockey Club, working with one vice-chairman from the Jockey Club and another from the National Hunt Committee. To ensure a certain continuity of office, the chairman was to hold office for five years, the vice-chairmen for two. The first chairman of the Turf Board was Major-General Sir Randle Feilden, the outstanding racing administrator of the post-war era.

The year 1965 saw the publication of the Duke of Norfolk's committee on the pattern of racing, the first serious attempt at long-term planning for the sport, and also the first tentative use of starting-stalls in Britain, a reform ultimately carried through in the face of much opposition. The following year the Jockey Club gave way to the gallant persistence of Mrs Florence Nagle, and women, barred for years by the medieval thinking of the rulers of British racing, became eligible to receive a trainer's licence. It was not until 1977 that women were first elected members of the Jockey Club.

In 1968, in order to streamline racing administration and to render it more efficient, the Jockey Club and the National Hunt Committee amalgamated, the new body, designated the Jockey Club (incorporating the National Hunt Committee), coming into force on 12 December 1968. Major-General Sir Randle Feilden became Senior Steward of this new body. The work of the stewards, two of whom retire annually, was divided into four main groups – Licensing, Racecourses and Rules; Discipline; Administration and Finance; Fixtures and Prize Money – certain stewards being made responsible for each group. Discipline is the responsibility of a committee under a disciplinary chairman.

The Jockey Club, which was incorporated by Royal Charter in 1970, no longer has responsibility for the activities at Newmarket, which include the racecourses, the properties and the investments. These have become the responsibility of the Newmarket Estates and Property Company. Newmarket racecourses have now the same relationship to the new Jockey Club as other racecourses.

Once the Levy Board took control of racing's finances, the role of the Jockey Club was bound to change. Its policies became increasingly administrative, depending on the implementation of the Rules of Racing, but all along it resisted attempts to divest it of power. It survived the all-party arrival of BRIC (Bloodstock and Racehorse Industries Confederation) in November 1974; it rode out the recommendations for a British Horseracing Authority contained in the Royal Commission on Gambling in July 1978; and it welcomed the appearance of the Horseracing Advisory Council in December 1979 by allowing the HAC chairman the right to attend meetings of the stewards, and by giving him one of its seats on the Levy Board.

The Jockey Club has made in recent years strenuous efforts to improve its image and to render the direction and organization of the sport more modern and more businesslike. However, this is the era of big business and professionalism, not of amateurs, however dedicated and gifted. It remains to be seen how durable is the power of the Jockey Club, a self-elected, self-perpetuating, essentially upper-class body.

JOCKEY CLUB, Members of

The Jockey Club and National Hunt Committee amalgamated as from 12 December 1968. The new body, designated the Jockey Club (incorporating the National Hunt Committee), took over the functions and powers of the old Jockey Club and National Hunt Committee as from 1 January 1969, when the stewards were as follows:

Maj.-Gen. Sir Randle Feilden (Senior Steward), T.F. Blackwell (Deputy Senior Steward), Maj. W.D. Gibson (Deputy Senior Steward), Duke of Devonshire, Capt. H.M. Gosling, Lt.-Col. J.D. Hornung, Earl Cadogan, J.J. Astor, Brig. F.B.B. Noble.

At the time of the amalgamation the Jockey Club comprised:

Patron: HM The Queen. Members: HRH Prince Philip, Duke of Edinburgh (honorary member), HRH the Duke of Gloucester (honorary member), HRH the Duke of Windsor (honorary member), Marquess of Abergavenny, Viscount Allendale,

J.J. Astor, Col. Julian Berry, T.F. Blackwell, Maj.-Gen. Sir George Burns, Earl Cadogan, Maj. E.M. Cameron, Sir Rex Cohen, Lt.-Gen. Sir George Collingwood, Lord Crathorne, Maj-Gen. J.A. d'Avigdor-Goldsmid, Gen. Sir Miles Dempsey, Earl of Derby, Duke of Devonshire, Sir William Dugdale, Bart., Earl of Durham, T.E.S. Egerton, Maj.-Gen. Sir Randle Feilden, Lt.-Col. D. Forster, Maj. W.D. Gibson, Earl of Halifax, J.O. Hambro, Sir Edward Hanmer, Bart., E. Holland-Martin, L. Brook Holliday, R.D. Hollingsworth, Lt.-Col. J.D. Hornung, Lord Howard de Walden, H.J. Joel, Lord Kilmany, Viscount Leverhulme, C.L. Loyd, Sir R. McAlpine, Capt. J. Macdonald-Buchanan, Maj. S.R. Macdonald-Buchanan, Lord Manton, Lord Margadale, P. Mellon (honorary member), Duke of Norfolk, J.P. Philipps, Lord Porchester, J. Rogerson, Earl of Rosebery, Duke of Roxburghe, Earl of Sefton, R.R. Shelley (honorary member), Rt. Hon. Christopher Soames, R. Stanley, Duke of Sutherland, Sir Richard Sykes, Bart., Brig. Lord Tryon, Sir Francis Weatherby, Maj.-Gen. Sir Harold Wernher, Bart., J.H. Whitney (honorary member), G.D. Widener (honorary member), Lord Willoughby de Broke, marquess of Zetland.

This was the composition of the National Hunt Committee at the time of the amalgamation:

Patrons: HM The Queen, HM Queen Elizabeth the Queen Mother. Members: HRH the Duke of Gloucester (honorary member), Marquess of Abergavenny, Maj. P.H.G. Bengough, Maj.-Gen. C.H. Blacker, Earl Cadogan, Maj. E.M. Cameron, Viscount Chelsea, E.R. Courage, Maj. D.R. Daly, Sir Humphrey de Trafford, H.W. Dufosee, Cmdr. H.S. Egerton, Maj.-Gen. Sir Randle Feilden, Capt. P.M. Forsythe Forrest, Maj. W.D. Gibson, Lt.-Col. Sir Martin Gilliat, Capt. H.M. Gosling, Earl of Halifax, Sir Edward Hanmer, Bart., J.R. Henderson, Maj. R. Hoare, E. Holland-Martin, H.J. Joel,

Lord Kilmany, G. Kindersley, Col. Sir Peter Grant-Lawson, Bart., Lord Leigh, Viscount Leverhulme, Lt.-Col. H.M. Llewellyn, J.A. Marshall, Lt.-Cmdr. R.J.B. Mildmay-White, Maj. J.C. Vernon Miller, Lt.-Col. R.B. Moseley, Brig. F.B.B. Noble, Duke of Norfolk, Lt.-Gen. Lord Norrie, Maj. H.M. Peacock, J.P. Philipps, Col. Sir John Carew-Pole, Bart., J. Rogerson, Earl of Rosebery, J.S. Schilizzi, Earl of Sefton, J.J. Straker, Maj.-Gen. V.W. Street,, J.R.H. Sumner, Col. John Thomson, Wing-Cmdr. P.D.O. Vaux, Col. G.R. Westmacott, W.H. Whitbread, J.H. Whitney (honorary member), Maj. D. Wigan, R.S. Wilkins, Lord Willoughby de Broke, Col. E.H. Wyndham.

Jockey Club Members (as at 1 January 1986), with date of election:
HRH Prince Philip* (1.12.47)
HRH the Prince of Wales* (16.6.80)
Lord Cadogan (17.7.39 NHC, 3.7.57 JC)
Lord Willoughby de Broke (9.12.40 NHC, 22.10.41 JC)
Lord Abergavenny (14.12.42 NHC, 30.4.52 JC)
Lord Derby (1.5.46)
Sir Harry Llewellyn (15.7.46 NHC)
Duke of Sutherland (15.10.47)
J. Rogerson (12.12.49 NHC, 1.5.68 JC)
Col. Sir John G. Carew Pole (11.12.50 NHC)
Lord Howard de Walden (30.4.52)
H.J. Joel (14.10.53)
Gen. Sir Cecil Blacker (13.12.54 NHC), Maj.-Gen. Sir George Burns (4.7.56)
Duke of Devonshire (4.7.56)
Lord Margadale (4.7.56)
W.H. Whitbread (16.7.56 NHC)
Maj. J.C. Vernon Miller (13.5.57 NHC)
Lord Allendale (29.10.58)
Lt.-Gen. Sir George Collingwood (29.10.58)
Sir John Astor (29.4.59)
J. Hambro (29.4.59)
J.A. Marshall (11.5.59)
Maj. W.D. Gibson (12.10.59 NHC, 5.12.66 JC)
Lord Leverhulme (9.10.61 NHC, 7.7.65 JC)
Sir Robin McAlpine (13.10.61)
Lord Zetland (17.10.62)

Lt.-Col. Sir Martin Gilliat (12.10.64 NHC)
L.B. Holliday (16.10.64)
Lord Porchester (16.10.64)
Sir Piers Bengough (1.3.65 NHC)
Capt. H.M. Gosling (1.3.65 NHC)
Sir William S. Dugdale (7.7.65)
J.R. Henderson (19.7.65 NHC)
R.S. Wilkins (19.7.65 NHC)
Sir John Thomson (11.10.65 NHC)
Maj. E.M. Cameron (6.12.65)
Brig. F.B.B. Noble (13.12.65 NHC)
Sir Rex Cohen (13.7.66)
T.E.S. Egerton (13.7.66)
R.D. Hollingsworth (5.12.66)
Capt. J. Macdonald-Buchanan (5.12.66)
Lord Chelsea (9.10.67 NHC)
Col. Julian Berry (1.5.68)
Maj.-Gen. Sir James d'Avigdor-Goldsmid (1.5.68)
C.L. Loyd (1.5.68)
Lord Manton (1.5.68)
Lord Soames (1.5.68)
P. Mellon* (1.5.68)
Lord McAlpine of Moffat (16.6.69)
James Morrison (16.6.69)
Lord Ranfurly (16.6.69)
R.N. Richmond-Watson (16.6.69)
R.R. Tweedie (16.6.69)
Lord Benson (8.12.69)
Brig. C.B. Harvey (8.12.69)
J.U. Baillie (12.10.70)
B.P. Jenks (12.10.70)
Sir Gordon Richards* (14.12.70)
Lt-Col. J.E.S. Chamberlayne (13.12.71)
J.L. Hislop (13.12.71)
Maj. V. McCalmont (13.12.71)
Sir Philip Oppenheimer (13.12.71)
Sir Michael Sobell (13.12.71)
J.B. Sumner (13.12.71)
P.M. Weatherby* (10.10.72)
C.D. Collins (11.12.72)
R.E. Sangster (11.12.72)
Lord Westbury (11.12.72)
L. Freedman (16.6.75)
R.R. Guest* (16.6.75)
T.D. Holland-Martin (16.6.75)
R.J. McAlpine (16.6.75)
A.J. Macdonald-Buchanan (16.6.75)
A. Mildmay-White (14.6.76)
Sir Thomas Pilkington (14.6.76)
Lord Scarbrough (14.6.76)
J.J. Warr (14.6.76)
George Weir (14.6.76)
R.A. Bethell (25.7.77)

E.S.M. Collingwood-Cameron (25.7.77)
Lord Fairhaven (25.7.77)
Sir Noel Murless (25.7.77)
A.M. Budgett (12.12.77)
J.B. Daly (12.12.77)
Ruth, Countess of Halifax (12.12.77)
Mrs P. Hastings (12.12.77)
Mrs H. Johnson Houghton (12.12.77)
David Sieff (12.12.77)
A.T.A. Wates (12.12.77)
Brig. H.J.L. Green* (12.12.77)
E. de Rothschild (11.12.78)
Lord Weinstock (11.12.78)
Dame Elizabeth Ackroyd (18.6.79)
Wentworth Beaumont (18.6.79)
Brig. Lord Grimthorpe (18.6.79)
Lord Halifax (18.6.79)
Sir Freddie Laker (18.6.79)
N.H. Phillips (18.6.79)
Lord Vestey (18.6.79)
Lord Hartington (5.12.80)
Mrs D. Brudenell-Bruce (14.12.81)
C.R. Saunders (14.12.81)
A.J. Struthers (14.12.81)
M.E. Wates (14.12.81)
P.S. Willett (14.12.81)
J.K. Barlow (13.12.82)
Lt.-Col. A.H. Parker Bowles (13.12.82)
Lord Ronaldshay (13.12.82)
C.H. Sporborg (13.12.82)
M.H. Wrigley (13.12.82)
Aga Khan* (13.12.82)
R.B. Waley-Cohen (12.12.83)
K. Abdulla* (12.12.83)
Capt. M. Lemos* (12.12.83)
P.G. Greenall (10.12.84)
M.B.J. Kimmins (10.12.84)
A.D.G. Oldrey (10.12.84)
Miss J. Thompson (10.12.84)
B. Hobbs (9.12.85)
Capt. W. Bulwer-Long (9.12.85)
P. Player (9.12.85)
Sheikh Maktoum Al-Maktoum* (9.12.85)
J. Weatherby* (9.12.85).
* honorary member
NHC – National Hunt Committee

The following are *ex officio* members of the Jockey Club:
The Queen's Representative at Ascot; the Queen's Racing Manager; the Manager of the Queen's Stud; the Stewards of the Turf Club, Ireland; the Chairman of the Curragh Race Committee; the Stewards of the Irish

National Hunt Steeplechase Committee; the President and four Stewards of the Société d'Encouragement pour l'Amélioration des Races de Chevaux en France; the Chairman of the Jockey Club, New York; the Chairman of Committee of the Australian Jockey Club, New South Wales; the Chairman of Committee of the Victoria Racing Club; the Chief Steward of the Jockey Club of Canada; the President of the New Zealand Racing Conference; the Chairman of the Executive Stewards of the Jockey Club of South Africa; the Chairman of the Royal Hong Kong Jockey Club.

Membership of the Standing Committees of the Jockey Club for 1986:

Administration and Finance: L. Freedman (chairman), E. de Rothschild, A. Struthers, M. Kimmins, N. Phillips.

Disciplinary: Sir Wm. Dugdale (chairman), C. Loyd, A. Mildmay-White, M. Wrigley, Lord Vestey.

Licensing: C.R. Saunders (chairman), R. Waley-Cohen, J. Barlow, J. Daly.

Race Planning: A. Wates (chairman), Mrs D. Brudenell-Bruce, Ruth, Countess of Halifax, P. Greenall.

Jockey Club representatives on the Levy Board are Lord Chelsea and Sir Thomas Pilkington, and on Tattersalls' Committee T.E.S. Egerton and Maj.-Gen. Sir James d'Avigdor-Goldsmid.

JOCKEYS ASSOCIATION OF GREAT BRITAIN

This is the body that represents the interests of professional riders both on the Flat and over jumps. The Flat Race Jockeys Association and the Professional National Hunt Jockeys Association were amalgamated in 1969.

Address: 1 Bridge Street, Newbury, Berkshire, RG14 6BL (Phone: 0635-44102).

JOCKEYS, Leading

See Appendix II

JOEL, Harry Joel (b. 1894)

The son of Mr J.B. Joel, Mr 'Jim' Joel served in World War I with the 15th/19th

Hussars. He owns the Childwick Bury Stud, St Albans, which he inherited from his father and restored to former glories. Despite the many high-class horses he has bred and raced, his first two Classic winners were separated by 23 years: Picture Play (1,000 Guineas) and Royal Palace (2,000 Guineas and Derby). These were followed by Light Cavalry (St Leger) and Fairy Footsteps (1,000 Guineas), though he had several placed including West Side Story (beaten a short head in the Oaks) and Connaught (second in the Derby). He also bred Welsh Pageant (Lockinge Stakes twice) and Major Portion (Middle Park Stakes, St James's Palace Stakes, Sussex Stakes and Queen Elizabeth II Stakes), and purchased Predominate (Goodwood Stakes three years running, Goodwood Cup) and the brilliant sprinter Song.

A bachelor, he is one of the most modest, kind and unassuming men and enjoys great popularity in the racing world. He is a member of the Jockey Club.

Racing colours: black, scarlet cap.

JOEL, Jack Barnato (1862-1940)

A man of humble origin, Mr Jack Barnato Joel went to South Africa as a young man and rapidly accumulated an immense fortune. Towards the close of the last century he returned to Britain and in 1900 registered his colours, black jacket, scarlet cap. From then on gold, diamonds, breeding and racing were his main interests in life. Because of his success in business and on the Turf, he was generally regarded as a lucky man. Mr Joel himself did not believe in luck; he believed in hard work and plenty of it.

In 1901 he engaged Charles Morton as private trainer, and the combination proved highly successful, as between 1903 and 1921 Mr Joel won no fewer than eleven Classic events. The Gold Cup was the one big race that always eluded him. He won the Derby with Sunstar in 1911 and Humorist in 1921. His other Classic successes were the 2,000 Guineas with Sunstar; 1,000 Guineas with Jest and Princess Dorrie; Oaks with Our

Lassie, Glass Doll, Jest and Princess Dorrie; and St Leger with Your Majesty and Black Jester.

In the closing stages of his racing career Mr Joel was notably less successful and the Childwick Bury Stud carried on by his son Jim Joel had to be revitalized.

JOEL, Solomon Barnato (1865-1931)

Usually referred to as 'Solly' Joel, Mr S.B. Joel made a fortune in South Africa as a young man, as did his brother Mr J.B. Joel. A forceful and rather self-assertive character, 'Solly' Joel raced on a big scale but was less shrewd and less successful than his brother. Pommern, who won the 'Triple Crown' in 1915, was his sole Classic winner. His most successful purchase was Polymelus for 4,000gns at the Newmarket October Sales. Within a month Polymelus had won the Duke of York Handicap at Kempton and the Cambridgeshire. Over the latter race Mr Joel and his friends won £100,000. Mr Joel himself had a final bet of £6,000 to £5,000 when the horses were at the post. Polymelus was five times champion sire.

JOEL, Stanhope Henry (1903-76)

Mr Stanhope Joel, son of Mr S.B. Joel, rose to the rank of Squadron-Leader in the RAF during the war. He lived in Bermuda and was seen in Britain rarely but nevertheless maintained considerable racing interests. The best horses he owned were Chamossaire (St Leger), Busted (Eclipse Stakes and King George VI and Queen Elizabeth Stakes), Matador (Stewards' Cup), Primera (Ebor Handicap, Churchill Stakes and Princess of Wales's Stakes), Caliban (Coronation Cup), Silver Tor (King's Stand Stakes), St Pauli Girl (second in the 1,000 Guineas and Oaks) and Saintly Song (St James's Palace Stakes). His wife won the Oaks with Lupe. On his death his colours were retained in the name of the Snailwell Stud, which he had bought in 1945.

JOHNSON, Ernest (b. 1948)

Ernie Johnson was apprenticed to Ian Balding at Kingsclere, had his first ride in 1965 and in 1967 was leading apprentice, with 39 winners, one of his victories being on Ovaltine in the Ebor Handicap. Balding at this time thought that Johnson would not get sufficient opportunities in his own stable and transferred his indentures to Sam Hall in Middleham, beginning a career which has alternated spells based in the North with periods in the South. In 1969 he got his big chance when given the ride on Blakeney in the Derby, in which he rode a faultless race. Three years later he was beaten a short head by Roberto when riding Rheingold for Barry Hills, whose stable he was associated with from 1969 to 1979, with one break when replaced on several runners by more senior jockeys, and a second when American Steve Cauthen joined the stable. Johnson's important winners for Hills were on Enstone Spark (1,000 Guineas), Rheingold (Dante Stakes), Proverb (Goodwood Cup) and Princess of Man (Musidora Stakes).

He won the Ebor again in 1968 on Alignment, and other major wins have come on Boismoss (Cesarewitch), Gold Pollen (Portland Handicap), Huntercombe (Middle Park Stakes), Blue Cashmere (Ayr Gold Cup), Super Nova (Chester Cup) and Jimmy the Singer (Stewards' Cup). His best season was 1978, with 86 winners. He completed the feat of at least one winner on every course in Britain in September 1974. Dwindling opportunities led him to take a contract in Ireland at the start of 1985, but the job lasted only a short time, he returned to England and at the end of the year left to ride in the Far East.

JOHNSON, Ian Ernest (b. 1955)

Ian Johnson was apprenticed to 'Frenchie' Nicholson and rode his first winner on Hornbeak at Warwick on 9 June 1973. The following year he gained his biggest success when travelling to Ireland and winning the local Cambridgeshire on Port Magee. He also had his best season in Britain in 1974, with 26 winners, and in

1975 rode Dominion into third place in the 2,000 Guineas for Arthur Budgett.

JOHNSTONE, William Raphael (1905-64)

Nicknamed 'Togo' before the war but more commonly referred to as 'Rae' after it, W.R. Johnstone was born in Australia. In 1931 he was champion jockey in Sydney and the following year he migrated to France at the invitation of M. Pierre Wertheimer. He headed the jockeys' list in France in three of his first six seasons there. In 1934 he accepted a retainer to ride for Lord Glanely in Britain. He won the 2,000 Guineas on Colombo, but he was sharply criticized for Colombo's defeat in the Derby and ceased to ride for Lord Glanely not long afterwards.

The following year Johnstone won the 1,000 Guineas on Mesa. He ought to have won the Oaks on her, too, instead of finishing a desperately unlucky third.

After the war, during which he lived an adventurous life in France, he enjoyed a period of resounding success. In 1947 he won the 1,000 Guineas and Oaks on Imprudence, and the following year the Derby on My Love. He was narrowly beaten in the 1949 Derby on Amour Drake but won again in 1950 on Galcador. That year he also won the 1,000 Guineas on Camarée, the Oaks on Asmena and the St Leger on Scratch II. He won the 1951 St Leger on Talma, the 1954 Oaks on Sun Cap and the 1956 Derby on Lavandin. At one time or another he won all the French Classic events and he had two victories in the Prix de l'Arc de Triomphe. At his best he was a brilliant rider and was always liable to be at his peak on the big occasion. He was admired in Britain – at any rate after the war – but the racing public never really took him to their hearts. Perhaps they could not forgive him for Colombo's defeat. He retired in 1957 and took up training.

JOINT RACING BOARD

The Joint Racing Board was founded in April 1968 as a forum for the joint discussion and problems facing the racing industry and to be a joint policy-making body of the Jockey Club and Levy Board. It was composed of the Senior Steward of the Jockey Club and the chairman of the Levy Board as co-chairmen, two members each from the Jockey Club and Levy Board, and the secretary of each organization as joint secretaries. The last meeting was held in October 1982, when the Levy Board chairman Sir Ian Trethowan suggested that formal meetings were no longer necessary. The Board was wound up, and its work has been replaced by regular, informal contracts.

JONES, Harry Thomson (b. 1925)

'Tom' Jones was educated at Eton and served in the Royals. He was assistant trainer to Bob Fetherstonehaugh for two years and to Sam Armstrong for four years before taking out a licence himself in 1951 to run a 'mixed' stable at Newmarket. Originally he was more noted for his National Hunt runners, even at the time he won the St Leger and Great Voltigeur Stakes with Athens Wood in 1971, the year he won the Yorkshire Oaks with Fleet Wahine. But gradually he switched the emphasis to Flat racing, and by the time he trained the high-class two-year-old filly Devon Ditty to win the Flying Childers Stakes and Cheveley Park Stakes in 1978 he had virtually given up training jumpers. He began the 1980s as one of the trainers with extensive interests for wealthy Arab owners, particularly Hamdan Al-Maktoum, for whom he has won the St Leger (Touching Wood), Gimcrack Stakes (Doulab) and Irish 1,000 Guineas (Al Bahathri).

JONES, Herbert (1881-1951)

Herbert Jones was a son of King Edward VII's first trainer, Jack Jones, who had a stable of jumpers at Epsom. Apprenticed to Richard Marsh, the royal trainer, at the age of ten, Herbert Jones rode his first winner in 1896. He was very little known to the public when in 1900 he was given the ride in the 2,000 Guineas on Diamond Jubilee, a high-class colt but temperamental and at times savage. The horse and Jones got on well together, and the combination won not only the Guineas but the Derby, Eclipse Stakes and St Leger. These successes established Jones's reputation, and in 1909 he won his second Derby in the royal colours, on Minoru, who also won the 2,000 Guineas. Jones had two other victories in the 2,000 Guineas and one in the Oaks. His final win was in 1923 on a horse of King George V's called Erne. He was 71 when he was found dead in the kitchen of his home at Girton.

JONES, Herbert (b. 1933)

Herbert Jones, who was apprenticed to Joe Thwaites and Jack Pearce, rode on the Flat from 1949 to 1963 and won races in Britain, India, Norway, Denmark and Sweden. In Britain he won the Ayr Gold Cup and the Ebor Handicap. He took out a licence to train on the outskirts of Malton in 1964 and moved into the town in 1977. His best horse, Jimsun, won the Earl of Sefton Stakes as a six-year-old.

JUDGE, THE

The Judge must occupy the judge's box at the time the horses pass the winning-post. He must announce his decision immediately, or after consulting the photo-finish print, and that decision shall be final unless an objection to the winner, or any placed horses, is made and sustained. This rule does not prevent a judge from correcting any mistakes, such correction being subject to confirmation by the stewards. Judges are licensed annually by the stewards of the Jockey Club.

JULIETTE MARNY
(1972, b f Blakeney – Set Free, by Worden II)

Juliette Marny completed the Epsom and Irish Oaks double for her owner, James Morrison, at whose Fonthill Stud she was bred. She also won the Lingfield Oaks Trial and passed the post first in the Princess Elizabeth Stakes at Epsom, only to be disqualified for hampering another runner in the last furlong. Not only was Set Free the first mare covered by Blakeney and Juliette Marny the product, but Juliette Marny was her sire's first runner in a Classic. Juliette Marny's daughter Jolly Bay won the Pretty Polly Stakes at Newmarket.

JULIO MARINER
(1975, b c Blakeney – Set Free, by Worden II)

Julio Mariner cost Marcos Lemos 40,000gns when bought from the Fonthill Stud as a yearling, and with three wins, including the St Leger, in which he became the first Classic winner for both his owner and his trainer Clive Brittain, he repaid the outlay. He also boosted the reputation of his dam, who, after the Oaks win of Julio Mariner's sister Juliette Marny, became the third mare this century to breed a Classic-winning brother and sister (after Scapa Flow and Ranai). Set Free's daughter Scintillate added further to the record. Julio Mariner was retired to stud after finishing unplaced in the Prix de l'Arc de Triomphe and began stallion duties at Newmarket in 1979 at a valuation of £800,000.

K

KALAGLOW
(1978 gr c Kalamoun – Rossitor, by Pall Mall)

For the first two years of his racing career Kalaglow raced under incorrect identification, as a result of a mistake which occurred ten years previously concerning the fillies Aglow and Rossitor. While wrongly described as being a son of Aglow, Kalaglow, who was bought as a yearling for 11,500gns, won all five races at two years, including the Horris Hill Stakes, and his first as a three-year-old, the Heath Stakes. He ran poorly in two more races, the Mecca-Dante Stakes and Derby, and was kept off the course by leg injury until the following year, when the true identity of his dam was established and he won four of his six races, including the Eclipse Stakes and King George VI and Queen Elizabeth Diamond Stakes. He retired to begin stud duties at Newmarket in 1983 with a valuation of £5 million.

KANDY
(1929, b f Alcantara II – Kiao Tchau by Chouberski)

Kandy was owned and bred in France by M.E. de Saint-Alary and trained by F. Carter. She won the 1,000 Guineas, ridden by E.C. Elliott, at 33-1 but was unplaced in her local equivalent.

KASHMIR II
(1963, br c Tudor Melody – Queen of Speed, by Blue Train)

Kashmir II was bred in Ireland by Mrs A. Levins Moore and sold as a yearling for 8,600gns to Dr J. Burkhardt acting for Mr P. Butler. Trained in France by C. Bartholomew, Kashmir II won three times as a two-year-old, and the following season won the Prix Djebel, and the 2,000 Guineas by inches from Great Nephew. Kashmir II retired to stud in France in 1967 and was responsible for the 1975 local Guineas winners Moulines (2,000) and Dumka (1,000), as well as the top-grade sprinter Blue Cashmere, his best produce trained in Britain. Kashmir II died late in 1980.

KEITH, Duncan (b. 1938)

Duncan Keith was born in Glasgow and served his apprenticeship with H.E. Smyth. He had a successful association with Walter Nightingall's stable, but his career was seriously interrupted by bad falls in 1964 and 1965, both times when riding London Melody. His first winner was in 1954, and he rode 656 winners in Britain before he gave up riding in August 1972 because of weight problems, after four years as stable jockey to Peter Walwyn. His most important wins for Nightingall were on Niksar (2,000 Guineas) and I Say (Coronation Cup), while for Walwyn he won the Cheveley Park Stakes and Sussex Stakes on Humble Duty, the Doncaster Cup and Goodwood Cup on Rock Roi (who was twice disqualified after passing the post first in the Ascot Gold Cup), the Sun Chariot Stakes on Lucyrowe, and the Observer Gold Cup on Linden Tree, who was also second in the Derby. He also won the Observer Gold Cup on Approval, and won the Victoria Cup twice. He started training at Winchester in 1974 but had to quit five years later after a dispute over the use of gallops, and for a short time trained abroad.

KELLEWAY, Gay Marie (b. 1963)

Daughter of Newmarket trainer Paul Kelleway, Gay rode her first winner as an amateur on Aberfield at Ripon on 3 June 1981. She rode eight winners as an amateur and turned professional in 1983, becoming apprenticed to her father. Four winners in her first season as a professional were ruled out by the Jockey Club on a technicality concerning her claim, but she has gone on to become the first female professional jockey to make her mark in Britain.

KELLEWAY, Paul Anthony (b. 1940)

Apprenticed on the Flat to Eddie Magner and Harry Wragg, Paul Kelleway became a successful jump jockey with 345 winners in thirteen seasons, including the Champion Hurdle and Cheltenham Gold Cup. He began training at Newmarket in 1977 and had his first winner with Port Justice at Leicester on 28 March 1977, after finishing second but getting the race on an objection. In his second season he won the Champion Stakes with Swiss Maid, and since then he has never been afraid to fly high with his horses. His other big wins have been in the King's Stand Stakes (African Song), Ayr Gold Cup (Sparkling Boy), Chester Cup (Donegal Prince) and French Oaks (Madam Gay), and there have been notable places, such as Media Luna's second place in the Oaks. His best season was 1978 with 26 winners.

KEMPTON PARK

Photographs of Kempton Park taken at the turn of this century show it to have been in remarkably pleasant and rural surroundings. The spread of suburbia has inevitably taken its hideous toll, but the course itself is still a pretty one in the summer, bearing in mind how close it is to London. An opportunity to restore some of Kempton's waning popularity was probably lost when Mr David Robinson could not get planning permission for his schemes after buying the course for £765,000 in 1969, whereupon he sold out for the same price to the Levy Board to be run by United Racecourses.

Unimaginative programmes have done nothing to arrest the decline of Kempton's traditional races – the Rosebery Stakes and Queen's Prize at the Easter meeting and Jubilee Handicap in May – and the course's biggest crowd-puller these days is the Boxing Day jumping meeting.

It is a right-handed triangular track, 1m 5f round and with only very gentle undulations. The straight 6f course, which intersects the back straight of the triangular course, is perfectly flat. The 10f Jubilee course, which has a slight downhill slope for the first 2f, joins the triangular course at the home turn.

KENNYMORE
(1911, b c John o' Gaunt – Croceum, by Martagon)

Kennymore won four races for £9,297, including the 2,000 Guineas, and was second in the St Leger. He died after a single season at stud.

KEYSOE
(1916, br f Swynford – Keystone II, by Persimmon)

Keysoe, bred and owned by Lord Derby, won four races for £8,087, including the St Leger in 1919, trained by the George Lambton and ridden by B. Carslake. She bred Caissot, winner of over £4,000, and Flittemere, grandam of Ballymoss.

KEYSTONE II
(1903, b f Persimmon – Lock and Key, by Janissary)

Lord Derby's Keystone II won the Oaks and bred six winners including Keysoe, winner of the 1919 St Leger, and the Derby runner-up Archaic.

KI MING
(1948, br c Ballyogan – Ulster Lily, by Apron)

Ki Ming won three races for £17,394, including the 2,000 Guineas, owned by Mr Ley On and trained by Michael Beary. He also won the Diadem Stakes. He failed as a sire and died in 1957.

KIMBERLEY, Alfred Anthony (b. 1942)

Tony Kimberley rode his first winner, Pinzari, at Nottingham on 3 June 1961, while apprenticed to Sir Gordon Richards, but it was much later, when he joined Jeremy Hindley at Newmarket, that his career blossomed. He won the Doncaster Cup on Crash Course and the Cambridgeshire on Sin Timon, and had his best season in 1977, with 39 winners. He was first jockey to Hindley for seven years, until Brian Taylor took over, and broke with the stable in the middle of 1983. He then became associated with Michael Stoute's stable and for him won the 1984 Northumberland Plate on Karadar.

KINCSEM

Kincsem, foaled in 1874, was by Cambuscan and was bred in Hungary. One of the greatest fillies in racing history, she ran 54 times and was never defeated, winning the Austrian Derby, Hungarian Oaks and St Leger, and the Goodwood Cup. Her descendants proved very successful in European racing but the family suffered heavy losses in both World Wars.

KINGSWAY (1940, b c Fairway – Yenna, by Ksar)

Kingsway won eight races for £4,931, including the 2,000 Guineas. He was exported to America in 1955 after eleven seasons in Britain, where his best produce was the St Leger runner-up Kingsfold.

KNOWN FACT (1977, b c In Reality – Tamerett, by Tim Tam)

Known Fact became the first Arab-owned Classic winner in Britain when he was awarded the 2,000 Guineas on the disqualification of Nureyev. The circumstances of his success for Khaled Abdulla, who bought him for $225,000 in his native America, tended to overshadow his undoubted ability for he had nothing to do with the interference that led to Nureyev's demotion. Known Fact won the Middle Park Stakes as a two-year-old and after the Guineas won the Waterford Crystal Mile and Queen Elizabeth II Stakes. He failed badly in his only race at four years and began stud duties in Berkshire as the winner of six races from eleven starts. He had his first runners in 1985.

L

LAD

The common term for stable employees is used for male and female, young and old, and also covers responsible individuals such as the head lad and travelling head lad.

LADY JOSEPHINE (1912, ch f Sundridge – Americus Girl, by Americus)

Lady Josephine is one of the most influential mares in the Stud Book, being the dam of Lady Juror and Mumtaz Mahal. Lady Juror, foaled in 1919, won three races worth over £8,000 and bred Fair Trial, a top-class miler who was later an outstanding sire, and Jurisdiction, second in the 1,000 Guineas. Lady Juror is also the ancestress of Tudor Minstrel (2,000 Guineas), Commotion (Oaks), Combat (unbeaten winner of nine races and a successful sire), Faux Tirage (winner of over £8,000 and a successful sire in New Zealand), Aristophanes (leading sire in Argentina) and Kashmir II (2,000 Guineas).

LA FLECHE

Foaled in 1889, Baron de Hirsch's La Flèche was by St Simon out of Quiver and was bred at the Royal Stud, Hampton Court. Bought as a yearling for 5,500gns, she proved a filly of the highest class, winning sixteen races worth over £34,000. Her victories included the Champagne Stakes, 1,000 Guineas, Oaks, St Leger, Cambridgeshire, Champion Stakes and Gold Cup. In the Derby she was beaten less than a length by Sir

Hugo and ought to have won, but her jockey, George Barrett, who was showing signs of incipient insanity, rode a deplorable race. At stud she bred John o' Gaunt, who was second in the Derby and sired that fine horse Swynford. Up till the end of her three-year-old season she was trained by John Porter, after that by Richard Marsh.

LAING, Douglas Raymond (b. 1923)

Ray Laing took up training later than most in his trade as it was not until 1978 that he took out a licence to train near Lambourn. He was born at Malton, where his father was a groom, and he worked locally for Captain Charles Elsey and at Newmarket for Basil Jarvis before being called up with the Royal Marine Engineers. He returned to racing to work for Ginger Dennistoun and then as travelling head lad to Syd Mercer before joining Peter Walwyn when the latter started training. Laing stayed with Walwyn for seventeen years before branching out on his own. His first winner was with Chukaroo at Sandown on 27 May 1978. Remarkably, his two richest successes have been in Ireland, with Cameroun (1984 Goffs Silver Flash Stakes) and Roaring Riva (1985 Phoenix Stakes). His best season in Britain was 1985, with 19 winners.

LAMBERT, Michael James (b. 1944)

Son of a Shropshire stud groom, Mick Lambert started racing with trainer George Owen and had spells in Newmarket, Hawick, the Midlands, Cheshire and Malton before joining Peter Easterby as travelling head lad. He began training near Malton in November 1981, and had his first Flat win with Rage Glen at Ayr the following March His best horses have been Fine Sun and Our Dynasty, and his best Flat seasons 1983 and 1984, with 12 winners. He left for Cyprus in 1986.

LAMBERT SIMNEL
(1938, b c Fair Trial – Simnel,
by Blandford)

Lambert Simnel was owned by the Duke of Westminster and trained by Fred Templeman. He won three races for £3,046, including the 2,000 Guineas. As a sire he was very undistinguished.

LAMBTON, Edward George
(1918-83)

Second son of George Lambton, 'Teddy' Lambton rode as an amateur before starting training at Kremlin House, Newmarket, for four years from 1945 and again from 1961. He handed in his licence unexpectedly in 1969 and was succeeded by his stable jockey Peter Robinson. Lambton won several big handicaps, including the Lincolnshire with Langton Abbot and Mighty Gurkha, the Magnet Cup (David Jack, also third in the St Leger), Ebor (Foxtrot) and Ayr Gold Cup (Compensation). He maintained a small number of horses in his own name with Robinson, the best being Mr Bigmore (named after a Newmarket bailiff) who won the Manchester Handicap and Goodwood Cup. He died in June 1983.

LAMBTON, George
(1860-1945)

George Lambton was the fifth son of the second Earl of Durham. After an undistinguished educational career at Eton and Cambridge, he became an outstanding amateur rider, winning the Grand Steeple-Chase de Paris on Parasang in 1888 and on one occasion being desperately unlucky not to win the Grand National. After a crashing fall at Sandown in 1892 he decided to take up training, this at a time when 'gentlemen' trainers were a rarity on the Turf.

In 1893 came the turning-point of his life when he was appointed trainer to the sixteenth Earl of Derby, who was intent on reviving the fortunes of the Stanley colours and of re-laying the foundations of the famous Knowsley Stud. Lambton had his first Classic success in 1896, when he won the Oaks for Lord Derby

with Canterbury Pilgrim, subsequently a most successful and influential broodmare. In 1906 he won the Oaks again, with Keystone II. In 1908 Lord Derby died suddenly and was succeeded by his eldest son, who was in due course to prove the greatest British owner-breeder of this century.

For the seventeenth Earl, Lambton won the 2,000 Guineas with Colorado (1926), the 1,000 Guineas with Canyon (1916), Ferry (1918) and Tranquil (1923), the Derby with Sansovino (1924) and Hyperion (1933), and the St Leger with Swynford (1910), Keysoe (1919) and Hyperion (1933). He also won the 1,000 Guineas in 1917 for Lord D'Abernon with Diadem. Other famous horses he trained included Stedfast, Phalaris, Pharos and Corrida. He was three times leading trainer.

In 1926 he was succeeded as Lord Derby's trainer by Frank Butters but remained as manager and five years later was re-appointed as trainer. It came as a shock when in 1933, the year of Hyperion's Derby victory, Lord Derby announced that at the age of 73 Lambton ought to be spared the burden and anxiety of running a big stable and replaced him with Colledge Leader. It is extremely doubtful if Lambton was gratified by Lord Derby's thoughtfulness. He became a public trainer and remained one till his death in 1945, among his patrons being M. Boussac.

A man of infinite charm, dandified in his dress to the last, Lambton loved and understood horses. He was a marvellous judge of a thoroughbred and, entrusted with buying yearlings, he laid the foundations of the Aga Khan's highly profitable racing empire. His autobiography *Men and Horses I Have Known* is widely regarded as the best book of racing memoirs ever written. His younger son, Edward, trained with varying success till he retired in 1969.

LANARK

Situated 25 miles from Glasgow and just over 30 from Edinburgh, Lanark provided modest racing for the Scottish faithful until its precarious financial position finally became untenable and closure was announced in December 1977. It was to no avail that it boasted two distinctions – for staging the longest handicap in the calendar, the William the Lion Handicap, and the oldest race in the world, the Lanark Silver Bell, instituted by King William the Lion (1165-1214).

LANE, Fred

A sound if unspectacular rider, Fred Lane rode a faultless race to win the 1932 Derby on April the Fifth. He had a long career in the saddle and was at his best in long-distance races. A quiet and unassuming character, he was much in demand to ride work at Newmarket even in late middle age.

LARKSPUR
(1959, ch c Never Say Die – Skylarking, by Precipitation)

Larkspur was bred by Mr Philip Love and bought for 12,200gns to be owned by Mr Raymond Guest and trained by Vincent O'Brien. He won the 1962 Derby but was probably lucky since about a quarter of the field came to grief in a pile-up on the descent to Tattenham Corner. Among the fallers was the favourite, Hethersett, who beat Larkspur without difficulty in the St Leger. Larkspur was exported to Japan in 1967 after standing in Ireland for four seasons where his best winner was Crazy Rhythm (Ebor Handicap).

LASSALLE
(1969, b c Bon Mot III – Windy Cliff, by Hard Sauce)

French-bred Lassalle cost Zenya Yoshida the equivalent of £23,000 at the Deauville yearling sales and reached his peak at four years when winning the top staying races in France and Britain, the Prix du Cadran and Ascot Gold Cup. He was placed in both races the following year, at the end of which he left for his owner's stud farm in Japan, retiring as the winner of six races and placed nine times.

LAVANDIN
(1953, b c Verso II – Lavande, by Rustom Pasha)

M. Pierre Wertheimer's Lavandin, trained by Alec Head and ridden by W.R. Johnstone, won the 1956 Derby. He is judged to have been one of the more moderate winners of that race this century. He failed to make much mark as a sire and was exported to Japan in 1962, three years before his daughter Blabla won the French Oaks.

LAWSON, Joseph
(1881-1964)

Joe Lawson was born in Durham and rode in a few races as a boy but soon became too heavy. In 1898 he joined Alec Taylor's stable at Manton and rapidly made his mark, becoming firstly travelling head lad and later Taylor's assistant.

When Taylor retired in 1927, Lawson was appointed to succeed him. Taylor was a difficult man to follow but Lawson used the same methods and proved an outstanding success. In 1931 he was leading trainer, with £93,899 in prize money, a record that stood until 1957.

Lawson trained at Manton for twenty years and then moved to Newmarket. It was there he had perhaps his greatest triumphs, winning the 1954 Derby and St Leger with Never Say Die. Altogether he had a dozen successes in Classic races, while he also won the Ascot Gold Cup on two occasions. His Classic winners were as follows:

2,000 Guineas: Orwell (1932); Pay Up (1936); Kingsway (1943); Court Martial (1945)
1,000 Guineas: Exhibitionnist (1937); Galatea II (1939); Dancing Time (1941)
Derby: Never Say Die (1954)
Oaks: Pennycomequick (1929); Exhibitionnist (1937); Galatea II (1939)
St Leger: Never Say Die (1954).

Among Lawson's many patrons were Lord Astor, Sir Abe Bailey, Sir Victor Sassoon, Mr Washington Singer, Mr Somerville Tattersall and Mr R.S. Clark. No publicity-seeker, he was much respected in the racing world for his skill and integrity.

LEAD

Metal weights, carried in weight-cloths attached to the saddle, to make up the difference between the jockey's weight and the poundage a horse is set to carry, are referred to by the term 'lead'.

LEADER, Colledge (1883-1938)

Colledge Leader was a son of Tom Leader who trained George Frederick to win the Derby in 1874. Like his brothers Tom, Harvey and Fred, Colledge became a trainer. He was appointed private trainer to Lord Derby in 1934 but died four years later. He won the 1,000 Guineas with Tide-way, and the Oaks and Gold Cup with that great mare Quashed.

LEADER, Harvey Cliff (1893-1972)

Harvey Leader, more commonly known as 'Jack' Leader, was a son of Tom Leader. He rode his first winner on the Flat at the age of twelve and for a short time rode under National Hunt Rules. He took out a licence to train in 1918 and gained his first big success in 1920, when he won the St Leger with Caligula. At one period he conducted a 'mixed' stable and won the 1926 Grand National with Jack Horner. He trained two brilliant sprinters in Diomedes and Shalfleet, while he won the Lincolnshire with Elton and the Cambridgeshire with Hidden Meaning and Dites. Towards the end of his career, he had a particularly brilliant spell with fillies, including winning the Musidora Stakes three years running, with Orabella II, Palatch and Exchange, the last two also winning the Yorkshire Oaks; in addition he trained Queen of Twilight (Jockey Club Stakes) and Bringley (Park Hill Stakes).

In his younger days he was a great supporter of hunting and polo at Newmarket, while his friendly, modest personality made him one of racing's most popular characters. He retired at the end of the 1971 season, handing over to Gavin Pritchard-Gordon, and died early the following year.

LEADER, Thomas Edward (1902-83)

Ted Leader, a son of Tom Leader, was originally apprenticed to his uncle, Harvey Leader, but it was as a rider under National Hunt Rules that he established his reputation, in particular riding many winners for his father, including Sprig in the 1927 Grand National. He also won the Cheltenham Gold Cup twice, and was once champion jockey under National Hunt Rules.

He took out a licence to train in 1934 and trained at Newmarket, apart from a period of war-time service with the RAF, until his retirement 40 years later. Before the war the best horse he trained was Wychwood Abbot, who won the Champion Stakes twice, Kempton Jubilee and Cambridgeshire. After the war he had a long association with Mr H.J. Joel, winning the Middle Park Stakes, Nunthorpe Stakes, St James's Palace Stakes twice, Goodwood Stakes three times, Goodwood Cup and National Stakes. He never trained a Classic winner for Mr Joel, but Major Portion was beaten a length in the 2,000 Guineas and West Side Story a short head in the Oaks. He also trained the popular stayer Predominate.

LEASE

The lease of a horse has to be registered with Messrs Weatherby, and the terms are agreed upon by the two parties concerned.

LEG

To say that a horse 'has a leg' is a colloquial way of saying that the horse in question is lame or is suffering from some sort of leg trouble.

LEICESTER

Leicester can hardly claim to be numbered among Britain's lovelier racecourses but it is one of the few courses with a straight mile, has an excellent watering system and provides modest but competitive sport for Midlands enthusiasts. It is a right-handed undulating track which is nearly 2m round. The straight mile, which joins the round course 5f from home, is mainly downhill for the first 4f, then uphill for the next 2f, gradually levelling off to the winning-post. The bends into the straight and after the winning-post have been cambered. Despite the undulations, it enjoys the reputation of being a fair, galloping course. The draw is unimportant.

LE KSAR
(1934, b c Ksar – Queen Iseult, by Teddy)

Le Ksar, owned by E. de Saint-Alary and trained in France by F. Carter, won the 2,000 Guineas at Newmarket at 20-1, and was second in the French 2,000 Guineas. He retired to stud in France and then stood for a few seasons in Britain before being exported to Argentina.

LEMBERG
(1907, b c Cyllene – Galicia, by Galopin)

Lemberg, owned and bred by 'Mr Fairie', the *nom de course* of Mr A.W. Cox, was a half-brother to Bayardo. Lemberg won the Derby, was second in the 2,000 Guineas and third in the St Leger. He also dead-heated for the Eclipse Stakes and won the Coronation Cup. He was trained by Alec Taylor at Manton. He was champion sire in 1922 and among his good winners were Lemonora (Grand Prix de Paris), Ellangowan (2,000 Guineas) and Taj Mah (1,000 Guineas).

LEMONORA
(1918, ch c Lemberg – Honora, by Gallinule)

Lemonora was trained by Alec Taylor at Manton and won the 1921 Grand Prix de Paris, being one of the very few British horses to win that race this century. His only other success was in the Newmarket Stakes. As a sire he proved extremely disappointing.

LEMOS, Captain Marcos D. (b. 1927)

Greek shipping magnate Marcos Lemos came into British racing in the mid-1960s, when his first horse won a hurdle race before breaking a leg and his second, that year's top-priced yearling, did the same before ever racing. Far from being put off, Captain Lemos expanded his racing interests by buying Warren Hill Stud in Newmarket in 1968 and the adjoining Ashley Heath Stud in 1974. Also in 1974 he bought Carlburg Stables in Newmarket to lease to his trainer, Clive Brittain, and made the switch to having all his horses in one stable. Previously he had his biggest successes with Petingo (Gimcrack, Middle Park, St James's Palace, Sussex Stakes), trained by Sam Armstrong, and Cavo Doro (Ballymoss Stakes and second in Derby), trained by Vincent O'Brien. The Brittain connection got off to a good start when Averof won the St James's Palace Stakes in 1974, and since then have come Julio Mariner (St Leger) and Pebbles (1,000 Guineas) among several good horses to carry his colours in an owner-trainer association which has survived the doldrums as well as enjoyed the good times.

Racing colours: royal blue, white hoop, striped cap.

LE MOSS
(1975, ch c Le Levanstell – Feemoss, by Ballymoss)

Le Moss became the first horse to complete the treble of Ascot Gold Cup, Goodwood Cup and Doncaster Cup in successive years when he achieved the feat in 1979 and 1980. The family is used to setting records; Le Moss's brother Levmoss is the only horse to have won the Ascot Gold Cup, Prix du Cadran and Prix de l'Arc de Triomphe. The McGrath family sold Le Moss as a yearling to Carlo d'Alessio for 26,000gns and paid ten times that sum to have him back at their Irish stud for his first season in 1981. He also finished second in the St Leger.

LENGTH

The length is the standard measure used in recording the results of races and represents the length of a horse from nose to tail, approximately 8ft.

LETHERBY, Dennis (b. 1947)

Dennis Letherby was apprenticed firstly to A.M. Smyth and then to Willie Stephenson. His most important success was in the Totalisator Spring Handicap on Barwin, and his best season was in 1966, when with 46 winners he was second leading apprentice. From 1975 to 1981 he rode abroad, mainly in Kenya before returning to ride briefly in the North of England in 1982. He returned to Kenya, where in January 1985 he was seriously injured in a fall, breaking his neck.

LEVERHULME, Philip William Bryce Lever, 3rd Viscount (b. 1915)

Lord Leverhulme served in the Cheshire Yeomanry and succeeded his father in 1949, the year he was appointed Lord Lieutenant of Cheshire. Elected to the National Hunt Committee in 1961, he was Senior Steward in 1968 and played a large part in the amalgamation with the Jockey Club, of which he was Senior Steward from 1973 to 1976. A steward at several northern courses, he is better known for his jumpers, notably Badanloch, who finished second in the Grand National, but his Flat-race horses have included the home-bred Hot Grove, second in the Derby.

Racing colours: green and yellow hoops, yellow sleeves, quartered cap.

LEVMOSS
(1965, b c Le Levanstell – Feemoss, by Ballymoss)

Levmoss was bred by the McGrath Trust Company and owned and trained by Seamus McGrath. He was a good staying three-year-old, finishing third in the French St Leger, but the following year proved himself outstanding by winning the Ascot Gold Cup, its French equivalent, the Prix du Cadran, and the 1½m Prix de l'Arc de Triomphe, beating four European Derby winners and the winners of the Grand Prix, French Oaks and King George VI and Queen Elizabeth Stakes. This victory took his earnings from eight victories to the equivalent of £142,226. He completed seven seasons at stud in Ireland before moving to France, where he died in 1977 after completing one season. His best produce were M-Lolshan (Irish St Leger) and Shafaraz (Prix du Cadran), and he was the broodmare sire of the dual Ascot Gold Cup winner Ardross.

LEWIS, Geoffrey (b. 1935)

Geoff Lewis, a Welshman, was apprenticed to Ron Smyth at Epsom and rode his first winner on Smyth's Eastern Imp over his local course in 1953. In 1969 he topped the hundred for the first time with his best-ever score of 146 winners, gave Lester Piggott a tough fight for the championship and rode his first Classic winners, Right Tack (2,000 Guineas and Irish 2,000 Guineas) and Prince Regent (Irish Sweeps Derby). That year he was back at Epsom riding for John Sutcliffe, having had a lengthy association with Peter Hastings-Bass and Ian Balding, for whom the best horses he rode included King's Troop, Secret Step, Silly Season, Berkeley Springs and Mill Reef. He rode for Sutcliffe for two years before joining Noel Murless for five years, during which 1971 was the highspot, in which he completed the great Epsom treble for the first time in racing history on Mill Reef (Derby), Lupe (Coronation Cup) and Altesse Royale (Oaks), the first trained by Balding and the last two by Murless.

Lewis moved to Bruce Hobbs' stable in 1976, and their major successes were with Grey Baron (Goodwood Cup), Tumbledownwind (Gimcrack Stakes) and Tachypous (Middle Park Stakes). Lewis, who had bought stables at Epsom in 1978 in preparation for training, retired in August 1979 but came back eleven days later when asked to ride Double Form in the Vernons Sprint and, having won that race, formally handed in his licence. His first runner on the Flat as a trainer, Concert Hall at Doncaster in March 1980, was a winner. His biggest success

Jockeys and Horses

A study in styles: above, Tod Sloan, a very early twentieth-century exponent of the modern jockeys' riding style, involving short stirrup leathers and a low crouch; and, below, on his way to the start on the Queen's Rejoicing, Gordon Richards, twenty-six times champion jockey and an unorthodox stylist who relied on power and vigour in a finish.

Three fine fillies: top, Sceptre, winner of every classic except the Derby, with her trainer Alec Taylor; centre, Dahlia (Lester Piggott) wins her second King George VI and Queen Elizabeth Diamond Stakes at Ascot, beating Highclere (right) and Dankaro (far right) in 1974; and, below, Oh So Sharp (Steve Cauthen), winner of the three British Classics she contested in 1985.

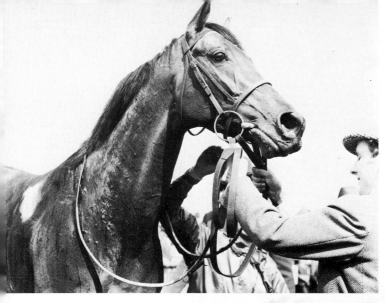

Giants from different eras: left, Brigadier Gerard, who was foaled in 1968 and was beaten only once in eighteen races; and, below, St Simon, foaled in 1881, one of the best racehorses in Turf history and a magnificent sire.

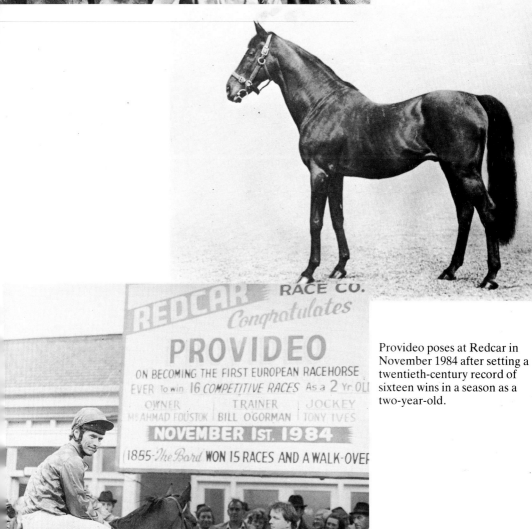

Provideo poses at Redcar in November 1984 after setting a twentieth-century record of sixteen wins in a season as a two-year-old.

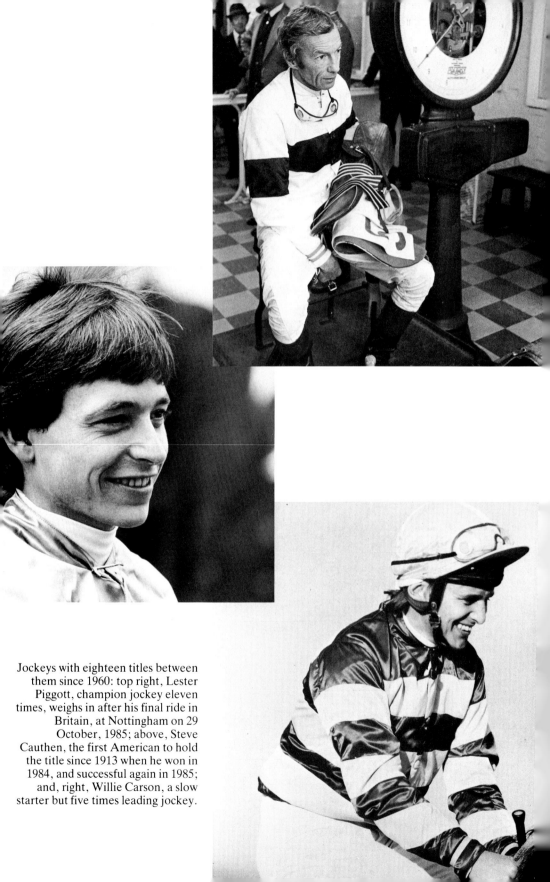

Jockeys with eighteen titles between them since 1960: top right, Lester Piggott, champion jockey eleven times, weighs in after his final ride in Britain, at Nottingham on 29 October, 1985; above, Steve Cauthen, the first American to hold the title since 1913 when he won in 1984, and successful again in 1985; and, right, Willie Carson, a slow starter but five times leading jockey.

as a trainer was with Yawa in the 1983 Grand Prix de Paris, and his best season in Britain was 1984, with 30 winners.

LIGHT BROCADE
(1931, br f Galloper Light – Trilogy, by Son-in-Law)

Light Brocade, trained by Frank Butters and ridden by Bernard Carslake, won the Oaks for Lord Durham. She won three other races for a total of £10,389, including the Cheveley Park Stakes, and was second in the 1,000 Guineas. She was a disappointing broodmare before her death in 1947.

LIGHT CAVALRY
(1977, b c Brigadier Gerard – Glass Slipper, by Relko)

Light Cavalry won four races for owner-breeder Jim Joel and trainer Henry Cecil, including the St Leger. After one successful outing as a two-year-old, and excepting his Classic outing, he raced exclusively at a mile and a half and at four years won the Princess of Wales's Stakes. He finished last in the 1981 King George VI and Queen Elizabeth Diamond Stakes and did not race again, being sold to stand at stud in the United States with a valuation of about $2.5m.

LILY AGNES

Lily Agnes, by Macaroni out of Polly Agnes and foaled in 1871, was a famous mare who bred the mighty Ormonde, winner of the 'Triple Crown' (1886), Farewell, winner of the 1,000 Guineas, and Ornament, dam of the great filly Sceptre who won every Classic bar the Derby.

LINDLEY, James Frederick (b. 1935)

Jimmy Lindley, apprenticed from 1949 to 1954 to Tom Masson, did not have an easy time of it with his weight and for a spell he rode under National Hunt Rules. Despite this, he had a fine record in major races, winning the 2,000 Guineas (Only For Life and Kashmir II), St Leger (Indiana), King George VI and Queen Elizabeth Stakes (Aggressor), Middle Park Stakes (Gustav, Track Spare, Tudenham), Coronation Cup (Charlottown), Queen Mary Stakes (three times), Ascot Gold Cup (Precipice Wood and Lassalle), and the Italian and Irish Oaks.

Towards the end of his career he rode in France, and his last ride was in Tokyo in November 1974. Since retiring he has taken up broadcasting and journalism, toured the world with a team of all-star jockeys and supervised Steve Cauthen's interests in Britain.

LINGFIELD PARK

Twenty-seven miles from London and 30 from Brighton, Lingfield Park is a pretty and popular course. It is a left-handed circuit of roughly 10f with pronounced gradients. The steep descent to the final bend makes it a particularly appropriate track for testing candidates for the Derby and the Oaks, and trials for these two Classics are among the most important races of the season.

The straight course of 7f 140yd is downhill the entire way. It joins the round course half a mile from the winning-post. Speed and a good action are the main requisites for a horse at Lingfield. On the straight course the draw favours high numbers except in heavy going when the reverse is the case. A lot of work has been done to improve the drainage but waterlogging will probably always be one of the dangers at the course, which was taken over by the bookmakers Ladbroke's in December 1974, when they bought it for around £500,000 from the Beckwith-Smith family. Ladbroke's found their enthusiasm had become stretched after seven years, and early in 1982 they sold out to a company run by Mr Ron Muddle.

LISTED RACES

The term 'listed race' is covered by one of the least informative entries in the Jockey Club definitions, being 'those races which in any particular year are approved as such by the stewards of the Jockey Club and are shown to be listed races in the Programme Books published under the authority of the Jockey Club'. In fact, they are important races which fall outside the category of Pattern races. Unlike the Pattern, listed races included handicaps until a decision was taken in 1985 to phase these out of the scheme, replacing them with condition races. Listed races in 1986 comprised:

Racing Post Mile, Doncaster, 1m
Cammidge Trophy, Doncaster, 6f
BonusPrint Easter Stakes (3yo), Kempton Park, 1m
Field Marshal Stakes, Haydock Park, 5f
Abernant Stakes, Newmarket, 6f
Ladbroke European Free Handicap (3yo), Newmarket, 7f
Gerry Fielden Stakes (3yo), Newmarket, 1m 1f
Princess Elizabeth Stakes (3yo), Epsom, 1m 110yds
Racal-Vodafone Blue Riband Trial Stakes (3yo), Epsom, 1½m
Pretty Polly Stakes (3yo), Newmarket, 1¼m
Coral Newmarket Stakes (3yo), Newmarket, 1¼m
Fairey Spring Trophy, Haydock Park, 7f 40yds
Cheshire Oaks (3yo), Chester, 1½m 65yds
Dee Stakes (3yo), Chester, 1¼m 85yds
Marley Roof Tiles Oaks Trial (3yo), Lingfield Park, 1½m
Sir Charles Clore Memorial Stakes (3yo), Newbury, 1¼m
Clive Graham Stakes, Goodwood, 1¼m
Schroder Life Predominate Stakes (3yo), Goodwood, 1½m
Sheraton Park Tower Lupe Stakes (3yo), Goodwood, 1¼m
Sandy Lane Stakes (3yo), Haydock Park, 6f
National Stakes (2yo), Sandown Park, 5f
Heron Stakes (3yo), Kempton Park, 1m
International Stakes (3yo), Kempton Park, 1m
Leisure Stakes, Lingfield Park, 6f
John of Gaunt Stakes, Haydock Park, 7f 40yds
Ballymacoll Stud Stakes (3yo), Newbury, 1¼m
Queen's Vase, Royal Ascot, 2m
Chesham Stakes (2yo), Royal Ascot, 6f
Racal-Vodafone Stakes, Kempton Park, 1¼m

Veuve Clicquot Champagne Stakes (2yo), Salisbury, 6f
Alington Stakes, Sandown Park, 5f
Bet With The Tote Trophy, Lingfield Park, 7f 140yds
Sun Page 3 Silver Cup, Lingfield Park, 1¾m
Hackwood Stakes, Newbury, 6f
Manton Rose Bowl Stakes (2yo), Newbury, 6f
Mecca Bookmakers Scottish Derby (3yo), Ayr, 1m 3f
Land of Burns Stakes, Ayr, 1¼m
Oak Tree Stakes, Goodwood, 7f
Alycidon Stakes, Goodwood, 1½m
Haydock Summer Trophy, Haydock Park, 1¼m 131yds
Sweet Solera Stakes (2yo), Newmarket, 7f
Washington Singer Stakes (2yo), Newbury, 7f
Goffs St Hugh's Stakes (2yo), Newbury, 5f
Lonsdale Stakes, York, 2m
Prince of Wales's Stakes (2yo), York, 5f
Galtres Stakes, York, 1½m
Hillsdown Holdings Select Stakes, Newmarket, 6f
March Stakes (3yo), Goodwood, 1¾m
Danepak Bacon Stakes (2yo), Newmarket, 1m
Virginia Stakes, Newcastle, 1¼m
BonusPrint Champion 2-Y-O Trophy, Ripon, 6f
B B A Atalanta Stakes, Sandown Park, 1m
Strensall Stakes, York, 7f
BonusPrint Sirenia Stakes (2yo), Kempton Park, 6f
Scarbrough Stakes, Doncaster, 5f
Sceptre Stakes, Doncaster, 1m
Doonside Cup, Ayr, 1m 3f
Harry Rosebery Challenge Trophy (2yo), Ayr, 5f
Firth of Clyde Stakes (2yo), Ayr, 6f
Harroways Stakes, Goodwood, 7f
Foundation Stakes, Goodwood, 1¼m
Somerville Tattersall Stakes (2yo), Newmarket, 7f
Grand Metropolitan Stakes (3yo), Ascot, 1m
Rockingham Stakes (2yo), York, 6f
Bentinck Stakes, Newmarket, 5f
Rochford Thompson Newbury Stakes (2yo), Newbury, 7f 60yds

Doncaster Stakes (2yo), Doncaster, 5f
George Stubbs Stakes, Newmarket, 1¾m
James Seymour Stakes, Newmarket, 1¼m
Ben Marshall Stakes, Newmarket, 1m
Jennings the Bookmakers Zetland Stakes
    (2yo), Newmarket, 1¼m
Remembrance Day Stakes, Doncaster, 6f

LITTLE WOLF
(1978, ch c Grundy – Hiding
Place, by Doutelle)

Bred and owned by Lord Porchester,
Little Wolf was trained by Dick Hern to
win seven races, including the 1983 Ascot
Gold Cup, which he won by five lengths.
He also won the Goodwood Cup that
year but in the process jarred a joint in
his near-fore and raced only once more,
again coming in lame on his reappearance
as a six-year-old. He began his first year
at stud in Berkshire in 1985.

LIVERPOOL

The future of Liverpool's racecourse at
Aintree, which had been in doubt since
the mid-1960s, was secured in 1983,
thanks to the efforts of the Levy Board,
Jockey Club, Seagram Distillers and the
public, but there seems to be no future for
Flat racing, which enjoyed fluctuating
fortunes from 1964, when two three-day
mixed meetings were augmented by three
days devoted entirely to Flat racing. In
1965 Flat racing occupied a place in the
spring and autumn mixed meetings; from
1966 to 1974 it was restricted to the
spring fixture with the exception of one
autumn venture in 1972; in 1975 a
two-day meeting was staged in June but
the proposed October mixed meeting was
scrapped; and the 1976 Grand National
meeting featured the last Flat race at
Liverpool. It seems highly likely that the
days when potential Classic horses ran at
Aintree are gone for ever, since the
economic prosperity of the course begins
and ends with the Grand National
meeting.

LODER, Major Eustace
(1867-1914)

Eustace Loder served in the 12th Lancers
for fifteen years. Not for nothing was he
known as 'Lucky Loder'. For 300gns he
bought Spearmint, who won both the
Derby and the Grand Prix de Paris. In
addition Major Loder owned and bred
Pretty Polly, one of the outstanding fillies
of this century.

LODER, Lt.-Col. Giles Harold
(1884-1966)

Lt.-Col. Giles Loder inherited Eyrefield
Stud in Co Kildare in 1914 from his
uncle, Major Eustace Loder. He was still
serving in the Scots Guards in 1920 when
he won the Derby with Spion Kop.
Loder's only other Classic winner in
Britain was Cresta Run, who won the
1,000 Guineas in 1927. Other good
horses to carry his colours included
Colorado Kid (Kempton Jubilee, Royal
Hunt Cup and Doncaster Cup); The
Cobbler (Coventry Stakes, Middle Park
Stakes, Victoria Cup and Wokingham
Stakes); and Arctic Explorer (Eclipse
Stakes). He also owned Foxbridge, who
had a wonderful record of success as a
sire in New Zealand.

At his stud the Colonel and his stud
managers gradually weeded out all the
other lines until the line attributed to
Admiration, the dam of Pretty Polly,
stood supreme.

At the time of his death at Cannes,
Lt.-Col. Loder had been a member of the
Jockey Club for 42 years. A shy, reserved
and kindly bachelor, he was noted for his
skill as a gardener and for his loyalty to
those who served him.

LOMAX, Mrs Rosemary Ann
(b. 1928)

Mrs Lomax rode over 40 point-to-point
winners and was secretary to a number of
trainers before she began her own stable
at Baydon, which until the rules were
changed in 1966, was conducted in the
name of her former husband, Ian Lomax,
a well-known cricketer who played for
Somerset. Her biggest triumph was to win
the 1970 Ascot Gold Cup with Precipice
Wood. She did not renew her licence in
1985.

LOMOND
(1980, b c Northern Dancer – My Charmer, by Poker)

Robert Sangster bought Lomond privately from his American breeders and gained the biggest of three wins with him in the 2,000 Guineas. Lomond did not win again after his Classic success; he finished second in the Irish 2,000 Guineas, beat four out of twenty in the Derby and flopped in the Sussex Stakes. He was retired to stud in Ireland to start his first season in 1984 at a fee of 65,000 Irish guineas.

LONG LOOK
(1962, b f Ribot – Santorin, by Greek Song)

Long Look, trained by Vincent O'Brien, won two races for £38,093, including the Oaks in the colours of her American breeder, Mr J.C. Brady. She was second in the Irish Oaks and third in the Prix Vermeille.

LORD LYON

Mr R. Sutton's Lord Lyon, by Stockwell, won the 2,000 Guineas, Derby and St Leger in 1866. In all he won seventeen of his 21 races and over £26,000 in stakes, a very big sum in those days. He was not a success at stud but sired the Grand Prix de Paris winner Minting and the Oaks winner Placida.

LORENZACCIO
(1965, ch c Klairon – Phoenissa, by The Phoenix)

Lorenzaccio was a useful two-year-old whose biggest wins came late in his career. He was in the frame in four decent juvenile races, two in France and the Champagne Stakes and Observer Gold Cup; he won the Prix Jean Prat at Chantilly at three and nothing at four, and ended his racing career with five wins as a five-year-old, including the Champion Stakes. After running unplaced in the Washington D.C. International, he returned to Britain to take up stud duties in 1971, and when he was exported to Australia six years later, the best of the offspring he left behind was the William Hill Sprint winner Ahonoora.

LOUVIERS
(1906, b c Isinglass – St Louvaine, by Carnage or Wolf's Crag)

Louviers, owned by Mr W. Raphael, was remarkable in being the first of two Derby seconds produced by the mating of his sire and dam, Louvois being the other. Louviers was beaten by a very short head by King Edward VII's Minoru in the 1909 Derby. He was not a success as a sire in Britain and was exported to Russia.

LOUVOIS
(1910, b c Isinglass – St Louvaine, by Carnage or Wolf's Crag)

Winner of the 2,000 Guineas and five other races for £12,754, Louvois was second in the Derby, being promoted on the disqualification of Craganour. He sired St Louis, winner of the 1922 2,000 Guineas.

LOVE IN IDLENESS
(1918, br f Bachelor's Double – Cornfield, by Isinglass)

Bred by Sir Gilbert Greenall, Love in Idleness was trained by Alec Taylor and owned by Mr J. Watson. She won the Oaks and Park Hill Stakes as well as seven other races for a total of £12,561. She bred six winners, of whom the best were Violator and Lo Zingaro.

LOVELY ROSA
(1933, b f Tolgus – Napoule, by Bachelor's Double)

Sir Abe Bailey's Lovely Rosa won two races, one over 5f and the Oaks, for a total of £8,422. At stud she bred Saracen, dam of Wilwyn, winner of 21 races including the inaugural Washington D.C. International.

LOWE, Professor Bruce

A well-known and influential theorist on bloodstock breeding during the latter part of the nineteenth century was the Australian Bruce Lowe. He traced the pedigrees of all the mares in the Stud Book of his own era back through the female line to their original foundation mares in the earlier volumes. He found there were about 50 of these original mares with living progeny in the direct female line. The descendants of each of these original mares comprised a family which he then classified according to the number of Derby, Oaks and St Leger winners it had produced. The first five families were designated 'Running Families' and were rated superior in racing merit to the remainder. Another group included those strong in the sire element and these he called 'Sire Families'. From these classifications certain rather complex deductions were made of how to breed a good horse and a successful stallion.

Lowe's laborious research revealed many hitherto unrecognized details about the manner in which the Thoroughbred had developed, and through his work knowledge of the subject was substantially increased.

The science of genetics has disproved Lowe's view that qualities such as prepotency in stallions can be guaranteed, and so modern breeders gain little practical assistance from his work. However, the family numbers are frequently used in private stud books, stallion registers and so forth.

LOWE, John (b. 1950)

Apprenticed to Jack Watts and his son Bill Watts at Newmarket, John Lowe moved to Richmond in Yorkshire when Watts junior changed stables in 1971 and stayed on after completing his apprenticeship until joining Steve Norton in 1981. Liverpool-born Lowe, a strong lightweight, gained his first winner in the 1968 Jubilee Handicap on Pally's Double and his most important in Britain on Sparkling Boy (Ayr Gold Cup), Full Extent (Gimcrack Stakes) and Leysh (Cambridgeshire). He also won the Prix Marcel Boussac on Goodbye Shelley in

1982. His best season was in 1977, with 86 winners.

LUCYROWE
(1966, b f Crepello – Esquire Girl, by My Babu)

Lucyrowe, owned by Mr Louis Freedman, who paid 9,000gns for her as a yearling, proved herself a brilliant filly up to $1\frac{1}{4}$m in 1969 and would in all probability have won the 1,000 Guineas had she not been badly knocked about in the early stages of a distinctly rough race. Her six wins for £22,202 included the Ebbisham Stakes, Coronation Stakes, Nassau Stakes and Sun Chariot Stakes. She was second to Habitat in the Wills Mile. Her first four foals were winners.

LUPE
(1967, b f Primera – Alcoa, by Alycidon)

Lupe, bred by her owner, Mrs Stanhope Joel, was unbeaten in six races spread over three seasons in Britain and suffered her only defeat when she went to France for the Prix Vermeille and finished sixth. Her best wins were at Epsom, where she won the Oaks and as a four-year-old the Coronation Cup. On retiring from racing she was bought by Daniel Wildenstein and has bred a number of good winners for him, including Leonardo da Vinci (White Rose Stakes), L'Ile du Rêve (Cheshire Oaks) and Legend of France (Earl of Sefton Stakes).

LYNCHRIS
(1957, b f Sayajirao – Scollata, by Niccolo dell'Arca)

Lynchris, who unfortunately succumbed to a stroke of lightning in America soon after her retirement from racing and export as a four-year-old, was a really good stayer who won the Irish Oaks, Yorkshire Oaks and Irish St Leger as well as three other races for a total of £15,960. She was originally bought as a yearling for 480gns and passed on to her trainer John Oxx for £600.

M

MA BICHE
(1980, b or br f Key to the Kingdom – Madge, by Roi Dagobert)

Born in the United States out of a French mare, Ma Biche was owned by Mme Alec Head and trained by her daughter Criquette when she won four races as a two-year-old, including the Prix Robert Papin and Cheveley Park Stakes. She was bought privately for a reputed £3 million by Maktoum Al-Maktoum before she ran as a three-year-old, remained with Mme Head at Chantilly and became the trainer's first Classic winning in Britain, taking the 1,000 Guineas. She ran three times more after the Newmarket Classic and retired to stud after winning her seventh race from eleven outings in the Prix de la Forêt.

McALPINE, Sir Robin (b. 1906)

Sir Robin McAlpine is a member of the Jockey Club, a former President of the Racehorse Owners' Association, a life member of the Council of the Thoroughbred Breeders' Association and a former steward at Ascot and Alexandra Park. He maintained a private stable, run by John Waugh at Newmarket until 1970, when his racing interests were transferred to France. He returned to British racing in the early 1980s with a few horses, and in 1984 won the Oaks with Circus Plume, whose dam is a daughter of his family's 1,000 Guineas winner Zabara.

Racing colours: McAlpine tartan, gold armlets and cap.

MACDONALD-BUCHANAN, Captain John (b. 1925)

Elected to the Jockey Club in 1966, John Macdonald-Buchanan served as a steward from 1970 to 1972 and as Senior Steward from 1979 to 1982. In between, for three years, he was the Jockey Club's representative on the Levy Board, and was chairman of Warwick racecourse from 1967 to 1979. He had served on many committees before assuming the highest position in the Jockey Club. His Flat horses are trained by Michael Stoute.

MACDONALD-BUCHANAN, Major Sir Reginald Narcissus (1898-1981)

Major Sir Reginald Macdonald-Buchanan served in the Scots Guards. A member of the Jockey Club, he was Senior Steward in 1953. For ten years he was a member of the Racecourse Betting Control Board. The best horse to carry his colours of black, white hoop and armlets was Abernant, who won fourteen races worth over £26,000. His wife, daughter of Lord Woolavington, inherited and maintained the wide breeding interests of her father at the Lavington, Egerton and Lordship Studs. She bred and owned the war-time Derby and Gold Cup winner Owen Tudor and bred Abernant.

McCORMACK, Matthew (b. 1939)

Born at Tullow, Co Carlow, Matt McCormack was a stable lad at Wetherby, at Newmarket with Cecil Boyd-Rochfort, Bernard van Cutsem and Noel Murless, and at Lambourn with Peter Walwyn before starting training near Wantage in 1980. His first Flat-race winner was Bincleaves at Newmarket on 1 May 1980. Two years later he won nine straight races with the two-year-old Horage, including the Coventry, July and Gimcrack Stakes, and the following season won the St James's Palace Stakes with him. His best season was 1985, with 22 winners.

McGLONE, Anthony David (b. 1963)

Tony McGlone rode his first winner in 1980 and ended that year with eleven wins. He completed his apprenticeship with Richard Hannon, for whose stable his father worked, and remained there when he came out of his time at the end of 1984. His biggest win has been with Melindra (Wokingham), and his best season was 1983, with 32 winners.

McGRATH, Joseph (1895-1966)

Mr Joseph McGrath played a leading part in the modern history of the Irish Turf. A patriotic Irishman, he fought for the freedom of his country during 'the Troubles' and was a member of the first Dáil and subsequently Minister of Labour and Minister of Commerce. He founded the famous and highly successful 'Irish Hospitals Sweep', was a leading owner and breeder in Ireland and was largely responsible for the modernizing of The Curragh racecourse.

In 1941 he bought the Brownstown Stud which he extended to cover 500 acres and contain 135 boxes. In 1944 he bought Nasrullah, reputedly for some 18,000gns, and sold him to an American syndicate for £130,000 in 1950. In both Britain and America Nasrullah proved one of the greatest stallions of his day. Mr McGrath won the 1951 Derby with Arctic Prince, whom he exported to America six years later. He also owned Windsor Slipper, the unbeaten winner of six races, including the Irish 'Triple Crown', Solar Slipper (Champion Stakes and third in the St Leger), Panaslipper (Irish Derby and second in the Epsom Derby), Silken Glider (Irish Oaks and second in the Epsom Oaks) and Le Levanstell (Sussex Stakes).

McGRATH, Seamus (b. 1923)

Seamus McGrath, son of Joseph McGrath, trained at Sandyford, Co Dublin. He took out his first licence in 1942 and among the big races he won were the Irish Derby (twice), Irish Oaks, Queen's Vase, St James's Palace Stakes, Royal Hunt Cup, Chesterfield Cup and Cambridgeshire, but his big triumph came in 1969, when he won the Ascot Gold Cup, Prix du Cadran and Prix de l'Arc de Triomphe with Levmoss. He was never afraid to take his best horses to France and in 1970 returned to win the local Oaks with Sweet Mimosa. At his peak he had 100 horses in training, but the numbers were reduced around 1980, and in 1983 he gave up training to concentrate on his business interests.

McHARGUE, Darrel (b. 1958)

American jockey Darrel McHargue rode for one season in Ireland for Dermot Weld, in 1983, and the following year for Luca Cumani at Newmarket. His style did not quite adapt to British conditions, and he had more than one brush with the stewards, though he did not let the stable down in the Extel Stakes, winning on Free Guest, or on one day at Newmarket when he won the Sun Chariot Stakes on the same filly and the Jockey Club Cup on Old Country. He lost the St Leger-winning ride on Commanche Run to Lester Piggott and returned to America at the end of the 1984 season.

McINTOSH, Norman (b. 1931)

Norman McIntosh enjoyed a long association with George Boyd, to whom he was apprenticed from 1948 to 1953 and for whom he rode until the trainer's retirement in 1969. McIntosh, a natural lightweight, rode his first winner in 1949 at Hamilton Park, and his best season was 1960, when he rode 37 winners. Big races he won included the Lincolnshire Handicap, Ayr Gold Cup and Northumberland Plate. He did not renew his licence in 1982.

MACKAY, Allan (b. 1959)

Born in Falkirk and originally apprenticed to Tommy Craig at Dunbar, Allan Mackay finished his time with Eric Eldin (later to be his father-in-law) at Newmarket. His first ride was a winner, on Lanark Birk at York on 8 October 1976. He lost his right to claim an allowance in 1983, the year he had his biggest success, on Grand Unit in the Bessborough Stakes, and his best total, 31 winners.

McKAY, Dennis James (b. 1945)

Dennis McKay was apprenticed to Jimmy Walsh and had his best season of 30 winners in 1969, when claiming an allowance. Among his winners was the Cesarewitch on Floridian. He won the race again the following year on Scoria, and in 1977 won the Lincoln Handicap on Blustery, while he has won the Wokingham Stakes twice.

McMAHON, Bryan Arthur (b. 1937)

Bryan McMahon began in racing at Newmarket, with Jack Waugh and Harvey Leader, but moved to the Midlands and took out a permit to train at Tamworth. He had his first winner in 1967 and progressed from a jumping licence to a mixed yard. His best seasons numerically were 1983 and 1985, with nineteen winners.

MADDEN, Herbert Otto (1872-1942)

Otto Madden was born in Germany of British parents. His father had ridden the famous Hungarian mare Kincsem in many of her races. His own career had its ups and downs – at one point he forfeited his licence for a season for 'consorting with persons of known bad character' – but he was four times champion jockey. He won the Derby on Jeddah, the 2,000 Guineas on Norman III, the Oaks on Musa and Sunny Jane, and the St Leger on Challacombe. He retired to take up training in 1909 but returned to the saddle in World War I before resuming his training career in 1919. In his closing years he was a popular and respected figure at Newmarket, being churchwarden at St Agnes. He left over £50,000 when he died.

MADDEN, Peter John (b. 1951)

Apprenticed to Doug Marks, Peter Madden made his base at Newmarket. His best season was as an apprentice in 1970, with 36 winners.

MADDOCK, Harold Russell (b. 1922)

Russ Maddock was born in Australia and rode his first winner there in 1936. He was eight times champion jockey in Queensland before trying his luck in Britain from 1961. He fractured his right leg twice, in October 1969 and March 1971, was forced to retire and returned to Australia. His most important British successes came in the Nunthorpe Stakes on Althrey Don, Princess Elizabeth Stakes on Pytchley Princess, and Vaux Gold Tankard and Yorkshire Cup on Quartette. He rode originally for Pat Rohan in the North and then Bernard van Cutsem at Newmarket.

MAHER, Daniel (1881-1916)

Danny Maher was an American jockey who came to Britain in 1900 with a big reputation which he certainly justified. He swiftly adapted his style to suit British courses and proved himself an artist of a very high order. Occasionally he overdid his favourite waiting tactics but at his best he was second to none. He rode three Derby winners – Rock Sand (1903), Cicero (1905) and Spearmint (1906) – as well as the other Classics at least once. A man of outstanding charm and intelligence, he was greatly liked by men such as Lord Rosebery and Lord Derby, but there was a strain of weakness in his character, and some of his racing friends did him little credit. He was inclined to burn the candle at both ends and in addition he was tubercular. His health had gone by 1914 when he returned to America.

MAHMOUD (1933, gr c Blenheim – Mah Mahal, by Gainsborough)

Mahmoud was bred and owned by the Aga Khan and trained by Frank Butters. He was a smallish, light grey colt with an Arab-like head. A high-class two-year-old when he won the Richmond Stakes, he improved through his second season, after being beaten by inches in the 2,000 Guineas, and he won the Derby on very firm going in the record time of 2 min 33.8 sec. He never won again and was hustled off to stud. In 1940 he was exported to America for £20,000. He did extremely well there and one year was champion sire.

MAIDEN

A 'maiden' on the Flat is a horse that has never won a race other than a National Hunt Flat race, a match or private sweepstakes or the Newmarket Challenge Cup or Whip. The term refers to a horse that has not won at the time of the race, except in the term 'maiden at closing', which refers to status at the time when entries for the race closed.

MAITLAND, David (b. 1947)

David Maitland was apprenticed to Gordon Smyth. He rode his first winner in 1965 and had his best season with 30 winners in 1966, including the Cambridgeshire on Dites. He won the Cambridgeshire again in 1974 on Flying Nelly, and the following year won the Royal Hunt Cup on Ardoon. He did not renew his licence in 1985.

MAKIN, Peter James (b. 1944)

Peter Makin worked for Arthur Budgett, George Forbes, Tom Yates and Toby Balding before taking out a licence to train at East Hendred in Berkshire in 1967. He moved to Ogbourne Maisey, Wiltshire, early in 1972. His best horses have been Rhodomantade (Victoria Cup) and Fine Blue (thirteen wins), though he achieved a double at Royal Ascot in 1984 with Hi-Tech Girl (Queen Mary Stakes) and Sea Falcon (Windsor Castle Stakes).

MAKTOUM, Hamdan Al-

Success eluded Hamdan Al-Maktoum on the same level as his brothers Sheikh Mohammed and Maktoum Al-Maktoum until Al Bahathri came along to win the Irish 1,000 Guineas, Coronation Stakes and Child Stakes, and to be narrowly beaten in the 1,000 Guineas in 1985. His other good winners have been Princes Gate (Westbury Stakes), Malaak (Cheshire Oaks) and Doulab (Gimcrack). He owns the Derrinstown Stud in Ireland and the Shadwell Stud at Newmarket.

Racing colours: royal blue, white epaulets, striped cap.

MAKTOUM, Maktoum Al- (b. 1942)

The eldest son of the ruler of Dubai and deputy Prime Minister of the United Arab Emirates, Maktoum Al-Maktoum won his first races in Britain with Shaab in 1979. Three years later he became the first of the three brothers to own an English Classic winner when Touching Wood, second in the Derby, won the English and Irish St Legers. He won the 1,000 Guineas in 1983 with Ma Biche (bought privately as a two-year-old), the 2,000 Guineas in 1985 with Shadeed, and the Irish Sweeps Derby in 1983 with Shareef Dancer. He owns the Gainsborough Stud in Berkshire and is developing a stud farm in Kentucky. He was elected an honorary member of the Jockey Club in December 1985.

Racing colours: royal blue, white chevron, light blue cap.

MANCHESTER

Manchester racecourse ceased to exist in 1964. The course, which had provided racing in a meander of the River Irwell since 1902, finally fell into the hands of property-developers, and the traditional end-of-season meeting was therefore transferred across the Pennines to Doncaster. One of Manchester's most notable records was to stage the first evening meeting in England, on 13 July 1951.

MANNA
(1922, b c Phalaris – Waffles, by Buckwheat)

Manna was bought as a yearling by Mr H.E. Morriss, a Shanghai bullion-broker, for 6,300gns. Trained by Fred Darling, Manna won four races for £23,534, including the 2,000 Guineas and Derby. He broke down in the St Leger and never ran again. The best horse he sired was Colombo, winner of the 2,000 Guineas and over £26,000 in stakes.

MANTON, Lord (b. 1924)

Elected to the Jockey Club in 1968, Lord Manton served as a steward from 1976 to 1979 and Senior Steward from 1982 to

1985. He rode 130 winners as an amateur between 1947 and 1964 and subsequently has been prominent in northern racing as a member of York Race Committee since 1963, director of Thirsk racecourse since 1970, and a local steward at Doncaster, York and Beverley.

MARCHETTA
(1907, ch f Marco – Hettie Sorrel, by Peter)

Marchetta was of no great merit as a racer but she founded one of the most famous families in modern racing. It has divided into two main branches descended from her daughters Rose Red (1924) and Sweet Lavender (1923). The Rose Red branch has produced Larkspur, Aurora, Alycidon, Borealis, Acropolis, Festoon, Celtic Ash, Altesse Royale and Bustino. From the Sweet Lavender branch come My Babu, Sayani, Ambiorix, Cagire II, Turn-to, Klairon, Atilla and English Prince. As time progresses, the branch from Sweet Lavender will probably be further distinguished by grouping together those horses descended from her granddaughter Perfume II (1938).

MARE

A mare is a female thoroughbred aged five years or upwards.

MARGUERITE VERNAUT
(1957, ch f Toulouse Lautrec – Mariebelle, by Mieuxcé)

Marguerite Vernaut, a very good Italian filly, won eight races in her native country, including the Gran Criterium and Gran Premio d'Italia, and in Britain won the Champion Stakes as a three-year-old. She is the grandam of the Premio Roma winner Montorselli and great-grandam of the Premio Presidente della Repubblica winner Máffei.

MARKS, Douglas (b. 1922)

Doug Marks was apprenticed to William Jarvis, and it was as a little-known claiming rider that he won the 1940 1,000 Guineas and Oaks on that temperamental filly Godiva. He rode under National Hunt Rules from 1946 to 1951 and took out a licence to train in 1949. At one time his stable was essentially a 'mixed' one but now he chiefly concentrates on the Flat. With Golden Fire he won the Chester Cup, Goodwood Stakes (twice) and Cesarewitch, and he also trained the good sprinters Shiny Tenth and Singing Bede. His stable is at Upper Lambourn.

MARSH, Alec (b. 1908)

Before the war, Alec Marsh was one of the leading amateur riders. For three years in succession he was top amateur under National Hunt Rules. At Aintree he won the Grand Sefton and the Foxhunters Chase. Altogether he rode in 960 races under National Hunt Rules and on the Flat, winning 163. In the war he served in the RAF and from 1946 to 1947 was starter to the Royal Calcutta Turf Club. He became a starter under Jockey Club Rules in 1947 and was Jockey Club Starter from 1953 until his retirement in 1971.

MARSH, Marcus Maskell
(1904-83)

Marcus Marsh, son of Richard Marsh, learnt the art of training from his father, Captain R.F.K. Gooch and Fred Darling before setting up on his own in Berkshire in 1929. In 1934 he enjoyed his first major success when he won the Derby and St Leger with Windsor Lad. In World War II he served in the RAF, was shot down and was a prisoner of war in Germany for nearly five years. After the war he was soon in his stride again in Newmarket and trained an outstanding sprinter in The Bug. On the retirement of Frank Butters he took over the Aga Khan's horses, and among the good winners he trained for him were Tulyar (1952 Derby, St Leger, Eclipse Stakes and King George VI and Queen Elizabeth Stakes) and Palestine (2,000 Guineas). He retired in 1964 and died in December 1983.

MARSH, Richard (1851-1933)

Richard Marsh was the son of a Kentish hop-farmer. He joined a Newmarket stable as a small boy but soon got too heavy to ride on the Flat. However, he did well over fences and hurdles. He first made his name as a trainer with jumpers belonging to the Duke of Hamilton, but he won the 1883 St Leger with Ossian and the 1,000 Guineas and Oaks in 1886 with Miss Jummy. He became trainer to the Prince of Wales, later King Edward VII, in 1893 and for him won the Derby with Persimmon (1896), Diamond Jubilee (1900) and Minoru (1909). Persimmon also won the St Leger, Eclipse Stakes and Gold Cup, Diamond Jubilee the 2,000 Guineas and St Leger, and Minoru the 2,000 Guineas. Marsh also won the Derby in 1898 for Mr J.W. Larnach with the 100-1 chance Jeddah, and in all won thirteen Classics.

Tall, hospitable and beautifully dressed, Marsh was never a man to spend much time in counting the pennies. He married a daughter of the famous Beckhampton trainer Sam Darling.

MARSHALL, William Cyril (b. 1918)

Bill Marshall served as a fighter pilot in the RAF during World War II, being awarded the DFC. After the war he rode as an amateur under National Hunt Rules till 1950, and from 1950 till 1957 as a professional. He took out a licence to train in 1950 and was successively stationed at Cheltenham, Marlborough, Whitsbury (from 1970) and Newmarket (from 1975). He made his name in the 1960s with proven performers bought from other stables and which he improved out of all recognition, notably My Swanee and Raffingora, who won thirteen good races between them, and Grey Mirage. His last season training in Britain was 1982, after which he retired to the West Indies.

MARSYAS II
(1940, ch c Trimdon – Astronomie, by Astérus)

Marcel Boussac's Marsyas II was an outstanding stayer in the immediate post-war era. In France he won the Prix du Cadran four times; in Britain he won the Queen Alexandra Stakes, Goodwood Cup and Doncaster Cup. He was not a stud success but got the Ascot Gold Cup winner Macip.

MARTIAL
(1957, ch c Hill Gail – Discipliner, by Court Martial)

Martial, a big powerful chestnut half-brother to Skymaster and El Gallo, was bred by Captain A.D. Rogers and sold for 2,400gns as a yearling. Owned by Mr R.N. Webster and trained by Paddy Prendergast, he won three races, including the Coventry Stakes and 2,000 Guineas for a total of £19,922. He was syndicated for stud but in 1967 was exported to Argentina, by which time his most notable offspring was the useful French miler The Marshal.

MARTIN, John Henry (1875-1944)

Born in New York and usually known as 'Skeets' Martin, he was one of the first American jockeys to ride with success in Britain. He won the Derby on Ard Patrick in 1902. The following year he won the 2,000 Guineas on Rock Sand. He was well enough off when he retired from racing but lost his money in property speculation and died penniless in Switzerland.

MASAKA
(1945, b f Nearco – Majideh, by Mahmoud)

Masaka, owned and bred by the Aga Khan, was a good but temperamental filly, winning six races worth £21,996. As a two-year-old she won the Queen Mary Stakes and July Stakes. The following season, ridden by Ken Gethin, she was favourite for the 1,000 Guineas but was in a wayward mood, stuck her toes in at the start and declined to race. However, ridden by Nevett, she won the Oaks and Irish Oaks. Her daughter Bara Bibi won the Park Hill Stakes at Doncaster, while her sprinter daughter Palsaka bred the smart French horse Silver Shark.

MASON, Ronald Edwin George (b. 1916)

Ron Mason served in World War II in the RAF. A man of some versatility, he was at one time a speedway rider and had interests in a haulage-contracting business. For a trainer with a small yard, at Guilsborough, Northants, he was remarkably successful after taking out a licence in 1959, especially at Royal Ascot, where he won the Royal Hunt Cup (Smartie), St James's Palace Stakes (Track Spare) and Queen Mary Stakes (Petite Path). He also won the Lincolnshire Handicap, Queen Elizabeth II Stakes, Totalisator Spring Handicap, Northumberland Plate, Middle Park Stakes and Ayr Gold Cup. He was the first trainer with a winner from starting-stalls in Britain, when Track Spare won at Newmarket in 1965. He was less successful in the 1970s and gave up training in 1981 to devote his attention to a stud farm he had bought in Queensland, Australia.

MASSINE (1920, b c Consols – Mauri, by Ajax)

The French horse Massine, who won the Ascot Gold Cup in 1924, was one of the best winners of that event between the two World Wars. He won eleven races in France, including the Prix de l'Arc de Triomphe, and amassed over 1m francs in stakes. He proved a high-class sire, among his winners being Mieuxcé (French Derby and Grand Prix), Strip The Willow (French Derby and Grand Prix), Laëken (French St Leger and sire of the great hurdler Sir Ken), Maravédis, sire of Souverain, who won the Ascot Gold Cup, Grand Prix and French St Leger, Chaudière (Prix du Cadran) and Féerie (French 1,000 Guineas and Oaks). Massine died in 1939.

MASSON, Thomas (1898-1969)

Tom Masson at one time rode show-horses and point-to-pointers for Bertram Mills of circus fame. He took out a licence to train in 1939 and ran a small 'mixed' stable at Lewes, during which period he earned the reputation of being particularly good with difficult and temperamental horses. He was a successful tutor of young riders, and Jimmy Lindley and Bobby Elliott were among his apprentices. He won the Ascot Stakes with Shatter and the Lingfield Derby Trial with Pindaric. The Queen was a patron of the stable. He died from injuries received in a car crash in 1969, and his son Michael took over the stable.

MATCH

A 'match' is a race between horses, the property of two different owners, on terms agreed by them. Competitive racing began on the principle of matches, but their popularity quickly waned once organized sport took over. In recent years matches have been staged for promotional and charitable purposes and for the publicity that a series of events between public personalities provided in the early years of women jockeys on the Flat.

MATCH III (1958, br c Tantième – Relance III, by Relic)

Owned and bred by M. François Dupré, Match III was out of the famous Relic mare Relance, dam of the Derby winner Relko and the French Derby winner Reliance. Match won seven races for the equivalent of £126,541, including the Prix Juigné, Prix Noailles, French St Leger, Grand Prix de Saint-Cloud, King George VI and Queen Elizabeth Stakes and Washington D.C. International. When his racing career was over, he was purchased to stand in Britain but unfortunately died all too young in 1965. He sired Murrayfield (Coventry Stakes) and Palatch (Yorkshire Oaks and dam of the French Derby second Patch). There is every indication from the stock he did produce that he would have made a great sire.

MATHET, François (1908-83)

One of France's finest trainers, François Mathet was an outstanding amateur rider in his native country, on the Flat and over jumps. He began training at Chantilly at the end of the second World War, and from 1949 until his death in January 1983 he was leading trainer for either races won or earnings every season. Often he led both categories and did so in his final season of 1982. He trained more than 3,000 winners for such owners as the Dupré, Volterra and Rothschild families, as well as the Aga Khan. He won the Prix de l'Arc de Triomphe twice with Tantième, and also with Sassafras and Akiyda. Sassafras also won the French Derby, as did Reliance, Tapalqué, Rheffic, Crystal Palace and Top Ville.

Mathet's first important success in Britain was with Phil Drake in the 1955 Derby. The following year he won the Oaks with Sicarelle; Bella Paola won the 1,000 Guineas and Oaks in 1958, and Relko gave him his second Derby success in 1963. Bella Paola also won the Champion Stakes, and Mathet trained Match III to win the King George VI and Queen Elizabeth Stakes. He won the Coronation Cup four times, with Tantième, Dicta Drake, Relko and Exceller, but the success of the last-named, in 1977, was Mathet's final important triumph in Britain, where he increasingly declined to send runners towards the end of his career.

MATTHIAS, John (b. 1953)

John Matthias started riding work for Ian Balding at the age of thirteen and remained with the Kingsclere stable until sacked from his retainer in 1982, though he continued to ride for the trainer on occasions after that. His most important winners for Balding came on Glint of Gold (Italian Derby, Grand Prix de Paris), Mrs Penny (Prix Vermeille, Cheveley Park Stakes) and Centurion (Cesarewitch). He rode his first winner on Garden Games at Beverley on 6 May 1972, and two years later won the season-long Crown Apprentice Championship. His best season was 1980, with 41 winners.

MAXWELL, William Farnham (b. 1905)

At the age of eighteen 'Freddie' Maxwell, who was born in Co Offaly, went to work in Aubrey Hastings's jumping stable at Wroughton and became a thoroughly competent steeplechase rider. Before World War II, in which he served in the RAF, he held a trainer's licence in Ireland, but from 1940 to 1953 he acted as assistant trainer to Evan Williams at Kingsclere. On the latter's retirement, he set up on his own. His main achievement was to win the Ascot Gold Cup three times, with Pandofell in 1961 and Fighting Charlie in 1965 and 1966. Other good races he won included the Doncaster Cup, Yorkshire Cup, July Cup, Queen's Prize, Portland Handicap and Northumberland Plate, and in 1970 he trained the very fast filly Cawston's Pride, winner of the Queen Mary Stakes and seven other juvenile races. He retired from training at the end of the 1977 season.

MEADOW COURT
(1962, ch c Court Harwell – Meadow Music, by Tom Fool)

Meadow Court was bred by Mrs Parker Poe and bought by Paddy Prendergast for 3,000gns as a yearling to be trained by him for a partnership of three American owners that included Mr Bing Crosby. He won three races for £101,668, including the Irish Derby and King George VI and Queen Elizabeth Stakes, while he was second in the Derby and the St Leger. He was syndicated for stud but his career as a stallion was most unsatisfactory and he was sent to Canada, where he resumed his racing career briefly in 1970.

MELD
(1952, b f Alycidon – Daily Double, by Fair Trial)

Meld, bred and owned by Lady Zia Wernher and trained by Cecil Boyd-Rochfort, was one of the outstanding fillies of the century. She was out of Daily Double, whose grandam was Double Life, the famous foundation mare of the Someries Stud. A bay combining superb quality with immense power, Meld met her only defeat in her initial race when she was second to her better-fancied stable companion, Corporal, in a 5f event at Newmarket. Thereafter she won five races worth £43,049.

As a three-year-old she ran four times, winning the 1,000 Guineas, Oaks, Coronation Stakes at Ascot and St Leger. At stud she proved disappointing until her son Charlottown won the 1966 Derby, but her unraced son Mellay became champion sire in New Zealand.

MELLOR, Mary Elain (b. 1943)

Wife of Stan Mellor and mother of two daughters, Elain Mellor became the most successful woman amateur jockey after the Jockey Club had allowed them to compete for the first time in 1972. She rode her first winner on Montanello at Carlisle on 3 July 1974 and was leading woman jockey in 1975, '77, '79, '81 and '83, and joint leader in '84. Her best seasons were 1977 and 1983, with eight winners. She retired from race-riding in 1985 to take up training on the Flat the following year.

MELLOR, Stanley Thomas Edward (b. 1937)

The most successful jump jockey in history, until John Francome took his record in 1984, Stan Mellor began training jumpers at Lambourn in 1972. He kept a few Flat-racers, and his first win on the level was with Aztec Star at Windsor on 7 May 1974. For a short time he changed the emphasis of his stable from jumpers to Flat-racers, but by the early 1980s the switch had been made back again. His biggest Flat success came in 1985 with Al Trui in the Stewards' Cup.

MERCER, Emmanuel Lionel (1930-59)

To the sincere sorrow of the racing world, 'Manny' Mercer was killed at Ascot on 26 September 1959. He was only 29 years of age. His mount, Priddy Fair, reared, slipped and fell on the way to the post. Mercer's head came into contact with a concrete support of the rails, and in addition he was kicked in the face by Priddy Fair as she struggled to regain her feet.

'Manny' Mercer was born in Stockport and apprenticed to Jim Russell at Mablethorpe. When Russell's licence was withdrawn in 1947, Mercer's indentures were transferred to George Colling. His first big success came in 1948, when he won the Lincolnshire Handicap on the 100-1 outsider Jockey Treble. At the time his riding weight was 5st 8lb. He rode 21 winners that season, sixteen in 1949 and lost his apprentice allowance early the following year. He had 37 winners in 1950. At this period E.C. Elliott was first jockey to George Colling, and Mercer owed a great deal to Elliott's advice and encouragement. To his death Mercer loyally continued to ride for George Colling's stable, despite several offers of far bigger retainers for his services.

He rode a good deal for owners for whom Jack Jarvis and Harry Wragg trained. In 1953 he won the 1,000 Guineas on Happy Laughter trained by Jarvis, and in 1954 the 2,000 Guineas on Darius trained by Wragg. Two years later he won the Irish Derby on Talgo and the Irish Oaks on Garden State, partnering the former into second place in the Prix de l'Arc de Triomphe behind Ribot. From the beginning of Wilwyn's three-year-old career that colt was always ridden by Mercer. The most notable of their nineteen victories together was in the first Washington D.C. International at Laurel, Maryland.

In eight seasons, from 1951 to 1958 inclusive, Mercer rode more than 100 winners four times and finished in the top four jockeys every year bar 1957, when he was fifth, and in 1955. He was second in 1954 and three times third. In 1958, his last full season, he had 125 winning rides. At the time of his death in 1959 he had ridden 100 winners.

A simple, loyal and friendly person, 'Manny' Mercer never pretended to have an eye for a horse or any particular interest in pedigrees, but he rode with style, sympathy and understanding. His judgement was as sound in a race as when driving one of the fast cars that gave him so much pleasure. He married Susan Wragg, the daughter of Harry Wragg, and their daughter Carolyn married Pat Eddery.

MERCER, Joseph (b. 1934)

A younger brother of the late 'Manny' Mercer, Joe Mercer served his apprenticeship with Major F.B. Sneyd, who at one time had both Eph and Doug Smith under his care. Mercer rode his first winner at Bath in 1950. He was top apprentice in 1952 and 1953, the latter being the first year when he was retained by the West Ilsley stable run by R.J. Colling and from 1962 by Major Dick Hern. During this time he was associated with the Astor horses, riding his first Classic winner in 1953 on Lord Astor's Ambiguity in the Oaks and his second on Mr J.J. Astor's Provoke in the 1965 St Leger. He also won the 1,000 Guineas and French Oaks on Highclere, another St Leger on Bustino and the Jockey Club Cup three times on High Line, as well as the Sussex Stakes, Yorkshire Oaks and Park Hill Stakes three times apiece. The most outstanding horse he rode was Brigadier Gerard, winner seventeen times in eighteen races including the 2,000 Guineas, Champion Stakes (twice) and King George VI and Queen Elizabeth Stakes.

It came as a great surprise in the summer of 1976 when it was announced Mercer would be replaced by Willie Carson as stable jockey at West Ilsley at the end of the year, the move being attributed to the insistence of the stable's owners and main patrons, Sir Michael Sobell and his son-in-law Sir Arnold Weinstock. Within a few weeks Mercer signed to be stable jockey to Henry Cecil and in his second season, 1979, won the 1,000 Guineas on One in a Million and was champion jockey for the only time, with 164 winners, his highest career total. In 1980 he won the St Leger on Light Cavalry and the Ascot Gold Cup, Goodwood Cup and Doncaster Cup on Le Moss, winning the Doncaster Cup for the eighth time. In 1981 he moved back to Berkshire to become stable jockey to Peter Walwyn and in one of the most popular results of the season won the St Leger on Cut Above, owned by Sir John Astor and trained by Dick Hern. Mercer retired at the end of 1985 and his last ride in Britain on Bold Rex in the November Handicap at Doncaster, was successful. His total of 2,810 winners in Britain has been bettered only by Sir Gordon Richards, Lester Piggott and Doug Smith.

MESA
(1932, b f Kircubbin – Mackwiller, by Verwood)

M. Pierre Wertheimer's Mesa, ridden by W.R. Johnstone and trained by P. Corbière, won the 1,000 Guineas and was third in the Oaks, where she had a very bad run and was desperately unlucky not to win. In her native France she won two minor races. She died at the age of nine, having bred three winners for Sir Malcolm McAlpine who bought her as a four-year-old.

MID-DAY SUN
(1934, b c Solario – Bridge of Allan, by Phalaris)

Mid-day Sun was the first horse to carry a woman's colours to victory in the Epsom Derby. After failing to make his reserve at the Doncaster sales, he was bought privately for 2,000gns on behalf of Miss L.M. Talbot, who shortly afterwards married Mr G.B. Miller, and her mother, Mrs J.A.W. Talbot.

Trained by Fred Butters, Mid-day Sun was a moderate two-year-old, won only once in eight races and in the Free Handicap was rated 34lb below the top-weight. However, he improved immensely during the winter. He won the Free Handicap from Exhibitionnist, who later won the 1,000 Guineas and Oaks, and he was third in the 2,000 Guineas. He won the Lingfield Derby Trial and, beautifully ridden by Michael Beary, won the Derby from the rank outsider Sandsprite. He won the Hardwicke Stakes at Royal Ascot and was unlucky in the St Leger, in which he was third behind Chulmleigh after being very badly hampered. That was his final race. The start of his stud career coincided with the war and he never got a full quota of mares. Largely through lack of opportunity, he failed to make the grade and in 1950 was exported to New Zealand, where he died in 1954. His best winner was Sterope, who twice won the Cambridgeshire.

MIGOLI
(1944, gr c Bois Roussel – Mah Iran, by Bahram)

The Aga Khan's grey colt Migoli was a game and consistent horse who was second in the Derby, trounced Tudor Minstrel in the Eclipse Stakes and in all won ten races for £22,950 in Britain. As a four-year-old he won the Prix de l'Arc de Triomphe, but that event did not then hold the immense prestige that it possesses today. As a sire Migoli proved disappointing though he got the Belmont Stakes winner Gallant Man, as a result of which he was exported to America, where he died in 1963.

MILLER, Mrs Lettice Butt

Mrs Miller was the owner, in partnership with her mother, Mrs J.A.W. Talbot, of the 1937 Derby winner, Mid-day Sun, the first Epsom Derby winner to carry the colours of a woman owner.

MILLER, Michael Melvyn (b. 1955)

Mick Miller was apprenticed to Sam and then Robert Armstrong from the age of fifteen and rode his first winner on Silky Moss at Catterick on 4 July 1974. He was with that stable for eight years, until joining Geoff Huffer at the end of 1979. He accepted a retainer from Ron Boss for 1985, but for the third time in his career a fall put him out of action. In 1978 he damaged his kidneys; in 1983 he broke a wrist and an ankle, and in 1985 he broke his pelvis. His most important success has been with First Movement in the Ayr Gold Cup, and his best season was 1982, with 24 winners.

MILL REEF
(1968, b c Never Bend – Milan Mill, by Princequillo)

A fractured near foreleg ended Mill Reef's brilliant racing career as a four-year-old, but the operation performed on the injury set up an equally marvellous stud career. Bred in the United States by his owner, Paul Mellon, Mill Reef was trained by Ian Balding and met defeat only twice in fourteen races, when My Swallow beat him in the Prix Robert Papin as a two-year-old and when Brigadier Gerard beat him in the 2,000 Guineas. His twelve wins, for a little more than £300,000 in prize money, included the top middle-distance races – the Prix de l'Arc de Triomphe, Derby, King George VI and Queen Elizabeth Stakes, Eclipse Stakes and Coronation Cup – as well as the Gimcrack and Dewhurst Stakes as a two-year-old. The only public regret about his career, other than that it ended prematurely, was that he and Brigadier Gerard never met after the Guineas, where the distance was probably less in Mill Reef's favour than his rival's.

When it became known that the operation to Mill Reef's injured leg had been a success, Mr Mellon, a noted anglophile, agreed to let the colt go to the National Stud at Newmarket, and a number of nominations were reserved for British breeders. The total valuation placed on him was about £1.5m, an indication of his owner's regard for Britain since he would have commanded a much higher figure in his native America. Champion sire in 1978, his third year with runners, Mill Reef is the sire of the Classic winners Shirley Heights (Derby and Irish Derby), Acamas (French Derby), Fairy Footsteps (1,000 Guineas), Wassl (Irish 2,000 Guineas) and Paris Royal (Italian Oaks), as well as the multi-Group One winning brothers Glint of Gold and Diamond Shoal (both owned by Mr Mellon), and Lashkari (Breeders' Cup Turf). Mill Reef suffered heart trouble in the summer of 1985, and when it deteriorated seriously late the following January, he was destroyed.

MINORU
(1906, br c Cyllene – Mother Siegel, by Friar's Balsam)

Minoru was the third and final Derby winner of King Edward VII. He also won the 2,000 Guineas. He was not the property of the King, being leased to him for racing by Colonel Hall Walker, later Lord Wavertree. At the end of his racing career Minoru was returned to his owner, who exported him to Russia, where he disappeared during the Revolution.

MITCHELL, Cyril

Cyril Mitchell was apprenticed to Victor Smyth at Epsom from 1929 to 1934, when he then also took out a licence to ride under National Hunt Rules. He was granted his first licence to train at Epsom in 1950, and his most important wins came between 1967 and 1974 with two horses owned by the broadcaster and journalist Peter O'Sullevan – the sprinter Be Friendly, whose victories included the King's Stand Stakes, Ayr Gold Cup, Vernons Sprint (twice) and Prix de l'Abbaye; and the stayer Attivo, who won the Northumberland Plate and Chester Cup. Mitchell retired in 1974 to live in the West Indies, leaving his son Philip to take over the stable.

MITCHELL, Philip (b. 1948)

Son of the Epsom trainer Cyril Mitchell, Philip became the most successful amateur Flat-race rider since the Second World War, winning 65 races from 128 rides and being champion five times, following his first ride at the age of sixteen and his first winner on Creditable at Haydock on 10 August 1966. He won the Moët & Chandon Silver Magnum, the top race for amateurs, four times before taking up training when his father retired at the end of the 1974 season. His winning totals on the Flat have increased steadily, the best being 1984 with 23 winners, and his biggest successes have been with Telsmoss (Newbury Autumn Cup), King's Glory (Lincoln) and Sylvan Barbarosa (Cork and Orrery).

MITCHELL, Victor John (b. 1919)

Vic Mitchell was apprenticed to George Digby at Exning and gained his most important win in the 1939 Lincolnshire Handicap on Squadron Castle. He served in the RAF during World War II, was shot down over Germany and was for three years a prisoner of war. He began training at Malton in 1964 and conducted small stables there, at Wiseton, Stockton, Worksop and York before he failed to renew his licence in 1983.

MOHAMMED, Sheikh, bin Rashid Al-Maktoum (b. 1948)

Youngest of the three sons of the ruler of Dubai and Defence Minister there, Sheikh Mohammed bought his first horses to race in Britain in 1976 and the following year won the Molecomb Stakes with Hatta. It was the first Pattern race success in a list that was to grow as his interests multiplied into a role as the biggest spender of the brothers, including his purchase of the world record-priced yearling, Snaafi Dancer, for $10.2m. Snaafi Dancer never ran, but Sheikh Mohammed has had plenty of success to compensate, his finest hour coming in 1985 when Oh So Sharp, whom he bred, won the 1,000 Guineas, Oaks and St Leger, and was narrowly beaten in the King George VI and Queen Elizabeth Diamond Stakes. Her successes helped Sheikh Mohammed to become leading owner in Britain for the first time, with a record total of £1,082, 668 from 115 wins by 69 horses.

His other major winners have been Jalmood, Awaasif, High Hawk, Kanz, Optimistic Lass, Head For Heights, Local Suitor, Bairn and Pebbles. He owns the Dalham Hall Stud at Newmarket, Aston Upthorpe, near Didcot and the Woodpark Stud in Ireland.

Racing colours: maroon, white sleeves, maroon cap, white star.

MOLONY, Tim (b. 1919)

Tim Molony, five times champion jockey under National Hunt Rules in a career from 1936 to 1958, took out a trainer's licence in 1960 to run a small 'mixed' stable at Wymondham, near Melton Mowbray. He retired from training at the end of 1980.

MONADE
(1959, br f Klairon – Mormyre, by Atys)

In the colours of Mr G. Goulandris and trained by J. Lieux, Monade won eight races in France including the Prix Vermeille. In Britain she won the Oaks and in all was placed eleven times from two to five years. She went to stud in the United States and has bred several winners, including Elect, Mariella and My Maravilla in Britain, and Que Mona (dam of the Champion Stakes runner-up Prima Voce) and Remedia (dam of the smart filly Too Chic) in America.

MON FILS
(1970, br c Sheshoon – Now What, by Premonition)

Mon Fils revelled in the soft ground for the 2,000 Guineas and pulled off a 50-1 success from Noble Decree. Mon Fils had won twice as a two-year-old under similar conditions, including when winning the Mill Reef Stakes, but he had only one more outing after the Guineas, finishing eighteenth in the Derby. Trained by Richard Hannon for all his races, he was sent to Vincent O'Brien after Epsom but tendon trouble caused his retirement. He spent two seasons at stud in Britain before being exported to France in 1975.

MONOLULU, PRINCE (c. 1885-1965)

Peter McKay, better known as Prince Ras Monolulu, was a big, powerful coloured man who came to Britain – from where is unknown – at the turn of the century. With his baggy trousers, umbrella and ostrich feathers, combined with his raucous and familiar cry of 'I gotta horse', he became by far the best-known racecourse tipster in the country. In fact he had become an accepted part of the British racing scene long before his death in 1965, when, despite his publishing his autobiography under the name of his famous cry, there was no more certainty about his history than during his lifetime.

MONTAVAL
(1953, b c Norseman – Ballynash, by Nasrullah)

Bred and owned by Mr R.B. Strassburger, Montaval won four races worth over 3,000,000 (old) francs in France, while in Britain he was second in the Derby and Eclipse Stakes and won the King George VI and Queen Elizabeth Stakes as a four-year-old. After Ascot he was sold to stand at stud in Ireland but his stay there was short and he was exported to Japan in 1961.

MOORE, Captain Charles (1880-1965)

Charles Moore, who owned a stud in Ireland, was appointed racing manager to King George VI in 1937 and on the King's death he held office as racing manager to the Queen till his retirement in 1963, when he was succeeded by Major Richard Shelley. One of Captain Moore's most important acts was to advise the King to appoint Captain (later Sir) Cecil Boyd-Rochfort as his trainer. Under Captain Moore's shrewd guidance the royal studs emerged from a long era of decline, and it was greatly to his credit that the Queen's horses enjoyed a wonderful period of success between 1954 and 1960, the Queen heading the list of winning owners in 1954 and 1957. He bought Malapert, dam of the Queen's 2,000 Guineas winner Pall Mall, for only 120gns. He conducted his duties with efficiency, charm and wit but could be brusque, even formidable, if he thought the occasion demanded it.

MOORE, George Thomas Donald (b. 1923)

This brilliant Australian jockey, who rode his first winner in 1940, had two short but spectacularly successful spells in Europe, the second for one season with Noel Murless's stable in 1967, winning the 2,000 Guineas and Derby on Royal Palace and the 1,000 Guineas on Fleet. He also won the King George VI and Queen Elizabeth Stakes on Busted. Altogether he rode 72 winners that season, at the conclusion of which he decided to return to Australia, there having been a number of threats to his life.

Moore, who combined power with gentle persuasion in his riding and who was a superb judge of pace, rode in France in 1959 and 1960 for Prince Aly Khan, and his victory on Taboun in the 1959 2,000 Guineas was his first ride in a British Classic race. He also won the French Derby and Grand Prix on Charlottesville, the Prix de l'Arc de Triomphe and Eclipse on Saint Crespin III, the Grand Prix de Saint-Cloud and Ascot Gold Cup on Sheshoon, the French 1,000 on Ginetta, the Irish 1,000 on Florentina, and the Gimcrack and Champagne Stakes on Paddy's Sister.

Awarded the OBE in January 1971, the year he retired from riding, he trained in France and Hong Kong with success. His son Gary has ridden with great success in both countries and in 1981 was brought from Hong Kong to ride the Prix de l'Arc de Triomphe winner Gold River. Twenty years earlier his father, George, had been summoned from Australia to ride fourth-placed Sovrango in the Derby for Harry Wragg, who won the race with Psidium.

MOORE, Reginald Patrick John (1921-77)

Pat Moore rode point-to-point winners in the early years after World War II and in 1952 took out a licence to train at Newmarket, continuing racing with farming. The best horse he trained on the Flat before his retirement in 1974 was Passenger, who won the William Hill Gold Cup and Bunbury Cup.

MORGANETTE

Morganette, foaled in 1884 and sired by Springfield, was a selling plater who had gone in the wind. At stud she bred Galtee More and Ard Patrick, who both won the Derby (1897 and 1902) and Blairfinde, winner of the Irish Derby.

MORRIS, Derek William (b. 1932)

This useful lightweight rider was apprenticed to Reg Day and Bobby Jones. He rode his first winner in 1947, and his best season was 1960 with 36 winners. His most important successes before his retirement from race-riding in 1976 came in the Lincoln Handicap, Queen's Prize, Rosebery Stakes, Portland Handicap and Newbury Autumn Cup.

MORRISS, Henry E. (d. 1951)

A bullion-broker with extensive business interests in the Far East, Mr Morriss won the 2,000 Guineas and Derby with Manna in 1925. He also bred the 1940 Derby winner Pont l'Evêque, whom he sold at the end of the colt's two-year-old season to his trainer, Fred Darling. With Pasch he won the 2,000 Guineas and Eclipse Stakes in 1938. He bought the Banstead Manor Stud at Cheveley, leaving his wife to undertake the management.

MORSTON (1970, ch c Ragusa – Windmill Girl, by Hornbeam)

Morston gave owner-breeder-trainer Arthur Budgett and the mare Windmill Girl their second Derby winner within four years, following Blakeney (who was by Hethersett). Morston, foaled in France when his dam was visiting Exbury, did not race at two years and became the first since Bois Roussel in 1938 to win the Derby on a one-race preparation, having won a minor event at Lingfield on his debut. Edward Hide, his Epsom jockey, had never sat on him before the big race, and after the event, in which he beat Cavo Doro by half a length, he left the course quickly in order to ride at Carlisle the following day. Morston did not race again; he sprained a near-fore tendon in mid-August and retired to stud in Britain for his first season in 1974. His best winners at stud have been Morcon (Prince of Wales's Stakes), Mr Fluorocarbon (Queen Anne Stakes), Valentinian (Prix Kergorlay) and Whitstead (Great Voltigeur Stakes).

MORTON, Charles (1855-1936)

Charles Morton learnt the business of training from Tom Parr, who had trained for Admiral Rous. Morton was neat in dress, quiet in speech and manner and extremely conscientious. His greatest period of success was during the 23 years he trained at Wantage for Mr J.B. Joel. Undoubtedly his most remarkable feat was to win the 1911 Derby with Sunstar, who had broken down the previous week and was so lame after the race that he could hardly hobble into the unsaddling enclosure.

Morton's Classis successes were as follows:

2,000 Guineas: Sunstar (1911)

1,000 Guineas: Jest (1913); Princess Dorrie (1914)

Derby: Sunstar (1911); Humorist (1921)

Oaks: Our Lassie (1903); Glass Doll (1907); Jest (1913); Princess Dorrie (1914)

St Leger: Your Majesty (1908); Black Jester (1914); Tranquil (1923).

MOSSBOROUGH
(1947, ch c Nearco – All Moonshine, by Bobsleigh)

Mossborough was bred by Lord Derby and was by no means an outstanding racehorse, winning five races worth £4,600, his main successes being in the Churchill Stakes at Ascot and the Liverpool Autumn Cup. He was also second in the Eclipse. As a sire, though, he exceeded all expectations, being champion sire once (1958) and second once before his death in 1971. His outstanding winners in Britain were Ballymoss and Noblesse; in Italy he was responsible for the 1,000 Guineas and Oaks winner Anticlea, and in the United States his son Cavan won the Belmont Stakes and over $135,000. Mares by Mossborough have produced the Ascot Gold Cup winners Sagaro (three times) and Shangamuzo, the Hardwicke Stakes winners Montcontour and Scorpio, as well as Exbury (Arc de Triomphe), Lady Berry (French St Leger) and Suffolk (Italian Derby).

MOWERINA

Mowerina (1876) is the most famous thoroughbred foaled in Denmark. By Scottish Chief, she ran for four seasons in Britain and won sixteen of her 34 races. A foundation mare of the Duke of Portland's stud, she bred Donovan (Derby and St Leger), Semolina (1,000 Guineas) and Raeburn (a good winner and third in the Derby). She died in 1906.

MR JINKS
(1926, gr c Tetratema – False Piety, by Lemberg)

Bred and owned by Major D. McCalmont and trained by 'Atty' Persse, Mr Jinks was a very good horse up to a mile. He won nine races worth £25,153, including the New Stakes, July Stakes, 2,000 Guineas and St James's Palace Stakes. He made a promising start as a sire but long before his death in 1952 his record was disappointing.

MRS BUTTERWICK

One of the smallest of Classic winners, Mrs Butterwick, by St Simon, stood just fifteen hands when she won the 1893 Oaks. From her the St Leger winner Singapore and that good sprinter Portlaw were descended. She also bred Phaleron, second in the 2,000 Guineas.

MRS McARDY
(1974, b f Tribal Chief – Hanina, by Darling Boy)

Bred by Lord Grimthorpe but sold in a package deal to trainer Mick Easterby as a yearling, Mrs McArdy raced for Mrs Edith Kettlewell and won eight races, easily the most important being the 1,000 Guineas. She won her last four of eight races as a two-year-old, took the Free Handicap before her major success and in two more victories became one of few recent Classic winners to run in a handicap when she won the Fen Ditton Handicap at Newmarket, carrying 10lb more than any other runner. At the end of her three-year-old campaign she was sold at the Newmarket December Sales for 154,000gns, a record for a horse in training, and was sent to the United States.

MULHALL, Joseph (b. 1933)

Born in Co Dublin, Joe Mulhall was apprenticed to Charlie Rogers but soon became too heavy for Flat racing and in 1954 came to Britain to ride under National Hunt Rules. Five years later he took out a trainer's licence at a yard within a stone's throw of York racecourse and remains there with a small string.

MULLION, Mr and Mrs J.R.

Mr Jim Mullion, a Scottish-born ship-owner, and his wife Meg, who bought the Ardenode Stud in 1956, have been most successful with their horses, which have been trained in Ireland, Britain and more recently France. Their earliest horses were trained by Paddy Prendergast who handled Mr Mullion's best winner so far, Ragusa, who won the Irish Derby, St Leger, Eclipse Stakes and King George VI and Queen Elizabeth Stakes. Other good winners in the Mullion colours include Paddy's Sister (Queen Mary Stakes, Gimcrack Stakes and Champagne Stakes), Court Harwell (second in St Leger), Floribunda (New Stakes, Nunthorpe Stakes and King George Stakes), Hardicanute (Timeform Gold Cup and Champagne Stakes), three Irish 1,000 Guineas winners in Gazpacho, Wenduyne and Sarah Siddons, and two Irish Sweeps Derby seconds in Lombardo and Exdirectory, as well as Ballymore (Irish 2,000 Guineas), Prominer (Royal Lodge Stakes and Hardwicke Stakes), Princess Pati (Irish Oaks) and Ukraine Girl (French 1,000 Guineas).

Mr Mullion's racing colours are white, Robertson tartan, sash and cap; those of his wife are white, red collar and cuffs, tartan cap.

MUMTAZ MAHAL
(1921, gr f The Tetrarch – Lady Josephine, by Sundridge)

Mumtaz Mahal was a filly whose tremendous speed as a two-year-old captured the imagination of the racing public. Commonly known as 'the Flying Filly', she was bred at the Sledmere Stud and as a yearling was sent up to Doncaster sales and bought for 9,100gns by George Lambton, on behalf of the Aga Khan.

She went to R.C. Dawson's stable at Whatcombe to be trained and in 1923

won successively and in brilliant style the Spring Stakes at Newmarket, Queen Mary Stakes at Ascot, National Breeders' Produce Stakes at Sandown, Molecomb Stakes at Goodwood and Champagne Stakes at Doncaster. Unwisely, as it turned out, she was started for the Imperial Produce Stakes at Kempton in the autumn when she was not at her best, and in heavy going was beaten half a length by Arcade, who received 7lb, to the astonishment and dismay of her many admirers.

Despite her obvious stamina limitations, she ran in the 1,000 Guineas and Coronation Stakes as a three-year-old and failed in both. However, she ended her career in appropriate style with decisive victories in the 6f King George Stakes at Goodwood and 5f Nunthorpe Stakes at York. Altogether she won seven races worth £13,933.

Considering her own excellence, her offspring, particularly her fillies, were disappointing on the racecourse, but it was a different story when her daughters were at stud, and through them she has exercised immense influence on blood-stock breeding throughout the world. There is only space to mention Mah Mahal, dam of the Derby winner Mahmoud, and Mumtaz Begum, dam of Nasrullah who was champion sire both in Britain and in the United States.

MURLESS, Sir Charles Francis Noel (b. 1910)

Noel Murless was born in Cheshire. He was always interested in horses and hunted and rode in point-to-points in his teens. He was first attached to Frank Hartigan's stable and rode with meagre success under National Hunt Rules. Later he assisted Hubert Hartigan, first at Penrith and then in Ireland. From those two shrewd and experienced Irish brothers he learnt a great deal.

He took out a licence to train in 1935, and his stable at Hambleton in Yorkshire was so successful after World War II that in 1947 he was invited to succeed the great Fred Darling at Beckhampton. He accepted, but he was never really happy and in 1952 he moved to Newmarket.

From then he never looked back and when he retired at the end of 1976 he was generally accepted as the foremost British trainer of the day.

He showed himself a master at preparing a horse for the right occasion, bringing his runners out fit to do themselves justice without being got ready on the racecourse, and throughout his career in the South he set his sights on the best races. Leading trainer nine times between 1948 and 1973, he set record stakes totals for a trainer in 1957, 1959 and 1967 (£256,899). His main successes were:

2,000 Guineas: Crepello (1957); Royal Palace (1967)

1,000 Guineas: Queenpot (1948); Petite Etoile (1959); Fleet (1967); Caergwrle (1968); Altesse Royale (1971); Mysterious (1973)

Derby: Crepello (1957); St Paddy (1960); Royal Palace (1967)

Oaks: Carrozza (1957); Petite Etoile (1959); Lupe (1970); Altesse Royale (1971); Mysterious (1973)

St Leger: Ridge Wood (1949); St Paddy (1960); Aurelius (1961)

King George VI and Queen Elizabeth Stakes: Aunt Edith (1966); Busted (1967); Royal Palace (1968)

Eclipse Stakes: Arctic Explorer (1957); St Paddy (1961); Busted (1967); Royal Palace (1968); Connaught (1970)

Gold Cup: Twilight Alley (1963)

Champion Stakes: Hugh Lupus (1956); Petite Etoile (1959); Lorenzaccio (1970)

Coronation Cup: Petite Etoile (1960-61); Royal Palace (1968); Caliban (1970); Lupe (1971).

A tall, thin, anxious-looking man who took his responsibilities very seriously, Murless was a great stableman with a flair for understanding the characteristics and capabilities of each individual horse under his care. The interests of his horses came first, even when it involved making an unpopular decision.

On his retirement his stable was taken over by his son-in-law, Henry Cecil. Murless was knighted in June 1977 and elected to the Jockey Club the following month. Apart from being a steward at Newmarket and York, he concentrated on his own stud in Yorkshire and the Wood Ditton Stud in Newmarket, whose affairs he managed.

MURRAY, Anthony Patrick (b. 1950)

Tony Murray is a son of Paddy Murray who rode winners under National Hunt Rules for Reg Hobbs just after World War II. Tony had a good grounding in the hunting field and show-ring while in the school holidays he used to ride gallops for Captain Tim Forster at Letcombe Bassett. On leaving school in 1965 he was apprenticed to 'Frenchie' Nicholson and in May 1966 rode his first winner, at Windsor. It was on the same course two years later that his career almost came to an end, his jaw being broken in 48 places in a bad fall. He made a good recovery and in 1970 moved to Newmarket to be first jockey to Doug Smith. Two years later he joined Ryan Price in the same capacity and in 1972 had his best-ever season with 122 winners, including Ginevra in the Oaks. He won the St Leger for Price on Bruni in 1975. His other important wins at this stage included the Nunthorpe Stakes (Sandford Lad) and Gimcrack and Champagne Stakes (Giacometti).

After turning down one offer to go to France he signed for Charles Millbank at Chantilly in 1976 and rode there for three seasons before joining Adrian Maxwell in Ireland in 1979, the year he won the Irish 2,000 Guineas and Eclipse Stakes on Dickens Hill. The following season he rode Tyrnavos (Irish Sweeps Derby) and Cairn Rouge (Irish 1,000 Guineas and Champion Stakes), and in 1982 he returned to Newmarket to ride for Michael Albina. Weight was always a problem for him and the following year he decided to retire to take up training, but he was back in 1984 as stable jockey to Tom Jones at Newmarket and for him gained further big-race successes with At Talaq (Grand Prix de Paris), Al Bahathri (Irish 1,000 Guineas, short-head second in 1,000 Guineas) and Doulab (Gimcrack Stakes), as well as for Jimmy FitzGerald on Kayudee (Cesarewitch).

MUSIDORA
(1946, b f Nasrullah – Painted Vale, by Gainsborough)

Musidora was bred by Mr F.F. Tuthill and bought for 4,700 gns as a yearling by Mr N.P. Donaldson. Trained by Captain Charles Elsey, she won four races for £24,007, including the 1,000 Guineas and Oaks. As a broodmare she proved disappointing, appearing only once in the pedigree of a high-class horse, as the third dam of the champion miler Homing.

MUSSON, William James (b. 1949)

Having trained in estate management, Willie Musson began training horses under permit at Bramley, near Guildford, in 1976, took out a licence two years later and trained his first winner on the Flat with Dropshot at Leicester on 29 May 1978. When the lease on his stables ran out, he moved to Newmarket in 1981. His best horse has been Ore, winner of the Henry II Stakes and second in the Ascot Gold Cup, and his best season was 1985, with nineteen winners.

MY BABU
(1945, b c Djebel – Perfume II, by Badruddin)

My Babu, originally named Lérins, was bred in France by Mr Peter Beatty. He was trained by 'Sam' Armstrong and in the colours of HH the Maharaja of Baroda won 10½ races worth £29,830, including the Woodcote Stakes, New Stakes, Craven Stakes, 2,000 Guineas and Victoria Cup. He went to stud in Ireland in 1950 but in 1956 was sold to go to the United States for £214,000. He sired the 1955 2,000 Guineas winner Our Babu, as well as Be Careful (Gimcrack Stakes, Champagne Stakes) and Primera (Ebor Handicap). He did well in America, where he died in 1970.

MY DEAR
(1915, b f Beppo – Silesia, by Spearmint)

Owned and bred by Mr A.W. Cox and trained by Alec Taylor, My Dear won eight races worth £8,358, including the Oaks (on the disqualification of Stony Ford), Champion Stakes and Liverpool Autumn Cup. At stud she bred three winners of over £6,000 in stakes.

MY LOVE
(1945, b c Vatellor – For My Love, by Amfortas)

My Love, owned in partnership by the Aga Khan and M. Léon Volterra, was trained in France by Richard Carver. He brought off a great double in 1948 when he won both the Derby and the Grand Prix de Paris. He was not a success as a sire in France and was exported to Argentina in 1954. The Derby of 1948 was most remarkable, since the part-owners of My Love also owned the second, Royal Drake (M. Volterra) and the third, Noor (Aga Khan).

MYROBELLA
(1930, gr f Tetratema – Dolabella, by White Eagle)

Myrobella was 30 years of age when she died at the National Stud in 1960. A beautiful grey filly, she was leased for racing to Lord Lonsdale and trained by Fred Darling. She did not stay beyond 6f but nevertheless won eleven races and £16,142 in stakes. As a two-year-old she headed the Free Handicap, being rated 7lb superior to Hyperion. Among her victories were the National Breeders' Produce Stakes, Champagne Stakes and July Cup. At stud her winners included Big Game, who won the 2,000 Guineas and became a successful sire; and Snowberry, who won the Queen Mary Stakes and was dam of the St Leger winner Chamossaire, grandam of the Grand Prix de Saint-Cloud winner Hopeful Venture, and third dam of the Derby winner Snow Knight.

MYSTERIOUS
(1970, ch f Crepello – Hill Shade, by Hillary)

Winner of her only race as a two-year-old, Mysterious was unbeaten in her first three outings the following year, including the 1,000 Guineas and Oaks, was second to Dahlia in the Irish Oaks but recovered winning form in the Yorkshire Oaks. Bred by her American owner George A. Pope and trained by Noel Murless, she retired to stud after being beaten twice in the autumn of 1973 and was sent to the United States after foaling to Brigadier Gerard in 1975. She has bred four minor winners from her first seven foals.

N

NAGLE, Florence (b. 1894)

Mrs Nagle came into racing in 1920, when she 'trained' her first winners, but it was not until, largely through her courage and indomitable persistence, the racing authorities were finally persuaded to yield and granted women licences to train in 1966 that her skill was officially recognized, since her horses had to run in the name of her head lad. Among the races she won as an owner were the Liverpool St Leger and Midland Cambridgeshire, and her Sandsprite was second in the 1937 Derby. She retired from training at the end of 1976.

NAMING OF HORSES

A name cannot be registered for a horse unless it is at least a yearling, except in the case of horses foaled elsewhere than in Great Britain, Ireland or the Channel Islands, or if the horse is outside these countries at the date of registration.

A name can only be registered for a horse at the Racing Calendar Office, with the following description – age, colour and sex, and the registered name of sire and dam. The application for a name must be accompanied by a certificate of age and markings signed by a vet. The name must contain no more than eighteen characters or spaces, and restrictions laid down by the Jockey Club include those of certain celebrated horses, those comprising solely of initial letters or numbers and those of well-known persons who have not given permission for their use.

Confusion surrounding horses of the same name which has been applied for in different countries has been overcome by applying a letter code, to denote the country of origin, as a suffix. Thus the stallions Bold Lad (Ire) and Bold Lad (USA) can be distinguished. But there remains the difficulty among different generations, as in Caerleon, the colt foaled in 1927 who won the Eclipse Stakes, and the colt of the same name, foaled in 1980, who won the French Derby and Benson & Hedges Gold Cup.

A name cannot be changed once the horse has run.

NARRATOR
(1951, b c Nearco – Phase, by Windsor Lad)

Narrator won four races worth £6,451 for his owner-breeder Major L.B. Holliday, including the Champion Stakes and Coronation Cup. Syndicated for stud, he sired many good winners including Night Off (1,000 Guineas and Cheveley Park Stakes), Nortia (Lingfield Oaks Trial, Nassau Stakes and Magnet Cup) and Narratus (Great Metropolitan and Chester Cup). Narrator died in 1969.

NASRAM II
(1960, b c Nasrullah – La Mirambule, by Coaraze)

Nasram II, a half-brother to the Irish Sweeps Derby winner Tambourine, was bred in America, raced there unsuccessfully as a two-year-old and was brought to France at three years. He won twice for Etienne Pollet in 1963, and the following year, when trained by Ernie Fellows, gained his one success from eight starts in the King George VI and Queen Elizabeth Stakes, where his front-running style on fast ground proved too much for the odds-on Santa Claus. Nasram II was syndicated to stud in France and sired the German Derby and Grosser Preis von Baden winner Athenagoras and the French 2,000 Guineas winner Zug, as well as the successful American stallion Naskra.

NASRULLAH
(1940, b c Nearco – Mumtaz Begum, by Blenheim)

Bred by the Aga Khan, Nasrullah was trained by Frank Butters, and won the

Coventry Stakes as a two-year-old, beating the future Derby winner Straight Deal, but in a gruelling race for the Middle Park Stakes he went under by a neck to Lord Rosebery's game filly Ribbon. That race left a permanent mark on Nasrullah and subsequently his temperament was unreliable. As a three-year-old he wore blinkers and was reluctant to go down to the start. It was perhaps unfortunate that owing to war-time restrictions he raced only at Newmarket, a course he had come to dislike. He was fourth in the 2,000 Guineas, third in the Derby and won the Champion Stakes. On his day and in the right mood he was undoubtedly high class. In all he won £3,348 in stakes.

Having stood for one season in Britain at a fee of £198, he was bought in August 1944 by the British Bloodstock Agency on behalf of the 'Nasrullah Syndicate' which in fact consisted solely of Messrs G. McElligott and Bert Kerr. For 19,000gns they passed him on to Mr Joseph McGrath.

As a sire Nasrullah was outstandingly and consistently successful. He headed the list in 1951 and was twice second and twice third. He sired Musidora (1,000 Guineas and Oaks), Nearula (2,000 Guineas), Belle of All (1,000 Guineas), and Never Say Die (Derby and St Leger). One of his first crop of runners was Noor, who went to America and won $346,940, on three occasions beating the allegedly unbeatable Citation.

It was a great loss to the British breeding industry when in 1950 Mr A.B. Hancock bought Nasrullah on behalf of an American syndicate for $340,000. In the United States Nasrullah was as successful as in Britain. Five times he was champion sire and three times second. Among his best American winners were Nashua, 'Horse of the Year' for 1955, Leallah, champion two-year-old filly of 1956, Bold Ruler, 'Horse of the Year' for 1957, Nadir, champion two-year-old of 1957, and Bald Eagle, twice winner of the Washington D.C. International at Laurel.

Nasrullah died in 1959. His sons Red God, Grey Sovereign and Princely Gift have done well as sires in Britain and Ireland, while Never Say Die sired the Derby winner Larkspur and the dual Classic winner Never Too Late. Bold Ruler did outstandingly well as a sire in the United States where he was champion sire eight times. Nasrullah's son Never Bend sired the Derby winner Mill Reef.

NATIONAL STUD

In 1915 Colonel W.Hall Walker, later Lord Wavertree, presented his stud at Tully, Co Kildare, to the British nation for the purpose of forming the National Stud. As well as the stud, the gift comprised six stallions, 43 top-grade mares, some foals, yearlings and hunters, 300 head of cattle, carthorses, forage – in fact everything on the land, including the famous Japanese garden, and in the buildings, including furniture and pictures. The difference between bloodstock values at that period and those existing today is shown by the fact that the total value of all livestock there was estimated to be £74,000. The first Director of the National Stud was Sir Henry Greer, a former army officer with long experience as both owner and breeder.

During World War II the disadvantages of having the British National Stud located in Eire became increasingly apparent, and in 1944 all the land at Tully became vested in Ireland, whose government established their own national stud, while the livestock were transferred to the stud at Gillingham in Dorset that had originally been established by Lord Furness, who had died in 1940. In 1949 the National Stud leased 600 acres of land at West Grinstead as an overflow.

From its inception until 1963 the National Stud was under the authority of the Ministry of Agriculture, but on 1 April that year responsibility for the stud was taken over by the Levy Board. It was then decided that the National Stud should not go on breeding in opposition to commercial studs and that the future function of the stud should be to concentrate on the standing of stallions and the holding of shares in top-class syndicated stallions. Accordingly in 1964 the broodmares, yearling fillies and filly-foals were dispersed, the yearling colts and colt-foals being permitted to continue through their racing career on lease to the Queen in the normal manner. Before the war the National Stud used to lease colts and fillies for racing purposes to the late Lord Lonsdale; on his death they were leased to King George VI, and following his death, to the Queen.

At the same time it was decided to build a new National Stud at Newmarket on land taken on a 999-year lease from the Jockey Club. By private treaty the National Stud at Gillingham was sold to Mr Simon Wingfield Digby.

The first stallions Never Say Die and Tudor Melody moved into the stud in 1966, and the following year the new buildings were officially opened by the Queen.

Since its inception there have been five Directors of the National Stud: Sir Henry Greer (1916-33); Mr Noble Johnson (1934-7); Mr Peter Burrell (1937-71); Lt.-Col. Douglas Gray (1971-5) and Mr Michael Bramwell (1975 to date).

National Stud stallions for 1986 are: Blakeney, Star Appeal, Royal Palace, Final Straw, Homing (at Highclere Stud), Jalmood and Rousillon.

Among the good horses bred at the National Stud were Blandford (sire of four Derby winners), Royal Lancer (St Leger), Big Game (2,000 Guineas), Chamossaire (St Leger and champion sire), Sun Chariot (1,000 Guineas, Oaks and St Leger), Myrobella (eleven races worth over £16,000 and dam of Big Game), Annetta (Irish 1,000), Carrozza (Oaks), Hopeful Venture (Grand Prix de Saint-Cloud and Hardwicke Stakes) and The Panther (2,000 Guineas).

In November 1985 came the report of the Levy Board's committee of inquiry into the future of the National Stud, chaired by Sir John Sparrow. Called in the light of current trends, particularly the inability of the National Stud to compete with high international prices for stallions, the inquiry recommended that the National Stud should not be privatised or closed, but that it should be developed to stand both top-class and commercial stallions, should broaden its scope by purchasing two high-quality NH stallions, and should do more to educate students and potential stud managers. The inquiry

also recommended that the stud should be reconstituted as a trust, possibly with charitable status.

NATIONAL TRAINERS' FEDERATION

The National Trainers' Federation was formed in the mid-1970s by amalgamation of the National Hunt Trainers' Association (formed 1964) and National Trainers' Association (formed 1969). Its objects are to promote the interests of trainers and to encourage a close liaison with the Jockey Club and all organizations connected with racing.

Registered office: 42 Portman Square, London W1H OAP (01-935 2055).

President: Major M.Pope. Chief Executive: Lt.-Col. R.Mackaness.

NEARCO
(1935, br c Pharos – Nogara, by Havresac II)

Nearco was among the best of many great horses bred in Italy by Signor Federico Tesio at his Dormello Stud. Nearco was a horse of perfect size and great quality. He was the unbeaten winner of fourteen races, thirteen in his native country plus the Grand Prix de Paris, in which he trounced the Derby winner Bois Roussel. Thought not to be a true stayer, Nearco employed his superb class and brilliant speed to win over nearly 2m.

Bought as a stallion for £60,000 by the bookmaker Mr M.H.Benson, he proved an outstanding sire in Britain. He was twice champion sire and between 1942 and 1956 was never lower than eighth on the list. Among the good horses he got were Dante (Derby), Nimbus (2,000 Guineas and Derby), Sayajirao (St Leger), Masaka (Oaks) and Neasham Belle (Oaks). The Derby winners Tulyar and Arctic Prince were out of Nearco mares, as were Aggressor and Vaguely Noble.

Nearco has had immense influence on bloodstock breeding in Europe and the United States, especially through his son Nasrullah. The Derby winners Dante, Nimbus, Never Say Die, Larkspur, Royal

Palace, Sir Ivor, Nijinsky, Mill Reef, Roberto, The Minstrel, Shirley Heights, Henbit, Golden Fleece, Secreto and Slip Anchor all have Nearco in the sire line.

NEARULA
(1950, b c Nasrullah – Respite, by Flag of Truce)

Nearula was bought for 3,000gns as a yearling by Captain Charles Elsey acting on behalf of Mr W.Humble. He was a very good two-year-old and won the Middle Park Stakes by four lengths. The following season he won the 2,000 Guineas by four lengths but his Derby preparation was interrupted by an injury to his foot and he was unplaced at Epsom behind Pinza. However, he won the St James's Palace Stakes and the Champion Stakes. Altogether he won seven races and £27,351 in stakes. His stud career was of brief duration as he died of a ruptured blood vessel in 1960 but he sired a Classic winner in Kythnos (Irish 2,000 Guineas).

NEASHAM BELLE
(1948, b f Nearco – Phase, by Windsor Lad)

Owned and bred by Major L.B.Holliday, Neasham Belle was a sister of the Champion and Eclipse Stakes winner Narrator. She won two races worth £15,630, including the Oaks. As a broodmare she proved disappointing, with three minor winners to her credit before she died in November 1971.

NEBBIOLO
(1974, ch c Yellow God – Novara, by Birkhahn)

Nebbiolo was put into training in Ireland with Kevin Prendergast by his breeder Niels Schibbye after he had been led out of the yearling sales unsold at 1,900gns, and his six wins included the 2,000 Guineas and Gimcrack Stakes. He also finished second in the Middle Park Stakes and third in the Irish 2,000 Guineas. He started at 20-1 for the Newmarket Classic and did not win again. He retired to stud in Ireland in 1978 but died two years later. From his limited opportunities he did well, his best winners including

Nepula (Hoover Fillies' Mile), Santella Man (Queen's Vase), Superlative (July Stakes and Flying Childers Stakes) and Alianna (second in Irish 1,000 Guineas).

NEIL GOW
(1907, ch c Marco – Chelandry, by Goldfinch)

Neil Gow was owned and bred by Lord Rosebery and was a beautiful chestnut horse, difficult to fault except for rather weak hocks. He was by nature high-mettled, inclined to be troublesome at the start, and gave his trainer many anxious moments. He was a brilliant two-year-old, his wins including the Champagne Stakes, and in 1910 he won the 2,000 Guineas, Danny Maher riding a superb race to beat Lemberg by a short head. Before the Derby, Neil Gow sprang a curb, missed his final gallop and was fourth to Lemberg. He met Lemberg again in the Eclipse Stakes and after a wonderful race they ran a dead-heat. In his St Leger preparation Neil Gow broke down and never ran again. He died after eight seasons at stud but nevertheless made a name for himself as a successful sire of broodmares. Of his sons, the Cambridgeshire winner Re-echo did extremely well as a sire in Argentina.

NELSON, Charles Robert (b. 1955)

Charlie Nelson worked for his father, Major Peter Nelson, and Tom Jones before beginning training in 1977 at the family's Upper Lambourn stables. His first winner was with Christmas Light at Pontefract on 18 July 1977. His first top-class horse was Millingdale Lillie (Fred Darling Stakes and second in Irish 1,000 Guineas), but the high-spot of his career was in 1983, when he won more than £100,000 in stakes with horses including Creag-an-Sgor in the Middle Park and Mahogany. Numerically his best season was 1980, with 32 winners.

NELSON, Major Peter Maurice (b. 1913)

From Marlborough and the RMC, where he distinguished himself at cricket and racquets, Peter Nelson joined the Royal Berkshire Regiment and was a regular soldier for fourteen years. He took out a trainer's licence in 1947 and, once established, was consistently successful, gaining his sole Classic win with Snow Knight in the 1974 Derby. Other good races he won included the Stewards' Cup, Coventry Stakes, Queen Mary Stakes, City and Suburban, Yorkshire Cup, King's Stand Stakes and Nunthorpe Stakes. His best horses included Whistler, Firestreak, Victorina, Knockroe and Bay Express. When he retired early in 1976, his son John took over his stables in Upper Lambourn for a year before his second son Charlie moved in.

NEOCRACY
(1944, b f Nearco – Harina, by Blandford)

Neocracy was the dam of two high-class horses, Tulyar (Derby, St Leger, Eclipse and King George VI and Queen Elizabeth Stakes) and Saint Crespin III (Imperial Produce Stakes, Eclipse Stakes and Prix de l'Arc de Triomphe). She won two of her five races and in all bred nine winners.

NESBITT, Stephen (1930-82)

Stephen Nesbitt was apprenticed to H.Lowe. He took out a trainer's licence in 1966 at Diggle, near Oldham, but moved to Ripon in 1971 and to Middleham in 1977. With a small stable of mainly moderate horses, his best winner was Ubedizzy, a useful sprinter. When he died in 1982, the licence was taken over by his widow Myra and in 1985 it passed to his son-in-law George Moore when the stable was bought by the football-pools winner Mr George Dawes.

NEVER SAY DIE
(1951, ch c Nasrullah – Singing Grass, by War Admiral)

Bred in the United States by Mr Robert Sterling Clark, though conceived in Ireland, Never Say Die was sent to Britain to be trained by Joe Lawson at Newmarket. Though a useful two-year-old, he appeared to be well below Classic

standard. However, he made immense improvement as a three-year-old and, ridden by Lester Piggott, then eighteen years of age, he won the Derby at 33-1 by two lengths. In the King Edward VII Stakes at Ascot he was beaten in a rough race, after which Piggott was suspended for the rest of the season. With Charlie Smirke in the saddle, he won the St Leger, his final race, by twelve lengths. As a token of his regard for the British Turf, Mr Clark presented Never Say Die to the National Stud. Though not consistently successful at stud, Never Say Die was champion sire in 1962, when his son Larkspur won the Derby. Never Say Die also sired a winner of the 1,000 Guineas and Oaks in Never Too Late, but his record went into decline after Larkspur. Never Say Die was put down in 1975, when his produce had won 309 races in Britain for a total of £400,527.

NEVER TOO LATE II
(1957, ch f Never Say Die – Gloria Nicky, by Alycidon)

Bred in America and trained in France by Etienne Pollet for Mrs Howell E.Jackson, Never Too Late II won the 1,000 Guineas and Oaks in 1960. She was also second in the Champion Stakes and won three races in France. She was retired to stud in America and bred six winners, including Fall In Love (second in the Cheveley Park Stakes) and Without Fear (leading sire in Australia).

NEVETT, William

When he rode Owen Tudor to victory in the Derby in 1941, Billy Nevett was a private in the Royal Army Ordnance Corps. Born in Lancashire, he was apprenticed to Dobson Peacock at Middleham in 1916 and became the outstanding rider in the North. He rode his thousandth winner in 1940. He won the Derby again on Ocean Swell in 1944 and for the third time on Dante in 1945. All his three Derby wins were gained in war-substitute races at Newmarket. His other Classic success was on the Aga Khan's Masaka in the 1948 Oaks. Runner-up to Gordon Richards four times in the jockeys' table, he had his best season in 1938 with 122 winners. On retirement at the end of 1956 he trained for a time at Ripon but soon found it considerably less profitable than riding and wisely gave it up.

NEWBURY

Newbury racecourse was primarily the inspiration, during his retirement, of John Porter, who had trained for many years at neighbouring Kingsclere. When travelling to London by rail, he often noticed a level stretch of land just south of the railway that seemed ideal for a racecourse. Mr L.H. Baxendale of Greenham was prepared to sell the land, but when Porter approached the Jockey Club with his plan, they proved coldly discouraging, and but for strong support from King Edward VII, once a patron of Porter's stable, the project would very likely have been dropped.

Fifty-six miles from London, Newbury owed much in the past to the excellence of the railway service, while the proximity of so many Berkshire and Wiltshire stables has always ensured a plentiful supply of runners. The general level of the sport is high, and the programmes are carefully thought out. The executive gives the impression of making every endeavour to please racegoers, and improvements, not least in the cheap enclosures, are constantly being made. It is not surprising that Newbury enjoys considerable popularity with the racegoing public.

It is arguable that Newbury's most popular race is a steeplechase, the Hennessy Cognac Gold Cup. On the Flat the Spring, Summer and Autumn Cups are well-established handicaps over 1m, 1½m and 1m 5f 60yd respectively. The Greenham Stakes is a significant trial for the 2,000 Guineas, and the Fred Darling Stakes an equivalent for the 1,000 Guineas, while the Lockinge Stakes is one of the most important mile races of the season.

During World War II Newbury became an important depot for military stores, and the whole racecourse was covered with roads, railway lines and vast stretches of concrete. It seemed improbable at the time that racing could ever take place there again, but as soon as hostilities were over, the task of clearing up was tackled with such commendable energy and determination that racing was resumed in 1949. Newbury's post-war recovery, its many improvements and the quality of the sport provided owed, and still owes, much to that shrewd and experienced racing official Mr Geoffrey Freer, for many years Clerk of the Course and now commemorated in a Pattern race run in August.

NEWCASTLE

The Newcastle course is attractively laid out in Gosforth Park. The amenities are modern and excellent. The track itself has the reputation of being a stiff one, particularly when the going is heavy. It is a left-handed circuit of 1m 6f with a run-in of just about 4f. The turns are well banked and can be taken at speed, thereby offering no respite for a tiring horse. The last 4f, except for the final 200yd which are level, is uphill. Stamina and resolution are the qualities a horse needs here.

The big race of the year is the Northumberland Plate, a 2m handicap which draws a very big crowd. Popularly known as the Pitmen's Derby, it was sponsored for a time in recent years by the coal industry, and remains one of the season's richest handicaps.

NEWMARKET

Newmarket is the headquarters of British Flat racing. Racing has been conducted there since the days of the Stuarts. In the time of James I hunting and hawking took pride of place over racing, but Charles II was a racing enthusiast and is the only king of England to have won a race on the Flat with himself as rider. He founded the Newmarket Town Plate and won it on two occasions. The famous Rowley Mile is named after him, as 'Old Rowley' was his nickname, derived from his favourite hack who bore that name.

Not only is Newmarket the main training centre but it is also the home of racing's governing body, the Jockey Club, whose premises are in the High Street. The Jockey Club owns Newmarket Heath and the two racecourses, thanks largely to the foresight and generosity of the fourth Duke of Portland, who was a member of the club for over 50 years and died at an advanced age in 1854. The main races run at Newmarket are the 2,000 Guineas and 1,000 Guineas at the Spring Meeting; the Middle Park Stakes and Cambridgeshire at the October Meeting; and the Dewhurst Stakes, Champion Stakes and Cesarewitch at the Houghton Meeting, also held in October. These races are all run on the Rowley Mile course. The July course was kept going during World War II and all the Classic races were run there bar the St Leger in 1940, 1941 and 1945. The first Classic races to be sponsored in Britain were run there in 1984, when both Guineas were backed by the General Accident insurance company.

Newmarket racecourse as a whole is shaped roughly like the letter Y with straight arms and the tail bent to the right. The tail is represented by the Beacon course which turns right at the junction into the July course on the right and the Rowley Mile course on the left.

The Rowley Mile course is one of the best, fairest and most testing in the country and is used for all except the summer meetings. All races up to 1m 2f inclusive are perfectly straight, with little rise or fall as far as 'the Bushes', about 2f from the finish. From that point the course runs downhill for a furlong to 'the Dip', the final furlong being uphill. Races exceeding 1m 2f start on the Beacon course and have a right-hand turn into the straight.

The surroundings at Newmarket tend to be severe and until recently amenities verged on the spartan; hence the money spent to try to give a 'cosier' atmosphere. Both the Rowley Mile course and the July course were laid out before the days when spectators came into the reckoning. Because of this much of the running in the Cesarewitch, for example, cannot be seen from the stands; in fact, watching that event has been described as 'hanging about in Suffolk to see a race that is run in Cambridgeshire.' As a palliative, the Sefton course was opened in 1958 but it was not popular and fell into disuse after 1974.

The lengths of the various courses are:
Rous course: 5f
Bretby course: 6f
Dewhurst Stakes course: 7f
Rowley Mile course: 1m
Cambridgeshire course: 1m 1f
Across the Flat: 1m 2f
Cesarewitch course: 2m 2f, 2m, 1m 6f, 1m 4f, finishing Across the Flat.

July course

Meetings in June, July and August are held on this charming course, which has a pleasant paddock with plenty of trees for shade. All races up to 1m inclusive are straight with a steadily increasing downhill gradient after 2f, the final furlong being uphill. Races of 1m 2f or over start on the Beacon course, turning right into the straight mile. The lengths of the courses are:
Chesterfield course: 5f
Bunbury Mile: 1m, 7f, 6f
Suffolk Stakes course: 1m 4f, 1m 2f
Summer course: 2m 24yd, 1m 6f 171yd

With extensive building work due to be carried out on the grandstands in 1986, all meetings for that year after the Guineas were scheduled to be staged on the July course.

NEWNES, William Anthony Paul (b. 1959)

Less than two years after winning a British Classic for the first time, Billy Newnes had his riding career halted by a three-year ban from the Jockey Club for accepting a £1,000 bribe from a professional punter, Harry Bardsley, who was warned off for 15 years for his part in the affair. In January 1984 Newnes was found guilty by the Jockey Club disciplinary committee for passing information to Bardsley regarding the chance of his mount Valuable Witness at Royal Ascot in 1983. The previous year Newnes, while with Henry Candy, was the leading apprentice, his career-best total of 57 winners including Time Charter's successes in the 1,000 Guineas and Champion Stakes, Crime of Passion's win in the Cherry Hinton Stakes and Quilted's victory in the Princess of Wales's Stakes. He missed the ride on Time Charter in the King George

VI and Queen Elizabeth Stakes in 1983 after a bad accident on the gallops, during which he was given the kiss of life, and suspension cost him further major wins on the filly in 1984. He remained in Candy's yard as a stable lad during his ban, which was considered by the Jockey Club disciplinary committee in February 1986, when it was reduced by six months to enable him to re-apply for a jockey's licence from 1 July 1986. Newnes rode his first winner on Pledge at Ascot on 29 April 1978.

NICHOLLS, David (b. 1956)

David Nicholls served his apprenticeship in Yorkshire with the Bastiman family and Clifford Watts and rode his first winner, Hunting Tower, at Chester on 13 July 1973. He rode 22 winners in 1977 but his average was in single figures until he began to ride regularly for David Chapman, for whom he rode the marvellous filly Soba; the Stewards' Cup was among their eleven successes together in 1982. The exploits of Soba got Nicholls noticed and he had his best season in 1984 with 47 winners. Breaking his leg playing football in the New Year 1985 threatened to halt his run, but he missed only a few weeks of the season and ended with 44 winners.

NICHOLSON, Herbert Charles Denton (1913-84)

'Frenchie' Nicholson was born in France where his father was huntsman to a French pack. He was apprenticed firstly to Charles Clout in France for three years and then he came to Britain, where he was six years with Stanley Wootton's stable at Epsom. Broad and strongly built, he was too heavy for the Flat but became a leading rider under National Hunt Rules, winning the Gold Cup and Champion Hurdle and twice riding four winners in a day at Cheltenham.

He began training at Cheltenham in 1946 and conducted a 'mixed' stable there until retiring in 1979 because of ill health. He deservedly earned a reputation as a fine trainer of young riders; his son David was a leading performer under National Hunt Rules, while Paul Cook,

Tony Murray, Pat Eddery and Walter Swinburn were among his apprentices.

NICK

Certain lines of thoroughbred blood appear to have an affinity for, and to produce particularly good results when mated to other specific lines. This phenomenon is usually termed a 'nick'. Earlier this century Phalaris did particularly well when mated with mares by Chaucer, and more recently many top-class horses have resulted from the mating of Nasrullah and his sons with mares by Princequillo, the best examples being Mill Reef, Secretariat and Seattle Slew.

NIGHT HAWK (1910, b c Gallinule – Jean's Folly, by Ayrshire)

Night Hawk won one race, the St Leger at 50-1, for Lord Wavertree. He was exported to Australia.

NIGHTINGALL, Walter (1895-1968)

Walter Nightingall came from a famous Epsom racing family. His father, whom he succeeded at the South Hatch stable at Epsom, was a successful trainer, and two Nightingalls rode winners of the Grand National. Walter Nightingall himself was apprenticed to his father. He took out a trainer's licence in 1926 when his father died, and his career was one of consistent success. Altogether he trained over 1,800 winners, having many victories under National Hunt Rules between the wars. He won the Derby in 1943 with Miss Dorothy Paget's Straight Deal and the 2,000 Guineas in 1965 with Mr W.Harvey's Niksar. After World War II he was appointed trainer to Sir Winston Churchill, for whom he won good races with Colonist II, High Hat, Vienna, Welsh Abbot and Tudor Monarch. He was a modest, friendly man of considerable charm; his horses were always out to win, and throughout his career he served the Turf with distinction.

NIGHT OFF
(1962, b f Narrator – Persuader, by Petition)

Bred and owned by Major L.B. Holliday, Night Off won the Cheveley Park Stakes in 1964 and the following year the 1,000 Guineas when trained by Walter Wharton. She bred three winners, the best being her first foal, Madame's Share, a useful two-year-old in 1970.

NIJINSKY
(1967, b c Northern Dancer – Flaming Page, by Bull Page)

No horse has done more to advance the status of Northern Dancer than his son Nijinsky. Bred in Canada by Edward Taylor and bought as a yearling by Charles Engelhard for $84,000, Nijinsky was trained by Vincent O'Brien in Ireland. He was an outstanding racehorse, winning all five races at two years, including the Dewhurst Stakes, and the Triple Crown at three, the first to do so since Bahram in 1935. He also won the Irish Sweeps Derby but after the St Leger met his first defeat, in the Prix de l'Arc de Triomphe, where he finished second to Sassafras. Had he won the Arc, he would have been retired, but he ran once more, and was again second, to Lorenzaccio in the Champion Stakes.

Nijinsky did not race after the Champion Stakes and went to stud in Kentucky with a valuation of almost $5.5m (then the equivalent of £2.25m), with shares trading at $170,000. In 1984 a nomination to Nijinsky (not a share) cost $450,000, such had been his success. Much of that had been due to the interest of Robert Sangster, whose chief yearling adviser, Vincent O'Brien, has trained many of Nijinsky's best offspring, including the Classic winners Golden Fleece (Derby), Caerleon (French Derby) and Kings Lake (Irish 2,000 Guineas), as well as Solford (Eclipse Stakes). Nijinsky's latest Classic winner is Shadeed (2,000 Guineas), following Caucasus (Irish St Leger), Green Dancer (French 2,000 Guineas) and Niniski (Irish St Leger), as well as the Oaks thirds African Dancer and Leap Lively. Green Dancer, Niniski and Quiet Fling (Coronation Cup) have raised Nijinsky to the status of a significant sire of sires, and in the United States his most recent Grade One stakes winners include the fillies Bemissed, De La Rose and Folk Art, and the colts Hostage, Nijinsky's Secret and Vision.

NIKSAR
(1962, ch c Le Haar – Niskampe, by Shikampur)

Niksar was bred in France by the Marquis de Nicolay and was bought for £4,650 at the Deauville Yearling Sales by Walter Nightingall, acting on behalf of Mr Wilfred Harvey, well known in the printing and publishing world. Niksar won the Kempton 2,000 Guineas Trial and the 2,000 Guineas and was fourth in the Derby and third in the Champion Stakes. At the close of his three-year-old career, he was sold for export to Australia.

NIMBUS
(1946, b c Nearco – Kong, by Baytown)

Nimbus was bred by Mr William Hill and sold for 5,000gns as a yearling to George Colling, who was acting on behalf of Mr H.A. Glenister, an official of the Midland Bank who gave Nimbus as a birthday present to his wife. As a two-year-old Nimbus showed high promise, and the following season he won the 2,000 Guineas and Derby, both by very narrow margins. It was the first time that the racecourse camera decided the Derby result. Apart from having a walk-over for a race at Haydock, Nimbus never ran after Epsom. He hardly came up to expectations as a sire and was exported to Japan in 1962. His best sons were Nucleus, second in the St Leger, and the Coronation Cup winner Nagami, while mares by Nimbus produced the smart sprinter African Sky and the Preakness Stakes winner Greek Money.

NOBLESSE
(1960, ch f Mossborough – Duke's Delight, by His Grace)

A brilliant filly at her best, Noblesse was bred by Mrs P.G. Margetts and as a yearling was bought on behalf of the American owner Mrs J.M. Olin for 4,200gns. Trained by Paddy Prendergast, she won four races and over £46,000 in prize money, her victories being the Blue Seal Stakes, Timeform Gold Cup, Musidora Stakes and Oaks. Her win in the 1963 Oaks was one of the easiest recorded in that event as she won in a canter by ten lengths. She went to stud in America, and all her five foals were winners, including Where You Lead, who finished second in the Oaks and bred Slightly Dangerous, also second in the Oaks.

NOCTURNAL SPREE
(1972, gr f Supreme Sovereign – Night Attire, by Shantung)

Nocturnal Spree, who cost 6,200gns as a yearling, ran only four times and won twice, a maiden race at The Curragh and the 1,000 Guineas at Newmarket. She split a pastern following her only race as a two-year-old, and after getting home first in a blanket finish for her Classic victory, she was fourth in the Irish equivalent. She split a pastern again in the summer and was retired to stud after being sold for 96,000gns at the 1975 Newmarket December Sales. Her first two foals were minor winners.

NOMINATIONS, Void

For many years the Jockey Club were worried by the question of nominations rendered void by the death of an owner. Backed by legal opinion, the Jockey Club had always acted on the principle that fees and forfeits incurred for horses entered under their rules could not be recovered under process of law, because if they were contracts, they were contracts by way of gambling and wagering, and thus without legal sanction. If a living owner evaded his forfeit liabilities, his name was published in the forfeit list in the *Racing Calendar*. As that deterrent could hardly be inflicted with decency on a dead man or on his executors, the 'Void Nominations' rule came into existence, stipulating that when an owner died, all entries for his horses ceased to exist.

The matter was under discussion in 1927 when Mr Edgar Wallace, the well-known author and journalist and a very keen racing man, suggested a 'friendly' action between the Jockey Club and himself. It was agreed that Mr Wallace should be sued in the High Court for the recovery of £4 in respect of a horse of his entered at Newmarket. In the Chancery Court the verdict was in favour of Mr Wallace, much to his disappointment, as when the action was pending he could not run any of his horses, since if he by chance won a race, the £4 in dispute would have been automatically appropriated. The case then was taken to the Court of Appeal where the Master of the Rolls and Lords Justices Lawrence and Russell found in favour of the Jockey Club. All expenses incurred by Mr Wallace were paid by the Jockey Club.

The change in the rule made possible by this action was carried through in 1929 and came in time for the 1931 Derby winner Cameronian, whose owner-breeder Lord Dewar died in April 1930 leaving the colt to his nephew Mr J.A.Dewar. Under the old rules nominations for Cameronian, including that in the Derby, would have been rendered void on Lord Dewar's death.

NOMINATOR

The 'nominator' is the person in whose name a horse is entered for a race.

NONOALCO
(1971, b c Nearctic – Seximee, by Hasty Road)

Nonoalco was bought as a yearling in the United States for $30,000 by an Englishman, George Blackwell, on behalf of a Mexican, Mme Maria-Felix Berger, to be trained in France by François Boutin; and he gained his most important success in Britain, in the 2,000 Guineas. His six other wins included the Prix

Morny and Prix de la Salamandre as a two-year-old and the Prix Jacques le Marois at three. He was reported to have been injured in the Prix du Moulin and did not race again. He spent one season at stud in France before going to Ireland in 1976, and was exported to Japan in 1981. A top-class miler at his best, he has sired similar good horses in the Classic winners Melyno (French 2,000 Guineas) and Katies (Irish 1,000 Guineas and Coronation Stakes), as well as Noalcoholic and Capricorn Belle.

NORFOLK, Lavinia, Duchess of (b. 1916)

A successful point-to-point rider before her marriage and a fine rider to hounds, Lavinia, Duchess of Norfolk knows every aspect of the racing game and has the reputation of an extremely shrewd judge both of a yearling and of the form-book. She took a keen personal interest in the running of the Arundel stable but her colours have not been prominent following the death of her husband in 1975.

Racing colours: sky blue and scarlet check, sky blue sleeves and scarlet cap.

NORFOLK, 16th Duke of (1908-75)

The Duke of Norfolk served first in the Royal Horse Guards and later in the Royal Sussex Regiment. For many years a member of the Jockey Club, he earned the reputation of being a thoroughly sound and extremely conscientious administrator. Apart from serving as a steward of the Jockey Club and as vice-chairman of the Turf Board, he headed the Norfolk Committee on the future pattern of racing and also a committee appointed to inquire into the problem of doping. He was Her Majesty's representative at Ascot from 1952 to 1972, during which time two new grandstands were built on the course and the quality of racing was constantly upgraded. His stewardship was not without controversy, particularly after a speech made over the racecourse public address system, to which Lord Wigg in particular took exception. He was also

drawn into public discussion after the Salisbury stewards reported the running of his filly Skyway to the Jockey Club stewards in 1970.

There were few more enthusiastic owner-breeders, and shortly before his death he had his greatest success when Ragstone won the Ascot Gold Cup. His other good winners included Ragtime, Sovereign Lord and Skymaster, while his post-war trainers at Arundel were the father and son William and Gordon Smyth and John Dunlop.

NORTHERN BABY (1976, b c Northern Dancer – Two Rings, by Round Table)

Bred in Canada, sold in the United States as a yearling for $120,000 and trained in France by François Boutin, Northern Baby gained the most significant of his five wins when he beat Town and Country in the Champion Stakes as a three-year-old. He was not so good at four years and was retired to stud in Ireland for one season before being exported to the United States in 1981. His first crop included the St James's Palace Stakes winner Bairn.

NORTON, Stephen Geoffrey (b. 1937)

Steve Norton comes from a South Yorkshire farming background and began training as a permit-holder, winning his first race, a selling hurdle, in 1966. He took out his first Flat-race licence in 1969 to train at Silkstone, near Barnsley, but began to make his presence felt when in the late 1970s he moved to a new yard built on the American barn principle at nearby High Hoyland. With the new yard came new owners, attracted by Norton's frequent trips to North America which brought US-bred yearlings to the stable for the first time in 1978. The best winner from that source was Full Extent (Gimcrack), and he was later to win important races with Goodbye Shelley (Prix Marcel Boussac) and Leysh (Cambridgeshire, beating stablemate Morwray Boy). Numerically his best season was 1982, with 49 winners.

NOTTINGHAM

No race of more than a passing significance is run at this long-established Midlands course, but sport there is usually quite brisk. The track is a left-handed circuit of about 1½m, which joins the straight mile about 4⅝f from the winning-post. The turns are reasonably easy, but in general the course is more suitable for a sharp, well-balanced horse than for a long-striding one. The few gradients are of a minor nature.

Nottingham Corporation bought the course in 1965 and three years later agreed to lease it to Racecourse Holdings Trust, thus ensuring the future of racing there.

NUMBER CLOTH

Every horse running in a race carries a saddlecloth bearing a number corresponding with that on the race-card. The cloth is given to the jockey when he weighs out and must be worn so that the number is clearly visible. Immediately he has weighed in after the race, he gives the number cloth to the official appointed to receive it.

NUNTHORPE STAKES

The traditional major 5f race run at the York August meeting began life in 1903 as a selling race, became a non-seller in 1922 and was renamed the William Hill Sprint Championship in 1976.

NUREYEV
(1977, b c Northern Dancer – Special, by Forli)

Nureyev was in the news from the day he was sold in the United States as a yearling for $1.3m to the day he was disqualified after passing the post first in the 2,000 Guineas on what proved to be his last public appearance. He first went into training with Peter Walwyn, but before he ran, owner Stavros Niarchos moved him to François Boutin in France. He won his only race as a two-year-old, and his one race before the Guineas, where he was controversially placed last because his jockey, Paquet, hampered and almost brought down the unplaced Posse 2f out. The race was awarded to Known Fact, who had had a clear run through the race. A viral infection kept Nureyev off the course during the summer, and he stood one season at stud in France, in 1981, before being exported to the United States. His first crop included the Irish Sweeps Derby runner-up Theatrical.

NURSERY

A nursery is a handicap confined to two-year-olds. Under Jockey Club Rules nurseries cannot take place before 1 July; top weight shall be not less than 9st 7lb and bottom weight not less than 7st 7lb.

O

O'BRIEN, David (b. 1956)

Son of Vincent O'Brien, David trained in accountancy for almost five years before becoming assistant to his father. He began training in a part of his father's yard in 1981, and his first batch of horses included Assert, winner of the Irish and French Derbys and the Benson & Hedges Gold Cup as a three-year-old. In 1984 he won the Epsom Derby, beating his father by a short head when Secreto got up to catch El Gran Señor, and in 1985 he won the Irish 2,000 Guineas with the filly Triptych.

O'BRIEN, Michael Vincent (b. 1917)

Vincent O'Brien's career has not been without its dramas and reverses, for he twice had his licence withdrawn by the Irish authorities, in 1954 for the inconsistent running of four jumpers and in 1960 after a dope test on Chamour, proved positive. But it is probably true to say that he is the greatest trainer in Irish racing history.

He rode a few winners as an amateur and took out a licence to train in 1944. At first his stable was concerned with National Hunt racing and he proved wonderfully skilful with steeplechasers and hurdlers, winning the Grand National three times, the Cheltenham Gold Cup four times and the Champion Hurdle three times. In the 1950s he turned his attention to the Flat with conspicuously successful results, mainly through the patronage of Robert Sangster and a combination of American owners and American-bred horses. His big wins in Britain are:

2,000 Guineas: Sir Ivor (1968); Nijinsky (1970); Lomond (1983); El Gran Señor (1984)

1,000 Guineas: Glad Rags (1966)

Derby: Larkspur (1962); Sir Ivor (1968); Nijinsky (1970); Roberto (1972); The Minstrel (1977); Golden Fleece (1982)

Oaks: Long Look (1965); Valoris (1966)

St Leger: Ballymoss (1957); Nijinsky (1970); Boucher (1972)

Coronation Cup: Ballymoss (1958); Roberto (1973)

Ascot Gold Cup: Gladness (1958)

Eclipse Stakes: Ballymoss (1958); Pieces of Eight (1966); Artaius (1977); Solford (1983); Sadler's Wells (1984)

King George VI and Queen Elizabeth Stakes: Ballymoss (1958); Nijinsky (1970); The Minstrel (1977)

Champion Stakes: Pieces of Eight (1966); Sir Ivor (1968)

Benson & Hedges Gold Cup: Roberto (1972); Caerleon (1983).

In France he has won the Prix de l'Arc de Triomphe with Ballymoss and twice with Alleged, the Derby with Caerleon, and the Grand Critérium with Sir Ivor. He has been leading trainer in Britain twice, in 1966 and 1977, and built a remarkable record in the Dewhurst Stakes, winning seven times between 1969 and 1983. The first five were ridden by Lester Piggott and the last two by Pat Eddery, while the last five ran in the colours of Robert Sangster.

Small, trim and self-possessed, O'Brien is first and foremost a perfectionist. No trouble is too great as far as the well-being of his horses is concerned, and on occasion this has led to rather less than harmonious relations with the Press.

OCEAN SWELL
(1941, b c Blue Peter – Jiffy, by Hurry On)

Bred and owned by Lord Rosebery, Ocean Swell is the only horse this century to have won the Derby and the Ascot Gold Cup. Trained by Jack Jarvis, he won a war-substitute Derby at Newmarket in 1944 and the Gold Cup the following year. He had not proved a stud success when he died after an accident in 1954.

OFFICIALS, Licences for

The following officials require a licence granted annually by the stewards of the Jockey Club: clerk of the course, handicapper, clerk of the scales, judge, starter and assistant, veterinary officer and assistant, stewards' secretary, inspector of courses, director of security and investigation officer of Racecourse Security Services, chief inspector and inspector of security, and jockeys' valet.

The clerk of the course is appointed for every meeting by the executive of that meeting, subject to the approval of the stewards, and is paid by the executive. All other officials are appointed for every meeting by the stewards of the Jockey Club and with the exception of veterinary officers are paid by the Jockey Club. No two offices for the same fixture can be held without permission from the stewards of the Jockey Club.

The Jockey Club stakeholders are stakeholders for all meetings.

Complaints against an official have to be made to the stewards in writing, signed by the complainant.

O'GORMAN, William Andrew (b. 1948)

Having ridden as an amateur on the Flat and as a professional over jumps, Bill O'Gorman was pitched into training on the death of his father Paddy in 1969. He had his first winner with Golden Masquerade at Newmarket on 28 June 1969, victory coming on a disqualification. A new ruling by the Jockey Club allowed trainers to ride their horses as professionals and O'Gorman became the first to take advantage when he won on Scarlet Wonder at Newmarket on 15 April 1975. In his first season training he won the Stewards' Cup with Royal Smoke, but things did not take off for his stable until 1977, when he began a reputation for multiple wins by taking seven races with Manor Farm Boy. Since then other prolific winners have been Abdu (nine), Brondesbury (six) and Provideo (sixteen). O'Gorman's best

horses have been sprinters, and he has won the Flying Childers Stakes (Superlative) and King's Stand Stakes (Sayf El Arab), while On Stage, Sayyaf and Mummy's Game have been other good sprinters. Numerically his best season was 1982, with 49 winners.

O'GORMAN, William Gerard (1913-69)

Paddy O'Gorman trained first at Exning from 1953, then at Newmarket from 1960. His best horses were Drum Beat (King's Stand Stakes), Epaulette (Stewards' Cup), Majority Rule (King's Stand Stakes) and Golden Horus (Gimcrack Stakes). He also won the Northumberland Plate, Britannia Stakes and Newbury Spring Cup. He died very suddenly in 1969 and the stable was taken over by his son, Bill O'Gorman.

OH SO SHARP (1982, ch f Kris – Oh So Fair, by Graustark)

Oh So Sharp, trained by Henry Cecil, was the first major British winner bred by Sheikh Mohammed, and his first Classic winner. She won all three races as a two-year-old, including the Hoover Fillies' Mile, and completed the fillies' Triple Crown at three – the 1,000 Guineas, Oaks and St Leger. Between her last two Classic successes she lost her unbeaten record to the colts Petoski (King George VI and Queen Elizabeth Diamond Stakes) and Commanche Run (Benson & Hedges Gold Cup), finishing second by less than a length each time. She was retired to stud after the St Leger.

OLDHAM, Gerald Anthony (b. 1925)

Gerry Oldham, an international financier living in Switzerland, served four years in the Coldstream Guards. Among the good horses he has owned are Lucero (Irish 2,000 Guineas), Talgo (Irish Derby), Fidalgo (Irish Derby and Chester Vase), Cynara (Queen Mary Stakes), Miralgo (Timeform Gold Cup and Hardwicke Stakes), Sovrango (Ormonde Stakes twice and Chester Vase), Espresso

(Grosser Preis von Baden twice and Vaux Gold Tankard), Salvo (Vaux Gold Tankard, Hardwicke Stakes, Yorkshire Cup, Grosser Preis von Baden and second in the Prix de l'Arc de Triomphe), Chicago (Cumberland Lodge Stakes and Gran Premio del Jockey Club, Milan), Intermezzo (St Leger), Stintino (third in the Derby) and Zino (2,000 Guineas), but his best-known runner was Sagaro, whom he bred and who is the only horse to win the Ascot Gold Cup three times. His early successes were as a patron of Harry Wragg's stable but in the 1970s he cut his interests in Britain to have his horses trained in France by François Boutin, who was responsible for Stintino. Sagaro and Zino, as well as good winners in France such as Romildo, Delmora and Tarona..

Racing colours: chocolate and white hoops, white cap.

OLDROYD, Geoffrey (b. 1946)

Geoff Oldroyd was apprenticed to Pat Rohan from 1961 to 1968 and rode his first winner in 1963 at Stockton. His best season was his last as an apprentice in 1968, when he rode 39 winners. Most of his riding career has been based in the North at Malton, and he began training near there in 1985. His first win was with his first runner, Low Flyer at Beverley in April 1985, which proved to be his only success of the season.

ONCIDIUM
(1961, b c Alcide – Malcolmia, by Sayani)

Oncidium was bred and owned by Lord Howard de Walden. He won five races and almost £30,000 in stakes, his successes including the Lingfield Derby Trial, Jockey Club Cup and Coronation Cup. He was much fancied for the Derby but finished unplaced behind Santa Claus. He was trained firstly by Jack Waugh and later, when he became difficult to train, by George Todd. He was exported to New Zealand and was a successful sire there before his death in 1975.

O'NEILL, Frank (1886-1960)

Frank O'Neill was one of the most successful of the many American jockeys who came to find fame and fortune in Europe before World War I. He settled in France and between 1910 and 1922 was champion jockey there in every year bar one. In 1910 he rode 156 winners, in 1911 163, and in 1913 162. He gained his first British Classic success in 1911, when he won the St Leger on Prince Palatine, on whom he won the Ascot Gold Cup the following season. After the war he won the 1920 Derby on Spion Kop, a lucky mount as the stable jockey Arthur Smith elected to ride Sarchedon. In 1924 he won the Oaks on Straitlace. That year he also won the Lincolnshire on Sir Gallahad, Kempton Jubilee on Parth and Queen Alexandra Stakes on Rose Prince.

He was not a stylist but a tough, determined rider who rode a strong finish and was inclined to be hard on his horses. On retirement he opened a bar in Paris that became a rendezvous for the Parisian racing world but returned to America in 1955 and died in New York.

ONE IN A MILLION
(1976, b f Rarity – Singe, by Tudor Music)

Bought for 18,500gns as a yearling and raced in the name of Helena Springfield Ltd, One in a Million became the first company-owned horse to win a Classic when successful in the 1,000 Guineas. She took first prize in her opening five races, including the Houghton Stakes at two years, but was awarded the Coronation Stakes at Royal Ascot on the controversial disqualification of Buz Kashi, to whom One in a Million finished second, being beaten on merit. One in a Million raced only once more and ran badly in the July Cup over 6f, after which she was retired to stud.

ONLY FOR LIFE
(1960, b c Chanteur II – Life Sentence, by Court Martial)

Only For Life was bought as a yearling for 1,600gns by Miss Monica Sheriffe. Trained by Jeremy Tree, he won three races for £36,666, including the 2,000 Guineas and King Edward VII Stakes. Before export to Japan in 1966, he sired

The Elk, winner of the Observer Gold Cup in 1968.

ON THE HOUSE
(1979, b f Be My Guest – Lora, by Lorenzaccio)

On The House failed to make her reserve at the yearling sales, remained in the ownership of her breeder, Sir Philip Oppenheimer, and gave him his first Classic success and trainer Harry Wragg his last when taking the 1,000 Guineas at 33-1 from Time Charter. On The House had won two of her four races as a two-year-old and finished second in the Cheveley Park Stakes. After the Guineas she won one of her four races, the Sussex Stakes, in which she beat the colts Sandhurst Prince and Achieved. She retired to stud in 1983 to be mated with the ill-fated Shergar.

ORBY
(1904, ch c Orme – Rhoda B, by Hanover)

Mr R.B. Croker's Orby, trained by Colonel F. MacCabe at Glencairn, Co Dublin, was the first Irish-trained horse to win the Derby, a feat he accomplished in 1907. Colonel MacCabe was a doctor who suspended his medical interests to become private trainer to Mr Croker. Orby sired a Derby winner in Grand Parade, but most of his descendants were noted for their speed rather than stamina.

ORLASS FAMILY

Orlass, foaled in 1914, was by Orby and won five races, all in Ireland over 5f. Though a sprinter herself, many of her descendants were top-class middle-distance performers and she had immense influence on Major L.B. Holliday's stud. Among her descendants are Hethersett, Neasham Belle, Narrator, None Nicer, Netherton Maid and Crisper, who all carried the Holliday colours. Other notable descendants are Gay Time, Elopement, Nucleus, Derring-Do, Flossy, Humble Duty and Peleid.

ORME
(1889, b c Ormonde – Angelica, by Galopin)

The Duke of Westminster's Orme was a top-class colt who was unable to run in the 2,000 Guineas and Derby owing to poisoning. It was never proved beyond doubt whether he was poisoned through malice or as a result of severe dental infection. The former is the more probable. In the St Leger he was unplaced behind La Flèche but beat her in the Eclipse the following year. He sired the 1899 'Triple Crown' winner Flying Fox who was exported to France and exercised great influence on bloodstock breeding there. He also sired the 1907 Derby winner Orby and Witch Elm, who won the 1,000 Guineas the same year. He was champion sire in 1899.

ORMONDE
(1883, b c Bend Or – Lily Agnes, by Macaroni)

Owned and bred by the first Duke of Westminster, Ormonde was trained by John Porter. He was unquestionably one of the greatest horses in British racing history and at two, three and four years of age was never beaten. Besides winning the 2,000 Guineas, Derby and St Leger, his victories included the Hardwicke Stakes (twice), Champion Stakes, Dewhurst Plate, Free Handicap and Imperial Gold Cup. His success was all the more remarkable in that for much of his career he suffered from respiratory trouble. His stud career proved an anti-climax. He was sold to Argentina and then to America, where he died in 1904.

ORMSTON, John Glaholme (b. 1909)

Jack Ormston, once a speedway rider, before World War II rode in steeplechases as an amateur and in point-to-points. He took out a licence to train in 1946 at stables in Richmond, Yorkshire. His most important success was with Reminiscence in the Portland Handicap, and his best-known horse was Le Garçon d'Or, who won each season between 1960 and 1972. He retired from training in November 1975.

ORPHEUS
(1917, b c Orby – Electra, by Eager)

Sir Hugo Cunliffe-Owen's Orpheus was third to Spion Kop in the Derby and won the Champion Stakes. He became extremely bad-tempered and was an indifferent sire although he did get one very good sprinter in Concerto.

ORWELL
(1929, b c Gainsborough – Golden Hair, by Golden Sun)

Orwell was bred by Lord Furness and bought as a yearling for 3,000gns by Mr Washington Singer. He won eight races worth over £29,000. He was trained by Joe Lawson at Manton and proved a brilliant two-year-old, his victories including the National Breeders' Produce Stakes. He was a hot favourite for the 2,000 Guineas, which he won, but he failed in the Derby and St Leger. He was not a success as a sire and died in 1948.

OSBORNE, John Howe
(1833-1922)

John Osborne was a member of a Suffolk family that migrated to Yorkshire. He had his first ride in 1846 and his last in 1892. Completely incorruptible, quite a rare quality in north-country jockeys at that time, he was for years the idol of Yorkshire, where he rode for the Ashgill stable at Middleham. He rode very short for those days and because of his style was known as 'the old pusher'. He won the Derby in 1869 on Pretender and was successful in the 2,000 Guineas six times, 1,000 Guineas and St Leger twice and Oaks once (on Apology, who also won the 1,000 Guineas and St Leger). He trained successfully at Brecongill in Middleham and rode work until the year of his death.

OUR BABU
(1952, b c My Babu – Glen Line, by Blue Peter)

Our Babu was bought for 2,700gns as a yearling by David Robinson and trained by Geoffrey Brooke. He won the Champagne Stakes, Middle Park Stakes and 2,000 Guineas. He was sold for export as a stallion to America in 1956, returned to Britain in 1963 and was sent to Japan in 1967.

OVERNIGHT DECLARATION

In every race there is a declaration of runners either four or three days before the race, and declarations may be cancelled up to 10 a.m. during the months of April to October inclusive, and up to 10.30 a.m. during the months of November to March inclusive, on the day before the race. The overnight declarations office is at Weatherbys, Sanders Road, Wellingborough, Northants.

OWEN TUDOR
(1938, b c Hyperion – Mary Tudor II, by Pharos)

Fred Darling's seventh and last Derby success was in 1941 with Owen Tudor, bred and owned by Mrs Macdonald-Buchanan and ridden by W. Nevett. Owen Tudor was not consistent but he was a good horse on his day and won a war-substitute Gold Cup in 1942. As a sire he got two exceptionally fast horses in Tudor Minstrel and Abernant; a champion middle-distance horse in Right Royal V, who slammed St Paddy in the King George VI and Queen Elizabeth Stakes; a fine stayer in Elpenor, who won the Ascot Gold Cup for M. Boussac; and a top-notch American racer in Tudor Era, winner of $22\frac{1}{2}$ races including the Man o' War Stakes. Owen Tudor, who did well as a sire of broodmares, was retired from stud in 1960 and died six years later.

OWNER

The term 'owner' includes 'part-owner' and 'lessee' but not 'lessor', and the lessor of a horse shall be deemed to have no interest in the horse unless he receives a share of the prize money won by the horse and contributes to the expense of running it. In the case of a partnership, it means all the partners, and in the case of a company-owned horse it means the company.

Owners' Contributions

Statistics published for the 1984 Flat season showed that from total prize money of £16,842,364, owners themselves contributed £5,157,852, or 30.6 per cent. The rest was made up of £6,378,565 (37.9 per cent) from the Betting Levy Board, £2,928,608 (17.4 per cent) from sponsors and £2,377,339 (14.1 per cent) from racecourse executives.

OWNERS, Leading: see Appendix II

OXLEY, John Elliott (1930-86)

John Oxley, after Eton and service in the King's Royal Rifle Corps, was assistant to Geoffrey Brooke from 1957 to 1958. He then went as assistant to George Colling and on the latter's death in 1959 took over the stable which he conducted at Hurworth House, Newmarket, until his retirement in 1975. In 1964 he won the Oaks with Sir Foster Robinson's Homeward Bound, who also won the Princess Elizabeth Stakes and Yorkshire Oaks. He won the Dante Stakes with Merchant Venturer, who was second in the Derby, and Hermes, the Yorkshire Cup with Cutter, the Coronation Stakes with Ocean, the King Edward VII Stakes with Mariner, the Great Voltigeur Stakes and Jockey Club Cup with Hermes, the Jockey Club Stakes with Torpid, and the Lincoln Handicap with Frankincense. Hermes, Cutter, Ocean, Mariner and Torpid were all owned by Mr R.D. Hollingsworth. Following an accident which confined him to a wheelchair, Oxley was ill for a long time before his death in January 1986.

P

PADDOCK

The 'paddock' usually refers to the area of ground on a racecourse that includes the parade ring, weighing-room and unsaddling enclosure. In most cases it is accessible only to those persons in the members' enclosure or in Tattersalls'.

PAGET, Miss Dorothy Wyndham (1905-60)

Miss Dorothy Paget was the second daughter of the first and last Baron Queenborough. A cousin of Mr John Hay Whitney, she inherited a huge fortune from her maternal grandfather, and this enabled her to race on a vast scale, both on the Flat and over jumps, for more than 30 years.

Extremely shy and retiring by nature, she was recognized as one of racing's eccentrics and for the last twenty years of her life she was a recluse, avoiding as far as possible human contact outside her own small and devoted female entourage. She was easily distinguished on the racecourse since she invariably wore a blue felt hat that owed nothing to current fashion, and a shapeless grey coat that extended nearly to her ankles. Her face, round, heavy and pale, was framed in lank dark hair. Stories circulated of her curious mode of life; of the odd hours that she kept and the gargantuan meals she was alleged to consume. Possibly she was never a really popular figure with the racing public, but she was respected for her independence, admired for the firm manner in which she successfully kept the Press at arm's length, and appreciated for the lavish patronage she gave to the Turf.

Being forthright and demanding, she was liable to terminate at short notice the services of trainers and jockeys. She was generous though, and those who possessed the knack of handling her successfully usually became genuinely fond of her. She betted on a very big scale indeed, many of her most audacious wagers being on second-rate jumpers at minor meetings under National Hunt Rules. Before World War II she was a staunch supporter of pony racing at Northolt.

Her most famous racehorse was the steeplechaser Golden Miller, winner of the Grand National and five Cheltenham Gold Cups. Considering the money spent on yearlings and the scope of her own stud, she was not particularly successful on the Flat, but she did win the 1943 Derby with Straight Deal, trained by Walter Nightingall, and that season was leading owner. Another good horse was Aldborough, winner of the Queen Alexandra Stakes and Doncaster Cup, and her last good horse was Nucleus, second to Meld in the St Leger. A notorious performer to carry her colours was Tuppence, who in three days before the Derby, was backed from 125-1 to 10-1. He finished eighteenth. At the time of her death Miss Paget's Flat-race horses were trained by Sir Gordon Richards, and following her death most of her horses and the Ballymacoll Stud in Ireland were bought by Sir Gordon's patron Mr Michael Sobell. Derby winner Troy was the grandson of one of the mares included in the deal.

PALACE MUSIC (1981, ch c The Minstrel – Come My Prince, by Prince John)

Palace Music made $130,000 as a yearling in the United States, and racing in the colours of Nelson Bunker Hunt for trainer Patrick Biancone, he became the first French-trained winner in Britain for eighteen months when holding Pebbles in the 1984 Champion Stakes. His previous form, having been unraced as a two-year-old, did not match up to that class, though he won two races in France in the spring of 1984. He won one race in France in 1985 and was third in the Champion Stakes won by Pebbles.

PALESTINE
(1947, gr c Fair Trial – Una, by Tetratema)

Bred by the Aga Khan, Palestine was trained by Marcus Marsh, and showed brilliant speed as a two-year-old, winning the Sandown Park Stud Produce Stakes, Coventry Stakes, National Breeders' Produce Stakes, Richmond Stakes, Gimcrack Stakes and Champagne Stakes.

As a three-year-old he was a really good horse up to 1m, winning the Henry VIII Stakes at Hurst Park, 2,000 Guineas, St James's Palace Stakes, Red Rose Stakes at Manchester and Sussex Stakes. He failed to stay in the Eclipse and finished fourth. Altogether he won eleven races and £38,515.

At stud he was perhaps not quite the success generally anticipated, but his winners included Pall Mall (2,000 Guineas), Palariva (£12,488), Zeus Boy (£11,615), Green Banner (Irish 2,000 Guineas) and Escort (Royal Lodge Stakes). Mares by Palestine have bred Enstone Spark (1,000 Guineas), Opaline II (Cheveley Park Stakes), Palatch (Yorkshire Oaks) and the smart sprinters Bay Express, Pentathlon and Silver Shark. Palestine died in 1974.

PALL MALL
(1955, ch c Palestine – Malapert, by Portlaw)

Captain Charles Moore, racing manager to King George VI and later to the Queen, bought Pall Mall's dam, Malapert, for the royal stud for 120gns. For three years she was covered by Kingstone but the produce were useless. Moore then sent her to Big Game, whose maternal grandsire is The Tetrarch's son Tetratema, and then to Palestine, whose maternal grandsire is likewise Tetratema. The result of the union with Palestine was Pall Mall.

Trained by Cecil Boyd-Rochfort, Pall Mall was a good, fast two-year-old, winning the New Stakes at Royal Ascot

and being placed in the July, Gimcrack and Champagne Stakes. As a three-year-old he won the Classic Trial Stakes at Thirsk and the 2,000 Guineas at 20-1. He also won the Lockinge Stakes at Newbury, while in the Sussex Stakes he was second to Major Portion, who had been second to him in the Guineas. As a four-year-old Pall Mall won the Lockinge Stakes again and the Midsummer Stakes at Newmarket. His seven victories were worth £20,542. He was a success at stud, where he died in 1978, his best offspring being Reform, winner of the St James's Palace Stakes, Sussex Stakes, Queen Elizabeth II Stakes, Champion Stakes and over £44,000 in prize money, Sallust, winner of seven races including the Sussex Stakes, and Sanedtki, whose ten wins in France, Britain and America included the Prix de la Forêt twice.

PAN II
(1947, b c Atys – Pretty Girl, by Tourbillon)

Owned by M.E. Constant and trained in France by Etienne Pollet, Pan II won the Ascot Gold Cup and Goodwood Cup in 1951. In France he won four races including the French St Leger.

PANDOFELL
(1957, b c Solar Slipper – Nadika, by Nosca)

Bred by Mr H.J. Joel, Pandofell was sold by him to Mr H.Warwick Daw for 600gns at the 1959 December Sales before he disclosed his great merits as a stayer. Pandofell was trained by Freddie Maxwell to win the Queen's Prize, Yorkshire Cup, Ascot Gold Cup and Doncaster Cup. All told he won eight races and over £20,000. Out-and-out stayers are rarely popular with breeders in Britain and he had not been long at stud here before he was sold for export to Russia. Before he left, in 1965, he sired a good but unpredictable stayer in Piaco, whose many successes included the Doncaster Cup and Northumberland Plate, and Pandora Bay, winner of the Ribblesdale Stakes and third in the Oaks.

PANORAMA
(1936, ch c Sir Cosmo – Happy Climax, by Happy Warrior)

Panorama was unbeaten in seven races at two years and won twice more before becoming one of the most successful sprinting sires in British racing history. When he died in 1955, his stock had won $463\frac{1}{2}$ races worth over £189,000, the best being Whistler and Delirium. Mares by Panorama have been responsible for Glad Rags (1,000 Guineas), Linacre (Irish 2,000 Guineas), Chamier (Irish Derby) and Bebe Grande (eight races at two years), as well as the 1,000 Guineas winners Pourparler and Fleet, Display (second in 1,000 Guineas) and Démocratie (Prix de la Forêt), who were all out of Review.

PAPPA FOURWAY
(1952, b c Pappageno II – Oola Hills, by Denturius)

Bred by the Ballykisteen Stud and trained by Bill Dutton, Pappa Fourway proved a brilliant sprinter, among twelve wins for almost £10,000 being the July Cup, King's Stand Stakes, Diadem Stakes and Tetrarch Stakes at Manchester, having cost less than £200 as a yearling. He was exported to the United States in 1956.

PAPYRUS
(1920, br c Tracery – Miss Matty, by Marcovil)

Owned by Mr Ben Irish, trained by Basil Jarvis and ridden by Steve Donoghue, Papyrus won nine races for £17,863, including six as a two-year-old and the Derby. In the autumn of 1923 he was sent to America to run in a match against their leading three-year-old Zev but in heavy conditions and ill-prepared for the surface he was soundly beaten. He changed hands for £25,000 at the end of 1923, failed to win again and was not a success as a sire before his death in 1941.

PARADE RING

Every racecourse must have a railed-off parade ring in the paddock where the horses parade after they have been saddled and where the jockeys assemble and mount. Only authorized persons are allowed entrance.

PARBURY
(1963, b c Pardal – Alconbury, by Alycidon)

Parbury came from a stoutly-bred family in which his first four dams were unsuccessful on the racecourse. He had his best season as a four-year-old, when after taking the Henry II Stakes, he won the Ascot Gold Cup in a close finish against Mehari, with the lame French-trained favourite Danseur third. Parbury, who won over six furlongs as a two-year-old and a mile and a half at three, won once in 1968, at the end of which season he was exported to Chile as a stallion. He was bred and owned by Major H.P. Holt and trained by Derrick Candy.

PARDAL
(1947, b c Pharis II – Adargatis, by Astérus)

Pardal was bred and owned by M.M. Boussac and though placed in the Prix Hocquart and Irish Derby, he did not win until he was four. He won twice in France and the Princess of Wales's Stakes, Great Yorkshire Stakes, Jockey Club Stakes and Lowther Stakes in Britain. He was not nearly such a good horse as his brother Ardan but proved a better sire.

Purchased as a stallion by Mr R.F. Watson and some associates, he stood at Newmarket until in his old age he was sent to Ireland, and he died there in 1969. His best winners were Psidium (Derby) and Parbury and Pardallo II, both successful in the Ascot Gold Cup. Eudaemon (£13,049), London Cry (£11,999), Firestreak (£11,459), Pardao (£45,810) and Decies (Irish 2,000 Guineas) were other good horses by Pardal.

PARDALLO
(1963, b c Pardal – Great Success II, by Niccolo Dell'Arca

Pardallo II reached his peak as a five-year-old when after a winter spent running over hurdles in France he was unbeaten in four outings on the Flat, including the Ascot Gold Cup. At Royal Ascot he beat two other French-trained horses, Samos III and Petrone. He stayed in training in 1969, but having won in the spring was unable to confirm his superiority over Samos in later races. Pardallo was bred and owned by Mme Suzy Volterra and trained by Charles Bartholomew.

PARDAO
(1958, ch c Pardal – Three Weeks, by Big Game)

Pardao was bred by the Sledmere Stud and bought as a yearling on behalf of Mrs C.O. Iselin for 7,000gns. He was trained by Cecil Boyd-Rochfort and won four races in Britain including the Lingfield Derby Trial and Gordon Stakes; he was also third in the Derby and fourth in the St Leger. At four he won the Jockey Club Cup (then 1½m) and was later sent to America, where at five he won two good handicaps. He retired to stud in Britain in 1964 and at once drew attention to himself by siring Sovereign, a very fast filly who won five races including the Coronation Stakes and Queen Mary Stakes. Pardao died in 1971, two years before his son Moulton gave him his biggest success in the Benson & Hedges Gold Cup.

PARK TOP
(1964, b f Kalydon – Nellie Park, by Arctic Prince)

Park Top was bred in 1964 by Mrs Joan Scott at the Buttermilk Stud, Oxfordshire, and as a yearling was bought at Newmarket by Bernard van Cutsem on behalf of the Duke of Devonshire for 500gns. She did not run as a two-year-old but from three years to six proved herself an outstanding racemare, winning thirteen races and being placed in eight for

prize money of £137,414 in Britain and France. At three she won the Ribblesdale Stakes and at four the Brighton Challenge Cup for the second year running, but at five she proved better than ever. Apart from winning a couple of races in France, she carried off the Coronation Cup, Hardwicke Stakes and King George VI and Queen Elizabeth Stakes. She ought to have won the Eclipse Stakes, too, but Geoff Lewis was well below his best form on that occasion and she was most unluckily beaten by Wolver Hollow. She was probably a shade unlucky, too, when second to Levmoss in the Prix de l'Arc de Triomphe, Piggott delivering his challenge just too late. She was clearly stale when subsequently runner-up in the Champion Stakes. In 1970 she won La Coupe at Longchamp but in the Coronation Cup was beaten by Caliban, Piggott riding a somewhat indifferent race. Park Top has been most disappointing at stud, producing only four foals, one of them the winner of a small race, before she was retired from the paddocks in 1980.

PARR, Thomas (1810–80)

Tom Parr was the owner-trainer of the remarkable Fisherman, whose 23 wins as a three-year-old in 1856 is the record for one season. Parr, whose Saucebox won the St Leger in 1855, treated most of his horses in the same fashion, believing that to win several modest races was better than to win no good ones.

PARSONS, John

John Parsons is believed to have been only sixteen years old when he rode Caractacus to victory in the 1862 Derby. After this singular triumph he vanished into obscurity.

PARTHIA
(1956, b c Persian Gulf – Lightning, by Hyperion)

Owned and bred by Sir Humphrey de Trafford, Parthia won four races as a three-year-old, including the Derby, but was beaten at odds-on in the St Leger, finishing fourth to Cantelo. He won two races as a four-year-old, including the

Jockey Club Cup, but his appetite for racing waned. He was the only Derby winner trained by Cecil Boyd-Rochfort and the only one ridden by Harry Carr. At stud his best produce were the fillies Sleeping Partner (Oaks), Parthian Glance (Ribblesdale Stakes), Every Blessing (Princess Elizabeth Stakes) and Parsimony (Cork and Orrery Stakes and July Cup). Parthia was exported in 1968 to Japan, where he died in 1970.

PASCH
(1935, b c Blandford – Pasca, by Manna)

Pasch was bred by the Banstead Manor Stud and owned by Mr H.E. Morriss. Trained by Fred Darling, he did not run as a two-year-old but the following season won the 2,000 Guineas and Eclipse and was third to his stable companion Bois Roussel in the Derby. He died after one season at stud with his most notable offspring Pasquinade, the dam of Royal Palm.

PASSPORT

A 'passport' under the Rules of Racing is the approved diagrammatic document of identity of a horse issued on the authority of the stewards of the Jockey Club or that of any recognized Turf Authority.

PATTERN RACES

Pattern races are those which the five major Turf authorities in Europe consider provide a balanced programme of high-class, non-handicap events for horses in each age-group run over all distances through the season, with the intention of providing a standard by which the best horses of each generation can be identified.

In 1965 a committee was appointed under the Duke of Norfolk to study the pattern of racing, and in 1967 a committee under Lord Porchester, called the Race Planning Committee, was set up to continue the work of the Duke of Norfolk's committee. Their findings were extended in 1970 to include France and Ireland, which agreed a system whereby Pattern races were split into three groups. In Group I are championship races,

including the Classics; in Group II are races just below championship standard which may include some weight penalties and allowances; and Group III races are those non-handicaps regarded as stepping-stones to the higher groups. The Group system was introduced in 1971, and in 1979, by which time West Germany and Italy had joined the International Pattern, ground rules were drawn up to cover the requirements for introducing new Pattern races or changing the conditions of existing ones. Changes are considered annually by the European Pattern Committee.

The British Flat Race Pattern Committee, as at 1 January 1986, comprises: Tim Holland-Martin (chairman), Mrs Dana Brudenell-Bruce, Paul Greeves, Charles Layfield, Peter Willet and Howard Wright.

Pattern races scheduled for Britain in 1986:

Group I – (20 races)

General Accident 1,000 Guineas (3yo), Newmarket, 1m

General Accident 2,000 Guineas (3yo), Newmarket, 1m

Every Ready Derby Stakes (3yo), Epsom, 1½m

Coronation Cup, Epsom, 1½m

Gold Seal Oaks (3yo), Epsom, 1½m

Gold Cup, Royal Ascot, 2½m

King's Stand Stakes, Royal Ascot, 5f

Coral-Eclipse Stakes, Sandown Park, 1¼m

Norcros July Cup, Newmarket, 6f

King George VI and Queen Elizabeth Diamond Stakes, Ascot, 1½m

Swettenham Stud Sussex Stakes, Goodwood, 1m

Sponsored Gold Cup, York, 1¼m

Yorkshire Oaks (3yo), York, 1½m

William Hill Sprint Championship, York, 5f

Holsten Pils St Leger Stakes (3yo), Doncaster, 1¾m 127yds

Tattersalls Cheveley Park Stakes (2yo), Newmarket, 6f

Tattersalls Middle Park Stakes (2yo), Newmarket, 6f

Dubai Champion Stakes, Newmarket, 1¼m

William Hill Dewhurst Stakes (2yo), Newmarket, 7f

William Hill Futurity Stakes (2yo), Doncaster, 1m

Group II – (29 races):

Trusthouse-Forte Mile, Sandown Park, 1m

General Accident Jockey Club Stakes, Newmarket, 1½m

Mecca-Dante Stakes (3yo), York, 1¼m 110yds

Yorkshire Cup, York, 1¾m

Juddmonte Lockinge Stakes, Newbury, 1m

King Edward VII Stakes (3yo), Royal Ascot, 1½m

Prince of Wales's Stakes, Royal Ascot, 1¼m

Queen Anne Stakes, Royal Ascot, 1m

St James's Palace Stakes (3yo), Royal Ascot, 1m

Coronation Stakes (3yo), Royal Ascot, 1m

Ribblesdale Stakes (3yo), Royal Ascot, 1½m

Hardwicke Stakes, Royal Ascot, 1½m

Princess of Wales's Stakes, Newmarket, 1½m

O C L Richmond Stakes (2yo), Goodwood, 6f

Vodafone Nassau Stakes, Goodwood, 1¼m

Walmac International Geoffrey Freer Stakes, Newbury, 1m 5f 60yds

Great Voltigeur Stakes (3yo), York, 1½m

Scottish Equitable Gimcrack Stakes (2yo), York, 6f

Lowther Stakes (2yo), York, 6f

Waterford Crystal Mile, Goodwood, 1m

Vernons Sprint Cup, Haydock Park, 6f

Park Hill Stakes (3yo), Doncaster, 1¾m 127yds

Laurent Perrier Champagne Stakes (2yo), Doncaster, 7f

Brian Swift Flying Childers Stakes (2yo), Doncaster, 5f

Rokeby Farms Mill Reef Stakes (2yo), Newbury, 6f

Hoover Fillies' Mile (2yo), Ascot, 1m

Queen Elizabeth II Stakes, Ascot, 1m

Royal Lodge Stakes (2yo), Ascot, 1m

Sun Chariot Stakes, Newmarket, 1¼m

Group III – (54 races):

Salisbury 2,000 Guineas Trial Stakes (3yo), Salisbury, 7f

Nell Gwyn Stakes (3yo), Newmarket, 7f

Earl of Sefton Stakes, Newmarket, 1m 1f

Charles Heidsieck Champagne Craven Stakes (3yo), Newmarket, 1m

Gainsborough Stud Fred Darling Stakes (3yo), Newbury, 7f 60yds

Clerical, Medical Greenham Stakes (3yo), Newbury, 7f

Lanes End John Porter Stakes, Newbury, 1½m

Guardian Classic Trial Stakes (3yo), Sandown Park, 1¼m

Westbury Stakes, Sandown Park, 1¼m

Insulpak Sagaro Stakes, Ascot, 2m

Palace House Stakes, Newmarket, 5f

Dalham Chester Vase (3yo), Chester, 1½m 65yds

Ormonde Stakes, Chester, 1m 5f 88yds

Highland Spring Derby Trial Stakes (3yo), Lingfield Park, 1½m

Tattersalls Musidora Stakes (3yo), York, 1¼m 110yds

Duke of York Stakes, York, 6f

Mappin & Webb Henry II Stakes, Sandown Park, 2m

Sears Temple Stakes, Sandown Park, 5f

Brigadier Gerard Stakes, Sandown Park, 1¼m

Diomed Stakes, Epsom, 1m 110yds

Coventry Stakes (2yo), Royal Ascot, 6f

Jersey Stakes (3yo), Royal Ascot, 7f

Queen Mary Stakes (2yo), Royal Ascot, 6f

Cork and Orrery Stakes, Royal Ascot, 5f

Norfolk Stakes (2yo), Royal Ascot, 5f

Van Geest Criterion Stakes, Newmarket, 7f

Harp Lager Lancashire Oaks (3yo), Haydock Park, 1½m

Pritchard Services Cherry Hinton Stakes (2yo), Newmarket, 6f

Anglia Television July Stakes (2yo), Newmarket, 6f

Child Stakes, Newmarket, 1m

Princess Margaret Stakes (2yo), Ascot, 6f

Beeswing Stakes, Newmarket, 7f

Gordon Stakes (3yo), Goodwood, 1½m

Molecomb Stakes (2yo), Goodwood, 5f

Goodwood Cup, Goodwood, 2m 5f

King George Stakes, Goodwood, 5f

Lanson Champagne Vintage Stakes (2yo), Goodwood, 7f

Trusthouse-Forte Hungerford Stakes, Newbury, 7f 60yds

Waterford Candelabra Stakes (2yo), Goodwood, 7f

Glen International Solario Stakes (2yo), Sandown Park, 7f

BonusPrint September Stakes, Kempton Park, 1m 3f 30yds

Doncaster Cup, Doncaster, 2¼m

May Hill Stakes (2yo), Doncaster, 1m

Kiveton Park Stakes, Doncaster, 7f

Scottish Equitable (Valdoe) Stakes, Goodwood, 1¼m

Cumberland Lodge Stakes, Ascot, 1½m

Trusthouse-Forte Diadem Stakes, Ascot, 6f

Jockey Club Cup, Newmarket, 2m

Cornwallis Stakes (2yo), Ascot, 5f

Princess Royal Stakes, Ascot, 1½m

Bisquit Cognac Challenge Stakes, Newmarket, 7f

Chevington Stud Rockfel Stakes (2yo), Newmarket, 7f

Matchmaker Horris Hill Stakes (2yo), Newbury, 7f 60yds

St Simon Stakes, Newbury, 1½m

PAWNEESE
(1973, b f Carvin – Plencia by Le Haar)

Pawneese added the Oaks to the 1,000 Guineas victory gained by Flying Water for their owner-breeder Daniel Wildenstein in 1976. Pawneese went further than her stablemate, because in the space of eight weeks she won not only the Oaks but also the French equivalent (Prix de Diane) and the King George VI and Queen Elizabeth Diamond Stakes, in which she made all the running and beat Bruni and Orange Bay, to add to her earlier two wins at Saint-Cloud. The disappointment of Pawneese's career was that she failed to reproduce her best in the autumn of her three-year-old career, being beaten in two races she might have been expected to win, and did not race again. She had one winner, Perreal, from her first three foals.

PAYNE, William John (b. 1910)

Bill Payne is the son of W.H. Payne, a noted National Hunt jockey and a successful trainer under both rules. 'Young' Bill Payne became a highly competent rider over fences and hurdles early in life and would have won the 1928 Grand National on Great Span if the saddle had not slipped two fences from home.

In World War II he served with the Yorkshire Dragoons, reaching the rank of major, and afterwards he assisted his father, who trained Zucchero to win the Coronation Cup and Tangle to win the King's Stand Stakes, until taking out a licence himself in 1955. His stables at Eastbury in Berkshire were small but the horses were cleverly placed and won at least their share of races until his retirement at the end of 1977. His son 'Pip' began training at Newmarket in 1986.

PAYNE-GALLWEY, Colonel Peter (1906-71)

Peter Payne-Gallwey joined the 11th Hussars after Eton and the RMC. In the 1930s he was one of the leading amateur riders, winning over 60 races including the Grand Military Gold Cup. He had a most distinguished war record, being awarded the DSO and two bars. He began training jumpers in 1949 – he had trained a good many winners in Egypt before the war – but gradually turned to the Flat. His stable at Upper Lambourn was small, and it was a great achievement to win the Stewards' Cup two years running, with Sky Diver in 1967 and 1968. He retired because of ill-health shortly before his death in November 1971.

PAY UP
(1933, br c Fairway – Book Debt, by Buchan)

Pay Up was bred and owned by Lord Astor and trained by Joe Lawson. He won three races for £11,344, including the Free Handicap and 2,000 Guineas but never raced again after finishing lame in the Derby, for which he was favourite. He sired the Grand National winner Nickel Coin but generally was a moderate sire.

PEACOCK, Matthew James (1879-1951)

A famous and much-loved Yorkshire character, noted for his blunt outspokenness and his hatred of humbug and dishonesty, 'Matt' Peacock assisted his father, Dobson Peacock, for many years at Manor House, Middleham, before taking out a trainer's licence himself in 1935. The best horse he trained was Dante, who won the Derby in 1945. The rumours and uncertainty that surrounded Dante's St Leger preparation – he was eventually withdrawn from the race – made Peacock a worried and unhappy man and he never quite regained his old buoyancy. A true Yorkshireman, his usual farewell after an Ascot or Newmarket meeting was 'Goodbye; now I'm off back to England.'

PEACOCK, Richard Dobson (1924-84)

Dick Peacock served in the Royal Scots Greys from 1942 to 1947. He assisted his father, Matt Peacock, at Middleham until taking over the licence on the latter's death in 1951. Among the many good races he won were the Cheveley Park Stakes, Gimcrack Stakes, Free Handicap, Northumberland Plate, Yorkshire Cup and King's Stand Stakes. The good horses he trained included Tudor Melody, Precast, Guide, Lindsay, Border Legend, Sweet Story and Fearless Lad. He died in July 1984 and until the end of the season the stable was run by his widow, 'Lennie'.

PEARCE, William James (b. 1950)

William Pearce, who rode in point-to-points, was assistant to Colin Davies, Richmond Sturdy and Dave Hanley before he acquired Hambleton House near Thirsk and began training in 1984. His first winner was with Sharlie's Wimpy at Ripon on 27 June 1984.

PEARL DIVER (1944, b c Vatellor – Pearl Cap, by Le Capucin)

Baron G. de Waldner's Pearl Diver, won the Derby in 1947 and returned for the St Leger but was only fourth. Though he won the Prix d'Harcourt as a four-year-old, he was well beaten in the Coronation Cup and Prix de l'Arc de Triomphe. He was bought to stand at stud in Britain but failed to make his mark as a sire and in 1957 was exported to Japan.

PEARL MAIDEN FAMILY

Foaled in 1918, Pearl Maiden, by Phaleron, was a famous broodmare though she, her dam and her grandam were all non-winners. Her offspring included Pearlweed (French Derby), Pearl Cap (French Oaks and Prix de l'Arc de Triomphe), Indus (French 2,000 Guineas) and Bipearl (French 1,000 Guineas). Among her descendants are Pearl Diver (Derby), Molvedo (Prix de l'Arc de Triomphe), Fine Pearl (French Oaks), Oncidium (Coronation Cup), Sleeping Partner (Oaks) and Averof (St James's Palace Stakes).

PEBBLES (1981, ch f Sharpen Up – La Dolce, by Connaught)

Pebbles achieved the rare distinction of winning Group One races in Britain for different owners while with the same trainer. She won the 1,000 Guineas for her breeder, Marcos Lemos, and after being sold in midsummer to Sheikh Mohammed and finishing second for him in the Champion Stakes that year, she won the Eclipse Stakes in 1985 (the first filly to do so), before an autumn campaign which brought her magnificent victories in the Champion Stakes (sponsored by her owner's family) and Breeders' Cup Turf race in New York. She is trained by Clive Brittain, for whom she proved a useful two-year-old by winning twice and finishing second in the Cheveley Park Stakes, and also finished second in the Coronation Stakes, where her early regular rider Philip Robinson chose to ride Katies, the winner. It was intended to keep her in training in 1986.

PECK, Charles (1873-1941)

A member of a famous racing family, Charles Peck trained his first winner in 1895 and acted for a good many years as private trainer to Mr S.B. Joel. His best winners were Pommern, who won the 2,000 Guineas, Derby and St Leger in 1915; Bachelor's Button, who beat Pretty Polly in the Ascot Gold Cup; and

Polymelus, who won the Cambridgeshire and became a most successful sire. After service with the Royal Horse Artillery in World War I, he trained for Mr S.B. Joel again in 1925 but in 1926 became private trainer to Mr Joel's brother Mr J.B. Joel. All told he trained 444 winners of £215,000 in stakes before retiring in 1928.

PECK, Robert (1845-99)

Robert Peck, father of Pommern's trainer Charles Peck, began and ended his training career at an early age. He started in his early twenties, was 28 when he won the Derby with Doncaster and the Oaks and St Leger with Marie Stuart, and 36 when he retired, a year after winning the Derby with Bend Or. He then founded a stud in Bedfordshire and managed two Newmarket stables, where his horses landed several huge gambles. He died at Scarborough in his native Yorkshire.

PELEID
(1970, b c Derring-Do – Winning Bid, by Great Captain)

Peleid, bred by his owner, Lt.-Col. W. Behrens, and trained by Bill Elsey, spent most of his three-year-old career in handicaps, winning three, until the St Leger, where he started at 28-1 and beat Buoy by 2½ lengths. He finished second in the John Porter Stakes on his first outing as a four-year-old but thereafter disappointed, and his one success came in Hungary, where he remained to take up stallion duties.

PENALTY

In some races penalties can be incurred by horses which win between the closing of entries, or the publication of weights in a handicap, and the running of the race concerned, in which they will then be compelled to carry additional weight. The scale of penalties varies considerably, and conditions for allotting penalties differ according to different races. In Group I Pattern races there are no penalties.

PENCILLER

This is a very old-fashioned slang term for those bookmakers on the rails

between Tattersalls and the members' enclosure. Most of their business is credit, and the bets are pencilled in a book by the clerk.

PENNYCOMEQUICK
(1926, br f Hurry On – Plymstock, by Polymelus)

Owned and bred by Lord Astor and trained by Joe Lawson, Pennycomequick won three races for £9,042, including the Oaks. She bred seven winners, including High Stakes, a gelding who won 34 races worth over £21,000. She was also the grandam of the Kentucky Derby winner Pensive.

PEPPIATT COMMITTEE

The Peppiatt Committee, under the chairmanship of Sir Leslie Peppiatt, a former President of the Law Society, was appointed in 1958 by the Home Secretary 'to investigate whether it is desirable and practicable that persons engaged in betting on horse races, otherwise than by means of the totalisator, should be required to make a contribution conducive to the improvement of breeds of horses or the sport of horse racing; and if so, to advise on the amount and on the means of securing it'. In due course the committee replied that this was indeed both desirable and practicable, their findings forming a most significant milestone in the history of British racing, leading to the levy on betting and the formation of the Betting Levy Board which now plays such a vital part in the sport.

PERDITA II
(1881, b f Hampton – Hermione, by Young Melbourne)

Winner of the Ayr Gold Cup before being bought on behalf of the Prince of Wales, later King Edward VII, by John Porter for £900, Perdita II bred two Derby winners, the brothers Persimmon and Diamond Jubilee, as well as a third brother, Florizel II, a smart stayer and sire of another Derby winner, Volodyovski.

PERKS, Stephen James (b. 1955)

Steve Perks was apprenticed to Reg Hollinshead in his native Midlands and rode his first winner as a sixteen-year-old, on Caernarvon Prince at Beverley on 9 June 1971. Next season he was champion apprentice with 41 winners. He had jobs at a number of stables after leaving Hollinshead in 1974 but returned to become stable jockey in 1981.

PERRYMAN, Richard (1903-76)

Dick Perryman was apprenticed to Fred Leader. He became a leading jockey between the wars, winning the 1,000 Guineas three times and Ascot Gold Cup twice. After being injured in a car crash, he retired from riding to start training at Newmarket in 1943, and his most successful phase came just after World War II when he won the St Leger with Chamossaire (1945) and the Derby and St Leger with Airborne (1946). He gave up training in 1967.

PERSIAN GULF (1940, b c Bahram – Double Life, by Bachelor's Double)

A half-brother to Precipitation, Persian Gulf won a war-time Coronation Cup and £2,123 in stakes. At stud he sired Parthia (Derby), Zabara (1,000 Guineas), Zarathustra (Irish Derby, Irish St Leger, Ascot Stakes, Ascot Gold Cup and Goodwood Cup), Queen of Sheba (Irish 1,000 and Royal Hunt Cup), Arabian Night (second in the Derby), Rustam (Champagne Stakes and successful sire) and Persian War (Champion Hurdle three times). He had a more impressive record at stud than on the racecourse, being third in the sires' list in 1959, fourth in 1952 and fifth in 1951 and 1954 before his death in 1964.

PERSIMMON (1893, b c St Simon – Perdita II, by Hampton)

Persimmon was bred by the Prince of Wales, later King Edward VII. He was a brother to Diamond Jubilee, winner of the 'Triple Crown' in 1900. He won the Derby and St Leger in 1896 and the following year the Eclipse Stakes and Gold Cup. He is the last Epsom Derby winner to have won the Ascot Gold Cup. He was a highly successful sire, the best of his offspring being the famous filly Sceptre, who came from his first crop. He died after an injury in 1908 and was leading sire four times.

PERSSE, Henry Seymour (1869-1960)

'Atty' Persse was 91 when he died. For around 50 years he was somewhere near the peak of the training profession. When he retired, he remarked in an interview, 'For nearly 70 years I've had the life of an amateur rider and an owner-trainer and I've loved every minute of it.' He once wrote 'Good trainers are born, not made. Without natural flair it is far better to keep away from racing stables and run a garage.' He himself possessed undoubted flair and could train trainers as well as horses; among his pupils were his brother-in-law Geoffrey Brooke and Cecil Boyd-Rochfort.

Educated at Cheltenham and Oxford, he was always mad about horses and avoided entry into the family business of whisky-distilling by going to America, where he rode a lot of winners. He returned to Britain in 1897 and won the National Hunt Chase on Marpessa. In 1906 he was third in the Grand National on Aunt May. A bad fall at Hurst Park eventually caused his retirement from race-riding and left him lame for life.

He started training in Ireland in 1902. In 1906 he moved to Britain, and in 1908 he bought the Chattis Hill Stables at Stockbridge. Under his skilful direction they became one of the most famous British racing establishments. As a trainer he was dedicated to his job and a severe disciplinarian. He was fully conscious of his responsibilities to his owners, avowed none to the public and did not much care for the Press. Above all he was a great trainer of two-year-olds and had the happy knack of preparing them so that they were rarely at a disadvantage first time out. 'The great thing in training a two-year-old,' he wrote, 'is to keep its speed, and if it loses it, it must be rested at once.' The most famous horse he trained was The Tetrarch, owned by his cousin Major Dermot McCalmont. A grey with curious white markings, hence his nickname of 'The Spotted Wonder', The Tetrarch was never beaten and was probably the fastest horse ever seen on the British Turf.

Persse won the 2,000 Guineas with Sweeper II, Tetratema and Mr Jinks, and the 1,000 Guineas with Silver Urn. His lucky race was the Kempton Jubilee, which he won on six occasions. One of his Jubilee winners was Bachelor's Double, who also won the Irish Derby, City and Suburban and Royal Hunt Cup. Val d'Assa and Queen of Sheba also won the Hunt Cup for him. Among the many fast two-year-olds that Persse produced were Thyestes, The Satrap, Portlaw, Doctor Dolittle, Queen of the Nore and Lindos Ojos. He won the Stewards' Cup with Tetrameter, Victoria Cup with Sir Archibald and The Yellow Dwarf and Coronation Cup with Apelle. He could train stayers, too, and landed a very big coup when Sanctum won the Cesarewitch. He also won the Chester Cup with St Mary's Kirk.

It was a great grief to Persse when his son John, whom he had hoped would carry on the stable, was killed in action in Italy in 1944. He decided to retire but eventually gave way to the entreaties of his friends and started up again at Kingsdown, Lambourn. He eventually retired for good on his wife's death in 1953. As he grew older, he mellowed considerably, and his sense of fun and his skill as a raconteur were a constant delight to all who knew him well. He left £152,000.

PETCH, Major Leslie (1900-83)

A farmer and auctioneer for most of his life, Major Leslie Petch revitalized the popularity of racing at York, Redcar and Catterick after taking up appointments as Clerk of the Course in 1955, 1946 and 1946 respectively. His first racing appointment was as a Judge in 1928. He earned the reputation of being one of the most imaginative and go-ahead officials in the sport, with a rare flair for publicity, and he always had the public spectacle and comfort of racegoers at heart. He relinquished the clerkship of York to his nephew John Sanderson in 1971 and the managership at the end of 1974. He was awarded the OBE in June 1975.

PETITE ETOILE (1956, gr f Petition – Star of Iran, by Bois Roussel)

Bred by the Aga Khan and Prince Aly Khan, Petite Etoile was trained by Noel Murless and proved herself one of the outstanding fillies of this century. Between 1958 and 1961 she won fourteen races over distances from 5f to $1\frac{1}{2}$m, her victories including the 1,000 Guineas, Oaks, Free Handicap, Sussex Stakes, Yorkshire Oaks, Champion Stakes and Coronation Cup (twice). She was second to Aggressor in the King George VI and Queen Elizabeth Stakes when Lester Piggott, who usually rode her to perfection, appeared to give her too much to do in the soft ground. Altogether she won £72,624 in stakes. In training she was high-mettled and often difficult; at stud she was almost a total failure, being difficult to get in foal and then difficult to keep in foal.

PETOSKI (1982, b or br c Niniski – Sushila, by Petingo)

Petoski was bred by Kirsten Rausing and bought by Marcia, Lady Beaverbrook, owner of Niniski, for 90,000gns as a yearling. He won his first two races as a two-year-old but was found wanting when tackling the top class, and as a three-year-old lost his good early form because of a virus before coming back to win the King George VI and Queen Elizabeth Diamond Stakes in a thrilling finish with Oh So Sharp. Petoski injured himself on the gallops while being prepared for an autumn campaign and missed the rest of the season but it was hoped to keep him in training as a four-year-old.

PHALARIS
(1913, br c Polymelus – Bromus, by Sainfoin)

Phalaris, owned by the seventeenth Earl of Derby, was a top-class sprinter who won fifteen races worth £5,475 during World War I. During his twelve years at stud he achieved remarkable success and has exerted tremendous influence on modern pedigrees all over the world. Twice champion sire, his sons included Pharos and Fairway, who were brothers, while his best daughter was their sister Fair Isle (1,000 Guineas). Distinguished members of the Phalaris male line include Pharis, Blue Peter, Nearco, Nasrullah, Nimbus, Dante, Royal Charger, Watling Street, Fair Trial, Court Martial, Palestine, Pall Mall, Sayajirao, Petition and many others.

PHAROS
(1920, b or br c Phalaris – Scapa Flow, by Chaucer)

Owned and bred by the seventeenth Earl of Derby, Pharos was a very good but not a great racehorse. He was full-brother to Fairway (St Leger) and Fair Isle (1,000 Guineas). Beaten a length in the Derby by Papyrus in 1923, Pharos ran for four seasons, winning fourteen of his 30 races, including the Champion Stakes, for £15,694 in stakes. He never won beyond 1¼m.

As a sire he was an outstanding success, firstly in Britain, later in France where he died aged 17. In Britain his best winners were Cameronian (2,000 Guineas and Derby), Firdaussi (St Leger) and Rhodes Scholar (Eclipse Stakes). He got Nearco in Italy and Pharis in France, both unbeaten winners of the Grand Prix. He was champion sire in Britain in 1931 and in France in 1935 and 1939.

PHIL DRAKE
(1952, br c Admiral Drake – Philippa, by Vatellor)

Mme Suzy Volterra's Phil Drake won the Derby and Grand Prix de Paris in 1955, a double previously achieved this century only by Spearmint and My Love and not yet repeated. Phil Drake did not run again after being unplaced in the King George VI and Queen Elizabeth Stakes. He died at the age of twelve having sired only one top-class horse, Dicta Drake, second in the Derby and winner of the Grand Prix de Saint-Cloud and Coronation Cup.

PHILIPPS, James Perrott (1905-84)

'Jim' Philipps served in the Leicestershire Yeomanry, Shropshire Yeomanry and Royal Artillery. Among many business interests, he was chairman of Tote Investors. A member of the Jockey Club and one-time president of the Thoroughbred Breeders' Association, he inherited his racing interests, including Dalham Hall Stud at Newmarket, on the death of his father, Lord Milford, in 1928. Among the good horses he bred and owned were Great Nephew (second in the 2,000 Guineas), Running Free (Free Handicap and Lingfield Oaks Trial), Pinzon (Paradise Stakes and Winston Churchill Stakes), Lalibela (Cheveley Park Stakes) and Welsh Saint (Cork and Orrery Stakes). He was a patron of Sir Jack Jarvis's stable and on the latter's death sent his horses to Bruce Hobbs in Britain, Vincent O'Brien in Ireland and Etienne Pollet in France. Dalham Hall Stud was sold to Sheikh Mohammed in 1983 and Mr Philipps' racing interests were drastically reduced. He committed suicide in September 1984 after being told he might have liver cancer.

PHOTOGRAPH

A 'photograph' under the Rules of Racing is the photograph taken when the horses pass the winning-post by the camera installed under the authority of the stewards of the Jockey Club. The Judge usually calls for a print of the finish if the distance between two horses is half a length or less.

The first finish ('photo-finish') to be decided by the camera was on 22 April 1947, in the Great Metropolitan Handicap at Epsom, to determine second place between Parhelion and Salubrious, who were separated by a head.

PIA
(1964, br f Darius – Peseta II, by Neckar)

Pia, bred and owned by Countess Margit Batthyany and trained by Bill Elsey, won four races outright, dead-heated for the Park Hill Stakes, and was placed four times for earnings of £36,797. At two years she won the Cherry Hinton Stakes and finished second in the Cheveley Park Stakes, and at three she won the Oaks. At stud she bred three winners, including the Chester Vase runner-up Palladium, and the useful French-trained filly Principia, who produced the tip-top sprinter-miler Chief Singer.

PICTURE PLAY
(1941, b f Donatello II – Amuse, by Phalaris)

Picture Play was bred and owned by Mr H.J. Joel and won three races including the 1,000 Guineas. She bred seven winners and has proved a wonderful servant to the Joel stud and others as the ancestress of West Side Story (second in the Oaks and third in the 1,000 Guineas), Crocket (seven wins for £19,321), Royal Palace (2,000 Guineas and Derby), Welsh Pageant (Lockinge Stakes twice), Selhurst (Hardwicke Stakes), Light Cavalry (St Leger) and Fairy Footsteps (1,000 Guineas).

PIGGOTT, Lester (b. 1935)

Racing is in Lester Piggott's blood as his father, Keith Piggott, was a capable jumping jockey and subsequently ran a small 'mixed' stable very shrewdly. Lester's grandfather, Ernest Piggott, rode two Grand National winners and married a sister of Mornington and Kempton Cannon who both rode Derby winners. As regards the bottom half of his pedigree, Lester's mother is a member of a famous racing family, aunt of Fred and Bill Rickaby. He strengthened the racing ties in 1960 when he married Susan Armstrong, daughter of the Newmarket trainer Sam Armstrong.

Lester was apprenticed to his father and rode his first winner at the age of twelve, on The Chase at Haydock on 18 August 1948.

Precociously brilliant as a boy, he managed to survive a period of rather nauseating adulation by the popular Press, but rather too frequently fearlessness, coupled with sheer determination to win, degenerated into recklessness and brought him into conflict with the authorities. He rode his first Derby winner, Never Say Die, at the age of eighteen, but a fortnight later, as the result of his riding of Never Say Die in the King Edward VII Stakes at Ascot, he was suspended and reported to the stewards of the Jockey Club.

In due course the stewards of the Jockey Club informed him that they had 'taken notice of his dangerous and erratic riding both this season and in previous seasons, and that in spite of continuous warnings, he continued to show complete disregard for the Rules of Racing and for the safety of other jockeys.' A statement was then issued that before any application for a renewal of his licence could be entertained – he had been suspended for the rest of the season – he must be attached to some trainer other than his father for six months. The trainer selected was Jack Jarvis.

Some people took the view that the stewards had been hard on Piggott, but the suspension proved a blessing in the long run and a turning-point for the better in his career. It must be emphasized that numerous brushes with authority never adversely affected his nerve or his confidence, nor did they ever diminish his immense popularity with the general public, who readily forgave his indiscretions because his sins were due to a burning ambition to win whatever the cost. Small punters felt he was essentially on their side.

In the course of time he learned to temper boldness and dash with respect for the rules and for the necks of his fellow riders. Tall for a jockey, he rode very short indeed – too short for control, some critics said – and with his behind stuck up in the air, he was easily recognizable even if not particularly elegant. Cool, and in consequence unmoved by the importance of the occasion, he was flexible in his methods and could ride a waiting race, as on Sir

Ivor in the 1968 Derby, as effectively as he could force the pace if he considered the occasion suitable. There was no stronger finisher in the game.

Perhaps because he has always been slightly hard of hearing, he has never been a notable conversationalist but he has the knack of summing up a person or a situation in a few trenchant words. Having been pitchforked into a tough adult world at an early age, he gives the impression of being 'hard-boiled' and unsentimental. He is reputed to be knowledgeable about money and to study the financial columns of the newspapers with close attention. He is certainly a 'character', and stories of his deeds and comments form part of the lore and legend of modern racing.

He had a long, successful, though not invariably smooth association with Noel Murless's stable which he elected to terminate in 1966 to ride freelance. He thus missed winning the Derby on Royal Palace. In 1968 he became frequently associated with Vincent O'Brien's stable, and its rise to prominence owed much to Piggott's ability. He won the Derby for O'Brien on Sir Ivor, Nijinsky, Roberto and The Minstrel, and the Prix de l'Arc de Triomphe twice on Alleged. The association ended in 1980, and the following year, when he joined Henry Cecil, Piggott was champion jockey for the first time since 1971. He survived a horrific accident in the starting-stalls that year, but rumours that he might retire from riding to start training at stables he had bought in Newmarket again proved unfounded. The all-time record of 27 Classic winners by Frank Buckle was passed in 1984, when he won the Oaks and St Leger, and the following year, having won his 29th Classic, on Shadeed in the 2,000 Guineas, he finally ended speculation and retired to start training at Newmarket in 1986. His other record totals as a jockey were nine wins in the King George VI and Queen Elizabeth Stakes, and 11 in the Gold Cup at Royal Ascot.

Piggott's 29 Classic victories in Britain were:

2,000 Guineas: Crepello (1957); Sir Ivor (1968); Nijinsky (1970); Shadeed (1985)

1,000 Guineas: Humble Duty (1970); Fairy Footsteps (1981)

Derby: Never Say Die (1954); Crepello (1957); St Paddy (1960); Sir Ivor (1968); Nijinsky (1970); Roberto (1972); Empery (1976); The Minstrel (1977); Teenoso (1983) – 9, all-time record

Oaks: Carrozza (1957); Petite Etoile (1959); Valoris (1966); Juliette Marny (1975); Blue Wind (1981); Circus Plume (1984)

St Leger: St Paddy (1960); Aurelius (1961); Ribocco (1967); Ribero (1968); Nijinsky (1970); Athens Wood (1971); Boucher (1972); Commanche Run (1984).

Champion apprentice in 1950 and 1951, he was champion jockey eleven times – 1960, 1964-71, 1981, 1982 – and his best season was in 1966, when he rode 191 winners. He was awarded the OBE in the 1975 New Year Honours List.

PILGRIMAGE
(1875, b f The Earl or The Palmer – Lady Audley, by Macaroni)

This famous mare had high racing ability and won both the 2,000 Guineas and the 1,000 Guineas. At stud she bred Canterbury Pilgrim, who won the Oaks and was dam of Swynford (St Leger) and other good winners, including Chaucer, who did extremely well as a sire. Pilgrimage was also dam of Jeddah (Derby) and Loved One, sire of the dams of the Derby winners Sunstar and Sansovino.

PILLION
(1923, b f Chaucer – Double Back, by Bachelor's Double)

Owned and bred by Mr A. de Rothschild, Pillion was trained by J. Watson to win three races worth £10,090, including the 1,000 Guineas. She was not a success as a broodmare, her most notable achievements being as grandam of Aldborough (Doncaster Cup) and third dam of Kythnos (Irish 2,000 Guineas).

PINZA
(1950, b c Chanteur II – Pasqua, by Donatello II)

Pinza was a big, powerful, slightly coarse colt bred by Fred Darling. As a yearling he was bought for 1,500gns on behalf of Sir Victor Sassoon and was sent to be trained by Norman Bertie at Newmarket. He proved himself a great racehorse at his best, though not perhaps an entirely sound one. He won five races for £47,401, including the Derby by four lengths, defeating the Queen's colt Aureole and giving Sir Gordon Richards his one and only victory in the race. He then won the King George VI and Queen Elizabeth Stakes in equally decisive fashion but broke down soon afterwards and never ran again. He was leading first-season sire in 1957 but his standing soon went into decline, and he could be regarded as a disappointment when he died in 1977. His best produce were Pindari (third in the St Leger), Pinturischio (Wood Ditton Stakes) and Violetta III (dam of Irish 1,000 Guineas winner Favoletta and Oaks runner-up Furioso).

PIPE, Martin Charles (b. 1945)

Son of a West-Country bookmaker, Martin Pipe kept point-to-pointers and trained under permit at Wellington, Somerset, before he took out a licence for the first time in 1977. Better noted for his success with jumpers, he has also won the Ascot Stakes with Right Regent and Windsor Castle Stakes with Atall Atall at the royal meeting. His best season on the Flat was 1983 with 12 winners.

PIPER, Edwin (1888-1951)

Edwin Piper won the 1913 Derby on the 100-1 outsider Aboyeur following the disqualification of the favourite, Craganour. Piper won the Ascot Stakes soon after on Rivoli, but he obtained little riding after World War I and gradually dropped out of the game.

PITT, Arthur John (b. 1935)

Arthur Pitt began training at Epsom in 1965 having been apprenticed to permit-holder Vivian Bishop, served in the RAVC and been travelling head lad to Jackie Sirett. He trained Persian War over hurdles for a time and has done well with a small team of horses. His best Flat-racers have been Ocean King (Cesarewitch) and Rocamadour (third in Eclipse).

PLACK
(1921, ch f Hurry On – Groat, by Junior)

Plack was bred by Lord Rosebery and, although an inveterate tail-swisher, was a good, tough, game filly. She won nine races worth £11,467, including the 1,000 Guineas (from Mumtaz Mahal), Newmarket Oaks and Jockey Club Cup. She was second in the Oaks. She bred four winners and Afterthought, whom she produced when in her nineteenth year, won the Jockey Club Cup and was second in the Oaks, Champion Stakes and Gold Cup. Afterthought is the grandam of Aunt Edith, winner of the King George VI and Queen Elizabeth Stakes.

PLAISANTERIE
(1882, b f Wellingtonia – Poetess, by Trocadero)

Plaisanterie, bred and trained in France, won sixteen races and achieved the rare feat of winning the Cesarewitch and Cambridgeshire in the same year. She was the grandam of the St Leger winner Tracery.

PLATE

1. A 'plate' is a race for which a prize or prizes of definite value are guaranteed by the race-fund, with the entrance fee, forfeit, subscription or other contribution of owners going to the race-fund. Any surplus over the advertised value of a plate was credited to the Joint Administrative Authority. Plates were abolished in the 1970s, but the concept resurfaced early in the 1980s under the name of 'guaranteed sweepstakes'.

2. A plate is a light shoe worn by a horse for racing. The expression 'to spread a plate' means that the shoe has widened out and protruded from under

the horse's foot. This can be a serious handicap in a race, and the shoe is removed and the horse replated if it is noticed in time.

3. Plate is also a colloquial term for the saddle, as in the phrase 'in the plate'.

PLUCKY LIEGE
(1912, b f Spearmint – Concertina, by St Simon)

One of the greatest mares of this century, Plucky Liège was bred by Lord Michelham, for whom she won four two-year-old races worth £1,811. She was first called Lucky Liège but this was changed on account of her owner's admiration for the defence of Liège in 1914.

Plucky Liège went to stud in France. The first of her offspring of any note was Sir Gallahad III, by Teddy. His successes included the French 2,000 Guineas and Lincolnshire Handicap. For two years he was at stud in France and sired Galaday II, dam of the 1,000 Guineas and Oaks winner Galatea II, and great-grandam of the Derby and St Leger winner Never Say Die. Sir Gallahad III then went to America, where he was champion sire four times.

Bull Dog and Quatre Bras were full brothers of Sir Gallahad III and like him they went to America. Bull Dog did almost as well as a sire there as his elder brother, and his son Bull Lea was champion sire five times, the best of his offspring being Citation, who won over a million dollars. Quatre Bras, who won ten races in America besides winning in France, did well as a sire, too, but his achievements were not on a par with those of his brothers.

Plucky Liège's son Admiral Drake won the Grand Prix de Paris and sired the Derby winner Phil Drake. Plucky Liège also bred the winners Marguerite de Valois, Chivalry, Elsa de Brabant, Noble Lady and Noor Jahan, while at the advanced age of 23 she produced Bois Roussel, who won the Derby in 1938.

POGROM
(1919, b f Lemberg – Popingaol, by Dark Ronald)

Pogrom was bred by Lord Astor and was trained by Alec Taylor. She won 6½ races worth £15,046, including the Oaks, Newmarket Oaks and Coronation Stakes. Her half-sister, Book Law, was second in the Oaks and won the St Leger. She was a failure at stud.

POLEMARCH
(1918, ch c The Tetrarch – Pomace, by Polymelus)

Polemarch was bred and owned by Lord Londonderry and was trained by Tom Green. He won five races for £9,125, including the Gimcrack Stakes and St Leger. He was one of three St Leger winners sired by The Tetrarch. He was exported to Argentina and did well·as a sire there.

POLLET, Etienne

Etienne Pollet was one of the outstanding French trainers of the post-war era, having begun training in 1942. His outstanding horse was Sea-Bird, winner of the Derby in 1965. His other successes in Britain included the 1,000 Guineas and Oaks (Never Too Late II), King George VI and Queen Elizabeth Stakes (Right Royal V), Ascot Gold Cup (Pan II) and 1,000 Guineas and Champion Stakes (Hula Dancer). He delayed his retirement for a year in order to complete the programme of Sea-Bird's son Gyr, who was runner-up in the 1970 Derby.

POLYGAMY
(1971, b f Reform – Seventh Bride, by Royal Record II)

Peter Walwyn, who had trained Mabel, Frontier Goddess and State Pension to finish second in the Oaks, achieved his first success in the race with Polygamy, bred at her owner Louis Freedman's Cliveden Stud. She won four other races and was narrowly beaten into second place by Highclere in the 1,000 Guineas. She ran only once more after the Oaks, finishing third in the Irish Oaks, and it

POLYMELUS
(1902, b c Cyllene – Maid Marian, by Hampton)

Polymelus was a very good middle-distance horse who was suspected of not being a genuine stayer. In 1906 Mr S.B. Joel bought him as a four-year-old, at the Newmarket October Sales, for 4,000gns. Before that season was over, Polymelus won the Duke of York Stakes at Kempton and then, with a 10lb penalty, the Cambridgeshire. He was a hot favourite for the Cambridgeshire, and Mr Joel and his friends won £100,000 in bets. As a sire Polymelus was an outstanding success. He was five times champion and got three Derby winners, Pommern, Fifinella and Humorist. His immense influence on thoroughbred breeding stemmed from the top-class sprinter Phalaris, sire of Fairway and Pharos.

POLYPHONTES
(1921, b c Polymelus – St Josephine, by St Denis)

Polyphontes was owned and bred by Mr S.B. Joel and won four races worth £26,566, including the Eclipse Stakes twice and the Ascot Derby. He proved a moderate sire.

POMMERN
(1912, Polymelus – Merry Agnes, by St Hilaire)

Pommern, owned by Mr S.B. Joel and trained by C. Peck, won a war-substitute 'Triple Crown' among his seven victories for £15,616. He was not a stud success.

PONTEFRACT

Set in countryside that has suffered greatly through industrialization, Pontefract is one of the minor Yorkshire meetings which draws heavily on its local popularity. Racing is known to have taken place there during the Civil War. In March 1644, a fortnight before the royalist stronghold of Pontefract Castle,

'the key to the north', surrendered to the Roundheads, a race-meeting was held there. In 1649 Pontefract Castle, which for 600 years had played its part in English history, was razed to the ground at the request of the prudent citizens of Pontefract who had conveniently changed from support of Charles I to support of Cromwell.

The track is left-handed, with a sharp bend into the 2f straight. It is noticeably undulating but the final 3f are uphill, rendering the course quite a test of stamina, particularly for two-year-olds. Low numbers are best in the draw, especially in sprint races. With a good draw, though, a swift start is essential to avoid being cut off as the runners crowd over to the rails. Originally a horseshoe shape, with a maximum distance of $1\frac{1}{2}$m, the track was developed into a circuit of about 2m in 1983, and the following year it was possible to stage one of Britain's longest races, over an extended 2m 5f, on the course with the longest closed circuit in the country.

The going in summer tended to become very hard, but in a deal negotiated with a nearby colliery a watering system was introduced in 1980, and this has added to the attraction of nearby motorways in encouraging runners from the South.

PONT L'EVEQUE
(1937, b c Barneveldt – Ponteba, by Belfonds)

Pont l'Evêque was bred by Mr H.E. Morriss who imported Ponteba, carrying Pont l'Evêque, from France in 1936. Trained by Fred Darling, Pont l'Evêque was a moderate two-year-old, and when, at the end of the season, Mr Morriss asked Darling to find a buyer, Darling decided to take a chance and bought the colt himself for £500.

Pont l'Evêque did well physically during the winter and won a race at Newbury in the spring with singular ease. Darling cabled Mr Morriss, who was in the Far East, offering him a half share in Pont l'Evêque for 2,500gns. Perhaps not surprisingly in the circumstances, Mr Morriss did not reply. Pont l'Evêque was beaten in the Newmarket Stakes but, starting at 10-1 and ridden by Sam Wragg, he won the Derby, run at Newmarket, by three lengths. In his only other race Pont l'Evêque was third in the Champion Stakes. In 1942 he was exported to Argentina but did only moderately as a sire there.

POPE, Major Michael Brownfield (b. 1917)

Major Michael Pope served in the Royal Horse Guards and the North Irish Horse during World War II. He began training in 1947 at stables at Streatley, Berkshire. He won the Wokingham Stakes (Golden Leg), Great Metropolitan (Luxury Hotel) and Queen's Prize (Royal Ridge), and also trained that game and consistent handicapper Birdbrook to win sixteen races. He retired from training in September 1973 and, as well as managing the stud and racing interests of Lord McAlpine, he became president of the newly formed National Trainers'· Federation from the start of 1974.

PORCHESTER, Lord (b. 1924)

Lord Porchester served in the Royal Horse Guards after being educated at Eton and the Royal Agricultural College at Cirencester. He is the Queen's racing manager (from 1969), a former chairman of the Flat Race Pattern Committee (until 1985) and a past president of the Thoroughbred Breeders' Association. One of the first top-class horses he owned was Tamerlane, whom he bought for 5,000gns and whose victories included the New Stakes, July Stakes and St James's Palace Stakes. Other good horses he has bred at his Highclere Stud and owned are Hiding Place (Nell Gwyn Stakes), Smuggler (Yorkshire Cup, Gordon Stakes), Matinee (Portland Handicap), Kittyhawk (Lowther Stakes) and Little Wolf (Ascot Gold Cup).

Racing colours: Eton Blue, black hooped cap.

PORTER, John (1838-1922)

Born at Rugeley, John Porter was one of the greatest trainers of the Victorian era. He was originally apprenticed to John Day in Sussex, and became head lad to William Goater when he took over the stable. Porter began training on his own account at the age of 25, when appointed private trainer to Sir Joseph Hawley. In 1867 the partnership moved to new stables at Kingsclere in Berkshire, which Porter bought on Sir Joseph Hawley's death in 1875. Porter won the Derby seven times – with Blue Gown, Shotover, St Blaise, Ormonde, Sainfoin, Common and Flying Fox – and had sixteen other Classic successes as well, with Ormonde, Common and Flying Fox winning the Triple Crown, and the filly La Flèche winning the 1,000 Guineas, Oaks and St Leger. He retired from training in 1905. Honest and conscientious but hardly noted for his humour, he was largely instrumental in planning the construction of Newbury racecourse.

PORTLAND, 4th Duke of (1768-1854)

The fourth Duke of Portland won the 1819 Derby with Tiresias. When he died in 1854, he had been a member of the Jockey Club for over 50 years. In 1831 he advanced money to the Jockey Club for the purchase at Newmarket of the Coffee Room, New Rooms and adjuncts. He owned part of Newmarket Heath and did much work at his own expense to improve the heath as a racing centre. Furthermore, he bought land surrounding the heath in case it should ever fall into the hands of persons hostile to racing.

In 1827 he was instrumental in establishing the Jockey Club's right to warn allegedly undesirable individuals off Newmarket Heath. There was a disputed bet, and the Jockey Club's decision on that matter greatly displeased a certain Mr Hawkins, who showed his feelings in a somewhat uncouth manner by swearing horribly at Lord Wharncliffe. The Jockey Club thereupon warned him off the heath. Mr Hawkins fought back gamely and brought an action against the Jockey Club. The case was defended by the Duke of Portland on behalf of the club, and the club's right to the action taken against Mr Hawkins was upheld by the judge.

Nowadays the Jockey Club takes no cognisance of betting disputes, which are settled by Tattersalls' Committee.

PORTLAND, 6th Duke of (1857-1943)

The sixth Duke of Portland was an ensign in the Coldstream Guards when he succeeded to the title and a fortune in 1879. He at once decided to revive the glories of the Welbeck Stud and wisely chose Mat Dawson as his trainer. On Dawson's advice he bought St Simon at the sale of Prince Batthyany's horses for 1,600gns. St Simon was undefeated on the racecourse but, owing to the rule then existing, he could not run in the 2,000 Guineas (his only Classic engagement) due to the death of his nominator, Prince Batthyany. There has never been a greater stallion than St Simon, who was champion sire on nine occasions.

Nor did the Duke's luck end with St Simon, as between 1888 and 1902 he won eleven Classics and two Ascot Gold Cups. He won the 2,000 Guineas with Ayrshire (1888), 1,000 Guineas with Semolina (1890) and Amiable (1894), Derby with Ayrshire (1888) and Donovan (1889), Oaks with Memoir (1890), Mrs Butterwick (1893), Amiable (1894) and La Roche (1900), and St Leger with Donovan (1889) and Memoir (1890). His Gold Cup winners were St Simon (1884) and William the Third (1902).

With the turn of the century the Duke's luck began to run out. He lost his enthusiasm for the Turf, and his colours were seldom seen in the last twenty years of his life. A generous, friendly and straightforward man, he dispersed much of the prize money he won on the Turf in charity.

POST

'Post' is a slightly muddling term as it is used to denote both the start and the finish of a race. 'Going down to the post' means a horse is cantering down to the start, while 'got his head in front on the post' denotes a horse taking the lead in the few strides before the winning-post.

POURPARLER (1961, b f Hugh Lupus – Review, by Panorama)

Bred by Commander Peter Fitzgerald, Pourparler was a half-sister to Fleet (1,000 Guineas) and Display (Coronation Stakes). She was bought for 7,000gns as a yearling by Beatrice, Lady Granard, and trained by Paddy Prendergast. She won the National Stakes, Lowther Stakes, 1,000 Guineas and £39,344 in prize money. She disappointed at stud.

PRATT, William Archer (1878-1957)

Willie Pratt was the son of the Cheltenham trainer Francis Pratt, whose wife was Fred Archer's sister. Willie was apprenticed to James Ryan at Newmarket and when he was fourteen he rode Cypria to dead-heat for the Cesarewitch with Red Eyes. Fifty years later he trained Whiteway to win the same race.

When still a boy he was appointed jockey to the powerful Rothschild stable in France, and between 1898 and 1903 he rode the winner of the Grand Prix on four occasions. In 1904 he was appointed trainer to M. Jean Stern and trained in France with success till 1940 when he returned to Britain and set up a small stable. During Walter Earl's serious illness in 1949, he took charge of the Stanley House stable and prepared that great stayer Alycidon to win the Goodwood and Doncaster Cups.

PRATT & Co

Messrs Pratt and Company, with offices in Haywards Heath managed by David Cameron, Clifford Griggs and Derek Hubbard, are stakeholders and also run the racecourses at Folkestone, Fontwell Park and Plumpton, having previously also acted for Cheltenham and the now-defunct Alexandra Park.

PRECIPICE WOOD (1966, gr c Lauso – Grecian Garden, by Kingstone)

Rosemary Lomax became the first woman trainer to have her name officially attached to the winner of a big race in

Britain when Precipice Wood won the Ascot Gold Cup in 1970. Precipice Wood won five other races but had a setback when being prepared for the Doncaster Cup and was retired to stand his first season at stud in 1971. Not unexpectedly, his best offspring were jumpers, including the Cheltenham Gold Cup winner Forgive n' Forget and the leading hunter chasers Compton Lad and Mr Mellors. Precipice Wood died in 1980.

PRECIPITATION
(1933, ch c Hurry On – Double Life, by Bachelor's Double)

Bred and owned by Lady Zia Wernher, Precipitation did not run as a two-year-old or compete in the Classics, but he was a top-class racehorse, his seven successes for £18,419 including the King Edward VII Stakes at Ascot, Jockey Club Stakes at Newmarket and Ascot Gold Cup. He ensured the survival of the Hurry On male line by siring Chamossaire, who won the 1945 St Leger and sired the Derby winner Santa Claus. Precipitation also sired Airborne (Derby and St Leger), Premonition (St Leger), Why Hurry (Oaks) and Sheshoon (Gold Cup). His son Summertime was a top stallion in New Zealand. Precipitation died in 1957.

PREDOMINATE
(1952, ch g Preciptic – Garryhinch, by Great Scot)

As a yearling Predominate was bought in Dublin for 1,150gns by Ken Cundell acting for Mrs G. Trimmer-Thompson. For her he won five races worth £2,580 at two, three and four years of age. He then went hurdling, winning two races. The following year Mr H.J. Joel bought him and it was decided to keep him for the Flat. Trained by Ted Leader, he was second in the Cesarewitch – he had been third in that race for his previous owner – and won the Queen Alexandra Stakes, the Goodwood Stakes three years running and, at nine years of age, the Goodwood Cup. He had thus won an important race at the big Goodwood meeting four years in succession. The Cup was his final race. In all, this gallant old gelding won

fourteen races and over £17,000 in prize money.

PREMONITION
(1950, b c Precipitation – Trial Ground, by Fair Trial)

Premonition was bred by the Dunchurch Lodge Stud and owned by Brigadier W.P. Wyatt. Trained by Cecil Boyd-Rochfort he won eight races worth over £27,000, including the St Leger, Blue Riband Trial Stakes, Voltigeur Stakes, Winston Churchill Stakes and Yorkshire Cup. He also finished first in the Irish Derby but was disqualified, unjustifiably so in the opinion of many of those who saw the race. He started joint favourite for the Epsom Derby with Pinza but ran disappointingly. He was not a success at stud.

PRENDERGAST, Patrick J. (1909-80)

Paddy Prendergast became one of the greatest Irish trainers but certainly came up the hard way. Before World War II he was a minor steeplechase jockey, riding for the most part mediocre horses at second-class meetings. After the war he got his chance as a trainer and seized it with both hands. For 30 years his career was one of almost unbroken success except for one rather sharp brush with the British racing authorities. One of the main reasons for this swift climb to fame was his skill in picking yearlings, and two very fast two-year-olds who helped to make his name, The Pie King and Windy City, were by no means fashionably bred. He was also helped by his skill in attracting a number of wealthy American patrons able to pay top prices at the sales. He won the Coventry Stakes six times and the Gimcrack Stakes four times, but his ability was not restricted to fast horses, and though he never won the Derby, he trained top-class middle-distance horses in Ragusa (St Leger, Irish Sweeps Derby, King George VI and Queen Elizabeth Stakes), Meadow Court (Irish Sweeps Derby, King George VI and Queen Elizabeth Stakes), Khalkis (Eclipse Stakes) and Noblesse (Oaks). He was the first Irish trainer to be leading trainer in Britain, in 1963, and repeated the feat in 1964 and 1965. His last major win was with Nikoli in the 1980 Irish 2,000 Guineas in the year of his death after a long illness.

His big winners in Britain were:

2,000 Guineas: Martial (1960)
1,000 Guineas: Pourparler (1964)
Oaks: Noblesse (1963)
St Leger: Ragusa (1963)
Chester Cup: Credo (1964)
Coventry Stakes: The Pie King (1953); Martial (1959); Typhoon (1960); Young Emperor (1965); Bold Lad (1966); Prince Tenderfoot (1969)
Queen Mary Stakes: Paddy's Sister (1959); Grizel (1968)
Eclipse Stakes: Khalkis (1963); Ragusa (1964)
King George VI and Queen Elizabeth Stakes: Ragusa (1963); Meadow Court (1965)
Sussex Stakes: Carlemont (1965)
Gimcrack Stakes: Windy City (1951); The Pie King (1953); Paddy's Sister (1959); Young Emperor (1965)
Champagne Stakes: Paddy's Sister (1959); Clear Sound (1961); Hardicanute (1964); Bold Lad (1966)
Middle Park Stakes: Bold Lad (1966)
Cheveley Park Stakes: Sixpence (1953); Display (1961)
Timeform Gold Cup: Noblesse (1962); Hardicanute (1964).

PRESCOTT, Sir Mark (b. 1948)

Sir Mark Prescott was just short of his 21st birthday when he took over training at Newmarket on the retirement of Jack Waugh through ill-health. He had previously been a pupil with Syd Kernick and Frank Cundell. His specific skill as a trainer has been in placing his horses, so that the Victoria Cup success of Heave To stands out as one of the few big-race triumphs, though he placed the two-year-old Spindrifter to win thirteen races in 1980. He had his first winner with Belle Royale at Stockton in April 1971, and that set the pattern for his frequent trips to the North. His best season numerically was 1981 with 36 winners.

PRETENDER
(1866, b c Adventurer – Ferina, by Venison)

Mr J. Johnstone's Pretender, trained by Tom Dawson at Tupgill, won the 2,000 Guineas and Derby in 1869. No North-country horse has won the Epsom Derby since, though Dante won a war-substitute Derby at Newmarket in 1945. Pretender made no mark as a sire.

PRETENDRE
(1963, ch c Doutelle – Limicola, by Verso II)

Bred by the Princess Royal, Prétendre was bought as a foal for 3,600gns by Mr J.A.C. Lilley, who sent him to be trained by Jack Jarvis. A big, impressive chestnut, Prétendre won six races, including the Dewhurst Stakes and Observer Gold Cup at two years, and was placed three times for total stakes of £44,414. He ran the race of his life in the Derby in which, ridden by Paul Cook, he was beaten a neck by Charlottown. At the end of 1966 he was sold for $425,000 through the British Bloodstock Agency to the American owner Mr Bunker Hunt. He was at stud in Lexington, USA, for three seasons and then alternated for two years between Britain and New Zealand, where he died in 1972. His son Cañonero won the Kentucky Derby and Preakness Stakes.

PRETTY POLLY
(1901, ch f Gallinule – Admiration, by Saraband)

Pretty Polly, one of the great fillies of racing history, was bred in Ireland by Major Eustace Loder. She was a big, powerful chestnut by Gallinule (who had gone wrong in his wind and was inclined to break blood vessels), out of Admiration, a very modest performer who won two minor events on the Flat in Ireland and was placed in a military steeplechase at Punchestown.

Pretty Polly went to Newmarket to be trained by Peter Gilpin. At first she gave out little promise and was very sluggish in her work but gradually she began to improve. Even so it came as a surprise to her trainer when she won her first race, the International Stakes at Sandown, by ten lengths. Before the season was over, she was the idol of the racing public, winning eight more races, including the National Breeders' Produce Stakes, Champagne Stakes, Cheveley Park Stakes and Middle Park Stakes. Not once was she in danger of defeat.

The following season she won the 1,000 Guineas, Oaks, Coronation Stakes at Ascot, Nassau Stakes at Goodwood, St Leger and Park Hill Stakes. At that point Major Loder decided he would like her to take on the best horses in France so she was sent to run in the Prix du Conseil Municipal at Longchamp. She had a bad train journey and, to the consternation of the racing world, was beaten by the unconsidered Presto II. Danny Maher, who rode her, said that, although she had won the St Leger in record time, she was not a true stayer. The Paris race was over $1\frac{1}{2}$m on heavy going.

On her return to Britain, Pretty Polly won the Free Handicap, giving weight and a beating to the Derby winner St Amant.

As a four-year-old she was unbeaten, winning the Coronation Cup, Champion Stakes, Limekiln Stakes and Jockey Club Cup. As a five-year-old she won the Coronation Cup and March Stakes but in the Ascot Gold Cup, her final race, she was beaten by a length by Bachelor's Button. She was not quite at her best that day and in addition her rider, Bernard Dillon, lost his head and disobeyed orders. Possibly the distance was a shade too far for her, too. Altogether she won 22 of her 24 races and over £37,000 in stakes.

She was too highly strung and nervous to make an ideal broodmare and was not a good mother, with the result that her offspring were inclined to be delicate when young. She never produced anything nearly as good as herself, but one daughter, Molly Desmond, won the Cheveley Park Stakes, and another, Polly Flinders, the National Breeders' Produce Stakes. However, her stud reputation has been ensured by the many glittering successes won by later descendants including St Paddy, Brigadier Gerard,

Donatello, Psidium, Vienna, Supreme Court and Only For Life. Pretty Polly died in 1931.

PRICE, Captain Henry Ryan (b. 1912)

Ryan Price began training under NH Rules in Sussex in 1937 but it was only after World War II, in which he served with the Commandos, that he became well known to the public. He made his reputation as a jumping trainer and won almost every big race, including the Grand National, Cheltenham Gold Cup and Champion Hurdle (three times). He trained a few Flat horses and won the Manchester November Handicap in 1957, Cesarewitch in 1963, 1966 and 1968, and Chester Cup in 1968. His move into Flat racing was completed in 1971, when he handed over all his jumpers to the care of Josh Gifford and announced his intention of concentrating on the Flat. Though he failed in his ambition to win the Derby, he did win the Oaks with Ginevra and St Leger with Bruni, as well as the Gimcrack Stakes, Champagne Stakes and Champion Stakes with Giacometti, and the Nunthorpe Stakes with Sandford Lad, proving his all-round skill as a trainer. He retired at the end of 1982, and his stables at Findon were taken over for a short time by his former assistant, Con Horgan.

PRIMERA (1954, b c My Babu – Pirette, by Deiri)

Foaled in 1954, Primera was bred by the Maharaja of Baroda. He raced until he was six and improved with age. Altogether he won nine races worth over £18,000, including the Churchill Stakes, Ormonde Stakes, Princess of Wales's Stakes (twice) and Ebor Handicap with 9st. As a sire he was not consistent but his fillies, who generally outshone his colts, included top-class performers in Aunt Edith (Nassau Stakes, Prix Vermeille, Yorkshire Cup and King George VI and Queen Elizabeth Stakes), Greengage (Coronation Stakes and over £18,000 in stakes), Lupe (Oaks and Coronation Cup) and Attica Meli

Trainers and Owners
The Aga Khan leads in Mahmoud, the third of his six Derby winners, at Epsom
in 1936. Mahmoud set a record time for the race and gave jockey Charlie Smirke
the second of his four Derby wins.

John Porter, right, who trained the winners of 23 British Classics, is pictured with Chevalier Ginistrelli, left, owner-trainer of Signorinetta.

Admiral Rous, a pillar of the Turf for almost 40 years in the 19th century.

Mat Dawson, trainer of 28 British Classic winners, portrayed by the popular periodical Baily's Magazine.

No. 79.   MEN OF THE DAY NO. 5.
"As straight as a reed."

BAILY'S MAGAZINE
of
Sports and Pastimes

VOL. XLIII

LONDON A.H.BAILY & C.º

1885.

Fred Darling, six times leading trainer, pictured with Sun Chariot, who in 1942 won three British Classics towards Darling's career total of 19.

Pat Eddery, left, and Vincent O'Brien have formed a powerful jockey and trainer combination since 1980.

Sir Noel Murless, whose record in big races is the best of any British trainer since the Second World War.

The Queen and Lord Rosebery, two of Britain's most successful owner-breeders this century, are seen at Epsom on Derby Day 1960.

Lester Piggott, Henry Cecil and Jim Joel: jockey, trainer and owner.

(Yorkshire Oaks, Park Hill Stakes and Doncaster Cup). Primera was exported to Japan in 1969, the year before Lupe gave him his sole Classic success in Britain.

PRINCE CHEVALIER
(1943, b c Prince Rose – Chevalerie, by Abbot's Speed)

Foaled in France, Prince Chevalier was a handsome colt and a top-class performer, winning the French Derby and finishing second in the Grand Prix (beaten a short head), French St Leger and Prix de l'Arc de Triomphe (beaten a head). Brought to Britain as a sire, he got the 1951 Derby winner Arctic Prince. Other good winners he sired were Doutelle, whose early death was such a loss to breeders, and Court Harwell, sire of the Irish Sweeps Derby winner Meadow Court. Prince Chevalier's best son in France was Charlottesville, who won the French Derby and Grand Prix and sired the 1966 Derby winner Charlottown. He died in 1961.

PRINCELY GIFT
(1951, b c Nasrullah – Blue Gem, by Blue Peter)

Princely Gift was bred by Mr A.E. Allnatt and bought for 5,000gns as a yearling by Sir Victor Sassoon. Trained by Noel Murless, he proved a high-class sprinter, winning nine races and over £6,000 in stakes. His best performance was to win the Portland Handicap with 9st 4lb. Standing at stud in Ireland, he did well as a stallion, particularly in siring a number of top-class horses who went on to become sires, notably Tesco Boy (a leading sire in Japan), Fabergé II (sire of Rheingold and Giacometti), Frankincense (£12,836), So Blessed (£19,616), Tribal Chief (sire of Mrs McArdy) and Sun Prince (£47,922). Princely Gift died in 1973.

PRINCE PALATINE
(1908, b c Persimmon – Lady Lightfoot, by Isinglass)

Prince Palatine was the best racing son of a great sire, Persimmon, and one of the finest stayers seen on the British Turf this century. Bred by Lord Wavertree and owned for most of his racing career by Mr T.R. Pilkington, he was not an entirely taking horse in appearance, being a very bad walker who suffered intermittently from foot trouble, and he always had an untidy mane and tail. He sometimes ran unaccountably badly, probably on account of his feet.

Trained by Beardsley at Whatcombe, he won eleven races worth £36,354, including the St Leger, Eclipse Stakes, Ascot Gold Cup (twice), Coronation Cup, Jockey Club Stakes and Doncaster Cup. In 1913 Mr J.B. Joel created a sensation by buying him for £45,000 just before the big Goodwood meeting. He was started in the Goodwood Cup but owing to foot trouble was quite unfit to run. Towards the finish, he was staggering from sheer exhaustion, and the race undoubtedly broke his heart.

Perhaps because of his terrible Goodwood ordeal, Prince Palatine was not a success as a sire, his career being divided between Britain, France and the United States before he was burnt to death at the age of sixteen in America. However, when in Britain he got Rose Prince (Cesarewitch and Queen Alexandra Stakes), who carried on the sire line through Prince Rose and his sons.

PRINCE REGENT
(1966, b c Right Royal V – Noduleuse, by Nosca)

Bred and owned by the Comtesse de la Valdène, Prince Regent was trained at Chantilly by E. Pollet. He won twice as a two-year-old and as a three-year-old swiftly proved his merit by victories in the Prix Greffulhe and Prix Lupin. His trainer confidently expected him to win the Derby but Deforge rode an ill-judged race and, despite making a remarkable late run from the rear of the field, he was only third to Blakeney and Shoemaker. In the Irish Sweeps Derby, which he won in great style, he was admirably ridden by Geoff Lewis and showed terrific acceleration in the final furlong to overhaul Ribofilio, who had looked all over a winner. His six wins and five places were worth a total of £153,283. He was at stud in Ireland for six seasons and spent three years in France before returning to Ireland in 1984. He was unable to maintain the bright start that brought Easy Regent (Critérium de Saint-Cloud) and Red Regent (City and Suburban Handicap) in his first crop. Red Regent sired Cajun (Middle Park Stakes) in his first crop.

PRINCE SIMON
(1947, b c Princequillo – Dancing Dora, by Sir Gallahad III)

Bred and owned by Mr William Woodward, chairman for many years of the New York Jockey Club, Prince Simon was an exceptionally handsome colt trained at Newmarket by Captain Cecil Boyd-Rochfort. Favourite for the 2,000 Guineas, he failed by a short head to catch Palestine. A hot favourite for the Derby, he was beaten a head by the French colt Galcador. In the King Edward VII Stakes at Ascot he started at 8-1 on and got beaten. He never ran again and left for stud in the United States having won two races for £2,565 but failing to live up to his reputation. His stud career proved a fiasco.

PRINCESS DORRIE
(1911, br f Your Majesty – Doris, by Loved One)

Bred and owned by Mr J.B. Joel, Princess Dorrie won two races, the 1,000 Guineas and Oaks for £9,900, after being beaten in all her eight races as a two-year-old. She was not a success at stud.

PRITCHARD-GORDON, Gavin Alexander (b. 1945)

Gavin Pritchard-Gordon took over the licence at Newmarket on the retirement in 1972 of Harvey Leader, to whom he had been assistant for six years. His first win was with Trillium at Warwick on 3 April 1972. Five years later he moved into the Stanley House Stables at Newmarket. In his original quarters the best horses he trained were Ardoon (Royal Hunt Cup) and Record Run (Prince of Wales's

Stakes), while the best from his present yard has been the French import Noalcoholic, who came to Newmarket to spend a short time before being sent to Australia as a stallion and stayed long enough to win the Lockinge and Sussex Stakes. Numerically his best season was 1979, with 58 winners.

PRIVY COUNCILLOR
(1959, ch c Counsel – High Number, by His Highness)

Bred and owned by Major Gerald Glover, Privy Councillor was trained by Tom Waugh. He was nothing out of the ordinary as a two-year-old, winning races at Birmingham, Leicester and Warwick, but he made immense improvement, and the following season after winning the Free Handicap with 8st 4lb, he won the 2,000 Guineas by three lengths, starting at 100-6 and ridden by W. Rickaby. The rest of his career was an anti-climax and he did not win again. He was exported to Japan in 1969, having done little of note as a stallion in Britain, though his daughter Sweet Councillor later bred the Eclipse Stakes winner Gunner B.

PRIZE MONEY

Levels of prize money in Britain are generally lower than in most major racing nations, especially in comparison with the United States, though the gap between France and Britain has been considerably narrowed in recent years. It must be remembered, though, that in many overseas countries either a Tote monopoly exists or bookmakers are allowed to bet only on the racecourses, and in consequence a far higher proportion of the profits from betting are ploughed into the sport. Where bookmakers do exist abroad, as in America and Australia, they tend to be strictly controlled and sharply taxed. Where off-course betting is illegal, except through government agencies, such as in Hong Kong, racecourse attendances are considerably boosted.

However, the arguments for increasing prize money in Britain have not always been well received. The Royal Commission on Gambling, which reported in July 1978, noted: 'The case for more prize money has been put far too high. We can see little evidence of the onset of the decline in the industry which we note has been confidently predicted for over 50 years. The number of horses in training has been consistently high ... there has been no decline in the number of trainers. We found the argument for increased prize money as a remedy for the low wages of stable staff particularly unconvincing.'

Until the advent of the Betting Levy Board in 1961, racecourse executives were responsible for the provision of prize money offered in races they staged, after taking into account the money provided by owners in the form of entry fees and forfeits. Increased wages costs and taxation imposed heavy burdens on racecourses and owners alike, with the result that racecourses were unable to raise prize money levels to any great degree, and their share has declined in the last twenty years. Prize money contributed by the Betting Levy Board and an increasing number of commercial sponsors have helped increase prize money, and since the arrival of the Pattern race system there has been a move towards rewarding the best races at the expense of those at the lower end of the ability scale. In 1963 the Betting Levy Board gave £382,738 towards prize money on the Flat; in 1984 they budgeted for £6,412,355. In 1970 total prize money was £3,418,764 – made up of £752,674 (22 per cent) contributed by owners to sweepstakes, £1,384,270 (40.5 per cent) from racecourses, £1,041,265 (30.5 per cent) from the Betting Levy Board and £240,555 (7 per cent) from sponsors. In 1984 total prize money was £16,842,364 – comprising £5,157,852 (30.6 per cent) from owners, £2,377,339 (14.1 per cent) from racecourses, £6,378,565 (37.9 per cent) from the Betting Levy Board and £2,928,608 (17.4 per cent) from sponsors.

PROVIDEO
(1982, br c Godswalk – Nadwa, by Tyrant)

Provideo, bred by his owner, Ahmed Foustok, became the first two-year-old to be voted Racehorse of the Year when he set a twentieth-century record for the number of juvenile wins in a season and equalled the 99-year-old record of The Bard by winning sixteen times. Unlike The Bard's, his season did not include a walk-over, and he had several very hard races, from which he emerged as courageous as on the first day of the season, when he won the Brocklesby Stakes at Doncaster. He equalled The Bard's record at Redcar on 1 November and even had a later outing in the United States, though unsuccessful. He was plagued by training troubles as a three-year-old and failed to win again. He was trained by Bill O'Gorman, whose meticulous planning enabled Provideo to surpass the recent achievements of thirteen juvenile wins by Nagwa (1975) and Spindrifter (1980).

PROVOKE
(1962, b c Aureole – Tantalizer, by Tantième)

Bred and owned by Mr J.J. Astor, Provoke took plenty of time to come to hand when sent to be trained by Dick Hern but he made rapid improvement as a three-year-old and won four races for total stakes of £45,622, his finest hour coming when at Doncaster, in torrential rain and on heavy going, he defeated the 11-4 on favourite Meadow Court by ten lengths in the St Leger at 28-1.

He never raced again. The following year he contracted a virus infection that afflicted his stable and was unable to run. He was then sold to Russia but died soon after his arrival there.

PSIDIUM
(1958, ch c Pardal – Dinarella, by Niccolo dell'Arca)

Mrs A. Plesch's Psidium, trained by Harry Wragg and ridden by R. Poincelet, won the Derby at 66-1. He went to Epsom having been beaten by eight of the field and ridden by his seventh different jockey. As he never ran again, it is a moot point whether he was a very good horse or whether his victory was one of those curious flukes that sometimes happen in racing. His two wins were worth £37,048, and he retired to stud in Newmarket in 1962, before being exported to Argentina in 1970. He sired only one horse to win more than £10,000 in a season in Britain – Sodium (St Leger and Irish Sweeps Derby) – but that horse's success in 1966 was almost enough to make Psidium leading sire.

Psidium's Derby victory was an example of the international character of modern racing. Bred in Ireland, Psidium was by the French-bred sire Pardal out of Dinarella, who was bred in Italy. Mrs Plesch was the wife of a Hungarian-born financier, Harry Wragg was British and Poincelet French.

PUNTER

The common term for anyone who bets on horse-racing.

Q

QUASHED
(1932, b f Obliterate – Verdict, by Shogun)

During the past 116 years only five fillies or mares have won the Gold Cup at Ascot: Brigantine (1869), Apology (1876), La Flèche (1894), Quashed (1936) and Gladness (1958). Quashed also won the Oaks and is the only winner of that race, bar the American-bred Cap and Bells, who is ineligible for inclusion in the Stud Book. Quashed was bred by Lady Barbara Smith and was out of Verdict, winner of the Cambridgeshire and Coronation Cup. Verdict was doubly half-bred as both her sire and her dam were thus classified.

Quashed was leased for racing to Lord Stanley, who sent her to be trained by Colledge Leader. Tall and leggy, she took a long time to come to hand, and her first victory was in a modest event at Gatwick only three weeks before the Oaks, in which at 33-1 she got up in the final stride to beat Ankaret by a short head. Later in the season she won the Prince Edward Handicap at Manchester and the Jockey Club Cup.

She was kept in training as a four-year-old with the Gold Cup as her main objective. She dead-heated for the Great Metropolitan, won the Ormonde Stakes at Chester and then crowned her career by winning a tremendous battle for the Gold Cup, defeating the American horse Omaha by inches. It was a gruelling contest and she thoroughly deserved the tribute paid to her by Mr Somerville Tattersall: 'the gamest mare of all time'.

The race took a lot out of her though, tough as she was, and she was never the same again, although she won the Jockey Club Cup for the second time in the autumn. She ran in the Gold Cup again the following year but could finish only third. Altogether her ten wins were worth a little short of £19,000. Unfortunately she was a stud failure and never bred a winner.

QUEEN OF SHEBA
(1948, b f Persian Gulf – Ojala, by Buen Ojo)

Queen of Sheba was bred and owned by Major D. McCalmont and trained by H.S. Persse. She won four races, including the Irish 1,000 Guineas, Cheshire Oaks and Royal Hunt Cup. Her wins were worth £7,919 and she was also second in the Irish Oaks. She bred nine winners, of whom the best were Menelek and Jibuti.

QUEENPOT
(1945, b f Big Game – Poker Chip, by The Recorder)

Queenpot was bred and owned by Sir Percy Loraine and trained by Fred Darling and Noel Murless. She won five races including the Molecomb Stakes at two and the following season the 1,000 Guineas. She bred seven winners from fifteen foals; none was of any consequence but Jellatina bred the champion French miler Northjet. Queenpot's unraced daughter Archduchess was the grandam of the Coventry Stakes winner Mark Royal.

QUEEN'S HUSSAR
(1960, b c March Past – Jojo, by Vilmorin)

Queen's Hussar was bred and owned by Lord Carnarvon and trained by 'Atty' Corbett. He won seven races, including the Sussex and Lockinge Stakes, for £21,105 in prize money. His original stud fee of £400 was not attractive, and he was offered at £250, at which price Brigadier Gerard was bred and Queen's Hussar's fee went up to £2,000. Brigadier Gerard was one of two produce who showed

235

higher racing ability than their sire, the other being Highclere (1,000 Guineas and French Oaks). Queen's Hussar died of a heart attack in January 1981.

QUICK AS LIGHTNING (1977, b f Buckpasser – Clear Ceiling, by Bold Ruler)

Brian Rouse won his first Classic when as fifth-choice jockey he drove Quick As Lightning to a narrow win in the 1,000 Guineas. Bred and owned by American Ogden Mills Phipps and trained by John Dunlop, Quick As Lightning won two of her three races as a two-year-old, including the Hoover Fillies' Mile, but failed to win again after the Guineas. She was fourth when favourite for the Oaks, and a neck second in the Coronation Stakes at Royal Ascot, after which she was retired to stud.

QUINN, Thomas Richard (b. 1961)

Richard Quinn became the third Paul Cole apprentice to take the title, following Robert Edmondson and David Dineley, when he rode 62 winners in 1984, his best season and an achievement made to look better by the fact that he lost his claim halfway through the season. From Willie Carson's birthplace of Stirling, he began his apprenticeship with Herbert Jones before joining Cole, and rode his first winner on Bolivar Baby at Kempton on 21 October 1981. Quinn has been given the opportunity on most of Cole's horses since 1984 and has won the Royal Lodge Stakes on Reach and Richmond Stakes on Nomination.

QUINTESSENCE (1900, b f St Frusquin – Margarine, by Petrarch)

Lord Falmouth's Quintessence, trained by Chandler, won the 1,000 Guineas, albeit fortuitously since only half the starting-gate worked properly and the runner-up Sun Rose was badly away, and was never beaten. She was the dam of five winners, including Paragon (Kempton Jubilee) and Clarissimus, who won the 2,000 Guineas and did extremely well as a sire in France.

R

RABELAIS
(1900, b c St Simon –
Satirical, by Satiety)

Rabelais was third in the 2,000 Guineas and fourth in the Derby, besides winning the Goodwood Cup. He was sold to France for £900 and, though very much on the small side, proved a sire of the highest order. His influence is immense as the St Simon line, pre-eminent at the turn of the century, was on the point of extinction in Britain so swiftly had it declined, and it was sustained only by Rabelais, who lived till his thirtieth year and sired the Derby winner Durbar II. From Rabelais, too, the mighty Ribot is descended, while he is also the grandsire of Nogara, dam of Nearco.

RACECOURSES

Flat racing is held on the following courses: Ascot, Ayr, Bath, Beverley, Brighton, Carlisle, Catterick Bridge, Chepstow, Chester, Doncaster, Edinburgh, Epsom, Folkestone, Goodwood, Hamilton Park, Haydock Park, Kempton Park, Leicester, Lingfield Park, Newbury, Newcastle, Newmarket (Rowley and July courses), Nottingham, Pontefract, Redcar, Ripon, Salisbury, Sandown Park, Thirsk, Warwick, Windsor, Wolverhampton, Yarmouth, York.

The following courses which staged Flat racing have closed since World War II (with dates of their last meeting): Alexandra Park (8 September 1970), Birmingham (21 June 1965), Bogside (10 April 1965, NH) Hurst Park (10 October 1962), Lanark (18 October 1977), Lewes (14 September 1964), Lincoln (21 May 1964), Manchester (9 November 1963), Stockton/Teesside Park (16 June 1981).

RACECOURSE ASSOCIATION LTD

The Racecourse Association is a company limited by guarantee not having a share capital and comprises all courses operating under the Rules of Racing. Administered from offices in Ascot, its primary object is to consider all questions affecting the welfare of racecourse owners and to watch over all matters affecting their rights. The association is constituted in three areas, Northern, Midland and Southern, each of which nominates three representatives to a board of directors, which is completed by a chairman (Gen Sir Peter Leng, since July 1985) and vice-chairman (Isidore Kerman).

Address: Winkfield Road, Ascot, Berkshire SL5 7HX (0990-25912).

RACECOURSE HOLDINGS TRUST LTD

Racecourse Holdings Trust Ltd was formed in 1964 and was originally set up to take over Cheltenham racecourse. The trust is a non-profit-making company, whose directors receive no fees, and is a wholly owned subsidiary of the Jockey Club, which owns its shares. The trust's object is to acquire at a fair and agreed price the shares in those racecourse companies whose shareholders are prepared to sell. Its acquisitions following Cheltenham have been Wincanton (1966), Nottingham (1967), Warwick (1967), Market Rasen (1968), Haydock Park (1979) and Liverpool (1983). Newmarket, which was owned by the Jockey Club, came under Racecourse Holdings Trust's administration in 1974.

Address: 42 Portman Square, London W1H OEN (01-486 4921).

RACECOURSE TECHNICAL SERVICES LTD

Racecourse Technical Services Ltd was formed in 1967 as a strengthening and modification of the Race Finish Recording Company Ltd. All shares in the

237

company are owned by the Levy Board, which meets the costs of the services provided, namely the photo-finish, film and video patrol and race-timing, the public-address system and on-course closed-circuit television. In 1968 Racecourse Technical Services took over from the Jockey Club the responsibility for starting-stalls. The board of directors includes a chairman and managing director, and representatives from the Levy Board, Jockey Club and Racecourse Association.

Address: 88 Bushey Road, Raynes Park, London SW20 0JH (01-947 3333).

RACEFORM LTD

Raceform Ltd print the official Jockey Club record of races run under their Rules in a weekly loose-leaf book giving the results of past races and comments on the appearance and performance of the competitors.

Address: 25 Shepherd Market, London W1 (01-499 4391).

RACEGOERS' CLUB

The Racegoers' Club was formed in June 1968 with the intention of starting a supporters' club for racing. Administered by the Racing Information Bureau, it reached a peak of 12,000 members and has since settled down to around 7,500. Its main objective is to get more people to go racing more often.

Most racecourses offer admission-price concessions to club members, and in addition numerous visits are organized to places of racing interest. Stable visits in Britain and overseas trips are the club's most popular activities.

The club owned its first horse in 1969, moved into syndication in 1971 and extended its scope into an Owners Group of 600 subscriptions in 1982.

Address: Racing Information Bureau, Winkfield Road, Ascot, Berkshire, SL5 7HX (0990-25912).

RACEHORSE OWNERS' ASSOCIATION

The Racehorse Owners' Association, formed in 1945, exists to promote the interests of owners, both Flat and jumping, and has approximately 4,000 members. Administration is conducted by a council, president, vice-president and director-general.

Address: 42 Portman Square, London W1H 9FF (01-486 6977).

RACEHORSE OF THE YEAR: see Appendix II

RACE MEETINGS, Regulations for

All racecourses have to be licensed, and all meetings have to be authorized by the stewards of the Jockey Club. Applications for fixtures for the following year have to be made to the Secretary of the Jockey Club by June of the current year. The application has to be accompanied by a statement of accounts for the preceding year made up to 31 December on a form prescribed by the stewards of the Jockey Club and obtainable at the Registry Office. This statement of accounts must be certified by a chartered accountant.

The conditions of every race before closing, and the full programme of every meeting, before it takes place, must be advertised in the *Racing Calendar*, and no alteration can be made in the conditions of any race after such publication, though a race may be declared void if the number of entries does not fulfil the advertised conditions.

At every meeting at which Flat races are advertised, one-half at least of the guaranteed prize money must be for races of a mile or over for three-year-olds and upwards, and of this sum not less than half shall be for races of $1\frac{1}{4}$m or upwards, but when more than one meeting is held at the same course during the current racing season, the apportionment may be calculated over each meeting or over all the meetings.

There must not be more than one selling or claiming race per day and, except with the permission of the stewards of the Jockey Club, each day there must be two races of a mile or more to the minimum aggregate distance of $2\frac{1}{2}$m, though neither shall be open to two-year-olds, and one of them must not be a handicap or selling race. In each day's programme of six races there must not be more than two for three-year-olds and upwards of less than 7f. When a seventh race is included, it may be of any distance. There must not be more than four handicaps on any programme, and if there are four, one must be an apprentice race or a seventh race.

RACING CALENDAR

The *Racing Calendar* is the official publication of the Jockey Club. It is printed by Messrs Weatherby and Sons and issued every Thursday. It contains particulars of every race, including the conditions, entries, handicaps, forfeit stages and final acceptances. It lists all race meetings, gives the registration of colours and names of horses, names of persons and horses on the Forfeit List, and reports all objections and disqualifications. All those persons requiring a licence from the Jockey Club are listed. Originally the first public intimation of any 'warning off' was the official notice in the *Racing Calendar* on the Thursday after the ban had come into force, but this information is now released as it happens, and the notice in the *Racing Calendar* is merely an official record of the action.

The first racing calendar was produced in 1727 by John Cheny of Arundel in the shape of a form book. On his death in 1751 his work was succeeded by *Heber's Calendar*, published by Reginald Heber, and the *Sporting Kalendar* of Mr Pond. Pond had the distinction of publishing the Laws of Racing for the first time in 1751, but his publication was seen off by Heber until the latter's death in 1769 brought further changes. Walker's volume of that year quickly gave way to the jointly published *Sporting Calendar* of William Tuting and Thomas Fawconer, but soon Tuting was persuaded by James Weatherby to break away from his partner. When Tuting died in 1773, James Weatherby produced his first *Racing Calendar*, and within two years he had beaten off the competition from Fawconer. Since 1778 the Weatherby family have preserved a monopoly in publishing the *Racing Calendar*, which

included rules for the conduct of racing for the first time in 1797.

RACING INFORMATION BUREAU

The Racing Information Bureau was established in January 1964 following the recommendations of a Levy Board study into the decline of racecourse attendances. Its original brief was 'to publicise and promote racing to all media, including national and provincial Press, television, radio and magazines, and to provide an efficient information service for racing correspondents and journalists at racecourses'.

The original director was David Hedges, who was succeeded by Tony Fairbairn in 1966, operating with three field PROs, a news editor and a feature editor. The bureau became the Jockey Club's PRO department in January 1969 but was relieved of the job in September 1981, since when it has moved from London to Ascot. With the Racecourse Association providing the major part of its funding, the emphasis has centred on the needs of racecourses and sponsors, with a separate brief to act for the Levy Board.

The Bureau administers the Racegoers' Club and in 1979 established a group sales unit to promote racecourse attendance by parties.

Address: Winkfield Road, Ascot, Berkshire, SL5 7HX (0990-25912).

RAGSTONE
(1970, br c Ragusa – Fotheringay, by Right Royal V)

There was no more popular result at Royal Ascot in 1974 than Ragstone's victory in the Gold Cup, for he was owned by the course's great administrator the Duke of Norfolk. It proved to be a poignant success too, for the following year the Duke of Norfolk died. Ragstone, trained by John Dunlop, won seven races in all, including the three in which he ran as a three-year-old, and the Henry II Stakes at four. He was retired to stud in Sussex after running badly in his last race that year but died in 1978 after only four seasons. His best offspring was Fingal's Cave, who was promoted to third place in the Eclipse Stakes and filled the same spot in the King George VI and Queen Elizabeth Diamond Stakes. He also sired the useful jumpers Janus, Ra Nova and Buckbe.

RAGUSA
(1960, b c Ribot – Fantan II, by Ambiorix II)

Ragusa was bred by Mr H.F. Guggenheim and was rather small and unprepossessing in his younger days. As Cecil Boyd-Rochfort, Mr Guggenheim's trainer, did not care much for him, he was sent up for sale as a yearling and bought by Paddy Prendergast on behalf of Mr J.R. Mullion for 3,800gns.

He proved a wonderful bargain. He won his only race as a two-year-old and the following season he won the Irish Derby, King George VI and Queen Elizabeth Stakes, Great Voltigeur Stakes and St Leger. In the Derby he was third behind Relko. As a four-year-old he won the Eclipse Stakes but ended his career when unplaced in the Prix de l'Arc de Triomphe. All told he won seven races and £146,650.

Syndicated to stand at the Ardenode Stud, Co Kildare, he died after an operation a month before his son Morston won the 1973 Derby. Other good winners by Ragusa were Ballymore (Irish 2,000 Guineas), Caliban (Coronation Cup), Homeric (second in St Leger and third in Arc de Triomphe) and Ragstone (Ascot Gold Cup). Tap on Wood, the 2,000 Guineas winner, is out of a Ragusa mare.

RAILS

Barriers defining the limits of a race track are known as rails. The term is also used to refer to the division between the Members' and Tattersalls' enclosures on a racecourse, where bookmakers, usually operating a credit business but barred from standing in the Members', take bets from their customers.

RAJPIPLA, Maharaja of
(1891-1951)

The Maharaja of Rajpipla won the Derby in 1934, ten years after he first registered his colours in Britain, with Windsor Lad, trained by Marcus Marsh and ridden by C. Smirke. Windsor Lad, whom he had bought for 1,300gns as a yearling, was his first runner in that race. The following month Windsor Lad, again ridden by Smirke, was a singularly unlucky loser of the Eclipse Stakes, and his owner was persuaded to sell him to Mr Martin Benson, a bookmaker, for £50,000. Windsor Lad was never beaten again.

RAMSHAW, George (b. 1938)

'Geordie' Ramshaw served his apprenticeship with Ron Smyth, for whom he rode his first winner, Fairy Princess, at Lingfield on Friday 13 May 1955. He rode successfully over hurdles in the 1960s and for Smyth won the Imperial Cup on Irish Imp and Triumph Hurdle on Blarney Beacon. Ramshaw remained associated with Epsom stables, and had his best season on the Flat in 1975, with sixteen winners. He did not renew his licence in 1985.

RANAI
(1925, b f Rabelais – Dark Sedge, by Prestige)

Ranai was one of Lord Derby's most successful mares. Bred in France, she was bought on behalf of Lord Derby at the Deauville Sales and won two races for him in France. At stud she bred ten winners including Watling Street (Derby) and Garden Path (2,000 Guineas). Her grandson Ruthless never won but became champion sire in New Zealand, and her great-grandson Latin Lover did well at stud in Australia.

RANDALL, Herbert
(1877-1959)

The son of Sir Henry Randall, a Northampton shoe-manufacturer, Herbert Randall rode firstly as an amateur, turning professional in 1902. He was associated with the famous filly Sceptre on whom he won the 2,000

Guineas, 1,000 Guineas and Oaks. He was also on her when she was fourth in the Derby but was not given the mount when she won the St Leger. The following season, 1903, he won the 1,000 Guineas on Quintessence. For several seasons he rode for Mr J.B. Joel, for whom he won the Oaks on Glass Doll in 1907. On that popular handicapper Dean Swift he won the City and Suburban in 1906 and 1908. He handed in his licence in 1914 and retired from the racing world.

RANDOM SHOT
(1967, b c Pirate King – Time and Chance, by Supreme Court)

Random Shot, bred and owned by Mrs G. Benskin and trained by Arthur Budgett, won six races and gained his biggest prize in the 1971 Ascot Gold Cup. He was beaten four lengths into second place but Rock Roi was disqualified after producing a positive sample at a dope test. Later that year Random Shot finished third in the Goodwood Cup, won by Rock Roi. Random Shot retired to stud in Ireland in 1973 and died in 1983.

RAYMOND, Bruce (b. 1943)

Bruce Raymond was apprenticed from 1959 to 1964 to Willie Stephenson, whose daughter he married in 1965. He rode his first winner on Arctic Bar at Birmingham on 19 June 1961 and was top apprentice in 1962 with thirteen winners. He was stable jockey for Humphrey Cottrill from 1965 to 1970, and rode for Michael Jarvis from 1970 until he left Britain in August 1985 to take up a three-year contract in Hong Kong, where he had his licence suspended until May '86 following a wide-ranging inquiry into corruption in February that year. His earliest big-race success was on Rainstorm in the 1962 Newbury Autumn Cup, and he has since won the Northumberland Plate (on Grey God and Totowah), July Cup and Nunthorpe Stakes (on Forlorn River), Ayr Gold Cup (Jon George), Vernons Sprint (Runnett) and Coronation Cup (Easter Sun). He never won a British Classic but was

second in the 1,000 Guineas and Oaks on St Pauli Girl. His best season was 1982, with 74 winners.

READER, Raymond (b. 1928)

Ray Reader was apprenticed to Walter Nightingall from 1946 to 1950 and rode his first winner, Radio Star, at Alexandra Park on 25 October 1948. He became a most experienced lightweight jockey, much in demand for major handicaps, and good races he won included the Stewards' Cup, Britannia Stakes (twice), Rosebery Stakes (twice) and Esher Cup (twice). His best season was 1950, with 29 winners. He rode his last winner in 1974 and retired four years later.

REAVEY, Edward John Bernard (1919-80)

Eddie Reavey served his apprenticeship first with Ernie Davey and then with Steve Donoghue. He rode his first winner on the Flat at Newcastle in 1936 but became too heavy and turned to riding under National Hunt Rules. He might well have ridden Zahia to victory in the 1948 Grand National but for taking the wrong course coming to the last fence. He took out a licence to train in 1956, and his stable at East Hendred, near Wantage, was noted for its skill at placing two-year-olds and sprinters. The best horse he trained was Polyfoto, who won the Nunthorpe Stakes and Prix d'Arenberg. When he died in 1980, his widow Jocelyn took over the stable. In 1983 she became Newmarket's first woman trainer when she moved into stables owned by Lord Matthews but her contract was not renewed after 1985, and she returned to Berkshire to train the following year.

RECOGNIZED MEETING

A 'recognized meeting' is one defined in the Jockey Club Rules as being authorized by a recognized Turf Authority.

REDCAR

The present seaside course was first used in 1871, but racing made a notable advance after the arrival in 1946 as Clerk of the Course and managing director of Major Leslie Petch, who had a commendable flair for publicity and knowing what his customers wanted. Sponsored handicaps became a feature of the programmes, and for a time the Vaux Gold Tankard, first run in 1959, was Europe's richest handicap. Prize money, which was £8,450 when Major Petch took over, had risen to £72,550 in 1964, when a new grandstand costing £260,000 was opened. John Sanderson succeeded Major Petch from 1972 to 1979, when John Cleverley became Clerk of the Course.

The track is a narrow, left-handed oval of about 1¾m, with a straight mile that joins the round course 5f from the winning post. There are virtually no gradients, and though the bends are on the sharp side their influence is counterbalanced by the long back straight and the run-in. The draw is not considered to be of significance.

RED GOD
(1954, ch c Nasrullah – Spring Ruin, by Menow)

Bred in America by Mr H.F. Guggenheim, Red God came to Britain to be trained by Cecil Boyd-Rochfort and as a two-year-old won the Richmond Stakes at Goodwood. At three and four years of age he raced in America, winning four races worth $29,000. He spent all but the last year of his stud career at the Loughtown Stud, Co Kildare, but died of a twisted gut in May 1979 after one season at the Milford Stud, Co Carlow.

Though he inherited problems of temperament from his sire, Nasrullah, and transmitted them to several offspring, he was a most successful sire. Most of his best runners were fast horses and included the French 2,000 Guineas winners Red Lord and Blushing Groom (who stayed well enough to finish third in the Derby), the Cheveley Park Stakes winner Jacinth (also second in the 1,000 Guineas), the Queen Mary Stakes winner Greenland Park and the Jersey Stakes winner Red Alert, as well as the sprinters Yellow God, Green God and St Alphage. Blushing Groom, St Alphage (who died prematurely) and Yellow God have done well as sires.

REFORM
(1964, b c Pall Mall – Country House, by Vieux Manoir)

Reform was a top-class miler who overcame an unpromising start to life. Bred by the Ballymacoll Stud Farm Ltd, he was an unprepossessing yearling and was not sent up for sale as it was reckoned he would do the stud no credit. Accordingly Michael Sobell kept him for himself and sent him to be trained by Sir Gordon Richards. He was fourth in his first race as a two-year-old and won the remaining six including the Berkshire Stakes at Newbury, Granville Stakes and Clarence House Stakes at Ascot, and Rous Memorial Stakes at Goodwood.

The following season he had seven races and won the St James Stakes, St James's Palace Stakes, Sussex Stakes, Queen Elizabeth II Stakes and Champion Stakes (beating Royal Palace in the last-named); he came second in the Greenham Stakes and Wills Mile. All told he won eleven of his fourteen races and £44,721. Reform died in March 1983, having sired top-class winners in Polygamy (Oaks), Roi Lear (French Derby), Admetus (twelve races including Washington D.C. International), Lancastrian (Prix Ganay) and Catalpa (Ribblesdale Stakes). His daughter Tenea, a maiden, was sold for a record 1.02m gns in December 1982.

REGISTRATION FEES

All fees relating to the registration of an owner and his horse are payable to the Jockey Club. They are reviewed annually, and for 1985 they were, exclusive of VAT:

Reservation of a horse's name, £7.
Registration of a horse's name: under two years old, £7; two and three years old, £18; four years old and upwards, £15.
Registration of a change of horse's name (when permitted), £50.
Registration of an owner's name, £14.
Registration of a recognized club and stud company, £50.

Registration of a recognized company, £190.

Registration of an agent for a recognized company, £14.

Registration of a syndicate agreement, £60.

Registration of a partnership, £12 for initial registration, £6 for each re-registration; £12 for each registration of a sale with contingencies.

Annual registration of colours, £9.50.

Annual registration of authority to act on behalf of an owner, £11.50.

Registration of transfer of engagements, £7.

REGISTRY OFFICE

The Registry Office is the office appointed for the purpose by the Jockey Club. The present office is at 42 Portman Square, London W1H 0EN (01-486 4921).

REID, John Andrew (b. 1955)

Born in Northern Ireland, John Reid began his apprenticeship with Leslie Crawford before moving to Verly Bewicke in Berkshire, both trainers with an emphasis on jumpers. He rode his first winner on Eyry at Goodwood on 16 May 1973. In 1978 he joined Fulke Johnson Houghton's stable and that year won the King George VI and Queen Elizabeth Stakes on Ile de Bourbon. The following year they won the Coronation Cup, and Reid was also successful for the stable on Pragmatic (Yorkshire Cup), Double Form (King's Stand Stakes) and Smartset (Cambridgeshire). He went on to his best season in 1980 with 79 winners, but the fortunes of the Johnson Houghton stable dipped and, having won his first Classic on On The House in the 1982 1,000 Guineas for Harry Wragg, Reid went freelance in 1984. That year he did well on Brian Swift's two-year-olds Prince Sabo (Flying Childers Stakes) and Primo Dominie (Richmond Stakes).

REIFF BROTHERS

Among the American jockeys who came to Europe at the turn of the century were Johnny Reiff and his elder brother Lester. Johnny Reiff first appeared on British racecourses as an angel-faced little boy in knickerbockers and an Eton collar, but he soon proved he was rather less innocent than he looked. In his youth he was a brilliant lightweight and won the Derby on Orby in 1907 and Tagalie in 1912. He also rode Craganour, who was first past the post in the 1913 Derby but was disqualified. Johnny Reiff went to France when the American millionaires started racing there and seldom came to Britain except for a major event. Lester, who was champion jockey in 1900 with 143 winners and won the Derby the following year on Volodyovski, was a fine rider who had a lot of trouble over weight. There is no doubt Lester was hand in glove with some big and disreputable American gamblers, and it came as no surprise when in October 1901 the Jockey Club imposed a ban on him. The Reiff brothers had been brought to Britain by an American trainer, Enoch Wishard, a confirmed doper of horses and the associate of some fairly desperate characters.

RELANCE III
(1952, ch f Relic – Polaire II, by Le Volcan)

Relance III, winner of seven races at two and three years, is one of the most celebrated mares of the twentieth century, being the dam of three top-class racers from the six consecutive winners she bred between 1957 and 1962 – Relko (French 2,000 Guineas, Epsom Derby, French St Leger, Prix Ganay, Coronation Cup and Grand Prix de Saint-Cloud), Match III (King George VI and Queen Elizabeth Stakes and Washington D.C. International) and Reliance II (French Derby, Grand Prix and French St Leger). Her unraced daughter Domination bred the useful sprinter Curravilla.

RELIANCE II
(1962, b c Tantième – Relance III, by Relic)

Reliance II, bred by François Dupré, and a brother to Match III and three-parts brother to Relko, did well to steer clear of Sea-Bird for most of his Classic season. His only defeat came when he finished second to Sea-Bird in the Prix de l'Arc de Triomphe. His five victories included the Prix Hocquart, French Derby, Grand Prix de Paris and French St Leger. When Match III died in 1965, Herbert Blagrave was instrumental in obtaining Reliance II for stud in Britain, where he was put down on humane grounds in August 1979. A large part of his stakes earnings came from France, where Recupéré won the Prix du Cadran. He sired two Goodwood Cup winners in Proverb and Tug of War, as well as Consol (Geoffrey Freer Stakes) and Assured (Cesarewitch), and was the maternal grandsire of Kris and Moorestyle.

RELIC
(1945, bl c War Relic – Bridal Colors, by Black Toney)

Relic was bred in America, where he won five races (maximum distance 7f) worth $72,300. In 1950 he retired to stud in the land of his birth, and his stock there won over 150 races and $1,113,000. In 1951 he was sent to France, and there his offspring won more than 300 races and 2,000,000 francs. His winners there included Buisson Ardent (French 2,000 Guineas), Venture VII (Prix Djebel), Mincio (French 2,000 Guineas) and Victorian Order and Texanita (both Prix d'Arenberg). He also sired the famous mare Relance III. He came to Britain in 1957 and died in 1970. His best winner in Britain, apart from French-trained Venture VII, was Pieces of Eight (Eclipse and Champion Stakes).

RELKO
(1960, b c Tanerko – Relance III, by Relic)

Relko was owned by M.F. Dupré and trained in France by F. Mathet. He won the Derby with Yves Saint-Martin in the saddle. Other successes included the French 2,000 Guineas, Prix Ganay, Prix Royal-Oak, Grand Prix de Saint-Cloud and Coronation Cup. He could only finish sixth in the Prix de l'Arc de Triomphe as a three-year-old.

After his Derby success Relko was to have run in the Irish Derby but was found to be lame at the start and had to be withdrawn.

On 11 July, two weeks after the Irish Derby, an announcement was made by the Jockey Club concerning positive reactions to routine dope tests at Epsom. No names were given at that stage, but it soon became known that Relko was one of the horses concerned. The following statement appeared in the *Racing Calendar* on 29 August 1963:

> The stewards of the Epsom Summer Meeting referred to the Stewards of the Jockey Club the reports which they have received from the club's analysts on the examination ordered to be made of Relko after winning the Derby Stakes on 29 May.
> The Stewards of the Jockey Club held their enquiry at the Registry Office on 28 August, when they heard evidence from the trainer, and other parties concerned including technical witnesses called on their behalf. They also took evidence from the Stewards' Advisory Committee.
> The Stewards were satisfied that a substance other than a normal nutrient was present in the horse.
> From the technical evidence they were not satisfied that it was administered with the intention of increasing its speed or improving its stamina, courage, or conduct in the race.
> They adjourned the case for further enquiry in conjunction with the police.

Finally, the following notice appeared in the *Racing Calendar* on 3 October:

> The Stewards of the Jockey Club, having considered the report on their further enquiries, are satisfied that the trainer and his employees have no case to answer under Rule 102(11).
> They found no evidence which would justify a disqualification of Relko under Rule 66(c).

In 1964 Lord Sefton bought a half share in Relko, who remained in training that season before coming to Britain to stand at stud, where he was put down on humane grounds in March 1982. His most significant winners were Relkino (Benson & Hedges Gold Cup), Olwyn (Irish Oaks), Breton (top juvenile in France), Tierceron (Gran Premio d'Italia), Relay Race (Hardwicke Stakes), Relfo (Ribblesdale Stakes), Give Thanks

(Irish Oaks), Karkour (Prix du Cadran) and Lanfranco (William Hill Futurity). He is also the broodmare sire of Fairy Footsteps (1,000 Guineas), Light Cavalry (St Leger), Swiftfoot (Irish Oaks) and Royal Heroine (Hollywood Derby).

RIBBON
(1940, b f Fairway – Bongrace, by Spion Kop)

Bred and owned by Lord Rosebery, Ribbon won five races for £2,333, including the Middle Park Stakes, beating Nasrullah, but she is better known for races in which she was beaten, since she was second in the 1,000 Guineas, Oaks and St Leger. Everyone, bar the Judge, thought she had won the St Leger and she was beaten a neck in both the 1,000 Guineas and the Oaks. She was not a success as a broodmare.

RIBERO
(1965, b c Ribot – Libra, by Hyperion)

Ribero was bred in America in 1965 by Mrs J.G. Rogers and as a yearling was bought by Mr Charles Engelhard for $50,000: 'The last of the cheap Ribots', Mr Engelhard is reputed to have said. Like his brother Ribocco, he was trained by Fulke Johnson Houghton and like Ribocco won the Irish Derby and Doncaster St Leger. Ribero did not retain his form as a four-year-old and was retired to stud after being withdrawn when refusing to enter the starting-stalls for the Coronation Cup. His stud career was unimpressive, with Ribecourt (Gran Premio d'Italia) and Vielle (second in the Oaks) his best winners, and he was sent to Japan in 1978.

RIBOCCO
(1964, b c Ribot – Libra, by Hyperion)

Bred in America by Mrs J.G. Rogers, Ribocco was bought for $35,000 as a yearling by Mr Charles Engelhard who sent him to Britain to be trained by Fulke Johnson Houghton. Among Ribocco's five victories were the Observer Gold Cup, Irish Derby and Doncaster St Leger. He was second in the Derby to Royal Palace and close-up third in the Prix de l'Arc de Triomphe. He was retired to stud in America after finishing seventh of nine in the Washington D.C. International at Laurel Park.

RIBOFILIO
(1966, b c Ribot – Island Creek, by Khaled)

Since World War II few horses have been more popular with the bookmakers than Ribofilio. Bred in America, he was bought by Mr Charles Engelhard for $100,000. Trained in Britain by Fulke Johnson Houghton, he was the outstanding two-year-old of 1968 and headed the Free Handicap. His career in 1969 proved an anti-climax. He was favourite for the 2,000 Guineas, Derby, Irish Derby and St Leger but lost the lot. In the 2,000 Guineas he had to be pulled up, and no satisfactory explanation exists for that lamentable display. At the end of the season he returned to America where he won as a four-year-old. At the end of his racing career he was exported as a stallion to South Africa.

RIBOT
(1952, b c Tenerani – Romanella, by El Greco)

Among the greatest racehorses of this century, Ribot was foaled in Britain at the National Stud but was bred in Italy by the Razza Dormello-Olgiata. He was the undefeated winner of sixteen races in three countries, on all types of going and over all distances. In Britain he won the King George VI and Queen Elizabeth Stakes, and in France he twice won the Prix de l'Arc de Triomphe. By no means outstanding in looks, he stood his first season at stud in Britain and had three seasons in Italy before being leased to America in 1960. The original lease was for five years but Ribot remained in America until his death there in April 1972. He was leading sire in Britain in 1963, '67 and '68.

Few of his stock were precociously brilliant, and they were best suited to European conditions. Rarely did a crop go by without at least one champion emerging. His European winners included Molvedo (Prix de l'Arc de Triomphe), Prince Royal II (Prix de l'Arc de Triomphe), Ragusa (St Leger, Irish Derby, King George VI and Queen Elizabeth Stakes, Eclipse Stakes), Ribocco (St Leger and Irish Derby), Ribero (St Leger and Irish Derby), Romulus (Sussex Stakes, Queen Elizabeth II Stakes), Long Look (Oaks), Boucher (St Leger) and Regal Exception (Irish Oaks).

In America his best winners were Tom Rolfe (Preakness Stakes), Dapper Dan (second in Kentucky Derby and Preakness Stakes), Graustark (seven out of eight races) and Arts and Letters (Belmont Stakes). Several of his sons have done well as sires throughout the world.

RICHARDS, Sir Gordon (b. 1904)

One of the outstanding personalities in British racing, Sir Gordon Richards, who was born in Shropshire as one of twelve children, was apprenticed to Martin Hartigan and rode his first winner at Leicester in 1921. He swiftly established himself and was champion for the first time in 1925. In 1926 he suffered a grave illness demanding convalescence in Switzerland, but he made a complete recovery and was champion again in 1927. From that point his career never looked back and when he eventually retired following a bad fall at Sandown in 1954, he had been champion 26 times and won fourteen Classics. His total of 4,870 winners is unapproached by any other rider in Britain. They came from 21,843 mounts, while the 269 winners he rode in 1947 formed another record. At one Chepstow meeting in 1933 he rode every winner except that of the last race on the second day. In 1932 he became first jockey to Fred Darling at Beckhampton, and remained with Noel Murless when he took over that stable in 1948, the pair remaining together when Murless moved to Newmarket in 1952.

Richards' most lasting ambition was to win the Derby, which he did at the 28th attempt, in 1953, the year before he retired. His Classic winners were:

2,000 Guineas: Pasch (1938); Big Game (1942); Tudor Minstrel (1947)
1,000 Guineas: Sun Chariot (1942); Queenpot (1948); Belle of All (1951)
Derby: Pinza (1953)
Oaks: Rose of England (1930); Sun Chariot (1942)
St Leger: Singapore (1930); Chulmleigh (1937); Turkhan (1940); Sun Chariot (1942); Tehran (1944).

Small, sturdy and short in the leg, he was hardly such a polished horseman as Steve Donoghue, and his style tended to be unorthodox. In a close finish he seemed to ride not only rather upright but often sideways and with a completely loose rein. Yet he retained entire control, and his mounts very rarely became unbalanced. He was uncannily good at the start, usually in the right place at the right moment, and above all possessed an overwhelming determination to win. He used his whip to encourage and not to chastise, and he seldom hit a horse. Success, combined with adulation from the Press and public, never turned his head or altered his pleasing personality. His standard of integrity was extremely high, and as both rider and trainer he was a most worthy representative of the best traditions of the Turf. He received his knighthood just before he rode Pinza to victory in the Derby.

He began training at Beckhampton in 1955 and moved to Ogbourne Maisey after one season and to Whitsbury in 1964. At the end of 1970 he retired to manage the horses owned by Sir Michael Sobell and Lady Beaverbrook. His best horses while training were Pipe of Peace (third in the 2,000 Guineas and Derby), Court Harwell (second in the St Leger), Reform (Champion Stakes) and Dart Board (third in the Derby).

RICKABY, William Anthony (b. 1917)

Bill Rickaby comes from a famous racing family. It was a Rickaby who trained the 1855 Derby winner, Wild Dayrell. Bill's grandfather, Frederick Rickaby, who won three Classics, was a well-known jockey, and so was Bill's father, Frederick Lester Rickaby, whose five Classic wins included two on Jest. Bill's brother Fred rode with much success until he became too heavy, when he became a trainer in South Africa; his aunt Iris is Lester Piggott's mother. Bill himself married Ryan Jarvis's sister.

Bill Rickaby was apprenticed to Walter Griggs and then George Lambton, riding his first winner in 1931 (when he beat his brother on the favourite by a length). Except for war service in the Royal Artillery in which he held the rank of major, he rode with success until he retired in 1968 to take up a racing appointment in Hong Kong. Few jockeys have been more popular or enjoyed such a high reputation for integrity. When he rode Silver Spray to victory at Newmarket on his last ride in public, he was given a memorable reception.

Big races he won included the 2,000 Guineas on Privy Councillor, 1,000 Guineas and Oaks on Sweet Solera and Eclipse Stakes on Busted. He also won the Irish Derby, Irish Oaks, Yorkshire Cup (twice), Goodwood Cup, July Cup, Jockey Club Cup (twice), Manchester Cup, Champion Stakes, Jockey Club Stakes, Goodwood Stakes, Lincolnshire Handicap and Jubilee Handicap. From 1949 to 1956 he had a particularly successful association with Jack Jarvis. In addition, he won important races in India and Scandinavia. His best season was 1953, when he rode 83 winners. Serious head injuries sustained in a car crash in Hong Kong in February 1970 cut short his administrative career, and he returned to Newmarket.

RIDDEN FOR HIRE

The Rules of Racing state that professional hunt servants, grooms, apprentices, stable-lads, and persons who are or who have been employed as paid servants in any capacity in private, hunting, racing, livery or horsedealers' stables, also persons who have ever received payment, directly or indirectly, for riding in a race are regarded as having 'ridden for hire' and are professional riders for the purposes of the rules.

RIDGE WOOD
(1946, br c Bois Roussel – Hanging Fall, by Solario)

Trained by Noel Murless for Mr G.R. Smith, Ridge Wood was bred by the Sledmere Stud and bought as a yearling for 4,000gns. He won seven races, including the St Leger, for £21,658. He had made little mark as a sire when he died in Ireland in 1956.

RIG

A rig is a horse who has one testicle which has not descended into the scrotum; more rare is the example in which neither testicle has descended. The condition may be inherited and is likely to cause aggressive behaviour unless treated by castration.

RIGHT BOY
(1954, gr c Impeccable – Happy Ogan, by Ballyogan)

One of the outstanding sprinters of the post-war era, Right Boy was bred in Ireland by Mr W.J. Byrne. Bought for 575gns by Bill Dutton, he was trained by him until his death in 1958 and then by Pat Rohan. He won sixteen races for £17,752, his victories including the King's Stand Stakes, Nunthorpe Stakes (twice), King George Stakes (twice), July Cup (twice) and Cork and Orrery Stakes (twice). A disappointing sire, he was put down in August 1977, with the best of his progeny – Reet Lass (Molecomb Stakes) and Village Boy (Richmond Stakes) – being at their peak as two-year-olds.

RIGHT ROYAL V
(1958, br c Owen Tudor – Bastia, by Victrix)

Bred in France in 1958 by Mme Jean Couturié, Right Royal V was trained by Etienne Pollet and proved himself an outstanding racehorse. In France he won the Grand Critérium, 2,000 Guineas, Prix Lupin and Derby. He was second to Molvedo in the Prix de l'Arc de Triomphe. In Britain he won the King George VI and Queen Elizabeth Stakes, completely outclassing the Derby and St Leger winner St Paddy.

He was syndicated to stand at stud in France, where he died in 1973. His most important winners were Salvo (Vaux Gold Tankard, Newbury Autumn Cup, Yorkshire Cup, Hardwicke Stakes, Grosser Preis von Baden), Ruysdael (Italian Derby), Prince Regent (Irish Sweeps Derby), Rex Magna (French St Leger) and Right Away (French 1,000 Guineas). Jacinth and Ragstone are out of Right Royal V mares.

RIGHT TACK
(1966, b c Hard Tack – Polly Macaw, by Polly's Jet)

Bred in Ireland by Mr P. Larkin, Right Tack was a far from fashionably bred colt, albeit a very good-looking one. Sold as a foal for 700gns, he was bought as a yearling for 3,200gns by Mr J.R. Brown, who sent him to be trained by John Sutcliffe junior. Right Tack went from strength to strength as a two-year-old, winning five of his six races including the Imperial and Middle Park Stakes, and being rated the second-best two-year-old in the Free Handicap.

As a three-year-old, he was beaten in the Greenham Stakes but then won in succession the 2,000 Guineas, Irish 2,000 Guineas and St James's Palace Stakes. He then contracted the cough and was well beaten in two races on his reappearance. His eight wins and three places were worth £59,843. Syndicated to stand at stud in Ireland, he was not a success and was exported to Australia in 1976.

RINGER

A slang term for a horse which is dishonestly substituted for another. Increased identification and surveillance have decreased the opportunity of a ringer being employed, but in June 1984 three men were found guilty of conspiracy to defraud when it was discovered that the two-year-old known as Flockton Grey, who won an auction race at Leicester on 29 March 1982 by twenty lengths on his first appearance, was the three-year-old Good Hand.

RIPON

This Yorkshire track, known as 'the garden racecourse', is within handy distance of Harrogate and York and the emphasis is on family racing. It is a right-handed, oval course, 1m 5f round, with a straight 6f joining the round course 5f from the winning post. It is undulating and somewhat sharp in character. The run-in is uphill for the first half, followed by a slight decline to within a few yards of the winning post, where the ground rises again. Low numbers in the draw may have a slight advantage on the straight course, but owing to the long bend soon after the start, high numbers are best in races over 1m.

ROARER

A slang term for a horse who has gone in his wind and makes an abnormal noise when breathing in.

ROBERTO
(1969, b c Hail to Reason – Bramalea, by Nashua)

Bred by American owner John Galbreath and trained in Ireland by Vincent O'Brien, Roberto won seven races in a career which had almost as many low points as highspots. The peaks were when he won the Derby by a short head from Rheingold under an inspired ride by Lester Piggott, and when he became the only horse to defeat Brigadier Gerard, with an equally thrilling ride from the American-based Braulio Baeza, who was making his British debut in the Benson & Hedges Gold Cup at York. Roberto also won the Coronation Cup as a four-year-old, but he was only seventh in the Prix de l'Arc de Triomphe as a three-year-old, and the following year, when his trainer caused controversy by withdrawing him on the morning of the Eclipse Stakes, for which he was odds-on, and the Benson & Hedges, he ran badly in the King George VI and Queen Elizabeth Stakes and did not race again. He was syndicated to stand at stud in America for a valuation of about £1.35m from 1974 and has done very well. His son Driving Home was a champion in Canada, and in Europe he has been responsible for Touching Wood

(St Leger), Sookera (Cheveley Park Stakes), Critique (Hardwicke Stakes), Real Shadai (Grand Prix de Deauville), Lear Fan (Prix Jacques le Marois), At Talaq (Grand Prix de Paris) and Bob Back (Prince of Wales's Stakes).

ROBERTSON, James Bell (1860-1940)

Mr J.B. Robertson was usually granted the courtesy title of 'Professor'. He was a veterinary surgeon who devoted his life to journalism. He was rightly regarded as the leading authority of his day on the breeding of the racehorse. A regular contributor to the *Sporting Chronicle*, *Sunday Times* and *Bloodstock Breeders' Review*, he did work of great value in relating the discoveries of the science of genetics to the special case of the Thoroughbred.

ROBINSON, Sir David (b. 1906)

David Robinson won the 2,000 Guineas with Our Babu in 1955, but it was from 1967, after he had made his fortune from television rentals, that he became Britain's biggest owner. At his peak he had 120 horses in training and three private trainers at Newmarket, the two most successful being Paul Davey and Michael Jarvis. He took the best advice in buying, and raced his horses in grades to win as many races as possible, setting a record for one owner of 115 winners of £114,735 in 1973. Retiring and shy of publicity, he refused to make the speech at the annual Gimcrack Dinner in 1968, though he did speak the following year. Ill health caused him to reduce his string considerably in 1975, and the following year the break-up of his interests was almost complete. He had his last winner in 1978. He continued to live near Newmarket but became a virtual recluse from 1978. He was knighted for his considerable services to charity and for the funding of Robinson College at Cambridge, having given away a reputed £26.5m by 1985. His one apparent failure in racing came after he bought Kempton Park in 1969: he was not granted

planning permission to extend the site beyond its use for racing, and he re-sold it to the Levy Board for the same price he paid. During his expansive stage as an owner he failed to win a Classic – Meadowville was second in the St Leger, and Yellow God and My Swallow second and third in the 2,000 Guineas – and his biggest successes came with two-year-olds and sprinters. His best horses included, apart from Yellow God and My Swallow, Deep Diver, So Blessed, Tudor Music, Green God, Bitty Girl and Flying Legs.

Racing colours: green, red sleeves, light blue cap.

ROBINSON, George William (b. 1934)

Irishman Willie Robinson was a distinguished rider under National Hunt Rules, and while based in Lambourn he won the Champion Hurdle on Anzio and Kirriemiur, Cheltenham Gold Cup on Mill House and Grand National on Team Spirit. Earlier he rode on the Flat and finished second in the 1958 Derby on Paddy's Point. He retired from riding in 1970 to begin training in Ireland. In his first full season he saddled King's Company to win the Irish 2,000 Guineas and Royal Ascot's Cork and Orrery Stakes, and he won the latter race again in 1980 with Kearney.

ROBINSON, James (1793-1865)

Born at Newmarket, Jem Robinson was a very fine rider, the equal of young Sam Chifney in technical skill and certainly his superior in respect of integrity. He rode six Derby winners, a number equalled by Steve Donoghue and only exceeded by Lester Piggott. His winners were Azor (1817), Cedric (1824), Middleton (1825), Mameluke (1827), Cadland (1828) and Bay Middleton (1836). He also rode the winner of the 2,000 Guineas a record nine times, the 1,000 Guineas five times, and the Oaks and St Leger twice each. His total of 24 Classic successes has been passed by only Frank Buckle and Lester Piggott. Robinson's riding career was ended in a racecourse accident at the age of 59, when he broke his thigh and thereafter was handicapped by one leg being four inches shorter than the other.

ROBINSON, Peter John (1936-78)

Peter Robinson was apprenticed for five years to Harry Wragg. He rode his first winner, Prince Yaky, at Birmingham on 22 June 1953 and two years later was champion apprentice with 46 winners. A strong jockey, capable of riding at 7st 9lb, he excelled in major handicaps and won the Lincolnshire Handicap three times, as well as the Ebor, Cambridgeshire, Royal Hunt Cup, Chester Cup and Ayr Gold Cup. His best season was in 1962, with 60 winners.

Associated with Jack Jarvis for two years, he became first jockey to Teddy Lambton in 1964 and took over the Newmarket stable when that trainer retired suddenly midway through 1969. That year Robinson won the Cambridgeshire with Prince de Galles, who was narrowly beaten in the following year's Lincoln Handicap and again won the Cambridgeshire. In 1972 Robinson did win the Lincoln, with Sovereign Bill, and in 1976 he won the Goodwood Cup with Mr Bigmore (named after Lambton's bailiff!). A promising career was cut short when in June 1978 Robinson suffered a heart attack and was found dead in his car returning from Salisbury races. His stable was taken over by Frankie Durr, to whom Robinson's son Philip became apprenticed.

ROBINSON, Philip Peter (b. 1961)

Philip Robinson followed his father as champion apprentice, but the latter sadly did not live to see it, as he died in 1978, a fortnight after Philip rode his first winner, on Busting at Yarmouth on 15 June. Robinson's indentures were transferred to Frankie Durr, and in 1979 he was leading apprentice, with 51 winners, and in 1980 with 59 winners, which remains his highest total in a season. In 1980 he gained major handicap wins with Karamita (Extel Stakes) and Swelter (Portland), but it was not long before he

was winning more important races. He gained several successes on the Continent, particularly with Prima Voce in Belgium's Grand Prix Prince Rose in 1983, and in 1984 he pulled off the English and Irish 1,000 Guineas double on Pebbles and Katies. He was retained by Pebbles' owner Marcos Lemos but in 1985 he accepted a retainer from Katies' trainer Mick Ryan, only to rejoin Lemos in 1986.

ROBSON, Robert (1765-1838)

Robert Robson made a great name for himself in the days when trainers held a comparatively low place in the social order and were in fact often referred to as 'training-grooms'. He was far less severe in his methods than most of his contemporaries and trained seven Derby winners, a number never exceeded and equalled only by John Porter and Fred Darling. In all he trained the winners of 34 Classics between 1793 and 1827 – twelve in the Oaks, nine in the 1,000 Guineas, seven in the Derby and six in the 2,000 Guineas, but none in the St Leger. His Derby winners were Waxy (1793), Tyrant (1802), Pope (1809), Whalebone (1810), Whisker (1815), Azor (1817) and Emilius (1823). On his retirement in 1828, ten years before he died, he was presented by leading members of the Turf with a handsome piece of plate in recognition of his professional skill and his character.

ROBSON, Thomas William (b. 1924)

Tommy Robson qualified at the Royal Veterinary College, Edinburgh, in 1950. A first-class amateur rider, he won the Scottish Grand National on two occasions. He took out a licence to train a mixed stable in 1954 at Penrith, Cumberland, and did well with horses bought cheaply out of Newmarket stables and rejuvenated. On the Flat his main successes were in the Chester Cup and Ascot Stakes with Harvest Gold, and he also won the Champion Hurdle with Magic Court. His success did not always meet official approval. His licence was not renewed in 1972, and he spent time as an assistant trainer and then adviser to the British Bloodstock Agency before resuming as private trainer to the Venezuelan Dr Jose Sahagun at Lambourn in 1981. Despite lavish spending on horses, the venture produced only five winners in two seasons, and at the end of 1982 Robson again retired from active training.

ROCHE, Christopher (b. 1950)

Christy Roche was leading apprentice in Ireland for four years while attached to Paddy Prendergast senior's stable, and he eventually became its retained rider. Following Prendergast's death, Roche became second jockey to Vincent O'Brien, and in 1982 he joined the latter's son David as stable jockey. Roche won five Irish Classics while with Prendergast – 2,000 Guineas (Ballymore, Nikoli), 1,000 Guineas (Sarah Siddons, More So) and St Leger (Mistigri) – and in his first season with David O'Brien won the Irish Sweeps Derby and French Derby on Assert. In Britain he has won the Yorkshire Oaks (Sarah Siddons), Ebor (Bonne Noel) and William Hill Futurity (Sandy Creek) but his greatest triumph came in 1984, when he won the Derby on Secreto by a short head from El Gran Señor, trained by David O'Brien's father, Vincent. Roche has been champion jockey in Ireland five times.

ROCKAVON
(1958, b c Rockefella – Cosmetic, by Sir Cosmo)

Bred by the Biddlesden Park Stud, Rockavon was bought as a foal for 420gns by Mr R.J. Donworth, who re-sold him as a yearling to Mr T.C. Yuill for 2,300gns. Trained by George Boyd, he won three modest events as a two-year-old, two at Hamilton Park and one at Stockton. As a three-year-old he brought off a very big surprise when he won the 2,000 Guineas at 66-1, ridden by Norman Stirk. His only other success that season was in a two-runner race at Newcastle. He was syndicated for stud and stood in Britain but failed to make any impression and was sent to France in 1970.

ROCKEFELLA
(1941, br c Hyperion – Rockfel, by Felstead)

Rockefella was a beautifully bred horse by Hyperion out of the dual Classic winner Rockfel. His racing record was modest but he did well as a sire, his winners including Rockavon (2,000 Guineas and £24,253), Outcrop (Yorkshire Oaks), Bounteous (Dewhurst Stakes and third in St Leger), Linacre (Irish 2,000 Guineas) and the brothers Gay Time, Elopement and Cash and Courage. Rockefella's daughter Angela Rucellai won the Italian 1,000 Guineas and Oaks and bred the Italian Derby winner Appiani II. Rockefella died in 1968.

ROCKFEL
(1935, b f Felstead – Rockliffe, by Santorb)

Bred and owned by Sir Hugo Cunliffe-Owen and trained by Captain O.M. Bell, Rockfel was a brilliant filly, though she began her career by finishing eighth in a selling race as a two-year-old. She rapidly improved and as a three-year-old won the 1,000 Guineas, Oaks, Champion Stakes and Aintree Derby. Her form at the end of the season showed she was far superior to the colts of her age. She retired to stud having won eight races for £23,431 but died from a twisted gut in 1941 after producing only one foal, Rockefella.

ROCK ROI
(1967, ch c Mourne – Secret Session, by Court Martial)

Rock Roi twice passed the winning-post first in the Ascot Gold Cup, in 1971 and 1972, but was disqualified on both occasions. Bred and owned by the Hue-Williams family and trained by Peter Walwyn from the age of three, he came into his own as a four-year-old. He was second in the Prix du Cadran and went one better at Royal Ascot but was stood down in favour of Random Shot, whom he beat by four lengths, when his post-race dope test proved positive for phenylbutazone ('bute'), a painkiller applied to offset stiffness. Walwyn was exonerated from blame and fined the minimum £100. Rock Roi went on to win the Goodwood Cup and Doncaster Cup. The following year he won the John Porter Stakes and Prix du Cadran, but after a hectic finish for the Ascot Gold Cup, in which he beat Erimo Hawk by a head, he was demoted because he had hampered the runner-up. He did not race again. Daniel Wildenstein bought a majority share in him in the summer of 1972, but on being prepared for autumn targets in France, he was injured in his box and started stud duties in 1973 in France.

ROCK SAND
(1900, br c Sainfoin – Roquebrune, by St Simon)

Bred and owned by Sir James Miller and trained by George Blackwell at Newmarket, Rock Sand was beaten only once in five races as a two-year-old, and the following year won the Triple Crown, as well as the St James's Palace Stakes. He won five times as a four-year-old. Soon after his racing career was over, Sir James Miller died and Rock Sand was sold for £25,000 to Mr August Belmont, president of the New York Jockey Club. He did well as a sire in America but was ultimately exported to France, where he died in 1914.

RODOSTO
(1930, ch c Epinard – Ramondie, by Neil Gow)

Princesse de Faucigny-Lucinge's Rodosto, trained by H. Count, won nine races, including the 2,000 Guineas in both Britain and France. The feat has been emulated since only by Djebel in 1940. Most of Rodosto's stud career was spent in France but when an old horse he was exported to Argentina. The best of his stock was Dogat, winner of the French 2,000 Guineas.

ROE, John Patrick (b. 1938)

Johnny Roe had been nine times Irish champion jockey before he rode his only British Classic winner on Nocturnal Spree in the 1975 1,000 Guineas.

Apprenticed to Seamus McGrath, he was a much-travelled rider, spending four years in Rhodesia before returning in 1963 to ride as second jockey to Vincent O'Brien. The year after, he rejoined McGrath; in 1965 he rode for Bernard van Cutsem at Newmarket, and the following year he started a renewed spell with O'Brien before joining Dermot Weld in the early 1970s. His British successes also included the Royal Hunt Cup, Cork and Orrery Stakes and Queen Alexandra Stakes. He began training at Shankill, Co. Dublin, in 1981.

ROGERS, John Michael (1925-85)

Mick Rogers came from a well-known Anglo-Irish racing family. He never had a big stable at The Curragh but won the Derby with Hard Ridden (1958) and Santa Claus (1964). In the summer of 1970 he announced his intention to retire from training but returned briefly in 1973. He spent some years in virtual retirement but emerged to become a prominent administrator for the Irish Turf Club before his sudden death in May 1985.

ROHAN, Hubert Patrick (b. 1933)

Born into a farming and horse-dealing family at Middleton, Co. Cork, Pat Rohan came to Britain in 1954 and from 1956 to 1958 assisted Bill Dutton, whose daughter he married in 1959. On Dutton's death in 1958, he took over the stable at Malton. Among the good horses he has trained are Right Boy, Sandiacre, Althrey Don and Tin Whistle, while his successes in important races include the Cork and Orrery Stakes (twice), July Cup (twice), Nunthorpe Stakes (twice), Brown Jack Stakes, Seaton Delaval Stakes (twice) and King George Stakes. With an astute eye for a cheap horse, Rohan made his early mark with sprinters, but like many Northern trainers he has found that even cheap horses are not guaranteed to win races, and from a peak of 52 winners in 1968, he slumped to six in 1983 before recovering to fifteen in 1985.

ROI HERODE
(1904, gr c Le Samaritain – Roxelane, by War Dance)

Roi Hérode, bred in France, was not top class and was something of a plodder but Mr E. Kennedy bought him for £2,000 with the object of sending him to stud in Ireland to revive the Herod sire line outside France. His first crop of runners included The Tetrarch, perhaps the fastest horse seen on the British Turf. Roi Hérode lived till he was 27 but never sired another horse of comparable ability.

ROLAND GARDENS
(1975, b c Derring-Do – Katricia, by Skymaster)

Roland Gardens gave trainer Duncan Sasse his first, and so far only, Classic success by winning the 2,000 Guineas at 28-1. He was bought for 3,200gns as a yearling and was trained by Robert Armstrong until Sasse's father, Tim, took a controlling interest after he had finished first in the Horris Hill Stakes only to be demoted to third for failing to keep a straight course, as a two-year-old. Before the Newmarket Classic he won the Blue Riband Trial at Epsom but won only once afterwards, in a minor race at Leicester as a four-year-old. At the end of his four-year-old career he was sold to stand at stud in South Africa.

ROMULUS
(1959, b c Ribot – Arietta, by Tudor Minstrel)

Bred by Mr P. Bull, Romulus was sold privately as a foal to Mr C. Engelhard. Trained by Fulke Johnson Houghton, he ran five times as a two-year-old, winning the Virginia Water Stakes at Ascot and being beaten a neck in the Champagne Stakes. As a three-year-old he developed into Europe's best miler, winning the Greenham Stakes, Queen Elizabeth II Stakes and Prix du Moulin de Longchamp. He was second in the 2,000 Guineas and fell in the Derby. In all he won £12,765 in Britain and 102,000 francs in France. He had not made his mark as a sire when he was exported to Japan in 1969, though he was represented by two above-average winners in Popkins and Petty Officer after his departure.

ROSEBERY, 5th Earl of
(1847-1929)

The fifth Earl of Rosebery is the only man to have won the Derby when holding office as Prime Minister. This he accomplished in 1894 with Ladas and 1895 with Sir Visto.

Lord Rosebery was a patron of the Turf from early manhood, though his fortunes were not always high and he twice gave up ownership. Most of his many good winners were bred at his Mentmore Stud, near Leighton Buzzard. The full range of his Classic successes is as follows:

2,000 Guineas: Ladas (1894); Neil Gow (1910); Ellangowan (1923)
1,000 Guineas: Chelandry (1897); Vaucluse (1915); Plack (1924)
Derby: Ladas (1894); Sir Visto (1895); Cicero (1905)
Oaks: Bonny Jean (1885)
St Leger: Sir Visto (1895).

Lord Rosebery retained his interest in racing till the end of his life, and his colours were carried to success for the last time only a week before his death.

ROSEBERY, 6th Earl of
(1882-1974)

The sixth Earl of Rosebery succeeded his father in 1929. In his youth he was a notable all-round sportsman; he captained Surrey at cricket, was just about the best heavyweight to hounds in the country and was on the fringe of international standard at polo. For more than 40 years he was one of the most active members of the Jockey Club, and his work as a racing administrator was notable for shrewdness and determination, backed up by a remarkable memory and a formidable power of repartee. He was not noted for his tolerance of fools and bores, and at one time was rated a somewhat formidable character, though he undoubtedly mellowed with age.

His association with trainer Jack Jarvis began in 1929 and ended with Jarvis's death in 1968, when his horses were taken over by Doug Smith. For the last three years of his life his trainer was Bruce Hobbs, who continued to train the hugely decreased string that Lady Rosebery kept on following her husband's death.

He twice won the Derby with horses bred at his Mentmore Stud – Blue Peter in 1939 and Ocean Swell in 1944. Blue Peter also won the 2,000 Guineas and Eclipse Stakes, Ocean Swell the Ascot Gold Cup. Lord Rosebery won the St Leger in 1931 with Sandwich, who was very unlucky not to win the Derby, and the Eclipse Stakes in 1932 with Miracle, who cost only 175gns as a yearling. In 1969 he won the Oaks for the only time with Sleeping Partner.

ROSE BOWL
(1972, b f Habitat – Roselière, by Misti IV)

Though only fourth in the 1,000 Guineas, Rose Bowl matured into a tip-top miler and 10f horse, with no peers among her own sex and few among the colts. As a three-year-old she won the Queen Elizabeth II Stakes and then beat Allez France in the Champion Stakes; the following year she won the Clive Graham Stakes, repeated her success in the Queen Elizabeth II Stakes and was beaten a neck by Vitigès when attempting the Champion Stakes double. She was the last big-race winner to carry the Engelhard colours, running in the name of Mrs Jane Engelhard following the death of her husband Charles. She was trained by Fulke Johnson Houghton. Her first foal, the filly Golden Bowl, won the Lupe Stakes and was narrowly beaten in the Cheshire Oaks.

ROSEDROP
(1907, ch f St Frusquin – Rosaline, by Trenton)

Rosedrop won the Oaks and was dam of the 'Triple Crown' winner and outstanding sire Gainsborough.

ROSE OF ENGLAND
(1927, br f Teddy – Perce-Neige, by Neil Gow)

Bred by Lady James Douglas, Rose of England was bought by Lord Glanely for 3,100gns as a yearling and won one race, the Oaks. At stud she bred Chulmleigh, who won the St Leger and was exported to Argentina, British Empire, who won over £5,000 in Britain and did very well as a sire in Argentina, Coastal Traffic, who was at stud successively in Ireland, France and America and then France again, and Faerie Queen, grandam of Arabian Night, who was second in the Derby and was sold to Argentina in 1955 for £41,000.

ROSE ROYALE II
(1954, b f Prince Bio – Rose of Yeroda, by Nearco)

Rose Royale II was bred by the Aga Khan and trained in France by Alec Head. She won the 1,000 Guineas and Champion Stakes in 1957 but was third on firm going when favourite for the Oaks. She was a well-beaten fifth in the Washington D.C. International and remained in America with the intention of mating her with Ribot, but shortly after she died.

ROSEWAY
(1916, br f Stornoway – Rose of Ayrshire, by Ayrshire)

Roseway won four races for £5,433, including the 1,000 Guineas, for her owner-breeder Sir Edward Hulton. She was also second in the Oaks, for which she started odds-on. She made little mark as a broodmare, though her daughter Roseola bred the French Classic runner-up and sire Tornado.

ROSY LEGEND
(1931, br f Dark Legend – Rosy Cheeks, by St Just)

Foaled in France, Rosy Legend won four races there and came to Britain as a five-year-old. Ten years later she was bought by Sir Eric Ohlson for 3,500gns. The foal she was carrying was the Derby winner Dante. She also bred the St Leger winner Sayajirao and five other winners of considerably lesser ability.

ROTHSCHILD, Anthony Gustav de (1887-1961)

Mr Anthony de Rothschild is one of the few British owners to have won the Grand Prix de Paris this century. This he did in 1919 with Galloper Light, whom he inherited from his father, Leopold. In 1926 he won the 1,000 Guineas with Pillion. He disposed of his bloodstock in 1944.

ROTHSCHILD, James Armand Edmond de (1878-1957)

Mr James de Rothschild was in his heyday one of the biggest and boldest punters on the British Turf. When he won the Cambridgeshire in 1919 with Brigand, he landed £80,000 in bets; when he won that race again two years later, with Milenko, the odds were shorter and he won only £30,000. He won the 1909 Ascot Gold Cup with Bomba, the last three-year-old to win that event, the 1911 1,000 Guineas with Atmah and the Grand Prix de Paris with Reine Lumière. A fabulous character of highly distinctive appearance, topped by an eye-glass, he was the only member of the Jockey Club to be awarded the DCM, a decoration for valour restricted to NCOs and other ranks.

ROUS, Admiral Henry John (1795-1877)

Admiral Rous dominated the British Turf from 1846 till his death. Vigorous, determined, utterly honest and extremely shrewd, he was a born leader with a single weakness – impetuosity. To his own detriment he had the unfortunate habit of writing hasty letters to the newspapers before he was fully conversant with the facts.

He served with credit in the Royal Navy, his outstanding feat being to bring the storm-battered frigate *Pique* safely home from Newfoundland to Spithead, a distance of some 1,500 miles, in twenty days, although *Pique* was rudderless and leaking at the rate of two feet of water an hour.

He was elected to the Jockey Club in 1821 and in periods of unemployment during naval service made a profound study of racing and in particular the rules of the sport. He was first elected a steward of the Jockey Club in 1838 and became, like Sir Charles Bunbury, 'a sort of perpetual president'. In 1850 he published *On The Laws and Practice of Horse-Racing*, a publication that established his position as the leading Turf authority of the day. The four main sections of his book dealt with the development of the Thoroughbred; the Newmarket Rules of Racing, with a clear and precise explanation of those rules; the duties of racing officials; and a list of difficult and complicated racing cases with judgement pronounced in each case.

He was an expert handicapper who was not easily hoodwinked. 'Every great handicap', he used to say, 'is a premium to fraud.' In 1855, when 60 years of age, he accepted the post of public handicapper but luckily he possessed the zest and industry required for this exacting job and used to sit up half the night studying form. With apparently inexhaustible energy he not only attended all important race-meetings but was out on Newmarket Heath most mornings, watching the horses work and jotting down in his notebook what he had seen.

At Newmarket he used to watch the races from the Bushes, 2f from the winning-post, as he reckoned it the ideal pitch from which to spot non-triers. If he saw what he thought was a bad case, he would roar at the jockey as he went by. If there was trouble at the start, he used to go down himself and sort it out. All this time he was a steward of the Jockey Club and it says much for his energy and integrity that he carried out his many tasks to the complete satisfaction of the majority. He certainly established a new high standard of handicapping.

Not the least of his services was to take in hand the Jockey Club financial position. This was anything but satisfactory but he succeeded in raising revenue derived from Newmarket from £3,000 a year to £18,000.

He detested heavy betting and strongly opposed lavish presents to jockeys, whom he felt should be kept in their place, and that place a fairly humble one. He retained his strength and vigour until he was over 80, and by and large racing never had a truer friend. Though for 25 years his word was law, he was never arrogant or overbearing in his determination to achieve a high standard in all that mattered. Some of his sayings remain applicable, such as his advice to owners: 'Keep yourself in the best company and your horses in the worst'.

ROUSE, Brian Albert (b. 1940)

Fulham-born Brian Rouse rode his first winner, Gay Bird, for Ted Smyth, to whom he was apprenticed at Epsom, at Alexandra Park on 29 July 1957 and rode his second, New Tack, for John Sutcliffe, who persuaded him back into racing, at Chepstow on 29 May 1972. That was the year he renewed his riding licence, after working for Brian Swift and Sutcliffe at Epsom, and he made enormous strides in the next few years, reaching 60 winners for the 1978 season, when he won the Northumberland Plate (for the second time) and Goodwood Cup on Tug of War and Cambridgeshire on Baronet. Two years later he won his first Classic, the 1,000 Guineas, on Quick As Lightning, who had been turned down by four other jockeys, and the Cambridgeshire again on Baronet. As well as becoming the best substitute rider when others were not available, he has notched some remarkable achievements including five consecutive winners at Lingfield on 9 July 1982 and a Royal Ascot double in 1983 in the Prince of Wales's Stakes and Hardwicke Stakes on Stanerra, whom he rode to win the Japan Cup that autumn. His best season was 1984, with 67 winners.

ROYAL CHARGER
(1942, ch c Nearco – Sun
Princess, by Solario)

Royal Charger was a handsome chestnut trained by Jack Jarvis for his breeder Sir John Jarvis. Royal Charger showed little promise early on but at three and four

years of age was a very good horse indeed. He was third in the 2,000 Guineas and won the Ayr Gold Cup with 9st 7lb. At the conclusion of his racing career he was sold to the Irish National Stud for 50,000gns. In 1953 he was sold for export to America. Among his winners were Happy Laughter (1,000 Guineas), Gilles de Retz (2,000 Guineas), Sea Charger (Irish St Leger), Royal Serenade (£10,791 in Britain and a good winner in America) and Turn-to (grandsire of Sir Ivor and Roberto). Royal Charger died in 1961.

ROYAL LANCER
(1919, b c Spearmint – Royal
Favour, by White Eagle)

Royal Lancer was bred by the National Stud, leased to Lord Lonsdale and trained by A. Sadler junior. He won six races for £14,779 including the St Leger at 33-1. He also won the Irish St Leger. He failed as a sire and ended up in South Africa. He was ridden in the St Leger by Bobby Jones, then a young apprentice. Jones was still waiting for his present when Lord Lonsdale died years later.

ROYAL MINSTREL
(1925, gr c Tetratema –
Harpsichord, by Louvois)

Bred in Ireland by Mr J.J. Maher, Royal Minstrel was an exceptionally handsome grey. Trained by Captain Cecil Boyd-Rochfort, first for Captain G.P. Gough and later for Mr J.H. Whitney, Royal Minstrel never ran as a two-year-old. The following season he was beaten by inches by Flamingo in the 2,000 Guineas. Up to 10f he was a really good horse, winning the Eclipse Stakes, in which he slammed Fairway, St James's Palace Stakes, Cork and Orrery Stakes and Victoria Cup. In a memorable duel for the July Cup he was just beaten by Lord Ellesmere's game little filly Tiffin, who was never defeated.

Royal Minstrel retired to stud in America, where he sired First Fiddle, winner of $398,000, and a good many other winners. He came back to Britain in 1938 but died two years later.

ROYAL PALACE
(1964, b c Ballymoss – Crystal Palace, by Solar Slipper)

Royal Palace was bred and owned by Mr H.J. Joel and trained by Noel Murless at Newmarket. He won two of his three races as a two-year-old, his most important success being in the Royal Lodge Stakes at Ascot, and the following year won the 2,000 Guineas and Derby. Owing to a mishap he had to miss the St Leger and was not at his best when third behind Reform in the Champion Stakes. As a four-year-old he was undefeated, his victories including the Coronation Cup, Eclipse Stakes and King George VI and Queen Elizabeth Stakes. His nine victories and one placing earned £166,063. He has had a chequered, mainly disappointing stud career, highlighted by the fillies Dunfermline (Oaks and St Leger), Royal Hive (Park Hill Stakes), Escorial (Musidora Stakes) and Antrona (Prix de Malleret). Royal Palace's stud fee of 5,000gns was reduced to 1,000gns in 1976, and to 500gns in 1981, after his owners had made a gift of him to the National Stud. He stood in Northumberland for three seasons before returning to Newmarket in 1984.

RUNNER

All horses which come under the starter's orders are designated 'runners'.

A runner is also the term used for employees of bookmakers whose job is to lay off excess commissions by transferring them to other bookmakers.

RUNNING REIN
(1841, b c The Saddler – Mab, by Duncan Grey)

Running Rein, belonging to Mr A. Wood, was first past the post in the 1844 Derby. However, it was later proved that he was a four-year-old called Maccabaeus. Thanks chiefly to the energy of Lord George Bentinck, the fraud was disclosed. Running Rein was disqualified and the race awarded to Colonel Peel's Orlando. The villain behind the plot was a disreputable gambler called Goodman Levy who fled the country when it was clear that the fraud had failed.

RUSSELL, Alexander John (b. 1918)

Alec Russell was apprenticed to J. Torterolo in France and rode his first winner in 1935 at Le Tremblay. After some 200 winners in France he had his first ride in Britain on 8 October 1949 and landed a gamble on Quixote in a selling handicap at Haydock Park. He remained to become senior jockey in the North of England until forced to retire in March 1974 after sustaining serious injuries when schooling the previous October. His best season was 1957, with 60 winners, of which six came at the meeting at Bogside on 19 July, the last time a jockey has gone through the card in Britain. The best horse he rode was Quorum, winner of the Sussex Stakes and second in the 2,000 Guineas. Other good races he won included the Zetland Gold Cup, Free Handicap and Jersey Stakes.

RUSSELL, James (d. 1961)

Born in Australia, James Russell trained with considerable success in South Africa before settling in Britain in 1928. He won the Lincolnshire Handicap in 1934 with Play On and in 1936 with Over Coat.

In April 1947 his licence was withdrawn when tests in respect of a horse of his, a winner at Lincoln, showed a positive reaction to dope. The following year he sued the stewards of the Jockey Club, alleging that his licence had been wrongfully withdrawn and claiming damages for alleged breach of contract. He also claimed damages for alleged libel in the *Racing Calendar*. The Lord Chief Justice, Lord Goddard, ruled there was no cause of action in libel but left to the jury the question of whether Russell had received a fair hearing from the stewards. On that point the jury failed to agree. Lord Goddard then said that in his opinion the defence submission was right and there was no case to go before the jury at all. Accordingly he dismissed the action with costs. Russell's appeal was dismissed in December 1948 by the Court of Appeal.

RUSTOM PASHA
(1927, b c Son-in-Law – Cos, by Flying Orb)

Bred by the Aga Khan, Rustom Pasha was by a great stayer, Son-in-Law, out of an extremely fast mare Cos. He himself proved a high-class middle-distance horse, his victories including the Eclipse Stakes and Champion Stakes. He was at stud first in France and then in Argentina. His daughter Rustom Mahal, out of Mumtaz Mahal, was the dam of Abernant. In the Derby Rustom Pasha started at 9-2 and was shouted home by his happy owner who was blissfully unaware that it was not Rustom Pasha winning but Blenheim, his 18-1 second-string.

RYAN, Michael John (b. 1941)

Mick Ryan took over Bernard van Cutsem's horses on the death of the latter, to whom he had been travelling head lad and assistant, in 1975, and when they were dispersed he continued training at Newmarket, moving to his present Cadland stables in 1978. Apprenticed to George Colling and Jack Watts, he had worked for George Archibald in the United States for four years before joining van Cutsem. He did well with runners in Holland for a Dutch patron, Mr W. Nuy, and broke through into the major races in 1984 with Katies, winner of the Irish 1,000 Guineas and Coronation Stakes at Royal Ascot, and contributing to his best season of 33 winners.

RYAN, William (b. 1960)

Willie Ryan followed Steve Perks and Kevin Darley as champion apprentices attached to Reg Hollinshead's stable, though he had to share the title with Gary Carter in 1985, with 37 winners from 392 rides. Son of the successful jockey Denis Ryan and grandson of the trainer Willie Stephenson, Ryan rode regularly for Gavin Pritchard-Gordon's stable in 1985.

S

SADDLE CLOTHS

Saddle cloths were first used in 1922.

SAGARO
(1971, ch c Espresso –
Zambara, by Mossborough)

Trained in France by François Boutin for
Gerry Oldham, Sagaro became the first
horse to win the Ascot Gold Cup three
times when he completed a hat-trick in
1977, after which he was sold to the Levy
Board for £175,000 and retired to stand
at the National Stud in Newmarket from
the following year. He was second in all
three races before Ascot in 1977, all to
Buckskin, but he turned the tables on that
rival when the unique triumph beckoned.
He proved himself Europe's leading
stayer for four years. As a three-year-old
he won the Grand Prix de Paris from
Bustino; at four he finished third in the
Prix du Cadran, France's equivalent to
the Gold Cup, before winning at Royal
Ascot; and at five he easily won the
Cadran as a prelude to the royal meeting.
Each time his Ascot Gold Cup jockey
was Lester Piggott, and each time it was
his last outing of the season. The modern
prejudice against stayers was evident in
Sagaro's stallion valuation. Having
stayed under the auspices of the National
Stud, he moved to Oxfordshire, Lin-
colnshire and Cheshire (from 1986) in a
short time. His early crops boasted Super
Sunrise (Chester Vase) and Sagamore
(Cambridgeshire) as his best winners. He
died of a heart attack in March 1986.

SAINT CRESPIN III
(1956, ch c Aureole –
Neocracy, by Nearco)

Bred by the Aga Khan and Prince Aly
Khan, Saint Crespin was a half-brother to
the Derby and St Leger winner Tulyar.
Trained in France by Alec Head, Saint
Crespin won four races including the
Imperial Produce Stakes, Eclipse Stakes
and Prix de l'Arc de Triomphe. He was
retired to stud in Ireland and before being
exported to Japan in 1970 sired a number
of smart fillies, including Dolina (Italian
Oaks), Casaque Grise (Prix Vermeille),
Mige (Cheveley Park Stakes) and Altesse
Royale (1,000 Guineas, Oaks and Irish
Oaks). His best colt was Shoemaker
(second in the Derby).

SAINT-MARTIN, Yves (b.
1941)

Yves Saint-Martin, the son of a civil
servant, rode his first winner in 1958,
while apprenticed to François Mathet,
and in the period since, he has been the
one French jockey who has consistently
mastered the intricacies of British
racecourses. He was champion jockey in
France for the first time in 1962, the year
he won the Oaks on Monade and King
George VI and Queen Elizabeth Stakes
on Match III. He stayed with the Mathet
stable until 1970, winning the 1963
Derby on Relko, and then took on a
retainer for Mr Daniel Wildenstein, for
whom he won three British Classics in
1976, the 1,000 Guineas (Flying Water),
Oaks (Pawneese) and St Leger (Crow).
Saint-Martin's other major British wins
have been in the 1,000 Guineas (1971,
Altesse Royale), 2,000 Guineas (1974,
Nonoalco), King George VI and Queen
Elizabeth Stakes (1976, Pawneese), and
Champion Stakes (1984, Palace Music).

In France, Saint-Martin has won their
1,000 Guineas seven times, 2,000
Guineas five times, Derby eight times,
Oaks five times and Grand Prix de Paris
four times. He has also won the Prix de
l'Arc de Triomphe four times – for
Mathet on Sassafras (1970), for Mr
Wildenstein on Allez France (1974) and
Sagace (1984), and for a more recent

retainer, the Aga Khan, on Akiyda (1982).

SALISBURY

Salisbury is one of the oldest racecourses in Britain and it is recorded that Queen Elizabeth I went to the races there in 1588, not long before Drake sailed from Plymouth to defeat the Spanish Armada. The big prize at Salisbury on that occasion was a golden bell valued at £50.

Situated on a hill a few miles outside the city, the track consists of fine old turf that provides admirable going, and it is rare for the ground to get really hard. The standard of racing is quite good, and fields are nearly always strong because of the proximity of so many Berkshire and Wiltshire stables. Many a good two-year-old has been introduced to racing at Salisbury, particularly in the days when Fred Darling trained at Beckhampton, Alec Taylor at Manton, and Noel Cannon at Druids Lodge, and the 1970s innovation of early-season trials for the 1,000 and 2,000 Guineas has added interest to the three-year-old races. In the heyday of the Bibury Club, which used to stage a three-day meeting in July, there were too many races for amateur riders to suit the public taste but that is a thing of the past.

The course consists of a mile track which is straight except for a slight right-hand elbow about 5f from the winning-post, and a right-handed loop which leaves the mile course at the elbow and rejoins it 7f from home. The $1\frac{3}{4}$m start is opposite the club enclosure, the horses running down the straight away from the stands, round the loop and back up the straight. The final 4f is uphill and calls for stamina, but the undulations and a sharp turn on the loop demand good balance and adaptability. High numbers in the draw usually have an advantage in races of 5f and 6f owing to the bend soon after the start, but a quick break is needed to avoid being cut off, and if the going is soft the advantage may transfer to the lower numbers.

SALIVA TEST

A laboratory test on a swab taken from the horse's mouth which will reveal the presence or otherwise of a prohibited substance, such as dope.

SALMON-TROUT
(1921, b c The Tetrarch – Salamandra, by St Frusquin)

Bred by Lord Furness, Salmon-Trout was bought by the Aga Khan as a yearling for 3,000gns and trained by Richard Dawson. He won five races for £15,830, including a sensational St Leger concerning which there were lurid stories linking the name of Salmon-Trout's jockey, Bernard Carslake, with that of a leading bookmaker who had laid Salmon-Trout heavily and was very hard hit by the result.

Salmon-Trout was not a great success as a sire although he did get two top-class horses in Salmon Leap (Coronation Cup and Goodwood Cup) and King Salmon (Coronation Cup and Eclipse Stakes). He was eventually exported to South Africa.

SALTASH
(1920, ch c Sunstar – Hamoaze, by Torpoint)

Bred by Lord Astor, Saltash was a brother to Buchan and half-brother to St Germans. Like Buchan, he won the Eclipse Stakes, as well as two other races, for total stakes of £11,113. He did well as a sire in Australia.

SALVO
(1963, ch c Right Royal V – Manera, by Macherio)

Salvo was bred in America and bought for $9,500 by Mr G.A. Oldham. Trained by Harry Wragg, he improved with age and won six races, the Craven Stakes, Vaux Gold Tankard, Newbury Autumn Cup, Yorkshire Cup, Hardwicke Stakes and Grosser Preis von Baden. He was also second in the John Porter Stakes, King George VI and Queen Elizabeth Stakes and Prix de l'Arc de Triomphe and gained total earnings of £73,677. He was at stud in Newmarket until being sent to West Germany.

SANDOWN PARK

Sandown Park, at Esher, is only fourteen miles from London. By British standards it is a modern racecourse, the first meeting having been held there in 1875. The three men who instituted racing at Sandown and laid out the course were Mr Hwfa Williams, his brother General Owen Williams, a Member of Parliament, a heavy gambler, and subsequently part-owner of The Bard, and Sir Wilfred Brett. Mr Hwfa Williams was the dominating personality and held office as chairman and Clerk of the Course for nearly 50 years.

The charm of Sandown, deservedly one of the most popular courses in the country, particularly in respect of racing over jumps, is based on the fact that the stands and enclosures are sited on a hill. It is possible to see nearly all the running by standing on the lawns in front of the stands, and on no other major course is viewing rendered so easy.

From the start Sandown proved a success and, with the support and encouragement of Mr Leopold de Roths-child, Mr Hwfa Williams decided to stage the first £10,000 race in Britain, the 1m 2f Eclipse Stakes. It was first run in 1886 and was won by Major H.T. Barclay's good horse Bendigo, who defeated the 1884 Derby dead-heater, St Gatien. In 1903 Ard Patrick, who had won the Derby the year before, defeated the famous filly Sceptre, winner of the other four Classics, and Rock Sand who won the Triple Crown in 1903. (It is an odd fact that the race had never been won by a filly until Pebbles in 1985.) Another memorable race came in 1910 when the Derby winner Lemberg ran a dead-heat with Neil Gow, winner of the 2,000 Guineas. In recent years the Eclipse has tended to be overshadowed by the King George VI and Queen Elizabeth Stakes at Ascot run later in the month. However, Tulyar, Ballymoss, Busted, Royal Palace, Mill Reef, Brigadier Gerard, Ela-Mana-Mou and Kalaglow have all won the two races in the same year.

The 5f National Stakes for two-year-olds, previously the National Breeders' Produce Stakes, has declined in status in recent years. The Tetrarch won this race after being virtually left at the post, and another famous winner was the Aga Khan's Bahram.

Sandown is a right-handed oval track of 1m 5f. The 4f run-in is uphill almost the entire way, and so is the straight 5f course. Sandown is a stiff course but a fair one, demanding the qualities of stamina and resolution. Because of the layout of the course, it is not possible to run 6f races there.

SANDWICH
(1928, b c Sansovino –
Waffles, by Buckwheat)

Sandwich, bred by Mr J.J. Maher, was a half-brother to the Derby winner Manna. Bought as a yearling for 3,600gns by Lord Rosebery and trained by Jack Jarvis, he won the Chester Vase, King Edward VII Stakes and St Leger for £17,019. He was a very unlucky loser of the Derby, Harry Wragg riding one of his less successful races and getting badly shut in in the straight. Sandwich did not add to his reputation as a four-year-old and failed as a sire.

SANGSTER, Robert (b. 1936)

From the humble beginnings of a small stud in Cheshire, Robert Sangster has helped to change the character of modern racing in Britain and internationally, as an owner and breeder. His patronage of United States sires, notably Northern Dancer and his sons, and his syndication of horses for racing and stallion purposes have transformed the commercial scene.

Much of this enormous effect has emanated from his association with Irish trainer Vincent O'Brien and the develop-ment, with various partners, of the Coolmore Stud complex in Ireland, as well as his own Swettenham Stud, which now sponsors the Sussex Stakes.

His first horses were trained by Eric Cousins and his first winner of conse-quence was Brief Star in the 1969 Ayr Gold Cup. He then forged the link with O'Brien, and has extended his interests to horses racing and at stud in England, Ireland, France, Germany, Italy, Aus-tralia, New Zealand, the United States and South Africa, the most recent development being to instil Michael Dickinson as Sweetenham Stud's private trainer at Manton, with runners from 1986.

Mr Sangster has been leading owner five times in the last nine years, in 1977, '78, '82, '83 and '84. Such domination has not been seen since the early pre-War days of the Aga Khan, and it is likely to be threatened only by the major Arab owners, whose buying power at the world's leading aution sales eclipses even Mr Sangster and his international syndicates, whose strategy is to produce at least one possible stallion for syndication each year.

His most important winners in Britain have been:

2,000 Guineas – Lomond (1983), El Gran Senor (1984)

Derby – The Minstrel (1977), Golden Fleece (1982)

Eclipsecg100 – Solford (1984)

King George VI and Queen Elizabeth Diamond Stakes – The Minstrel (1977)

Benson & Hedges – Hawaiian Sound (1978), Assert (1982), Caerleon (1983)

Ascot Gold Cup – Gildoran (1984, 1985).

He has also won the Dewhurst Stakes five times (The Minstrel, Try My Best, Monteverdi, Storm Bird, El Gran Senor) in eight years, and the Cheveley Park Stakes three times (Durtal, Sookera, Woodstream). All these big-race winners were trained by Vincent O'Brien except Durtal, Hawaiian Sound and Gildoran (Barry Hills), Assert (David O'Brien) and Sookera (Dermot Weld). Assert also won the French Derby, and Caerleon emulated the success a year later. Mr Sangster has also won the French 1,000 Guineas, with River Lady, and the Prix de l'Arc de Triomphe, with Alleged (twice) and Detroit. In Ireland he has won the 2,000 Guineas and 1,000 Guineas twice each, the Sweeps Derby three times, and the Oaks and St Leger once each.

Mr Sangster's early big-race winners were usually ridden by Lester Piggott, but in 1980 he took on Pat Eddery as contract jockey. He was also responsible for bringing Steve Cauthen from the United States and Brent Thomson from Australasia to ride for him in Britain. As well as sponsoring the Sussex Stakes, he backs the Vernons Sprint Cup through his family football pools firm, and after several attempts won it in 1985 with Orojoya.

Racing colours: Emerald green, royal blue sleeves, white cap, emerald green spots.

SANSOVINO
(1921, b c Swynford –
Gondolette, by Loved One)

Bred by Lord Derby, Sansovino was trained by George Lambton and as a two-year-old won both his races, the Ham Stakes at Goodwood and Gimcrack Stakes. The following season he ran with promise when close-up third in the Newmarket Stakes and shortly afterwards did a very impressive gallop at Newmarket. Immediately after the gallop one of the jockeys who had taken part, pawned his wife's jewellery and put every penny he raised on Sansovino for the Derby.

The going at Epsom was very heavy, and rain fell in torrents throughout Derby day. The conditions, though, suited Sansovino and, ridden by Tommy Weston, he won by six lengths. It was the first time for 137 years that the race had been won by an earl of Derby.

Sansovino ran twice at Ascot, winning the Prince of Wales's Stakes and finishing unplaced in the Hardwicke Stakes. He was unplaced in the St Leger but he had been coughing not long before the race. As a four-year-old he had leg trouble and was never really right but proved his speed by beating Diophon, winner of the 2,000 Guineas, over a mile at Lingfield. He was unplaced in the City and Suburban and is the last Derby winner to have competed in that event.

As a sire he was a shade disappointing but got Sandwich (St Leger), Jacopo (a top-class two-year-old and successful sire in America), Monument (Coronation Cup), Buckleigh (Jockey Club Cup), Sans Peine (Goodwood Cup) and Sansonnet (dam of Tudor Minstrel). Sansovino died in 1940.

SANTA CLAUS
(1961, b c Chamossaire – Aunt Clara, by Arctic Prince)

Santa Claus was bred by Dr F.A. Smorfitt and sold for 800gns as a foal, before being bought as a yearling for 1,200gns on behalf of Mr J. Ismay. Trained at The Curragh by Mick Rogers, he won four races for £138,127, including the Derby, Irish 2,000 Guineas and Irish Derby. He was second in the King George VI and Queen Elizabeth Stakes and Prix de l'Arc de Triomphe. He was valued at £400,000 when retired to the Airlie Stud, Co. Dublin, where he stood till his sudden death in February 1970. His two Classic winners were the brother and sister Reindeer (Irish St Leger) and Santa Tina (Irish Oaks), but other good winners included Yaroslav (Royal Lodge Stakes) and Bonne Noel (Ebor Handicap).

SANTORB
(1921, br c Santoi – Countess Torby, by Morganatic)

Bred by Captain Charles Moore, Santorb was a very good stayer, winning 8½ races for £8,446, including the Ascot Gold Cup, Doncaster Cup and Newbury Summer Cup. He was at stud in Britain for four years before being exported to Hungary but left his mark by siring Rockliffe, dam of Rockfel.

SASSE, Duncan Jonathan Grant (b. 1951)

Duncan Sasse had a remarkable start to his training career. After working in France, Newmarket, Australia and Lambourn, he began training at Lambourn in 1974 and won the Eclipse Stakes with Coup de Feu that season. His first win was with Great Echo at Pontefract on 10 April 1974. In 1978 he won the 2,000 Guineas with Roland Gardens, but results flagged after that, the stable failed to get into double figures after winning fourteen races in 1979 and in the autumn of 1985 Sasse left to train in Italy.

SASSOON, Sir Ellice Victor (1881-1961)

Sir Victor Sassoon was educated at Harrow and Cambridge and succeeded to the baronetcy in 1924. In World War I he served in the RFC. A member of a famous Jewish family that emigrated from Baghdad to India early in the nineteenth century, his business interests were mainly concerned with E.D. Sassoon and Co. bankers, merchants and mill-owners.

For over 30 years Sir Victor was in truth a pillar of the Turf. He came into the sport almost by accident. In India he got to know Jimmy Crawford, the son of an Ayrshire blacksmith and a successful amateur rider on the Indian Turf. In 1922 Crawford came to Britain to train for Mr M. Goculdas, a Bombay cotton magnate. Goculdas got into financial difficulties, and Sassoon took over his racing interests, consisting of over 100 horses in India and a number in Britain. In India he raced as 'Mr Eve', and when he established a stud at Newmarket he named it the Eve Stud.

In 1925 he began to launch out on the Turf and spent what was then considered a fortune on yearlings. He bought the Fitzroy House stables at Newmarket and installed Jimmy Crawford as his trainer. The 1925 yearlings included the highly strung Gay Crusader colt Hot Night who ran second to Call Boy in the Derby. When Crawford died, Sir Victor divided his horses between Basil Jarvis, Joe Lawson and Matt Peacock, while he also sent some to Jack Rogers in Ireland.

In 1937 Sir Victor enjoyed his first British Classic successes when he won the 1,000 Guineas and Oaks with Exhibitionnist, trained by Lawson. She was by Solario out of Lady Wembley, a mare bought by Crawford for only 750gns. The same year Sir Victor won the Irish 2,000 Guineas and Irish Derby with Phideas. He had won the Irish 'Triple Crown' two years previously with Museum. In 1936 he purchased the French horse Mieuxcé, who, although disappointing as a sire of winners, did well as a sire of broodmares.

Sir Victor's peak of success came

between 1953 and 1960, when he won the Derby on four occasions. Considering his many expensive purchases, it is ironical that two of his Derby winners, Pinza (1953) and Hard Ridden (1958), cost only 1,500gns and 270gns respectively. Pinza, trained by Norman Bertie, also won the King George VI and Queen Elizabeth Stakes. Hard Ridden, trained by Mick Rogers, won the Irish 2,000 Guineas before his Epsom triumph. Noel Murless trained Sir Victor's two other Derby winners, Crepello (1957) and St Paddy (1960). Crepello also won the 2,000 Guineas and St Paddy the St Leger and Eclipse Stakes. Sir Victor won the 1,000 Guineas in 1956 with Honeylight trained by Captain Charles Elsey. She was a half-sister to Crepello and to the 1963 Gold Cup winner Twilight Alley.

Like a good many rich men, Sir Victor was not always easy to get on with but, considering his contribution to racing and the invaluable financial advice he could have given, it seems odd that he was never elected to the Jockey Club.

SASSOON, Lady (b. 1920)

Lady Sassoon carried on the breeding and racing interests of her husband, Sir Victor Sassoon, when he died in 1961, including the Sassoon Studs which incorporated the Beech House Stud and Eve Stud at Newmarket, Thornton Stud in Yorkshire and the Killeen Stud in Co. Meath. But in 1971 the Beech House Stud and most of the Sassoon bloodstock were sold to Mr Louis Freedman, and the famous peacock blue and old-gold hooped colours gradually disappeared from the racecourse. Good horses owned by Lady Sassoon included Twilight Alley (Ascot Gold Cup), The Creditor (Jersey Stakes, Lockinge Stakes and Queen Elizabeth II Stakes), Sweet Moss (Dee Stakes, Dante Stakes, Gordon Stakes and Rous Memorial Stakes), Soft Angels (Royal Lodge Stakes) and Sucaryl (News of the World Stakes).

SAUCY SUE
(1922, b f Swynford – Good and Gay, by Bayardo)

Saucy Sue was one of Lord Astor's best fillies. She won eight races for £25,284 from ten starts, including the 1,000 Guineas, Oaks and Coronation Stakes. She bred only one winner, Truculent.

SAYAJIRAO
(1944, br c Nearco – Rosy Legend, by Dark Legend)

Bred by Sir Eric Ohlson, Sayajirao was a brother of the Derby winner Dante. As a yearling he was purchased by the Maharaja of Baroda for the record sum of 28,000gns. Trained by Sam Armstrong, he was backward as a two-year-old but the following season won the Lingfield Derby Trial, Irish Derby, Warren Stakes at Goodwood and St Leger. In addition he was third in both the 2,000 Guineas and the Derby. As a four-year-old he won the Hardwicke Stakes and was just beaten by Petition in the Eclipse Stakes. In all he won £19,342 in stakes from his six wins.

At stud Sayajirao was rather slow to make his mark, and the fact that a good many of his stock needed time and were out-and-out stayers did not increase his popularity with commercial breeders. His best winners were Indiana (Chester Vase, Great Voltigeur Stakes and St Leger), Gladness (Ascot Gold Cup, Goodwood Cup, Ebor Handicap), Lynchris (Irish Oaks, Yorkshire Oaks, Irish St Leger) and I Say (Coronation Cup). He died in 1966.

SCAPA FLOW
(1914, ch f Chaucer – Anchora, by Love Wisely)

Scapa Flow was a famous mare belonging to the Earl of Derby. Her sons and daughters won 63 races worth £85,649. She herself had competed in selling races. Two of her offspring, Fairway (sire of Blue Peter) and Fair Isle, were Classic winners, while Pharos (sire of Nearco and Pharis II) was a champion sire both in Britain and in France.

SCEPTRE
(1899, b f Persimmon – Ornament, by Bend Or)

Sceptre was one of the best and bravest fillies to race in Britain. Foaled in 1899, she was bred by the Duke of West-minster, who died later that year. She came up for sale as a yearling and was bought for 10,000gns, a huge sum in those days, by Mr Robert Sievier, a journalist and adventurer who was a bold and occasionally unscrupulous gambler.

As a two-year-old, trained by Charles Morton, she won the Woodcote Stakes at Epsom and July Stakes at Newmarket but had trained off when she was beaten in the Champagne Stakes at Doncaster.

The following year Sievier himself trained her. Narrowly beaten in the Lincolnshire Handicap, when she was far below her best, she won both the 2,000 Guineas and the 1,000 Guineas. Her preparation for the Derby suffered interruption for a day or two at a critical stage, and as she was a thick-winded filly this may have cost her the race, in which she finished fourth to Ard Patrick. However, she won the Oaks two days later.

Sievier, hard up despite the filly's successes, at once packed her off to Paris for the Grand Prix, in which, indifferently ridden, she was unplaced. On her return she was sent to Royal Ascot, where she was fourth in the Coronation Stakes and won the St James's Palace Stakes. Thus she had five races against top-class opposition in under a month.

She was then afforded a brief rest but returned at Goodwood where she was beaten in the Sussex Stakes and won the Nassau Stakes. She won the St Leger but her greedy owner pulled her out again two days later for the Park Hill Stakes and she was beaten.

Next year a gamble in the Lincolnshire with her failed, and Sievier then sold her for £25,000 to William Bass, who sent her to Alec Taylor to be trained. She was in very poor condition when she arrived at Manton but Taylor gradually built her up and she won the Hardwicke Stakes at Ascot. She was beaten a neck by Ard Patrick in a wonderful race for the Eclipse and then won in succession the Jockey Club Stakes, Duke of York Stakes, Champion Stakes and Limekiln Stakes. As a five-year-old she was past her best but in her three outings was third in the Hardwicke Stakes and Ascot Gold

Cup, and second in the Coronation Cup. Altogether she won thirteen races worth over £38,000. The real tragedy of her career was the death of her breeder, the Duke of Westminster. If she had carried his colours and been trained by John Porter, she would have been treated with far greater consideration and would probably have never been beaten.

Sceptre, who in later life was owned by Mr Somerville Tattersall, Mr John Musker and Lord Glanely, lived till she was 28. At stud her offspring were disappointing in respect of racing ability, but her descendants, in particular through her daughter Maid of the Mist, who was bought by Lord Astor, have played a notable part in Turf history, not only in Britain but in France, America and Australia. Her record of having won four Classics outright is unlikely to be equalled let alone beaten.

SCINTILLATE
(1976, b f Sparkler – Set Free, by Worden II)

Set Free became the third mare this century to breed two Classic winners who were sister and brother when Julio Mariner won the St Leger three years after Juliette Marny, Set Free's first foal, had won the Oaks. Set Free was emulating Scapa Flow (dam of Fairway and Fair Isle) and Ranai (dam of Watling Street and Garden Path), and in 1979 her daughter Scintillate, by the miler Sparkler, added to her record by winning the Oaks. No other mare has produced two winners of the Oaks in the twentieth century; no other mare this century has produced three Classic winners, the previous one being Araucaria, who was born in 1862. Scintillate won one other race, the Sandleford Priory Stakes at Newbury, on her pre-Oaks outing, and showed modest form in two races after Epsom. Her second foal, Alshinfarah, won a Pattern race in Germany at two years.

SCOTT, John (1794-1871)

The outstanding trainer of the mid-Victorian era, John Scott was born at Chippenham, near Newmarket. A trainer from 1815, he moved to the Whitewall stable at Malton in 1825 and was the most successful Yorkshire trainer of all time. Between 1827 and 1863 he won the St Leger sixteen times, a record that is unlikely to be broken. He also trained five Derby winners, eight Oaks winners, seven winners of the 2,000 Guineas and four of the 1,000 Guineas. His Derby winners were Mündig (1835), Attila (1842), Cotherstone (1843), Daniel O'Rourke (1852) and West Australian (1853). For eighteen years his brother William was stable jockey. In many ways a likeable and entertaining man, John Scott was inclined to be just a bit too crafty at times.

SCOTT, William (1797-1848)

Born at Chippenham, near Newmarket, William Scott was one of the greatest riders of his time. He won the Derby four times – on St Giles (1832), Mündig (1835), Attila (1842) and Cotherstone (1843). He rode nine winners of the St Leger, four of them in succession, and he also had three victories in the Oaks. Fourteen of his Classic winners were for his brother John, but their association ended in 1844. Drink was William Scott's weakness, and in the latter part of his career he was frequently unfit to ride. If he had not been blind drunk, he would have won the 1846 Derby on his own horse Sir Tatton Sykes. (Jockeys could own horses in those days.) He rode for the last time in 1847.

SCOTTISH UNION
(1935, b c Cameronian – Trustful, by Bachelor's Double)

Scottish Union was bred by the Sledmere Stud and sold by them as a yearling for 3,000gns to Mr J.V. Rank. Trained by Noel Cannon, he won six races for £21,587, including the Middle Park Stakes, St James's Palace Stakes, St Leger and Coronation Cup. He was second in the 2,000 Guineas and Derby and third in the Ascot Gold Cup. At stud he got plenty of winners but not one that was outstanding, the best being the gallant stayer Strathspey, whose victories

included the Cesarewitch and Goodwood Stakes. Scottish Union also sired the dual Champion Hurdle winner National Spirit.

SCRATCH

'To scratch a horse' means to take it out of a race for which it has been entered. Once taken out at the Racing Calendar Office, a horse cannot be reinstated.

SCRATCH II
(1947, ch c Pharis II – Orlamonde, by Astérus)

Bred by M. Marcel Boussac, Scratch II won the Solario Stakes and St Leger in Britain, and in France the Prix Greffulhe, French Derby and Prix Jean Prat. After four seasons at stud in France, during which he sired the French Oaks winner Dushka, he was exported to Argentina.

SCUTTLE
(1925, b f Captain Cuttle – Stained Glass, by Tracery)

Bred by King George V, Scuttle was the King's only Classic winner, carrying off the 1,000 Guineas among her five victories for £11,800. She was second in the Oaks. She made little mark at stud before her death in 1934.

SEA-BIRD II
(1962, ch c Dan Cupid – Sicalade, by Sicambre)

Sea-Bird II was bred and owned by M. Jean Ternynck and trained by Etienne Pollet at Chantilly. He came from an unprepossessing family, since not one of the first five dams in his pedigree won under Rules on the Flat, but he proved himself one of the best horses of this century, his victories in 1965 including the Derby, Prix Greffulhe, Prix Lupin, Grand Prix de Saint-Cloud and Prix de l'Arc de Triomphe. He won both the Derby and the Arc de Triomphe with contemptuous ease. Altogether he won the equivalent of £225,000 in stakes. His solitary defeat was as a two-year-old when second to his stable-companion Grey Dawn in the Grand Critérium. He did not run as a four-year-old and was leased for five years to stand at stud in America. The lease was renewed for two years, but before he could stand at stud in Europe he died in April 1973. He was not the stud failure that some observers have suggested, having one brilliant offspring, the filly Allez France, and several very good ones, such as Gyr (second in the Derby), Dubassof (American Derby), Sea Pigeon (Ebor, two Chester Cups, two Champion Hurdles), Little Current (Belmont Stakes and Preakness Stakes), Great Heron (second in Irish 2,000 Guineas) and Guillemot (third in Irish Sweeps Derby).

SEAGRAVE, John (b. 1933)

John Seagrave served his apprenticeship with Billy Smallwood and Ernie Davey from 1947 to 1955 and rode his first winner at Lincoln in September 1948, but it was not until almost twenty years later that he regularly rode decent horses for Rufus Beasley, Pat Rohan and Bill Elsey. In 1973, at the age of 39, he landed his first major retainer, with Paul Davey, one of Mr David Robinson's private trainers. He returned to the North of England in 1975, was badly injured in a fall in 1978 but resumed the following year until forced to retire in the spring of 1984 as a result of injuries sustained in a fall the previous October. In the first seventeen years of his career he rode a total of 81 winners, in the last nineteen he rode 849, his best season being 1969, with 76 winners. His biggest successes came with Music Boy (Gimcrack Stakes), Roman Warrior (Ayr Gold Cup) and Princely Son (Vernons Sprint), while he finished second in the St Leger on Meadowville.

SECOND DAM

Refers to the horse's grandmother. Likewise third dam, fourth dam etc are counted back on the female side of the pedigree.

SECRETO
(1981, b c Northern Dancer – Betty's Secret, by Secretariat)

Secreto became Northern Dancer's third winner of the Derby, after Nijinsky and The Minstrel, and like them he returned to the United States after his three-year-old career. Secreto cost $340,000 as a yearling, went into training in Ireland with David O'Brien and won a small race on his only outing as a two-year-old. At three he had three runs, winning at The Curragh on his reappearance, finishing third to Sadler's Wells in the Irish 2,000 Guineas and getting up close home in a driving finish to beat El Gran Señor by a short head at Epsom. All manner of big summer objectives came and went without Secreto and he never ran again, being retired to stud in Kentucky with a reputed valuation of $30m.

SEFTON, 7th Earl of (1898-1972)

Lord Sefton served in the Royal Horse Guards from 1917 to 1930 and from 1939 to 1945. Interested in most forms of sport, he was a prominent figure in the coursing world and until World War II was rated one of the best heavyweights across Leicestershire. He played a leading part in public life in Lancashire, his home county, and was lord mayor of Liverpool in 1944-5. He was for many years one of the most active members of the Jockey Club and held office as Senior Steward. He was in no small degree responsible for the gradual modernization of racing at Newmarket, and the now-disused Sefton course was named after him. However, his sale of Liverpool racecourse to the Topham family was not one of his most popular decisions, and the much-later turbulent history of the course reflected badly on him.

His best horses were Bob Cherry (Cork and Orrery Stakes), Titian (Kempton 2,000 Guineas Trial), Kipling (Gordon Stakes), Gaul (King Edward VII Stakes and Jockey Club Stakes) and St Lucia (Coronation Stakes).

SELENE
(1919, b f Chaucer – Serenissima, by Minoru)

Selene was bred by Lord Derby. She was a tough, game filly, winning 15½ races, worth £14,386, including the Park Hill Stakes and Liverpool Autumn Cup. As a broodmare she was outstanding, among her offspring being Hyperion (Derby, St Leger and six times champion sire), Sickle (a leading two-year-old, placed in the 2,000 Guineas and a highly influential sire in America), Pharamond (Middle Park Stakes and a leading sire in America), Hunter's Moon (Newmarket Stakes and a leading sire in Argentina) and All Moonshine (dam of the very successful sire Mossborough). Selene bred ten winners of 30 races worth £47,345 and made her most recent appearance in the female line of a top-class winner as the fourth dam of Mountain Lodge (Irish St Leger in 1983).

SELLING RACE

In a selling race the conditions demand that every horse running, if a loser, may be claimed, and if the winner, must be offered for sale by auction. The lowest price at which the winner can be sold is laid down in the Rules of Racing and varies according to the value of the race. For a long time, if at the auction the winner was sold for more than the stipulated selling price, the surplus went to the owner of the second horse, but this occasionally stirred claims of bidding-up, and the rule was changed to allow the surplus to go to the race-fund. Now, the winning owner receives 10% of any surplus up to £2,000, 25% between £2,000 and £3,000 and 50% above £3,000, with the rest going to the race-fund. A loser in a selling race can be claimed for the stipulated claiming price. The claim has to be made in writing to the Clerk of the Scales within ten minutes of the all-right signal. The horse goes to the person submitting the highest claim; if there are equal claims, the successful one will be determined by lot. No horse can be claimed by its owner, and a horse which is claimed must go to a trainer other than the one who prepared it for the race. Any surplus above the claiming price is divided between the racecourse and the Jockey Club.

SEMBLAT, Charles Henri (1897-1972)

A leading jockey in France, Charles Semblat won the 2,000 Guineas in 1937 on Le Ksar. He was for a time trainer to the French industrialist M. Marcel Boussac. In 1950, the year M. Boussac's Galcador won the Derby, Asmena the Oaks and Scratch II the St Leger, Semblat headed the trainers' list in Britain with eleven winners of £57,044 but not once did he set foot in Britain. He won the St Leger again in 1951, with Talma II, and when his partnership with M. Boussac ended three years later, he had won the French Derby five times and the Prix de l'Arc de Triomphe four times for his patron.

SERENISSIMA (1913, b f Minoru – Gondolette, by Loved One)

Serenissima was one of Lord Derby's most famous mares. A half-sister to the Derby winner Sansovino, she bred eight winners of 40 races worth over £47,000, including Selene (£14,000 and dam of Hyperion), Tranquil (1,000 Guineas, St Leger and Jockey Club Cup) and Bosworth (Ascot Gold Cup).

SEXTON, Graham (b. 1948)

Graham Sexton was a most successful apprentice with Harry Wragg from 1963 to 1968 and had his best season in 1967, with 29 winners. Among good races he has won are the Royal Hunt Cup (Regal Light), Newbury Autumn Cup (Salvo), St Simon Stakes (Little Wolf and Richmond Stakes (Godstone). He can claim to have ridden a winner on every course in Britain since his first at Wolverhampton in April 1966.

SHADEED (1982, b c Nijinsky – Continual, by Damascus)

Shadeed, who cost $800,000 as a yearling, was made winter favourite for the Derby after winning the second of two races as a two-year-old. On the way to Epsom he won the Craven Stakes impressively and the 2,000 Guineas in a close struggle with Bairn (when Lester Piggott stood in for the suspended Walter Swinburn). In the Derby he was most disappointing but he was found to be off colour. He returned in the autumn and beat a strong field, including Teleprompter and Bairn, in the Queen Elizabeth II Stakes. He was retired to Kentucky to stand his first season at stud in 1986.

SHANGAMUZO
(1973, ch c Klairon – French Fern, by Mossborough)

Shangamuzo, who cost 3,000gns as a yearling, was trained by Gavin Hunter to win five races as a three-year-old, including the King George V Handicap at Royal Ascot, and the Doncaster Cup from eleven races at four years. As a five-year-old he moved to Michael Stoute's stable and won the Ascot Gold Cup, in a year when the race was not so strongly contested as some in the series. After Ascot he was placed in the Goodwood Cup, Doncaster Cup and Jockey Club Cup, but he was below his best as a six-year-old and, after finishing a remote fourth in the Ascot Gold Cup, was exported to Brazil.

SHANTUNG
(1956, b c Sicambre – Barley Corn, by Hyperion)

Bred by Baron Guy de Rothschild, Shantung won three races in France. He started favourite for the Derby and was desperately unlucky. Coming down the hill he collided with another runner, and his rider, thinking the colt had broken a leg, pulled him back to last, preparatory to pulling him up. But Shantung was not injured and ran on to such purpose in the straight that he finished third, only two lengths behind Parthia, the winner.

Shantung was at stud for one season in France before moving to Newmarket, where he stayed until his death in July 1983, after being retired for a few years.

La Bamba, third in the Oaks and Prix de l'Arc de Triomphe, came from his French crop, while in Britain he sired several top-class fillies, including Ginevra (Oaks), Full Dress II (1,000 Guineas), Lacquer (Irish 1,000 Guineas) and Saraca (Prix Vermeille). Felicio (Grand Prix de Saint-Cloud) and Canadel (Prix

de la Salamandre) were among his best sons.

SHEATHER, Ronald (b. 1932)

One of several talented apprentices raised by Ernie Davey, Ron Sheather rode in the United States before rejoining Davey for a year in 1970. He then rode work for Toby Balding for six years and then for Barry Hills before taking out a trainer's licence in February 1978 at Newmarket. His first win was with Sombreuil at Ayr on 21 July 1978. Though he came late to training, it was not long before he got a big-race winner, Saher in the 1981 Lincoln, but his big break-through came with the arrival of the two-year-old Chief Singer in 1983. That year he won the Coventry Stakes and the following season the St James's Palace Stakes, July Cup and Sussex Stakes, earning the bulk of his trainer's £212,174 winnings and contributing to his best season of sixteen winners. In 1985 he won the Northumberland Plate with Trade Line.

SHEDDEN, Lewis Horace (1902-77)

'Tommy' Shedden was assistant trainer to his father for five years and then from 1925 to 1935 head lad to Bobby Renton. He took out a licence to train in 1935 and remained at his stable at Wetherby until ill-health forced him to retire in 1977. He died within a few weeks of the season's end. His biggest triumphs were in the 1951 Yorkshire Cup with Orderly Ann and the 1969 Cesarewitch with Floridian. His stables were taken over by one of his patrons, Peter Asquith, who trained until 1983.

SHERGAR
(1978, b c Great Nephew – Sharmeen, by Val de Loir)

Shergar's life was short but sensational. He won the Derby by ten lengths, the biggest margin ever recorded; he was syndicated to stand at stud in Ireland at a valuation of £10m, the highest ever asked for a Derby winner; and before he could start his second season he was kidnapped and never seen again. The IRA were blamed for his disappearance, but no ransom was paid, and his body has not been found.

Bred by the Aga Khan, Shergar was trained by Michael Stoute. He had two races as a two-year-old, winning a small event at Newbury and finishing second in the William Hill Futurity. He won his first five races as a three-year-old – the Sandown Classic Trial, Chester Vase, Derby, Irish Sweeps Derby (in which Lester Piggott deputized for the suspended Walter Swinburn) and King George VI and Queen Elizabeth Diamond Stakes (where he beat Madam Gay and Fingal's Cave). The only Derby winner to run in the St Leger since Nijinsky in 1970, Shergar started odds-on but was beaten more than 2f out and finished fourth to Cut Above. Shergar did not run again, though it had been expected that he would tackle the Prix de l'Arc de Triomphe.

He died with one crop to represent him, including Authaal, who went through the ring for 325,000 Irish guineas as a foal and made a European yearling record of 3.1m Irish guineas when bought on behalf of Sheikh Mohammed.

SHESHOON
(1956, ch c Precipitation – Noorani, by Nearco)

Bred by the Aga Khan and Prince Aly Khan, and raced by the latter at the time of his death in 1960, Sheshoon was a half-brother to Charlottesville. His $7\frac{1}{2}$ successes included the Ascot Gold Cup, Grand Prix de Saint-Cloud and Grosser Preis von Baden. He was just beaten in the Prix du Cadran. He was syndicated and spent the whole of his stud career at the Limestone Stud in Lincolnshire, where he was put down on humane grounds in October 1979. Despite standing in Britain, almost all his chief money-earners were abroad, the most important being three French St Leger winners – Sassafras (also French Derby and Prix de l'Arc de Triomphe), Pleben and Samos III – Stintino (Prix Lupin and third in the Derby) and two winners of the Critérium des Pouliches, Véla and

Oak Hill. His best son in Britain was Mon Fils (2,000 Guineas).

SHIRLEY HEIGHTS
(1975, b c Mill Reef – Hardiemma, by Hardicanute)

Bred and owned by Lord Halifax, Shirley Heights won two Derbys and bred two Derby winners from his first three crops of racing age. He has been a welcome tonic to British breeding since he went to stud in Norfolk in 1979 as no more than an average Epsom Derby winner. He won two of his six races as a two-year-old, including the Royal Lodge Stakes, and won his last four the following year, before injury to a tendon while being prepared for the St Leger brought about his retirement. He won the Heathorn Stakes narrowly from Ile de Bourbon, the Mecca-Dante Stakes by a length and a half from Julio Mariner, the Derby with a late challenge to beat Hawaiian Sound, and the Irish Sweeps Derby in a blanket finish with Exdirectory and Hawaiian Sound.

Shirley Heights' first crop, born in 1980, included the good winners Acclimatise (Nassau Stakes and second in Oaks) and High Hawk (Ribblesdale Stakes, Park Hill Stakes); his second included Darshaan (French Derby) and Head for Heights (Princess of Wales's Stakes, King Edward VII Stakes); and his third brought his sire line's success in the Epsom Derby to the third generation by the victory of Slip Anchor.

Hardiemma, Shirley Heights' dam, won two small races in the North of England before being sold as a three-year-old for 9,000gns. A year later she was bought for 12,000gns by Lord Halifax, with the intent of sending her to Mill Reef. Shirley Heights was the outcome, but when he was a yearling Hardiemma (in foal again to Mill Reef) was sold for 15,000gns. The new owner sold Hardiemma's Mill Reef foal for 250,000gns following her upgrading to the status of a Derby-winning producer!

SHORT STORY
(1923, b f Buchan – Long Suit, by Lemberg)

Bred by Lord Astor, Short Story won two races for £9,400, including the Oaks. She was also third in the 1,000 Guineas and Park Hill Stakes. Of her progeny, Birthday Book won over £6,000 in stakes.

SHOTOVER
(1879, ch f Hermit – Stray Shot, by Toxophilite)

The Duke of Westminster's Shotover is one of the six fillies who have won the Derby, a feat she accomplished in the year that fillies won all five Classics. She also won the 2,000 Guineas but was beaten a neck at odds-on by St Marguerite in the 1,000 Guineas two days later, and was third in the St Leger.

SHOW

A list of betting odds is often described as a 'show'. The opening list is known as the first show, at which price some punters stipulate their bets will be made, thereby hoping to gain greater odds about a horse they expect to shorten in price.

SICARELLE
(1953, b f Sicambre – Royale Maîtresse, by Vatellor)

Bred in France by Mme Suzy Volterra and trained by François Mathet, Sicarelle won three races, including the Oaks. She made little impression in her remaining races.

SICKLE
(1924, br c Phalaris – Selene, by Chaucer)

Bred by Lord Derby, Sickle was a half-brother to Hyperion. A good two-year-old and third in the 2,000 Guineas, he was exported to America and became a leading sire, later to appear in the pedigrees of Native Dancer and Sea-Bird II.

SIEVIER, Robert Standish
(1860-1939)

Bob Sievier was born in a cab and led a stormy life. A big gambler who landed many successful coups but was almost always short of money, he bought the famous filly Sceptre for 10,000gns at the dispersal of the Duke of Westminster's bloodstock. This was a record price for a yearling at the time. Trained as a three-year-old by Sievier, Sceptre won every Classic bar the Derby, in which she was fourth, in 1902. Her owner, though, was broke at the end of the season and had to sell her.

Sievier ran his horses honestly enough, and his warning-off in 1904 was the work of his enemies, of whom he had many, for in other aspects of his life he seldom appeared hampered in his conduct by the possession of moral scruples. He was allowed to resume as an owner in 1907, but a later licence to train was withdrawn because of his activity as a publisher. His paper *The Winning Post* reflected his scurrilous nature, and he was frequently involved in litigation.

SIGNORINETTA
(1905, b or br f Chaleureux – Signorina, by St Simon)

Bred, owned and trained at Newmarket by Cavaliere Odoardo Ginistrelli, an Italian, Signorinetta brought off one of the surprises of the century when she won the Derby at 100-1. Two days later she won the Oaks. She never won another race and when bought by Lord Rosebery made little lasting mark in Britain as a broodmare, though her son The Winter King bred Barneveldt (Grand Prix de Paris), who in turn sired the Derby winner Pont l'Evêque. In both her Epsom triumphs she was ridden by W. Bullock.

SILLY SEASON
(1962, br c Tom Fool – Double Deal, by Straight Deal)

Bred in America by his owner, Mr Paul Mellon, Silly Season was trained by Ian Balding and won over £61,000 in prize money, his seven successes including the Coventry Stakes, Dewhurst Stakes, St

James's Palace Stakes, Champion Stakes and Lockinge Stakes. In the 2,000 Guineas he was beaten by a length by Niksar. He was also very narrowly beaten in the Sussex Stakes, Rous Memorial Stakes and Queen Elizabeth II Stakes. Three of his best winners at stud – Fair Season (Horris Hill Stakes), Martinmas (Greenham Stakes) and Rowantree (Fred Darling Stakes) – were trained by Ian Balding, though his best produce was Lunchtime (Dewhurst Stakes). He died in February 1981, having been a prolific sire of winners though few were of outstanding quality.

SILVER RING

This is the enclosure below Tattersalls' on a racecourse. It was originally so called because the price of admission was less than a pound, but as inflation has risen and patrons have moved up into the more expensive enclosures, several courses have done away with this facility.

SILVER URN
(1919, ch f Juggernaut – Queen Silver, by Queen's Birthday)

Bred and owned by Mr B.W. Parr and trained by 'Atty' Persse, Silver Urn won three races for £10,004, including the 1,000 Guineas. She bred five winners but they were not of great account.

SIME, Joseph Francis (b. 1923)

Joe Sime, for many years after World War II the most successful northern jockey, served his apprenticeship with Dawson Waugh and rode his first winner in 1941 at Newmarket, on his first ride in public. He was never troubled by his weight and up to his retirement in 1969 could go to scale at 7st 8lb. His best season was in 1960 when he rode 108 winners. He was leading apprentice in 1943, 1944 and 1946. Few jockeys boasted a better record in big handicaps and he won the Lincolnshire Handicap three times, Wokingham Stakes three times, Ebor Handicap four times, Cesarewitch three times, Vaux Gold

Tankard twice and Manchester November Handicap twice, as well as the Northumberland Plate, Ayr Gold Cup, William Hill Gold Cup, Portland Handicap and Royal Hunt Cup. Many of these were for Sam Hall, the Middleham trainer.

SIMPSON, Rodney (b. 1945)

South Londoner Rod Simpson was apprenticed to Cyril Mitchell, John Tilling and Frank Muggeridge before he joined Alec Kerr, to whom he became head lad. His first chance to look after horses on his own came as private trainer to the Zandona family in Berkshire, and he had his first win with Lady Tartown at Warwick on 9 June 1979. Early in 1981 Simpson moved into South Hatch stables at Epsom, from where he had his biggest win with Bajan Sunshine in the 1983 Cesarewitch. The horse had been sold to leave the yard straight after the race, and late that year Simpson had to move out of the stables, which had been sold. He moved to Upper Lambourn early in 1984 and in his first season trained Fortune's Guest to win the Queen's Prize and fourteen other winners for his best total.

SINCLAIR, Auriol (b. 1918)

Miss Sinclair conducted most efficiently a 'mixed' stable at Lewes from 1950, though she has actually held a licence only since 1966 when women were first permitted to train. Before that she controlled the stable though the licence was held by her head man. The stable won the Wokingham Stakes in 1958 with Magic Boy, and the Rosebery Stakes in 1963 with Wilhelmina Henrietta. In 1981 Miss Sinclair moved her stable to Tenterden in Kent.

SINGAPORE
(1927, b c Gainsborough – Tetrabbazia, by The Tetrarch)

Bred by Sir Alec Black and bought by Lord Glanely for 12,500gns as a yearling, Singapore won three races for £13,000, including the St Leger, and was narrowly beaten in the Ascot Gold Cup. Before being exported to Brazil, he sired the St Leger winner Chulmleigh and Indian Call, the dam of Ballymoss.

SIRETT, Jack (b. 1905)

Jack Sirett served his apprenticeship with Stanley Wootton. He was a highly successful lightweight jockey and between 1924 and 1953 rode more than 800 winners, being in demand for the major handicaps, of which he won the Wokingham Stakes three times, Free Handicap three times, Victoria Cup twice, City and Suburban and Cesarewitch. He took out a licence to train in 1954 and remained at Epsom until his retirement at the end of 1973. The best horse he trained was the sprinter St Alphage.

SIR GALLAHAD III
(1920, b c Teddy – Plucky
Liège, by Spearmint)

Bred in France by Captain J.D. Cohn, Sir Gallahad III won ten races in France, including their 2,000 Guineas, while in Britain he won the Lincolnshire Handicap. Exported to America after one season at stud in France, he became an outstandingly successful stallion, being leading sire four times.

SIR IVOR
(1965, b c Sir Gaylord – Attica,
by Mr Trouble)

Sir Ivor was bred in America by Mrs Alice Headley Bell and sold as a yearling for $42,000 to Mr Raymond Guest. An exceptionally handsome colt trained in Ireland by Vincent O'Brien, he was a top-class two-year-old, winning the National Stakes at The Curragh and Grand Critérium at Longchamp. In 1968 he had nine races and won the Ascot 2,000 Guineas Trial, 2,000 Guineas, Derby, Champion Stakes and Washington D.C. International Stakes at Laurel Park. He was second in the Irish Derby, Prix Henry Delamarre and Prix de l'Arc de Triomphe and third in the Eclipse Stakes. A courageous horse with great power of acceleration, he achieved the rare feat of winning in Ireland,

France, Britain and America. His owner left him in Ireland to stand at stud for two seasons before he moved to Kentucky in 1971. His two crops in Ireland produced two Derby seconds, Cavo Doro and Imperial Prince, but his crops in America have brought better fillies than colts among his top-class racers. They include Ivanjica (French 1,000 Guineas, Prix Vermeille and Prix de l'Arc de Triomphe), Val's Girl (second in Oaks), Lady Capulet (Irish 1,000 Guineas), Godetia, (Irish 1,000 Guineas and Irish Oaks) and Northern Princess (Ribblesdale Stakes). His best colts have been Malinowski (Craven Stakes), Bates Motel (nine wins and $752,120) and St Hilarion (Gran Premio d'Italia and Gran Premio del Jockey Club), a fairly disappointing list for such a smart racer.

SIR PETER TEAZLE
(1784, br c Highflyer –
Papillon, by Snap)

Sir Peter Teazle won the 1787 Derby for the twelfth Earl of Derby, who named him in compliment to his second wife as she had made a great reputation on the stage in the part of Lady Teazle, in *The School for Scandal*. Sir Peter Teazle had never run before the Derby. He proved a highly successful sire, getting four Derby winners (Sir Harry, Archduke, Ditto and Paris), four St Leger winners (Ambrosio, Fyldener, Paulina and Petronius) and two winners of the Oaks (Hermione and Parisot).

SKULL CAP

No jockey is permitted to ride in a race unless he is wearing a skull cap of the pattern approved by the stewards of the Jockey Club. They were introduced for the first time for Flat racing in September 1956, and their design has been carefully improved to conform with specifications of the British Standards Institute.

SLEEPING PARTNER
(1966, gr f Parthia – Old
Dutch, by Fastnet Rock)

Sleeping Partner was bred by her owner, Lord Rosebery, and gave him his only success in the Oaks, for which she was trained by Doug Smith following the death of Sir Jack Jarvis. She won three other races, including the Lingfield Oaks Trial and Ribblesdale Stakes, and was placed six times for total earnings of £39,245. She failed in her one race in 1970 and was retired to stud where she died without produce.

SLIEVE GALLION
(1904, bl c Gallinule –
Reclusion, by St Florian)

Bred and owned by Captain (later Sir) Henry Greer, Director of the National Stud, Slieve Gallion won the 2,000 Guineas and was third to Orby when odds-on for the Derby. He ran only once after Epsom, winning the St James's Palace Stakes. He was then exported to Austria for £15,000.

SLIP ANCHOR
(1982, b c Shirley Heights –
Sayonara, by Birkhahn)

Slip Anchor gave Lord Howard de Walden, one of Britain's few remaining large-scale owner-breeders, his first Classic success by winning the Derby. He was also a first Derby winner for sire Shirley Heights, trainer Henry Cecil and jockey Steve Cauthen (who became the first rider to win both the Kentucky Derby and the Epsom Derby, following his success on Affirmed in his native United States). Slip Anchor, whose dam was purchased in Germany, won the second of his two outings in small races at two years and improved greatly in his second season when allowed to force the pace over a distance of ground. He won the Heathorn Stakes and Lingfield Derby Trial before spreadeagling his field at Epsom, where he beat Law Society unchallenged by seven lengths. A setback in training prevented his being prepared for the St Leger, but he reappeared in September at Kempton Park, when beaten narrowly by the four-year-old Shernazar, and then finished second to Pebbles in the Champion Stakes. It was intended to keep him in training in 1986.

SLOAN, James Furman
(1874-1933)

'Tod' Sloan was a brilliant American jockey who came to Britain at the turn of the century and was largely instrumental in revolutionizing race-riding over here. His style – short leathers and a pronounced, streamlined crouch – was ridiculed to start with, and critics referred to him as a 'monkey up a stick', but before long he proved that his methods were far more effective than the traditional British ones embodying long leathers and an upright seat.

Sloan had a wonderful understanding with horses and was a superb judge of pace. Unfortunately he mixed habitually with some of the least desirable characters in the racing world. It was no surprise when in 1900 the authorities told him it would be pointless to apply for a licence the following season. In the short time that he rode in Britain he was on 254 winners, but only one in a Classic, Sibola, in the 1899 1,000 Guineas. He remained in Britain until 1915, when he was deported to America for a gaming offence, and he died in poverty.

SMIRKE, Charles James
William (b. 1906)

Charlie Smirke was apprenticed to Stanley Wootton. At his best – and he was always at his best on big occasions – he was the equal of any jockey riding. His long career in the saddle had its ups and downs, and from 1928 till 1933 he was banned by the Jockey Club after an incident at the start of a race at Gatwick. As an apprentice he was retained by the Aga Khan, and the association lasted, on and off, for 30 years. He rode in his first Derby in 1924 and his last 35 years later, winning on Windsor Lad (1934), Mahmoud (1936), Tulyar (1952) and Hard Ridden (1958). He also won the 1,000 Guineas on Rose Royale II (1957), 2,000 Guineas on My Babu (1948) and Palestine (1950) and St Leger on Windsor Lad (1934), Bahram (1935) and Tulyar (1952). He rode for the last time in 1959.

In temperament he was almost aggressively self-confident and never displayed the slightest sign of nerves. Possibly he was a bit too brash and cocky to win the affection of the racing community as a whole, but many admired his superb skill, his cheerfulness in bad times and an impudent sense of humour that could never be entirely subdued.

SMITH, Denys (b. 1924)

Denys Smith began training in 1961, when most of the horses in his Bishop Auckland, Co Durham, stable were jumpers. He took out his first Flat licence in 1964 and won with his third runner, Miss Autumn, at Liverpool. His biggest success over jumps was with Red Alligator in the 1968 Grand National. The following year he won the Lincoln and William Hill Gold Cup with Foggy Bell, and in 1972 the Middle Park Stakes with Tudenham. His most important success since was with Mandrake Major in the 1976 Flying Childers Stakes. His best season was 1979 with 53 winners.

SMITH, Douglas (b. 1917)

Doug Smith, younger brother of Eph Smith, had a long, honourable and successful career in the saddle before he retired in 1967 to take up training at Newmarket, from which he retired in 1979, blaming the economic situation.

As a small boy he was apprenticed to Major F.B. Sneyd and rode his first winner in 1931. Like his brother, he was never beset by problems of weight, and season after season he rode with consistent success. In particular he excelled at Newmarket, and there has probably never been a better rider over the Rowley Mile. On five occasions – 1954, 1955, 1956, 1958 and 1959 – he was champion jockey. He rode 3,112 winners from 20,079 mounts, his best season being 1947 when his winners totalled 173. He survived some serious accidents towards the close of his career, but his nerve and his dash remained unaffected.

He never won an Epsom Classic as a jockey but won the 2,000 Guineas on Our Babu and Pall Mall, and 1,000 Guineas on Hypericum and Petite Etoile. A wonderfully sound judge of pace, he was usually at his best in long-distance

races and won the Ascot Gold Cup (twice), Ascot Stakes (twice), Doncaster Cup (six times), Goodwood Cup (three times), Cesarewitch (six times), Jockey Club Stakes (six times) and Northumberland Plate (three times). Probably the best horse he rode was that great stayer Alycidon, winner of the Ascot, Goodwood and Doncaster Cups.

Quiet, modest and level-headed, Doug Smith was noted for his loyalty to his patrons, and his association with Lord Derby was one of the longest in modern racing history.

In 1969 he trained his only Classic winner when he won the Oaks with Lord Rosebery's Sleeping Partner, having taken over that owner's horses on the death of Sir Jack Jarvis. The arrangement was terminated in 1971. His other important winners were Owen Anthony (City and Suburban), who gave him a winner with his first runner, Golden Mean (Royal Hunt Cup), Miss Paris (Fred Darling Stakes), Honeyblest (Diadem Stakes) and Derrylin (Horris Hill Stakes in a dead-heat).

SMITH, Eric Ephraim (1915-72)

Eph Smith was the son of a sporting Berkshire farmer. He showed riding ability at a precociously early age and was apprenticed to Major F.B. Sneyd. He made the most of his early chances and, untroubled by problems of weight, enjoyed a successful career in the saddle for more than 30 years, when ill-health forced him to retire in 1965 after riding 2,313 winners.

He won the 2,000 Guineas and Derby on Blue Peter and the St Leger on Premonition. He won the Ascot Gold Cup (twice), Eclipse Stakes, King George VI and Queen Elizabeth Stakes, Cesarewitch (three times), Cambridgeshire, Ascot Stakes (five times), Goodwood Stakes (four times, including three on Mr H.J. Joel's popular stayer Predominate), Lincolnshire Handicap (three times) and Manchester November Handicap (twice). His best season was in 1947, when he rode 144 winners. Quiet and unflamboyant, he never permitted success to go to his head or the fact that he was always hard of hearing to affect his career. His body was found in a river near Newmarket in August 1972, and a verdict of death by misadventure was returned.

SMITH, Stanley (b. 1913)

Stan Smith served his apprenticeship with George Batchelor in France, his first winner being at Le Tremblay in 1927. He began to ride in Britain in 1949 and also had a lot of experience in India, where he won the Derby in two successive years. His best season in Britain was in 1963, when he was retained by Lord Rosebery and won 41 races, including the Blue Riband Trial Stakes and Stewards' Cup. The following year he won the City and Suburban. He retired in 1969 but remained a work-rider at Newmarket.

SMYLY, Captain Richard Mark (b. 1943)

Mark Smyly rode as an amateur and spent two years with Tim Forster and four as assistant to Peter Walwyn before starting to train on his own account at Lambourn in 1975. Two years later he had his biggest success to date, with Blustery in the Lincoln. His best season numerically was 1982, with sixteen winners.

SMYTH, Gordon Richard (b. 1926)

For fifteen years Gordon Smyth assisted his father, William, and succeeded him in 1961 as trainer at the Duke of Norfolk's Arundel stable. At the end of 1965 he took over Jack Gosden's stable at Lewes and the following year won the Derby with Charlottown. Other big races he won included the Coronation Cup, Gimcrack Stakes, Stewards' Cup, Rosebery Stakes, Richmond Stakes (twice) and Oxfordshire Stakes. In July 1977 he left Britain to train in Hong Kong.

SMYTH, Herbert Edwin (b. 1911)

For twelve years Ted Smyth assisted his father, Herbert Smyth, who was Willie

Smyth's elder brother and one of racing's most notable characters and a peerless raconteur. Ted Smyth served in the RAF during World War II and began training at Epsom in 1951. Good races he won before his retirement at the end of 1976 included the Wokingham Stakes, Lowther Stakes, Newbury Spring Cup, Brighton Cup and Acorn Stakes. His apprentice Alan Bond was champion in 1974 and 1975.

SMYTH, Paul (b. 1936)

Paul Smyth assisted his father, Victor, before taking over the stable at Epsom in 1965. He gave up training in 1974 to become an off-course bookmaker.

SMYTH, Ronald Victor (b. 1915)

Ron Smyth, son of Herbert Smyth and brother of Ted, was for many years a successful rider under National Hunt Rules and was champion jockey in 1941-2. He rode the winner of the Champion Hurdle on three occasions. Since 1947 he has been running a 'mixed' stable at Epsom, and among the good races he has won are the Stewards' Cup, King Edward VII Stakes, Free Handicap, Jubilee Handicap, Cesarewitch and Great Metropolitan. His most recent big-race successes have been with the top-class handicapper Tremblant, who in 1985 won the Victoria Cup, Bunbury Cup and Cambridgeshire (carrying 9st 8lb). He has a good record with apprentices, the most notable being Geoff Lewis.

SMYTH, Victor Henry James (1901-84)

Vic Smyth, younger brother of Herbert, was a successful and respected jockey who won the Oaks on Brownhylda in 1923, the year he won the Ascot Gold Cup on Happy Man. He began training at Epsom in 1926 and won the 1952 1,000 Guineas with Zabara. His son Paul took over his stable in 1965.

SNAITH, William (b. 1928)

Willie Snaith was apprenticed to Sam Armstrong from 1943 to 1950 and was leading apprentice in 1949. During the early 1950s he was one of the most successful jockeys, though he never won a Classic, and he reached his peak with 73 winners in 1954. Retained in turn by Armstrong and Major L.B. Holliday, he also rode for Captain Cecil Boyd-Rochfort. His important successes included the Stewards' Cup (twice), Royal Hunt Cup, July Cup, Sussex Stakes, Gimcrack Stakes, Nunthorpe Stakes (twice), Champagne Stakes and Dewhurst Stakes. His success dwindled from 1966 but he continued to ride until early 1975 and remained a work-rider at Newmarket.

SNOW KNIGHT
(1971, ch c Firestreak – Snow Blossom, by Flush Royal)

Snow Knight, who changed hands for 5,200gns as a yearling, lost more races than he won in Britain, where he was trained by Peter Nelson, but greatly enhanced his reputation when he became the first Derby winner to continue his racing career in North America. He won twice as a two-year-old and was narrowly beaten in the Champagne Stakes. Placed behind Bustino in Classic trials at Sandown and Lingfield, he revelled on the firm ground in the Derby, led 5f out and beat Imperial Prince by two lengths. Snow Knight was beaten in his next five races as a three-year-old, the last three being in Canada, where he was sent after Edward Taylor headed a syndicate which bought him for more than £520,000.

As a four-year-old Snow Knight won six of his nine races and was nominated champion grass horse in the United States, where he won the Man o' War Stakes; he also won the Canadian International Championship. Since retiring to stud in Canada alongside Northern Dancer at Windfields Farm in Ontario, Snow Knight's best offspring have raced in Europe – Awaasif (Yorkshire Oaks, third in the Arc de Triomphe) and Ivano (Earl of Sefton Stakes) – though he is also responsible for Northern Blossom, the champion three-year-old filly in Canada in 1983.

SOBELL, Sir Michael (b. 1892)

Sir Michael Sobell is well known in the business and financial world. His first interest in racing was with jumpers but from the late 1950s, mainly through the influence of Sir Gordon Richards, his first trainer, he veered towards the Flat. His first horse on the Flat was London Cry whom he bought at the December Sales for 3,500gns and whose subsequent successes included the Chesterfield Cup and Cambridgeshire. In 1960 Sobell bought the Ballymacoll Stud, Co Meath, from the executors of the late Miss Dorothy Paget, and there he has bred countless good-class winners owned outright or in partnership with his son-in-law Lord Weinstock. The best are: Admetus (twelve wins, including Washington D.C. International), Cistus (second in French Oaks), Dart Board (third in Derby), Lancastrian (Prix Ganay), Open Day (King Edward VII Stakes), Prince Bee (second in Irish Sweeps Derby), Reform (eleven wins including Champion Stakes), Sallust (Sussex Stakes), Sun Prince (St James's Palace Stakes), Sun Princess (Oaks and St Leger), Troy (Derby, Irish Sweeps Derby, King George VI and Queen Elizabeth Stakes) and Homeric (Lingfield Derby Trial).

One of the few remaining owner-breeders on a large scale, Sir Michael has had his horses trained mainly by Dick Hern since Sir Gordon Richards' retirement, and as owner of the West Ilsley stable was able to bring about the removal of long-time stable jockey Joe Mercer for 1977 in favour of Willie Carson. He sold the stable to the Queen in December 1982 and has since had horses trained by Ian Balding, as well as in France. He was leading owner in 1979.

Racing colours: pale blue, yellow and white checked cap.

SOCIETE d'ENCOURAGEMENT POUR L'AMELIORATION DES RACES DE CHEVAUX EN FRANCE

This is the governing body of French racing and corresponds to a combination of the Jockey Club and Weatherbys. The

Romanet family, father Jean and son Louis, have been its most recent guiding lights.

Address: 11 rue du Cirque, Paris 75382, Cedex 08.

SODIUM
(1963, b c Psidium – Gambade, by Big Game)

Sodium was bred by the Kilcarn Stud and as a yearling was bought for 3,500gns by George Todd on behalf of Mr R.J. Sigtia. He did not win a race during his first season but showed promise. As a three-year-old he was not consistent but a good horse on his day, winning the Brighton Derby Trial, Irish Sweeps Derby and St Leger. He was second in the King George VI and Queen Elizabeth Stakes and fourth in the Derby. He was disappointing as a four-year-old and was sold to stand at stud in France, where he made little mark.

SOLARIO
(1922, br c Gainsborough – Sun Worship, by Sundridge)

Solario was bred by Lord Dunraven, sold as a yearling for 3,500gns to Sir John Rutherford and trained by Reg Day. He might have won the Derby but for losing lengths at the start when he got caught in a loose tape. He won the St Leger and the following year the Coronation Cup and Ascot Gold Cup so that his six wins were worth £20,935. His owner died in 1932 and he was sent up for sale at Newmarket in December, fetching 47,000gns, a very big price in those days. He got two Derby winners – Mid-day Sun (1937) and Straight Deal (1943) – as well as Dastur (second in the 2,000 Guineas, Derby and St Leger) and Exhibitionnist (1,000 Guineas and Oaks). He was champion sire in 1937 and died in 1945.

SOLAR SLIPPER
(1945, b c Windsor Slipper – Solar Flower, by Solario)

Bred and owned by Mr Joseph McGrath, Solar Slipper was out of Solar Flower, winner of over £10,000 in stakes. Solar Slipper himself won five races for £5,822, including the Champion Stakes, and was third in the St Leger. Before being exported to America in 1956 he sired Panaslipper (Irish Derby and second in Epsom Derby) and Pandofell (Ascot Gold Cup).

SON-IN-LAW
(1911, br c Dark Ronald – Mother-in-Law, by Matchmaker)

A handsome horse bred and owned by Sir Abe Bailey, Son-in-Law had his racing career hampered by World War I but he proved himself a fine stayer, winning the Goodwood Cup, Cesarewitch and Jockey Club Cup (twice) among eight wins for £5,546. As a sire of stayers he was outstanding and sired the Ascot Gold Cup winners Foxlaw, Bosworth and Trimdon, the last-named winning that race twice. Foxlaw carried on the tradition by siring the Gold Cup winners Foxhunter and Tiberius, while Epigram (by Son-in-Law) sired the similar winner Souepi. Son-in-Law also sired Rustom Pasha, winner of the Eclipse Stakes and Champion Stakes, and Straitlace, winner of the Oaks. Before his death at the age of 30 he had sired the winners of 650 races and was leading sire in 1924 and 1930.

SON OF LOVE
(1976, ch c Jefferson – Mot d'Amour, by Bon Mot III)

Son of Love had an unusual record for a Classic winner, beginning with the fact that he was bought by his French owner for the equivalent of £4,700 as a two-year-old at the Auteuil horses in training sale. He won two of his seven races for trainer Robert Collet as a two-year-old, coming into his own at a mile and 10f, but lost his first ten as a three-year-old until he came to Britain for the St Leger. In a driving finish with another French runner, Soleil Noir, Son of Love and Alain Lequeux got up close home to win by a short head in a big field of seventeen. Son of Love did not win again. He went to the United States after the St Leger and returned to France to run as a four-year-old but showed nothing like his previous form.

SOUEPI
(1948, br c Epigram – Sousse, by Bala Hissar)

Bred by Mr G.R. Digby and Mohammed Bey Sultan, Souepi did not win until the age of four but proved a fine stayer, winning 5½ races for £23,046, including the Gold Vase, Ascot Gold Cup and Goodwood Cup. He dead-heated for the Doncaster Cup. Retiring as a six-year-old, he was sold for the trifling sum of 2,100gns to go to Chile.

SOVEREIGN PATH
(1956, gr c Grey Sovereign – Mountain Path, by Bobsleigh)

Sovereign Path proved a bargain for owner-trainer Ron Mason, who bought him for 700gns as a yearling. He won eight races worth over £10,000, including the Lockinge Stakes and Queen Elizabeth II Stakes. Syndicated for £48,000 to stand at stud in Ireland, he had sired the winners of 750 races and £1m when he died in December 1977. Among his many good winners were: Spanish Express (Middle Park Stakes), Petite Path (Queen Mary Stakes and Ayr Gold Cup), Regal Light (Royal Hunt Cup), King of Peace (Ascot Stakes), Supreme Sovereign (Free Handicap and Lockinge Stakes), Wolver Hollow (Eclipse Stakes), Humble Duty (Cheveley Park Stakes and 1,000 Guineas) and He Loves Me (Cork and Orrery Stakes). Sons of Sovereign Path who have done well as stallions include Wolver Hollow, Spanish Express (in Japan), Sovereign Edition (in New Zealand), Supreme Sovereign and Town Crier.

SPEARMINT
(1903, b c Carbine – Maid of the Mint, by Minting)

Spearmint was bred by Sir Tatton Sykes at Sledmere and sold as a yearling for 300gns to Major Eustace Loder. He was lightly raced but won the Derby, trained by Peter Gilpin and ridden by Danny Maher, and eleven days later the Grand Prix de Paris. He sired the 1920 Derby winner Spion Kop, also trained by Gilpin, Royal Lancer (St Leger), the Irish Classic winners Zionist and Spelthorne, and that fine broodmare Plucky Liège.

SPION KOP
(1917, b c Spearmint – Hammerkop, by Gallinule)

Bred and owned by Colonel Giles Loder, Spion Kop was trained by Peter Gilpin. He failed to win in six races as a two-year-old, but after finishing second in the Free Handicap, with only 7st 4lb, he improved with distance and, though in the Derby he was less fancied than his stable-companion Sarchedon, the race was run at a terrific pace under exceptionally fast conditions and he outstayed his rivals. Ridden by Frank O'Neill, he won by two lengths from Archaic.

In the Grand Prix Spion Kop was unplaced behind his stable-companion Comrade and never won another race. As a sire he was inconsistent but among his offspring were Felstead (Derby), Kopi (Irish Derby and quite a successful sire in France), Bongrace (good staying mare) and The Bastard, who, as The Buzzard, made a great reputation as a sire in Australia. Spion Kop died in 1941.

SPLIT PASTERN

A split pastern represents a fracture of the largest digital bone between the fetlock and coronet. Recovery depends on the extent and severity of the injury but complete recovery is usually effected after rest.

SPORTING SILK

This is old-fashioned journalese for 'running'. For example, 'Lord Crooksby's promising juvenile is due to sport silk for the first time in the Plodders Plate at Pontefract.' Rarely seen nowadays, when other euphemisms are found, but reference is still made to 'silks', which are the jacket and cap worn by a jockey.

SPRINTER

A horse whose best distance is 5-7f is commonly described as a sprinter.

STAKEHOLDERS

Stakeholders are appointed by the Jockey Club and collect all entrance fees and other sums due under the conditions of races, as well as arrears and other fees due under the rules.

The stakeholders shall not allow a jockey to be weighed out for any horse till such a horse's entrance fee for that race, and the arrears for every horse belonging to that owner or standing in his name, the jockey's fee and any arrears claimed under the Rules of Racing, have been paid, or the stakeholders shall themselves be liable.

Fifteen days after the end of the meeting the stakeholders must render an account and pay out all stakes and added money to the persons entitled to receive them, as well as fillies' premiums and all sums related to horses sold, bought in or claimed.

Stakeholders appointed by the Jockey Club are Messrs Weatherby and Messrs Pratt and Co.

ST AMANT
(1901, b c St Frusquin – Lady Loverule, by Muncaster)

Leopold de Rothschild's St Amant was a horse of uncertain temperament who won the 2,000 Guineas in 1904 and then led from start to finish in the Derby, which was run during a terrible thunderstorm. The rest of his career, bar a win in the Jockey Club Stakes, was disappointing, and he was overshadowed by a contemporary, Pretty Polly. He made little mark as a sire.

STANDISH, Sir Frank (c 1746-1812)

Sir Frank Standish owned three Derby winners, Spread Eagle (1795), Didelot (1796) and Archduke (1799), and two Oaks winners, Yellow Filly (1786) and Parisot (1796). It was for poisoning Sir Frank's Eagle colt by placing arsenic in a drinking trough at Newmarket that Daniel Dawson, the agent of two bookmakers called Bland, was hanged at Cambridge in 1812.

STARKEY, Greville Michael Wilson (b. 1939)

Greville Starkey was apprenticed to Tom Jones at Newmarket and, having ridden his first winner at Pontefract in June 1956, was leading apprentice the following year, with 45 winners. For eight years he was associated with John Oxley's stable but that ended in 1969 and for four years he rode for Henry Cecil, until they split suddenly in April 1974. To this time his most important victories had been in the Oaks (Homeward Bound), Dante Stakes (three times), Ascot Gold Cup (Fighting Charlie), Goodwood Cup, Jockey Club Cup and Lincoln Handicap (Frankincense). In 1975 he became stable jockey to Guy Harwood, and their success has grown year by year with wins in the 2,000 Guineas (To-Agori-Mou), Eclipse Stakes and King George VI and Queen Elizabeth Stakes (Kalaglow), Waterford Crystal Mile (Sandhurst Prince, Rousillon), Sussex Stakes (Rousillon), Lincoln Handicap (Cataldi) and William Hill Futurity (Alphabatim, Bakharoff).

Starkey has also won for other trainers the Derby (Shirley Heights), Oaks (Fair Salinia), Ascot Gold Cup (Shangamuzo), Eclipse Stakes and Prix de l'Arc de Triomphe (Star Appeal), Champion Stakes (Swiss Maid), Lincoln Handicap (Fair Season) and Flying Childers Stakes (three times).

As a reflection of the increased demand on his services following this late rush to the top of his profession, he rode 100 winners in a season for the first time in 1978, ending with his best seasonal score, 107 winners. Increasingly used by trainers abroad, Starkey has crossed swords with local stewards with greater regularity than most jockeys, his determination not always keeping him within the rules, and in 1983 he spent more than three weeks out of action as a result of his indiscretions.

STARTER

A starter is licensed annually by the stewards of the Jockey Club. He is appointed to act at meetings by the Joint Administrative Authority and Jockey

Club and is paid by them in accordance with the terms of his employment.

The starter obtains a list of the runners and the draw from the clerk of the scales in the weighing-room. He gives all orders necessary for securing a fair start. When using the flag to start a Flat race, as opposed to the stalls, he must start the horses as far as possible in a line; he is permitted to start them a reasonable distance behind the starting-post if necessary.

After the starter has called over the names of the runners and the draw, the horses take their place in the order drawn, and when all the horses are in the stalls, he gives orders for a white flag to be raised. The field is then 'under starter's orders'.

If the starter reckons that for some reason or other a horse is unable to start, he must at once notify the clerk of the scales that the number must be withdrawn and must tell him whether the horse has come under starter's orders or not.

A starter has power to remove an unruly horse from the place allotted in the draw if the race is started by flag, and the horse is placed at such a distance to one side that it cannot gain an advantage or prejudice the chances of the other horses and jockeys in the race. Permission may be given by a starter for a horse to be held, or he may himself order an unruly horse to be held, but in all such cases the horse must be held 'at a stand' behind the other runners. Should an unruly horse cause delay, it may be 'left'. In a race from starting stalls the starter has power to remove an unruly horse but it cannot be allowed to start from outside the stalls. In such cases the horse will be withdrawn, usually without coming under starter's orders.

If a starter thinks that through a faulty action of the starting stalls a fair start has not been effected, he declares it a false start and by means of a re-call flag orders the jockeys to return to the post. Unless one rider returns to the start, the race is declared void. Any horse which completes the course after a false start is withdrawn.

A start in front of the starting-post or on a wrong course or before the appointed time is void.

A starter can fine up to £50 any rider guilty of misconduct at the start; if he does, he must report the fact to the stewards. He must also report to the stewards any case of a jockey whom he considers guilty of misconduct at the start.

A starter must report to the stewards for transmission to the Racing Calendar Office all cases in which he has dispensed with starting stalls or had to withdraw a runner, together with his reasons.

The starting-stalls team will include, in addition to the starter's assistant, the appropriate number of handlers divided into groups of two men who are accustomed to working together. The loading procedure is set out in a Jockey Club instruction. Any horse which fails to enter the stalls is reported to the stewards and must undergo a test before he is allowed to race from stalls again. A horse which fails a second test is reported to the stewards of the Jockey Club.

Jockeys whose behaviour causes difficulty or delay can be dealt with in the same manner as in cases of misconduct at the starting-gate. Trainers whose horses are not properly trained to stalls can be reported by the starter to the stewards.

STARTER'S ORDERS

A horse comes under the starter's orders when the white flag is raised on the official's instruction. From this moment the horse is considered to be a starter, and withdrawal after this point entails loss of all bets placed on the horse. Withdrawal prior to coming under starter's orders renders the horse a non-runner, and stakes on all bets (except ante-post) are returned.

STARTING GATE

A barrier of elasticated webbing, stretched across the course and which when operated by a lever swung upwards and away from the runners, was used for the first time at Newmarket in 1897.

STARTING STALLS

A mobile mechanism which comprises compartments with mechanically operated doors is used to start all but a handful of Flat races. Though they had long been in operation in the United States, starting stalls were viewed with some disquiet in Britain, and their introduction for the first time in public, in the Chesterfield Stakes at Newmarket on 8 July 1965, was the start of a 'trial' run. Opposition was gradually overcome, and the use of stalls has become an integral part of a race. Fewer than half a dozen Flat race meetings a season do not have starting stalls and have to be started by flag following dismantling of the old-style starting-gate structures.

STAYER

A horse is described as a stayer if it needs $1\frac{1}{2}$m or more to show its best form. In recent times, as prize money for mile to middle-distance races has been increased, stayers have lost their attraction, particularly among commercial breeders, and to be described as such often sounds the death-knell for a stallion's prospects.

STEADY AIM (1943, b f Felstead – Quick Arrow, by Casterari)

Steady Aim ran only three times and won twice for £6,816, including the Oaks for her owner-breeder, Sir Alfred Butt. She bred seven winners but they were of no particular distinction, except Immortal, who won the Newbury Spring Cup. Steady Aim's daughter Petitioner bred ten winners from eleven foals in America, including Pas de Nom (dam of the unbeaten Danzig).

STEDFAST (1908, ch c Chaucer – Be Sure, by Surefoot)

Bred by the sixteenth Earl of Derby, Stedfast was one of the best winners owned by his successor. He won twenty races, worth £26,479, including the Coronation Cup, Hardwicke Stakes and Jockey Club Stakes. He was second in the 2,000 Guineas and Derby. He sired the Oaks winner Brownhylda but otherwise his stud record was very disappointing.

STEPHENSON, William (b. 1911)

Willie Stephenson was brought up in Co Durham and apprenticed to Major W.V.

Beatty at Newmarket. Shortly after his sixteenth birthday he rode Niantic to dead-heat for the Cambridgeshire. He rode from 1925 to 1945 before starting training at Royston. He conducted a successful 'mixed' stable and won the Derby in 1951 with Arctic Prince and Grand National in 1959 with Oxo. He also trained the great hurdler Sir Ken, winner of the Champion Hurdle three years running. He was also noted for his handling of apprentices, of whom Des Cullen, Dennis Letherby, 'Buster' Parnell, Bruce Raymond and Denis Ryan were the most successful. Stephenson was responsible for re-starting the Doncaster Bloodstock Sales with Ken Oliver in 1962; he founded the Tudor Stud (named after his Eclipse and Sussex Stakes winner King of the Tudors) but handed in his trainer's licence in 1980.

STEPHENSON, William Arthur (b. 1920)

Arthur Stephenson, a cousin of Willie Stephenson, was a farmer when he began training at Bishop Auckland, Co Durham, in 1959, after having held a permit since 1946. His stable comprises mainly jumpers, and though he started training on the Flat in 1960, it was not until 1967 that he won more than £10,000 in stakes in a season. That year he won the Nunthorpe Stakes and July Cup with Forlorn River, whose son Rapid River won the Gimcrack Stakes for the stable five years later.

STERN, George (1882-1928)

George Stern was born in France of British parents and was bi-lingual. In his prime he was fully the equal of any jockey in France or Britain and was a particularly strong finisher. He could look after himself under any circumstances, and any rough stuff in a race was liable to be repaid with considerable interest. He rode for the most part in France but won the 2,000 Guineas on Sunstar (1911) and Kennymore (1914), the Derby on Sunstar (1911) and the St Leger on Troutbeck (1906). He rode a terribly rough race in the 1907 Ascot Gold Cup on Eider, who dead-heated with The White Knight, and inevitably Eider was disqualified. A good many people had thought that Stern's riding on Troutbeck in the St Leger had merited similar official action. After he finished riding he trained for M. Marcel Boussac and others.

STEWARDS OF MEETINGS

There must be at least four stewards at every meeting, appointed by the racecourse but approved by the stewards of the Jockey Club.

Should there not be four stewards or their deputies present, the clerk of the course shall, without delay, see that any vacancy or vacancies are filled, so that there shall be four persons to act.

The stewards of a meeting have full power to make (and if necessary, to vary) all such arrangements for the conduct of the meeting as they think fit.

They have power, under exceptional circumstances, to abandon the meeting, or to abandon any races, or to postpone any races to the following day or days within the original fixture, provided that all races originally advertised for any day shall be included in that day's programme.

The stewards have control over, and free access to, all stands, rooms, enclosures and other places used for the purposes of the meeting.

They shall exclude from all places under their control every disqualified person and have power to exclude at their discretion any person from all or any places under their control.

The stewards have power to enquire into, regulate, control, take cognisance of and adjudicate upon the conduct of all officials and of all owners, nominators, trainers, jockeys, grooms, persons attendant upon horses and all persons frequenting the stands or other places used for the purpose of the meeting.

When in the opinion of the stewards any person has committed any breach of the Rules of Racing they have power at their discretion to impose upon such person a fine not exceeding £550.

When in the opinion of the stewards there is a reasonable suspicion that any person has committed any breach of the Rules of Racing which in their opinion ought to be considered by the stewards of the Jockey Club, or where in their opinion any person has committed any breach of the Rules of Racing and in their opinion some fine or punishment in excess of £550 ought to be imposed upon such person, or in their opinion a jockey has committed a breach of the rule that requires suspension of longer than fourteen days, they have power at their discretion to report the matter to the stewards of the Jockey Club.

The stewards have power by notices exhibited on the number board or elsewhere and by any form of public address system at the racecourse to state and announce that an objection has been lodged, the subject and nature thereof, and also their decision in respect of such objection, or of any other matter coming within their jurisdiction.

The stewards have power to call for proof that a horse is neither itself disqualified in any respect, nor nominated by, nor the property, wholly or in part, of a disqualified person; and in default of such proof being given to their satisfaction they may declare the horse disqualified. They have power to prevent from running any horse which cannot be shown to be qualified under these rules or under the conditions of the race.

The stewards have power at any time to order an examination by such person or persons as they think fit, of any horse entered for a race, or which has run in a race. Where such an examination includes the taking of samples for subsequent analysis, the samples may be of any body fluid, tissue, excreta, hair or skin scrapings.

The stewards, as such, shall not entertain any dispute relating to bets.

STEWARDS OF THE JOCKEY CLUB

See JOCKEY CLUB.

STEWART, Alexander Christie (b. 1955)

Educated at Gordonstoun, Alec Stewart was assistant to Gavin Hunter and Tom Jones before he took out a licence to train at Newmarket in 1983. His first winner was Opale at Catterick on 4 June 1983, and the same filly gave him his first Classic success when she won the Irish St Leger the following year. He had the backing of the Maktoum family from the start of his career, and after clocking totals of six, thirteen and 22, he swapped Newmarket stables with Jeremy Hindley for the 1986 season.

ST FRUSQUIN
(1893, br c St Simon – Isabel, by Plebeian)

Leopold de Rothschild's St Frusquin was one of the best sons of St Simon. He won eleven races, including the 2,000 Guineas, worth over £33,000. In the Derby he was beaten by a neck by another son of St Simon, Persimmon. St Frusquin was twice champion sire and twice runner-up.

ST GERMANS
(1921, b c Swynford – Hamoaze, by Torpoint)

St Germans was bred by Lord Astor. Trained by Alec Taylor, he was second in the Derby, like his half-brothers Buchan and Tamar, but won nine races, including the Doncaster and Coronation Cups. He was exported to America where he was a great success as a sire, among his offspring being the Kentucky Derby winner but stud failure Twenty Grand.

STILL, Raymond (b. 1946)

As an apprentice to Sam Armstrong, Ray Still had his best season in 1968, with 38 winners, three years after riding his first winner, at Pontefract. A natural lightweight, he has had his biggest successes in major handicaps, among them the Victoria Cup (on Heave Ho) and Ebor Handicap (Big Hat). He is a regular visitor to India, but a fall there in December 1979 put him out for the whole of 1980, since when he has not found it easy to secure rides.

STIRK, Norman

Norman Stirk was apprenticed to Alec Boyd and rode his biggest winners for the latter's brother George Boyd, to whose Dunbar stable he was attached. Stirk

rode his first winner on Las Vegas in August 1946 at Newmarket, and gained two of his most important winners on the same course, with Rockavon, 66-1 winner of the 2,000 Guineas in 1961, and Rexequus in the 1959 Cambridgeshire. He also won the Northumberland Plate in 1960 on New Brig, having had his best season in 1959, with 29 winners. He rode for the last time in 1969.

ST LOUIS
(1919, b c Louvois – Princess Sterling, by Florizel II)

Bred in Ireland by Mr J.J. Maher, St Louis won two races for £11,084, including the 2,000 Guineas. He made little mark as a sire.

STOCKTON

Racing at Stockton, whch had been held since 1724 came to a close on 16 June 1981, and two months later the racecourse company went into liquidation. It ended a chequered recent history for the course, which changed its name to Teesside Park in 1967, 'to identify the track more closely with the Great Teesside Development', but reverted to 'Stockton' in 1980 when that grand scheme failed. In between, the course had opened a National Hunt track in October 1967, suspended unprofitable Flat racing in 1973 and 1974, and spent £1m in 1979 on a new weighing-room, stables and Tote block, most of the money coming from the Department of the Environment in compensation when a new road scheme was put into effect. The course closed with an overdraft of £700,000, unable to withstand heavy bank interest charges.

The course, 11m from Darlington and 34 from Newcastle, was a left-handed, oval-shaped track with a straight run-in of half a mile. The 5f and 6f courses both started on separate spurs and neither was straight. The 5f course bent left to join the round course 4f from the winning-post. The 6f course had a straight run of 2f before joining the round course on the home turn. It was reckoned a fast track with easy turns and no place for the plodder. Low numbers were strongly favoured in races over 5f and 6f, to a lesser degree over 7f and 1m.

STOCKWELL
(1849, ch c The Baron – Pocahontas, by Glencoe)

One of the great stallions of the nineteenth century, Stockwell was bought by Lord Exeter as a yearling for £180. He won the 2,000 Guineas and St Leger but was a sick horse when he failed in the Derby. He was a magnificent stamp of weight-carrying thoroughbred and at stud fully earned his title of 'Emperor of Stallions', transmitting to his stock the stoutness for which he was famous. On seven occasions he was champion sire and four times runner-up. He sired three Derby winners – Blair Athol, Lord Lyon and Doncaster – and in 1866 the first three in the Derby were sired by him. Stockwell is the ancestor of the Phalaris male line, one of the most powerful in Britain today. To him also traces the line of The Boss, a dominating sprinting influence in breeding, and that of Teddy, to whom French and American bloodstock owe so much. He died in 1870, the victim of an unfortunate accident. While covering a mare, he fell backwards; part of his tail broke off, and the other part punctured his bowels.

STONE, Keith (b. 1942)

Head lad to Peter Easterby for fifteen years, Keith Stone branched out on his own at Malton in 1978. His first win was with French Touch at Doncaster on 28 May 1979, and since then he has done consistently well with a small string, his best season being 1985 with eighteen winners.

STOUTE, Michael Ronald (b. 1945)

It took Michael Stoute one season to make his mark and only ten for him to join the best and most successful trainers in the country. He came to Britain from his native Barbados at the age of nineteen to become pupil-trainer to Pat Rohan, and then had spells with Doug Smith and Tom Jones before starting training at Newmarket in 1972. He had his first winner with Sandal (owned by his father) at Newmarket on 28 April 1972 and the following year won the Stewards' Cup (Alphadamus) and Ayr Gold Cup (Blue Cashmere). It was not long before he was winning some of the major condition races, and his first Classic came with Fair Salinia (Oaks) in 1978, the year he also won the Ascot Gold Cup (Shangamuzo).

In 1980 he was leading trainer for winners, with 101 (his best came five years later with 120), and in 1981 he was leading trainer for stakes, thanks to the peerless Shergar (Derby, Irish Sweeps Derby and King George VI and Queen Elizabeth Stakes). He won the Irish Derby again in 1983 with Shareef Dancer for the Maktoum family, who are among his chief patrons. He had his third British Classic success with Shadeed (2,000 Guineas) in 1985. Other good horses he has trained include Triple First (Sun Chariot Stakes), Marwell (King's Stand Stakes), Final Straw (Champagne), Girandole (Goodwood Cup), Shaftesbury (Ebor), Sally Brown (Yorkshire Oaks) and Optimistic Lass (Musidora Stakes). Not all his recent important wins have been in condition races, for he has won the Northumberland Plate (twice), Chester Cup and Stewards' Cup since 1980.

ST PADDY
(1957, b c Aureole – Edie Kelly, by Bois Roussel)

St Paddy was Sir Victor Sassoon's fourth and last Derby winner. Bred by his owner, he won nine races and was placed three times for earnings of £101,527. Besides the Derby he won the St Leger, Hardwicke Stakes and Eclipse Stakes. In the King George VI and Queen Elizabeth Stakes in 1961 he was slammed by Right Royal V. He was widely regarded as a high-class horse but not a great battler in a struggle. He retired to stud in Newmarket and, though Parnell (fourteen wins) gave him his only success in a Classic, the Irish St Leger, he went close with Connaught, second in the Derby, St Pauli Girl, second in the 1,000 Guineas and Oaks, and Patch, second in the

French Derby. St Paddy had been retired for three years when he was destroyed on humane grounds in May 1984.

STRAIGHT DEAL
(1940, b c Solario – Good Deal, by Apelle)

Bred by Miss Dorothy Paget, Straight Deal was trained by Walter Nightingall. He won twice as a two-year-old and was second in the Coventry Stakes and Dewhurst Stakes. The following year he won a race at Windsor, was sixth in the 2,000 Guineas and then, ridden by Tommy Carey, won the Derby by a head from Umiddad with Nasrullah close-up third.

After the Derby he won a $1\frac{1}{2}$m race at Ascot. He started favourite for the St Leger but finished third behind two good fillies, Herringbone and Ribbon. That was his last race. Possibly because he had a lot of unfashionable blood on his dam's side, he was always rather neglected by breeders but he got three good staying fillies in Ark Royal (£12,400), Kerkeb (£7,373) and Above Board (£5,110). He also got Aldborough (Doncaster Cup and Queen Alexandra Stakes), Sicilian Prince (French St Leger) and Royal Highway (Irish St Leger). His daughters have done well at stud, producing such as Silly Season, Doutelle and Kythnos. Straight Deal died in 1969.

STRAITLACE
(1921, br f Son-in-Law – Stolen Kiss, by Best Man)

Bred by Lady Sykes and sold for 17,000gns as a yearling to Sir Edward Hulton, Straitlace was a very high-class performer and, trained by Dawson Waugh, she won eleven races, including the Oaks and Coronation Stakes, and £24,131. On her owner's death she was bought by Mr E. Esmond for 17,000gns – a record for a broodmare. The best of her offspring was Lovelace, who won ten races in France and was second in the

French Derby and Eclipse Stakes.

ST SIMON
(1881, b c Galopin – St Angela, by King Tom)

St Simon, perhaps the greatest of British stallions, was bred by Prince Batthyany, a Hungarian who had made Britain his home. The Prince was the owner of Galopin, who won the Derby in 1875. In 1883 the Prince dropped dead from a heart attack just outside the Jockey Club Luncheon Room at Newmarket, half an hour before Galliard, a son of Galopin, won the 2,000 Guineas. Because of his owner's death, St Simon came up for sale when he was a two-year-old at Newmarket in July. His only Classic entry, in the 2,000 Guineas, had been rendered void on account of the death of his nominator according to the rule at that time. For 1,600gns he was bought by the young Duke of Portland, whose trainer was the famous Mat Dawson.

St Simon had not run at the time of his purchase. He won twice at Goodwood and then carried off the Devonshire Nursery at Derby under top weight. At Doncaster he won the Prince of Wales Nursery by eight lengths from twenty opponents, to some of whom he was conceding 44lb. He finished the season by defeating the Duke of Westminster's good two-year-old, Duke of Richmond, in a match.

The following year he received a walk-over in the Epsom Gold Cup and won the Ascot Gold Cup by twenty lengths. He next won a gold cup over a mile at Gosforth Park and concluded his racing career by winning the Goodwood Cup by twenty lengths. He was kept in training at the age of four but broke down on the gallops before his intended reappearance.

St. Simon's stud fee to start with was 50gns but rose to 500gns, a very big sum for those days. His stud record remains unsurpassed. He was champion sire nine times and finished in the first three on five other occasions. Six times he was leading sire of winning broodmares. He sired the winners of seventeen Classics and, overall, the winners of 571 races worth

£553,150. He dropped dead at the advanced age of 27.

He stood just on sixteen hands but was so perfectly proportioned that he looked smaller than he was. He possessed outstanding quality, shoulders so sloped that he seemed to be short in the back, and great length from hip to hock. He was higher at the croup than at the withers. His constitution was exceptionally robust, and to the day of his death he was very rarely off-colour. He possessed exceptional vitality, sweated freely and was highly strung and quick tempered. Many of these characteristics he transmitted to his stock, among the outstanding members of which were the Derby-winning brothers Persimmon and Diamond Jubilee, and the Oaks-winning sisters Memoir and La Flèche.

STUBBS, Ralph William (b. 1945)

Bill Stubbs, who began training in 1976, occupied a number of stables in the North before moving to his present yard, Tupgill Park at Middleham, in 1984, when he had his best season with thirteen winners.

STUD BOOK

The *General Stud Book* and the annual volumes of *Races Past* (more recently discontinued by the Jockey Club in favour of the records kept by Raceform) have been described as 'the twin pillars that support the evolution of the Thoroughbred'. The former provides the pedigrees of broodmares and their foaling records; the latter provided evidence of the racecourse tests upon which the selection of the most suitable animals for breeding purposes must be based. The British stud book is unique in that it is the property of a private firm, Messrs Weatherby.

STURDY, Richmond Chartres (b. 1912)

Richmond Sturdy first took out a licence in 1936 with stables at Shrewton, Wiltshire, but it was not until 1970 that he had a major success, with Tintagel II in the Ebor Handicap. He relinquished his licence in 1983.

SUN CAP
(1951, gr f Sunny Boy III – Cappellina, by Le Capucin)

The French filly Sun Cap, owned by Mme R. Forget and trained by Reginald Carver, won the Oaks in 1954. She was subsequently purchased on behalf of Lady Macdonald-Buchanan and bred five minor winners, of whom the most successful was the staying handicapper Imperial Crown.

SUN CASTLE
(1938, b c Hyperion – Castle Gay, by Buchan)

Sun Castle won three races for £4,697, including a war-time St Leger. He died before he could take up stud duties.

SUN CHARIOT
(1939, br f Hyperion – Clarence, by Diligence)

One of the greatest fillies of this century, Sun Chariot was bred by the National Stud, then situated in Ireland. Leased to King George VI for her racing career, she was trained by Fred Darling. At first she gave little sign of ability, and it was proposed to send her back to Ireland, but there was delay in securing an export licence and in the meantime she began to reveal her merit.

Standing 15.2 hands, she was a robust, well-balanced, long, low filly with a faultless action. By nature she was unpredictable, quick-tempered and self-willed. As a two-year-old she was unbeaten, her successes including the Queen Mary Stakes and Middle Park Stakes. At Salisbury, in her first race the following season, she was in waspish, unco-operative mood and sustained the one defeat of her career. Early in May she won a small race at Salisbury and, starting even-money favourite for the 1,000 Guineas, she won impressively.

In the Oaks she was in a thoroughly difficult mood. She spoiled three starts, and when at length the starter got them off, she darted away to the left. When the others had gone a furlong, she had covered about 50yd, but she won all the same. She gave her finest display in the St

Leger, winning with contemptuous ease from the colts that had occupied the first three places in the Derby.

At the stud she bred seven winners, including Blue Train, a very good horse who was never beaten but whose career was curtailed by leg trouble, Gigantic, winner of the Imperial Produce Stakes and a successful sire in New Zealand, Landau, who won the Rous Memorial Stakes at Ascot and Sussex Stakes and did quite well as a sire in Australia, and Pindari, winner of the Solario Stakes, King Edward VII Stakes and Great Voltigeur Stakes. Sun Chariot died in 1963.

SUNDRIDGE
(1898, ch c Amphion – Sierra, by Springfield)

Sundridge was unsound in his wind and began his career in selling-races. However, he stayed in training for five years and won sixteen short-distance races worth over £6,000. He went to stud at a fee of 9gns but was champion sire in 1911 and top sire of winning broodmares in 1923. He sired the Derby winner Sunstar, whose dam also ran in sellers, and also Jest, who won the 1,000 Guineas and Oaks and was dam of the Derby winner Humorist. His sons Sun Briar and Sunreigh, full brothers, exercised great influence on American bloodstock.

SUNNY JANE
(1914, ch f Sunstar – Maid of the Mist, by Cyllene)

Lord Astor's Sunny Jane won two races for £1,141, including the Oaks, and was second in the 1,000 Guineas. She was exported to America but before leaving Britain bred the 2,000 Guineas runner-up Bright Knight.

SUN PRINCESS
(1980, b f English Prince – Sunny Valley, by Val de Loir)

Sun Princess, bred by her owner, Sir Michael Sobell, and trained by Dick Hern, was among a number of top-class fillies who stayed in training as four-year-olds in 1984 but disappointed. Yet judged on her three-year-old career there have been few better among her sex at middle-distances since World War II. She won the Oaks (by twelve lengths), Yorkshire Oaks and St Leger (emulating the Classic record of Hern's filly Dunfermline) and finished no worse than third in her other three races that year, including third to Time Charter in the King George VI and Queen Elizabeth Diamond Stakes, and second, beaten a length by All Along, in the Prix de l'Arc de Triomphe.

SUNSTAR
(1908, ch c Sundridge – Doris, by Loved One)

Sunstar was by the sprinter Sundridge, who had gone in his wind, out of a mare who had run in selling races. Bred and owned by Mr J.B. Joel and trained by Charles Morton, he proved a good, game horse. He won the 2,000 Guineas and then, despite having broken down in a gallop the week before Epsom, the Derby. He was so lame after the Derby that he could hardly hobble to the unsaddling enclosure and never ran again. He was a successful sire and, though never champion, got the winners of 440 races worth over £229,000. At one stage of his stud career there was a rumpus among breeders about the very large number of mares he was allowed to cover, but he was an exceptionally virile horse and thrived on his exertions. His most important produce were Buchan and Craig an Eran.

SUN STREAM
(1942, ch f Hyperion – Drift, by Swynford)

Bred by her owner Lord Derby, Sun Stream was trained by Walter Earl. She won five races for £15,670, including the 1,000 Guineas and Oaks. At stud she bred four winners of no particular distinction.

SUPREME COURT
(1948, br c Persian Gulf or Precipitation – Forecourt, by Fair Trial)

Bred by Mr T. Lilley and given to his wife when he failed to reach a modest reserve as a yearling, Supreme Court was trained by Evan Williams. He won five races and £36,950 in stakes. He was unbeaten as a three-year-old, when his victories included the King George VI and Queen Elizabeth Festival of Britain Stakes, King Edward VII Stakes and Chester Vase. The best horse he sired was Pipe of Peace, winner of the Middle Park Stakes and third in the 2,000 Guineas and Derby. He proved a good sire of broodmares, their numbers including the dams of D'Urberville, Hopeful Venture, Random Shot and Rheingold. He died in 1962.

SUTCLIFFE, John Robert (b. 1940)

John Sutcliffe, whose father John started training at Epsom after his son had taken out a licence and won the 1971 Grand National with Specify, rode as an amateur and professional under National Hunt Rules. He began training at Epsom in 1962 and rapidly made a name for himself. In 1969 he won the 2,000 Guineas and Irish 2,000 Guineas with Right Tack, who the previous year had won the Imperial Stakes and Middle Park Stakes. In 1968 he also won the Wills Mile with Jimmy Reppin, who had been third in the 2,000 Guineas.

In 1969 he did even better, as Right Tack, besides his other successes, won the St James's Palace Stakes, while Jimmy Reppin won the Sussex Stakes, Queen Elizabeth II Stakes and £7,000 Prix Perth in France. In 1970 he trained the useful two-year-old Mummy's Pet (Norfolk Stakes, Temple Stakes and second in Middle Park Stakes). His more recent major wins have been in handicaps, with The Adrianstan (Victoria Cup), My Hussar and Tender Heart (both Royal Hunt Cup), Anji (Ebor Handicap) and Last Tango (Ayr Gold Cup). His best season was 1970 with 32 winners.

SWALLOW TAIL
(1946, b c Bois Roussel – Schiaparelli, by Schiavoni)

Bred and owned by Lord Derby, Swallow Tail earned £12,258 from six victories including the Royal Lodge Stakes, Chester Vase and King Edward VII Stakes. In a finish of heads he was third to Nimbus and Amour Drake in the Derby. When his racing career was over, he was exported to Brazil and did well as a sire.

SWANNELL, Major David William Ashburnham (b. 1918)

David Swannell served in the Durham Light Infantry for eighteen years. At one time Clerk of the Course at Beverley and county stand secretary at York, he was an official handicapper from 1956 until his retirement in 1983, when he held the senior post as Jockey Club handicapper on the Flat. He was instrumental in starting a racing museum at York and was the driving force behind the National Horseracing Museum which opened in Newmarket in 1983.

SWEEPER II
(1909, ch c Broomstick – Ravello, by Sir Hugo)

The American-bred Sweeper II, trained by 'Atty' Persse, won the 2,000 Guineas for Mr H.B. Duryea. He started a hot favourite for the Derby but finished down the course and was also unplaced in the St Leger.

SWEEPSTAKE

A sweepstake is a race in which the entrance fees, forfeits, subscriptions and other contributions go to the winner or placed horses.

'Private sweepstakes', which have gone out of fashion, denote a race which is not advertised prior to closing and for which only owners with certain qualifications may enter horses. An example is the Arundel Castle Private Sweepstake – known to the vulgar as 'The Castle Carve-Up' – which was run at Goodwood for the last time in 1965.

SWEET SOLERA
(1958, ch f Solonaway – Miss Gammon, by Grandmaster)

Bred by Mrs D.M. Walker, Sweet Solera was bought as a yearling for 1,850gns by Reg Day for his patron Mrs S.M. Castello and proved an outstanding bargain. She won six races and £40,165 in stakes, her victories including the Cherry Hinton Stakes, 1,000 Guineas and Oaks. She was not an outstanding broodmare, breeding four winners (in Italy, Holland, France and Britain), of whom Bon Appetit (Prix Vanteaux) was the best.

SWIFT, Brian (1937-85)

Brian Swift, son of the well-known bookmaker Jack Swift, served his apprenticeship with Jack Reardon at Epsom and rode with fair success as a professional for nine years. Among races he won were the Prix d'Arenberg, New Stakes and King's Stand Stakes. For eighteen months he assisted the Epsom trainer Staff Ingham before setting up on his own in 1967. For a time he trained the subsequent three-times Champion Hurdle winner Persian War but made his name for training two-year-olds, sprinters and milers. Tribal Chief and Decoy Boy were two of his earliest top two-year-olds, while he won the Stewards' Cup with Ahonoora and the Lincoln Handicap with The Hertford. In 1984 he won the Coventry Stakes with Primo Dominie, at 146,000gns the most expensive yearling he had bought, and that year he trained 27 winners. Sadly, it was his last season because in February 1985 he died following a heart attack. His widow Sylvia ran the stable briefly before it was taken over by Geoff Lewis.

SWINBURN, Walter Robert (b. 1937)

Wally Swinburn was apprenticed to 'Sam' Armstrong from 1951 to 1958, riding his first winner in May 1953 at Warwick. His best season in Britain was 1961, when he rode 39 winners. However, after a much-travelled career, including spells in India, Britain and France, he rode a record of 101 winners in Ireland in 1977. He gained his first Classic success in Europe in 1972 on Pidget (Irish 1,000 Guineas) when based in France, and later won the same race on Prince's Polly (1982) and the Irish Oaks on Blue Wind (1981). His first important winner in Britain was By Thunder! (Ebor Handicap), on whom he won the Yorkshire Cup the following year, and he was associated with the career of the Sussex Stakes winner Romulus. He retired from riding at the end of 1982 and spent a year as assistant to Dermot Weld in Ireland before buying the Genesis Green Stud in Newmarket in 1984.

SWINBURN, Walter Robert John (b. 1961)

Walter Swinburn, son of former jockey Wally Swinburn, had the benefit of an apprenticeship with the two master tutors in British racing, 'Frenchie' Nicholson and Reg Hollinshead. He rode his first winner on Paddy's Luck at Kempton on 12 July 1978. When Nicholson retired in 1980, Swinburn moved to Hollinshead and at the end of that year he was appointed stable jockey to Michael Stoute for 1981, six months after losing his claim. The move paid off handsomely for Swinburn, who in his first season with Stoute won the Derby on Shergar, though he missed the ride in the Irish Sweeps Derby because of suspension. He won the Sweeps Derby in 1983 on Shareef Dancer, but 1981 was not the only time a ban cost Swinburn; he forfeited the winning ride on Shadeed in the 1985 2,000 Guineas for the same reason and to the same jockey, Lester Piggott. In contrast, Swinburn rode All Along to win the 1983 Arc de Triomphe after Piggott had been one of several jockeys to turn down the ride, and he went on to ride the filly to three major autumn wins in North America. The following year he failed to please All Along's connections, including owner Daniel Wildenstein, and became one of a number of jockeys cast aside by the Paris art-dealer. He missed 100 winners by one in 1984, his best season.

SWISS MAID
(1975, b f Welsh Pageant –
Hornton Grange, by
Hornbeam)

Swiss Maid had an inauspicious introduction to her career. Unraced as a two-year-old, she was withdrawn at the start of her intended first outing. But trainer Paul Kelleway cured her aversion to the stalls and on her eleventh outing as a three-year-old she won her fifth and easily most important prize of the season, the Champion Stakes, where she beat the Derby runner-up Hawaiian Sound by a length and a half. Previously she had won the Sun Chariot Stakes over the same Newmarket course and distance. She had nine races as a four-year-old, being placed only twice, when third in the Hardwicke Stakes and second in the Sussex Stakes. She went through the sale ring three times, each occasion reflecting the ups and downs of her career. As a yearling she fetched 6,000gns; as a three-year-old her stable retained her for 325,000gns, a European record for a filly in training; and as a four-year-old she made 290,000gns when sold to the United States.

SWYNFORD
(1907, br c John o' Gaunt –
Canterbury Pilgrim, by
Tristan)

Swynford was bred and owned by Lord Derby and was a big, powerful colt. He was trained by George Lambton and took a long time to come to hand; in fact his first victory was in the Hardwicke Stakes at Ascot as a three-year-old. From that point he began to improve rapidly, and after an easy win in the Liverpool Cup he won a controversial St Leger, beating the Derby winner Lemberg.

As a four-year-old his successes included the Hardwicke Stakes, Princess of Wales's Stakes and Eclipse Stakes. He was a long-striding, freegoing horse that did best when permitted to force the pace, and his defeat by Lemberg in the Coronation Cup was due to the fact that Frank Wootton for some unexplained reason abandoned his usual tactics and rode a waiting race on him.

In September 1911 Swynford smashed a fetlock in a half-speed gallop. Fortunately skilled veterinary treatment saved him for stud, as he was champion sire in 1923, second in 1924 and 1925 and third in 1921. He sired the Derby winner Sansovino and five other Classic winners, all fillies: Tranquil (1,000 Guineas and St Leger), Keysoe (St Leger), Saucy Sue (1,000 Guineas and Oaks), Ferry (1,000 Guineas) and Bettina (1,000 Guineas). He also sired Blandford, who got four Derby winners and one year was champion sire in Britain and France.

SYNDICATION OF STALLIONS

The practice of syndicating stallions has become common since World War II and has largely superseded the old system, as far as top-class stallions are concerned, of standing them at a fixed covering fee. The syndication of a stallion involves its capitalization in 40 shares (in the United States it is usually 32) – most stallions cover 40 mares each season – and the offer of some or all of the shares for sale. A breeder who buys a share has the right to send a mare to the stallion each season or to dispose of the nomination for a particular year to another breeder for as long as the stallion is at stud or remains the property of the syndicate. General management of the stallion is usually vested in a small committee of shareholders. Whereas in 1950 a Classic-class winner of impeccable breeding would have been sold to 40 shareholders at a rate of £2,500 per share, the going rate when Shareef Dancer was syndicated in the autumn of 1983 was $1m a share!

T

TABOUN
(1956, b c Tabriz – Queen of Basrah, by Fair Trial)

Taboun was bred by the Aga Khan and Prince Aly Khan. Raced in the colours of Prince Aly Khan and trained by Alec Head, he won the Prix Robert Papin as a two-year-old, and the following year won the 2,000 Guineas when favourite. Odds-on for the French 2,000 Guineas, he was unlucky in running and finished second. His stud career in Ireland was brief as he died at the age of six as a result of an accident.

TAGALIE
(1909, gr f Cyllene – Tagale, by Le Sancy)

Owned by Mr Walter Raphael, a rich London financier, and trained at Newmarket by Dawson Waugh, Tagalie is the only grey filly to have won the Derby, which she did when ridden by Johnny Reiff. She ran less well for George Stern when odds on for the Oaks and was unplaced. Earlier she had won the 1,000 Guineas at 20-1. She made no lasting impression as a broodmare, though her son Allenby finished second in the 2,000 Guineas.

TAJ MAH
(1926, b f Lemberg – Taj Mahal, by The Tetrarch)

Bred by the Aga Khan, Taj Mah won four races for her owner, Mr S.

Guthmann, while trained in France by J. Torterolo. She won the 1,000 Guineas at 33-1 on her only outing in Britain.

TALGO
(1953, b c Krakatao – Miss France, by Jock II)

Talgo was bred by Brigadier C.M. Stewart and sold as a yearling for 1,350gns to Mr Gerry Oldham to be trained by Harry Wragg. He won the Irish Derby and was second to Ribot in the Prix de l'Arc de Triomphe. Talgo was exported to Mexico in 1963.

TALMA II
(1948, ch c Pharis – Thaouka, by Astérus)

Talma II was bred by M. Boussac and distinguished himself when he came over for the St Leger. Despite deplorable behaviour in the paddock he was the best backed horse on the day and won in truly remarkable style by what the judge estimated to be ten lengths, but what appeared to be more like twenty. Neither before that race nor after it did he show comparable form, though he was placed in the Prix du Cadran and finished third when favourite for the Ascot Gold Cup. His St Leger victory will for ever remain the subject of much conjecture.

TAMBOURINE II
(1959, b c Princequillo – La Mirambule, by Coaraze)

Bred in the United States and trained in France by Etienne Pollet, Tambourine II was unraced as a two-year-old but won three races the following year, including the inaugural running of the Irish Sweeps Derby in a close finish with Arctic Storm. Tambourine was taken out of training that autumn because of tendon trouble and retired to stud in France.

TAP ON WOOD
(1976, ch c Sallust – Cat O'Mountaine, by Ragusa)

Steve Cauthen won his first British Classic on Tap on Wood in the 2,000

Guineas, which he took by half a length from Kris. Tap on Wood, trained by Barry Hills, ran only twice more – in contrast to an unusually heavy two-year-old campaign of thirteen races, of which he won seven including the National Stakes at The Curragh – in the Derby, where he finished twelfth, and a 7f race at Doncaster which he won from R.B. Chesne. A virus infection kept Tap on Wood away from a return against Kris in the autumn, and he began his career as a stallion at the Irish National Stud in 1980 with a valuation of £1m, and was sold for a reported £1.6 million to stand at stud in Japan from 1986. He was leading first-season sire in 1983, and his best winners have been Ibadiyya (in France), Mahogany (Fred Darling Stakes) and Rappa Tap Tap (Blue Seal Stakes).

TATTERSALLS

The firm of Tattersalls is famous all over the world for the sale of bloodstock. The founder was a Yorkshireman, Richard Tattersall (1724-95). When he was 21 he journeyed south to seek his fortune and by 1766 had amassed sufficient capital to construct premises of his own that he hoped would become the acknowledged centre suitable for the sale of horses.

The land he had set his eyes on was at Hyde Park Corner, and he secured a 99-year lease from Earl Grosvenor, a leading figure on the Turf of that period. The project prospered and 'The Corner', where sales were held twice weekly, soon became a rendezvous for fashionable London. Apart from the stables, kennels were built for the sale of hounds and dogs, and stands for the sale of carriages. A special room was set aside for members of the Jockey Club.

In 1865 the firm moved rather less than a mile westwards to a new site at Knightsbridge Green, where sales were carried out on Mondays and occasional Thursdays until 1939. The scene at these Monday sales has been immortalized by H.M. Bateman in his cartoon 'The man who bid half a guinea at Tattersalls'.

After World War II the site was sold, the famous Rotunda with the statue of the fox removed to Newmarket, the sale yard

and boxes demolished. In its place arose an office block in which Tattersalls had their London office until the whole operation was moved to Newmarket in 1977.

Towards the close of the eighteenth century, Tattersalls were conducting sales in the High Street at Newmarket outside the Jockey Club Rooms. This practice continued until about 1860, when land behind Queensbury House, about 200yd from the present sales paddock, was rented. In 1870 the sales were transferred to Park Paddocks, the existing site, and have been held there without interruption since that date. In recent years land adjacent to Park Paddocks has been acquired and many improvements have been made, in particular the construction of the covered sales ring that was first used in the autumn of 1965.

The present senior partner of Tattersalls is Michael Watt, who took over from his cousin Captain Kenneth Watt in 1984.

The principal sales of yearlings were moved from Doncaster, where they had been held in conjunction with the St Leger meeting, after 1957 because of leasing problems, and Tattersalls' British sales are now confined to Newmarket. Principal sales are the Highflyer (in early October), October, autumn (late-October) and December, which have been extended to cover almost two weeks.

As the demand for British bloodstock from overseas buyers has risen in recent years, so has Tattersalls' turnover. In 1982 it was 43m gns; in 1983 it rose to 64m gns, and in 1984 it reached 80m gns. Tattersalls-sold horses won five European Classics in 1984, and Kala Dancer, purchased for 11,000gns as a yearling, was top weight in the European Free Handicap.

Record prices at Tattersalls:
Foal: 490,000gns – ch f Golden Fleece – Chemise, 1 December 1984, bought by T.A. Vigors.
Yearling: 1,550,000gns – ch c Hello Gorgeous – Centre Piece, 27 September 1983, bought by British Bloodstock Agency.

Horse in training: 1,020,000gns – Tenea, 3yo filly, 30 November 1982, bought by British Bloodstock Agency.

Broodmare: 820,000gns – Dunette, 7yo mare covered by Golden Fleece, 30 November 1983, bought by British Bloodstock Agency.

TATTERSALLS COMMITTEE

Tattersalls Committee is the authority recognized by the Jockey Club to settle all matters of dispute relating to bets. The members hear claims and disputes, whether by bookmaker or punter and, if a sum of money is owing, will make an order for payment. If this is not complied with, they will inform the Jockey Club, who in turn may 'warn off' an individual for non-payment. The present rules allow for up to fourteen members; two are appointed by the Jockey Club, and the remainder co-opted by the committee subject to approval by the stewards of the Jockey Club. The current set-up has been in existence since 1929, when the Jockey Club suggested an amalgamation of committees which covered London and Newmarket. Meetings are held in the Café Royal, London, but applicants must first approach the secretary.

Chairman: Maj.-Gen. Sir J. d'Avigdor-Goldsmid. Secretary: Peter Guard, PO Box 13, 7-9 Hatherley Road, Reading, Berks RG1 5QD (0734-65402)

TATTERSALLS' ENCLOSURE

Tattersalls' enclosure on a racecourse is situated next to the club or members' stand, and it is there that the main volume of on-course betting takes place. The public who pay to go into Tattersalls' have access to the paddock.

TAYLOR, Alec (1862-1943)

Alec Taylor, nicknamed 'The Wizard of Manton', was beyond argument one of the greatest trainers of this century. His grandfather, Thomas, had trained at Manton and so had his father, 'Old Alec', who won the 1878 Derby with Sefton. When 'Old Alec' died in 1894, he left Manton to 'Young Alec' and his half-brother Tom. The two worked in partnership for some years but in 1902 'Young Alec' assumed control of the entire Manton property.

'Old Alec' had been hard on his horses and was reputed to give his yearlings a two-mile gallop before Christmas! His son was the most patient of men, regarding horses as mere babies till they were three. Most of his patrons were rich men who could afford to wait, and frequently a policy of patience and restraint earned handsome dividends. The list of famous races that Alec Taylor won is notable both for its length and for the small proportion of two-year-old events included.

Taylor trained the winners of 1,003 British races worth over £839,000. He also trained Lemonora, who won the Grand Prix de Paris. His Classic winners were Challacombe (1905 St Leger), Bayardo (1909 St Leger), Lemberg (1910 Derby), Rosedrop (1910 Oaks), Kennymore (1914 2,000 Guineas), Gay Crusader (1917 2,000 Guineas, Derby and St Leger), Sunny Jane (1917 Oaks), Gainsborough (1918 2,000 Guineas, Derby and St Leger), My Dear (1918 Oaks), Bayuda (1919 Oaks), Craig an Eran (1921 2,000 Guineas), Love in Idleness (1921 Oaks), Pogrom (1922 Oaks), Saucy Sue (1925 1,000 Guineas and Oaks), Short Story (1926 Oaks), and Book Law (1927 St Leger). He was leading trainer on twelve occasions, seven of them in succession from 1917 to 1923. After his retirement in 1927, he used to say that the best horse he ever trained was Picaroon, the cause of whose untimely death when in training was never discovered.

A bachelor, dignified, frugal and reserved, Alec Taylor looked more like a country banker of the old school than the popular conception of a trainer of racehorses. He always preferred to carry his own bag than take a taxi and when he died he left close on £600,000.

TAYLOR, Brian (1939-84)

Brian Taylor, whose most notable riding achievement was to win the 1974 Derby on Snow Knight, was killed as a result of a fall while racing in Hong Kong in

Races

Gold Cup glory: above, Bend Or, ridden by Fred Archer, beats Robert the Devil by a neck in an epic race for the Epsom Gold Cup in 1881; and, below, Sagaro, ridden by Lester Piggott, beats Buckskin in the 1977 Gold Cup at Royal Ascot to become the first horse to win the race three years in succession.

Ancient and modern starting: above, chaos at Kempton Park in 1951, when the six-strand tape was in use; and, below, starting stalls in operation for the first time in Britain for the Chesterfield Stakes at Newmarket on 8 July, 1965.

More than just another Classic winner for Lester Piggott as Commanche Run beats Baynoun (Steve Cauthen) in the 1984 St Leger at Doncaster, giving Piggott an all-time record of 28 British Classic successes.

The race of the century as, above, Grundy (Pat Eddery) beats Bustino (Joe Mercer) in the 1975 King George VI and Queen Elizabeth Diamond Stakes at Ascot; and, below, the ambition of a lifetime as Slip Anchor (Steve Cauthen) wins the 1985 Ever Ready Derby at Epsom for his owner-breeder Lord Howard de Walden.

December 1984, a few months after he retired from riding in Europe and shortly before he was due to return to Britain to concentrate on running his stud near Newmarket. Born in Southend to a family which had no connection with racing, he was apprenticed to Harvey Leader from 1953 to 1962, rode his first winner on Creole at Yarmouth in September 1956 and remained with the stable until Leader retired at the end of 1971. They were especially successful with fillies, winning the Musidora Stakes with Orabella II, Palatch and Exchange in successive years, as well as the Yorkshire Oaks with the latter two, and Park Hill Stakes with Bringley. Taylor later had retainers from John Winter and Peter Robinson before becoming stable jockey to Ryan Prince from 1976 to 1980, during which time he had his best season, with 108 winners in 1976. His last ride in Britain (Barra Head, Newmarket, 4 August 1984) and his last ride in Europe (Bedtime, Deauville, a week later) were both successful.

TEASER

The teaser is a humble but important member of every stud where a stallion holds court. His job is to tell the stud groom whether a mare is in use or not by her reaction to an entire horse on the other side of a trying, or teasing board. He therefore bears much responsibility for the incidence of fertility.

TEENOSO
(1980, b c Youth – Furioso, by Ballymoss)

Teenoso gave Geoffrey Wragg a flying start to his training career when he succeeded his father Harry in 1983, for the Derby winner was among those horses the long-time assistant took over. He had shown promise but been unplaced in his three races as a two-year-old, and revelled in the early-season soft ground the following year, progressing from being beaten in a Haydock maiden event to winning a Newmarket maiden, the Lingfield Derby Trial and the Derby (where he beat Carlingford Castle by

three lengths). Teenoso was third in his two races after the Derby in 1983, in a hotly contested Irish Sweeps Derby and when the weights were against him in the Great Voltigeur Stakes. He went lame on his off-fore after the York race but returned to racing as a four-year-old and enhanced his reputation by winning the Ormonde Stakes and Grand Prix de Saint-Cloud, and reached new heights by winning the King George VI and Queen Elizabeth Diamond Stakes, showing he was not beholden to soft ground. The Ascot race brought out Teenoso's regular rider Lester Piggott at his best, as they beat the highly rated three-year-old Sadler's Wells. Injury to his off-fore led to Teenoso's withdrawal from the Arc de Triomphe 24 hours before the race, and he did not run again. Syndication at a valuation of £12m failed to fill, and Teenoso retired to begin his first season as a stallion at the Highclere Stud in 1985 at an estimated valuation of £4m.

TEHRAN
(1941, b c Bois Roussel – Stafaralla, by Solario)

Tehran was bred by Prince Aly Khan and while owned in turn by him and the Aga Khan he won six races including the St Leger. He was second in the Derby and Ascot Gold Cup and third in the 2,000 Guineas. By far the best horse he sired was Tulyar, winner of the Derby and St Leger and unbeaten as a three-year-old when Tehran was leading sire. Tehran also sired Amante (Irish Oaks), Mystery IX (Eclipse Stakes), Tabriz (sire of Taboun) and Raise You Ten (Yorkshire, Goodwood and Doncaster Cups). He died in 1966.

TELEVISED RACING

The Derby was first televised in 1932, being viewed at the Metropole in Victoria, London, and had its first live television broadcast in 1938, but it was not until 1946 that direct coverage of the sport began. It gradually increased and gained impetus when the independent network was introduced, until a peak coverage of 826 races (176 on the Flat and 122 jumping by BBC, and 375 Flat and 153 jumping by ITV) was reached in 1974. With allowance for meetings abandoned because of bad weather, coverage of at least 760 races a year was maintained until 1983, when ITV, which had encouraged midweek coverage and two fixtures on a Saturday, cut down coverage because of a reaction to small viewing-figures in comparison with other possible programmes. This was brought to a head by Central TV's decision not to televise 54 races in 1983 and was followed by the removal to Channel 4 of midweek coverage in 1984 and Saturday's from late 1985. The BBC have maintained their level of coverage.

Increased television coverage has been one of the factors in a general decrease in racecourse attendances in the last twenty years, but the disadvantage is partly offset by the interest which it stimulates among the general public, the volume of off-course betting which it creates, and the sponsorship of races which it attracts.

In May 1964 a television committee set up by the Racecourse Association recommended that, in relation to television, the object of the Association was to negotiate block contracts with the BBC and with independent television authorities. This object has not been achieved. Its purpose was not merely to benefit those courses whose meetings were being televised but to form a fund in which those courses whose meetings were not televised would share. In the meantime, racecourses continue to negotiate their own contracts, many of which are of a long-term character.

See also Appendix III.

TEMPLEMAN, Simeon (1805-84)

Sim Templeman was a Yorkshire-born jockey who had remarkable success in the Classics for one who was not regarded in the highest class of riders. He won the Derby on Bloomsbury, Cossack and Surplice, the Oaks on Miami, Cymba and Marchioness, and the St Leger on Newminster, including the Epsom double in 1847.

TENERANI (1944, br c Bellini – Tofanella, by Apelle)

This good Italian horse was bred by Federico Tesio, using a mare he had bought in Britain as a yearling for 140gns. He won fourteen races in Italy, including their Derby, while in Britain he won the Queen Elizabeth Stakes at Ascot and the Goodwood Cup. He was a stallion at the National Stud in Britain until 1960 and in Italy until his death in 1965. His place in racing history is assured as sire of that great racehorse and outstanding sire Ribot. He also sired Fighting Charlie, twice winner of the Ascot Gold Cup, and Tenterhooks (Gold Vase and Goodwood Cup).

TERESINA (1920, ch f Tracery – Blue Tit, by Wildfowler)

Bred by Lady Sykes, Teresina was bought as a yearling for 7,700gns on behalf of the Aga Khan. She was a good and genuine racemare, winning the Jockey Club Stakes and Goodwood Cup, besides being placed in the Oaks, St Leger, Eclipse Stakes and Cesarewitch. She bred eight winners of 24 races, including Theresina (Irish Oaks), and her son Alibhai, who never ran, was a great success as a sire in the United States.

TETRATEMA (1917, gr c The Tetrarch – Scotch Gift, by Symington)

Owned and bred by Major Dermot McCalmont, Tetratema was a very fast grey horse. As a two-year-old he was unbeaten in five races. He won the 2,000 Guineas but failed to stay in the Derby and the Eclipse. After the Eclipse he was kept to sprinting and was never beaten again. Altogether he won thirteen races worth £21,778. He was leading sire in 1929. His best colts were Mr Jinks, Royal Minstrel and Theft, his best fillies, Tiffin, Myrobella and Four Course. Tetratema died in 1939.

THE BASTARD
(1926, b c Spion Kop –
Valescure, by Swynford)

The Bastard belonged to Lord Rosebery and his most important success was the Yorkshire Cup. He won a race at Newmarket at 100-1 when the Tote was just beginning to operate and book-makers were offering extravagant prices. He was exported to Australia where, with surprising refinement, he was re-named The Buzzard. He proved an outstanding success as a sire there before being retired in 1950.

THE MINSTREL
(1974, ch c Northern Dancer –
Fleur, by Victoria Park)

The Minstrel typifies the strength of modern American breeding, being by Northern Dancer out of a half-sister to Northern Dancer's son Nijinsky. The Minstrel also exemplifies the manner in which valuations can rise to enormous heights in a short time if a colt makes the grade sufficiently to be regarded as a stallion prospect. He fetched $200,000 (£85,500) as a yearling when bought on behalf of Robert Sangster in the United States, and returned there to stand at stud at a valuation of $9m. Trained in Ireland by Vincent O'Brien, The Minstrel was undefeated in his three races as a two-year-old, including the Dewhurst Stakes; he was third in the 2,000 Guineas and second, beaten a short head, in the Irish equivalent, and ended his career unbeaten in three races – the Derby, (where his courage under strong pressure from Lester Piggott brought a neck win over Hot Grove), Irish Sweeps Derby, and King George VI and Queen Elizabeth Diamond Stakes, where he beat Orange Bay by a short head. He did not race again, though he was in training for the Prix de l'Arc de Triomphe. Import restrictions in America because of disease forced his premature departure, and he had his first season at stud in 1978. Several members of his early crops have returned to Europe, and they include the Classic winners L'Emigrant (French

2,000 Guineas) and Crusader Castle (Italian St Leger), the useful fillies Silverdip, Treizième, Kanz and Malaak, the Champion Stakes winner Palace Music and Bakharoff, the top two-year-old of 1985.

THE PANTHER
(1916, br c Tracery – Countess
Zia, by Gallinule)

Bred at the National Stud, sold for 3,600gns as a yearling to Sir Alec Black and trained by G. Manser, The Panther showed high promise as a two-year-old, but it was regarded as a rather silly joke when his owner, who knew little about racing, sent him up to the Newmarket Sales in 1918 with a reserve of 40,000gns on him. 'This will give a chance to all comers,' Sir Alec Black observed. 'If he passes out of the ring unsold, there will be no further opportunity to buy him.' There was no bid.

The Panther won the 2,000 Guineas and started 6-5 favourite for the Derby. His temper that day was abominable and he ran badly. He also failed in the Irish Derby and Champion Stakes. He was exported to Argentina where he sired winners of more than £60,000 in stakes. In 1929 he was repatriated to Britain but died two years after his return.

THE TETRARCH
(1911, gr c Roi Hérode –
Vahren, by Bona Vista)

The Tetrarch may well have been the fastest horse seen on a British racecourse this century. Bred in Ireland by Mr Edward Kennedy, he was by Roi Hérode, a grey, and he himself when in training was iron-grey with a number of curious white marks as if some joker had thrown a bucket of whitewash at him. Hence his nicknames of 'The Rocking Horse' and 'The Spotted Wonder.

He was bought as a yearling for 1,300gns by the Stockbridge trainer 'Atty' Persse who passed him on to his cousin Major Dermot McCalmont. As a two-year-old he ran seven times and was unbeaten. He won all his races very

easily, bar the National Breeders' Produce Stakes at Sandown which he won by
a neck after being left. In the autumn he
injured a foreleg and was never able to
run again. Some of his trials at home were
fantastic, and in June he took on two very
smart older sprinters over 5f and beat
them pulling up by ten lengths on 45lb
worse terms than weight for age!

The Tetrarch hated restraint, and his
rider Steve Donoghue was convinced he
would never have been a stayer.
Nevertheless, The Tetrarch sired three St
Leger winners in five years: Caligula,
Polemarch and Salmon-Trout. Unfortunately, although champion sire in 1919,
he was far from keen on stud duties. He
got 130 foals, of whom 80 were winners,
and from 1926 till his death in 1935 he
was sterile. His best son was the very fast
Tetratema; his best daughter was the
brilliant Mumtaz Mahal.

THE WHITE KNIGHT
(1903, b c Desmond – Pekla,
by Buckshot)

The White Knight won the Gold Cup at
Ascot in 1907 and 1908. In the former
year he dead-heated with the French
horse Eider, but George Stern on Eider
rode a disgracefully rough race, and Eider
was disqualified. The White Knight was a
sad failure as a sire and ended his days in
Argentina.

THIRSK

Thirsk, 24 miles from York, is an
agreeable and well-run course which
enjoys an unusually large number of
Saturday meetings in comparison with
other tracks of similar standing. It is a
left-handed track of just over 1m 2f, with
a straight 6f course which joins the round
course 4f from the winning post. The 6f
straight is mildly undulating throughout,
so that, although the rest of the track is
flat and the turns are easy, it is not ideal
for the long-striding or awkward galloper.
In sprint races high numbers are
favoured.

THOM, David Trenchard (b.
1925)

David Thom served as a Royal Marine

Commando in World War II and took
out a trainer's licence in 1959, making his
name first with NH horses such as
Master Mascus and Prince Hansel, who
was also a useful Flat-race stayer,
winning the Doncaster Cup. Thom won
other good long-distance races with
Narratus (Great Metropolitan and
Chester Cup) but has proved equally
adept at preparing fast two-year-olds at
his stable at Exning, near Newmarket.

THOMAS, Myrddin Lloyd (b.
1945)

Born in Wales, 'Taffy' Thomas was
apprenticed to Geoffrey Barling for five
years, and stayed on as stable jockey for
four years until joining Ryan Jarvis in
1968. He rode for Jarvis for ten years
before turning freelance. He rode his first
winner on Weather Way at Hurst Park in
August 1962, and three years later had
his first important success on Piaco in the
Northumberland Plate. Subsequent big
handicaps he has won include the Lincoln
(Quizair), Stewards' Cup (Royal Smoke
and Import), Cambridgeshire (Emerilo
and Sagamore) and Cesarewitch (Cider
with Rosie). Major conditions races
which have come his way include the
Dante Stakes (Activator and Lucky
Sovereign), Vernons Sprint (Absalom)
and King's Stand Stakes (Sayf El Arab).
His best season was in 1977, with 98
winners.

THOMSON, Brent (b. 1958)

Though born in New Zealand, Brent
Thomson made his name as a jockey in
Australia and came to Britain for the first
time in the summer of 1984 at the request
of Robert Sangster. He returned the
following year for the whole season with
a retainer for the owner, and midway
through the year Barry Hills agreed that
Thomson would be his stable jockey in
1986. Though he had ridden almost 1,000
winners before he came to Britain,
adapting to the different techniques was
not easy, but in his first year he won the
William Hill Sprint on Committed, and in
1985 he rode the winners of 64 races,
including the Ascot Gold Cup (Gildoran),
Ormonde Stakes (Seismic Wave), Ver-

nons Sprint (Orojoya) and Champagne Stakes (Sure Blade).

THORNTON, Christopher William (b. 1949)

Chris Thornton worked for Sam Armstrong at Newmarket and Theo Grieper in Germany before becoming assistant to Sam Hall at Middleham in 1973. He was granted the licence on Hall's death in July 1977 and has remained there with Guy Reed his major patron. Reed's dependence on the stock of his good horse Warpath has led to the stable having a preponderance of slow-maturing, often staying horses in the stable. Thornton's first win was with Sioux and Sioux at Edinburgh on 11 July 1977, and his biggest success was with Path of the Peace in the Manchester Handicap in 1980. His best season was his second, with 35 winners, and perhaps his best horse has been Shotgun, fourth in the Derby.

THOROUGHBRED, Origins of

The origin of the Thoroughbred is veiled in mystery. It is, however, safe to say that a period of intensive and remarkably rapid evolution took place between the middle of the seventeenth century and the first quarter of the nineteenth. During this era, the average height of a racehorse increased by six inches, and there were corresponding increases in strength, length of stride and speed.

It was that uncouth, ramshackle monarch James VI who established Newmarket as the racing centre of England, while the incentive to the nobility to breed improved horses was provided by Charles II, who was devoted to racing and was probably happier at Newmarket than anywhere else. After Charles II's death, Tregonwell Frampton was trainer-manager to William III, Queen Anne, George I and George II, and he knew more about breeding and training horses than any man of his day .

Though no one can say with any certainty how the British Thoroughbred was evolved, it is safe to assume that the faster and lighter native breeds were mated with horses imported from the East, from Italy and from Spain. Arabian blood was particularly favourite. Several leading seventeenth century breeders were confident that Arabian stallions got the best racehorses, but a good many breeders used Barbs since the best Arabians were extremely expensive. Barbs came from Barbary, that part of North Africa which comprises modern Tunisia.

The General Stud Book listed 103 stallions which were imported or of wholly foreign pedigree. About half of these were Arabians, the rest Turks or Barbs. Three of them founded dynasties that have survived to modern times – the Darley Arabian, the Byerley Turk and the Godolphin Arabian.

Of the three the Darley Arabian has easily surpassed the other two in numbers, and from him stem the male lines of Blandford, St Simon, Phalaris, Teddy, The Boss, Son-in-Law, and Gainsborough.

The Darley Arabian, a bay with a white blaze and four white feet, was foaled in 1700 and exported to England in 1704 by the British Consul in Aleppo, Mr Richard Darley, who sent him to his brother in Yorkshire. The Darley Arabian lived till he was 30, and it is impossible to exaggerate the extent of his influence.

The origins of the Byerley Turk are more obscure, and he may have been a spoil of war. Colonel Byerley used him as his charger and rode him at the Battle of the Boyne. His sire line has been carried on by The Tetrarch and Tourbillon this century.

The Godolphin Arabian was foaled in 1724 and died at Lord Godolphin's stud, Gogmagog, near Cambridge, at the age of 29. One story related that he was discovered pulling a water-cart in Paris. More probably he was one of four Arabian horses given to the King of France by the Bey of Tunis. Three were turned loose in the Brittany forests, while the fourth was acquired by Mr Edward Coke, who passed him on to Lord Godolphin. The Godolphin Arabian's influence has been great, and in 1891 the editors of the General Stud Book wrote that there 'is not a superior horse now on the Turf without a cross of the Godolphin Arabian, nor has there been for many years past'. He is represented today by the sire line of Hurry On and Precipitation.

Much uncertainty covers the identity of the mares who were the foundation stock of the Thoroughbred. Seventy-eight mares were listed in Volume I of the General Stud Book but this list contained a number of duplications. In any case it is impossible to state with any certainty the origins and pedigrees of these mares.

THOROUGHBRED BREEDERS' ASSOCIATION

The principal object of the Thoroughbred Breeders' Association is to encourage, by means of the provision of educational and research facilities, the science of producing and improving the Thoroughbred horse. The association has its own organization and staff through which breeders, Government departments and other bodies can obtain information and to which members can go for information and advice. Most recent achievements have been to encourage the introduction of the European Breeders' Fund and more opportunities for mares in jump racing.

Address: Stanstead House, The Avenue, Newmarket, Suffolk CB8 9AA (0638-661321). Secretary: Sam Sheppard.

THUNDERHEAD II
(1949, ch c Merry Boy – Herodiade, by Tourbillon)

Thunderhead II was bred in France, where he was trained by Etienne Pollet and won twice. He came to Britain to win the 2,000 Guineas by five lengths at 100-7. He was also second in the French 2,000 Guineas. When his racing days were over, he was exported to South Africa.

THURSBY, Sir George (1869-1941)

An extremely good rider by any standard, Sir George Thursby is the only amateur rider to have been placed in the Derby,

which he achieved when second in 1904 on John o' Gaunt and again on Picton two years later.

TIBERIUS
(1931, br c Foxlaw – Glenabatrick, by Captain Cuttle)

Sir Abe Bailey's Tiberius was a fine stayer, winning the Ascot Gold Cup and Goodwood Cup among his seven successes for £9,565. He was also placed in the Derby and St Leger. He made little mark as a sire except under NH Rules.

TIC-TAC

'Tic-tac' is the system of sign language used by bookmakers' employees to signal the amount of money being wagered on horses in the various enclosures or off the course. They usually wear white gloves and use a well-guarded, pre-arranged code signalled with hands and arms.

TIDE-WAY
(1933, br f Fairway – Drift, by Swynford)

Bred by Lord Derby, Tide-way won three races worth over £10,000, including the 1,000 Guineas. She was dam of Gulf Stream, winner of the Gimcrack Stakes and Eclipse Stakes and second in the Derby.

TIFFIN
(1926, b f Tetratema – Dawnwind, by Sunstar)

Lord Ellesmere's Tiffin was an exceptionally fast and game little filly who remained unbeaten in eight races before an accident in training ended her career. She won five races worth over £13,000 as a two-year-old and headed the Free Handicap. The following season she won all the three races in which she competed, showing superb courage in beating Royal Minstrel in a memorable race for the July Cup. Bad luck dogged her to the end and she died after producing her first foal, Merenda, who was a Royal Ascot winner as a two-year-old.

TIME CHARTER
(1979, b f Saritamer – Centrocon, by High Line)

Time Charter gained a deservedly high and popular reputation with fine efforts in top-class races at the ages of three, four and five, resulting in nine wins for more than £410,000 in first-prize money. She won twice at two years, the Oaks and Champion Stakes at three, the King George VI and Queen Elizabeth Diamond Stakes at four, and the Coronation Cup at five. She was ridden by apprentice Billy Newnes in her first two seasons and, following his injury and later suspension, by Joe Mercer and Steve Cauthen. Time Charter also went close in two other Group One races; she was beaten a little more than a length into fourth place in the 1983 Arc de Triomphe and the following year did not get the run of the race when beaten a neck by Sadler's Wells in the Eclipse Stakes. The only notable produce of her sire Saritamer, Time Charter retired after the 1984 Arc and was sent to Shirley Heights as her first mate.

TO-AGORI-MOU
(1978, br c Tudor Music – Sarah van Fleet, by Cracksman)

To-Agori-Mou, an impressive individual who outraced his modest pedigree, was bought for 20,000gns as a yearling by Guy Harwood for Mrs Andry Muinos, who also had the good fortune to own Ela-Mana-Mou in his early days. To-Agori-Mou won three races as a two-year-old, including the Solario Stakes, and finished second his other two, including to Storm Bird in the Dewhurst Stakes. He remained in the first two as a three-year-old until his ninth race of the season and his first over 10f, in the Champion Stakes. Over a mile he was a tip-top racer, winning the 2,000 Guineas, St James's Palace Stakes, Waterford Crystal Mile and Queen Elizabeth II Stakes. Inferior pedigree probably contributed to failure to sell him as a stallion in Europe, and at the end of 1981 he was

sent to the United States.

TOBOGGAN
(1925, b f Hurry On – Glacier, by St Simon)

Bred by Lord Derby, Toboggan won seven races worth over £25,000, including the Oaks, Coronation Stakes and Jockey Club Stakes. At stud Bobsleigh was the only winner she produced, though her daughter Hydroplane II produced the top-class American horse Citation.

TODD, George Edward (1894-1974)

George Todd was one of the most astute trainers of this century, being a good judge of a yearling and a sound trainer of stayers who was able to maintain the enthusiasm of many horses for several years. He was wounded on the Somme in World War I and entered racing on his return, working with H. Lines for five years and then two years with Tom Coulthwaite. From 1921 he conducted a highly successful 'mixed' stable and over the years a high proportion of his fancied runners 'collected'. He specialized in elderly handicappers who more often than not were ridden by boys rather than leading jockeys. Towards the end of his career, though, he trained some high-class horses and in 1966 won the St Leger and Irish Derby with Sodium. Other good winners included Oncidium (Coronation Cup), Roan Rocket (St James's Palace Stakes and Sussex Stakes), Parthian Glance (Yorkshire Oaks, Park Hill Stakes and Ribblesdale Stakes), Trelawny (Chester Cup, Ascot Stakes twice, Queen Alexandra Stakes twice, Goodwood Cup), Dramatic (Stewards' Cup and Lincolnshire) and River Chanter (Dewhurst Stakes).

He trained at Manton, near Marlborough, from 1947 until his retirement in 1973, only a few months before his death in January the following year.

TOLLER, James Arthur Richard (b. 1954)

Son of the former handicapper and

present Clerk of the Course Charles Toller, James began training at Newmarket in 1980 after learning the trade with Bernard van Cutsem and Luca Cumani in Britain and in the United States and Australia. His first winner was with Mosse at Bath on 1 June 1981, on the course where his father officiates. His best season was 1982 with seven winners.

TOMPKINS, Mark Harding (b. 1951)

Mark Tompkins began training at Newmarket in late October 1979 after the retirement of Ryan Jarvis, to whom he had been assistant for $2\frac{1}{2}$ years. Lusitanica was one of his best early horses, winning seven times in two seasons, including the Tennent Trophy, and finishing second in the Ebor Handicap. His best seasons were 1983 and 1985, with seventeen winners.

TOTE, The: see Horserace Totalisator Board

TOUCHING WOOD (1979, b c Roberto – Mandera, by Vaguely Noble)

Touching Wood became the first British Classic winner for a member of the Maktoum family when he won the St Leger for Maktoum Al-Maktoum. Bought for $200,000 as a yearling and trained by Tom Jones, Touching Wood was placed in his first four races, including second to Golden Fleece in the Derby, before he won his first race, the Welsh Derby. Placed then in the Gordon Stakes and Great Voltigeur Stakes, he ended the season, and his career, by winning the St Leger and the Irish equivalent, the first to do so since Trigo in 1929 and the first Doncaster winner to attempt it in that time. Though at one time it seemed that Touching Wood would continue in training as a four-year-old, he began his first season at his owner's Newmarket stud in 1983.

TRACERY (1909, br c Rock Sand – Topiary, by Orme)

Tracery was bred in America by his owner Mr August Belmont and, brought to Britain, proved top-class, winning six races for £19,717 including the St Leger, Eclipse Stakes, Champion Stakes and St James's Palace Stakes, besides finishing third in the Derby. In the Ascot Gold Cup he was brought down by a man who ran out on to the course. He retired to stud in Britain in 1914 and sired Papyrus (Derby), The Panther (2,000 Guineas) and Transvaal (Grand Prix de Paris). In 1920 he was sold for 53,000gns to Argentina, but after Papyrus had won the Derby in 1923, he was brought back by a British syndicate but died the following year.

TRADE UNIONISM

Racing and the trade unions have not always made perfect bedfellows, especially where trainers and stable lads are concerned; elements in one suspect the other of interfering where it is not required, and in the other they sometimes feel their members are being exploited.

Relations reached their lowest point in 1975, when stable lads at Newmarket belonging to the Transport and General Workers Union, which has had an agreement with the town's trainers since 1937, went on strike as a result of a pay dispute. The strike began on 30 April and ended on 24 July only after the Newmarket Trainers Federation had reversed an earlier decision not to go to arbitration.

The Newmarket strike affected a minority of the town's 600 stable lads and did not gain support in other training areas. It led to some ugly scenes particularly before the 2,000 Guineas at Newmarket. Willie Carson was pulled from his horse by demonstrators, whose presence meant the big race had to be started by flag and who also clashed with racegoers, including some well-known faces from the 'establishment', intent on putting forward their opinions with action rather than words.

The strike ended with an agreement that the previous basic rate of pay, £30.83 a week, would be raised to a minimum of £37 (many stable lads in Newmarket already received more than the basic, hence the lack of majority support). There were soon more far-reaching changes, for in the wake of the strike the Stable Lads Association was founded in Lambourn, the National Joint Council for Stable Staff was set up as a voluntary body to negotiate wages and conditions between trainers and employees, and the insistence of Levy Board chairman Sir Desmond Plummer that the structure for a national minimum wage for all stable staff should be agreed, before £1m of extra prize money would be released, concentrated wavering minds wonderfully.

The NJCSS operates under a chief negotiator, at present Mr Sandy Lamdale, and comprises representatives of the National Trainers Federation, the Transport and General Workers Union and the Stable Lads Association. There is no limit on the numbers each section can send to a meeting, and they meet as and when required, with most deliberation done between September and December in preparation for the 1 February date for an annual agreement. Their findings, which relate to a minimum level and not actual pay, have no legal enforcement, but the Jockey Club's instructions say they are 'satisfied it is in the interest of horse-racing that the terms and conditions of service of employees or those engaged in training race horses should be fair and reasonable'. It is in the Jockey Club's power to withdraw a trainer's licence if he does not comply with the instruction, and a routine check of a certain number of trainers is made each year.

Latest conditions negotiated by the NJCSS include: a national minimum rate for 40 hours for stable staff nineteen years old (eighteen in Newmarket) and over, with one year's service, £83.08 (from 1 February 1985); normal working week 40 hours (excluding meal breaks) from Monday morning to 12.45 p.m. Saturday; one weekend in three off;

overtime paid at time and a half per hour Monday to Saturday, double time per hour Sunday; four weeks paid annual holiday; minimum allowance of £12.75 for two consecutive days working away from home, £16 a day up to a maximum of seven days for racing abroad; ratio of horses to lads generally recommended to be three to one.

The TGWU are also represented among the great majority of starting-stalls handlers employed by Racecourse Technical Services, who also negotiate with the Association of Cinematographic Television and Allied Technicians for camera staff and public-address announcers, and the Association of Scientific, Technical and Managerial Staffs for a small number of workshop employees.

TRAINERS

Every person who wishes to train a horse to run under the Rules of Racing must obtain an annual licence from the stewards of the Jockey Club. For this they pay a fee, at the moment £4 but which the stewards of the Jockey Club decide from time to time, and of which £1 is allocated to the Jockey Club Charities.

Under the Rules, every trainer must conduct his business with reasonable care and skill, and with due regard to the interests of his owners, and the safety of his employees.

Every owner or part-owner who has a horse in his stable must enter into a training agreement which has to be registered at the Racing Calendar Office. This registration gives the trainer certain safeguards concerning the payment of an owner's bills.

When a horse has run under the Rules of Racing and been found on examination to have received a substance (other than a normal nutrient) which could have affected its racing performance at the time of running, the trainer shall be fined not less than £550 or, at the discretion of the stewards of the Jockey Club, his licence may be withdrawn.

Hiring of stable staff is strictly

controlled and trainers cannot take on an employee from another stable without a reference from the trainer concerned, and the stewards of the Jockey Club maintain a register of the names of stable employees.

Applications for a trainer's licence must be accompanied by details of numbers of horses likely to be trained and the establishment at which training will commence. Inspection of the stables takes place before a licence is granted by the Jockey Club. Types of training licence were altered in 1975. Previously a trainer who operated both on the Flat and over jumps had to have separate licences; since 1975 licences have been split into those for Flat races, steeplechases and hurdle races; for Flat races only, and for steeplechases and hurdle races only.

TRAINERS Leading: see Appendix II

TRAINING CENTRES

Training in modern times has tended to become a more centralized affair than it used to be. The maintenance of private gallops has become increasingly expensive, and trainers find it cheaper and more convenient to have their stables at a recognized centre such as Newmarket, Epsom, or the Lambourn district of Berkshire in the South, and Malton or Middleham in the North. There the gallops are maintained and used on a communal basis, trainers usually paying a fee in respect of each horse under their care. In addition, at these centres the best veterinary and transport services are readily available, while trainers and jockeys going to a distant meeting can share the cost of hiring an aircraft.

Apart from a concentration at the centres above, the major pre-war changes have involved the loss of major stables in Scotland, and the growth of important stables in Sussex at Arundel and Pulborough.

In the old days some of the craftier trainers with owners who liked to bet favoured secluded stables in the remoter parts of Salisbury Plain. Secrets could be kept there, particularly as the discipline among employees used to be very strict indeed. Nowadays it is almost impossible to obtain stable labour at any place remote from a town of reasonable size. The lads will not stand it; nor will their wives.

TRANQUIL
(1920, b f Swynford – Serenissima, by Minoru)

Bred by Lord Derby, Tranquil was a very fine performer, winning eight races for almost £22,000, including the 1,000 Guineas, St Leger and Jockey Club Cup. She was not a great success as a broodmare but produced three winners of seven races.

TREE, Arthur Jeremy (b. 1925)

Jeremy Tree served in the Life Guards for four years and after spells in a City merchant bank and as assistant pupil to Dick Warden at Newmarket, he began training in 1952, spending one season at Newmarket before succeeding Noel Murless at Beckhampton the following year.

His first winner was Court Life at Birmingham in April 1952, and three years later he had his first major success, with Double Bore in the Goodwood Cup. His first Classic winner was Only For Life in the 2,000 Guineas for Miss Monica Sheriffe, whose Sharpo he trained to win the William Hill Sprint in three successive years. Tree has also won the Oaks with Juliette Marny and Scintillate, while Known Fact was awarded the 2,000 Guineas on a disqualification. He won the Prix de l'Arc de Triomphe in similar fashion in 1985, when Rainbow Quest passed the post second to Sagace but was awarded the race on the latter's demotion for interference.

Other good horses he has trained include The Elk (Observer Gold Cup), Persian Road (Ebor Handicap), Monet (Stewards' Cup), Gustav (Middle Park Stakes), Double Jump (National Stakes, Prix Robert Papin and Gimcrack Stakes),

Minor Portion (City and Suburban), D'Urberville (King's Stand Stakes), Swing Easy (King's Stand Stakes and Nunthorpe Stakes), John Cherry (Chester Cup and Cesarewitch), Quiet Fling (Coronation Cup), Bright Finish (Yorkshire Cup), Bassenthwaite (Middle Park Stakes) and Valuable Witness (Goodwood Cup).

TRELAWNY
(1956, br g Black Tarquin – Indian Night, by Umidwar)

This famous stayer was bred by the Astor Studs but after winning three races as a three-year-old he was sold for 2,500gns and raced on the Flat trained by Syd Mercer and George Todd, and over hurdles by Fred Rimell. He was probably the most popular horse since Brown Jack, and twice pulled off the double of the Ascot Stakes and Queen Alexandra Stakes at the royal meeting. He also won the Chester Cup, Brown Jack Stakes and Goodwood Cup. Altogether he won eleven races on the Flat worth more than £19,000 in addition to the Spa Hurdle at Cheltenham.

TRETHOWAN, Sir Ian (b. 1922)

A former journalist and television presenter who became director general of the BBC, Sir Ian was appointed chairman of the Betting Levy Board in 1982 and was re-appointed for a further three-year term in 1985 until 30 September 1988.

TRIGO
(1926, b c Blandford – Athasi, by Farasi)

Trigo, owned by Mr W. Barnett and trained at Whatcombe by R.C. Dawson, after being in Ireland as a two-year-old, won the Derby, St Leger and Irish St Leger among his six successes for £27,101. He was a stud failure before his death in 1946.

TRIMDON
(1926, b c Son-in-Law – Trimestral, by William the Third)

Trimdon was bred by Lord Durham and, unraced until the age of four, he became an outstanding stayer, winning five races for £13,705 – the Ascot Gold Cup twice, Gold Vase, Queen's Prize and Yorkshire Cup. A three-parts brother to the Gold Cup winner Foxhunter, he was not a stud success but sired the great French stayer Marsyas II whose record of four victories in the Prix du Cadran (French Gold Cup) is unlikely to be equalled. Trimdon also sired Trimbush, who won fourteen races, including the Doncaster Cup.

TRIPLE CROWN

To earn the mythical 'Triple Crown' a three-year-old must win the 2,000 Guineas, Derby and St Leger. The following have done so:
1853 – West Australian
1865 – Gladiateur
1866 – Lord Lyon
1886 – Ormonde
1891 – Common
1893 – Isinglass
1897 – Galtee More
1899 – Flying Fox
1900 – Diamond Jubilee
1903 – Rock Sand
1915 – Pommern
1917 – Gay Crusader
1918 – Gainsborough
1935 – Bahram
1970 – Nijinsky
Lack of recent winners is an indication of the modern-day specialization, which means the Triple Crown is now rarely attempted.

TRISTAN
(1878, ch c Hermit – Thrift, by Stockwell)

Tristan was an extremely good horse and a very tough one but remarkably bad-tempered. All courses and all distances came alike to him and he won 25 races, including the Gold Cup. At one Royal Ascot meeting he won three long-distance races; shortly after that he won the 6f July Cup. In the nineteenth century horses were frequently more robust and certainly more versatile than they are today. Tristan was at stud in France, Britain and Austria-Hungary, and sired Canterbury Pilgrim, winner of the Oaks and an influential broodmare.

TROUTBECK
(1903, b c Ladas – Rydal Mount, by St Serf)

The Duke of Westminster's Troutbeck was beaten only once in nine races as a three-year-old, in the Derby, but he won the St Leger. He failed as a sire in both Britain and America.

TROY
(1976, b c Petingo – La Milo, by Hornbeam)

A perforated gut took the life of Troy in May 1983, only three months after the abduction of another easy Derby winner, Shergar. Troy was bred at Sir Michael Sobell's Ballymacoll Stud in Ireland and was trained by Dick Hern and ridden by Willie Carson. He raced eleven times, and his eight wins and three places earned a European record of £450,494, leading to his syndication for stud at a further European record valuation of £7.2m. He reached that status by winning two of his four races as a two-year-old and finishing second in the Royal Lodge Stakes, and winning his first six races at three years, including the elusive mile-and-a-half treble of the Derby (the 200th running and by seven lengths), Irish Sweeps Derby (by four lengths) and King George VI and Queen Elizabeth Diamond Stakes (from French-trained Gay Mécène). He then tackled 10½f and won the Benson & Hedges Gold Cup but on his final outing he was beaten when odds-on for the Prix de l'Arc de Triomphe, finishing third to Three Troikas. Troy retired to the Highclere Stud in Berkshire and had four crops to represent him, the last curtailed by his death. He had his first Classic success with Helen Street (Irish Oaks) and also sired Walensee (Prix Vermeille),

Trojan Fen (Queen Anne Stakes) and Ilium (Yorkshire Cup).

TUBING

'Tubing' assists a horse with respiratory trouble. It consists of an operation on the animal's throat, a metal tube being inserted through which it breathes instead of through the normal nasal route. It is a process rarely used nowadays.

TUDOR MELODY
(1956, br c Tudor Minstrel – Matelda, by Dante)

Tudor Melody was one of the bargains of post-war racing, being bought as a yearling for 610gns. He won five races as a two-year-old and was placed top of the Free Handicap. He was then exported to America, where he raced for two seasons, winning twice. He returned to Europe and went to stud in Ireland in 1961, before moving to the National Stud at Newmarket within months of his son Kashmir II winning the 1966 2,000 Guineas. Tudor Melody was put down in August 1978, due to failing health, which had restricted him to eleven mares in each of his last four seasons. His other important winners were Golden Horus and Tudor Music (both Gimcrack Stakes), Magic Flute (Cheveley Park Stakes), Tarim (German Derby) and Welsh Pageant (Lockinge Stakes twice).

TUDOR MINSTREL
(1944, br c Owen Tudor – Sansonnet, by Sansovino)

Tudor Minstrel was bred and owned by Mr J.A. Dewar and was the last of the many great horses trained by Fred Darling. On paper he had a stayer's pedigree, but the dominating influence in his make-up was tremendous speed.

An immensely powerful bay, Tudor Minstrel was unbeaten as a two-year-old, and the following season he won a small race at Bath before carrying off the 2,000 Guineas by eight lengths. Prematurely hailed by the racing Press as 'the horse of the century', he started 7-4 on for the Derby, but failed to stay and finished a moderate fourth behind Pearl Diver. Some people criticized Gordon Richards' riding, saying that, if he had permitted the hard-pulling Tudor Minstrel to stride along in front instead of endeavouring to restrain him, he might have won. That was soon proved invalid as after winning the St James's Palace Stakes at Ascot, Tudor Minstrel was beaten in the Eclipse Stakes by Migoli. No attempt on this occasion was made to restrain Tudor Minstrel, who turned for home six lengths clear but was in trouble 2f from home.

Tudor Minstrel ended his career with eight wins worth £24,629, and up to a mile he was brilliant. Had he been kept to that distance, he might never have been beaten. As a sire he failed to come up to the highest expectations and was never higher in the list than seventh. He was exported to America in 1959 and retired from stud duties in 1970. He sired Classic winners in Toro (French 1,000 Guineas) and Tomy Lee (Kentucky Derby), and his son Tudor Melody was a top-class racehorse and sire.

TULK, Paul (b. 1938)

Paul Tulk was apprenticed to 'Sam' Armstrong from 1953 to 1959 and remains associated with that Newmarket stable as assistant to Armstrong's son Robert. Tulk rode his first winner on Carpet Light at Worcester in June 1955, and his most important wins came in the next two years, on Curry (Cesarewitch) and Ennis (Nunthorpe Stakes). His best season was 1967 when he rode 30 winners. He was retained by owner Robin McAlpine for twelve years until he went freelance in 1970, and spent some time in the Far East before his return to Britain in 1976.

TULYAR
(1949, br c Tehran – Neocracy, by Nearco)

Tulyar was the fifth and last of the Aga Khan's Derby winners. Bred by his owner, he was by the St Leger winner Tehran, who was otherwise not greatly distinguished as a sire. Trained by

Marcus Marsh, he was no more than a useful stayer as a two-year-old, his main success being in the Buggins Farm Nursery at Haydock Park. In the Free Handicap he was rated 19lb inferior to Windy City.

As a three-year-old he was a very different proposition and was never beaten, winning in succession the 7f Henry VIII Stakes at Hurst Park, Ormonde Stakes at Chester, Lingfield Derby Trial, Derby, Eclipse Stakes, King George VI and Queen Elizabeth Stakes and St Leger. He may rarely have been spectacular, but as a three-year-old no , rival ever got to the bottom of him. He won £76,417 from nine wins, beating the British earnings record so long held by Isinglass, who raced till he was five.

The Aga Khan sold Tulyar to the Irish National Stud for approximately £250,000. In 1955 he was sold to an American sydicate. He left Ireland in 1956 and became gravely ill soon afterwards. At one time his life was despaired of but he recovered. He was a disappointing stallion, though after his death in 1972 he became better noted as a broodmare sire. His best racers were the fillies Ginetta (French 1,000 Guineas), Fiorentina (Irish 1,000 Guineas) and Castle Forbes (top two-year-old filly in USA), in addition to the Eclipse runner-up Tulyartos.

TURKHAN
(1937, b c Bahram – Theresina, by Diophon)

Bred by the Aga Khan, Turkhan won three races for £5,980, including the St Leger and Irish Derby, and was second in the Derby. He was not a great success as a sire, but his mares did quite well. He was exported to France in 1952.

TWILIGHT ALLEY
(1959, ch c Alycidon – Crepuscule, by Mieuxcé)

Bred by the Sassoon Studs, Twilight Alley was a big chestnut, standing well over seventeen hands, three-parts brother to the dual Classic winner Crepello. He took a long time to come to hand and never ran as a two-year-old. At the age of three he won his only race, the Cranbourn Chase Stakes at Ascot. He ran three times the following season, finishing second in the Henry II Stakes, winning the Ascot Gold Cup and breaking down in the King George VI and Queen Elizabeth Stakes in which he split a pastern and had to be pulled up. He retired to the Beech House Stud, Newmarket, at a fee of 400gns but cut little ice as a stallion, his most notable success being with Midnight Court (Cheltenham Gold Cup).

U

UDAIPUR
(1929, br f Blandford – Uganda, by Bridaine)

Bred by the Aga Khan, Udaipur won four races for £15,047, including the Oaks and Coronation Stakes. She bred seven winners before her death in 1949, including Umiddad (Gold Cup) and Dust Devil (Jockey Club Stakes).

UJIJI
(1939, b c Umidwar – Theresina, by Blandford)

Bred by the Aga Khan and sold for 400gns privately as a yearling, Ujiji was a half-brother to Turkhan. He won eight races for £3,634, including the Gold Cup, and was third in the Derby. An undistinguished sire, he was exported to Sweden.

UMIDDAD
(1940, b c Dastur – Udaipur, by Blandford)

Umiddad was bred by the Aga Khan and won seven races for £3,942, including the Dewhurst Stakes and Gold Cup, and was second in the Derby. He did little good as a sire either in Britain or later in France.

UNDER STARTER'S ORDERS

The horses come under the starter's orders when they are all in the starting-stalls or, if the race is to be started by flag, when the starter has taken up his position. At this stage the starter orders that a white flag be raised, and from this point all bets stand. A horse withdrawn after it has come under starter's orders is deemed to be a loser.

UNSADDLING ENCLOSURE

The winner and placed horses are unsaddled after a race in an enclosed area immediately in front of the weighing-room, known as the unsaddling enclosure or winners' enclosure.

USHER, Mark Donald Ian (b. 1958)

Mark Usher was assistant trainer to Barry Hills, Robert Armstrong and Henry Candy before he took out a trainer's licence in 1983 at stables in Lambourn leased from Tom Marshall on his retirement. His first win was with Portogon at Thirsk on 21 May 1983, and the game front-runner continued to be a mainstay of the stable, which had six winners in its first season, twelve in its second and nineteen in its third.

V

VAGUELY NOBLE
(1965, b c Vienna – Noble Lassie, by Nearco)

Vaguely Noble was bred by Major L.B. Holliday, who died before he ran, and raced for Mr Brook Holliday. As a two-year-old, trained by W. Wharton, his successes included the Observer Gold Cup, which he won by seven lengths. In view of demands for death duties, less than two months afterwards he came up for sale at Newmarket, and although he held no Classic engagements, he was bought for the record public auction price for a thoroughbred of 136,000gns. The purchaser was an American plastic surgeon, Dr Robert Franklyn, who the following spring sold a half-share to another American, Nelson Bunker Hunt.

After the sale Vaguely Noble went for a time to P.J. Prendergast in Ireland, but he was soon transferred to Etienne Pollet in France. The main objective for 1968 was Europe's richest racing prize, the Prix de l'Arc de Triomphe, and Vaguely Noble justified his enormous purchase price by winning it in the manner of an outstanding racehorse.

That was the end of his racing career, his six wins having earned the equivalent of £148,641, and he retired to stud in the United States. He was not the type to sire fast-maturing stock but it was fortunate that many of his produce found their way to Europe, and he was an immediate success at stud, becoming leading sire in Britain in 1973 and 1974. His Classic winners are: Dahlia (Irish Oaks, as well as King George VI and Queen Elizabeth Stakes twice), Empery (Derby), Exceller (Prix Royal-Oak, as well as Coronation Cup and several races in USA), Gonzales (Irish St Leger) and Noble Dancer (Norwegian St Leger). His daughter Nobiliary was second in the Derby, and other good winners sired by Vaguely Noble include Noble Decree (Observer Gold Cup), Ace of Aces (Sussex Stakes) and Lemhi Gold (Jockey Club Gold Cup in New York).

Empery and Exceller have been joined by Gay Mécène and Royal and Regal as sons of Vaguely Noble who have sired at least one Pattern-race winner in Europe. The Classic winners Touching Wood, L'Emigrant and Golden Fleece, as well as the top American filly Sabin, are out of Vaguely Noble mares.

VALETS

Jockeys' valets form a valuable section of the racing community. They travel from meeting to meeting, look after the jockeys, keep their equipment in order and provide any that is required. They are licensed by the Jockey Club but are paid by the jockeys on a scale according to the number of rides they have in a day. At one time it was difficult for an outsider to become a valet as the business was often kept within families, but today at least two former jockeys have taken up the trade. In recent years there has been a trend for a small number of jockeys to look after themselves and dispense with the service and cost of a valet.

VALORIS
(1963, br f Tiziano – Vali, by Sunny Boy III)

Charles Clore's Valoris won only two races, both Classics, the Irish 1,000 Guineas and Epsom Oaks. Trained in Ireland by Vincent O'Brien, she was ridden by Lester Piggott at Epsom, and his decision to take the mount rather than ride Varinia for Noel Murless led to his break with the Newmarket stable. She has been a good broodmare, her daughters Vincennes and Val's Girl finishing second in the Irish and Epsom Oaks respectively, and her son Valinsky finishing second in the Grand Prix de Paris.

VASEY, Melton Avril (1906-86)

The famous Northern family of Vasey severed its link with racing when Avril Vasey retired from training at Middleham in 1972. He rode under National Hunt Rules from 1923 till 1932 and for a time he assisted his father Melton Vasey. Although he held a jumping trainer's licence as far back as 1925, it was not until 1952 that he began to train on the Flat. His successes included the Ayr Gold Cup and Free Handicap.

VAUCLUSE (1912, b f Dark Ronald – Valve, by Velasquez)

Owned and bred by Lord Rosebery, Vaucluse won one race, the 1,000 Guineas. She bred five winners including a very good staying mare in Bongrace.

VAYRANN (1978, br c Brigadier Gerard – Val Divine, by Val de Loir)

Vayrann had his finest hour when he won the Champion Stakes as a three-year-old, though his victory was not confirmed for eight months and was in doubt for some time after that. The Champion Stakes was the last of five wins for the colt owned by his breeder, the Aga Khan, and trained by François Mathet, but traces of a prohibited substance, anabolic steroids, were found in a routine urine sample taken after the Newmarket race. Disqualification looked automatic under the Jockey Club's strict rules on the subject, but the disciplinary committee of the Jockey Club, at their inquiry on 7 June 1982, were unable to find evidence that the substance had been administered to Vayrann; they held that it could have been self-produced (though they were unable to say definitely that it was) and that no breach of the rules had been proved. Vayrann kept the race. He remained in training as a four-year-old but in his second race broke down on his off-fore and was retired to stud in France to stand his first season in 1983.

VEDAS (1902, b or br c Florizel II – Agnostic, by Rosicrucian)

Mr W.F. de Wend-Fenton's Vedas, trained by W. Robinson, won the 2,000 Guineas. Because of injury he was unable to compete in the Derby but he resumed racing the following year and won two handicaps.

VERDICT (1920, b f Shogun – Finale, by Pericles)

Lord Coventry's Verdict was doubly half-bred, both her sire Shogun and her dam Finale being so classified, and it was not until 1969 that her family was allowed into the Stud Book. Verdict was a good, game mare and won eight races, including the Cambridgeshire, in which she beat the French horse Epinard in a memorable race, and the Coronation Cup. At stud she bred Quashed, one of the gamest mares ever seen on the British Turf and winner of the Oaks and Ascot Gold Cup, and her family has included two fine sprinters in Lucasland and So Blessed, both winners of the July Cup.

VERNEUIL (1874, ch c Mortemer – Regalia, by Stockwell)

At Royal Ascot in 1878 the French-bred horse Verneuil, trained by Tom Jennings, won the Gold Vase, Gold Cup and Alexandra Plate, all run over two miles or more, without being headed for a single stride in any of those races. Horses had to be tough in those days!

VETERINARY OFFICER and VETERINARY SURGEON

A veterinary officer and his assistant at a race-meeting are licensed officials of the Jockey Club who, for example, act on their behalf in the collection of samples for forensic analysis. The veterinary surgeon, on the other hand, is engaged by the executive of the racecourse and is responsible for the treatment of sick or injured horses.

VICTORIA CLUB

A London sporting club, whose members are chiefly bookmakers and professional backers. The Victoria Club call-over, at which prices for forthcoming big races were set, gradually lost its importance in the late 1960s, when the major bookmaking firms began to advertise their ante-post prices daily in the Sporting Press

VIGORS, Nicholas Ashmead Cliffe (b. 1947)

Nick Vigors, a nephew of the bloodstock agent and stud-owner Tim Vigors, assisted Geoffrey Brooke and Jeremy Tree before he took out his first training licence in 1970 near Lewes. He had his first win with Ballynockan at Brighton on 27 May 1970. The following year he moved to Upper Lambourn. His best horse has been All Friends, twice winner of the Diomed Stakes at Epsom, and his best season was 1981, with 21 winners.

VIMY
(1952, b c Wild Risk – Mimi, by Black Devil)

Bred in France by Pierre Wertheimer, Vimy won $3\frac{1}{2}$ races, including the King George VI and Queen Elizabeth Stakes, and was beaten a short head in the French Derby. He was bought by the Irish National Stud but was not a great success and was exported to Japan in 1964. He sired the Eclipse winner Khalkis, Vimadee (Irish St Leger) and the dams of Busted and High Top.

VIRAGO
(1851, ch f Pyrrhus the First – Virginia, by Rowton)

Virago was a famous filly who as a three-year-old won those two popular handicaps at Epsom, the 10f City and Suburban and the $2\frac{1}{4}$m Great Metropolitan, on the same afternoon. She later won the 1,000 Guineas, Nassau Stakes, Goodwood Cup and Doncaster Cup, proving herself perhaps the greatest racemare of the nineteenth century. She bred the Cesarewitch winner Thalestris.

VITIGES
(1973, ch c Phaeton – Vale, by Verrières)

Vitigès, who cost the equivalent of £6,600 as a yearling, divided his racing career between France and Britain and has done the same at stud. He was trained by George Philippeau to win four of his seven races as a two-year-old, including the Prix Robert Papin and Prix Morny, and one of his first seven, the Prix Djebel, as a three-year-old, when he also finished second to Wollow in the 2,000 Guineas and sixth in the Derby. He came to Britain to be trained by Peter Walwyn for his last race in 1976, and won the Champion Stakes by heading Rose Bowl close home. Vitigès disappointed in his three races as a four-year-old and retired to stud at Newmarket in 1978. He was repatriated to France in 1983, with Tants (Lingfield Oaks Trial) his most significant winner.

VOLODYOVSKI
(1898, b or br c Florizel II – La Reine, by Rosicrucian)

Known by the bookmakers as 'Bottle of Whisky', Volodyovski won five races as a two-year-old but only one afterwards, the Derby, for the American Mr W.C. Whitney, trained by an American John Higgins, and ridden by an American Lester Reiff. He was narrowly and unluckily beaten in a very rough race for the St Leger. He failed completely as a sire.

VOLTIGEUR
(1847, b c Voltaire – Martha Lynn, by Mulatto)

One of the best horses ever trained in the North, Lord Zetland's Voltigeur won his only race as a two-year-old, and on his next outing won the Derby. He won the St Leger on a run-off and two days later beat The Flying Dutchman in the Doncaster Cup. From Voltigeur the mighty St Simon was descended in tail-male.

VUILLIER, Colonel Jean-Joseph (d. 1931)

Colonel Vuillier, a French cavalry officer who became an expert on bloodstock breeding, closely examined the pedigrees of 650 leading racehorses from the early days of the sport of racing down to the 1920s and from his observations made certain conclusions.

The pedigree of each horse under his scrutiny was examined down to the twelfth generation. There are 4,096 individuals in the twelfth generation and to each of these Colonel Vuillier allowed a value of one. Two points were allowed to each of the 2,048 individuals in the eleventh generation, and so on down to the two parents, who each had a value of 2,048. By applying this method to the 650 horses selected, he obtained an aggregate value for each ancestor and calculated not merely the individuals that ought to appear in the pedigree of 'a standard good horse' but also their proportions or 'dosages'. Put in the briefest and simplest terms, he reckoned that, when a stallion or mare was lacking in any of the constituents of 'a standard good pedigree', a mate ought to be selected that would correct the 'dosage' in the expected offspring. Colonel Vuillier died in 1931 soon after the publication of his last book, *Les Croisements Rationnels dans la Race Pure*.

W

WAFFLES
(1917, b f Buckwheat – Lady Mischief, by St Simon)

Waffles was a most influential mare, though she herself was never broken. She stood barely fifteen hands. Her first foal, Bunworry, won four races and was then sent to India before ending in Federico Tesio's Italian stud where she bred Bernina (Italian 2,000 Guineas, 1,000 Guineas and Oaks and grandam of the Gold Cup winner Botticelli), Bozzetto (three times champion sire in Italy), Brueghel (a leading sire in Australia) and Saucy Silver, dam of an American Grand National winner.

Waffles bred two British Classic winners, Manna (2,000 Guineas and Derby) and Sandwich (St Leger). She also bred the notorious Tuppence who was the top-priced yearling of 1931, was heavily backed in Hyperion's Derby, never won a race and was sent to Russia.

WAINWRIGHT, Stanley (b. 1928)

'Snowy' Wainwright took out a licence to train in 1966, in Malton, where he had served his apprenticeship with Captain Charles Elsey and been travelling head lad to Rufus Beasley. His first winner was Nevison's Lad at Hamilton in June 1966, and his biggest success was with Music Boy in the 1975 Gimcrack Stakes. He had his licence withdrawn for five years in 1980, following a Jockey Club inquiry into the running of Foresters Lad, beaten in a Beverley seller in June 1980.

WALDRON, Philip (b. 1959)

Apprenticed to Ian Balding from 1965, Philip Waldron stayed with the yard for nine years, during which he rode his first winner on Aldie at Bath on 5 July 1969, was champion apprentice in 1970 with 59 winners and had his best season, with 64 winners, in 1971. He left to become first jockey to Henry Candy in 1975 and did particularly well on Master Willie (Benson & Hedges Gold Cup, Coronation Cup, Eclipse), Centroline (Jockey Club Cup), Assured (Cesarewitch), Quay Line (Park Hill Stakes), Nicholas Bill (Jockey Club Cup) and Wind and Wuthering (Dewhurst) before leaving the yard at the end of 1981 for a retainer to ride Esal Commodities horses. The move did not work out well; Waldron soon lost the support of one of the firm's trainers, and Time Charter emerged at the Candy stable. Waldron continued to ride for Geoff Lewis, for whom he won the Grand Prix de Paris in 1983 on Yawa, but the following year his score dipped to 23, his lowest since his first season as an apprentice, and in 1985 it fell to eighteen.

WALK-OVER

A race in which only a single horse is declared a runner is known as a walk-over. The jockey of the horse in question must weigh out, mount at the appointed time, canter past the stands and then return to the unsaddling enclosure where he must unsaddle the horse and then be weighed in. The owner of the horse takes the prize money allotted for the other places.

WALLABY II
(1955, b c Fast Fox – Wagging Tail, by Tourbillon)

Bred in France by Baron Geoffroy de Waldner, Wallaby II was beaten favourite for the Epsom Derby but won the French St Leger and as a four-year-old won the Ascot Gold Cup, just beating Alcide. He was sent to Japan as a stallion and died there in 1967.

WALLINGTON, Harold George (1898-1972)

Harold Wallington rode many winners under National Hunt Rules before taking out a licence to train in 1937 at Epsom. He had considerable successes in important handicaps, winning the Royal Hunt Cup and William Hill Gold Cup with Faultless Speech, the Cambridgeshire and William Hill Gold Cup with Hasty Cloud, and the Victoria Cup (twice) with Alf's Caprice. He retired in 1969, passing control to his son Harold, and died in August 1972.

WALLINGTON, Harold (1939-78)

Assistant to his father from 1963, Harold Wallington took over the licence in 1969 but gave up the Epsom stables in 1973 because of estate duty commitments and became secretary to the Racehorse Owners' Association. His biggest success as a trainer was to emulate his father's success in the Victoria Cup win with Mon Plaisir. He was found drowned in August 1978.

WALLS, Tom Kirby (1883-1949)

The son of a builder and for a short time a constable in the Metropolitan Police, Tom Walls went on the stage in 1905 and became a highly successful light comedian, earning immense popularity in the series of Aldwych farces in which he appeared with Ralph Lynn and Robertson Hare. His first managerial venture was a farce aptly named *Tons of Money* which ran for two years. He later became a director and star in films.

He was always devoted to sport, to racing in particular, and trained a small string of horses at Epsom. His big triumph was to own and train the 1932 Derby winner April the Fifth. It gave him almost equal pleasure to train Crafty Alice, on whom his son, then an officer in the 5th Inniskilling Dragoon Guards, won the Grand Military Gold Cup at Sandown.

WALWYN, Fulke (b. 1910)

Fulke Walwyn was for a brief period a regular soldier in the 9th Lancers. He was a top-class rider under National Hunt Rules, first as an amateur and later as a professional, winning the Grand National in 1936 on Reynoldstown. He has proved an outstanding trainer of chasers and hurdlers and at one period trained Flat-racers for Miss Dorothy Paget, for whom he won the Doncaster Cup and Queen Alexandra Stakes with Aldborough.

WALWYN, Peter Tyndall (b. 1933)

Peter Walwyn was educated at Charterhouse, and entered racing in 1953 as assistant for three years to Geoffrey Brooke. He then helped his cousin Mrs Helen Johnson Houghton until taking out a licence in October 1960 to train at Lambourn. In 1965 he moved to his present stables at Seven Barrows. A great enthusiast and a tremendously hard worker, he has developed his stable from very small numbers into one of the best in the country, becoming leading trainer in 1974, when he won the Oaks with Polygamy, and 1975, when he won the Derby with Grundy. His other British Classic winner is Humble Duty (1,000 Guineas). He has a good record with fillies, including Mabel, Lucyrowe, May Hill, Frontier Goddess and Pasty, while his top-class colts have also included Crozier, Orange Bay, Oats and Classic Example (all Jockey Club Stakes), Habat (Middle Park Stakes), Record Token (Victoria Cup and Vernons Sprint), Formidable (Middle Park Stakes), Lunchtime (Dewhurst Stakes), Linden Tree (Observer Gold Cup), Stalker (Gimcrack and Middle Park Stakes) and, the most unfortunate of them all, Rock Roi, who, though he won the Goodwood and Doncaster Cups, was twice disqualified after passing the post first in the Ascot Gold Cup, once for traces of a prohibited painkiller in his urine sample and once for hampering the runner-up.

Walwyn has always displayed intense loyalty to his stable jockeys, notably Duncan Keith and Pat Eddery, and he has been well served by head lads who have become successful trainers in their own right, such as Ray Laing and Matt McCormack. His best season was 1975, with 121 winners.

WARNING OFF

When anyone commits a breach of the Rules of Racing, the Jockey Club stewards have the power to declare him, or her, a disqualified person, the official term for being 'warned off'. Anyone reported to the Jockey Club by Tattersalls Committee shall be declared a disqualified person.

A disqualified person cannot act as a steward or official at any recognized race meeting, or act as an authorized agent. He cannot enter, run, train or ride a horse in a race. He cannot enter any racecourse premises, and he can be employed in a racing stable only by permission of the Jockey Club stewards. He cannot be involved in the syndication of racehorses.

WARWICK

This Midlands course provides opportunities for moderate horses to make some contribution towards their keep. It is a broad, oval, left-handed circuit of $1\frac{3}{4}$m with a run-in of $2\frac{1}{2}$f. The 5f course has a pronounced left-handed elbow where it links up with the round course on the home turn. The elbow naturally confers an advantage on horses drawn with low numbers.

In 1985, the course brought together Lester Piggott and John Francome for the first, and only, time as jockeys in a match race that drew a crowd of more than 7,000 on a wet Saturday night.

WATERLOO
(1969, ch f Bold Lad (Ire) – Lakewoods, by Hyperion)

Bred by the Stanley family, Waterloo gave trainer Bill Watts and sire Bold Lad (Ire) their first Classic winner when beating Marisela in the 1,000 Guineas. She had won four of her six races as a two-year-old over sprint distances, including the Queen Mary Stakes and Cheveley Park Stakes, and after the Guineas she won the Falmouth Stakes at Newmarket but was second in the Coronation Stakes at Royal Ascot and a lesser race at York. At the end of her three-year-old career she was sold to the United States, where she has bred several winners, including Water Woo (successful in France) and Water Cay (winner of the 1985 Donnington Castle Stakes in Britain).

WATLING STREET
(1939, b c Fairway – Ranaï, by Rabelais)

Watling Street was the third and last Derby winner owned by the seventeenth Earl of Derby, He won a war-substitute Derby at Newmarket in 1942. He was not a success as a sire in Britain. In 1951 he was exported to the United States but died within a year of his arrival.

WATTS, John (1861-1902)

Jack Watts was one of the best riders in the late Victorian era. He won nineteen Classics, including the St Leger five times, and the 1,000 and 2,000 Guineas, and Derby four times each. He won the Derby on Merry Hampton (1887), Sainfoin (1890), Ladas (1894) and Persimmon (1896). He received his early schooling from Tom Cannon, and his style, quiet, cool-headed and unspectacular, reflected the methods of his tutor. He was extremely reserved in manner and even after winning the Derby on Persimmon in the royal colours barely permitted himself the luxury of a transitory smile. He founded a remarkable line of trainers, since his son, grandson and great-grandson have all trained at Newmarket.

WATTS, John Evelyn (1887-1959)

John Watts was the son of Jack Watts, the Victorian jockey. After a short riding career he started training at Newmarket in 1907. In 1911 he went to Germany to manage a stable associated with the German Government's stud, but returned to Britain just before the outbreak of war, in which he served overseas with the Suffolk Yeomanry.

In 1922 he moved to Primrose Cottage, Newmarket, to train for Mr Frank Curzon, who controlled numerous London theatres, and for him won the 1927 Derby with Call Boy. When Mr Curzon died, a few weeks after the Derby, Watts returned to his original stable at Lansdowne House.

In 1935 Watts moved to France to train for M. Boussac, with whose famous mare Corrida, who whose destined to be stolen by the Germans and was never recovered, he won the Prix de l'Arc de Triomphe (twice), Grand Prix de Marseille (twice), Berlin Grosser Preis, Ostend Grand National, Prix du Président de la République and Hardwicke Stakes at Ascot.

For a second time war interrupted Watts' career in Europe. He returned to Britain and from 1942 till he retired ten years later trained for Mr H.J. Joel, for whom he won the 1,000 Guineas with Picture Play.

WATTS, John Frederick (b. 1911)

The third generation of the Watts family of Newmarket trainers was also known as Jack. Having been assistant to his father, as well as Colledge Leader and William Pratt, and served for five years in the RAF Regiment during the war, he took out a licence to train in 1950. He succeeded George Colling as Lord Derby's trainer and for his patron trained Alcove (Cesarewitch) and Tudor Treasure (St James's Palace Stakes). The arrangement terminated in 1963, the year before he won the St Leger with Mr Charles Engelhard's Indiana.

Other good horses Watts trained before his retirement in 1973 were Super Sam (Extel Handicap), Visp (Queen Mary Stakes), Ovaltine (Ebor and Goodwood Cup) and Black Prince II (third in Derby).

WATTS, John William (b. 1942)

Bill Watts, son of John Frederick Watts, became the fourth generation of his family to train at Newmarket when, after a brief career with Raceform, he took

charge of his father's overflow yard in 1965 and two years later started on his own account. He trained at Newmarket for only three seasons before moving to Richmond, Yorkshire, in December 1970. His first winners as a trainer came on 6 April 1968, when Prospect Pleases won over hurdles at Leicester and Rasping was successful on the Flat at Catterick.

His first major success came in his last year at Newmarket, with Calpurnius in the Royal Hunt Cup, but in his first year in Yorkshire he won the Cheveley Park Stakes with Waterloo, who went on to win the following year's 1,000 Guineas. In 1978 he sent out Mountain Cross to take both the Ascot Stakes and the Queen Alexandra Stakes at the royal meeting. Numerically his best season was 1977, with 57 winners, but his richest success came in 1985 when Teleprompter won the Arlington Million in Chicago.

WAUGH, Jack Alfred James (b. 1911)

From 1927 to 1932 Jack Waugh assisted his father, R.T. (Tom) Waugh, who was then training at Newmarket, while from 1932 to 1939 he was with Basil Jarvis. After three years' service in the Royal Artillery during the war, he took out a licence to train on the retirement of his uncle Dawson Waugh at the end of 1942. He followed the family tradition by being unspectacular, highly conscientious and an excellent stableman. Among the scores of good races he won were the July Cup (twice), Cheveley Park Stakes, Ribblesdale Stakes (twice), Wokingham Stakes, Coventry Stakes, Queen Mary Stakes, Royal Lodge Stakes, Park Hill Stakes and News of the World Stakes. His outstanding horses included Matador, Lucasland, Queensberry, Amerigo, Almiranta and Star Moss. Waugh gave up training in 1970 and became stud manager for the Macdonald-Buchanan family.

WAUGH, John Alexander (b. 1931)

John Waugh is the son of Alec Waugh, who trained in Germany prior to World War I and in Austria and Germany from

1920 to 1933, when he returned to Britain. John Waugh assisted his father for a time at Newmarket and was then assistant to George Colling from 1951 to 1957 and to Reg Day from 1958 to 1960. From 1960 to 1970 he trained at Fitzroy House, Newmarket, for Sir Robin McAlpine and family and on relinquishing his licence continued to manage their stud. In 1974 he also became manager of the Someries Stud in Newmarket.

WAUGH, Mathew Dawson (1872-1955)

Dawson Waugh, named after his godfather, the famous Mathew Dawson, was a son of James Waugh. His brother Willie succeeded John Porter at Kingsclere, two other brothers trained at Newmarket, and a sister was mother of that fine trainer Frank Butters.

Dawson Waugh assisted John Porter for some years and then trained in Hungary for a spell. In 1903 he became private trainer at Newmarket to Mr W. Raphael, for whom he won the 1,000 Guineas and Derby in 1912 with the grey filly Tagalie, and the 2,000 Guineas in 1913 with Louvois. Waugh eventually parted company with Mr Raphael, and after World War I his chief patrons were Sir Edward Hulton, for whom he won the Oaks with Straitlace, and Lord Howard de Walden. Little interested in betting, he was a man of great kindliness and the utmost integrity. There was no stable where apprentices were better cared for, and among his protégés were Harry Blackshaw and Joe Sime.

WAUGH, Thomas Alexander (b. 1915)

Tom Waugh, younger brother of Jack Waugh, assisted his father, R.T. Waugh, as well as both Fred and Frank Butters, and Harvey Leader before in 1956 he set up on his own at Newmarket. He trained Privy Councillor, winner in 1962 of the Free Handicap and 2,000 Guineas. His best subsequent season was 1971, when he won the Northumberland Plate with Tartar Prince and the Flying Childers Stakes with Rose Dubarry. He retired from training at the end of the 1980 season.

WAVERTREE, William Hall Walker, Lord (1856-1933)

Lord Wavertree, formerly Colonel W. Hall Walker, was an eccentric, somewhat peppery individual who was rarely satisfied for long with his jockey or his trainer. A fervent student of the stars, he observed their course with the closest attention, and all his important decisions were based on what they appeared to foretell. Unfortunately they advised him to sell Prince Palatine, who proceeded to win the St Leger and two Ascot Gold Cups. Lord Wavertree bred the 2,000 Guineas and Derby winner Minoru, who was leased for racing to King Edward VII. He presented Tully to the British Government as a National Stud (it is now the Irish National Stud), and it was his flow of eloquent persuasiveness that induced the Aga Khan to take up racing on a princely scale.

WEATHERBY, E.W. (1905-67)

Bill Weatherby became secretary to the Jockey Club and Keeper of the Match Book in 1953. The previous occupant of the post had been Sir Francis Weatherby, who in turn had succeeded Bill Weatherby's father.

In the 1960s Bill Weatherby was at the centre of the many changes that were taking place in British racing. All the reforms – in particular the overnight declaration of runners – threw more and more work on the firm of Weatherbys' and called for an ever-increasing degree of modernization and mechanization. Bill Weatherby, the most loyal and conscientious of men, was under a considerable strain, and his health began to suffer. In 1967 he collapsed and died at London Airport on his way to see the Irish Derby.

WEATHERBY, Sir Francis (1885-1969)

Sir Francis Weatherby served with the Oxfordshire Yeomanry in World War I. A distinguished cricketer in his youth, he succeeded Mr Mansfield Weatherby as secretary to the Jockey Club in 1930, and held the post until 1952, when he was elected an honorary member of the Jockey Club. He did much to keep racing ticking over during World War II.

WEATHERBY, Simon Maxwell (1938-83)

On the retirement of Peter Weatherby in 1972, Simon Weatherby became the youngest member of the distinguished family to be appointed secretary to the Jockey Club, at the age of 34. A skilled administrator, he continued to work through a long and painful illness until his death in January 1983.

WEATHERBY & SONS

Messrs Weatherby and Sons, whose administrative headquarters are on a modern site in Wellingborough, Northants, and also occupy offices at 42 Portman Square, London W1, act as agents to the Jockey Club. A member of the Weatherby family held office as secretary to the Jockey Club continuously from 1770 until Simon Weatherby's death in 1983, when he was succeeded by Christopher Foster. As well as providing the secretariat for the Jockey Club, they are publishers, on behalf of the Jockey Club, of the *Racing Calendar* and proprietors and compilers of the *General Stud Book*, the authoritative register of all British and Irish thoroughbred bloodstock.

Over the years the continuity of government with regard to racing has been supplied by members of the Weatherby family, whose role in Turf affairs has been compared with that of those invaluable civil servants who serve and advise successive members of the Cabinet. As a family, the Weatherbys possess qualities associated with the best type of civil servant, too: experience, discretion, loyalty, a dislike of publicity and, in most cases, a Winchester education. Like civil servants, they are frequently subjected to criticism and it is periodically alleged that they conduct their immensely profitable business in a somewhat rigid and old-fashioned manner. They are also occasionally accused of being allergic to change or innovation in the conduct of the sport.

Whatever the justice of these complaints, the Weatherby family has played an important and estimable part in the development and control of racing in this country and they can justly claim to be, in the words of a modern racing historian, 'the very machinery of the Turf'.

WEBSTER, Stuart Graham (b. 1957)

Stuart Webster was apprenticed to Tommy Fairhurst, for whom he rode his first winner, Hei'land Jamie at Pontefract on 20 May 1974. His best season came as an apprentice, with 25 winners in 1976, and two years after that he turned freelance in the North.

WEIGHING-ROOM

The Jockey Club have laid down strict rules about who shall enter the racecourse building known as the weighing-room, where jockeys change and prepare for a race and are weighed in and out. Unless special permission is granted by the stewards, the only persons allowed into the weighing-room are officials of the meeting, the owner, trainer and rider, or anyone having care of a horse in a race, and jockeys' valets. There are even more stringent rules applied to the riders' dressing-rooms, which are forbidden to all but officials of the meeting, riders and their valets.

WEIGHT, Heaviest recorded

At York in 1788 Mr Maynard's mare beat Mr Baker's horse in a 1m match for 100gns, both competitors carrying 30 stone.

WEIGHTS AND PENALTIES

Weights carried in each race are determined either by the conditions of the event, which stipulate the weights according to age, sex, races won or prize money won, or a combination; or by the handicapper, in the case of such races. It is the trainer's responsibility to see that his horse carries the correct weight.

Minimum weights carried on the Flat have changed over the years. In 1925, for example, the minimum weight was 6st,

ALLOWANCE, ASSESSED IN LB, WHICH 3 YEAR OLDS WILL RECEIVE FROM
4 YEAR OLDS, AND 2 YEAR OLDS WILL RECEIVE FROM 3 YEAR OLDS

		MARCH APRIL		MAY		JUNE		JULY		AUGUST		SEPT.		OCT.		NOV.
		March & 1-15	16-30	1-15	16-31	1-15	16-30	1-15	16-31	1-15	16-31	1-15	16-30	1-15	16-31	
5 furlongs	2	32	31	29	27	26	25	25	23	21	20	19	18	17	16	15
	3	12	12	11	10	9	8	7	6	5	4	3	2	1	—	—
6 furlongs	2	—	—	30	29	29	28	27	26	26	24	22	21	21	20	18
	3	15	14	13	12	11	10	9	8	7	6	5	4	3	2	1
7 furlongs	2	—	—	—	—	—	—	—	—	—	—	24	23	23	22	21
	3	16	15	14	13	12	11	10	9	8	7	6	5	4	3	2
1 mile	2	—	—	—	—	—	—	—	—	—	—	27	27	26	25	24
	3	18	17	16	15	14	13	12	11	10	9	8	7	6	5	4

ALLOWANCE, ASSESSED IN LB, WHICH 3 YEAR OLDS WILL RECEIVE FROM 4 YEAR OLDS

		MARCH APRIL		MAY		JUNE		JULY		AUGUST		SEPT.		OCT.		NOV.
		March & 1-15	16-30	1-15	16-31	1-15	16-30	1-15	16-31	1-15	16-31	1-15	16-30	1-15	16-31	
9 furlongs	3	18	17	16	15	14	13	12	11	10	9	8	7	6	5	4
1¼ miles	3	19	18	17	16	15	14	13	12	11	10	9	8	7	6	5
11 furlongs	3	20	19	18	17	16	15	14	13	12	11	10	9	8	7	6
1½ miles	3	20	19	18	17	16	15	14	13	12	11	10	9	8	7	6
13 furlongs	3	21	20	19	18	17	16	15	14	13	12	11	10	9	8	7
1¾ miles	3	21	20	19	18	17	16	15	14	13	12	11	10	9	8	7
15 furlongs	3	22	21	20	19	18	17	1£6	15	14	13	12	11	10	9	8
2 miles	3	22	21	20	19	18	17	16	15	14	13	12	11	10	9	8
2¼ miles	3	23	22	21	20	19	18	17	16	15	14	13	12	11	19	9
2½ miles	3	25	24	23	22	21	20	19	18	17	16	15	14	13	12	11

unless the 5lb apprentice allowance was claimed, and 5st in races for apprentices alone. In 1948 it was 6st 7lb, unless apprentice allowances of up to 7lb were claimed, and 6st in apprentice-only races. Today the fact that jockeys are generally heavier than in the past has been acknowledged to some extent with a minimum weight of 7st 7lb, unless the apprentice allowance is claimed.

Maximum top weight in three-year-old handicaps and nurseries is 9st 7lb, and in all other handicaps 10st. These are exceeded only when a penalty is added to a horse's original handicap weight under the conditions of the race.

A recent innovation in handicaps has been the facility to raise the weights at the four-day declaration stage and the overnight stage if the highest-weighted horse left in is below the maximum weight allowed by the conditions. At the four-day stage weights are raised to a top weight of 9st 7lb in nurseries and three-year-old handicaps, and 9st 10lb in all other races. At the overnight stage the top weight is 9st 7lb. Penalties are added after the weights have been raised, so that a horse may carry more than the stipulated maximum.

Winners of Flat races confined to apprentices do not incur weight penalties as a result of that win, except in further races confined to apprentices or where the conditions of the race specifically say so. Extra weight penalties are not incurred for winning matches or private sweepstakes, or the Newmarket Challenge Cup or Whip. Extra weight is allotted only for winning, not for being placed. Nor can horses receive weight allowances or be relieved from extra weight, for having been beaten in one or more races, though maidens can be given an allowance for not having won within a specified time, or races of a specified value or distance.

Geldings are not permitted a weight allowance in races with guaranteed prize money of £3,000 or more. The allowance for fillies traditionally has been 3lb, but some races stipulate more, and there is evidence to suggest the allowance should be at least 5lb to enable fillies to compete against colts on something approaching equal terms.

The idea that horses of different ages should carry different weights in order to equalize their chances was formulated in 1850 by Admiral Rous on a scale of weight for age, allowing younger horses to carry less weight than their elders. Rous revised his scale in 1873, and with only minor alterations this was used as a guide to Clerks of the Course until a further revision by the Jockey Club senior Handicapper Major David Swannell in 1976 translated the differences from actual weights to be carried to an allowance in pounds.

The current scale of weight for age, drawn up in pounds with the year split into fortnights, is:

WELLS, John (1833-73)

John Wells was closely associated with Sir Joseph Hawley, for whom he rode the Derby winners Beadsman (1858), Musjid (1859) and Blue Gown (1868). Tall for a jockey and in late life distinctly portly, he was nicknamed 'Tiny'. No stylist, he was capable, obedient and honest, and was twice champion jockey. His retainer was only £100 but he was generously rewarded when he won a good race.

WEST AUSTRALIAN (1850, b c Melbourne – Mowerina, by Touchstone)

West Australian was bred and owned by John Bowes and is regarded as the first

Triple Crown winner of the 2,000 Guineas, Derby and St Leger. As a four-year-old he won the Ascot Gold Cup. He was not a success as a sire but Hurry On was descended from him in tail-male.

WESTMINSTER, 1st Duke of (1825-99)

Hugh Lupus Grosvenor, first Duke of Westminster, was reputedly the richest man in Britain. He was one of the foremost owner-breeders in the last twenty years of the nineteenth century and won the 2,000 Guineas (Shotover, Ormonde and Flying Fox), 1,000 Guineas (Farewell), Derby (Bend Or, Shotover, Ormonde and Flying Fox) and St Leger (Ormonde and Flying Fox). Thus he owned two 'Triple Crown' winners in Ormonde, one of the best horses of the century, and Flying Fox. He also bred the famous filly Sceptre, winner of every Classic bar the Derby, who was sold as a yearling after his death. A tall, upright man of patrician appearance, dignified, reserved and self-contained, he was an exceptional horseman and knew as much as any man about the breeding, training and riding of thoroughbreds.

WESTON, Tommy (1903-81)

Tommy Weston was brought up in a hard school; he served his apprenticeship in a Yorkshire stable controlled by a book-maker. He became one of the outstanding riders of the inter-war era, combining great dash and courage with the best of hands. Even in his prime, though, he was liable to be somewhat erratic. He rode for Lord Derby for eleven years, a tribute to his character and ability, and for him rode eight Classic winners among his eleven victories in such races, which included the Derby on Sansovino and Hyperion and St Leger on Hyperion and Fairway. A distinct personality, he was always popular with the racing community, not least on account of his lively sense of humour. He served with credit in the Royal Navy during World War II and returned to win the Lincolnshire Handicap on Langton Abbot and the 2,000 Guineas on Happy Knight in 1946. He rode his last winner in 1950 and for the remainder of his life lived less than prosperously in Newmarket.

WEYMES, Ernest (b. 1935)

Ernie Weymes assisted his father for seven years before taking out a licence in 1958. His stables are at Middleham, Yorkshire.

WHALEBONE
(1807, b c Waxy – Penelope, by Trumpator)

Whalebone won the 1810 Derby for the Duke of Grafton. That famous writer 'The Druid' described him in the following somewhat unflattering terms: 'Whalebone was as shabby to the eye as old Prunella herself. He had rather a Turkish pony look, and was broad and strong, with a shortish neck. His own feet grew very pumiced and his mares lost their speed early.' Whalebone, who stood just over fifteen hands, may not have been handsome but he exercised a profound influence on bloodstock breeding.

WHARTON, Walter (b. 1924)

Walter Wharton for some years worked with his father, who was well known in Yorkshire fox-hunting and horse-dealing circles. He started to train in 1951 in Wetherby and in 1964 was appointed trainer to Major Lionel Holliday at Newmarket. For four seasons he did particularly well, winning the Ebor Handicap with Proper Pride, 1,000 Guineas with Night Off and Observer Gold Cup with Vaguely Noble, but at the end of 1967 the stables were sold and Wharton moved to Richmond, Yorkshire, to become a public trainer. He left for Melton Mowbray in December 1970 and had his biggest success since then when Tom Sharp won the 1984 Cesarewitch. He maintains a mixed yard, and his many successes over jumps include the Topham Trophy at Liverpool.

WHELAN, Dermot (b. 1918)

Dermot Whelan, nicknamed 'Boggy', was apprenticed to Martin Hartigan and later was for ten years with R.V. Smyth's stable and for five with W. Payne. He served in the Royal Armoured Corps during World War II and took out a licence to train at Epsom in 1955. A wit and a notable raconteur, he won the Cheshire Oaks twice, Wokingham Stakes, Chesterfield Cup, Kempton Jubilee, Northumberland Plate (twice) and Goodwood Cup before retiring from training at the end of 1983.

WHITAKER, Richard Mawson (b. 1942)

From riding point-to-point winners and training jumpers under permit from 1976, Richard Whitaker took out a full licence for the first time in October 1977 at stables on the outskirts of Leeds. His first Flat win was with Sandra's Secret at Stockton on 3 June 1980. His best season on the Flat was 1984, with fifteen winners, and the following year he moved to stables at Wetherby.

WHITNEY, John Hay (1904-82)

'Jock' Whitney, United States Ambassador to Great Britain from 1957 to 1961, was for 60 years a patron of British racing. The most famous horse to carry his colours in Britain was the brilliant steeplechaser Easter Hero, but he won the Eclipse Stakes in 1929 with Royal Minstrel and towards the end of his life did well with horses trained by Jeremy Tree, including Persian Road, Gulf Pearl, D'Urberville, Swing Easy, Quiet Fling and Bright Finish. In 1976 he won both legs of the Autumn Double, with Intermission (Cambridgeshire) and John Cherry (Cesarewitch). Following his death in February 1982 his racing and breeding interests were dispersed, though Tree took over some on his own account.

WHY HURRY
(1940, ch f Precipitation – Cybiane, by Blandford)

Bred by Mr J.V. Rank and trained by Noel Cannon, Why Hurry won two races for £2,123, including the Oaks. At stud she produced six rather moderate winners.

WIGG, George Edward Cecil, Lord (1900-83)

Lord Wigg served as an NCO in the Royal Tank Regiment from 1919 to 1937. In 1940 he re-joined the Army, retiring in 1946 as a colonel in the Royal Army Educational Corps.

From 1945 until 1967 he was Labour MP for Dudley, earning the reputation of being an expert on defence questions and all matters connected with betting and racing. He played a notable part in the passage of the Betting and Gaming Act, 1960. A strong and outspoken personality, he always aroused feelings of either admiring loyalty or intense dislike among those who knew him; nor were his enemies by any means confined to his political opponents.

In November 1967 Colonel Wigg, as he then was, was serving as Paymaster General in Mr Harold Wilson's Government and was commonly believed to occupy a position of considerable power behind the throne. However, he left politics, was made a life peer and was appointed to succeed Field Marshal Lord Harding as chairman of the Betting Levy Board. He had always been a racing enthusiast and had gained experience of racing administration during his term of service with the Racecourse Betting Control Board (1958-61) and the Horserace Totalisator Board (1961-4).

As chairman of the Levy Board, he showed immense energy and drive. There were occasions when it might have been to his own benefit, and to the benefit of the sport, too, if he had numbered urbanity and tact among his virtues, but he was combative by nature and trod, without necessity at times, on a good many toes. All sections of the racing world, though, while not always approving of his views or his methods, agreed that he had the good of the Turf at heart.

He served two terms of office with the Levy Board, ending in 1972, the first being more notable than the second, if only because by the conclusion of the second he and some members of the Establishment had fallen out once too often. By that time, however, he had ensured that the spending of money on Jockey Club recommendations had been made accountable to the Home Secretary, as the law required but not as had become practice. He also revolutionized the raising of levy revenue since the principle of collection was changed from a charge on betting offices to one on bookmakers' turnover. During his term the Levy Board acquired Epsom and Sandown racecourses, and Epsom Downs were secured for use by the local trainers. He was always mindful of stable staff, and not the least of his achievements was the introduction of measures to improve the safety and security of all who work in racing. With the bookmakers he conducted a curious love-hate relationship. If it ever came to a showdown with the bookmakers, his years of experience in the toughest parliamentary in-fighting suggested he would be odds-on to win, but his last racing appointment, which he held until his death in August 1983, was as president of the Betting Office Licensees' Association, the new job to which he had moved ten years previously on leaving the Levy Board.

WIGHAM, Michael (b. 1958)

Son of former jump jockey Percy Wigham and brother of Cliff Wigham, who made his riding career in Italy, Michael Wigham was apprenticed to Reg Hollinshead, for whom he rode his first winner, Highland Jig, at Leicester on 22 September 1975, and his first big-race winner, Remainder Man, in the 1978 Free Handicap. In 1978, when he had his best season with 56 winners, he also won the Lincoln (Captain's Wings), Royal Hunt Cup (Fear Naught) and Newbury Autumn Cup (Piccadilly Line) but at the end of the year he went freelance for four years until he joined Stan Mellor as stable jockey in 1982. His biggest subsequent success came for Mellor on Al Trui in the 1985 Stewards' Cup.

WIGHTMAN, William Gilbert Rowell (b. 1914)

Bill Wightman worked for two years in Laing Ward's stable near Winchester and then trained ponies before taking out a licence to train under Rules in 1937. He moved shortly to Upham, Hants, and has trained there ever since, but for service in the Royal Artillery in World War II when he had the ill luck to be captured by the Japanese and returned to Britain weighing less than 8st.

He started training again and quickly established his reputation through the exploits of that fine chaser Halloween, who twice won the King George VI Chase. Nowadays his stable is devoted chiefly to the Flat, and he has a good record in major handicaps, having won the Extel Handicap (Fraxinus), Portland (Privateer, Walk By), Ayr Gold Cup (Somersway), Cambridgeshire (Flying Nelly), Stewards' Cup (Import), Chester Cup (Charlotte's Choice) and Lincoln (King's Ride).

WILDENSTEIN, Daniel (b. 1917)

An international art dealer and historian, Daniel Wildenstein had his first major success as an owner in France when Don II won the local 2,000 Guineas in 1969. He considered Britain an unlucky hunting ground until Lianga gave him his first win in this country in the 1975 July Cup. Lianga returned later that year to win the Vernons Sprint Cup, and Mr Wildenstein's interest in the British scene grew quickly, though his star filly Allez France, winner of the French 1,000 Guineas in 1973 and Prix de l'Arc de Triomphe the following year, never showed her best form here.

Still, Mr Wildenstein became leading owner in Britain in 1976, largely thanks to the three Classic winners, Flying Water (1,000 Guineas), Pawneese (Oaks) and Crow (St Leger), all trained at Chantilly by Angel Penna, who had succeeded Albert Klimscha as the Wildenstein trainer.

In 1978 Mr Wildenstein had his first horses trained in England, by Peter Walwyn, who won for him that year the Coronation Cup (Crow) and Prix du Cadran (Buckskin), but the owner was not best pleased with Pat Eddery's riding of Buckskin in that year's Ascot Gold Cup, and with Walwyn standing by his

retained rider, the Wildenstein horses were moved to Henry Cecil. It was the first of three partings of the way between the owner and a top British jockey.

Lester Piggott was replaced by Steve Cauthen after Vacarme's 1983 disqualification in the Richmond Stakes, and Walter Swinburn, having won the Arc de Triomphe and a million-dollar bonus in North America on All Along in 1983, was sacked from riding the filly late the following year after being beaten in the United States. Mr Wildenstein has shown that while he is paying the piper, he will call the tune.

Patrick Biancone became the Wildenstein trainer in France in 1978, when Penna left to train the owner's horses in America, and in 1984 he trained Palace Music to win the Champion Stakes and Sagace the Arc de Triomphe within a fortnight. Sagace was also first past the post in the 1985 Arc but was demoted for interference and the race awarded to Rainbow Quest – ridden by Pat Eddery. The irony was not lost on British observers at Longchamp, especially since only two months before Mr Wildenstein had removed to France all his horses trained by Cecil, whose achievements for the owner included winning the Mecca-Dante Stakes with Hello Gorgeous, Simply Great and Claude Monet.

Racing colours: Royal blue, light blue epaulets, light blue cap.

WILLIAMS, Robert James Royston (b. 1953)

Robert Williams spent six years with Barry Hills before beginning training at Newmarket in 1981. His first win was with Great Light at Nottingham on 7 April 1981. In 1983 he moved into Marriott Stables when William Hastings-Bass left for Australia. Numerically Williams' best season was his second, in 1982, with 22 winners.

WILLIAMSON, Bill (1922-79)

Bill Williamson was among the best Australian jockeys to ride in Britain, though because of his modesty and apparent dislike of self-advertisement, his ability did not always receive full recognition.

He rode his first winner in Australia in 1937 and in due course established a big reputation there. He came to Europe in 1960, spending two years with Seamus McGrath in Ireland before moving to Britain, though he continued to be in demand with Irish trainers. Apart from several Irish Classics, for McGrath he won the Ascot Gold Cup (Levmoss), Sussex Stakes (Le Levanstell) and Cambridgeshire (Tarqogan), for John Oxx the Yorkshire Oaks (Lynchris) and Champion Stakes (Arctic Storm) and for Paddy Prendergast the Timeform Gold Cup (Hardicanute) and Doncaster Cup (Canterbury).

His two Classic winners were Abermaid and Night Off in the 1,000 Guineas – Abermaid trained by Harry Wragg, for whom he also won the Ormonde Stakes twice with Sovrango and Timeform Gold Cup with Miralgo, and Night Off owned by the Holliday family, for whom he won the Observer Gold Cup with Vaguely Noble. He returned to ride Vaguely Noble to win the Prix de l'Arc de Triomphe in 1968, and the following year won the same race on Levmoss. He rode in France for a short time in 1971 but the following year was retained by David Robinson, for whom he won the Nunthorpe Stakes on Deep Diver, before retiring from riding at the end of 1973.

He became racing manager to Ravi Tikkoo, for whom he had ridden Steel Pulse to win the Irish Sweeps Derby in 1972, but returned to Australia in 1976 and became an official with the Victoria Turf Club. He died in Melbourne in January 1979.

WILLOUGHBY de BROKE, John Henry Peyto Verney, 20th Baron (b. 1896)

Lord Willoughby de Broke served with the 17th/21st Lancers in World War I, and in World War II with the Auxiliary Air Force. In his youth he rode as an amateur. He was elected to the Jockey Club in 1941 and became one of its most active and outspoken members. He was a steward of the Jockey Club from 1944 to 1946 and again from 1954 to 1956. He also served three terms of office as

steward of the National Hunt Committee. From 1948 to 1954 he was chairman of Tattersalls Committee. Well-known in the Midlands, he was a long-time chairman of Cheltenham and Wolverhampton Racecourses and held a similar position with the Race-Finish Recording Co Ltd. He has bred and owned numerous winners, in training with Harvey Leader and then Gavin Pritchard-Gordon, but none of outstanding merit.

WILMOT, Miss Norah (1889-1980)

Miss Norah Wilmot assisted her father, Sir Robert Wilmot, from 1911 to 1931. After his death she gallantly carried on the stable at Binfield, Berkshire, though it was not until 1966 that the Jockey Club, thanks to the efforts of Miss Wilmot herself and even more so to those of Mrs Nagle, gave way and women were permitted to hold a licence. Till then Miss Wilmot, who numbered the Queen among her patrons, had to run the stable in the name of her assistant or head lad. Among the good races she won, but for which she was not officially recognized, were the Goodwood Cup, Doncaster Cup, Newbury Spring Cup, Newbury Autumn Cup, Brown Jack Stakes and Blue Riband Trial Stakes. She did, however, get the credit as the first woman officially to train a winner on the Flat in Britain. Her filly Pat won at Brighton on 3 August, 1966, the day after she was granted her licence. A familiar and greatly liked personality, she gave up training at the end of the 1979 season, at the age of 90. She died the following year.

WILSON, David Adam (b. 1940)

Born in Scotland and educated at Harrow, David Wilson was assistant to John Sutcliffe senior until the latter's death in 1975, and after five years out of racing he returned to train from Sutcliffe's yard from the middle of 1980 until forced to move to another part of Epsom in 1984 because of leasing difficulties. His biggest success has been with Gamblers Dream in the Crocker Bulteel Handicap at Ascot.

WILSON, John Murrin (b. 1933)

'Jock' Wilson was apprenticed to Jack Reardon from 1948 to 1953 and rode his first winner in 1949. A lightweight jockey, much in demand in handicaps, he won the Cambridgeshire, Northumberland Plate, Newbury Spring Cup, Royal Hunt Cup, Portland Handicap and Newbury Spring Cup. His best season was 1954, with 38 winners. He injured his back in a fall at exercise in 1978 and was forced to retire a year later. He eventually took a public house in Reigate.

WILSON, John Stoddart (b. 1956)

A former amateur rider under National Hunt Rules, John Wilson began training under permit at Motherwell in 1975 and became a public trainer in 1980. He took over the Cree Lodge Stables at Ayr in November 1984 and trains a mixed string, with the emphasis on jumpers.

WILWYN
(1948, b c Pink Flower – Saracen, by Donatello II)

Bred by his owner Mr R.C. Boucher and trained by George Colling, Wilwyn won twenty races in Britain, including the Free Handicap, Great Yorkshire Stakes and Rous Memorial Stakes, but he is most notable for being the winner of the first Washington D.C. International Stakes at Laurel Park, Maryland, in 1952. He was exported to South Africa in 1959, having sired the Yorkshire Oaks winner Tenacity (dam of a similar winner in Parthian Glance) and the useful sprinter Ampney Princess.

WINDMILL GIRL
(1961, b f Hornbeam – Chorus Beauty, by Chanteur II)

Bred by Major L.B. Holliday, Windmill Girl won the Ribblesdale Stakes and was second in the Oaks. She made her name in the history books as the dam of two Derby winners: Blakeney (by Hethersett) and Morston (by Ragusa). She became the eleventh mare to breed two such winners and the first for 71 years. The previous ten comprised six with sets of brothers: Flyer, Horatia, Arethusa, Penelope, the Canopus mare and Perdita II, and four with sets of half-brothers: Mr Tattersall's Highflyer mare, Arctic Lass, Emma and Morganette.

WINDSOR

With the advent of the M4 motorway, Windsor has become more accessible than ever for metropolitan racegoers. The introduction of evening meetings in 1966 has made this a popular venue, though the racing tends to be of a modest but competitive nature, and viewing is far from easy.

The course, at Rays Meadow, dating from 1866, is bounded on the north, east and south by the Thames and the Mill Stream. The track is a figure-of-eight, just over 1¾m round and almost level. The bends are on the sharp side, but there is a long run-in of 6f with only a slight elbow. High numbers are favoured in the draw on the sprint course, but they must be well away to avoid being cut off at the elbow.

WINDSOR LAD
(1931, b c Blandford – Resplendent, by By George!)

Windsor Lad was one of the best Derby winners of the inter-war period. He was bred by Mr Dan Sullivan and bought as a yearling for 1,300gns by Marcus Marsh acting on behalf of the Maharajah of Rajpipla.

As a two-year-old Windsor Lad was rated 18lb below Colombo in the Free Handicap. He improved out of all knowledge during the winter and the following season won the Chester Vase, Newmarket Stakes and then the Derby. He ought to have won the Eclipse Stakes, too, but ridden by Smirke, who had won the Derby on him, he got hopelessly boxed in in the straight and was most unluckily beaten by King Salmon. He was never beaten again afterwards.

Soon after the Eclipse, as the result of some rather complicated negotiations, he became the property of a bookmaker, Mr Martin Benson, who is said to have written out a cheque for £50,000. Windsor Lad won the St Leger in Mr Benson's colours and as a four-year-old the Coronation Cup and Eclipse. Altogether he won ten races worth £36,257. His stud career was dogged by ill-health, and after much suffering he had to be put down in 1943. His only produce of note were the unbeaten Windsor Slipper (successful in the Irish Triple Crown) and Phase, one of the linchpins of Major L.B. Holliday's stud.

WINTER, John Rous (b. 1929)

John Winter, younger brother of Fred Winter, the famous rider and successful trainer of jumpers, was apprenticed to their father Fred, and later was his assistant, finally taking over the Newmarket stable in 1965. He has won the July Cup with Realm and the Wokingham Stakes with Spaniards Mount, but most of his best horses have been owned by Mr Daniel Prenn, including Mehari (Prix Kergorlay), Folle Rousse (Prix Robert Papin), Balliol (Cork and Orrery Stakes) and Danton (Newbury Autumn Cup). Winter has involved himself more than most trainers in Turf politics and was largely responsible for the introduction of the Bloodstock and Racehorse Industries Confederation (BRIC), a forerunner of the Racing Industry Liaison Committee (RILC) and the present Horseracing Advisory Council (HAC).

WOLLOW
(1973, b c Wolver Hollow – Wichuraiana, by Worden II)

Wollow was bought for 7,000gns as a yearling on behalf of Italian owner Carlo d'Alessio and more than paid his way in training with Henry Cecil by winning nine of his eleven races. He was unbeaten before he tackled 12f for the only time in the Derby, where he got a bad run and finished fifth to Empery. Previously Wollow had won his four races as a two-year-old, including Doncaster's Champagne Stakes and the Dewhurst Stakes, and after winning the Greenham Stakes on his first outing at three, he beat Vitigès in the 2,000 Guineas. After the

Derby he finished second in the Eclipse Stakes but was awarded the race when Trepan failed the post-race dope test; he won the Sussex Stakes and Benson & Hedges Gold Cup but beat only four of the nineteen runners in the Champion Stakes and was retired to stud at Newmarket with a valuation of £1.4m. He stood his first season in 1977 but was exported to Japan in 1981, leaving behind plenty of winning offspring but none of any great consequence.

WOLVERHAMPTON

Racing at Wolverhampton is not of a generally high standard but every effort is made to give patrons value for money. Amenities are first-rate and include a parade-ring in front of the stands, accessible to all enclosures, saddling boxes in view of all enclosures, and refreshment rooms where the racing can be followed from behind glass.

It is a left-handed level course with separate tracks for Flat racing, hurdle racing and steeplechasing. The Flat course is nearly 1m 5f round, with easy turns and a run-in of 5f. The 5f 190yd straight course joins the round course at the home turn. High numbers in the draw are thought to hold a slight advantage on the straight course.

WOLVER HOLLOW
(1964, b c Sovereign Path – Cygnet, by Caracalla II)

Bred by the Gaybrook Park Stud and formerly owned by Mrs C.O. Iselin, who died in 1970 at the age of 102, Wolver Hollow was for his first three seasons in training under the care of Sir Cecil Boyd-Rochfort and on the latter's retirement by Henry Cecil. A big, tall colt who took a long time to come to hand, Wolver Hollow won four races and was placed in a further twelve, gaining his main success as a five-year-old when, ridden by Piggott, he won the Eclipse Stakes. Whether he would have won if Lewis had not ridden a poor race on Park Top is open to question. The previous autumn Wolver Hollow had run a fine race to finish second in the Cambridgeshire with 9st 8lb, having finished third in the race as a three-year-old with 8st 1lb. In five seasons at stud in Britain he had a patchy career, his best offspring being Wollow (2,000 Guineas), Furry Glen (Irish 2,000 Guineas) and Charlie Bubbles (Hardwicke Stakes), before he was exported to Japan in 1981. He was champion sire in 1976.

WOOD, Charles (1856-1945)

Charlie Wood was a leading jockey in the late-Victorian era. He left home at the age of eleven and for seven years was attached to Joseph Dawson's stable at Newmarket. He won ten Classics, including the Derby three times – once in a dead-heat. During the first phase of his riding career his integrity was frequently questioned. Sherrard's Newmarket stable was in fact controlled jointly by Wood and Sir George Chetwynd – the latter lived by betting although he had acted as Senior Steward of the Jockey Club. Matters came to a head after the Earl of Durham had made scathing comments on Sherrard's stable in a Gimcrack Dinner speech. Sir George sued Lord Durham for libel, and as a result of the evidence in that case, Wood forfeited his licence to ride. That was in 1889; he resumed in 1897 and that year won the Derby on Galtee More, ten years after he had been champion jockey. He retired in 1900, and 45 years later died at Eastbourne, very comfortably off.

WOOD, Michael (b. 1957)

Barnsley-born Michael Wood was apprenticed to his local trainer Steve Norton and rode his first winner on Mary Mod at Ripon on 17 August 1974, after which he had to survive an objection. His indentures were later transferred to Gordon Richards at Penrith, until he went freelance, based at Malton, in 1980. His best season was 1985 with eighteen winners.

WOODLAND, Percy (1884-1958)

Percy Woodland had an incomparable record as a rider, winning two French Derbys and two Grand Nationals, while he also won the Grand Steeple-Chase de

Paris twice. After World War I he became a leading trainer under National Hunt Rules, though not before he had won the Lincolnshire Handicap in 1920.

WOOLAVINGTON, James Buchanan, Lord (1849-1935)

James Buchanan, first and last Lord Woolavington, was a shrewd, industrious Scot who amassed a huge fortune as a distiller of whisky. He left more than £7,000,000 when he died in 1935. He won the Derby with Captain Cuttle in 1922 and Coronach in 1926. Both were sired by Hurry On, whom he had bought for 500gns and who was the best horse he owned. His racing interests were carried on by his daughter Catherine, Lady Macdonald-Buchanan.

WOOL WINDER (1904, b c Martagon – St Windeline, by Enoch)

Colonel E.W. Baird's Wool Winder was second to Orby in the Derby. He appeared somewhat unlucky to lose, and unkind rumours circulated in respect of his rider, Otto Madden. That was the only race in which he was beaten as a three-year-old, and he proved a very easy winner of the St Leger. He was exported to Austria as a stallion.

WOOTTON, Frank (1893-1940)

Frank Wootton is the only man to have been a leading jockey on the Flat and over the jumps as well.

His father, Richard, trained with success in his native Australia, South Africa and Britain. Frank Wootton came to Britain with his father and was twelve when at Folkestone in 1906 he rode his first winner. He rode fifteen other winners that season and the following year won the Cesarewitch on Demure, thereby landing a big gamble for the horse's Australian owner and his friends.

His progress to the top of his profession was swift, and he captured the imagination of the public in a manner only equalled this century by Steve

Donoghue, Gordon Richards and Lester Piggott. Extremely intelligent, he not only was a brilliant horseman but had an almost uncanny ability in summing up the form and characteristics, not only of the horse he was riding but of the others in the race. Like most Australian jockeys, he liked to stick to the rails. In a riding career on the Flat that because of increasing weight lasted only seven years, he rode 882 winners from 3,866 mounts, showing the remarkable figure of 23 per cent of winning rides. He was champion jockey in 1909, '10, '11 and '12. He never won the Derby, but won the Oaks, St Leger and Grand Prix de Paris. He rode seven winners at Royal Ascot in 1912.

In World War I he served in Mesopotamia and rode the winner of the Baghdad Grand National. In the early 1920s he rode under National Hunt Rules, chiefly over hurdles, and won 61 races in 1921. He rode in one Grand National but came to grief. For a few years he trained at Epsom, turning out more than 100 winners. He returned to Australia in 1933 and died in Sydney.

WOOTTON, Stanley Thomas (1897-1986)

Stanley Wootton, Australian by birth, was a son of the trainer Richard Wootton and brother of Frank Wootton.

Stanley Wootton was a fine jockey but became too heavy. He served with distinction in World War I and between the wars trained with much success at Treadwell House, Epsom. Few of his horses were of great distinction, and many of them were selling platers, but they were cleverly placed and won more often than not when the money – and sometimes it was big money – was down. He always showed himself to be far-sighted, a great organizer, a disciplinarian and above all completely unflappable, his cool comments on any situation being made with a somewhat old-fashioned precision of speech. Like his father, he possessed the art of producing fine jockeys, sometimes from unpromising material. Perhaps the most famous of his pupils was Charlie Smirke, while Staff Ingham achieved distinction

first on the Flat, later over hurdles, and for many years was a successful trainer with something of the Wootton touch about his methods.

In 1925 Wootton bought the greater part of Walton Downs, Epsom, for £35,000. In 1969 he agreed to assign to the Levy Board the Walton Downs gallop so there is every prospect that Epsom will be preserved for all time for racing and training.

WRAGG, Geoffrey (b. 1930)

Geoff Wragg trained the Derby winner, Teenoso, in his first season with a licence, 1983, but the record was not so outstanding as at first sight for he had been assistant to his father Harry for the best part of 30 years. Teenoso went on to win the King George VI and Queen Elizabeth Diamond Stakes in 1984, when Wragg trained the winners of 22 races, compared with 27 in his first season. In 1985 he trained 26 winners.

WRAGG, Harry (1902-85)

The eldest and most accomplished of three brothers, Harry Wragg was the coolest and most calculating rider of his time. Intelligent, thoughtful and with unusual power of concentration, he was a superb judge of pace and excelled in waiting tactics, hence his nickname of 'The Head Waiter'. He was the only jockey to break Gordon Richards' run as champion from 1931 to 1953, when, with Richards injured, he was leading rider in 1941. His Classic victories were:

2,000 Guineas: Garden Path (1944)
1,000 Guineas: Campanula (1934); Herringbone (1943); Sun Stream (1945)
Derby: Felstead (1928); Blenheim (1930); Watling Street (1942)
Oaks: Rockfel (1938); Commotion (1941); Sun Stream (1945); Steady Aim (1946)
St Leger: Sandwich (1931); Herringbone (1943).

He also rode the winner of the Eclipse Stakes on five occasions.

Having ridden his first winner in 1919, Wragg retired in 1946 to take up training at Newmarket the following year, and he followed with 26 years as a trainer. When he handed over to his son Geoffrey at the end of 1982, the only Classic he had not won as a trainer was the Oaks. He won the 1,000 Guineas with Abermaid (1962), Full Dress II (1969) and On The House (1982), 2,000 Guineas with Darius (1954), Derby with Psidium (1961) and St Leger with Intermezzo (1969).

Wragg's attention to detail as a jockey was translated to his training career, and he was in the forefront of many new ideas. In the stables he would weigh his horses to gauge their fitness; on the gallops he would time their work; and he was one of the first trainers to take advantage of easier modern travel, sending horses to Ireland, where he won several Classics, and to the Continent, where he won the Grosser Preis von Baden four times in the 1960s. He died in October 1985.

WRAGG, Samuel (1909-83)

Sam Wragg, younger brother of Harry Wragg, won the 1940 Derby on Pont l'Evêque. He also won the Oaks on Châtelaine and 1,000 Guineas on Rockfel. Perhaps the best horse he rode was Star King, winner of the Gimcrack and Richmond Stakes before becoming an influential stallion in Australia. Wragg retired from riding in 1953, the year his brother Arthur died.

Y

YANKEE

'Yankee' is a popular form of bet in which four horses are backed in six doubles, four trebles and an accumulator.

YARMOUTH

This well-run course, where the stands face the sea, has always been a popular one, particularly with East Coast holidaymakers. A high proportion of the runners come from Newmarket, just over 70m distant, and an above-average two-year-old will occasionally make his début here.

It is a left-handed track, with a level, straight mile, 1½m round, and there is a slight rise round the turn into the back straight and a corresponding decline into the finishing straight. High numbers are slightly favoured in the draw on the straight course. The soil is sandy and quick-draining so the going is rarely heavy.

YATES, David (b. 1944)

Champion apprentice in 1963, David 'Flapper' Yates had the best part of his riding career in the years immediately after, when he won the Cesarewitch, Goodwood Stakes (twice) and Chester Cup on Golden Fire, and the Chester Cup on Narratus. He also won the Extel Handicap on Fraxinus and Doncaster Cup on Prince Hansel. When opportunities diminished in Britain, he rode abroad, until he returned in 1977 to ride for a further five seasons.

YEARLING

A horse of either sex is a yearling during the twelve months from 1 January after it is born. A Jockey Club rule barring the racing of yearlings was introduced in 1859 but entries for the Classics had to be made when the horse was a yearling – in the case of the St Leger almost two years before the race – until 1965, when the closing date of the first four Classics was put back to the February of the horse's two-year-old career.

YELLOW JACK

Yellow Jack was a good horse of the 1850s who had the unfortunate propensity of always finding one competitor just better than himself in every race in which he ran, including the 2,000 Guineas and Derby in 1856. For many years a horse who habitually ran second was sometimes referred to as 'a regular Yellow Jack' but the saying has gone out of fashion.

YORK

As Newmarket was the main racing centre in the South in the eighteenth century, so was York the meeting where the best horses in the North used to run. York races were first run on Knavesmire in 1731, and they are still held on that famous expanse of common land twenty minutes' walk from the centre of the city.

In 1767 the men who ran York races decided to call themselves the Gimcrack Club to perpetuate the memory of a famous and popular grey horse named Gimcrack who won 26 races. The Gimcrack Stakes, founded in 1841, is run at the August meeting, and the owner of the winner is traditionally the guest of honour at the Gimcrack Club Dinner in December when he makes the main speech of the evening, usually dealing with certain aspects of the state of the British Turf. It was at York in 1851 that one of the most famous matches in British racing history was run, that between The Flying Dutchman and Voltigeur.

Not for nothing is York called the 'Ascot of the North'. It is managed in a most enterprising and go-ahead fashion, the amenities are excellent and the standard of racing first-class. Its prestige has been enhanced in the last twenty years with the building of a new grandstand in 1965 and the energetic management of Major Leslie Petch and his nephew John Sanderson. The most heavily sponsored course in the country, York was voted Racecourse of the Year three times in the early 1980s in a poll of Racegoers' Club members.

The big meeting is the three-day one in August when among the main events are the Ebor Handicap of $1\frac{3}{4}$m, the 5f Nunthorpe Stakes, the Great Voltigeur Stakes of $1\frac{1}{2}$m, a notable St Leger trial, the Yorkshire Oaks of $1\frac{1}{2}$m for three-year-old fillies, the 6f Gimcrack Stakes for two-year-olds, the 5f Lowther Stakes for two-year-old fillies, and the $10\frac{1}{2}$f Benson & Hedges Gold Cup. The other important fixture is the three-day meeting in May, with the Yorkshire Cup of $1\frac{3}{4}$m and two significant Classic trials, the Dante Stakes and Musidora Stakes.

There is no enclosed circuit but the 2m course is left-handed, wide, flat and with easy, sweeping turns. There is a 6f straight, and the 7f course joins the round course just under 5f from home. All in all, the track provides an essentially fair test of the Thoroughbred.

YORK, Frederick Augustus, Duke of (1763-1827)

Frederick, Duke of York, one of the unattractive and unsatisfactory sons of George III, won the Derby twice, with Prince Leopold in 1816, who actually ran in the name of Mr Warwick Lake, the Duke's Master of Horse, and with Moses in 1822. The Duke was not unsuccessful on the Turf but he was an inveterate gambler and left behind a mountain of debts when he died. To discharge these, the Government is said to have ceded Cape Breton to his creditors.

YOUR MAJESTY (1905, b c Persimmon – Yours, by Melton)

Mr J.B. Joel's Your Majesty started favourite for the St Leger and won by half a length from White Eagle. He made no mark as a sire in Britain but after six years was exported to Argentina, where he did well.

Z

ZABARA
(1949, ch f Persian Gulf – Samovar, by Caerleon)

Bred by Lady Wyfold and trained by Victor Smyth, Zabara ran in the colours of Sir Malcolm McAlpine. She won six races and £28,848, her victories including the 1,000 Guineas, Coronation Stakes, Imperial Stakes and Cheveley Park Stakes. She was second in the Oaks. As a broodmare she proved rather disappointing, though her four moderate winning produce included Golden Fez, dam of the Oaks winner Circus Plume for the McAlpine family.

ZARATHUSTRA
(1951, bl c Persian Gulf – Salvia, by Sansovino)

Bred and owned by Sir Harold Gray, Zarathustra was trained in Ireland by Michael Hurley at two and three, and by Cecil Boyd-Rochfort at Newmarket at four and five. He won thirteen races from 5f to 2m 5f, including the Irish Derby, Irish St Leger, Ascot Stakes, Goodwood Cup and Ascot Gold Cup. Unfortunately he was slow to make his mark as a sire, and this good and versatile horse was sold for export to Japan, where he died three years later, in 1967. His only notable offspring in Britain was Crozier, winner of the Jockey Club Stakes and Doncaster Cup.

ZETLAND, Thomas Dundas, 2nd Earl of (1795-1873)

The second Earl of Zetland owned an outstanding Derby winner in Voltigeur, whom he bought for 1,000gns with a 500gns contingency if Voltigeur won the 1850 Derby. Shortly before the Derby Lord Zetland discovered that forfeits of £400 were due from Voltigeur's nominator and that, unless these were paid, Voltigeur would be unable to run. With aristocratic disdain for the feelings and pockets of the thousands who had backed his horse, Lord Zetland gave orders for Voltigeur to be scratched. Servants and tenants on the Zetland estates who had had their limit on the horse were in despair and sent a deputation to Lord Zetland's brother-in-law, Mr Williamson, who agreed to see what he could do. Mr Williamson induced Lord Zetland to change his mind, and Voltigeur won at 16-1. Lord Zetland's coachman won £200, a goodly sum in those days, and nearly as much as Lord Zetland, no betting man, won himself. Thousands of Freemasons punted on Voltigeur as Lord Zetland was then the head of British Freemasonry. His other Classic winner was Vedette, who won the 2,000 Guineas in 1857.

ZINFANDEL
(1900, ch c Persimmon – Medora, by Bend Or)

Zinfandel was a horse of outstanding ability and might have won the Derby but for the rule then existing that prevented him from running on account of the death of his nominator, Colonel McCalmont. He passed into the possession of Lord Howard de Walden, for whom he won the Coronation Cup, beating Rock Sand and Sceptre, who had won seven Classic races between them. He also won the Ascot Gold Cup. There is a racing legend that when he won the Gold Cup, his owner was seated under a tree in the paddock, perusing the score of an opera.

ZINO
(1979, b c Welsh Pageant – Cyriana, by Salvo)

Zino was bred by his owner Gerry Oldham and trained in France by François Boutin. He won three of his five races as a two-year-old, including the Critérium de Maisons-Laffitte, and was second in the other two, including the Prix de la Salamandre. First time out at three he won the Prix Djebel by six lengths, and in the 2,000 Guineas he got the better of a close struggle with Wind and Wuthering. Zino did not win again, but he ran well when second in the Prix Jean Prat and third in the Prix Jacques le Marois before running the one bad race of his career, when last of fourteen in the Champion Stakes. He was retired to stud in France and stood his first season in 1983.

Appendix I

COURSES AND THEIR RESULTS

ASCOT

Royal Enclosure, Ascot, Berkshire. SL5 7JN. (0990-22211)
Clerk of the Course: Captain Nicky Beaumont

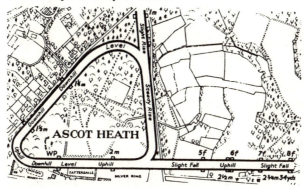

Right-handed course with electrical timing apparatus.

EFFECT OF DRAW: Low numbers slightly favoured when stalls on stands side on straight course; high numbers slightly favoured on round course.

Best Times

DISTANCE	TIME	AGE	WEIGHT		GOING	HORSE	DATE	
5f	59·27	3	8	8	Firm	Amber Rama	June 19,	1970
5f	1.0·75	2	8	11	Firm	Brondesbury	June 17,	1982
6f	1.13·29	4	9	0	Firm	Indian King	June 17,	1982
6f	1.13·64	2	8	11	Firm	Vacarme (disq.)	June 18,	1983
7f	1.26·52	6	8	7	Firm	Manchesterskytrain	Sept. 28,	1985
7f	1.27·3	2	8	11	Firm	Tour D'Or (USA)	Sept. 28,	1984
8f (rnd)	1.38·80	3	9	0	Firm	Shadeed	Sept. 28,	1985
8f (rnd)	1.40·92	2	8	7	Fast	Untold	Sept. 26,	1985
8f (str)	1.39·53	3	7	13	Firm	Richboy	June 19,	1970
		3	8	10	Firm	Final Chord	June 21,	1974
10f	2.3·31	4	9	1	Firm	Trepan	June 15,	1976
12f	2.26·96	5	8	9	Firm	Stanerra	June 17,	1983
16f	3.24·76	4	9	4	Firm	Bally Russe	June 14,	1966
20f	4.18·81	4	9	0	Firm	Gildoran	June 21,	1984
22f 34y	4.53·69	5	7	3	Firm	Gurkha	July 17,	1964

Race Results

Autobar Victoria Cup   7f

Handicap. First run in present form 1908. Run at Hurst Park until 1963. Run as Top Rank Club Victoria Cup 1972-77. Run at Newbury 1964, 1977; at Newmarket 1970. No race 1941-45, 1983 (waterlogged).

	OWNER	TRAINER	JOCKEY	RAN	SP
1930 Ecilath, 4-7-4	B. Davis	B. Davis	J. Sirett	21	13-2
1931 Fleeting Memory, 6-8-7	S. Joel	W. Earl	R. Perryman	18	8-1
1932 Knight Error, 6-7-11	A. Wilson	P. Whitaker	F. Fox	17	100-7
1933 Fonab, 4-8-1	J. Dewar	F. Darling	G. Richards	23	5-1
1934 Alluvial, 6-8-8	J.B. Joel	C. Peck	B. Carslake	18	4-1
1935 Precious Pearl, 4-7-5	J. Baylis	G. Lambton	J. Dines	19	10-1
1936 Hairan, 4-8-12	Aga Khan	Frank Butters	C. Smirke	18	20-1
1937 Fairplay, 4-7-8	R. Middlemas	P. Allden	P. Maher	18	17-2
1938 Phakos, 4-8-8	E. Esmond	J. Jarvis	E. Smith	18	100-8
1939 Unbreakable, 4-9-2	J. Widener	C. Boyd-Rochfort	P. Beasley	19	7-1
1940 Time Step, 4-8-4	J. Whitney	J. Anthony	R. Ruttle	21	100-8
1946 Honeyway, 5-9-7	Lord Milford	J. Jarvis	E. Smith	17	3-1
1947 Fairey Fulmar, 4-8-7	G. Tachmindji	O. Bell	T. Gosling	16	10-1
1948 Petition, 4-9-3	Sir A. Butt	Frank Butters	K. Gethin	19	7-2
1949 My Babu, 4-9-7	Maharaja of Baroda	F. Armstrong	C. Smirke	14	7-1
1950 Star Signal, 5-8-0	Mrs F. Wignall	G.J. Houghton	P. Evans	14	25-1
1951 Fastnet Rock, 4-8-2	Lord Rosebery	J. Jarvis	E. Mercer	21	100-6
1952 Star Signal, 7-7-9	Mrs F. Wignall	R. Poole	P. Evans	15	100-7
1953 Orgoglio, 4-8-7	P. Bull	C. Elsey	K. Gethin	15	100-7
1954 Chivalry, 5-7-9	P. Hatvany	T. Rimell	D. Forte	15	100-6
1955 Alf's Caprice, 4-7-9	E. Pacitto	H. Wallington	D. Smith	19	9-1
1956 Coronation Year, 5-8-9	A. Thomas	A. Thomas	K. Gethin	25	25-1
1957 Dionisio, 4-8-3	P. Bull	C. Elsey	E. Hide	14	7-1
1958 Red Letter, 4-8-5	Lady Davidson	W. Smyth	G. Lewis	17	10-1
1959 Alf's Caprice, 8-7-13	E. Pacitto	H. Wallington	E. Cracknell	20	20-1
D.T.J, 5-7-9	H. Price	W. Lyde	W. Snaith	—	20-1
1960 Sanctum, 4-8-4	F. Rowe	A. Smyth	A. Breasley	20	9-1
1961 Bass Rock, 7-7-12	Lord Rosebery	J. Jarvis	P. Robinson	21	7-1
1962 Spaniards Close, 5-9-3	Mrs B. Davis	F. Winter	D. Smith	21	20-1
1963 Tudor Treasure, 5-9-0	D. Murray	E. Cousins	D. Leah	35	100-7
1964 Blazing Scent, 5-7-11	R. Capon	G. Todd	R. Hutchinson	19	25-1
1965 Princelone, 4-9-7	A. Allen	W. Nightingall	D. Keith	9	10-1
1966 Enrico, 4-9-10	D. Robinson	J. Thompson	L. Piggott	14	11-2
1967 Hadrian, 4-7-11	D. Molins	W. Nightingall	A. Murray	17	9-1
1968 Rome, 4-8-6	J. Ismay	K. Cundell	B. Taylor	15	20-1
1969 Town Crier, 4-8-10	E. de Rothschild	P. Walwyn	D. Keith	14	6-1
1970 Welsh Pageant, 4-9-6	H.J. Joel	N. Murless	A. Barclay	14	4-1
1971 Mon Plaisir, 4-9-8	Mrs A. Turner	H. Wallington	G. Lewis	23	3-1
1972 Heave To, 4-7-13	Lord Fairhaven	M. Prescott	R. Still	10	9-2
1973 Royal Prerogative, 4-8-7	L.B. Holliday	Denys Smith	W. Carson	18	7-2
1974 Galiano, 5-8-8	J. Stallard	B. Hills	W. Carson	11	100-30
1975 Rhodomantade, 4-8-3	J. Carrington	P. Makin	G. Baxter	20	22-1
1976 Record Token, 4-9-4	Sir H. Ingram	P. Walwyn	P. Eddery	14	6-1
1977 Duke Ellington, 4-9-1	C. Olley	H.R. Price	B. Taylor	16	18-1
1978 Private Line, 5-8-13	G. Greenwood	C. Brittain	E. Hide	16	25-1
1979 The Adrianstan, 4-8-6	S. Powell	J. Sutcliffe	J. Mercer	18	25-1
1980 Kampala, 4-9-3	Mrs D. McCalmont	P. Walwyn	P. Eddery	16	8-1
1981 Columnist, 4-9-13	J. Whitney	J. Tree	P. Eddery	14	8-1
1982 Indian King, 4-9-3	J. Levy	G. Harwood	G. Starkey	13	4-1
1984 Mummys Pleasure, 5-8-9	A. Piller	P. Haslam	B. Raymond	13	14-1
1985 Tremblant, 4-8-5	K. Abdullah	R. Smyth	W. Carson	22	8-1

Prince of Wales's Stakes   1¼m

Three-year-olds and upwards. 3-y-o 8st, 4-y-o & upwards 9st 1lb, fillies allowed 3lb (plus penalties). First run 1920. Run over 1m 5f for three-year-olds only 1920-39. No race 1940-67 until revived with new conditions. Group Two.

	OWNER	TRAINER	JOCKEY	RAN	SP
1968 Royal Palace, 4-9-5	H.J. Joel	N. Murless	A. Barclay	2	1-4
1969 Connaught, 4-9-2	H.J. Joel	N. Murless	A. Barclay	5	11-10
1970 Connaught, 5-9-4	H.J. Joel	N. Murless	A. Barclay	4	10-11
1971 Arthur, 4-9-2	Lady Rosebery	J. Dunlop	R. Hutchinson	4	5-4
1972 Brigadier Gerard, 4-9-2	Mrs J. Hislop	W. Hern	J. Mercer	7	1-2
1973 Gift Card, 4-9-5	Countess Batthyany	A. Penna	L. Piggott	5	7-2
1974 Admetus, 4-9-5	Sir M. Sobell	J. Cunnington	M. Philipperon	7	6-1

		OWNER	TRAINER	JOCKEY	RAN	SP
1975	Record Run, 4-9-2	S. Grey	G. Pritchard-Gordon	P. Eddery	6	12-1
1976	Anne's Pretender, 4-9-1	Sir C. Clore	H.R. Price	L. Piggott	8	100-30
1977	Lucky Wednesday, 4-9-1	C. St George	H. Cecil	J. Mercer	5	5-6
1978	Gunner B, 5-9-1	Mrs P. Barrett	H. Cecil	J. Mercer	7	4-5
1979	Crimson Beau, 4-9-1	H. Spearing	P. Cole	L. Piggott	7	11-2
1980	Ela-Mana-Mou, 4-9-4	S. Weinstock	W. Hern	W. Carson	10	100-30
1981	Hard Fought, 4-9-4	L.B. Holliday	M. Stoute	W.R. Swinburn	9	3-1
1982	Kind of Hush, 4-9-1	A. Shead	B. Hills	S. Cauthen	7	4-1
1983	Stanerra, 5-8-12	F. Dunne	F. Dunne	B. Rouse	11	7-1
1984	Morcon, 4-9-1	Lord Rotherwick	W. Hern	W. Carson	5	11-8
1985	Bob Back, 4-9-7	A. Balzarini	M. Jarvis	B. Raymond	4	33-1

St James's Palace Stakes   1m

Three-year-olds. 9st, fillies allowed 3lb. First run 1834. Run at Newmarket 1941. No race 1940, 1942-45. Group Two.

		OWNER	TRAINER	JOCKEY	RAN	SP
1930	Christopher Robin, 9-0	Lieut-Col G. Loder	V. Gilpin	P. Beasley	6	100-7
1931	Cameronian, 9-0	J. Dewar	F. Darling	F. Fox	6	8-15
1932	Andrea, 9-0	Duke of Marlborough	P. Whitaker	T. Weston	10	100-8
1933	Canon Law, 9-0	Lord Astor	J. Lawson	R. Dick	9	9-2
1934	Flamenco, 9-0	Lord Rosebery	J. Jarvis	H. Wragg	4	100-9
1935	Bahram, 9-0	Aga Khan	Frank Butters	F. Fox	5	1-8
1936	Rhodes Scholar, 8-7	Lord Astor	J. Lawson	R. Dick	5	2-1
1937	Goya II, 9-0	M. Boussac	G. Lambton	E.C. Elliott	6	9-4
1938	Scottish Union, 9-0	J. Rank	N. Cannon	B. Carslake	8	4-7
1939	Admiral's Walk, 8-7	Sir J. Jarvis	J. Jarvis	E. Smith	6	6-5
1941	Orthodox, 9-0	J. Rank	N. Cannon	D. Smith	7	6-1
1946	Khaled, 9-0	Aga Khan	Frank Butters	G. Richards	5	2-1
1947	Tudor Minstrel, 9-0	J. Dewar	F. Darling	G. Richards	3	6-100
1948	Black Tarquin, 9-0	W. Woodward	C. Boyd-Rochfort	E. Britt	5	5-1
1949	Faux Tirage, 9-0	J. Dewar	N. Murless	G. Richards	8	11-10
1950	Palestine, 9-0	Aga Khan	M. Marsh	C. Smirke	4	4-7
1951	Turco II, 9-0	W. Woodward	C. Boyd-Rochfort	W.H. Carr	10	7-1
1952	King's Bench, 9-0	A. Tompsett	M. Feakes	G. Richards	7	3-1
1953	Nearula, 9-0	W. Humble	C. Elsey	E. Britt	6	4-6
1954	Darius, 9-0	Sir P. Loraine	H. Wragg	E. Mercer	7	evens
1955	Tamerlane, 9-0	Lord Porchester	N. Bertie	A. Breasley	5	8-11
1956	Pirate King, 9-0	Maj L. Holliday	H. Cottrill	D. Smith	6	6-1
1957	Chevastrid, 8-7	J. McGrath	S. McGrath	J. Eddery	5	8-1
1958	Major Portion, 9-0	H.J. Joel	T. Leader	E. Smith	5	evens
1959	Above Suspicion, 8-7	The Queen	C. Boyd-Rochfort	W.H. Carr	5	9-4
1960	Venture VII, 9-0	Aly Khan	A. Head	G. Moore	2	1-33
1961	Tudor Treasure, 8-7	Lord Derby	J. Watts	D. Smith	9	11-4
1962	Court Sentence, 8-7	H.J. Joel	T. Leader	E. Smith	8	100-8
1963	Crocket, 9-0	D. van Clief	G. Brooke	D. Smith	10	9-2
1964	Roan Rocket, 9-0	T. Frost	G. Todd	L. Piggott	8	5-4
1965	Silly Season, 9-0	P. Mellon	I. Balding	G. Lewis	12	5-1
1966	Track Spare, 9-0	R. Mason	R. Mason	J. Lindley	7	100-9
1967	Reform, 9-0	M. Sobell	Sir G. Richards	A. Breasley	5	4-6
1968	Petingo, 9-0	M. Lemos	F. Armstrong	L. Piggott	3	10-11
1969	Right Track, 9-0	J.R. Brown	J. Sutcliffe	G. Lewis	4	4-6
1970	Saintly Song, 9-0	S. Joel	N. Murless	A. Barclay	6	11-10
1971	Brigadier Gerard, 9-0	Mrs J. Hislop	W. Hern	J. Mercer	4	4-11
1972	Sun Prince, 9-0	Sir M. Sobell	W. Hern	J. Lindley	5	7-4
1973	Thatch, 9-0	J. Mulcahy	V. O'Brien	L. Piggott	2	evens
1974	Averof, 9-0	M. Lemos	C. Brittain	B. Taylor	7	7-4
1975	Bolkonski, 9-0	C. d'Alessio	H. Cecil	G. Dettori	8	4-5
1976	Radetzsky, 9-0	C. Elliot	C. Brittain	P. Eddery	8	16-1
1977	Don, 9-0	E. Ryan	W. Elsey	E. Hide	7	11-2
1978	Jaazeiro, 9-0	R. Sangster	V. O'Brien	L. Piggott	8	5-2
1979	Kris, 9-0	Ld Howard de Walden	H. Cecil	J. Mercer	5	11-10
1980	Posse, 9-0	O.M. Phipps	J. Dunlop	P. Eddery	8	11-2
1981	To-Agori-Mou, 9-0	Mrs A. Muinos	G. Harwood	G. Starkey	8	2-1
1982	Dara Monarch, 9-0	Mrs L. Browne	L. Browne	M.J. Kinane	9	7-2
1983	Horage, 9-0	A. Rachid	M. McCormack	S. Cauthen	7	18-1

	OWNER	TRAINER	JOCKEY	RAN	SP
1984 Chief Singer, 9-0	J. Smith	R. Sheather	R. Cochrane	8	85-40
1985 Bairn, 9-0	Sheikh Mohammed	L. Cumani	L. Piggott	8	6-4

Coventry Stakes   6f

Two-year-olds. 8st 11lb, fillies allowed 3lb. First run 1890. Run over 5f before 1955.
Run at Newmarket 1941-44. No race 1940. Group Three.

	OWNER	TRAINER	JOCKEY	RAN	SP
1930 Lemnarchus	Lord Ellesmere	F. Darling	F. Fox	12	9-2
1931 Cockpen	Lord Woolavington	F. Darling	F. Fox	8	13-8
1932 Manitoba	Lord Woolavington	F. Darling	G. Richards	12	13-8
1933 Medieval Knight	J. Dewar	F. Darling	G. Richards	9	8-13
1934 Hairan	Aga Khan	F. Butters	G. Richards	9	4-9
1935 Black Speck	J. Rank	H. Cottrill	T. Burns	11	7-1
1936 Early School	Lord Astor	J. Lawson	R. Dick	18	11-4
1937 Mirza II	Aga Khan	F. Butters	C. Smirke	11	4-11
1938 Panorama	Mrs J. Corrigan	C. Boyd-Rochfort	P. Beasley	12	2-9
1939 Turkhan	Aly Khan	F. Butters	C. Smirke	16	100-8
1941 Big Game	King George VI	F. Darling	H. Wragg	5	2-9
1942 Nasrullah	Aga Khan	F. Butters	G. Richards	7	7-4
1943 Orestes	Miss D. Paget	W. Nightingall	T. Carey	11	13-8
1944 Dante	Sir E. Ohlson	M. Peacock	W. Nevett	6	11-8
1945 Khaled	Aga Khan	F. Butters	G. Richards	8	9-1
1946 Tudor Minstrel	J. Dewar	F. Darling	G. Richards	6	2-13
1947 The Cobbler	Lieut-Col G. Loder	F. Darling	G. Richards	12	4-5
1948 Royal Forest	Maj R. M-Buchanan	N. Murless	G. Richards	14	5-1
1949 Palestine	Aga Khan	F. Butters	G. Richards	12	1-2
1950 Big Dipper	Mrs J. Bryce	C. Boyd-Rochfort	W.H. Carr	11	2-1
1951 Kings Bench	A. Tompsett	M. Feakes	G. Richards	11	4-6
1952 Whistler	Maharanee of Baroda	P. Nelson	E. Britt	7	2-5
1953 The Pie King	R. Bell	P. Prendergast	T. Gosling	12	11-2
1954 Noble Chieftain	Maj L. Holliday	H. Cottrill	F. Barlow	8	11-8
1955 Ratification	Sir M. McAlpine	V. Smyth	W. Carr	7	100-30
1956 Messmate	Lord Milford	J. Jarvis	E. Mercer	17	20-1
1957 Amerigo	Lord Howard de Walden	J.A. Waugh	E. Smith	10	7-4
1958 Hieroglyph	Mrs J. Hanes	C. Boyd-Rochfort	W.H. Carr	14	10-1
1959 Martial	R. Webster	P. Prendergast	W. Swinburn	13	11-10
1960 Typhoon	N. McCarthy	P. Prendergast	R. Hutchinson	9	evens
1961 Xerxes	Mrs D. McCalmont	G. Brooke	D. Smith	17	9-2
1962 Crocket	D. van Clief	G. Brooke	D. Smith	14	9-4
1963 Showdown	Mrs D. Prenn	F. Winter	D. Smith	12	6-1
1964 Silly Season	P. Mellon	I. Balding	G. Lewis	19	13-2
1965 Young Emperor	Mrs P. Poe	P. Prendergast	L. Piggott	13	9-4
1966 Bold Lad	Lady Granard	P. Prendergast	D. Lake	16	4-6
1967 Mark Royal	B. Schmidt-Bodner	P. Norris	A. Breasley	16	13-2
1968 Murrayfield	Mrs P. Hastings	I. Balding	G. Lewis	16	15-2
1969 Prince Tenderfoot	Mrs P. Poe	P. Prendergast	W. Williamson	10	15-8
1970 Mill Reef	P. Mellon	I. Balding	G. Lewis	5	4-11
1971 Sun Prince	M. Sobell	W. Hern	J. Mercer	10	20-1
1972 Perdu	A. Holland	T. Corbett	J. Lindley	7	16-1
1973 Doleswood	F. Tory	R. Akehurst	F. Durr	12	20-1
1974 Whip It Quick	G. van der Ploeg	W. Marshall	G. Lewis	18	11-1
1975 Galway Bay	J. Mullion	I. Balding	L. Piggott	10	2-1
1976 Cawstons Clown	J. Murrell	N. Adam	M.L. Thomas	12	11-2
1977 Solinus	D. Schwartz	V. O'Brien	L. Piggott	17	7-4
1978 Lake City	H. Demetriou	H.R. Price	B. Taylor	20	7-1
1979 Varingo	PTP Plant Hire	H.R. Price	B. Taylor	18	11-8
1980 Recitation	A. Bodie	G. Harwood	G. Starkey	13	11-1
1981 Red Sunset	P. Burns	G. Harwood	G. Starkey	16	14-1
1982 Horage	A. Rachid	M. McCormack	P. Eddery	8	85-40
1983 Chief Singer	J. Smith	R. Sheather	R. Cochrane	14	20-1
1984 Primo Dominie	P. Wetzel	B. Swift	J. Reid	8	4-7
1985 Sure Blade	Sheikh Mohammed	B. Hills	B. Thomson	12	3-1

Ribblesdale Stakes   1½m

Three-year-old fillies. 8st 7lb (plus penalties). First run 1919. Run over 1m for three and four-year-olds 1919-39; over 1½m for maiden three-year-olds 1948-49; for three-year-old fillies from 1950. No race 1940-47. Group Two.

	OWNER	TRAINER	JOCKEY	RAN	SP
1930 Flying Argosy, 3-8-0	W. Vincent	H. Powney	T. Weston	8	7-4
1931 Doctor Dolittle, 3-8-12	A. Basset	H. Persse	H. Beasley	9	6-4
1932 Rose en Soleil, 4-9-7	Lord Howard de Walden	D. Waugh	J. Childs	7	9-2
1933 Versicle, 3-8-4	Lord Stanley	G. Lambton	T. Weston	8	100-8
1934 The Blue Boy, 4-9-4	Sir W. Portal	M. Hartigan	J. Childs	5	11-10
1935 Easton, 4-9-12	Lord Woolavington	F. Darling	G. Richards	6	1-4
1936 Can-Can, 3-7-11	T. Blackwell	G. Barling	P. Evans	11	100-8
1937 Rhodes Scholar, 4-9-12	Lord Astor	J. Lawson	R. Jones	11	11-10
1938 River Prince, 3-8-5	Duke of Marlborough	C. Boyd-Rochfort	P. Beasley	10	6-1
1939 Ombro, 3-8-4	Lord Portal	C. Boyd-Rochfort	T. Burns	11	5-1
1950 La Baille, 8-10	Mohamed Bey Sultan	M. Marsh	C. Smirke	9	15-2
1951 Chinese Cracker, 8-10	Mrs G. Blagrave	H. Blagrave	A. Breasley	9	7-4
1952 Esquilla, 8-10	M. Boussac	C. Semblat	W.R. Johnstone	13	9-2
1953 Skye, 8-6	Lord Rosebery	J. Jarvis	W. Rickaby	12	4-1
1954 Sweet One, 8-10	Lord Milford	J. Jarvis	W. Rickaby	8	100-8
1955 Ark Royal, 8-10	R. Hollingsworth	G. Colling	D. Smith	11	2-1
1956 Milady, 8-10	Maj H. Holt	M. Marsh	C. Smirke	13	100-8
1957 Almeria, 8-6	The Queen	C. Boyd-Rochfort	W.H. Carr	9	13-8
1958 None Nicer, 9-0	Maj J. Holliday	W. Hern	S. Clayton	12	11-2
1959 Cantelo, 9-0	W. Hill	C. Elsey	E. Hide	8	5-4
1960 French Fern, 8-6	Maj H. Broughton	J.A. Waugh	G. Lewis	8	8-1
1961 Futurama, 8-6	G. Oldham	H. Wragg	A. Breasley	12	9-2
1962 Tender Annie, 8-6	Mrs J. Bryce	P. Prendergast	G. Bougoure	15	5-4
1963 Ostrya, 8-6	Lord Howard de Walden	J.A. Waugh	J. Lindley	8	100-9
1964 Windmill Girl, 8-10	Lieut-Col Sir J. Darell	A. Budgett	A. Breasley	15	9-4
1965 Bracey Bridge, 8-6	M. Wickham-Boynton	N. Murless	L. Piggott	9	5-1
1966 Parthian Glance, 8-6	Mrs W. Riley-Smith	G. Todd	R. Hutchinson	13	11-2
1967 Park Top, 8-10	Duke of Devonshire	B. van Cutsem	R. Maddock	12	9-2
1968 Pandora Bay, 8-10	Maj C. Nathan	G. Barling	M.L. Thomas	9	11-4
1969 Sleeping Partner, 9-4	Lord Rosebery	D. Smith	J. Gorton	10	7-4
1970 Parmelia, 8-6	Lord Howard de Walden	N. Murless	A. Barclay	12	9-1
1971 Fleet Wahine, 8-10	R. Ohrstrom	H.T. Jones	G. Starkey	10	9-1
1972 Star Ship, 8-10	C. St George	H.R. Price	A. Murray	7	13-8
1973 Miss Petard, 8-10	P. Williams	R. Jarvis	M.L. Thomas	9	12-1
1974 Northern Princess, 8-10	S. Yoshida	J. Hindley	A. Kimberley	8	9-2
1975 Gallina, 8-10	S. Fraser	V. O'Brien	L. Piggott	6	7-1
1976 Catalpa, 8-10	Lord Howard de Walden	H. Cecil	A. Bond	7	16-1
1977 Nanticious, 8-10	Mrs B. Firestone	D. Weld	W. Swinburn	9	15-2
1978 Relfo, 8-10	Lord Granard	P. Prendergast	C. Roche	12	12-1
1979 Expansive, 8-10	The Queen	W. Hern	W. Carson	7	11-2
1980 Shoot A Line, 8-11	R. Budgett	W. Hern	W. Carson	9	5-2
1981 Strigida, 8-7	Lord Howard de Walden	H. Cecil	L. Piggott	9	5-1
1982 Dish Dash, 8-7	J. Bryce	R. Armstrong	B. Raymond	10	6-1
1983 High Hawk, 8-7	Sheikh Mohammed	J. Dunlop	W. Carson	14	7-1
1984 Ballinderry, 8-7	K. Abdullah	J. Tree	T. Ives	9	9-2
1985 Sally Brown, 8-7	R. Cowell	M. Stoute	W.R. Swinburn	10	7-1

Queen Mary Stakes   5f

Two-year-old fillies 8st 8lb. First run 1921. Run at Newmarket 1941-44. No race 1940. Group Three.

	OWNER	TRAINER	JOCKEY	RAN	SP
1930 Atbara	Lieut-Col G. Loder	V. Gilpin	P. Beasley	26	20-1
1931 Diamalt	Mrs V. Sainsbury	A. Holland	H. Wragg	27	100-9
1932 Supervisor	F. Darling	F. Darling	G. Richards	29	3-1
1933 Maureen	Lord Woolavington	F. Darling	G. Richards	24	5-2
1934 Caretta	Lord Lonsdale	F. Darling	G. Richards	25	6-4
1935 Fair Ranee	Vicomte de Fontarce	R. Dawson	S. Donoghue	20	100-8

	OWNER	TRAINER	JOCKEY	RAN	SP
1936 Night Song	J. Whitney	C. Boyd-Rochfort	P. Beasley	35	4-1
1937 Queen of Simba	Aga Khan	F. Butters	C. Smirke	31	20-1
1938 Belle Travers	T. Land	F. Butters	D. Smith	29	3-1
1939 Snowberry	Lord Lonsdale	F. Darling	G. Richards	28	4-1
1941 Sun Chariot	King George VI	F. Darling	H. Wragg	12	11-8
1942 Samovar	Lord Wyfold	H. Persse	M. Beary	10	100-6
1943 Fair Fame	Mrs B. Lavington	H. Leader	F. Lane	12	15-2
1944 Sun Stream	Lord Derby	W. Earl	H. Wragg	10	100-30
1945 Rivaz	Aga Khan	F. Butters	E.C. Elliott	5	4-7
1946 Apparition	Mrs R. M-Buchanan	F. Darling	G. Richards	14	11-8
1947 Masaka	Aga Khan	F. Butters	C. Smirke	18	4-1
1948 Coronation V	M. Boussac	C. Semblat	E.C. Elliott	28	7-2
1949 Diabletta	Aga Khan	F. Butters	W. Johnstone	18	7-4
1950 Rose Linnet	Mrs A. Johnston	R. Day	D. Smith	16	10-1
1951 Primavera	Lord Milford	J. Jarvis	E. Mercer	20	100-6
1952 Devon Vintage	Lady Wyfold	R.J. Colling	E. Mercer	23	100-8
1953 Sybil's Niece	Lord Milford	J. Jarvis	E. Mercer	24	100-6
1954 Bride Elect	Maj L. Holliday	H. Cottrill	F. Barlow	16	6-1
1955 Weeber	J. Olding	P. Nelson	A. Breasley	16	10-1
1956 Pharsalia	Maj L. Holliday	H. Cottrill	L. Piggott	19	100-7
1957 Abelia	Col B. Hornung	N. Murless	L. Piggott	14	11-2
1958 A.20	H. Clifton	F. Sutherland	W. Rickaby	23	5-1
1959 Paddy's Sister	Mrs J. Mullion	P. Prendergast	G. Moore	21	15-8
1960 Cynara	G. Oldham	H. Wragg	W. Carr	17	evens
1961 My Dream	D. Robinson	G. Brooke	D. Smith	11	2-1
1962 Shot Silk	Lieut-Col D. Cripps	G. Brooke	D. Smith	14	100-8
1963 Lerida	Mrs R. M-Buchanan	J.A. Waugh	J. Lindley	15	9-2
1964 Brassia	A. Plesch	V. O'Brien	J. Purtell	17	7-2
1965 Visp	E. Benjamin	J. Watts	J. Lindley	10	6-4
1966 Petite Path	R. Mason	R. Mason	J. Lindley	13	33-1
1967 Sovereign	R. Moller	H. Wragg	R. Hutchinson	12	10-11
1968 Grizel	Col W. Stirling	P. Prendergast	W. Williamson	13	5-2
1969 Farfalla	D. van Clief	D. Smith	A. Murray	13	13-2
1970 Cawston's Pride	L. Hall	F. Maxwell	B. Taylor	11	2-1
1971 Waterloo	Mrs R. Stanley	J.W. Watts	E. Hide	11	9-2
1972 Truly Thankful	G. van der Ploeg	H.R. Price	A. Murray	14	14-1
1973 Bitty Girl	D. Robinson	M. Jarvis	B. Raymond	13	11-2
1974 Highest Trump	Lord Petersham	D. Weld	J. Roe	10	5-2
1975 Rory's Rocket	Mrs W. Slaytor	P. Ashworth	A. Murray	18	33-1
1976 Cramond	Mrs S. Eldin	R. Boss	J. Mercer	12	25-1
1977 Amaranda	R. Moller	H. Wragg	L. Piggott	13	4-6
1978 Greenland Park	Greenland Park Ltd	W. Hastings-Bass	H. White	21	15-2
1979 Abeer	K. Abdullah	J. Tree	W. Carson	14	7-1
1980 Pushy	Lord Tavistock	H. Cecil	J. Mercer	17	7-1
1981 Fly Baby	Malden Farms Ltd	R. Hannon	P. Cook	11	40-1
1982 Widaad	M. Al-Maktoum	M. Stoute	W.R. Swinburn	16	13-8
1983 Night of Wind	P. Durkan	M. McCormack	B. Raymond	15	50-1
1984 Hi-Tech Girl	Intercraft	P. Makin	G. Starkey	17	16-1
1985 Gwydion	S. Niarchos	H. Cecil	S. Cauthen	14	2-1

Royal Hunt Cup   1m

Handicap. First run 1843. Run over 7f 166yds before 1930; over 7f 155yds 1930-55. No race 1940-44.

	OWNER	TRAINER	JOCKEY	RAN	SP
1930 The McNab, 4-7-8	J. Dewar	F. Darling	F. Fox	22	100-7
1931 Grand Salute, 4-7-5	Lord Glanely	T. Hogg	G. Richards	18	5-1
1932 Totaig, 3-7-3	V. Emanuel	G. Duller	B. Rosen	31	33-1
1933 Colorado Kid, 4-8-5	Lieut-Col G. Loder	V. Gilpin	C. Buckham	28	100-8
1934 Caymanas, 4-8-4	C. Ewing	C. Easterbee	C. Ray	29	50-1
1935 Priok, 4-7-4	H. B-Hankey	P. Whitaker	S. Middleton	37	66-1
1936 Guinea Gap, 5-8-5	Lady Nuttall	H. Cottrill	R. Jones	31	28-1
1937 Fairplay, 4-8-3	R. Middlemas	P. Allden	P. Maher	33	18-1
1938 Couvert, 5-7-12	H. Blagrave	H. Blagrave	C. Richards	29	100-8
1939 Caerloptic, 4-8-12	Sir A. Bailey	H. Cottrill	M. Beary	24	100-8
1945 Battle Hymn, 3-7-11	J. Whitney	C. Boyd-Rochfort	P. Maher	14	20-1

	OWNER	TRAINER	JOCKEY	RAN	SP
1946 Friar's Fancy, 5-7-12	O. Watney	T. Leader	E. Smith	16	15-2
1947 Master Vote, 4-7-6	H. Blagrave	H. Blagrave	T. Sidebotham	28	25-1
1948 Master Vote, 5-8-10	H. Blagrave	H. Blagrave	W. Johnstone	27	100-7
1949 Steptoe, 4-8-12	J. Townley	P. Beasley	J. Caldwell	29	100-6
1950 Hyperbole, 5-8-8	J. Rank	N. Cannon	A. Breasley	20	10-1
1951 Val d'Assa, 4-8-8	Maj D. McCalmont	H. Persse	N. Sellwood	23	100-6
1952 Queen of Sheba, 4-8-4	Maj D. McCalmont	H. Persse	F. Barlow	29	100-7
1953 Choir Boy, 4-7-8	The Queen	C. Boyd-Rochfort	D. Smith	21	100-6
1954 Chivalry, 5-8-3	P. Hatvany	T. Rimell	D. Forte	26	33-1
1955 Nicholas Nickleby, 4-7-9	J. Gerber	F. Armstrong	W. Snaith	22	50-1
1956 Alexander, 4-8-11	The Queen	C. Boyd-Rochfort	W.H. Carr	27	13-2
1957 Retrial, 5-8-2	Lady Z. Wernher	C. Boyd-Rochfort	P. Robinson	18	100-7
1958 Amos, 4-7-1	L. Carver	S. Mercer	P. Boothman	17	20-1
1959 Faultless Speech, 4-8-1	H. Wallington	H. Wallington	G. Lewis	23	8-1
1960 Small Slam, 5-8-2	P. King	G. Barling	R.P. Elliott	26	28-1
1961 King's Troop, 4-8-4	Mrs P. Hastings	P. Hastings-Bass	G. Lewis	39	100-7
1962 Smartie, 4-7-9	R. Mason	R. Mason	J. Sime	31	22-1
1963 Spaniard's Close, 6-8-6	Mrs B. Davis	F. Winter	L. Piggott	38	25-1
1964 Zaleucus, 4-8-2	Maj D. McCalmont	G. Brooke	D. Smith	30	100-7
1965 Casabianca, 4-8-7	Lieut-Col J. Hornung	N. Murless	L. Piggott	26	100-9
1966 Continuation, 4-7-9	S. McGrath	S. McGrath	J. Roe	30	25-1
1967 Regal Light, 4-7-6	Mrs L. Lazarus	S. Hall	G. Sexton	15	100-9
1968 Golden Mean, 5-8-4	S.H. Lee	D. Smith	F. Durr	26	28-1
1969 Kamundu, 7-8-6	J. Banks	F. Carr	L. Piggott	24	7-1
1970 Calpurnius, 4-7-13	C. Engelhard	J.W. Watts	G. Duffield	18	33-1
1971 Picture Boy, 6-7-13	K. MacKenzie	G. Todd	J. Wilson	18	11-1
1972 Tempest Boy, 4-8-1	Lieut-Col P. Hesse	J. Sutcliffe	R. Hutchinson	20	20-1
1973 Camouflage, 5-7-9	J. Edwards	J. Dunlop	D. Cullen	20	14-1
1974 Old Lucky, 4-8-8	N.B. Hunt	B. van Cutsem	W. Carson	30	8-1
1975 Ardoon, 5-8-3	F. Feeney	G. Pritchard-Gordon	D. Maitland	18	9-1
1976 Jumping Hill, 4-9-7	G. Pope Jr	N. Murless	L. Piggott	16	6-1
1977 My Hussar, 5-8-10	L. Goldschlager	J. Sutcliffe	W. Carson	15	10-1
1978 Fear Naught, 4-8-0	W. Norton	J. Etherington	M. Wigham	19	12-1
1979 Pipedreamer, 4-8-5	Mrs J. Brookes	H. Candy	P. Waldron	24	12-1
1980 Tender Heart, 4-9-0	Esal Commodities	J. Sutcliffe	J. Mercer	20	13-2
1981 Teamwork, 4-8-6	A. Ward	G. Harwood	G. Starkey	20	8-1
1982 Buzzards Bay, 4-8-12	Mrs V. McKinney	H. Collingridge	J. Mercer	20	14-1
1983 Mighty Fly, 4-9-3	Mrs V. Tory	D. Elsworth	S. Cauthen	31	12-1
1984 Hawkley, 4-8-6	S. Dinsmore	P. Haslam	T. Williams	18	10-1
1985 Come On The Blues, 6-8-2	M. Lemos	C. Brittain	C. Rutter	27	14-1

Coronation Stakes   1m

Three-year-old fillies. 9st (plus penalties). First run 1870. No race 1940-45. Group Two.

	OWNER	TRAINER	JOCKEY	RAN	SP
1930 Quarrat-al-Ain, 8-10	Aga Khan	R. Dawson	M. Beary	14	6-1
1931 Sunny Devon, 8-4	Lord Astor	J. Lawson	R. Dick	9	3-1
1932 Udaipur, 9-3	Aga Khan	Frank Butters	M. Beary	10	6-1
1933 Betty, 8-10	Lord Astor	J. Lawson	R. Dick	11	10-11
1934 Foxcroft, 8-4	M. Field	C. Boyd-Rochfort	J. Childs	11	5-1
1935 Ankaret, 8-10	Mrs G. Miller	Fred Butters	F. Fox	13	5-1
1936 Traffic Light, 8-10	Lord Astor	J. Lawson	R. Dick	18	5-1
1937 Gainsborough Lass, 8-10	Sir J. Jarvis	J. Jarvis	E. Smith	17	4-1
1938 Solar Flower, 8-10	Sir A. Butt	Frank Butters	G. Richards	14	100-8
1939 Olein, 8-11	Lord Glanely	B. Jarvis	T. Lowrey	11	6-1
1946 Neolight, 8-11	J. Dewar	F. Darling	G. Richards	7	15-8
1947 Saucy Sal, 8-11	Mrs G. Blagrave	H. Blagrave	W.R. Johnstone	9	20-1
1948 Fortuity, 8-4	J. Musker	M. Marsh	E. Britt	8	20-1
1949 Avila, 8-11	King George VI	C. Boyd-Rochfort	M. Beary	15	11-2
1950 Tambara, 9-0	Aga Khan	M. Marsh	C. Smirke	7	6-5
1951 Belle of All, 9-0	H. Tufton	N. Bertie	G. Richards	11	15-8
1952 Zabara, 9-0	Sir M. McAlpine	V. Smyth	K. Gethin	7	6-5
1953 Happy Laughter, 9-0	H. Wills	J. Jarvis	W. Rickaby	7	7-4
1954 Festoon, 9-0	J. Dewar	N. Cannon	J. Mercer	6	11-8
1955 Meld, 9-0	Lady Z. Wernher	C. Boyd-Rochfort	W.H. Carr	5	4-9

	OWNER	TRAINER	JOCKEY	RAN	SP
1956 Midget II, 9-0	P. Wertheimer	A. Head	W.R. Johnstone	7	5-6
1957 Toro, 9-0	Aga Khan	A. Head	J. Massard	11	3-1
1958 St Lucia, 9-0	Lord Sefton	P. Hastings-Bass	G. Lewis	8	100-8
1959 Rosalba, 9-0	J. Astor	R.J. Colling	J. Mercer	8	11-8
1960 Barbaresque, 9-0	W. Guest	W. Clout	G. Moore	6	9-2
1961 Aiming High, 9-0	The Queen	N. Murless	L. Piggott	6	100-8
1962 Display, 9-0	Lady Granard	P. Prendergast	G. Bougoure	8	3-1
1963 Fiji, 9-0	Lady Halifax	J. Oxley	G. Starkey	7	7-2
1964 Ocean, 8-7	R. Hollingsworth	J. Oxley	G. Starkey	6	7-1
1965 Greengage, 9-0	R. Watson	G. Richards	A. Breasley	8	5-4
1966 Haymaking, 9-0	C. Nicholson	R.J. Houghton	J. Mercer	8	100-7
1967 Fleet, 9-0	R. Boucher	N. Murless	G. Moore	8	15-8
1968 Sovereign, 9-0	R. Moller	H. Wragg	R. Hutchinson	6	3-1
1969 Lucyrowe, 9-0	L. Freedman	P. Walwyn	D. Keith	10	15-8
1970 Humble Duty, 9-0	Lady Ashcombe	P. Walwyn	D. Keith	3	4-6
1971 Magic Flute, 9-0	Lord Howard de Walden	N. Murless	G. Lewis	4	85-40
1972 Calve, 9-0	Lord Granard	P. Prendergast	L. Piggott	7	12-1
1973 Jacinth, 9-0	Lady Butt	B. Hobbs	J. Gorton	9	15-8
1974 Lisadell, 9-0	J. Mulcahy	V. O'Brien	L. Piggott	8	7-2
1975 Roussalka, 9-0	N. Phillips	H. Cecil	L. Piggott	11	9-1
1976 Kesar Queen, 9-0	R. Tikkoo	A. Breasley	Y. Saint-Martin	8	7-2
1977 Orchestration, 9-0	V. McCalmont	A. Maxwell	P. Eddery	10	12-1
1978 Sutton Place, 8-8	Mrs T. Donahue	D. Weld	W. Swinburn	14	14-1
1979 One In A Million, 9-4	Helena Springfield Ltd	H. Cecil	L. Piggott	12	10-11
1980 Cairn Rouge, 9-4	D. Brady	M. Cunningham	A. Murray	8	6-5
1981 Tolmi, 9-0	G. Cambanis	B. Hobbs	E. Hide	10	4-1
1982 Chalon, 9-0	M. Riordan	H. Cecil	L. Piggott	8	9-4
1983 Flame of Tara, 9-0	Miss P. O'Kelly	J. Bolger	D. Gillespie	6	11-2
1984 Katies, 9-4	T. Ramsden	M. Ryan	P. Robinson	10	11-2
1985 Al Bahathri, 9-4	H. Al-Maktoum	H.T. Jones	A. Murray	7	4-6

Gold Cup   2½m

Three-year-olds and upwards (except 3-y-o fillies). 3-y-o 7st 8lb, 4-y-o & upwards 9st, fillies allowed 3lb. First run 1807. Run as Emperor's Plate 1845-53. Run over 2¼m at Newmarket 1941-44. No race 1940, 1964 (waterlogged). Group One.

	OWNER	TRAINER	JOCKEY	RAN	SP
1930 Bosworth, 4-9-0	Lord Derby	Frank Butters	T. Weston	7	3-1
1931 Trimdon, 5-9-4	Brig-Gen C. Lambton	J. Lawson	J. Childs	10	3-1
1932 Trimdon, 6-9-4	Brig-Gen C. Lambton	J. Lawson	J. Childs	9	15-2
1933 Foxhunter, 4-9-0	E. Esmond	J. Jarvis	H. Wragg	10	25-1
1934 Felicitation, 4-9-0	Aga Khan	Frank Butters	G. Richards	10	9-2
1935 Tiberius, 4-9-0	Sir A. Bailey	J. Lawson	T. Weston	6	100-30
1936 Quashed 4-8-11	Lord Stanley	C. Leader	R. Perryman	9	3-1
1937 Precipitation, 4-9-0	Lady Z. Wernher	C. Boyd-Rochfort	P. Beasley	12	2-1
1938 Flares, 5-9-0	W. Woodward	C. Boyd-Rochfort	R. Jones	10	100-7
1939 Flyon, 4-9-0	Lord Milford	J. Jarvis	E. Smith	9	100-6
1941 Finis, 6-9-0	Sir H. C-Owen	O. Bell	H. Wragg	7	4-1
1942 Owen Tudor, 4-9-0	Mrs R. M-Buchanan	F. Darling	G. Richards	9	5-2
1943 Ujiji, 4-9-0	A. Allnatt	J. Lawson	G. Richards	8	8-1
1944 Umidadd, 4-9-0	Aga Khan	Frank Butters	G. Richards	5	5-4
1945 Ocean Swell, 4-9-0	Lord Rosebery	J. Jarvis	E. Smith	10	6-1
1946 Caracalla II, 4-9-0	M. Boussac	C. Semblat	E.C. Elliott	7	4-9
1947 Souverain, 4-9-0	F. Schmitt	H. Delavaud	M. Lollierou	6	6-4
1948 Arbar, 4-9-0	M. Boussac	C. Semblat	E.C. Elliott	8	4-6
1949 Alycidon, 4-9-0	Lord Derby	W. Earl	D. Smith	7	5-4
1950 Supertello, 4-9-0	W. Harvey	J.C. Waugh	D. Smith	13	10-1
1951 Pan II, 4-9-0	E. Constant	E. Pollet	R. Poincelet	11	100-8
1952 Aquino II, 4-9-0	Maharanee of Baroda	F. Armstrong	G. Richards	6	4-1
1953 Souepi, 5-9-0	G. Digby	G. Digby	E.C. Elliott	10	11-2
1954 Elpenor, 4-9-0	M. Boussac	E.C. Elliott	J. Doyasbere	11	100-8
1955 Botticelli, 4-9-0	Marchese della Rocchetta	Marchese della Rocchetta	E. Camici	9	9-4
1956 Macip, 4-9-0	M. Boussac	E.C. Elliott	S. Boullenger	10	6-1
1957 Zarathustra, 6-9-0	T. Gray	C. Boyd-Rochfort	L. Piggott	9	6-1

	OWNER	TRAINER	JOCKEY	RAN	SP
1958 Gladness, 5-8-11	J. McShain	V. O'Brien	L. Piggott	8	3-1
1959 Wallaby II, 4-9-0	Baron de Waldner	P. Carter	F. Palmer	6	9-4
1960 Sheshoon, 4-9-0	Aly Khan	A. Head	G. Moore	6	7-4
1961 Pandofell, 4-9-0	H. Daw	F. Maxwell	L. Piggott	10	100-8
1962 Balto, 4-9-0	A. Reuff	M. Bonaventure	F. Palmer	7	7-4
1963 Twilight Alley, 4-9-0	Lady Sassoon	N. Murless	L. Piggott	7	100-30
1965 Fighting Charlie, 4-9-0	Lady M. Bury	F. Maxwell	L. Piggott	7	6-1
1966 Fighting Charlie, 5-9-0	Lady M. Bury	F. Maxwell	G. Starkey	7	15-8
1967 Parbury, 4-9-0	Maj H. Holt	D. Candy	J. Mercer	7	7-1
1968 Pardallo II, 5-9-0	Mme L. Volterra	C. Bartholomew	W. Pyers	9	13-2
1969 Levmoss, 4-9-0	S. McGrath	S. McGrath	W. Williamson	6	15-8
1970 Precipice Wood, 4-9-0	R.J. McAlpine	Mrs R. Lomax	J. Lindley	6	5-1
1971 Random Shot, 4-9-0	Mrs G. Benskin	A. Budgett	G. Lewis	10	11-1
1972 Erimo Hawk, 4-9-0	Y. Yamamoto	G. Barling	P. Eddery	8	10-1
1973 Lassalle, 4-9-0	Z. Yoshida	R. Carver	J. Lindley	7	2-1
1974 Ragstone, 4-9-0	Duke of Norfolk	J. Dunlop	R. Hutchinson	6	6-4
1975 Sagaro, 4-9-0	G. Oldham	F. Boutin	L. Piggott	8	7-4
1976 Sagaro, 5-9-0	G. Oldham	F. Boutin	L. Piggott	7	8-15
1977 Sagaro, 6-9-0	G. Oldham	F. Boutin	L. Piggott	6	9-4
1978 Shangamuzo, 5-9-0	Mrs E. Charles	M. Stoute	G. Starkey	10	13-2
1979 Le Moss, 4-9-0	C. d'Alessio	H. Cecil	L. Piggott	6	7-4
1980 Le Moss, 5-9-0	C. d'Alessio	H. Cecil	J. Mercer	8	3-1
1981 Ardross, 5-9-0	C. St George	H. Cecil	L. Piggott	4	30-100
1982 Ardross, 6-9-0	C. St George	H. Cecil	L. Piggott	5	1-5
1983 Little Wolf, 5-9-0	Lord Porchester	W. Hern	W. Carson	12	4-1
1984 Gildoran, 4-9-0	R. Sangster	B. Hills	S. Cauthen	9	10-1
1985 Gildoran, 5-9-0	R. Sangster	B. Hills	B. Thomson	12	5-2

King Edward VII Stakes   1½m

Three-year-old colts and geldings. 8st 8lb (plus penalties). First run 1926. No race 1940-45, 1964 (waterlogged). Group Two.

	OWNER	TRAINER	JOCKEY	RAN	SP
1930 Pinxit, 8-10	Sir C. Hyde	N. Scobie	B. Carslake	8	9-4
1931 Sandwich, 8-10	Lord Rosebery	J. Jarvis	H. Wragg	3	1-3
1932 Dastur, 8-10	Aga Khan	Frank Butters	M. Beary	6	4-9
1933 Sans Peine, 8-3	E. Esmond	J. Jarvis	E. Smith	7	20-1
1934 Berestoi, 8-10	W. Smith	M. Peacock	W. Nevett	8	4-1
1935 Field Trial, 8-10	Lord Astor	J. Lawson	R. Dick	7	8-11
1936 Precipitation, 8-4	Lady Z. Wernher	C. Boyd-Rochfort	P. Beasley	10	2-1
1937 Solfo, 9-1	J. Courtauld	B. Jarvis	T. Lowrey	7	8-11
1938 Foroughi, 8-3	Aga Khan	Frank Butters	H. Wragg	11	100-8
1939 Hypnotist, 8-10	W. Woodward	C. Boyd-Rochfort	P. Beasley	10	evens
1946 Field Day, 8-3	Prince Aly Khan	Frank Butters	G. Richards	8	5-2
1947 Migoli, 8-10	Aga Khan	Frank Butters	G. Richards	5	1-4
1948 Vic Day, 8-10	H. Blagrave	H. Blagrave	W.R. Johnstone	14	13-2
1949 Swallow Tail, 8-10	Lord Derby	W. Earl	D. Smith	7	4-5
1950 Babu's Pet, 8-10	Maharaja of Baroda	G. Duller	T. Burn	4	20-1
1951 Supreme Court, 9-0	Mrs V. Lilley	E. Williams	E.C. Elliott	9	6-4
1952 Castleton, 8-10	T. Carey	T. Carey	D. Smith	10	100-6
1953 Skyraider, 8-10	Prince Aly Khan	A. Head	R. Poincelet	9	13-2
1954 Rashleigh, 8-10	C. Steuart	N. Murless	G. Richards	8	5-1
1955 Nucleus, 8-10	Miss D. Paget	C. Jerdein	L. Piggott	10	4-1
1956 Court Command, 8-6	Mrs V. Lilley	N. Murless	L. Piggott	12	100-7
1957 Arctic Explorer, 8-10	G. Loder	N. Murless	L. Piggott	8	6-1
1958 Restoration, 8-6	The Queen	C. Boyd-Rochfort	W.H. Carr	10	6-1
1959 Pindari, 8-10	The Queen	N. Murless	L. Piggott	12	13-8
1960 Atrax, 8-10	M. Boussac	H. Nicholas	R. Poincelet	12	4-1
1961 Aurelius, 8-10	Mrs V. Lilley	N. Murless	L. Piggott	10	11-4
1962 Gaul, 8-10	Lord Sefton	P. Hastings-Bass	G. Lewis	9	20-1
1963 Only For Life, 8-10	Miss M. Sheriffe	J. Tree	J. Lindley	7	3-1
1965 Convamore, 8-10	E. More O'Ferrall	R. Smyth	J. Mercer	12	13-2
1966 Pretendre, 8-10	J. Lilley	J. Jarvis	P. Cook	8	1-2
1967 Mariner, 8-10	R. Hollingsworth	J. Oxley	G. Starkey	10	8-1
1968 Connaught, 8-6	H.J. Joel	N. Murless	A. Barclay	5	1-2

	OWNER	TRAINER	JOCKEY	RAN	SP
1969 Vervain, 8-10	D. McCalmont	P. Nelson	E. Hide	6	10-1
1970 Great Wall, 8-6	D. Sung	A. Breasley	W. Williamson	5	9-4
1971 Seafriend, 8-10	Mrs J. Mullion	P. Prendergast	J. Mercer	7	3-1
1972 Lord Nelson, 8-6	T. Frost	G. Todd	W. Williamson	6	16-1
1973 Klairvimy, 8-10	Mrs B. Allen-Jones	D. Weld	R. Parnell	7	10-1
1974 English Prince, 9-0	Mrs V. Hue-Williams	P. Walwyn	P. Eddery	6	8-11
1975 Sea Anchor, 8-10	R. Hollingsworth	W. Hern	J. Mercer	8	4-1
1976 Marquis de Sade, 8-10	C. St George	H.R. Price	B. Taylor	5	6-1
1977 Classic Example, 8-10	F. Hue-Williams	P. Walwyn	P. Eddery	10	14-1
1978 Ile de Bourbon, 8-6	A. McCall	R.J. Houghton	J. Reid	10	11-1
1979 Ela-Mana-Mou, 8-6	Mrs A. Muinos	G. Harwood	G. Starkey	9	11-10
1980 Light Cavalry, 8-6	H.J. Joel	H. Cecil	J. Mercer	10	9-2
1981 Bustomi, 8-6	Lady Beaverbrook	W. Hern	W. Carson	10	13-2
1982 Open Day, 8-6	Sir M. Sobell	W. Hern	W. Carson	11	100-30
1983 Shareef Dancer, 8-6	M. Al-Maktoum	M. Stoute	W.R. Swinburn	7	10-1
1984 Head For Heights, 8-6	Sheikh Mohammed	W. Hern	W. Carson	10	5-1
1985 Lanfranco, 8-6	C. St George	H. Cecil	S. Cauthen	10	13-8

Hardwicke Stakes 1½m

Four-year-olds and upwards. 8st 9lb, fillies allowed 3lb (plus penalties). First run 1879. No race 1940-45, 1964 (waterlogged). Group Two.

	OWNER	TRAINER	JOCKEY	RAN	SP
1930 Alcester, 4-9-7	Lord Harwood	W. Jarvis	J. Childs	9	10-1
1931 Orpen, 3-8-5	Sir J. Rutherford	J. Lawson	R.A. Jones	11	8-11
1932 Goyescas, 4-9-10	M. Boussac	B. Jarvis	S. Donoghue	12	9-2
1933 Limelight, 4-9-10	King George V	W. Jarvis	J. Childs	8	7-1
1934 Cotoneaster, 4-9-7	E. Thornton-Smith	F. Templeman	G. Nicholl	9	9-1
1935 J.R. Smith, 3-7-9	M. Field	C. Boyd-Rochfort	G. Richards	9	4-1
1936 Corrida, 4-9-7	M. Boussac	J. Watts	E.C. Elliott	11	8-1
1937 Mid-day Sun, 3-8-8	Mrs G. Miller	Fred Butters	M. Beary	5	2-1
1938 Maranta, 4-8-4	Sir A. Bailey	J. Lawson	T. Weston	7	11-4
1939 Pointis, 3-7-7	Prince Aly Khan	Frank Butters	D. Smith	11	12½-1
1946 Priam II, 5-9-12	M. Boussac	C. Semblat	E.C. Elliott	4	4-11
1947 Nirgal, 4-9-10	M. Boussac	C. Semblat	E.C. Elliott	5	2-1
1948 Sayajirao, 4-9-10	Maharaja of Baroda	F. Armstrong	C. Smirke	3	13-8
1949 Helioscope, 3-7-6	Lady Z. Wernher	C. Boyd-Rochfort	J. Sime	8	20-1
1950 Peter Flower, 4-8-8	Lord Rosebery	J. Jarvis	W. Rickaby	4	6-5
1951 Saturn, 4-8-12	Lord Derby	G. Colling	D. Smith	5	9-2
1952 Dynamiter, 4-9-1	M. Boussac	J. Glynn	E.C. Elliott	4	7-2
1953 Guersant, 4-9-1	G. de Rothschild	G. Watson	P. Blanc	4	evens
1954 Aureole, 4-9-1	The Queen	C. Boyd-Rochfort	E. Smith	4	8-11
1955 Elopement, 4-9-1	Sir V. Sassoon	N. Murless	L. Piggott	2	6-5
1956 Hugh Lupus, 4-8-12	Lady Vernon	N. Murless	W.R. Johnstone	6	100-30
1957 Fric, 5-9-1	M. Calmann	J. Lawson	J. Deforge	6	11-10
1958 Brioche, 4-9-4	W. Humble	C. Elsey	E. Britt	5	7-2
1959 Impatient, 4-8-8	Sir H. Wernher	J. Gosden	J. Lindley	5	10-1
1960 Aggressor, 5-8-12	Sir H. Wernher	J. Gosden	J. Lindley	5	7-2
1961 St Paddy, 4-9-4	Sir V. Sassoon	N. Murless	L. Piggott	4	4-9
1962 Aurelius, 4-9-4	Mrs V. Lilley	N. Murless	A. Breasley	4	8-13
1963 Miralgo, 4-8-12	G. Oldham	H. Wragg	W. Williamson	3	100-30
1965 Soderini, 4-8-12	L. Lawrence	S. Ingham	G. Lewis	9	3-1
1966 Prominer, 4-8-8	J. Mullion	P. Prendergast	D. Lake	6	4-1
1967 Salvo, 4-8-8	G. Oldham	H. Wragg	R. Hutchinson	8	7-4
1968 Hopeful Venture, 4-8-8	The Queen	N. Murless	A. Barclay	6	4-6
1969 Park Top, 5-8-9	Duke of Devonshire	B. van Cutsem	G. Lewis	4	11-8
1970 Karabas, 5-8-12	Lord Iveagh	B. van Cutsem	L. Piggott	5	11-8
1971 Ortis, 4-8-12	C. Vittadini	P. Walwyn	D. Keith	8	9-2
1972 Selhurst, 4-8-10	H.J. Joel	N. Murless	G. Lewis	5	11-4
1973 Rheingold, 4-9-0	H. Zeisel	B. Hills	Y. Saint-Martin	4	1-5
1974 Relay Race, 4-8-10	Sir R. Macdonald-Buchanan	H. Cecil	L. Piggott	5	10-11
1975 Charlie Bubbles, 4-8-10	L. Sainer	P. Walwyn	P. Eddery	11	12-1
1976 Orange Bay, 4-9-0	C. Vittadini	P. Walwyn	P. Eddery	5	9-2
1977 Meneval, 4-9-0	Mrs G. Getty	V. O'Brien	L. Piggott	7	2-1
1978 Montcontour, 4-8-12	Mrs H. Hausmann	M. Zilber	Y. Saint-Martin	8	25-1
1979 Obraztsovy, 4-8-9	R. Sangster	H.R. Price	B. Taylor	6	9-4

	OWNER	TRAINER	JOCKEY	RAN	SP
1980 Scorpio, 4-9-0	G. Oldham	F. Boutin	P. Paquet	7	2-1
1981 Pelerin, 4-8-12	Sir P. Oppenheimer	H. Wragg	B. Taylor	9	7-1
1982 Critique, 4-8-9	G. Vanian	H. Cecil	L. Piggott	8	7-2
1983 Stanerra, 5-8-9	F. Dunne	F. Dunne	B. Rouse	10	4-1
1984 Khairpour, 5-8-12	G. Chittick	R.J. Houghton	S. Cauthen	7	13-2
1985 Jupiter Island, 6-8-9	Lord Tavistock	C. Brittain	L. Piggott	4	85-40

Wokingham Handicap   6f

Three-year-olds and upwards. First run 1874. No race 1940-44, 1964 (waterlogged).

	OWNER	TRAINER	JOCKEY	RAN	SP
1930 Grandmaster, 5-7-5	Lord Glanely	T. Hogg	G. Richards	17	5-1
1931 Heronslea, 4-8-7	W.R. Smith	M. Peacock	J. Taylor	22	100-30
1932 Concerto, 4-8-6	Sir H. Cunliffe-Owen	O. Bell	H. Wragg	15	9-2
1933 Concerto, 5-9-3	Sir H. Cunliffe-Owen	O. Bell	H. Wragg	24	4-1
1934 Coroado, 4-8-9	F. Lundgren	W. Easterby	H. Gunn	18	11-4
1935 Theio, 3-7-5	Sir L. Philipps	J. Jarvis	E. Smith	23	33-1
1936 Cora Deans, 4-7-11	Sir V. Sassoon	B. Jarvis	S. Donoghue	26	7-1
1937 Kong, 4-6-12	Sir C. Hyde	N. Scobie	F. Sharpe	31	33-1
1938 Bold Ben, 4-8-9	A. Berry	F. Armstrong	E.C. Elliott	26	9-1
1939 America, 4-8-12	F. Wilmot	H. Jellis	R.A. Jones	28	20-1
1945 Portmara, 4-7-5	D. Morris	M. Beary	D. Smith	10	20-1
1946 The Bug, 3-8-7	N. Wachman	H. Wellesley	C. Smirke	21	7-1
1947 Lucky Jordan, 4-7-6	Mrs G. Gilroy	A. Boyd	J. Sirett	24	33-1
1948 White Cockade, 4-7-7	R. Glasspool	T. Leader	J. Sirett	32	33-1
1949 The Cobbler, 4-9-4	G. Loder	N. Murless	G. Richards	35	4-1
1950 Blue Book, 3-7-11	H. Morris	M. Marsh	E. Britt	24	100-6
1951 Donore, 4-8-5	Sir H. de Trafford	C. Boyd-Rochfort	W.H. Carr	23	100-9
1952 Malka's Boy, 4-8-10	H. Elvin	W. Nightingall	L. Piggott	22	100-6
1953 Jupiter, 3-7-3	Lord Lambton	P. Beasley	J. Sirett	22	22-1
1954 March Past, 4-9-0	Mrs G. Trimmer-Thompson	K. Cundell	W. Rickaby	16	15-2
1955 The Plumber's Mate, 4-6-9	Lord Ashcombe	H. Smyth	D. Keith	19	25-1
1956 Light Harvest, 4-7-12	D. Forster	J.A. Waugh	J. Sime	28	100-6
1957 Dionisio, 4-8-10	P. Bull	C. Elsey	E. Britt	8	5-1
1958 Magic Boy, 5-7-5	D. Miller	M. Bolton	D. Greening	22	20-1
1959 Golden Leg, 4-7-1	E. McAlpine	M. Pope	R.P. Elliott	29	33-1
1960 Silver King, 4-7-11	J. Phang	S. Hall	J. Sime	29	15-2
1961 Whistler's Daughter, 4-8-6	T. Lucas	S. Hall	J. Sime	28	10-1
1962 Elco, 4-8-13	T. Langton	D. Whelan	W. Williamson	35	20-1
1963 Marcher, 3-7-12	R. Zelker	D. Hanley	R. Hutchinson	27	100-8
1965 Nunshoney, 3-7-2	G. Todd	G. Beeby	D. East	25	33-1
1966 My Audrey, 5-8-2	Mrs D. Rosenfield	E. Cousins	G. Cadwaladr	33	20-1
1967 Spaniard's Mount, 5-8-6	B. Schmidt-Bodner	J. Winter	D. Smith	19	100-6
1968 Charicles, 3-7-6	P. Bull	E. Lambton	D. East	21	100-7
1969 Sky Rocket, 4-7-3	A. Pope	M. Pope	P. Eddery	21	20-1
1970 Virginia Boy, 4-7-4	B. Schmidt-Bodner	D. Smith	D. McKay	13	100-9
1971 Whistling Fool, 5-7-7	B. Schmidt-Bodner	D. Smith	D. McKay	21	11-2
1972 Le Johnstan, 4-9-5	S. Powell	J. Sutcliffe	G. Lewis	17	9-1
1973 Plummet, 4-8-2	M. Myers	J.E. Sutcliffe	W. Carson	21	11-1
1974 Ginnies Pet, 4-8-6	J. Jackson	J.E. Sutcliffe	L. Piggott	22	7-1
1975 Boone's Cabin, 5-10-0	R. Sangster	V. O'Brien	L. Piggott	20	6-1
1976 Import, 5-9-4	H. Cayzer	W. Wightman	M.L. Thomas	12	4-1
1977 Calibina, 5-8-5	E. Badger	P. Cole	G. Baxter	13	14-1
1978 Equal Opportunity, 4-7-12	P. Wentworth	P. Arthur	R. Curant	24	20-1
1979 Lord Rochford, 4-8-8	B. Shine	B. Swift	S. Raymont	28	16-1
1980 Queen's Pride, 4-7-13	Mrs L. d'Ambrumenil	P. Cole	G. Baxter	29	28-1
1981 Great Eastern, 4-9-8	Mrs A. Struthers	J. Dunlop	W. Carson	29	16-1
1982 Battle Hymn, 3-7-7	Mrs D. Abbott	G. Harwood	A. Clark	24	16-1
1983 Melindra, 4-7-5	Miss A. Winfield	D. Elsworth	A. McGlone	27	7-1
1984 Petong, 4-9-6	T. Warner	M. Jarvis	B. Raymond	28	11-1
1985 Time Machine, 4-7-12	T. Harty	P. Hughes	W. Carson	30	10-1

King's Stand Stakes   5f

Three-year-olds and upwards. 3-y-o 8st 9lb, 4-y-o & upwards 9st 3lb, fillies allowed 3lb. First run 1901. No race 1940-45, 1964 (waterlogged). Group One.

		OWNER	TRAINER	JOCKEY	RAN	SP
1930	Oak Ridge, 7-10-0	F. Cundell	L Cundell	H. Beasley	5	11-8
1931	Stingo, 4-10-7	D. Gant	W. Lowe	H. Wragg	14	2-1
1932	Lemnarchus, 4-10-3	Lord Ellesmere	F. Darling	G. Richards	9	7-2
1933	Gold Bridge, 4-10-3	A. Macomber	W. Beatty	H. Beasley	11	11-10
1934	Gold Bridge, 5-10-3	Lord Beatty	W. Beatty	E.C. Elliott	10	11-2
1935	Shalfleet, 4-9-7	H. Leader	H. Leader	H. Jelliss	15	5-4
1936	Sweet Polly, 4-9-4	L. Long	L. Cundell	G. Richards	10	7-1
1937	Ticca Gari, 3-7-11	Aly Khan	Frank Butters	A. Dupuit	17	5-1
1938	Foray, 4-9-1	M. Field	C. Boyd-Rochfort	P. Beasley	8	3-1
1939	Mickey The Greek, 5-9-9	N. Frieze	H. Leach	H. Wragg	21	20-1
1946	Vilmorin, 3-8-0	J. Read	J. Lawson	C. Richards	7	10-1
1947	Greek Justice, 3-8-6	J. Dewar	F. Darling	G. Richards	10	100-30
1948	Squander Bug, 5-9-1	Mrs E. Moss	M. Collins	W. Rickaby	15	33-1
1949	Abernant, 3-8-6	Maj R. M-Buchanan	N. Murless	G. Richards	7	4-6
1950	Tangle, 3-8-0	Lady Baron	W. Payne	E. Smith	3	3-1
1951	Stephen Paul, 3-8-6	J. Olding	H. Persse	N. Sellwood	12	7-2
1952	Easter Bride, 3-7-11	W. Rimell	T. Rimell	E. Fordyce	5	7-1
1953	Fairy Flax, 4-9-2	R. Clark	J. Lawson	A. Breasley	13	20-1
1954	Golden Lion, 3-8-4	W. Barrett	C. Mitchell	B. Swift	11	10-1
1955	Pappa Fourway, 3-9-0	Mrs E. Goldson	W. Dutton	W.H. Carr	5	4-7
1956	Palariva, 3-8-3	Aga Khan	A. Head	R. Poincelet	14	6-1
1957	Right Boy, 3-8-6	G. Gilbert	W. Dutton	L. Piggott	8	4-1
1958	Drum Beat, 5-8-9	J. Gerber	W. O'Gorman	A. Breasley	5	2-1
1959	Chris, 3-8-10	H. Hartley	W. Nevett	J. Sime	8	9-4
1960	Sound Track, 3-8-6	Lady Hemphill	A. O'Brien	A. Breasley	8	8-1
1961	Silver Tor, 3-8-0	S. Joel	R. Fetherstonhaugh	G. Lewis	8	7-4
1962	Cassarate, 3-7-11	Countess M. Batthyany	V. O'Brien	N. Sellwood	7	5-1
1963	Majority Blue, 3-8-6	J. Muldoon	W. O'Gorman	L. Piggott	9	100-8
1965	Goldhill, 4-9-1	R. Johnson	M.H. Easterby	J. Etherington	11	10-1
1966	Roughlyn, 5-9-9	J. Pickering	W. Francis	G. Cadwaladr	10	20-1
1967	Be Friendly, 3-8-3	P. O'Sullevan	C. Mitchell	A. Breasley	10	3-1
1968	D'Urberville, 3-8-3	J. Whitney	J. Tree	J. Mercer	12	4-1
1969	Song, 3-8-8	B. Jenks	D. Candy	J. Mercer	8	evens
1970	Amber Rama, 3-8-8	A. Plesch	F. Mathet	Y. Saint-Martin	11	4-1
1971	Swing Easy, 3-8-8	J. Whitney	J. Tree	L. Piggott	9	7-1
1972	Sweet Revenge, 5-9-4	Mrs B. Attenborough	T. Corbet	G. Lewis	7	7-2
1973	Abergwaun, 5-9-1	C. St George	V. O'Brien	L. Piggott	8	7-4
1974	Bay Express, 3-8-9	P. Cooper	P. Nelson	B. Taylor	10	9-4
1975	Flirting Around, 4-9-4	Mme A. Hausmann	R. Carver	Y. Saint-Martin	12	9-2
1976	Lochnager, 4-9-3	C. Spence	M.W. Easterby	E. Hide	13	6-4
1977	Godswalk, 3-8-9	R. Sangster	V. O'Brien	L. Piggott	11	4-6
1978	Solinus, 3-8-9	D. Schwartz	V. O'Brien	L. Piggott	8	4-6
1979	Double Form, 4-9-3	Baroness H. Thyssen	R.J. Houghton	J. Reid	13	12-1
1980	African Song 3-8-9	G. Kaye	P. Kelleway	P. Eddery	14	10-1
1981	Marwell, 3-8-6	E. Loder	M. Stoute	W.R. Swinburn	12	5-4
1982	Fearless Lad, 3-8-9	G. Soulsby	R.D. Peacock	E. Hide	14	10-1
1983	Sayf El Arab, 3-8-9	M. Dabaghi	W. O'Gorman	M.L. Thomas	16	33-1
1984	Habibti, 4-9-0	M. Mutawa	J. Dunlop	W. Carson	11	4-5
1985	Never So Bold, 5-9-3	D. Kessly	R. Armstrong	L. Piggott	15	4-1

King George VI and Queen Elizabeth Diamond Stakes   1½m

Three-year-olds and upwards. 3-y-o 8st 8lb, 4-y-o & upwards 9st 7lb, fillies allowed 3lb. First run 1951 as King George VI and Queen Elizabeth Festival of Britain Stakes. Run as King George VI and Queen Elizabeth Stakes 1952-74. Group One.

		OWNER	TRAINER	JOCKEY	RAN	SP
1951	Supreme Court, 3-8-4	Mrs V. Lilley	E. Williams	E.C. Elliott	19	100-9
1952	Tulyar, 3-8-6	Aga Khan	M. Marsh	C. Smirke	15	3-1
1953	Pinza, 3-8-4	Sir V. Sassoon	N. Bertie	G. Richards	13	2-1

	OWNER	TRAINER	JOCKEY	RAN	SP
1954 Aureole, 4-9-4	The Queen	C. Boyd-Rochfort	E. Smith	17	9-2
1955 Vimy, 3-8-4	P. Wertheimer	A. Head	P. Poincelet	10	10-1
1956 Ribot, 4-9-4	Marchese della Rochetta	U. Penco	E. Camici	9	2-5
1957 Montaval, 4-9-7	R. Strassburger	G. Bridgland	F. Palmer	12	20-1
1958 Ballymoss, 4-9-7	J. McShain	V. O'Brien	A. Breasley	8	7-4
1959 Alcide, 4-9-7	Sir H. de Trafford	C. Boyd-Rochfort	W.H. Carr	11	2-1
1960 Aggressor, 5-9-7	Sir H. Wernher	J. Gosden	J. Lindley	8	100-8
1961 Right Royal V, 3-8-7	Mme. J. Couturié	E. Pollet	R. Poincelet	4	6-4
1962 Match III, 4-9-7	F. Dupré	F. Mathet	Y. Saint-Martin	11	9-2
1963 Ragusa, 3-8-7	J. Mullion	P. Prendergast	G. Bougoure	10	4-1
1964 Nasram II, 4-9-7	Mrs H. Jackson	E. Fellows	W. Pyers	4	100-7
1965 Meadow Court, 3-8-7	G. Bell	P. Prendergast	L. Piggott	12	6-5
1966 Aunt Edith, 4-9-4	Lieut-Col J. Hornung	N. Murless	L. Piggott	5	7-2
1967 Busted, 4-9-7	S. Joel	N. Murless	G. Moore	9	4-1
1968 Royal Palace, 4-9-7	H.J. Joel	N. Murless	A. Barclay	7	4-7
1969 Park Top, 5-9-4	Duke of Devonshire	B. van Cutsem	L. Piggott	9	9-4
1970 Nijinsky, 3-8-7	C. Engelhard	V. O'Brien	L. Piggott	6	40-85
1971 Mill Reef, 3-8-7	P. Mellon	I. Balding	G. Lewis	10	8-13
1972 Brigadier Gerard, 4-9-7	Mrs J. Hislop	W. Hern	J. Mercer	9	8-13
1973 Dahlia, 3-8-4	N.B. Hunt	M. Zilber	W. Pyers	12	10-1
1974 Dahlia, 4-9-4	N.B. Hunt	M. Zilber	L. Piggott	10	15-8
1975 Grundy, 3-8-7	C. Vittadini	P. Walwyn	P. Eddery	11	4-5
1976 Pawneese, 3-8-5	D. Wildenstein	A. Penna	Y. Saint-Martin	10	9-4
1977 The Minstrel, 3-8-8	R. Sangster	V. O'Brien	L. Piggott	11	7-4
1978 Ile de Bourbon, 3-8-8	D. McCall	R.J. Houghton	J. Reid	14	12-1
1979 Troy, 3-8-8	Sir M. Sobell	W. Hern	W. Carson	7	2-5
1980 Ela-Mana-Mou, 4-9-7	S. Weinstock	W. Hern	W. Carson	10	11-4
1981 Shergar, 3-8-8	Aga Khan	M. Stoute	W.R. Swinburn	7	2-5
1982 Kalaglow, 4-9-7	A. Ward	G. Harwood	G. Starkey	9	13-2
1983 Time Charter, 4-9-4	R. Barnett	H. Candy	J. Mercer	9	5-1
1984 Teenoso, 4-9-7	E. Moller	G. Wragg	L. Piggott	13	13-2
1985 Petoski, 3-8-8	Marcia, Lady Beaverbrook	W. Hern	W. Carson	12	12-1

Hoover Fillies' Mile   1m

Two-year-old fillies. 8st 10lb (plus penalties). First run 1973. Run as Green Shield Stakes 1973, Argos Star Fillies' Mile 1975-77. No race 1974 (waterlogged). Group Two.

	OWNER	TRAINER	JOCKEY	RAN	SP
1973 Escorial, 8-11	The Queen	I. Balding	L. Piggott	11	7-4
1975 Icing, 9-1	Lady Iveagh	P. Prendergast	C. Roche	6	5-1
1976 Miss Pinkie, 9-1	H.J. Joel	N. Murless	L. Piggott	8	5-1
1977 Cherry Hinton, 9-1	R. Moller	H. Wragg	L. Piggott	8	10-11
1978 Formulate, 9-1	Mrs D. Butler	H. Cecil	J. Mercer	9	5-4
1979 Quick As Lightning, 8-12	O.M. Phipps	J. Dunlop	W. Carson	9	9-1
1980 Leap Lively, 8-12	P. Mellon	I. Balding	J. Matthias	7	9-2
1981 Height of Fashion, 9-2	The Queen	W. Hern	J. Mercer	8	15-8
1982 Acclimatise, 8-9	J. Hambro	B. Hobbs	A. Murray	8	3-1
1983 Nepula, 8-9	S. Al-Qemlas	G. Huffer	B. Crossley	8	3-1
1984 Oh So Sharp, 8-10	Sheikh Mohammed	H. Cecil	L. Piggott	8	6-5
1985 Untold, 8-7	R. Cowell	M. Stoute	W.R. Swinburn	9	6-4

Queen Elizabeth II Stakes   1m

Three-year-olds and upwards, 3-y-o 8st 7lb, 4-y-o & upwards 9st, fillies allowed 3lb (plus penalties). First run 1955. Run at Newbury 1960, 1963. No race 1974 (waterlogged). Group Two.

	OWNER	TRAINER	JOCKEY	RAN	SP
1955 Hafiz II, 3-8-4	Aga Khan	A. Head	R. Poincelet	8	9-4
1956 Cigalon, 3-8-1	Comte de Kerouara	M. d'Okhuysen	S. Boullenger	11	8-1
1957 Midget II, 4-8-8	P. Wertheimer	A. Head	A. Breasley	7	5-6

	OWNER	TRAINER	JOCKEY	RAN	SP
1958 Major Portion, 3-8-4	H.J. Joel	T. Leader	E. Smith	4	1-3
1959 Rosalba, 3-8-2	J. Astor	J. Colling	J. Mercer	6	5-2
1960 Sovereign Path, 4-8-11	R. Mason	R. Mason	W.H. Carr	4	13-8
1961 Le Levanstell, 4-8-11	J. McGrath	S. McGrath	W. Williamson	6	20-1
1962 Romulus, 3-8-4	C. Engelhard	R.J. Houghton	W. Swinburn	7	7-4
1963 The Creditor, 3-8-4	Lady Sassoon	N. Murless	L. Piggott	9	5-4
1964 Linacre, 4-8-11	F.M. O'Ferrall	P. Prendergast	L. Piggott	5	11-10
1965 Derring-Do, 4-8-11	Mrs H. Renshaw	A. Budgett	A. Breasley	6	9-4
1966 Hill Rise, 5-9-1	G. Pope, Jnr	N. Murless	L. Piggott	6	7-2
1967 Reform, 3-8-8	M. Sobell	Sir G. Richards	A. Breasley	4	6-5
1968 World Cup, 3-8-4	J. Mullion	P. Prendergast	W. Williamson	5	7-2
1969 Jimmy Reppin, 4-9-1	Mrs S. Bates	J. Sutcliffe	G. Lewis	6	13-8
1970 Welsh Pageant, 4-9-1	H.J. Joel	N. Murless	A. Barclay	5	100-30
1971 Brigadier Gerard, 3-8-8	Mrs J. Hislop	W. Hern	J. Mercer	3	2-11
1972 Brigadier Gerard, 4-9-7	Mrs J. Hislop	W. Hern	J. Mercer	4	4-11
1973 Jan Ekels, 4-9-0	A. Bodie	G. Harwood	J. Lindley	5	5-1
1975 Rose Bowl, 3-8-4	Mrs C. Engelhard	R.J. Houghton	W. Carson	5	9-2
1976 Rose Bowl, 4-9-4	Mrs C. Engelhard	R.J. Houghton	W. Carson	8	13-8
1977 Trusted, 4-9-0	Duchess of Norfolk	J. Dunlop	W. Carson	7	20-1
1978 Homing, 3-8-7	Lord Rotherwick	W. Hern	W. Carson	11	9-2
1979 Kris, 3-9-0	Ld Howard de Waldern	H. Cecil	J. Mercer	7	8-11
1980 Known Fact, 3-9-0	K. Abdullah	J. Tree	W. Carson	7	3-1
1981 To-Agori-Mou, 3-9-0	Mrs A. Muinos	G. Harwood	L. Piggott	6	5-4
1982 Buzzards Bay, 4-9-0	Mrs V. McKinney	H. Collingridge	W.R. Swinburn	10	50-1
1983 Sackford, 3-8-7	A. Bodie	G. Harwood	G. Starkey	9	11-2
1984 Teleprompter, 4-9-0	Lord Derby	J.W. Watts	W. Carson	6	11-2
1985 Shadeed, 3-9-0	M. Al-Maktoum	M. Stoute	W.R. Swinburn	7	9-4

AYR

Racecourse Office, 2 Whitletts Road, Ayr. KA8 0JE (0292-264179)
Joint Clerks of the Course: Bill McHarg, David McHarg

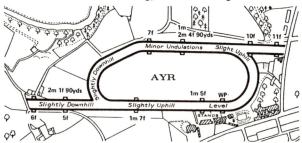

Left-handed course.
EFFECT OF DRAW: High numbers favoured when stalls on stands side on straight course, but low numbers slightly favoured on soft going.

Best Times

DISTANCE	TIME	AGE	WEIGHT	GOING	HORSE	DATE	
5f	57·68	7	7 7	Firm	Red Desire	July 21,	1972
5f	57·8	2	8 0	Hard	Monte Christo	May 17,	1946
6f	1.10·2	3	8 11	Hard	Toronto	May 18,	1946
		3	6 9	Good	The Country Lane	Sept. 18,	1969
6f	1.9·73	2	7 10	Good	Sir Bert	Sept. 17,	1969
7f	1.24·56	5	8 5	Firm	Secret Gilf	May 29,	1982
7f	1.26·5	2	8 6	Firm	Ludham	July 19,	1966
8f	1.36	4	7 13	Firm	Sufi	Sept. 16,	1959
8f	1.39·92	2	8 6	Firm	Calypso	Sept. 18,	1959

DISTANCE	TIME	AGE	WEIGHT	GOING	HORSE	DATE	
10f	2.5·38	4	9 5	Firm	Chil The Kite	July 24,	1976
11f	2.15·94	6	8 9	Firm	Empire Way	Sept, 17	1959
13f	2.46·34	4	9 7	Firm	Plenty Spirit	May 28,	1977
15f	3.12·76	7	8 11	Firm	Cagirama	July 18,	1966
17f 90y	3.45	4	6 13	Good	Curry	Sept. 16,	1955
18f	3.48·4	4	7 3	Hard	Danger	July 18,	1949
20f 90y	4.33·86	4	8 6	Good	Charles Stuart	July 8,	1983

Race Results

Ladbrokes Ayr Gold Cup   6f

Handicap. First run 1804. Run as Ayr Gold Cup before 1972; Burmah Castrol Ayr Gold Cup 1972-8. No race 1939-45.

	OWNER	TRAINER	JOCKEY	RAN	SP
1930 Heronslea, 3-8-6	W. Smith	M. Peacock	J. Taylor	10	5-1
1931 Heronslea, 4-9-11	W. Smith	M. Peacock	J. Taylor	16	8-1
1932 Solenoid, 3-8-9	Mrs C. Mackean	G. Poole	J. Marshall	14	7-1
1933 Ken Hill, 9-7-8	Sir L. Green	T. Green	E. Fox	11	10-1
1934 Figaro, 4-9-1	J. Leach	J. Leach	H. Jellis	13	7-2
1935 Greenore, 6-9-3	Lady Ludlow	O. Bell	S. Wragg	14	5-1
1936 Marmaduke Jinks, 4-6-13	Mrs C. Robinson	H. Peacock	A. Richardson	15	20-1
1937 Daytona, 4-9-0	Sir G. Bullough	J. Jarvis	M. Beary	19	100-8
1938 Old Reliance, 3-9-2	Sir J. Jarvis	J. Jarvis	E. Smith	13	8-1
1946 Royal Charger, 4-9-7	Sir J. Jarvis	J. Jarvis	E. Smith	19	2-1
1947 Kilbelin, 4-7-13	C. Blyth	B. Bullock	W.H. Carr	12	6-1
1948 Como, 6-8-9	Capt J. Fielden	G. Armstrong	J. Marshall	9	10-1
1949 Irish Dance, 6-9-1	H. Stockdale	H. Whiteman	E. Britt	16	4-1
1950 First Consul, 4-9-7	Maharaja of Rajpipla	F. Armstrong	C. Smirke	17	2-1
1951 Fair Seller, 5-9-4	E. Davey	E. Davey	R. Sheather	15	10-1
1952 Vatellus, 4-8-7	A. Bird	J. Pearce	H. Jones	13	10-1
1953 Blue Butterfly, 4-8-9	F.M. O'Ferrall	H. Wragg	E. Mercer	16	11-2
1954 Orthopaedic, 3-8-1	Mrs M. Moss	J. Gosden	J. Lindley	18	11-2
1955 Hook Money, 4-7-11	R. Clark	A. Budgett	W. Elliott	10	4-1
1956 Precious Heather, 4-7-7	A. Bird	J. Gosden	E. Hide	16	5-1
1957 Jacintha, 6-7-7	G. Munro	W. Lyde	E. Larkin	17	100-7
1958 Rhythmic, 3-8-5	Maj A. Straker	W. Dutton	F. Durr	22	20-1
1959 Whistling Victor, 3-7-8	R. Galloway	G. Laurence	J. Sime	16	7-1
1960 Dawn Watch, 5-7-2	W. Kendrick	E. Cousins	L.C. Parkes	23	100-9
1961 Klondyke Bill, 3-8-7	A. Comerford	C. Benstead	E. Smith	17	100-8
1962 Janeat, 3-7-11	G. Turnbull	A. Vasey	B. Henry	25	25-1
1963 Egualita, 3-8-0	R. Sigtia	S. Hall	F. Durr	18	10-1
1964 Compensation, 5-8-10	Mrs G. Lambton	E. Lambton	P. Robinson	18	10-1
1965 Kamundu, 3-8-1	M. Higgins	E. Cousins	G. Cadwaladr	20	100-8
1966 Milesius, 4-7-12	G. Boyd	G. Boyd	N. McIntosh	24	25-1
1967 Be Friendly, 3-8-9	P. O'Sullevan	C. Mitchell	G. Lewis	33	100-8
1968 Petite Path, 4-7-6	Mrs R. Mason	R. Mason	J. Higgins	21	100-7
1969 Brief Star, 3-7-0	R. Sangster	E. Cousins	L.C. Parkes	23	10-1
1970 John Splendid, 3-8-10	A. Struthers	J. Dunlop	R. Hutchinson	19	10-1
1971 Royben, 3-8-7	A. Kennedy	A. Breasley	W. Williamson	28	9-1
1972 Swinging Junior, 3-8-11	N. Angus	N. Angus	Rchd Hutchinson	20	14-1
1973 Blue Cashmere, 3-8-2	R. Clifford-Turner	M. Stoute	E. Johnson	19	7-1
1974 Somersway, 4-7-12	T. Parrington	W. Wightman	D. Cullen	23	16-1
1975 Roman Warrior, 4-10-0	J. Brown	N. Angus	J. Seagrave	23	8-1
1976 Last Tango, 5-7-5	R. McRobert	J. Sutcliffe	L. Charnock	18	6-1
1977 Jon George, 3-8-4	Mrs G. Newsome	M.W. Easterby	B. Raymond	25	22-1
1978 Vaigly Great, 3-9-6	T. Sellier	M. Stoute	G. Starkey	24	5-1
1979 Primula Boy, 4-7-7	Kavli	W. Bentley	W. Higgins	22	40-1
1980 Sparkling Boy, 3-9-2	R. Orloff	P. Kelleway	J. Lowe	24	15-1
1981 First Movement, 3-7-10	Mrs D. Thompson	G. Huffer	M. Miller	21	14-1
1982 Famous Star, 3-7-7	S. Moubarak	M. Albina	Paul Eddery	14	13-2
1983 Polly's Brother, 5-8-3	Mrs C. Geraghty	M.H. Easterby	K. Hodgson	28	11-1
1984 Able Albert, 4-8-6	Mrs A. Henson	M.H. Easterby	M. Birch	29	9-1
1985 Camps Heath, 4-7-9	A. Whiteside	F. Durr	W. Woods	25	14-1

BATH

The Racecourse, Lansdown, Bath. (0225-24609)
Clerk of the Course: Captain Charles Toller

Left-handed course.
EFFECT OF DRAW: Low numbers slightly favoured up to 1m.

Best Times

DISTANCE	TIME	AGE	WEIGHT	GOING	HORSE	DATE	
5f	1.1·6	3	9 0	Firm	Pert Lad	June 2,	1980
5f	1.1·2	2	8 11	Firm	Avon Valley	July 3,	1971
5f 167y	1.9·3	4	7 3	Firm	Make Me Happy	June 3,	1985
5f 167y	1.10·3	2	8 11	Hard	Cheri Berry	Aug. 26,	1981
7f 8y	1.27·8	{ 4	8 3	Firm	Diplomatic Cloak	Sept. 2,	1961
		{ 3	8 4	Firm	Star Flare	July 28,	1980
7f 8y	1.28·6	2	9 0	Firm	Hunting Tower	Aug. 3,	1970
8f 8y	1.39·4	5	7 11	Firm	Traditional Miss	Aug. 27,	1980
8f 8y	1.41·8	2	9 0	Firm	Aberader	Sept. 19,	1977
10f 50y	2.8·8	3	8 11	Hard	Sirenivo	July 19,	1979
11f 150y	2.26·3	3	9 0	Firm	Mubarak of Kuwait	April 27,	1982
13f 12y	2.48·4	3	8 0	Firm	Assembly Ball	July 7,	1973
17f 27y	3.44	6	8 10	Hard	Morgan's Choice	July 13,	1983
17f 194y	4.0·5	3	7 11	Good	Baytree	Aug. 30,	1969

BEVERLEY

19 North Bar Within, Beverley, North Humberside. HU17 8DB. (0482-867488)
Clerk of the Course: John Cleverly

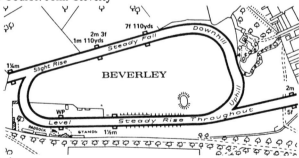

Right-handed course.
EFFECT OF DRAW: High numbers strongly favoured over 5f when stalls on far side.

Best Times

DISTANCE	TIME	AGE	WEIGHT	GOING	HORSE	DATE	
5f	1.1	4	7 4	Firm	Noble Native	Aug. 27,	1970
5f	1.2	2	8 11	Firm	Persian Breeze	June 13,	1974
		2	8 8	Firm	Fimi	Aug. 27,	1981
7f	1.25·2	5	7 6	Firm	Billsborrow	Aug. 28,	1969
7f	1.25·8	2	8 11	Firm	Wicked Will	July 26,	1980
8f	1.36·4	3	8 5	Firm	Dorset Cottage	June 4,	1985
8f	1.38·8	2	8 9	Firm	Foghorn	Sept. 23,	1970
10f	2.2·2	4	7 9	Firm	Coffee House	Aug. 30,	1979
12f	2.31	3	8 6	Firm	Corrals Bond	Aug. 29,	1979
16f	3.30·9	3	9 3	Firm	Amerian	Sept. 5,	1978
19f	4.13·8	4	9 10	Firm	Happy Worker	July 28,	1979

BRIGHTON

The Racecourse, Brighton, Sussex. BN2 2XZ (0273-682912/603580)
Clerk of the Course: Cliff Griggs

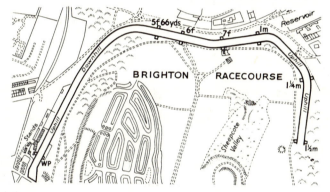

Left-handed course.
EFFECT OF DRAW: Low numbers favoured.

Best Times

DISTANCE	TIME	AGE	WEIGHT	GOING	HORSE	DATE	
5f 66y	1.0·1	5	10 3	Firm	St. Alphage	Aug. 28,	1968
5f 66y	1.1·2	2	9 3	Good	Anton Pillar	Sept. 28,	1983
		2	9 2	Firm	Homing Angel	Oct. 2,	1985
6f	1.7·95	3	7 12	Firm	Sound Of The Sea	Sept. 16,	1982
6f	1.9·6	2	9 7	Firm	Myra's Special	Sept. 18,	1985
7f	1.19·8	3	8 12	Firm	Last Case	June 9,	1966
7f	1.21·7	2	9 6	Firm	Picatrix	Oct. 2,	1985
8f	1.31·8	3	7 12	Firm	Loose Cover	June 9,	1966
		4	9 0	Firm	Soueida	Sept. 19,	1963
8f	1.33·8	2	8 10	Firm	Arbutus	Sept. 19,	1963
10f	1.57·2	3	9 0	Firm	Get the Message	April 30,	1984
12f	2.25·8 (flag)	4	8 2	Firm	New Zealand	July 4,	1985

CARLISLE

Blackwell House, The Racecourse, Carlisle, Cumbria (0228-22504)
Clerk of the Course: Major Tim Riley

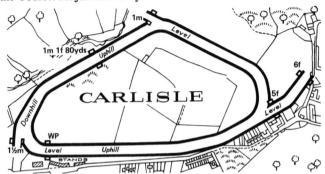

Right-handed course.
EFFECT OF DRAW: High numbers slightly favoured.

Best Times

DISTANCE	TIME	AGE	WEIGHT		GOING	HORSE	DATE	
5f	59.8	4	8	3	Firm	Miss Taurus	July 15,	1971
		3	9	3	Firm	Bollin Emily	July 5,	1984
5f	1.0·8	2	9	5	Hard	Erudite	June 29,	1960
6f	1.11·8	6	8	13	Firm	Night Patrol	Aug. 27,	1970
6f	1.13·8	2	8	11	Firm	Off Scent	Sept. 13,	1973
8f	1.38·4	3	8	0	Firm	Nasr	June 7,	1984
8f	1.44·6	2	8	8	Firm	Blue Garter	Sept. 9,	1980
9f 80y	1.56·8	3	8	0	Firm	K-Battery	July 5,	1984
10f	2.8	3	8	1	Hard	War Eagle	July 5,	1962
12f	2.28·1	3	8	0	Firm	Auchinlea	July 4,	1985

CATTERICK BRIDGE

The Racecourse, Catterick Bridge, Richmond, North Yorkshire (0748-811478)
Clerk of the Course: John Sanderson

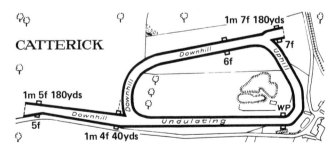

Left-handed course.
EFFECT OF DRAW: Low numbers slightly favoured over 5f.

Best Times

DISTANCE	TIME	AGE	WEIGHT	GOING	HORSE	DATE	
5f	58.3	3	7 10	Firm	Cree Bay	June 4,	1982
5f	58.3	2	8 10	Firm	A Star Is Born	May 31,	1978
5f	1.10·4	3	8 8	Firm	Triad Treple	May 31,	1984
6f	1.11·4	2	9 4	Firm	Captain Nick	July 11,	1978
7f	1.23	{ 4	7 12	Firm	Royal Ziska	June 9,	1973
		{ 4	9 7	Firm	Maazi	July 25,	1985
7f	1.24·1	2	8 11	Firm	Lindas Fantasy	Sept. 18,	1982
12f 40y	2.33·4	3	8 3	Firm	Watet Khet	June 4,	1982
13f 180y	2.54·8	3	8 5	Firm	Geryon	May 31,	1984
15f 180y	3.20·8	4	7 11	Firm	Bean Boy	July 8,	1982

CHEPSTOW

Chepstow Racecourse plc, 17 Welsh Street, Chepstow. NP6 5YH (02912-2260)
Clerk of the Course: John Hughes

Left-handed course.
EFFECT OF DRAW: Low numbers slightly favoured up to 1m.

Best Times

DISTANCE	TIME	AGE	WEIGHT	GOING	HORSE	DATE	
5f	56.8	3	8 4	Firm	Torbay Express	Sept. 15,	1979
5f	58.1	2	7 4	Hard	Mayo Moonlight	Aug. 31,	1981
6f	1.8·9	4	9 3	Hard	Numismatist	July 5,	1983
7f	1.19·9	3	9 10	Firm	Prince Titian	Aug. 29,	1978
7f	1.21·4	2	8 11	Hard	Dijla	Aug. 31,	1981
8f	1.31·8	{ 6	9 6	Firm	Traditional Miss	June 27,	1981
		{ 6	9 6	Firm	Traditional Miss	Aug. 31,	1981
10f	2.4·1	5	8 9	Hard	Leonidas	July 5,	1983
12f	2.31	{ 5	8 11	Hard	The Friend	Aug. 29,	1983
		{ 7	9 6	Hard	Maintop	Sept. 27,	1984
16f	3.32·4	5	11 6	Hard	Yeled	Aug. 30,	1983

CHESTER

The Racecourse, Chester. CH1 2LY (0244-23170)
Clerk of the Course: Captain Charles Toller

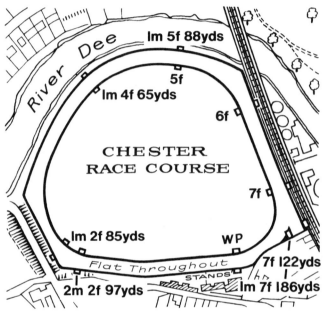

Left-handed course with electrical starting apparatus.
EFFECT OF DRAW: Low numbers favoured up to 7f 122yds.

Best Times

DISTANCE	TIME	AGE	WEIGHT		GOING	HORSE	DATE	
5f	59.2	3	10	0	Firm	Althrey Don	July 10,	1964
5f	1.0·4	2	8	11	Firm	Cynara	May 31,	1960
6f	1.12·8	4	7	5	Good	Welsh Warrior	July 27,	1968
6f	1.13·4	2	9	3	Good	Stung	July 27,	1968
7f	1.26·22	3	8	1	Firm	Numas	May 8,	1980
7f	1.26·60	2	8	5	Firm	No Faith	Sept. 1,	1979
7f 122y	1.32·4	3	8	8	Firm	Joey	Sept. 2,	1972
7f 122y	1.35	2	9	0	Firm	Double Value	Sept. 1,	1972
10f 10y	2.6·2	6	9	7	Good	Colonel Blimp	July 27,	1968
10f 85y	2.9·90	3	8	8	Firm	Playboy Jubilee	May 8,	1980
12f 65y	2.36·56	3	8	12	Firm	Henbit	May 6,	1980
13f 88y	2.48·6	3	8	3	Firm	Rock Roi	July 18,	1970
15f 186y	3.25	3	8	6	Firm	Seacourt	Sept. 1,	1972
18f 77y	3.59·2	6	8	0	Firm	Curry	May 8,	1957

Race Results

Dalham Chester Vase   1½m 65yds

Three-year-old colts and fillies. 8st 12lb, fillies allowed 3lb (plus 4lb maiden allowance). First run 1907. Run as Chester Vase before 1984. For three and four-year-olds until 1959. No race 1940-45, 1969 (waterlogged), 1983 (waterlogged). Group Three.

		OWNER	TRAINER	JOCKEY	RAN	SP
1959	Fidalgo, 8-6	G. Oldham	H. Wragg	S. Clayton	9	10-1
1960	Mr Higgins, 8-10	P. Winstone	H. Cottrill	W.H. Carr	6	10-1
1961	Sovrango, 8-10	G. Oldham	H. Wragg	J. Mercer	10	7-1
1962	Silver Cloud, 8-6	T. Blackwell	J. Jarvis	R. Hutchinson	6	5-1
1963	Christmas Island, 8-10	Lord Ennisdale	P. Pendergast	L. Piggott	7	100-8
1964	Indiana, 8-6	C. Engelhard	J.F. Watts	J. Mercer	8	11-4
1965	Gulf Pearl, 8-10	J. Whitney	J. Tree	J. Lindley	6	7-1
1966	General Gordon, 8-6	Lord Rosebery	J. Jarvis	P. Cook	9	6-1
1967	Great Host, 8-10	L. Gelb	P. Prendergast	D. Lake	7	2-1
1968	Remand, 8-10	J. Astor	W. Hern	J. Mercer	4	4-11
1970	Politico, 8-12	Mrs O. Phipps	N. Murless	A. Barclay	6	5-2
1971	Linden Tree, 8-12	Mrs D. McCalmont	P. Walwyn	D. Keith	5	11-2
1972	Ormindo, 8-8	G. Oldham	H. Wragg	B. Taylor	6	12-1
1973	Proverb, 8-8	Lt-Col J. Chandos-Pole	B. Hills	E. Johnson	7	33-1
1974	Jupiter Pluvius, 8-8	T. Blackwell	B. Hobbs	J. Gorton	8	11-2
1975	Shantallah, 8-12	R. More O'Ferrall	H. Wragg	B. Taylor	7	15-2
1976	Old Bill, 8-8	R. Moller	H. Wragg	B. Taylor	6	33-1
1977	Hot Grove, 8-12	Lord Leverhulme	R.J. Houghton	L. Piggott	6	100-30
1978	Icelandic, 8-12	P. Prendergast	P. Prendergast	C. Roche	4	8-1
1979	Cracaval, 8-8	A. Shead	B. Hills	S. Cauthen	6	4-1
1980	Henbit, 8-12	Mrs A. Plesch	W. Hern	W. Carson	5	evens
1981	Shergar, 8-12	Aga Khan	M. Stoute	W.R. Swinburn	10	4-11
1982	Super Sunrise, 8-12	J. Maxwell	G. Hunter	P. Cook	8	10-1
1984	Kaytu, 8-8	R. Khan	W. Hern	W. Carson	7	11-2
1985	Law Society, 8-12	S. Niarchos	V. O'Brien	P. Eddery	5	5-2

Ladbroke Chester Cup   2¼m 97yds

Handicap. First run 1824. Run as Chester Cup before 1972. No race 1940-45, 1969 (waterlogged), 1983 (waterlogged).

		OWNER	TRAINER	JOCKEY	RAN	SP
1930	Mountain Lad, 5-7-11	H. Sutton	R. Gooch	F. Lane	18	20-1
1931	Brown Jack, 7-9-6	Sir H. Wernher	I. Anthony	M. Beary	19	100-8
1932	Bonny Brighteyes, 4-7-3	Mrs C. Robinson	M. Peacock	J. Dines	17	20-1
1933	Dick Turpin, 4-7-10	R.F. Watson	M. Hartigan	G. Richards	14	9-1
1934	Blue Vision, 7-7-11	M. Evans	I. Anthony	F. Fox	20	100-6
1935	Damascus, 4-7-1	G. Lambton	G. Lambton	H. Foster	17	10-1
1936	Cho-sen, 4-7-2	Mr W. Ahern	W. Higgs	J. Dines	13	100-7
1937	Faites vos Jeux, 6-7-4	Lady Nuttall	H.L. Cottrill	P. Maher	17	8-1
1938	Mr Grundy, 4-7-5	Sir A. Bailey	J. Lawson	G. Richards	17	10-1
1939	Winnebar, 5-7-12	Sir F. Eley	F. Templeman	G. Richards	18	100-8
1946	Retsel, 4-7-9	H. Lester	G. Todd	G. Richards	8	4-1
1947	Asmodee II, 4-9-1	P. Duboscq	W. Halsey	T. Burns	14	10-1
1948	Billet, 4-8-3	B. Hilliard	H. Wragg	W. Nevett	12	5-1
1949	John Moore, 5-6-10	W. Chapman	H. Weatherill	A. Carson	16	25-1
1950	Heron Bridge, 6-9-7	J. Davies	D. Rogers	T. Burns	15	11-2
1951	Wood Leopard, 4-7-5	Lord Durham	R.J. Colling	J. Egan	19	20-1
1952	Le Tellier, 7-8-11	J. Westoll	G. Barling	G. Littlewood	14	6-1
1953	Eastern Emperor, 5-9-2	Lord Milford	J. Jarvis	W. Rickaby	13	2-1
1954	Peperium, 4-8-6	C. Elsey	C. Elsey	E. Britt	16	13-2
1955	Prescription, 4-8-9	Lord Rosebery	J. Jarvis	W. Rickaby	23	8-1
1956	Golovine, 6-8-2	Begum Aga Khan	H. Wragg	P. Robinson	18	9-2
1957	Curry, 6-8-0	F. Honour	F. Armstrong	J. Gifford	11	11-4
1958	Sandiacre, 6-8-5	M. Cowley	W. Dutton	L. Piggott	15	15-2
1959	Agreement, 5-9-4	The Queen	C. Boyd-Rochfort	W.H. Carr	14	3-1

	OWNER	TRAINER	JOCKEY	RAN	SP
1960 Trelawny, 4-7-11	Mrs L. Carver	S. Mercer	F. Durr	16	100-6
1961 Hoy, 5-8-0	C. Spencer	L. Dale	G. Lewis	16	15-2
1962 Golden Fire, 4-7-9	Mrs G. Ridley	D. Marks	D. Yates	19	7-1
1963 Narratus, 5-7-5	D. Symonds	D. Thom	D. Yates	21	8-1
1964 Credo, 4-8-3	L. Gelb	P. Prendergast	P. Cook	13	4-1
1965 Harvest Gold, 6-7-11	T. Marshall	T. Robson	F. Durr	10	11-2
1966 Aegean Blue, 4-8-7	Lieut-Cmdr P. Emmet	R.J. Houghton	L. Piggott	22	22-1
1967 Mahbub Aly, 6-8-1	Lord Rotherwick	W. Hern	P. Cook	14	7-1
1968 Major Rose, 6-8-7	R. Heaton	H.R. Price	L. Piggott	15	11-4
1970 Altogether, 4-7-0	W. Bolton	W. Murray	W. Bentley	13	33-1
1971 Random Shot, 4-8-1	Mrs G. Benskin	A. Budgett	F. Durr	21	6-1
1972 Eric, 5-7-0	J. Ismay	V. Cross	A. Cressy	16	22-1
1973 Crisalgo, 5-7-7	J. Hanson	J.A. Turner	W. Bentley	10	12-1
1974 Attivo, 4-7-5	P. O'Sullevan	C. Mitchell	R. Werham	7	6-1
1975 Super Nova, 5-7-7	J. Mitchell	W. Hall	E. Johnson	15	11-2
1976 John Cherry, 5-9-4	J. Whitney	J. Tree	L. Piggott	15	5-1
1977 Sea Pigeon, 7-8-8	P. Muldoon	M.H. Easterby	M. Birch	15	7-1
1978 Sea Pigeon, 8-9-7	P. Muldoon	M.H. Easterby	M. Birch	13	10-1
1979 Charlotte's Choice, 4-8-4	R. Green	W. Wightman	W. Carson	13	10-1
1980 Arapahos, 5-9-5	R. Sangster	B. Hills	S. Cauthen	10	7-2
1981 Donegal Prince, 5-8-4	J. McGonagle	P. Kelleway	P. Young	15	12-1
1982 Dawn Johnny, 5-8-8	Sir G. White	M. Stoute	W.R. Swinburn	16	14-1
1984 Contester, 4-8-2	P. Winfield	P. Cundell	G. Baxter	19	22-1
1985 Morgans Choice, 8-7-11	C.J. Hill	C.J. Hill	W. Carson	16	13-2

Ormonde Stakes   1m 5f 88yds

Four-year-olds and upwards. 9st, fillies allowed 3lb (plus penalties). Before 1936 run over 5f for two-year-olds; 1955-57 for three-year-olds over 1¼m 10yds. No race 1940-45, 1969 (waterlogged), 1983 (waterlogged). Group Three.

	OWNER	TRAINER	JOCKEY	RAN	SP
1936 Quashed, 4-8-11	Lord Stanley	C. Leader	R. Perryman	9	7-4
1937 Young England, 4-8-11	R. Bownass	M. Peacock	W. Nevett	11	10-1
1938 Senor, 4-8-11	W. Barnett	R. Dawson	J. Crouch	5	7-2
1939 Tricameron, 3-7-2	E. de Rothschild	L. Robert	A. Tucker	6	7-1
1946 High Stakes, 4-8-7	Lord Astor	J. Lawson	C. Richards	4	4-5
1947 Turkish Tune, 4-8-8	W. Buckley	D. Rogers	W. Wells	7	11-4
1948 Goyama, 5-9-3	M. Boussac	C. Semblat	E.C. Elliott	5	11-2
1949 Alycidon, 4-9-0	Lord Derby	W. Earl	D. Smith	4	4-5
1950 Olein's Grace, 4-8-11	P. McCarthy	D. Rogers	E.C. Elliott	6	7-4
1951 Cagire II, 4-9-0	Mrs E. Williams	E. Williams	E.C. Elliott	7	9-4
1952 Tulyar, 3-7-9	Aga Khan	M. Marsh	D. Smith	4	13-8
1953 Wyandank, 4-8-11	Miss M. Cox	J. Lawson	E. Mercer	5	9-1
1954 Stem King, 4-8-11	S. Joel	R. Perryman	D. Smith	5	4-1
1955 North Cone, 3-8-12	Lord Ellesmere	G. Barling	E. Smith	10	4-1
1956 Stephanotis, 3-8-12	A. Plesch	H. Leader	K. Gethin	8	9-4
1957 Hindu Festival, 3-8-12	C. Myerscough	P. Prendergast	T. Gosling	5	3-1
1958 Doutelle, 4-8-9	The Queen	C. Boyd-Rochfort	W.H. Carr	6	11-8
1959 Primera, 5-9-0	C. Dracoulis	N. Murless	L. Piggott	6	11-8
1960 Light Horseman, 4-8-4	Lord Ennisdale	P. Prendergast	R. Hutchinson	4	4-1
1961 Alcaeus, 4-8-9	Sir R. Brooke	P. Prendergast	A. Breasley	4	4-11
1962 Sovrango, 4-8-12	G. Oldham	H. Wragg	W. Williamson	6	11-10
1963 Sovrango, 5-9-3	G. Oldham	H. Wragg	W. Williamson	7	11-4
1964 Arctic Vale, 5-9-3	Mrs E. Goring	P. Prendergast	L. Piggott	3	6-5
1965 Indiana, 4-8-12	C. Engelhard	J.F. Watts	J. Lindley	4	4-11
1966 Biomydrin, 4-8-7	Lady Sassoon	N. Murless	L. Piggott	8	11-2
1967 David Jack, 4-8-12	J. Fisher	E. Lambton	L. Piggott	4	8-13
1968 Hopeful Venture, 4-8-12	The Queen	N. Murless	A. Barclay	3	evens
1970 Blakeney, 4-9-2	A. Budgett	A. Budgett	E. Johnson	5	9-4
1971 Quayside, 4-8-6	T. Robson	Denys Smith	L. Piggott	4	6-4
1972 Selhurst, 4-8-4	H.J. Joel	N. Murless	G. Lewis	7	9-4
1973 Ormindo, 4-8-12	G. Oldham	H. Wragg	B. Taylor	5	13-2
1974 Crazy Rhythm, 6-8-9	K. Dodson	S. Ingham	G. Lewis	5	3-1
1975 Rouser, 4-8-4	Mrs J. de Rothschild	B. Hobbs	G. Lewis	6	11-8
1976 Zimbalon, 4-8-6	R. Hollingsworth	W. Hern	J. Mercer	4	13-8
1977 Oats, 4-9-0	A. Oldrey	P. Walwyn	P. Eddery	7	7-4
1978 Crow, 5-9-0	D. Wildenstein	P. Walwyn	P. Eddery	7	5-4

	OWNER	TRAINER	JOCKEY	RAN	SP
1979 Remainder Man, 4-8-10	Mrs D. Jardine	R. Hollinshead	J. Mercer	4	7-4
1980 Niniski, 4-9-4	Lady Beaverbrook	W. Hern	W. Carson	5	4-7
1981 Pelerin, 4-9-4	Sir P. Oppenheimer	H. Wragg	B. Taylor	5	11-8
1982 Six Mile Bottom, 4-8-10	E. Moller	H. Wragg	S. Cauthen	6	12-1
1984 Teenoso, 4-9-4	E. Moller	G. Wragg	P. Eddery	5	11-8
1985 Seismic Wave, 4-8-10	R. Sangster	B. Hills	B. Thomson	8	7-1

DONCASTER

The Grandstand, Leger Way, Doncaster, South Yorkshire. DN2 6BB (0302-20066)
Clerk of the Course: Pat Firth

Left-handed course with electrical starting apparatus.
EFFECT OF DRAW: High numbers favoured when stalls on stands side on straight course and going is soft.

Best Times

DISTANCE	TIME	AGE	WEIGHT		GOING	HORSE	DATE	
5f	58·2	3	8	8	Firm	Sir Gatric	Sept. 10,	1959
5f	58·4	2	9	0	Good	D'Urberville	Sept. 13,	1967
5f 152y	1.6·2	3	9	2	Good	Welsh Abbot	Sept. 12,	1958
5f 152y	1.8	2	8	10	Good	Crown Flatts	Oct. 25,	1947
6f	1.10·2	4	7	9	Firm	Ryecroft	May 16,	1959
6f	1.11·2	2	8	11	Firm	Paddy's Sister	Sept. 9,	1959
7f	1.22·6	3	9	4	Hard	Pinolil	June 3,	1963
7f	1.24·4	2	9	0	Good	Chebs Lad	Sept. 12,	1969
8f (str)	1.37	3	8	0	Good	Lovestone	Sept. 12,	1958
8f (str)	1.39·6	2	7	8	Firm	Corinthian	Oct. 21	1955
8f (rnd)	1.35·6	4	8	1	Hard	Old Tom	June 3,	1963
8f (rnd)	1.38·32	2	9	0	Firm	Sandy Creek	Oct. 28,	1978
10f 56y	2.6·4	4	8	7	Firm	Silver Cloud	Sept. 12,	1963
12f	2.30·2	5	9	2	Firm	Saraceno	Oct. 24,	1970
14f 127y	3.2·92	3	8	10	Good	Eastern Mystic	Sept. 11,	1985
18f	3.52·7	3	7	6	Firm	Protection Racket	Sept. 10,	1981

Race Results

William Hill Lincoln Handicap   1 m

First run 1853. Run at Lincoln as Lincolnshire Handicap 1853-1964. Run at Pontefract 1942-45. Run as Lincoln Handicap 1965-68; Irish Sweeps Lincoln Handicap 1969-78.

Year	Horse	OWNER	TRAINER	JOCKEY	RAN	SP
1930	Leonidas II, 5-8-0	M. Boussac	S. Darling	H. Southey	31	66-1
1931	Knight Error, 5-7-7	Capt A. Wilson	P. Whitaker	F. Fox	35	100-9
1932	Jerome Fandor, 4-6-13	A. McKinlay	H. Peacock	W. Christie	36	40-1
1933	Dorigen, 4-9-1	G. Lambton	G. Lambton	T. Weston	28	25-1
1934	Play On, 4-7-8	M. Simon	J. Russell	J. Dines	26	100-9
1935	Flamenco, 4-9-0	Lord Rosebery	J. Jarvis	E. Smith	34	8-1
1936	Over Coat, 5-7-12	H. Selby	J. Russell	T. Weston	34	10-1
1937	Marmaduke Jinks, 5-8-0	Mrs C. Robinson	H. Peacock	D. Smith	32	33-1
1938	Phakos, 4-8-3	E. Esmond	J. Jarvis	E. Smith	27	8-1
1939	Squadron Castle, 6-7-7	S. Oxenham	W. Smallwood	V. Mitchell	38	40-1
1940	Quartier Maitre, 5-8-1	Mrs A. Bendir	I. Anthony	G. Richards	21	7-2
1941	Gloaming, 4-7-4	S. Raphael	G. Lambton	D. Dick	19	100-7
1942	Cuerdley, 4-9-4	E. Pilcher	R. Renton	J. Taylor	20	3-1
1943	Lady Electra, 4-8-10	W. Richardson	C. Ray	R. Colven	17	9-2
1944	Backbite, 5-7-8	A. Tully	A. Boyd	M. Pearson	24	33-1
1945	Double Harness, 4-6-10	J. Hetherton	C. Elsey	D. Stansfield	25	33-1
1946	Langton Abbot, 4-8-2	T. Best	E. Lambton	T. Weston	37	7-1
1947	Jockey Treble, 5-6-0	S. Oxenham	W. Smallwood	E. Mercer	46	100-1
1948	Commissar, 8-8-9	R. Budgett	A. Budgett	W. Rickaby	58	33-1
1949	Fair Judgment, 4-7-10	C. Gordon	J. Jarvis	E. Smith	43	6-1
1950	Dramatic, 5-8-13	A. Saunders	G. Todd	G. Richards	40	7-1
1951	Barnes Park, 5-8-0	H. Lane	G. Boyd	J. Sime	35	33-1
1952	Phariza, 5-6-12	C. O-Lee	J. Powell	D. Forte	40	33-1
1953	Sailing Light, 4-7-11	Mrs M. Farr	G. Armstrong	A. Roberts	41	100-8
1954	Nahar, 7-8-0	Aly Khan	A. Head	J. Massard	32	100-7
1955	Military Court, 5-8-2	Begum Aga Khan	H. Wragg	E. Mercer	29	8-1
1956	Three Star II, 8-6-13	G. Graham	H. Davison	D.W. Morris	41	40-1
1957	Babur, 4-7-13	Capt S. Lord	C. Elsey	E. Hide	32	25-1
1958	Babur, 5-9-0	Capt S. Lord	C. Elsey	E. Britt	37	25-1
1959	Marshal Pil, 5-7-13	Dr S. Lip	S. Hall	P. Robinson	32	15-2
1960	Mustavon, 5-6-13	Mrs L. McVey	S. Hall	N. McIntosh	31	8-1
1961	Johns Court, 6-7-7	K. Wheldon	E. Cousins	B. Lee	37	25-1
1962	Hill Royal, 4-7-9	D. Murray	E. Cousins	J. Sime	40	50-1
1963	Monawin, 8-7-9	R. Mason	R. Mason	J. Sime	40	25-1
1964	Mighty Gurkha, 5-7-8	Mrs G. Lambton	E. Lambton	P. Robinson	45	33-1
1965	Old Tom, 6-8-7	J. Ellis	M.H. Easterby	A. Breasley	38	22-1
1966	Riot Act, 4-8-3	Mrs J. Bryce	F. Armstrong	A. Breasley	49	8-1
1967	Ben Novus, 5-7-10	I.N. Peatt	W. Hide	P. Robinson	24	22-1
1968	Frankincense, 4-9-5	Lady Halifax	J. Oxley	G. Starkey	31	100-8
1969	Foggy Bell, 4-7-11	J. Forrester	Denys Smith	A. Barclay	25	20-1
1970	New Chapter, 4-8-1	C. Goulandris	F. Armstrong	A. Barclay	23	100-9
1971	Double Cream, 4-8-9	R. Dennis	W. Elsey	E. Hide	26	30-1
1972	Sovereign Bill, 6-8-12	W. Barr	P. Robinson	E. Hide	21	9-2
1973	Bronze Hill, 4-7-9	Mrs E. Smith	M.H. Easterby	M. Birch	26	50-1
1974	Quizair, 5-7-13	W. MacDonald	R. Jarvis	M.L. Thomas	26	28-1
1975	Southwark Star, 4-7-3	T. Hammond	G. Peter-Hoblyn	R. Fox	24	33-1
1976	The Hertford, 5-8-6	B. Shine	B. Swift	G. Lewis	26	20-1
1977	Blustery, 5-7-11	R. Lorenz	M. Smyly	D. McKay	26	20-1
1978	Captain's Wings, 5-7-10	M. House	R. Boss	M. Wigham	25	13-2
1979	Fair Season, 5-8-10	Col J. Berry	I. Balding	G. Starkey	23	8-1
1980	King's Ride, 4-8-12	D. Clark	W. Wightman	G. Baxter	18	10-1
1981	Saher, 5-8-12	J. Smith	R. Sheather	R. Cochrane	19	14-1
1982	Kings Glory, 4-8-3	C. Heard	P. Mitchell	B. Crossley	26	11-1
1983	Mighty Fly, 4-8-4	Mrs V. Tory	D. Elsworth	S. Cauthen	26	14-1
1984	Saving Mercy, 4-8-9	M. Benacerraf	D. Weld	W.R. Swinburn	26	14-1
1985	Cataldi, 4-9-10	K. Abdullah	G. Harwood	G. Starkey	26	10-1

Park Hill Stakes   1¾m 127yds

Three-year-old fillies. 8st 9lb (plus penalties). First run 1839. Run at Newmarket 1941. No race 1939-40, 1942-45. Group Two.

	OWNER	TRAINER	JOCKEY	RAN	SP
1930 Glorious Devon, 8-13	Lord Glanely	T. Hogg	G. Richards	10	7-2
1931 Volume, 8-0	Lord Astor	J. Lawson	F. Lane	8	8-1
1932 Fury, 7-11	Sir E. Hanmer	M. Peacock	W. Nevett	5	9-2
1933 Typhonic, 9-3	Maj. J. Courtauld	B. Jarvis	G. Richards	7	7-2
1934 Poker, 8-3	J. de Rothschild	F. Pratt	G. Bezant	3	7-2
1935 Foxlair, 8-0	Mrs C. Glorney	L. Cundell	S. Donoghue	6	3-1
1936 Traffic Light, 8-3	Lord Astor	J. Lawson	J. Sirett	5	11-10
1937 Nadushka, 8-10	G. Fairhurst	V. Gilpin	H. Wragg	11	10-1
1938 Gainly, 8-0	W. Woodward	C. Boyd-Rochfort	M. Beary	10	9-2
1941 Bright Lady, 7-7	T. Venn	V. Hobbs	J. Hine	6	11-2
1946 Procne, 8-4	Miss J. Clayton	C. Elsey	E. Britt	4	2-1
1947 Mitrailleuse, 8-8	Lord Astor	R.J. Colling	G. Richards	8	9-4
1948 Vertencia, 8-8	W. Hill	A. Smyth	M. Beary	9	100-8
1949 Sea Idol, 8-4	A. Hedley	J. Lawson	E. Smith	12	100-7
1950 La Baille, 9-0	Mohamed Bey Sultan	M. Marsh	C. Smirke	14	100-6
1951 Verse, 8-8	J. Rank	N. Cannon	A. Breasley	5	10-1
1952 Moon Star, 8-8	W. Woodward	C. Boyd-Rochfort	W.H. Carr	14	5-2
1953 Kerkeb, 9-0	Aga Khan	N. Marsh	C. Smirke	9	9-2
1954 Bara Bibi, 9-0	Aga Khan	N. Murless	C. Smirke	14	100-9
1955 Ark Royal, 9-0	R. Hollingsworth	G. Colling	E. Mercer	5	4-1
1956 Kyak, 8-4	R. Hollingsworth	G. Colling	E. Mercer	10	100-6
1957 Almeria, 9-0	The Queen	C. Boyd-Rochfort	W.H. Carr	5	2-7
1958 Cutter, 9-0	R. Hollingsworth	G. Colling	E. Mercer	8	100-8
1959 Collyria, 9-0	Sir V. Sassoon	N. Murless	E. Smith	7	33-1
1960 Sunny Cove, 9-0	M. Sobell	Sir G. Richards	A. Breasley	6	5-1
1961 Never Say, 9-0	J. Astor	J. Colling	J. Mercer	8	7-2
1962 Almiranta, 9-0	Lord Howard de Walden	J.A. Waugh	W.H. Carr	9	7-2
1963 Outcrop, 9-0	Maj J. Priestman	G. Barling	E. Smith	9	4-1
1964 Cursorial, 9-0	Maj L. Holliday	W. Wharton	J. Mercer	5	100-6
1965 Bracey Bridge, 9-0	M. Wickham-Boynton	N. Murless	L. Piggott	5	7-2
1966 Parthian Glance, 9-0	Mrs W. Riley-Smith	G. Todd	L. Piggott	7	4-5
1967 Pia, 9-0	Countess M. Batthyany	W. Elsey	E. Hide	7	7-2
Pink Gem, 9-0	H.J. Joel	N. Murless	G. Moore	—	2-1
1968 Bringley, 9-0	R. Midwood	H. Leader	B. Taylor	8	3-1
1969 Aggravate, 9-0	L. van Moppes	A. Budgett	E. Johnson	6	8-1
1970 Parmelia, 9-0	Lord Howard de Walden	N. Murless	A. Barclay	5	8-11
1971 Example, 9-0	The Queen	I. Balding	L. Piggott	8	11-2
1972 Attica Meli, 9-0	L. Freedman	N. Murless	G. Lewis	7	5-4
1973 Reload, 9-0	R. Moller	H. Wragg	A. Murray	9	100-30
1974 Mil's Bomb, 9-0	L. Freedman	N. Murless	G. Lewis	10	11-10
1975 May Hill, 9-0	G. Williams	P. Walwyn	P. Eddery	7	13-8
1976 African Dancer, 9-0	Sir P. Oppenheimer	H. Wragg	A. Murray	9	6-1
1977 Royal Hive, 9-0	L. Freedman	H. Cecil	J. Mercer	3	8-15
1978 Idle Waters, 9-0	R. Crutchley	R.J. Houghton	J. Reid	10	9-1
1979 Quay Line, 9-0	W. Barnett	H. Candy	P. Waldron	5	3-1
1980 Shoot a Line, 9-0	R. Budgett	W. Hern	W. Carson	8	1-2
1981 Alma Ata, 9-0	Mrs D. Zurcher	L. Cumani	T. Ives	13	25-1
1982 Swiftfoot, 9-0	Lord Rotherwick	W. Hern	W. Carson	6	4-6
1983 High Hawk, 9-0	Sheikh Mohammed	J. Dunlop	W. Carson	7	2-1
1984 Borushka, 9-0	Aga Khan	R.J. Houghton	K. Darley	13	13-2
1985 I Want To Be, 9-0	Sheikh Mohammed	J. Dunlop	L. Piggott	7	6-5

Portland Handicap   5f 140yds

First run 1855. Run as Coronation Handicap 1937. Run over 6f at Newmarket 1941. Run as William Hill Portland Handicap 1972-80. No race 1939-40, 1942-45.

	OWNER	TRAINER	JOCKEY	RAN	SP
1930 Polar Bear, 3-7-2	Mrs J. Joel	H. Cottrill	J. Dines	18	10-1
1931 Xandover, 4-9-7	J. Schwob	B. Jarvis	C. Elliott	11	11-4
1932 Polar Bear, 5-8-8	Mrs J. Joel	C. Peck	B. Carslake	22	100-6

	OWNER	TRAINER	JOCKEY	RAN	SP
1933 Valkyrie, 4-7-5	O. Watney	C. Leader	T. Barber	20	100-7
1934 Rosemary's Pet, 5-8-12	J. Joel	C. Peck	B. Carslake	16	6-1
1935 Shalfleet, 4-9-7	Maj J. Walker	H. Leader	H. Jellis	23	8-1
1936 Shalfleet, 5-9-2	Maj J. Walker	H. Leader	H. Jellis	23	10-1
1937 Carissa, 3-8-3	Sir V. Sassoon	H. Peacock	S. Donoghue	25	100-8
1938 The Drummer, 6-7-3	W. Carr	W. Carr	D. Smith	27	7-1
1941 Comatas, 4-8-11	Miss K. Farrar	O. Bell	W. Nevett	15	100-7
1946 The Shah, 4-7-5	D. Scott	B. Bullock	J. Sime	14	7-1
1947 Good View, 5-8-0	A. Halford	E. Parker	M. Beary	17	100-7
1948 Gold Mist, 3-7-12	Capt. A. Wills	N. Murless	C. Richards	18	20-1
1949 Le Lavandou, 5-7-7	Lieut-Col J. Innes	G. Houghton	P. Evans	28	25-1
1950 Paramount, 4-8-9	Sir H. de Trafford	M. Marsh	C. Smirke	19	100-7
1951 Reminiscence, 4-8-10	Mrs J. Rank	W. Nightingall	C. Smirke	25	100-6
1952 Stephen Paul, 4-9-3	J. Olding	H. Persse	G. Richards	20	100-30
1953 Reminiscence, 6-8-8	L. Bland	J. Ormston	E. Britt	29	100-7
1954 Vilmoray, 4-9-0	A. Green	B. Bullock	A. Shrive	25	100-7
1955 Princely Gift, 4-9-4	Sir V. Sassoon	N. Murless	L. Piggott	12	5-2
1956 Epaulette, 5-8-2	J. Gerber	F. Armstrong	W. Snaith	19	8-1
1957 Refined, 3-8-10	Lady M. van Cutsem	P. Prendergast	D. Smith	18	9-1
1958 Welsh Abbot, 3-9-2	Sir W. Churchill	W. Nightingall	S. Clayton	14	100-9
1959 New World, 6-7-3	R. Shaw	G. Balding	D. Greening	11	25-1
1960 Accompanist, 5-7-6	Mrs A. Palmer	F. Maxwell	D.W. Morris	12	7-1
1961 Winna, 4-7-2	Lieut-Col N. Frieze	H. Wragg	L.C. Parkes	16	100-8
1962 Harmon, 3-8-2	Mrs J. Aspinall	P. Beasley	A. Breasley	18	9-1
1963 Marcher, 3-8-9	R. Zelker	D. Hanley	R. Hutchinson	20	100-6
1964 Comefast, 5-7-13	H. Walton	J. Vickers	E. Hide	17	9-1
1965 Go Shell, 3-8-7	Lord Derby	B. van Cutsem	D. Smith	14	100-7
1966 Audrey Joan, 3-7-3	Mrs D. Rosenfeld	E. Cousins	A. Barclay	21	20-1
1967 Florescence, 3-8-13	J. Mullion	F. Armstrong	W. Williamson	15	100-9
1968 Gold Pollen, 3-7-7	W. Gaskin	R. Jarvis	E. Johnson	12	11-4
1969 Mountain Call, 4-8-11	I. Kornberg	B. van Cutsem	L. Piggott	20	11-4
1970 Virginia Boy, 4-7-1	B. Schmidt-Bodner	D. Smith	D. McKay*	15	9-1
1971 Royben, 3-8-6	A. Kennedy	A. Breasley	W. Williamson	17	13-2
1972 Privateer, 6-8-1	D. Colebrook	W. Wightman	E. Hide	13	8-1
1973 Supreme Gift, 3-8-6	R. Pritchard	B. Swift	J. Wilson	15	100-30
1974 Matinee, 3-8-11	Lord Porchester	J. Clayton	F. Durr	20	10-1
1975 Walk By, 3-8-10	Mrs F. Fleetwood-Hesketh	W. Wightman	E. Hide	16	9-1
1976 Hei'land Jamie, 5-7-13	W. Paul	N. Adam	T. McKeown	11	20-1
1977 Jon George, 3-7-12	Mrs G. Newsome	M.W. Easterby	W. Carson	12	11-2
1978 Goldhills Pride, 4-8-10	H. Ford	T. Craig	K. Leason	13	8-1
1979 Oh Simmie, 4-7-0	D. Coppenhall	R. Hollinshead	B. Jones	21	10-1
1980 Swelter, 4-8-2	G. Greenwood	F. Durr	P. Robinson	20	8-1
1981 Touch Boy, 5-8-11	G. Mullins	J. Berry	T. Ives	21	16-1
1982 Vorvados, 5-8-13	Miss F. Gallichan	M. Haynes	L. Piggott	14	6-1
1983 Out of Hand, 4-7-3	J. Baxter	D. Dale	S. Dawson	15	14-1
1984 Dawn's Delight, 6-7-8	K. Ivory	K. Ivory	L. Charnock	22	20-1
1985 Lochtillum, 6-8-1	J. Douglas-Home	J. Douglas-Home	R. Cochrane	17	14-1

Doncaster Cup $2\frac{1}{4}$m

Three-year-olds and upwards. 3-y-o 8st, 4-y-o & upwards 8st 13lb, fillies allowed 3lb (plus penalties). First run in 1766 as Doncaster Gold Cup. No race 1939-45. Group Three.

	OWNER	TRAINER	JOCKEY	RAN	SP
1930 Brown Jack, 6-9-11	Sir H. Wernher	I. Anthony	J. Childs	5	11-10
1931 Singapore, 4-9-12	Lord Glanely	T. Hogg	G. Richards	6	13-8
1932 Foxhunter, 3-7-8	E. Esmond	J. Jarvis	G. Richards	6	13-8
1933 Colorado Kid, 4-8-6	Lieut-Col G. Loder	V. Gilpin	G. Richards	2	4-9
1934 Alcazar, 3-8-8	W. Woodward	C. Boyd-Rochfort	J. Childs	3	30-100
1935 Black Devil, 4-9-9	W. Woodward	C. Boyd-Rochfort	J. Childs	5	4-6
1936 Buckleigh, 4-9-2	Lord Glanely	T. Hogg	G. Richards	6	7-2
1937 Haulfryn, 4-9-2	F. Minoprio	R. Metcalfe	G. Richards	6	8-1
1938 Epigram, 5-10-0	J. Rank	N. Cannon	B. Carslake	5	7-4
1946 Marsyas II, 6-9-9	M. Boussac	C. Semblat	E.C. Elliott	4	1-7
1947 Trimbush, 7-9-6	Mrs F. Senior	P. Vasey	D. Smith	7	10-1
1948 Auralia, 5-9-7	Mrs A. Johnston	R. Day	D. Smith	9	6-1

	OWNER	TRAINER	JOCKEY	RAN	SP
1949 Alycidon, 4-9-7	Lord Derby	W. Earl	D. Smith	4	2-7
1950 Aldborough, 5-9-9	Miss D. Paget	F. Walwyn	D. Smith	8	6-1
1951 Fast Fox, 4-9-4	Baron de Waldner	P. Carter	F. Palmer	7	3-1
1952 Aquino II, 4-9-7	Maharanee of Baroda	F. Armstrong	G. Richards	7	2-1
1953 Souepi, 5-9-9	G. Digby	G. Digby	E.C. Elliott	7	5-1
Nick la Rocca, 4-9-4	F. Williams	R.J. Colling	J. Mercer	–	100-7
1954 Osborne, 7-9-6	Brig W. Wyatt	C. Boyd-Rochfort	W.H. Carr	9	5-1
1955 Entente Cordiale, 4-9-4	Lord Derby	G. Colling	D. Smith	4	5-2
1956 Atlas, 3-8-3	The Queen	C. Boyd-Rochfort	W.H. Carr	8	11-4
1957 French Beige, 4-9-4	R. Dennis	H. Peacock	G. Littlewood	4	5-1
1958 Agreement, 4-9-4	The Queen	C. Boyd-Rochfort	D. Smith	7	25-1
1959 Agreement, 5-9-9	The Queen	C. Boyd-Rochfort	W.H. Carr	4	11-4
1960 Exar, 4-9-7	C. Vittadini	N. Murless	L. Piggott	2	6-100
1961 Pandofell, 4-9-7	H. Daw	F. Maxwell	L. Piggott	5	9-4
1962 Bonnard, 4-8-12	Marchese della Rocchetta	J. Clayton	R. Hutchinson	6	6-1
1963 Raise You Ten, 3-7-11	P. Widener	C. Boyd-Rochfort	D. Smith	4	5-1
1964 Grey of Falloden, 5-9-0	Lord Astor	W. Hern	J. Mercer	6	8-1
1965 Prince Hansel, 4-8-12	J. Barker	D. Thom	D. Yates	6	2-1
1966 Piaco, 3-7-11	Mrs O. Watney	G. Barling	M.L. Thomas	6	11-8
1967 Crozier, 4-8-12	A. Oldrey	P. Walwyn	F. Durr	6	20-1
1968 The Accuser, 4-8-12	Lord Rotherwick	W. Hern	J. Mercer	4	2-1
1969 Canterbury, 4-8-12	J. Olin	P. Prendergast	W. Williamson	8	100-30
1970 Magna Carta, 4-8-12	The Queen	I. Balding	G. Lewis	4	6-4
1971 Rock Roi, 4-8-12	Col F. Hue-Williams	P. Walwyn	D. Keith	5	4-11
1972 Biskrah, 5-9-0	Lady Beaverbrook	A. Breasley	J. Mercer	5	4-1
1973 Attica Meli, 4-8-11	L. Freedman	M. Murless	G. Lewis	4	4-11
1974 Proverb, 4-9-0	Lieut-Col J. Chandos-Pole	B. Hills	W. Carson	3	1-2
1975 Crash Course, 4-9-0	Mrs J. Hindley	J. Hindley	A. Kimberley	3	4-7
1976 Sea Anchor, 4-9-3	R. Hollingsworth	W. Hern	J. Mercer	4	2-5
1977 Shangamuzo, 4-8-12	Mrs E. Charles	G. Hunter	P. Eddery	5	33-1
1978 Buckskin, 5-9-2	D. Wildenstein	H. Cecil	J. Mercer	6	5-2
1979 Le Moss, 4-9-2	C. d'Alessio	H. Cecil	J. Mercer	5	4-11
1980 Le Moss, 5-9-2	C. d'Alessio	H. Cecil	J. Mercer	4	4-6
1981 Protection Racket, 3-7-6	S. Fradkoff	J. Hindley	J. Lowe	4	8-11
1982 Ardross, 6-9-2	C. St George	H. Cecil	L. Piggott	8	2-9
1983 Karadar, 5-8-5	Aga Khan	M. Stoute	W.R. Swinburn	8	2-1
1984 Wagoner, 4-8-5	A. Oldrey	P. Walwyn	T. Ives	4	10-1
1985 Spicy Story, 4-8-9	P. Mellon	I. Balding	S. Cauthen	8	7-4

Laurent Perrier Champagne Stakes   7f

Two-year-olds. 9st, fillies allowed 3lb. First run 1823. Run over 6f before 1962, and as Champagne Stakes before 1975. Run at Newbury 1941. No race 1939-40, 1942-45. Group Two.

	OWNER	TRAINER	JOCKEY	RAN	SP
1930 Portlaw, 9-0	Sir A. Bailey	H. Persse	H. Beasley	8	5-4
1931 Orwell, 9-0	W. Singer	J. Lawson	R.A. Jones	5	1-4
1932 Myrobella, 8-11	Lord Lonsdale	F. Darling	G. Richards	8	11-8
1933 Blazonry, 9-0	Lord Howard de Walden	D. Waugh	R. Perryman	8	11-2
1934 Kingsem, 9-0	Sir C. Hyde	N. Scobie	S. Donoghue	7	8-1
1935 Mahmoud, 9-0	Aga Khan	Frank Butters	F. Fox	11	13-8
1936 Foray, 9-0	M. Field	C. Boyd-Rochfort	P. Beasley	10	7-4
1937 Portmarnock, 9-0	Sir H. de Trafford	C. Boyd-Rochfort	P. Beasley	8	11-2
1938 Panorama, 9-0	Mrs J. Corrigan	C. Boyd-Rochfort	P. Beasley	7	8-13
1941 Big Game, 9-0	King George VI	F. Darling	H. Wragg	6	1-2
1946 Petition, 9-0	Sir A. Butt	Frank Butters	H. Wragg	3	2-7
1947 Lerins (re-named My Babu), 9-0	Maharaja of Baroda	F. Armstrong	E. Britt	4	21-20
1948 Abernant, 9-0	Maj R. M-Buchanan	N. Murless	G. Richards	3	2-5
1949 Palestine, 9-0	Aga Khan	Frank Butters	G. Richards	3	1-9
1950 Big Dipper, 9-0	Mrs J. Bryce	C. Boyd-Rochfort	W.H. Carr	7	4-7
1951 Orgoglio, 9-0	P. Bull	C. Elsey	E. Britt	7	100-8
1952 Bebe Grande, 8-11	J. Gerber	F. Armstrong	W. Smith	5	4-9
1953 Darius, 9-0	Sir P. Loraine	H. Wragg	E. Mercer	6	7-4
1954 Our Babu, 9-0	D. Robinson	G. Brooke	D. Smith	9	100-8
1955 Rustam, 9-0	Lady Wyfold	G. Brooke	D. Smith	3	8-15
1956 Eudaemon, 9-0	Mrs E. Foster	C. Elsey	E. Britt	4	5-2

	OWNER	TRAINER	JOCKEY	RAN	SP
1957 Kelly, 9-0	J. Olding	N. Cannon	J. Purtell	5	10-1
1958 Be Careful, 8-11	W. Hill	C. Elsey	E. Hide	5	4-7
1959 Paddy's Sister, 8-11	Mrs J. Mullion	P. Prendergast	G. Moore	6	8-15
1960 Ambergris, 8-11	Sir P. Loraine	H. Wragg	J. Lindley	9	7-2
1961 Clear Sound, 9-0	Mrs M. Sheehan	P. Prendergast	R. Hutchinson	8	3-1
1962 King of Babylon, 9-0	R. Dennis	W. Elsey	E. Hide	10	100-7
1963 Talahasse, 9-0	H. Loebstein	T. Corbett	A. Breasley	7	4-7
1964 Hardicanute, 9-0	J. Mullion	P. Prendergast	G. Bougoure	11	7-1
1965 Celtic Song, 9-0	M. Rayne	P. Prendergast	L. Piggott	8	2-1
1966 Bold Lad, 9-0	Lady Granard	P. Prendergast	D. Lake	5	8-11
1967 Chebs Lad, 9-0	H. Brown	W. Gray	B. Connorton	6	7-1
1968 Ribofilio, 9-0	C. Engelhard	R.J. Houghton	L. Piggott	7	7-2
1969 Saintly Song, 9-0	S. Joel	N. Murless	A. Barclay	6	11-4
1970 Breeder's Dream, 9-0	D. Robinson	M. Jarvis	F. Durr	6	4-1
1971 Crowned Prince, 8-11	F. McMahon	B. van Cutsem	L. Piggott	8	11-10
1972 Otha, 9-0	N.B. Hunt	B. van Cutsem	W. Carson	5	11-4
1973 Giacometti, 9-0	C. St George	H.R. Price	A. Murray	8	8-11
1974 Grundy, 9-0	C. Vittadini	P. Walwyn	P. Eddery	10	13-8
1975 Wollow, 9-0	C. d'Alessio	H. Cecil	G. Dettori	8	11-4
1976 J.O. Tobin, 9-0	G. Pope Jnr	N. Murless	L. Piggott	6	4-9
1977 Sexton Blake, 9-0	T. Motley	B. Hills	W. Carson	6	5-2
1978 R.B. Chesne, 9-0	C. St George	H. Cecil	J. Mercer	7	8-13
1979 Final Straw, 9-0	J. Wigan	M. Stoute	P. Cook	9	9-2
1980 Gielgud, 9-0	C. St George	H. Cecil	J. Mercer	10	11-2
1981 Achieved, 9-0	R. Sangster	V. O'Brien	P. Eddery	8	11-4
1982 Gorytus, 9-0	Mrs J. Mills	W. Hern	W. Carson	5	8-13
1983 Lear Fan, 9-0	A. Salman	G. Harwood	A. Clark	4	1-4
1984 Young Runaway, 9-0	Spyros Niarchos	G. Harwood	G. Starkey	6	5-2
1985 Sure Blade, 9-0	Sheikh Mohammed	B. Hills	B. Thomson	5	5-4

Holsten Pils St Leger Stakes   1¾m 127yds

Three-year-old colts and fillies. 9st, fillies allowed 3lb. First run 1776. Run at Newmarket 1915-18, 1942-44; at Thirsk 1940; at Manchester 1941; at York 1945. No race 1939. Run over 1¾m 132yds 1826-1969. Run as St Leger before 1984. Group One.

	OWNER	TRAINER	JOCKEY	RAN	SP
1900 Diamond Jubilee	Prince of Wales	R. Marsh	H. Jones	11	2-7
1901 Doricles	L. de Rothschild	A. Hayhoe	K. Cannon	13	40-1
1902 Sceptre, 8-11	R. Sievier	R. Sievier	F. Hardy	12	100-30
1903 Rock Sand	Sir J. Miller	G. Blackwell	D. Maher	5	2-5
1904 Pretty Polly, 8-11	Maj E. Loder	P. Gilpin	W. Lane	6	2-5
1905 Challacombe	W. Singer	A. Taylor	O. Madden	8	100-7
1906 Troutbeck	Duke of Westminster	W. Waugh	G. Stern	12	5-1
1907 Wool Winder	Col E. Baird	H. Enoch	W. Halsey	12	11-10
1908 Your Majesty	J. Joel	C. Morton	Wal Griggs	10	11-8
1909 Bayardo	'Mr Fairie'	A. Taylor	D. Maher	7	10-11
1910 Swynford	Lord Derby	G. Lambton	F. Wootton	11	9-2
1911 Prince Palatine	T. Pilkington	H. Beardsley	F. O'Neill	8	100-30
1912 Tracery	A. Belmont	J. Watson	G. Bellhouse	14	8-1
1913 Night Hawk	Col Hall-Walker	W. Robinson	E. Wheatley	12	50-1
1914 Black Jester	J. Joel	C. Morton	Wal Griggs	18	10-1
1915 Pommern	S. Joel	C. Peck	S. Donoghue	7	1-3
1916 Hurry On	J. Buchanan	F. Darling	C. Childs	5	11-10
1917 Gay Crusader	'Mr Fairie'	A. Taylor	S. Donoghue	3	2-11
1918 Gainsborough	Lady Douglas	A. Taylor	J. Childs	5	4-11
1919 Keysoe, 8-11	Lord Derby	G. Lambton	B. Carslake	10	100-8
1920 Caligula	M. Goculdas	H. Leader	A. Smith	14	100-6
1921 Polemarch	Lord Londonderry	T. Green	J. Childs	9	50-1
1922 Royal Lancer	Lord Lonsdale	A. Sadler	R. Jones	24	33-1
1923 Tranquil, 8-11	Lord Derby	C. Morton	T. Weston	13	100-9
1924 Salmon-Trout	Aga Khan	R. Dawson	B. Carslake	17	6-1
1925 Solario	Sir J. Rutherford	R. Day	J. Childs	15	7-2
1926 Coronach	Lord Woolavington	F. Darling	J. Childs	12	8-15
1927 Book Law, 8-11	Lord Astor	A. Taylor	H. Jelliss	16	7-4

		OWNER	TRAINER	JOCKEY	RAN	SP
1928	Fairway	Lord Derby	Frank Butters	T. Weston	13	7-4
1929	Trigo	W. Barnett	R. Dawson	M. Beary	14	5-1
1930	Singapore	Lord Glanely	T. Hogg	G. Richards	13	4-1
1931	Sandwich	Lord Rosebery	J. Jarvis	H. Wragg	10	9-1
1932	Firdaussi	Aga Khan	Frank Butters	F. Fox	19	20-1
1933	Hyperion	Lord Derby	G. Lambton	T. Weston	14	6-4
1934	Windsor Lad	M. Benson	M. Marsh	C. Smirke	10	4-9
1935	Bahram	Aga Khan	Frank Butters	C. Smirke	8	4-11
1936	Boswell	W. Woodward	C. Boyd-Rochfort	P. Beasley	13	20-1
1937	Chulmleigh	Lord Glanely	T. Hogg	G. Richards	15	18-1
1938	Scottish Union	J. Rank	N. Cannon	B. Carslake	9	7-1
1940	Turkhan	Aga Khan	Frank Butters	G. Richards	6	4-1
1941	Sun Castle	Lord Portal	C. Boyd-Rochfort	G. Bridgland	16	10-1
1942	Sun Chariot, 8-11	King George VI	F. Darling	G. Richards	8	9-4
1943	Herringbone, 8-11	Lord Derby	W. Earl	H. Wragg	12	100-6
1944	Tehran	Aga Khan	Frank Butters	G. Richards	17	9-2
1945	Chamossaire	S. Joel	R. Perryman	T. Lowrey	10	11-2
1946	Airborne	J. Ferguson	R. Perryman	T. Lowrey	11	3-1
1947	Sayajirao	Maharaja of Baroda	F. Armstrong	E. Britt	11	9-2
1948	Black Tarquin	W. Woodward	C. Boyd-Rochfort	E. Britt	14	15-2
1949	Ridge Wood	G. Smith	N. Murless	M. Beary	16	100-7
1950	Scratch II	M. Boussac	C. Semblat	W. Johnstone	15	9-2
1951	Talma II	M. Boussac	C. Semblat	W. Johnstone	18	7-1
1952	Tulyar	Aga Khan	M. Marsh	C. Smirke	12	10-11
1953	Premonition	Brig W. Wyatt	C. Boyd-Rochfort	E. Smith	11	10-1
1954	Never Say Die	R. Clark	J. Lawson	C. Smirke	16	100-30
1955	Meld, 8-11	Lady Z. Wernher	C. Boyd-Rochfort	W.H. Carr	8	10-11
1956	Cambremer	R. Strassburger	G. Bridgland	F. Palmer	13	8-1
1957	Ballymoss	J. McShain	V. O'Brien	T.P. Burns	16	8-1
1958	Alcide	Sir H. de Trafford	C. Boyd-Rochfort	W.H. Carr	8	4-9
1959	Cantelo, 8-11	W. Hill	C. Elsey	E. Hide	11	100-7
1960	St. Paddy	Sir V. Sassoon	N. Murless	L. Piggott	9	4-6
1961	Aurelius	Mrs V. Lilley	N. Murless	L. Piggott	13	9-2
1962	Hethersett	Maj L. Holliday	W. Hern	W. Carr	15	100-8
1963	Ragusa	Mrs J. Mullion	P. Prendergast	G. Bougoure	7	2-5
1964	Indiana	C. Engelhard	J.F. Watts	J. Lindley	15	100-7
1965	Provoke	J. Astor	W. Hern	J. Mercer	11	28-1
1966	Sodium	R. Sigtia	G. Todd	F. Durr	9	7-1
1967	Ribocco	C. Engelhard	R.J. Houghton	L. Piggott	9	7-2
1968	Ribero	C. Engelhard	R.J. Houghton	L. Piggott	8	100-30
1969	Intermezzo	G. Oldham	H. Wragg	R. Hutchinson	11	7-1
1970	Nijinsky	C. Engelhard	V. O'Brien	L. Piggott	9	2-7
1971	Athens Wood	Mrs J. Rogerson	H.T. Jones	L. Piggott	8	5-2
1972	Boucher	O. Phipps	V. O'Brien	L. Piggott	7	3-1
1973	Peleid	Col W. Behrens	W. Elsey	F. Durr	13	28-1
1974	Bustino	Lady Beaverbrook	W. Hern	J. Mercer	10	11-10
1975	Bruni	C. St George	H.R. Price	A. Murray	12	9-1
1976	Crow	D. Wildenstein	A. Penna	Y. Saint-Martin	15	6-1
1977	Dunfermline, 8-11	The Queen	W. Hern	W. Carson	13	10-1
1978	Julio Mariner	M. Lemos	C. Brittain	E. Hide	14	28-1
1979	Son of Love	A. Rolland	R. Collet	A. Lequeux	17	20-1
1980	Light Cavalry	H.J. Joel	H. Cecil	J. Mercer	7	3-1
1981	Cut Above	Sir J. Astor	W. Hern	J. Mercer	7	28-1
1982	Touching Wood	M. Al-Maktoum	H.T. Jones	P. Cook	15	7-1
1983	Sun Princess, 8-11	Sir M. Sobell	W. Hern	W. Carson	10	11-8
1984	Commanche Run	I. Allan	L. Cumani	L. Piggott	11	7-4
1985	Oh So Sharp, 8-11	Sheikh Mohammed	H. Cecil	S. Cauthen	6	8-11

William Hill Futurity Stakes   1m

Two-year-old colts and fillies. 9st, fillies allowed 3lb. First run 1961. Run as Timeform Gold Cup 1961-64; Observer Gold Cup 1965-75. Group One.

		OWNER	TRAINER	JOCKEY	RAN	SP
1961	Miralgo, 8-12	G. Oldham	H. Wragg	W. Williamson	13	10-1
1962	Noblesse, 8-12	Mrs J. Olin	P. Prendergast	G. Bougoure	12	11-10
1963	Pushful, 8-12	Maj L. Holliday	S. Meaney	W.H. Carr	10	100-6

	OWNER	TRAINER	JOCKEY	RAN	SP
1964 Hardicanute, 8-12	J. Mullion	P. Prendergast	W. Williamson	11	13-8
1965 Pretendre, 8-12	J. Lilley	J. Jarvis	R. Hutchinson	13	6-1
1966 Ribocco, 8-12	C. Engelhard	R.J. Houghton	L. Piggott	11	4-9
1967 Vaguely Noble, 8-12	L.B. Holliday	W. Wharton	W. Williamson	8	8-1
1968 The Elk, 8-12	Miss M. Sheriffe	J. Tree	W. Pyers	11	10-1
1969 Approval, 8-12	Sir H. de Trafford	H. Cecil	D. Keith	9	5-1
1970 Linden Tree, 8-12	Mrs D. McCalmont	P. Walwyn	D. Keith	9	25-1
1971 High Top, 8-11	Sir J. Thorn	B. van Cutsem	W. Carson	13	11-2
1972 Noble Decree, 9-0	N.B. Hunt	B. van Cutsem	L. Piggott	10	8-1
1973 Apalachee, 9-0	J. Mulcahy	V. O'Brien	L. Piggott	10	evens
1974 Green Dancer, 9-0	Mme P. Wertheimer	A. Head	F. Head	10	7-2
1975 Take Your Place, 9-0	C. d'Alessio	H. Cecil	G. Dettori	11	4-1
1976 Sporting Yankee, 9-0	Wm Hill Racing Ltd	P. Walwyn	P. Eddery	6	9-2
1977 Dactylographer, 9-0	P. Niarchos	P. Walwyn	P. Eddery	12	100-30
1978 Sandy Creek, 9-0	A. McClean	C. Collins	C. Roche	11	15-1
1979 Hello Gorgeous, 9-0	D. Wildenstein	H. Cecil	J. Mercer	7	11-8
1980 Beldale Flutter, 9-0	A. Kelly	M. Jarvis	P. Eddery	7	14-1
1981 Count Pahlen, 9-0	Mrs A. Villar	B. Hobbs	G. Baxter	13	25-1
1982 Dunbeath, 9-0	M. Riordan	H. Cecil	L. Piggott	8	4-7
1983 Alphabatim, 9-0	K. Abdullah	G. Harwood	G. Starkey	9	9-2
1984 Lanfranco, 9-0	C. St George	H. Cecil	L. Piggott	10	100-30
1985 Bakharoff, 9-0	K. Abdullah	G. Harwood	G. Starkey	9	2-1

William Hill November Handicap   1½m

First run 1876. Run at Manchester as Manchester November Handicap 1876-1963. Run at Pontefract 1942-45. No race 1954 (waterlogged). Transferred to Doncaster and run as Manchester Ovaltine Handicap 1964-66; Manchester Handicap 1967-75.

	OWNER	TRAINER	JOCKEY *	RAN	SP
1930 Glorious Devon, 3-7-5	Lord Glanely	T. Hogg	G. Richards	28	25-1
1931 North Drift, 4-7-6	J. Downing	M. Vasey	C. Dowdall	42	8-1
1932 Hypostyle, 3-7-5	Mrs C. Beatty	H. Fergusson	A. Richardson	18	20-1
1933 Jean's Dream, 3-7-5	A. Boazman	M. Peacock	J. Dines	28	20-1
1934 Pip Emma, 3-7-9	Lord Rosebery	J. Jarvis	E. Smith	29	100-7
1935 Free Fare, 7-8-4	B. Warner	E. Gwilt	S. Wragg	19	22-1
1936 Newton Ford, 4-8-4	A. Boazman	M. Peacock	W. Nevett	21	100-8
1937 Solitaire, 6-8-1	Sir E. Hoyle	H. Peacock	J. Taylor	31	25-1
1938 Pappageno, 3-8-6	G. Hartigan	M. Hartigan	G. Richards	26	100-7
1939 Tutor, 3-8-3	Lord Rosebery	J. Jarvis	E. Smith	24	9-2
1940 Beinn Dearg, 5-8-2	Lord Zetland	H. Peacock	W. Nevett	20	9-1
1941 Crown Colony, 5-7-9	Lord Glanely	J. Lawson	C. Richards	18	100-6
1942 Golden Boy, 4-8-11	W. Carr	W. Carr	D. Smith	17	10-1
1943 Mad Carew, 4-7-6	Mrs W. Robottom	P. Vasey	J. Sime	21	33-1
1944 Kerry Piper, 3-8-0	Sir H. Bruce	F. Armstrong	C. Spares	19	25-1
1945 Oatflake, 3-7-13	W. Barnett	F. Armstrong	E. Britt	23	100-8
1946 Las Vegas, 4-8-8	Sir W. Chaytor	A. Boyd	H. Wragg	23	20-1
1947 Regret, 4-6-3	Mrs F. Senior	P. Vasey	J. Walker	34	66-1
1948 Sports Master, 3-6-13	D. Morris	J. Beary	D. Greening	40	20-1
1949 Fidonia, 5-9-2	A. Halford	E. Parker	W.H. Carr	41	40-1
1950 Coltbridge, 4-7-6	D. Thomson	S. Hall	J. Sime	37	100-6
1951 Good Taste, 7-7-13	J. Bullock	S. Hall	W. Nevett	21	28-1
1952 Summer Rain, 3-7-13	Lord Milford	J. Jarvis	P. Evans	24	100-6
1953 Torch Singer, 4-6-5	J. Hanson	S. Hall	D. Ward	25	40-1
1955 Tearaway, 5-6-11	J. Hanson	S. Hall	W. Bentley	38	40-1
1956 Trentham Boy, 5-7-6	T. Degg	J. Gosden	J. Gifford	26	100-6
1957 Chief Barker, 4-6-5	N. Cohen	H.R. Price	D. Walker	40	33-1
1958 Paul Jones, 3-8-2	Col P. Wright	A. Budgett	J. Mercer	30	100-7
1959 Operatic Society, 3-8-9	R. Agar-Walker	C. Benstead	K. Gethin	49	18-1
1960 Dalnamein, 5-7-10	J. Phang	S. Hall	H.J. Greenaway	30	28-1
1961 Henry's Choice, 4-8-2	W. Harrison	P. Beasley	E. Hide	29	100-8
1962 Damredub, 5-8-1	T. Degg	J. Gosden	M. Germon	35	20-1
1963 Best Song, 4-9-6	H. Allen	J. Gosden	J. Lindley	31	100-7
1964 Osier, 4-7-10	D. Montagu	B. van Cutsem	D. Smith	28	20-1
1965 Concealdem, 6-8-10	G. Taylor	J. Gosden	R. Hutchinson	18	100-8
1966 Polish Warrior, 3-7-3	Col P. Wright	A. Budgett	A. Barclay	26	100-6
1967 Bugle Boy, 4-7-8	Miss E. Rigden	A. Budgett	A. Barclay	25	22-1

		OWNER	TRAINER	JOCKEY	RAN	SP
1968	Zardia, 4-7-8	S. Gillatt	A. Vasey	R. Still	29	25-1
1969	Tintagel II, 4-9-0	Mrs R. Sturdy	R. Sturdy	L. Piggott	21	15-2
1970	Saraceno, 5-9-2	G. Oldham	H. Wragg	G. Sexton	21	15-2
1971	Misty Light, 3-8-5	R. Scully	F. Armstrong	J. Mercer	20	25-1
1972	King Top, 3-7-11	Lady Halifax	J. Oxley	W. Carson	16	6-1
1973	Only For Jo, 3-7-4	D. Toomey	R. Smyth	I. Jenkinson	22	13-1
1974	Gritti Palace, 5-7-0	Mrs J. Fisher	P. Robinson	R. Fox	21	7-2
1975	Mr Bigmore, 3-9-1	E. Lambton	P. Robinson	G. Starkey	12	100-30
1976	Gale Bridge, 3-8-12	J. Byrne	H.R. Price	B. Taylor	14	10-1
1977	Sailcloth, 3-7-7	Lord Porchester	W. Hastings-Bass	M.L. Thomas	20	13-2
1978	Eastern Spring, 4-7-10	Miss F. Vittadini	L. Cumani	M. Wigham	21	17-2
1979	Morse Code, 4-8-3	A. Budgett	J. Dunlop	P. Cook	14	11-2
1980	Path of Peace, 4-8-5	Miss L. Gold	C. Thornton	J. Bleasdale	22	14-1
1981	Lafontaine, 4-8-7	Mrs J. Bigg	C. Brittain	G. Duffield	20	16-1
1982	Double Shuffle, 3-9-0	D. Sieff	G. Pritchard-Gordon	G. Duffield	17	12-1
	Turkoman, 3-8-7	M. Pote	D. Sasse	D. McKay	—	20-1
1983	Asir, 3-8-7	Yazid & Ahmed Ltd	G. Harwood	G. Starkey	25	10-1
1984	Abu Kadra, 3-8-12	M. Salem	M. Stoute	W.R. Swinburn	23	25-1
1985	Bold Rex, 3-8-7	Lord Granard	J. Dunlop	J. Mercer	24	20-1

EDINBURGH

The Racecourse, Musselburgh, Midlothian, Scotland (031-665-2859, race days only; 0292-264179, admin)
Clerk of the Course: David McHarg

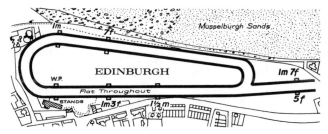

Right-handed course.
EFFECT OF DRAW: Low numbers strongly favoured when stalls on stands side on straight course; high numbers favoured on round course.

Best Times

DISTANCE	TIME	AGE	WEIGHT		GOING	HORSE	DATE	
5f	57·4	4	7	2	Firm	Palm Court Joe	July 4,	1977
5f	58·6	2	8	10	Firm	Baroda	Sept. 20,	1949
7f	1.26	6	9	0	Firm	Show Of Hands	April 19,	1982
7f	1.28·3	2	8	8	Firm	Roxburgh Belle	July 5,	1976
8f	1.38·3	4	8	13	Firm	Churchillian	July 11,	1977
8f	1.41·6	2	8	9	Firm	Pipecay	Sept. 20,	1949
11f	2.19·7	3	8	10	Firm	Old Court	July 4,	1977
12f	2.32·2	5	7	9	Good	Glengrigor	April 15,	1946
15f	3.10·4	3	8	0	Good	Cunningham	Sept. 21,	1953

EPSOM

United Racecourses Ltd., Racecourse Paddock, Epsom, Surrey. (03727-26311)
Clerk of the Course: Mark Kershaw

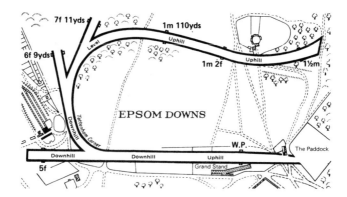

Left-handed course with electrical timing apparatus.
EFFECT OF DRAW: High numbers favoured over 5f; low numbers strongly favoured at
1m 100yds to 1¼m.

Best Times

DISTANCE	TIME	AGE	WEIGHT		GOING	HORSE	DATE	
5f	53·6	4	9	5	Firm	Indigenous	June 2,	1960
5f	55·2	2	8	9	Firm	Cerise	June 4,	1954
6f	1.7·91	5	7	7	Firm	Moor Lane	June 7,	1973
6f	1.8·4	2	9	0	Hard	My Babu	Aug. 4,	1947
7f	1.20·15	4	8	7	Firm	Capistrano	June 7,	1972
7f	1.22·44	2	9	0	Hard	Leonardo	Sept. 5,	1964
8f 110y	1.41·31	4	9	3	Firm	Hardgreen	June 4,	1980
10f	2.3·5	5	7	13	Good	Crossbow	June 7,	1967
12f	2.33·1	4	9	0	Firm	Bustino	June 7,	1975
18f	3.54	4	6	8	Firm	Gay Ballad	April 23,	1957

Race Results

Ever Ready Derby Stakes   1½m

*Three-year-old colts and fillies. 9st, fillies allowed 5lb. First run 1780. Run at
Newmarket 1915-18, 1940-45. Group One.*

		OWNER	TRAINER	JOCKEY	RAN	SP
1780	Diomed	Sir C. Bunbury	—	S. Arnull	9	6-4
1781	Young Eclipse	Maj D. O'Kelly	—	Hindley	15	10-1
1782	Assassin	Lord Egremont	F. Neale	S. Arnull	13	5-1
1783	Saltram	Mr Parker	F. Neale	Hindley	6	5-2
1784	Sergeant	Col D. O'Kelly	—	J. Arnull	11	3-1
1785	Aimwell	Lord Clermont	—	Hindley	10	7-1
1786	Noble	Mr Panton	F. Neale	J. White	15	30-1
1787	Sir Peter Teazle	Lord Derby	—	S. Arnull	17	2-1
1788	Sir Thomas	Prince of Wales	F. Neale	W. South	11	5-6
1789	Skyscraper	Duke of Bedford	—	S. Chifney, Sn.	11	4-7
1790	Rhadamanthus	Lord Grosvenor	—	J. Arnull	10	5-4
1791	Eager	Duke of Bedford	—	Stephenson	9	5-2
1792	John Bull	Lord Grosvenor	—	F. Buckle	7	6-4
1793	Waxy	Sir F. Poole	Robson	W. Clift	13	12-1
1794	Daedalus	Lord Grosvenor	—	F. Buckle	4	6-1
1795	Spread Eagle	Sir F. Standish	—	A. Wheatley	11	3-1
1796	Didelot	Sir F. Standish	—	J. Arnull	11	—
1797	colt by Fidget	Duke of Bedford	—	J. Singleton	7	10-1

		OWNER	TRAINER	JOCKEY	RAN	SP
1798	Sir Harry	J. Cookson	F. Neale	S. Arnull	10	7-4
1799	Archduke	Sir F. Standish	—	J. Arnull	11	12-1
1800	Champion	Mr Wilson	—	W. Clift	13	7-4
1801	Eleanor	Sir C. Bunbury	—	Saunders	11	5-4
1802	Tyrant	Duke of Grafton	Robson	F. Buckle	9	7-1
1803	Ditto	Sir H. Williamson	—	W. Clift	6	7-2
1804	Hannibal	Lord Egremont	F. Neale	W. Arnull	8	3-1
1805	Cardinal Beaufort	Lord Egremont	—	D. Fitzpatrick	15	20-1
1806	Paris	Lord Foley	—	J. Shepherd	12	5-1
1807	Election	Lord Egremont	—	J. Arnull	13	3-1
1808	Pan	Sir H. Williamson	—	F. Collinson	10	25-1
1809	Pope	Duke of Grafton	Robson	T. Goodison	10	20-1
1810	Whalebone	Duke of Grafton	Robson	W. Clift	11	2-1
1811	Phantom	Sir J. Shelley	—	F. Buckle	16	5-1
1812	Octavius	R. Ladbroke	—	W. Arnull	14	7-1
1813	Smolenski	Sir C. Bunbury	—	T. Goodison	12	evens
1814	Blücher	Lord Stawell	—	W. Arnull	14	5-2
1815	Whisker	Duke of Grafton	Robson	T. Goodison	13	8-1
1816	Prince Leopold	W. Lake	—	W. Wheatley	11	20-1
1817	Azor	J. Payne	Robson	J. Robinson	13	50-1
1818	Sam	T. Thornhill	W. Chifney	S. Chifney, Jn.	16	7-2
1819	Tiresias	Duke of Portland	—	W. Clift	16	5-2
1820	Sailor	T. Thornhill	W. Chifney	S. Chifney, Jn.	15	4-1
1821	Gustavus	J. Hunter	—	S. Day	13	2-1
1822	Moses	Duke of York	—	T. Goodison	12	6-1
1823	Emilius	J. Udny	Robson	F. Buckle	11	11-8
1824	Cedric	Sir J. Shelley	—	J. Robinson	17	9-2
1825	Middleton	Lord Jersey	Edwards	J. Robinson	18	7-4
1826	Lapdog	Lord Egremont	Bird	G. Dockeray	19	50-1
1827	Mameluke	Lord Jersey	Edwards	J. Robinson	23	9-1
1828	Cadland	Duke of Rutland	—	J. Robinson	15	4-1
1829	Frederick	W. Gratwicke	J. Forth	J. Forth	17	40-1
1830	Priam	W. Chifney	W. Chifney	S. Day	23	4-1
1831	Spaniel	Lord Lowther	—	W. Wheatley	23	50-1
1832	St. Giles	R. Ridsdale	—	W. Scott	22	3-1
1833	Dangerous	I. Sadler	—	J. Chapple	25	30-1
1834	Plenipotentiary	S. Batson	—	P. Conolly	23	9-4
1835	Mündig	J. Bowes	J. Scott	W. Scott	14	6-1
1836	Bay Middleton	Lord Jersey	—	J. Robinson	21	7-4
1837	Phosphorus	Lord Berners	—	G. Edwards	17	40-1
1838	Amato	Sir G. Heathcote	R. Sherwood	J. Chapple	23	30-1
1839	Bloomsbury	W. Ridsdale	W. Ridsdale	S. Templeman	21	25-1
1840	Little Wonder	D. Robertson	W. Forth	W. Macdonald	17	50-1
1841	Coronation	A. Rawlinson	—	P. Conolly	29	5-2
1842	Attila	Col Anson	J. Scott	W. Scott	24	5-1
1843	Cotherstone	J. Bowes	J. Scott	W. Scott	23	13-8
1844	Orlando	Col Peel	Cooper	E. Flatman	29	20-1
1845	The Merry Monarch	W. Gratwicke	J. Forth	F. Bell	31	15-1
1846	Pyrrhus the First	J. Gully	J. Day	S. Day	27	8-1
1847	Cossack	T. Pedley	J. Day	S. Templeman	32	5-1
1848	Surplice	Lord Clifden	J. Kent	S. Templeman	17	evens
1849	The Flying Dutchman	Lord Eglinton	Fobert	Marlow	26	2-1
1850	Voltigeur	Lord Zetland	R. Hill	J. Marson	24	16-1
1851	Teddington	Sir J. Hawley	A. Taylor	J. Marson	33	3-1
1852	Daniel O'Rourke	J. Bowes	J. Scott	F. Butler	27	25-1
1853	West Australian	J. Bowes	J. Scott	F. Butler	28	6-4
1854	Andover	J. Gully	J. Day	A. Day	21	7-2
1855	Wild Dayrell	F. Popham	Rickaby	R. Sherwood	12	evens
1856	Ellington	Admiral Harcourt	T. Dawson	T. Aldcroft	24	20-1
1857	Blink Bonny	W. I'Anson	W. I'Anson	Charlton	30	20-1
1858	Beadsman	Sir J. Hawley	G. Manning	J. Wells	23	10-1
1859	Musjid	Sir J. Hawley	G. Manning	J. Wells	30	9-4
1860	Thormanby	J. Merry	M. Dawson	H. Custance	30	4-1
1861	Kettledrum	Col Towneley	Oates	Bullock	18	16-1
1862	Caractacus	C. Snewing	Zachary	J. Parsons	34	40-1
1863	Macaroni	R. Naylor	Godding	T. Challoner	31	10-1
1864	Blair Athol	W. I'Anson	W. I'Anson	J. Snowden	30	14-1
1865	Gladiateur	Count de Lagrange	T. Jennings	H. Grimshaw	29	5-2
1866	Lord Lyon	R. Sutton	J. Dover	H. Custance	26	5-6

		OWNER	TRAINER	JOCKEY	RAN	SP
1867	Hermit	H. Chaplin	Bloss	J. Daley	30	66-1
1868	Blue Gown	Sir J. Hawley	J. Porter	J. Wells	18	7-2
1869	Pretender	J. Johnstone	T. Dawson	J. Osborne	22	11-8
1870	Kingcraft	Lord Falmouth	M. Dawson	T. French	15	20-1
1871	Favonius	Baron de Rothschild	J. Hayhoe	T. French	17	9-1
1872	Cremorne	H. Savile	W. Gilbert	C. Maidment	23	3-1
1873	Doncaster	J. Merry	P. Peck	F. Webb	12	45-1
1874	George Frederick	W. Cartwright	T. Leader	H. Custance	20	9-1
1875	Galopin	Prince Batthyany	J. Dawson	Morris	18	2-1
1876	Kisber	A. Baltazzi	J. Hayhoe	C. Maidment	15	4-1
1877	Silvio	Lord Falmouth	M. Dawson	F. Archer	17	100-9
1878	Sefton	W. Crawford	A. Taylor	H. Constable	22	100-12
1879	Sir Bevys	Mr Acton	J. Hayhoe	G. Fordham	23	20-1
1880	Bend Or	Duke of Westminster	R. Peck	F. Archer	19	2-1
1881	Iroquois	P. Lorillard	J. Pincus	F. Archer	15	11-2
1882	Shotover	Duke of Westminster	J. Porter	T. Cannon	14	11-2
1883	St. Blaise	Sir F. Johnstone	J. Porter	C. Wood	11	5-1
1884	St. Gatien	J. Hammond	R. Sherwood	C. Wood	15	100-8
	Harvester	Sir J. Willoughby	J. Jewitt	S. Loates	—	100-7
1885	Melton	Lord Hastings	M. Dawson	F. Archer	12	75-40
1886	Ormonde	Duke of Westminster	J. Porter	F. Archer	9	4-9
1887	Merry Hampton	'Mr Abington'	M. Gurry	J. Watts	11	100-9
1888	Ayrshire	Duke of Portland	G. Dawson	F. Barrett	9	5-6
1889	Donovan	Duke of Portland	G. Dawson	T. Loates	13	8-11
1890	Sainfoin	Sir J. Miller	J. Porter	J. Watts	8	100-15
1891	Common	Sir F. Johnstone	J. Porter	G. Barrett	11	10-11
1892	Sir Hugo	Lord Bradford	T. Wadlow	F. Allsopp	13	40-1
1893	Isinglass	H. McCalmont	J. Jewitt	T. Loates	11	4-9
1894	Ladas	Lord Rosebery	M. Dawson	J. Watts	7	2-9
1895	Sir Visto	Lord Rosebery	M. Dawson	S. Loates	15	9-1
1896	Persimmon	Prince of Wales	R. Marsh	J. Watts	11	5-1
1897	Galtee More	J. Gubbins	S. Darling	C. Wood	11	1-4
1898	Jeddah	J. Larnach	R. Marsh	O. Madden	18	100-1
1899	Flying Fox	Duke of Westminster	J. Porter	M. Cannon	12	2-5
1900	Diamond Jubilee	Prince of Wales	R. Marsh	H. Jones	14	6-4
1901	Volodyovski	W. Whitney	J. Huggins	L. Reiff	25	5-2
1902	Ard Patrick	J. Cubbins	S. Darling	J. Martin	18	100-14
1903	Rock Sand	Sir J. Miller	G. Blackwell	D. Maher	7	4-6
1904	St. Amant	L. de Rothschild	A. Hayhoe	K. Cannon	8	5-1
1905	Cicero	Lord Rosebery	P. Peck	D. Maher	9	4-11
1906	Spearmint	Maj E. Loder	P. Gilpin	D. Maher	22	6-1
1907	Orby	R. Croker	Col McCabe	J. Reiff	9	100-9
1908	Signorinetta	E. Ginistrelli	E. Ginistrelli	W. Bullock	18	100-1
1909	Minoru	King Edward VII	R. Marsh	H. Jones	15	7-2
1910	Lemberg	'Mr Fairie'	A. Taylor	B. Dillon	15	7-4
1911	Sunstar	J. Joel	C. Morton	G. Stern	26	13-8
1912	Tagalie	W. Raphael	D. Waugh	J. Rieff	20	100-8
1913	Aboyeur	A. Cunliffe	T. Lewis	E. Piper	15	100-1
1914	Durbar II	H. Duryea	T. Murphy	M. MacGee	30	20-1
1915	Pommern	S. Joel	C. Peck	S. Donoghue	17	11-10
1916	Fifinella	E. Hulton	R. Dawson	J. Childs	10	11-2
1917	Gay Crusader	'Mr Fairie'	A. Taylor	S. Donoghue	12	7-4
1918	Gainsborough	Lady J. Douglas	A. Taylor	J. Childs	13	8-13
1919	Grand Parade	Lord Glanely	F. Barling	F. Templeman	13	33-1
1920	Spion Kop	Maj G. Loder	P. Gilpin	F. O'Neill	19	100-6
1921	Humorist	J. Joel	C. Morton	S. Donoghue	23	6-1
1922	Captain Cuttle	Lord Woolavington	F. Darling	S. Donoghue	30	10-1
1923	Papyrus	B. Irish	B. Jarvis	S. Donoghue	19	100-15
1924	Sansovino	Lord Derby	G. Lambton	T. Weston	27	9-2
1925	Manna	H. Morriss	F. Darling	S. Donoghue	27	9-1
1926	Coronach	Lord Woolavington	F. Darling	J. Childs	19	11-2
1927	Call Boy	F. Curzon	J. Watts	E.C. Elliott	23	4-1
1928	Felstead	Sir H. C-Owen	O. Bell	H. Wragg	19	33-1
1929	Trigo	W. Barnett	R. Dawson	J. Marshall	26	33-1
1930	Blenheim	Aga Khan	R. Dawson	H. Wragg	17	18-1
1931	Cameronian	J. Dewar	F. Darling	F. Fox	25	7-2
1932	April the Fifth	T. Walls	T. Walls	F. Lane	21	100-6
1933	Hyperion	Lord Derby	G. Lambton	T. Weston	24	6-1
1934	Windsor Lad	Maharaja of Rajpipla	M. Marsh	C. Smirke	19	15-2

	OWNER	TRAINER	JOCKEY	RAN	SP
1935 Bahram	Aga Khan	Frank Butters	F. Fox	16	5-4
1936 Mahmoud	Aga Khan	Frank Butters	C. Smirke	22	100-8
1937 Mid-day Sun	Mrs G. Miller	Fred Butters	M. Beary	21	100-7
1938 Bois Roussel	P. Beatty	F. Darling	E.C. Elliott	22	20-1
1939 Blue Peter	Lord Rosebery	J. Jarvis	E. Smith	27	7-2
1940 Pont l'Eveque	F. Darling	F. Darling	S. Wragg	16	10-1
1941 Owen Tudor	Mrs R. M-Buchanan	F. Darling	W. Nevett	20	25-1
1942 Watling Street	Lord Derby	W. Earl	H. Wragg	13	6-1
1943 Straight Deal	Miss D. Paget	W. Nightingall	T. Carey	23	100-6
1944 Ocean Swell	Lord Rosebery	J. Jarvis	W. Nevett	20	28-1
1945 Dante	Sir E. Ohlson	M. Peacock	W. Nevett	27	100-30
1946 Airborne	J. Ferguson	R. Perryman	T. Lowrey	17	50-1
1947 Pearl Diver	Baron de Waldner	C. Halsey	G. Bridgland	15	40-1
1948 My Love	Aga Khan	R. Carver	W. Johnstone	32	100-9
1949 Nimbus	Mrs M. Glenister	G. Colling	E.C. Elliott	32	7-1
1950 Galcador	M. Boussac	C. Semblat	W. Johnstone	25	100-9
1951 Arctic Prince	J. McGrath	W. Stephenson	C. Spares	33	28-1
1952 Tulyar	Aga Khan	M. Marsh	C. Smirke	33	11-2
1953 Pinza	Sir V. Sassoon	N. Bertie	G. Richards	27	5-1
1954 Never Say Die	R. Clark	J. Lawson	L. Piggott	22	33-1
1955 Phil Drake	Mme L. Volterra	F. Mathet	F. Palmer	23	100-8
1956 Lavandin	P. Wertheimer	A. Head	W. Johnstone	27	7-1
1957 Crepello	Sir V. Sassoon	N. Murless	L. Piggott	22	6-4
1958 Hard Ridden	Sir V. Sassoon	J. Rogers	C . Smirke	20	18-1
1959 Parthia	Sir H. de Trafford	C. Boyd-Rochfort	W.H. Carr	20	10-1
1960 St Paddy	Sir V. Sassoon	N. Murless	L. Piggott	17	7-1
1961 Psidium	Mrs A. Plesch	H. Wragg	R. Poincelet	28	66-1
1962 Larkspur	R. Guest	V. O'Brien	N. Sellwood	26	22-1
1963 Relko	F. Dupré	F. Mathet	Y. Saint-Martin	26	5-1
1964 Santa Claus	J. Ismay	J.M. Rogers	A. Breasley	17	15-8
1965 Sea Bird II	J. Ternynck	E. Pollet	T.P. Glennon	22	7-4
1966 Charlottown	Lady Z. Wernher	G. Smyt	A. Breasley	25	5-1
1967 Royal Palace	H.J. Joel	N. Murless	G. Moore	22	7-4
1968 Sir Ivor	R. Guest	V. O'Brien	L. Piggott	13	4-5
1969 Blakeney	A. Budgett	A. Budgett	E. Johnson	26	15-2
1970 Nijinsky	C. Engelhard	V. O'Brien	L. Piggott	11	11-8
1971 Mill Reef	P. Mellon	I. Balding	G. Lewis	21	100-30
1972 Roberto	J. Galbreath	V. O'Brien	L. Piggott	22	3-1
1973 Morston	A. Budgett	A. Budgett	E. Hide	25	25-1
1974 Snow Knight	Mrs N. Phillips	P. Nelson	B. Taylor	18	50-1
1975 Grundy	C. Vittadini	P. Walwyn	P. Eddery	18	5-1
1976 Empery	N.B. Hunt	M. Zilber	L. Piggott	23	10-1
1977 The Minstrel	R. Sangster	V. O'Brien	L. Piggott	22	5-1
1978 Shirley Heights	Lord Halifax	J. Dunlop	G. Starkey	25	8-1
1979 Troy	Sir M. Sobell	W. Hern	W. Carson	24	7-1
1980 Henbit	Mrs A. Plesch	W. Hern	W. Carson	24	7-1
1981 Shergar	Aga Khan	M. Stoute	W.R. Swinburn	18	10-11
1982 Golden Fleece	R. Sangster	V. O'Brien	P. Eddery	18	3-1
1983 Teenoso	E. Moller	G. Wragg	L. Piggott	21	9-2
1984 Secreto	L. Miglietti	D. O'Brien	C. Roche	17	14-1
1985 Slip Anchor	Ld Howard de Walden	H. Cecil	S. Cauthen	14	9-4

Derby Times

	Min	Sec		Min	Sec		Min	Sec		Min	Sec		Min	Sec
1846	2	55	1859	2	59	1872	2	45.5	1885	2	44.2	1898	2	47
1847	2	52	1860	2	55	1873	2	50	1886	2	45.6	1899	2	42.8
1848	2	48	1861	2	45	1874	2	46	1887	2	43	1900	2	42
1849	3	00	1862	2	45.5	1875	2	48	1888	2	43	1901	2	40.8
1850	2	50	1863	2	50.5	1876	2	44	1889	2	44.4	1902	2	42.2
1851	2	51	1864	2	43	1877	2	50	1890	2	49.8	1903	2	42.8
1852	3	02	1865	2	46	1878	2	56	1891	2	56.8	1904	2	42.4
1853	2	55.5	1866	2	50	1879	3	02	1892	2	44	1905	2	39.4
1854	2	52	1867	2	52	1880	2	46	1893	2	43	1906	2	36.8
1855	2	54	1868	2	43.5	1881	2	50	1894	2	45.8	1907	2	44
1856	3	04	1869	2	52.5	1882	2	45.6	1895	2	43.4	1908	2	39.8
1857	2	45	1870	2	45	1883	2	48.4	1896	2	42	1909	2	42.4
1858	2	54	1871	2	50	1884	2	46.2	1897	2	44	1910	2	35.2

	Min	Sec		Min	Sec		Min	Sec		Min	Sec
1911	2	36.8	1930	2	38.2	1949	2	42	1968	2	38.73
1912	2	38.8	1931	2	36.6	1950	2	36.8	1969	2	40.3
1913	2	37.6	1932	2	43.2	1951	2	39.4	1970	2	34.68
1914	2	38.6	1933	2	34	1952	2	36.4	1971	2	37.14
1915	2	32.6	1934	2	34	1953	2	35.6	1972	2	36.09
1916	2	36.6	1935	2	36	1954	2	35.8	1973	2	35.92
1917	2	40.6	1936	2	33.8	1955	2	39.8	1974	2	35.04
1918	2	33.2	1037	2	37.6	1956	2	36.4	1975	2	35.35
1919	2	35.8	1938	2	39.2	1957	2	35.4	1976	2	35.69
1920	2	34.8	1939	2	36.8	1958	2	41.2	1977	2	36.44
1921	2	36.2	1940	2	30.8	1959	2	36	1978	2	35.3
1922	2	34.6	1941	2	32	1960	2	35.8	1979	2	36.59
1923	2	38	1942	2	29.6	1961	2	36.4	1980	2	34.77
1924	2	46.6	1943	2	30.4	1962	2	37.6	1981	2	44.21
1925	2	40.6	1944	2	31	1963	2	39.4	1982	2	34.27
1926	2	47.8	1945	2	26.6	1964	2	41.98	1983	2	49.07
1927	2	34.4	1946	2	44.6	1965	2	38.41	1984	2	39.12
1928	2	34.4	1947	2	38.4	1966	2	37.63	1985	2	36.23
1929	2	36.4	1948	2	40	1967	2	38.36			

Coronation Cup 1½m

Four-year-olds and upwards. 9st, fillies allowed 3lb. Run at Newbury 1941; at Newmarket 1943-45. No race 1940, 1942. Group One.

		OWNER	TRAINER	JOCKEY	RAN	SP
1930	Plantago, 5-9-6	W. Singer	J. Lawson	C. Ray	6	7-2
1931	Parenthesis, 4-9-3	Lord Woolavington	F. Darling	F. Fox	11	9-4
1932	Salmon Leap, 5-9-6	Mrs A. James	G. Lambton	T. Weston	8	7-2
1933	Dastur, 4-9-3	Aga Khan	Frank Butters	E.C. Elliott	4	7-4
1934	King Salmon, 4-9-3	Sir A. Brooke	O. Bell	H. Wragg	3	7-4
1935	Windsor Lad, 4-9-3	M. Benson	M. Marsh	C. Smirke	4	evens
1936	Plassy, 4-9-3	Lord Derby	C. Leader	P. Perryman	8	11-8
1937	Cecil, 6-9-6	Sir A. Bailey	J. Lawson	T. Weston	8	100-8
	His Grace, 4-9-3	J. Rank	R. Dawson	G. Richards	—	100-9
1938	Monument, 5-9-6	Duke of Marlborough	C. Boyd-Rochfort	P. Beasley	7	9-2
1939	Scottish Union, 4-9-3	J. Rank	N. Cannon	G. Richards	6	85-40
1941	Winterhalter, 4-9-3	Aga Khan	Frank Butters	D. Smith	6	7-2
1943	Hyperides, 4-9-0	Lord Rosebery	J. Jarvis	E. Smith	7	7-4
1944	Persian Gulf, 4-9-0	Lady Z. Wernher	C. Boyd-Rochfort	R. Jones	6	5-2
1945	Borealis, 4-9-0	Lord Derby	W. Earl	H. Wragg	4	5-2
1946	Ardan, 5-9-3	M. Boussac	C. Semblat	E.C. Elliott	3	5-6
1947	Chanteur II, 5-9-3	P. Magot	H. Count	R. Brethes	5	1-3
1948	Goyama, 5-9-3	M. Boussac	C. Semblat	E.C. Elliott	5	5-2
1949	Beau Sabreur, 4-9-0	A. MacNaughton	C. Brabazon	W. Cook	3	9-4
1950	Amour Drake, 4-8-7	Mme L. Volterra	R. Carver	R. Poincelet	6	15-8
1951	Tantieme, 4-8-7	F. Dupré	F. Mathet	J. Doyasbere	5	2-7
1952	Nuccio, 4-8-7	Aga Khan	A. Head	R. Poincelet	5	3-1
1953	Zucchero, 5-8-10	G. Rolls	W. Payne	L. Piggott	10	100-7
1954	Aureole, 4-8-7	The Queen	C. Boyd-Rochfort	E. Smith	8	5-2
1955	Narrator, 4-8-7	Maj L. Holliday	H. Cottrill	F. Barlow	12	100-30
1956	Tropique, 4-8-7	Baron de Rothschild	G. Watson	P. Blanc	6	13-8
1957	Fric, 5-8-10	M. Calmann	P. Lallie	J. Deforge	8	7-2
1958	Ballymoss, 4-8-7	J. McShain	V. O'Brien	A. Breasley	5	evens
1959	Nagami, 4-8-7	Mrs A. Plesch	H. Wragg	L. Piggott	3	5-4
1960	Petite Etoile, 4-8-4	Aly Khan	N. Murless	L. Piggott	3	1-3
1961	Petite Etoile, 5-8-7	Aga Khan	N. Murless	L. Piggott	5	2-5
1962	Dicta Drake, 4-8-7	Mme L. Volterra	F. Mathet	Y. Saint-Martin	7	2-1
1963	Exbury, 4-8-7	Baron de Rothschild	G. Watson	J. Deforge	9	11-8
1964	Relko, 4-8-7	F. Dupré	F. Mathet	Y. Saint-Martin	7	4-6
1965	Oncidium, 4-8-11	Lord Howard de Walden	G. Todd	A. Breasley	10	11-2
1966	I Say, 4-8-10	L. Freedman	W. Nightingall	J. Lindley	7	10-1
1967	Charlottown, 4-8-10	Lady Z. Wernher	G. Smyth	D. Keith	7	11-8
1968	Royal Palace, 4-8-10	H.J. Joel	N. Murless	A. Barclay	4	4-9
1969	Park Top, 5-9-0	Duke of Devonshire	B. van Cutsem	L. Piggott	7	11-4
1970	Caliban, 4-9-0	S. Joel	N. Murless	A. Barclay	4	8-1
1971	Lupe, 4-8-11	Mrs S. Joel	N. Murless	G. Lewis	6	5-2

	OWNER	TRAINER	JOCKEY	RAN	SP
1972 Mill Reef, 4-9-0	P. Mellon	I. Balding	G. Lewis	4	2-15
1973 Roberto, 4-9-0	J. Galbreath	V. O'Brien	L. Piggott	5	4-9
1974 Buoy, 4-9-0	R. Hollingsworth	W. Hern	J. Mercer	5	4-1
1975 Bustino, 4-9-0	Lady Beaverbrook	W. Hern	J. Mercer	6	11-10
1976 Quiet Fling, 4-9-0	J. Whitney	J. Tree	L. Piggott	6	5-2
1977 Exceller, 4-9-0	N.B. Hunt	F. Mathet	G. Dubroeucq	6	13-8
1978 Crow, 5-9-0	D. Wildenstein	P. Walwyn	P. Eddery	5	9-4
1979 Ile de Bourbon, 4-9-0	Sir P. Oppenheimer	R.J. Houghton	J. Reid	4	4-6
1980 Sea Chimes, 4-9-0	J. Thursby	J. Dunlop	L. Piggott	4	5-4
1981 Master Willie, 4-9-0	R. Barnett	H. Candy	P. Waldron	5	1-2
1982 Easter Sun, 5-9-0	Lady Beaverbrook	M. Jarvis	B. Raymond	8	20-1
1983 Be My Native, 4-9-0	K. Hsu	R. Armstrong	L. Piggott	6	8-1
1984 Time Charter, 5-8-11	R. Barnett	H. Candy	S. Cauthen	6	100-30
1985 Rainbow Quest, 4-9-0	K. Abdullah	J. Tree	P. Eddery	7	8-15

Gold Seal Oaks Stakes 1½m

*Three-year-old fillies. 9st. First run 1779. Run at Newmarket 1915-18, 1940-45. Run
as Oaks Stakes 1779-1983. Group One.*

	OWNER	TRAINER	JOCKEY	RAN	SP
1900 La Roche	Duke of Portland	J. Porter	M. Cannon	14	5-1
1901 Cap and Bells II	F. Keen	S. Darling	M. Henry	21	9-4
1902 Sceptre	R. Sievier	R. Sievier	H. Randall	14	5-2
1903 Our Lassie	J. Joel	C. Morton	M. Cannon	14	6-1
1904 Pretty Polly	Maj E. Loder	P. Gilpin	W. Lane	4	8-100
1905 Cherry Lass	W.H. Walker	W. Robinson	H. Jones	12	4-5
1906 Keystone II	Lord Derby	G. Lambton	D. Maher	12	5-2
1907 Glass Doll	J. Joel	C. Morton	H. Randall	14	25-1
1908 Signorinetta	E. Ginistrelli	E. Ginistrelli	W. Bullock	13	3-1
1909 Perola	W. Cooper	G. Davies	F. Wootton	14	5-1
1910 Rosedrop	Sir W. Bass	A. Taylor	C. Trigg	11	7-1
1911 Cherimoya	W.B. Cloete	C. Marsh	F. Winter	21	25-1
1912 Mirska	J. Prat	T. Jennings	J. Childs	14	33-1
1913 Jest	J. Joel	C. Morton	F. Rickaby	12	8-1
1914 Princess Dorrie	J. Joel	C. Morton	W. Huxley	21	11-4
1915 Snow Marten	L. Neumann	P. Gilpin	W. Griggs	11	20-1
1916 Fifinella	E. Hulton	R. Dawson	J. Childs	7	8-13
1917 Sunny Jane	Maj W. Astor	A. Taylor	O. Madden	11	4-1
1918 My Dear	A. Cox	A. Taylor	S. Donoghue	15	3-1
1919 Bayuda	Lady Douglas	A. Taylor	J. Childs	10	100-7
1920 Charlebelle	A. Cunliffe	H. Braime	A. Whalley	17	7-2
1921 Love in Idleness	J. Watson	A. Taylor	J. Childs	22	5-1
1922 Pogrom	Lord Astor	A. Taylor	E. Gardner	11	5-4
1923 Brownhylda	Vicomte de Fontarce	R. Dawson	V. Smyth	12	10-1
1924 Straitlace	Sir E. Hulton	D. Waugh	F. O'Neill	12	100-30
1925 Saucy Sue	Lord Astor	A. Taylor	F. Bullock	12	30-100
1926 Short Story	Lord Astor	A. Taylor	R. Jones	16	5-1
1927 Beam	Lord Durham	Frank Butters	T. Weston	16	4-1
1928 Toboggan	Lord Derby	Frank Butters	T. Weston	13	100-15
1929 Pennycomequick	Lord Astor	J. Lawson	H. Jelliss	13	11-10
1930 Rose of England	Lord Glanely	T. Hogg	G. Richards	15	7-1
1931 Brulette	Lieut-Col C. Birkin	F. Carter	E.C. Elliott	15	7-2
1932 Udaipur	Aga Khan	Frank Butters	M. Beary	12	10-1
1933 Chatelaine	E. T-Smith	F. Templeman	S. Wragg	14	25-1
1934 Light Brocade	Lord Durham	Frank Butters	B. Carslake	8	7-4
1935 Quashed	Lord Stanley	C. Leader	H. Jelliss	17	33-1
1936 Lovely Rosa	Sir A. Bailey	H. Cottrill	T. Weston	17	33-1
1937 Exhibitionnist	Sir V. Sassoon	J. Lawson	S. Donoghue	13	3-1
1938 Rockfel	Sir H. C-Owen	O. Bell	H. Wragg	14	3-1
1939 Galatea II	R. Clark	J. Lawson	R. Jones	21	10-11
1940 Godiva	Lord Rothermere	W. Jarvis	D. Marks	14	7-4
1941 Commotion	J. Dewar	F. Darling	H. Wragg	12	8-1
1942 Sun Chariot	King George VI	F. Darling	G. Richards	12	1-4
1943 Why Hurry	J. Rank	N. Cannon	E.C. Elliott	13	7-1
1944 Hycilla	W. Woodward	C. Boyd-Rochfort	G. Bridgland	16	8-1

		OWNER	TRAINER	JOCKEY	RAN	SP
1945	Sun Stream	Lord Derby	W. Earl	H. Wragg	16	6-4
1946	Steady Aim	Sir A. Butt	Frank Butters	H. Wragg	10	7-1
1947	Imprudence	Mme P. Corbiere	J. Lieux	W. Johnstone	11	7-4
1948	Masaka	Aga Khan	Frank Butters	W. Nevett	25	7-1
1949	Musidora	N. Donaldson	C. Elsey	E. Britt	17	4-1
1950	Asmena	M. Boussac	C. Semblat	W. Johnstone	19	5-1
1951	Neasham Belle	Maj L. Holliday	G. Brooke	S. Clayton	16	33-1
1952	Frieze	A. Keith	C. Elsey	E. Britt	19	100-7
1953	Ambiguity	Lord Astor	J. Colling	J. Mercer	21	18-1
1954	Sun Cap	Mme R. Forget	R. Carver	W. Johnstone	21	100-8
1955	Meld	Lady Z. Wernher	C. Boyd-Rochfort	W.H. Carr	13	7-4
1956	Sicarelle	Mme L. Volterra	F. Mathet	F. Palmer	14	3-1
1957	Carrozza	The Queen	N. Murless	L. Piggott	11	100-8
1958	Bella Paola	F. Dupré	F. Mathet	M. Garcia	17	6-4
1959	Petite Etoile	Aly Khan	N. Murless	L. Piggott	11	11-2
1960	Never Too Late II	Mrs H. Jackson	E. Pollet	R. Poincelet	10	6-5
1961	Sweet Solera	Mrs S. Castello	R. Day	W. Rickaby	12	11-4
1962	Monade	G. Goulandris	J. Lieux	Y. Saint-Martin	18	7-1
1963	Noblesse	Mrs J. Olin	P. Prendergast	G. Bougoure	9	4-11
1964	Homeward Bound	Sir F. Robinson	J. Oxley	G. Starkey	18	100-7
1965	Long Look	J. Brady	V. O'Brien	J. Purtell	18	100-7
1966	Valoris	C. Clore	V. O'Brien	L. Piggott	13	11-10
1967	Pia	Countess M. Bathyany	W. Elsey	E. Hide	12	100-7
1968	La Lagune	H. Berlin	F. Boutin	G. Thiboeuf	14	11-8
1969	Sleeping Partner	Lord Rosebery	D. Smith	J. Gorton	15	100-6
1970	Lupe	Mrs S. Joel	N. Murless	A. Barclay	16	100-30
1971	Altesse Royale	Col F. Hue-Williams	N. Murless	G. Lewis	11	6-4
1972	Ginevra	C. St George	H.R. Price	A. Murray	17	8-1
1973	Mysterious	G. Pope Jnr	N. Murless	G. Lewis	10	13-8
1974	Polygamy	L. Freedman	P. Walwyn	P. Eddery	15	3-1
1975	Juliette Marny	J. Morrison	J. Tree	L. Piggott	12	12-1
1976	Pawneese	D. Wildenstein	A. Penna	Y. Saint-Martin	14	6-5
1977	Dunfermline	The Queen	W. Hern	W. Carson	13	6-1
1978	Fair Salinia	S. Hanson	M. Stoute	G. Starkey	15	8-1
1979	Scintillate	J. Morrison	J. Tree	P. Eddery	14	20-1
1980	Bireme	R. Hollingsworth	W. Hern	W. Carson	11	9-2
1981	Blue Wind	Mrs B. Firestone	D. Weld	L. Piggott	12	3-1
1982	Time Charter	R. Barnett	H. Candy	W. Newnes	13	12-1
1983	Sun Princess	Sir M. Sobell	W. Hern	W. Carson	15	6-1
1984	Circus Plume	Sir R. McAlpine	J. Dunlop	L. Piggott	15	4-1
1985	Oh So Sharp	Sheikh Mohammed	H. Cecil	S. Cauthen	12	6-4

FOLKESTONE

The Racecourse, Westenhanger, Hythe, Kent. (0303-66407/68449)
Clerk of the Course: Major David Cameron

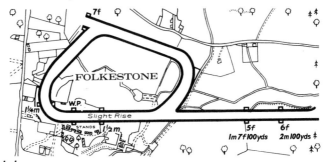

Right-handed course.
EFFECT OF DRAW: Low numbers slightly favoured on straight course; high numbers favoured on round course.

Best Times

DISTANCE	TIME	AGE	WEIGHT	GOING	HORSE	DATE	
5f	58·8	3	6 10	Good	Tammany	Aug. 12,	1963
5f	58·8	2	8 11	Hard	Merry Monk	July 6,	1971
6f	1.10·5	4	8 5	Firm	Zipperdi-Doo-Dah	Mar. 31,	1976
6f	1.11	2	7 13	Hard	Fashion Model	Aug. 31,	1970
7f	1.22·3	3	9 1	Firm	Telwaah	July 16,	1985
7f	1.28·8	2	7 8	Firm	Lord Rochford	July 2,	1977
1m 1f 130y	1.57·8	4	8 11	Firm	Lord Raffles	June 2,	1980
10f	1.59·7	3	9 8	Firm	Shardari	July 2,	1985
12f	2.33·8	3	8 4	Firm	Santella King	June 28,	1983
		3	9 5	Firm	Royal Cracker	July 17,	1984
15f	3.15·1	6	7 6	Firm	Bonds Best	April 14,	1980
15f 100y	3.18·8	3	7 13	Firm	Coral Heights	July 17,	1984
16f 100y	3.32·5	6	7 13	Firm	North West	July 21,	1981
		3	8 5	Firm	On Her Own	Aug. 11	1981

GOODWOOD

Goodwood, Chichester, Sussex. PO18 0PX. (0243-774107)
Clerk of the Course: Rod Fabricius

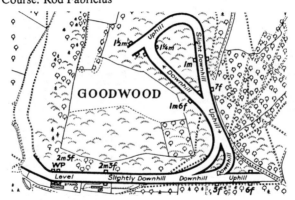

Right-handed loop course with electrical timing apparatus.
EFFECT OF DRAW: Low numbers slightly favoured when stalls on stands side on straight course; high numbers favoured 7f to 1½m.

Best Times

DISTANCE	TIME	AGE	WEIGHT	GOING	HORSE	DATE	
5f	56·92	4	9 0	Firm	Tina's Pet	July 29,	1982
5f	58·07	2	8 10	Firm	Kafu	July 27,	1982
6f	1.9·58	3	8 4	Firm	Soba	July 27,	1982
6f	1.11·05	2	8 11	Fast	Vacarme (disq.)	July 27,	1983
7f	1.24·7	3	7 13	Yielding	Alcindoro	Sept. 14,	1970
7f	1.26·77	2	9 0	Firm	Trojan Fen	July 28,	1983
8f	1.37·51	6	9 7	Firm	Noalcoholic (FR)	July 27,	1983
8f	1.40·66	2	8 13	Firm	Bonnie Isle	Sept. 18,	1978
10f	2.5·31	6	9 1	Firm	Prominent	Aug. 25,	1973
11f 200y	2.35·1	3	8 3	Good	Karabas	July 30,	1968
12f	2.32·73	4	9 1	Firm	Capstan	July 30,	1982
14f	2.58·83	3	9 1	Firm	Capstan	Aug. 29,	1981
19f	4.10·57	5	8 9	Good	Mister Lord (USA)	May 24,	1984
20f 193y	4.35·08	4	9 0	Firm	Mr Bigmore	July 29,	1976
21f	4.32·28	5	9 7	Firm	Little Wolf	July 28,	1983

Race Results

William Hill Stewards' Cup   6f

Handicap. First run 1840. Run at Newmarket as Stewards Handicap 1941. No race 1940, 1942-45. Run as Stewards' Cup 1840-1969; Spillers Stewards' Cup 1970-80; Tote Stewards' Cup 1981.

	OWNER	TRAINER	JOCKEY	RAN	SP
1930 Le Phare, 4-8-1	Aga Khan	R. Dawson	M. Beary	28	100-6
1931 Poor Lad, 4-7-11	Sir H. C-Owen	O. Bell	S. Wragg	15	9-1
1932 Solenoid, 3-7-10	Mrs C. Mackean	G. Poole	T. Barber	21	33-1
1933 Pharacre, 4-7-5	Capt A. Wills	Fred Butters	F. Fox	26	22-1
1934 Figaro, 4-8-5	J. Leach	J. Leach	T. Weston	22	100-7
1935 Greenore, 6-8-8	Lady Ludlow	O. Bell	S. Wragg	17	7-1
1936 Solerina, 4-8-11	C. Mackean	H. Cottrill	E. Smith	20	10-1
1937 Firozepore, 3-8-3	R. Strassburger	F. Darling	G. Richards	30	100-8
1938 Harmachis, 5-7-6	Mrs G. Farrand	B. Bullock	P. Evans	25	100-7
1939 Knight's Caprice, 4-8-6	Col T. Clarke	R. Dawson	J. Canty	23	100-8
1941 Valthema, 4-7-2	H. Jennings	Frank Butters	K. Robertson	15	100-8
1946 Commissar, 6-7-12	A. Budgett	E. Stedall	A. Richardson	15	10-1
1947 Closeburn, 3-8-10	R. White	N. Murless	G. Richards	19	100-7
1948 Dramatic, 3-7-7	A. Saunders	G. Todd	E. Smith	16	9-1
1949 The Bite, 4-7-7	Mrs W. Armstrong	J. Wood	H. Packham	21	33-1
1950 First Consul, 4-8-13	Maharaja of Rajpipla	F. Armstrong	E. Britt	21	100-9
1951 Sugar Bowl, 4-7-12	J. Gerber	F. Armstrong	W. Snaith	21	100-6
1952 Smokey Eyes, 5-8-10	D. Robinson	R. Jarvis	C. Smirke	18	100-7
1953 Palpitate, 4-7-13	F. Armstrong	F. Armstrong	W. Snaith	22	5-1
1954 Ashurst Wonder, 4-6-11	R. Merrick	L. Hall	A. Shrive	28	50-1
1955 King Bruce, 4-8-11	W. Tarry	P. Hastings-Bass	W. Rickaby	26	100-6
1956 Matador, 3-9-2	S. Joel	J.A. Waugh	E. Smith	24	100-8
1957 Arcandy, 4-8-9	Mrs M. Linde	G. Beeby	T. Gosling	16	100-7
1958 Epaulette, 7-9-0	J. Gerber	W. O'Gorman	F. Durr	20	33-1
1959 Tudor Monarch, 4-7-13	Sir W. Churchill	W. Nightingall	G. Lewis	21	25-1
1960 Monet, 3-8-5	Sir P. Dunn	J. Tree	J. Lindley	18	20-1
1961 Skymaster, 3-8-12	W. Kelly	G. Smyth	A. Breasley	22	100-7
1962 Victorina, 3-8-9	Sir B. Mountain	P. Nelson	W. Williamson	26	10-1
1963 Creole, 4-9-1	Lord Rosebery	J. Jarvis	S. Smith	25	20-1
1964 Dunme, 5-7-12	J. Simmons	R. Read	P. Cook	20	9-1
1965 Potier, 3-8-5	T. Blackwell	J. Jarvis	R. Hutchinson	20	100-7
1966 Patient Constable, 3-7-7	I. Allen	R. Smyth	R. Reader	25	33-1
1967 Sky Diver, 4-7-5	J. Fane	P. Payne-Gallwey	D. Cullen	31	20-1
1968 Sky Diver, 5-7-6	J. Fane	P. Payne-Gallwey	T. Sturrock	18	100-6
1969 Royal Smoke, 3-7-9	I. Allen	W. O'Gorman	M.L. Thomas	15	100-7
1970 Jukebox, 4-8-11	D. Morris	H. Wallington	L. Piggott	24	100-6
1971 Apollo Nine, 4-9-5	P. Nelson	P. Nelson	J. Lindley	26	14-1
1972 Touch Paper, 3-8-2	A. Villar	B. Hobbs	P. Cook	22	25-1
1973 Alphadamus, 3-7-11	Mrs J. Mountfield	M. Stoute	P. Cook	27	16-1
1974 Red Alert, 3-9-2	B. Firestone	D. Weld	J. Roe	25	16-1
1975 Import, 4-8-0	Maj H. Cayzer	W. Wightman	M.L. Thomas	21	14-1
1976 Jimmy the Singer, 3-7-8	Mrs S. Bates	B. Lunness	E. Johnson	17	15-1
1977 Calibina, 5-8-5	E. Badger	P. Cole	G. Baxter	24	8-1
1978 Ahonoora, 3-8-0	E. Alkhalifa	B. Swift	P. Waldron	23	50-1
1979 Standaan, 3-7-10	A. Richards	C. Brittain	P. Bradwell	16	5-1
1980 Repetitious, 3-7-2	Mrs A. Trimble	G. Harwood	A. Clark	28	15-1
1981 Crews Hill, 5-9-9	C. Henry	F. Durr	G. Starkey	30	11-1
1982 Soba, 3-8-4	Mrs M. Hills	D. Chapman	D. Nicholls	30	18-1
1983 Autumn Sunset, 3-8-2	J. McCaughey	M. Stoute	W. Carson	23	6-1
1984 Petong, 4-9-10	T. Warner	M. Jarvis	B. Raymond	26	8-1
1985 Al Trui, 5-8-1	M. Saunders	S. Mellor	M. Wigham	28	9-1

O C L Richmond Stakes   6f

Two-year-olds. 8st 11lb, fillies allowed 3lb. First run 1877. Run as Richmond Stakes before 1983. No race 1940-45. Group Two.

	OWNER	TRAINER	JOCKEY	RAN	SP
1930 Four Course, 9-5	Lord Ellesmere	F. Darling	F. Fox	11	8-13
1931 Spenser, 9-8	S. Tattersall	J. Lawson	R.A. Jones	7	11-10
1932 Solar Boy, 8-12	Sir F. Eley	F. Templeman	F. Fox	7	6-1
1933 Colombo, 9-7	Lord Glanely	T. Hogg	S. Donoghue	8	30-100
1934 Bobsleigh, 8-7	Lord Derby	C. Leader	T. Weston	11	1-3
1935 Mahmoud, 9-7	Aga Khan	Frank Butters	F. Fox	11	2-1
1936 Perifox, 9-2	W. Woodward	C. Boyd-Rochfort	P. Beasley	12	5-2
1937 Unbreakable, 9-7	J. Widener	C. Boyd-Rochfort	P. Beasley	8	11-10
1938 Chancery, 8-12	J. Walker	H. Leader	B. Carslake	13	5-2
1939 Moradabad, 8-7	Aga Khan	Frank Butters	C. Smirke	8	10-11
1946 Petition, 9-0	Sir A. Butt	Frank Butters	H. Wragg	4	1-5
1947 Birthday Greetings, 8-7	Miss D. Paget	H. Jelliss	J. Simpson	10	11-10
1948 Star King, 9-0	W. Harvey	J.C. Waugh	S. Wragg	10	8-11
1949 Palestine, 9-0	Aga Khan	Frank Butters	G. Richards	3	6-100
1950 Grey Sovereign, 9-0	F. Measures	G. Beeby	W.H. Carr	7	5-2
1951 Gay Time, 8-7	J. Rank	N. Cannon	A. Breasley	4	100-7
1952 Artane, 8-7	J. O'Connell	P. Prendergast	G. Richards	5	13-8
1953 The Pie King, 9-0	R. Bell	P. Prendergast	G. Richards	6	8-13
1954 Eubulides, 9-0	P. Bull	C. Elsey	E. Britt	7	6-5
1955 Ratification, 9-0	Sir M. McAlpine	V. Smyth	W. Rickaby	4	11-8
1956 Red God, 9-0	H. Guggenheim	C. Boyd-Rochfort	W.H. Carr	5	7-2
1957 Promulgation, 9-0	H.J. Joel	T. Leader	E. Smith	7	11-8
1958 Hieroglyph, 9-0	Mrs J. Hanes	C. Boyd-Rochfort	W.H. Carr	7	9-4
1959 Dollar Piece, 9-0	P. Winstone	H. Cottrill	J. Mercer	4	100-6
1960 Typhoon, 9-0	N. McCarthy	P Prendergast	R. Hutchinson	5	4-11
1961 Sovereign Lad, 9-0	Duke of Norfolk	G. Smyth	G. Lewis	7	8-1
1962 Romantic, 9-0	G. Loder	N. Murless	L. Piggott	5	8-11
1963 Gentle Art, 9-0	Sir A. Jarvis	J. Jarvis	R. Hutchinson	5	8-11
1964 Ragtime, 9-0	Duke of Norfolk	G. Smyth	R. Hutchinson	3	13-8
1965 Sky Gipsy, 9-0	R. Hibbert	G. Smyth	R. Hutchinson	3	3-1
1966 Hambleden, 9-0	Lord Carnarvon	T. Corbett	A. Breasley	7	2-1
1967 Berber, 9-0	Sir M. Sobell	G. Richards	A. Breasley	3	8-11
1968 Tudor Music, 9-0	D. Robinson	M. Jarvis	F. Durr	3	5-1
1969 Village Boy, 9-0	Mrs A. Hurlstone	G. Todd	W. Williamson	5	9-2
1970 Swing Easy, 9-0	J. Whitney	J. Tree	L. Piggott	5	4-5
1971 Sallust, 8-11	Sir M. Sobell	W. Hern	J. Mercer	10	2-1
1972 Master Sing, 9-0	B. Jenks	D. Candy	J. Mercer	7	13-8
1973 Dragonara Palace, 8-11	Mrs B. Stein	B. Hills	L. Piggott	7	4-9
1974 Legal Eagle, 8-11	P. Gallagher	W. Marshall	G. Baxter	6	4-1
1975 Stand To Reason, 8-11	Lord Ranfurly	B. Hills	W. Carson	9	12-1
1976 J.O. Tobin, 8-11	G. Pope Jnr	N. Murless	L. Piggott	5	8-11
1977 Persian Bold, 8-11	R. Vahabzadeh	A. Ingham	L. Piggott	5	4-6
1978 Young Generation, 8-11	A. Ward	G. Harwood	G. Starkey	5	12-1
1979 Castle Green, 8-11	Sir G. White	M. Stoute	P. Cook	5	20-1
1980 Another Realm, 8-11	Mrs D. Goldstein	F. Durr	J. Mercer	10	16-1
1981 Tender King, 8-11	Esal (Commodities) Ltd	J. Sutcliffe	P. Waldron	7	11-4
1982 Gallant Special, 8-11	W. Hawn	R. Armstrong	L. Piggott	4	4-6
1983 Godstone, 8-11	Esal (Commodities) Ltd	P. Haslam	G. Sexton	9	14-1
1984 Primo Dominie, 8-11	P. Wetzel	B. Swift	J. Reid	6	10-11
1985 Nomination, 8-11	F. Salman	P. Cole	T. Quinn	10	8-1

Swettenham Stud Sussex Stakes   1m

Three-year-olds and upwards. 3-y-o 8st 10lb, 4-y-o & upwards 9st 7lb, fillies allowed 3lb. First run 1841. For three-year-olds before 1959; for three and four-year-olds 1960-74. Run as Sussex Stakes before 1984. No race 1940-45. Group One.

	OWNER	TRAINER	JOCKEY	RAN	SP
1930 Paradine, 3-9-1	W. Cazalet	J. Lawson	R. Jones	7	13-8
1931 Inglesant, 3-8-5	S. Tattersall	J. Lawson	R. Jones	6	10-11

	OWNER	TRAINER	JOCKEY	RAN	SP
1932 Dastur, 3-9-3	Aga Khan	Frank Butters	M. Beary	2	8-15
1933 The Abbot, 3-8-13	King George V	W. Jarvis	J. Childs	7	11-2
1934 Badruddin, 3-9-3	Aga Khan	Frank Butters	F. Fox	3	2-5
1935 Hairan, 3-8-12	Aga Khan	Frank Butters	R. Perryman	7	6-4
1936 Corpach, 3-8-2	Lord Astor	J. Lawson	G. Richards	5	4-1
1937 Pascal, 3-9-3	H. Morris	F. Darling	G. Richards	6	5-2
1938 Faroe, 3-9-1	Lord Derby	C. Leader	R. Perryman	6	20-1
1939 Olein, 3-9-5	Lord Glanely	B. Jarvis	T. Lowrey	7	7-4
1946 Radiotherapy, 3-9-3	T. Lilley	F. Templeman	G. Richards	6	7-4
1947 Combat, 3-9-3	J. Dewar	F. Darling	G. Richards	2	8-13
1948 My Babu, 3-9-8	Maharaja of Baroda	F. Armstrong	C. Smirke	2	1-3
1949 Krakatao, 3-9-1	Lord Feversham	N. Murless	G. Richards	2	2-11
1950 Palestine, 3-9-8	Aga Khan	N. Marsh	C. Smirke	4	1-2
1951 Le Sage, 3-9-3	S. Sanger	T. Carey	G. Richards	7	6-4
1952 Agitator, 3-9-1	J. Dewar	N. Murless	G. Richards	5	8-15
1953 King of the Tudors, 3-8-10	F. Dennis	W. Stephenson	C. Spares	4	11-10
1954 Landau, 3-9-1	The Queen	N. Murless	W. Snaith	4	6-4
1955 My Kingdom, 3-8-9	J. Armstrong	W. Nightingall	D. Smith	5	13-2
1956 Lucero, 3-9-1	G. Oldham	H. Wragg	E. Mercer	6	8-1
1957 Quorum, 3-9-1	T. Farr	W. Lyde	A.J. Russell	4	10-11
1958 Major Portion, 3-9-7	H.J. Joel	T. Leader	E. Smith	5	8-11
1959 Petite Etoile, 3-9-4	Aly Khan	N Murless	L. Piggott	6	1-10
1960 Venture VII, 3-8-4	Aga Khan	A. Head	G. Moore	6	13-8
1961 Le Levanstell, 4-8-10	J. McGrath	S. McGrath	G. Williamson	11	100-7
1962 Romulus, 3-8-4	C. Engelhard	R.J. Houghton	W. Swinburn	8	9-1
1963 Queen's Hussar, 3-8-3	Lord Carnarvon	T. Corbett	R. Hutchinson	10	25-1
1964 Roan Rocket, 3-8-5	T. Frost	G. Todd	L. Piggott	8	4-6
1965 Carlemont, 3-8-3	L. Gelb	P. Prendergast	R. Hutchinson	11	7-2
1966 Paveh, 3-8-3	P. Widener	T. Ainsworth	R. Hutchinson	7	5-1
1967 Reform, 3-8-3	M. Sobell	Sir G. Richards	A. Breasley	10	evens
1968 Petingo, 3-8-4	M. Lemos	F. Armstrong	L. Piggott	6	6-4
1969 Jimmy Reppin, 4-9-4	Mrs S. Bates	J. Sutcliffe	G. Lewis	5	7-4
1970 Humble Duty, 3-8-4	Jean, Lady Ashcombe	P. Walwyn	D. Keith	5	11-8
1971 Brigadier Gerard, 3-8-7	Mrs J. Hislop	W. Hern	J. Mercer	5	4-6
1972 Sallust, 3-8-10	Sir M. Sobell	W. Hern	J. Mercer	3	9-2
1973 Thatch, 3-8-10	J. Mulcahy	V. O'Brien	L. Piggott	7	4-5
1974 Ace of Aces, 4-9-7	N.B. Hunt	M. Zilber	J. Lindley	10	8-1
1975 Bolkonski, 3-8-10	C. d'Alessio	H. Cecil	G. Dettori	9	1-2
1976 Wollow, 3-8-10	C d'Alessio	H. Cecil	G. Dettori	9	10-11
1977 Artaius, 3-8-10	Mrs G. Getty II	V. O'Brien	L. Piggott	11	6-4
1978 Jaazeiro, 3-8-10	R. Sangster	V. O'Brien	L. Piggott	6	8-13
1979 Kris, 3-8-10	Ld Howard de Walden	H. Cecil	J. Mercer	7	4-5
1980 Posse, 3-8-10	O.M. Phipps	J. Dunlop	P. Eddery	9	8-13
1981 King's Lake, 3-8-10	Mme J. Binet	V. O'Brien	P. Eddery	9	5-2
1982 On The House, 3-8-7	Sir P. Oppenheimer	H. Wragg	J. Reid	13	14-1
1983 Noalcoholic, 6-9-7	W. du Pont III	G. Pritchard-Gordon	G. Duffield	11	18-1
1984 Chief Singer, 3-8-10	J. Smith	R. Sheather	R. Cochrane	5	4-7
1985 Rousillon , 4-9-7	K. Abdullah	G. Harwood	G. Starkey	10	2-1

Goodwood Cup   2m 5f

Three-year-olds and upwards. 3-y-o 7st 10lb, 4-y-o & upwards 9st, fillies allowed 3lb (plus penalties). First run 1812. No race 1940-45. Group Three.

	OWNER	TRAINER	JOCKEY	RAN	SP
1930 Brown Jack, 6-9-7	Sir H. Wernher	I. Anthony	S. Donoghue	5	4-9
1931 Salmon Leap, 4-9-3	Mrs A. James	G. Lambton	T. Weston	6	5-2
1932 Brulette, 4-9-4	Lord Woolavington	F. Darling	G. Richards	5	5-2
1933 Sans Peine, 3-7-11	E. Esmond	J. Jarvis	E. Smith	5	20-1
1934 Loosestrife, 5-9-6	P. Johnson	E. Richards	G. Richards	4	11-2
1935 Tiberius, 4-9-7	Sir A. Bailey	J. Lawson	T. Weston	3	2-9
1936 Cecil, 5-9-6	Sir A. Bailey	J. Lawson	T. Weston	9	13-8
1937 Fearless Fox, 4-9-2	A. Smith	J. Jarvis	E. Smith	6	6-1
1938 Epigram, 5-9-6	J. Rank	N. Cannon	B. Carslake	11	6-1
1939 Dubonnet, 4-8-1	J. Hornung	B. Jarvis	T. Lowrey	5	6-4

	OWNER	TRAINER	JOCKEY	RAN	SP
1946 Marsyas II, 6-9-11	M. Boussac	C. Semblat	E.C. Elliott	4	1-3
1947 Monsieur l'Amiral, 6-9-2	Mrs I. Henderson	E. Charlier	C. Smirke	4	1-2
1948 Tenerani, 4-8-12	F. Tesio	N. Bertie	E. Camici	4	100-30
1949 Alycidon, 4-8-12	Lord Derby	W. Earl	D. Smith	5	30-100
1950 Val Drake, 4-8-12	Mme L. Volterra	R. Carver	R. Roincelet	4	4-1
1951 Pan II, 4-8-12	E. Constant	E. Pollet	R. Poincelet	4	5-6
1952 Medway, 4-8-12	P. Bartholomew	F. Winter	D. Smith	4	5-1
1953 Souepi, 5-9-0	G. Digby	G. Digby	E.C. Elliott	8	2-1
1954 Blarney Stone, 5-9-0	M. McAlpine	V. Smyth	W. Rickaby	5	13-2
1955 Double Bore, 4-9-0	J. Tree	J. Tree	T. Gosling	8	9-1
1956 Zarathustra, 5-9-0	T. Gray	C. Boyd-Rochfort	W. Carr	4	10-11
1957 Tenterhooks, 3-7-10	Lord Allendale	C. Elsey	E. Britt	7	2-1
1958 Gladness, 5-8-11	J. McShain	V. O'Brien	L. Piggott	4	1-2
1959 Dickens, 3-7-10	Lady Z. Wernher	C. Boyd-Rochfort	D. Smith	4	9-4
1960 Exar, 4-9-0	C. Vittadini	N. Murless	L. Piggott	4	4-9
1961 Predominate, 9-9-0	H.J. Joel	T. Leader	E. Smith	4	11-4
1962 Sagacity, 4-9-0	Lady Cholmondeley	C. Boyd-Rochfort	W.H. Carr	4	5-1
1963 Trelawny, 7-9-0	Mrs L. Carver	G. Todd	A. Breasley	4	8-13
1964 Raise You Ten, 4-9-0	P. Widener	C. Boyd-Rochfort	S. Clayton	5	evens
1965 Apprentice, 5-9-0	The Queen	C. Boyd-Rochfort	S. Clayton	5	8-1
1966 Gaulois, 3-7-10	The Queen	C. Boyd-Rochfort	R. Hutchinson	7	15-2
1967 Wrekin Rambler, 4-9-0	G. Murphy	Sir G. Richards	A. Breasley	5	2-1
1968 Ovaltine, 4-9-0	G. Cooper	J.F. Watts	B. Taylor	7	5-2
1969 Richmond Fair, 5-9-0	T. Blackwell	B. Hobbs	J. Gorton	3	5-4
1970 Parthenon, 4-9-0	Sir R. Macdonald-Buchanan	H. Cecil	G. Starkey	5	3-1
1971 Rock Roi, 4-9-0	Col F. Hue-Williams	P. Walwyn	D. Keith	5	4-6
1972 Erimo Hawk, 4-9-0	Y. Yamamoto	G. Barling	P. Eddery	4	10-11
1973 Proverb, 3-7-10	Lt-Col J. Chandos-Pole	B. Hills	E. Johnson	4	6-4
1974 Proverb, 4-9-0	Lt-Col J. Chandos-Pole	B. Hills	L. Piggott	4	4-5
1975 Girandole, 4-9-0	J. Hattersley	M. Stoute	L. Piggott	8	7-2
1976 Mr Bigmore, 4-9-0	E. Lambton	P. Robinson	G. Starkey	6	3-1
1977 Grey Baron, 4-9-3	P. Parnell	B. Hobbs	G. Lewis	8	11-4
1978 Tug of War, 5-9-0	Mrs Y. Perry	D. Whelan	B. Rouse	5	20-1
1979 Le Moss, 4-9-7	C. d'Alessio	H. Cecil	J. Mercer	5	1-2
1980 Le Moss, 5-9-7	C. d'Alessio	H. Cecil	J. Mercer	5	4-7
1981 Ardross, 5-9-7	C. St George	H. Cecil	L. Piggott	6	2-9
1982 Heighlin, 6-9-0	J. Burr	D. Elsworth	S. Cauthen	8	8-1
1983 Little Wolf, 5-9-7	Lord Porchester	W. Hern	W. Carson	7	4-9
1984 Gildoran, 4-9-7	R. Sangster	B. Hills	S. Cauthen	4	9-4
1985 Valuable Witness, 5-9-0	S. Niarchos	J. Tree	P. Eddery	7	11-10

Extel Handicap   1¼m

Three-year-olds. First run 1962. Run as News of the World Handicap 1962-69.

	OWNER	TRAINER	JOCKEY	RAN	SP
1962 Tamerlo, 9-0	M. Sobell	Sir G. Richards	A. Breasley	26	100-7
1963 Fraxinus, 7-7	Mrs W. Wightman	W. Wightman	D. Yates	21	25-1
1964 French Possession, 7-9	R. Dennis	G. Brooke	D. Smith	19	20-1
1965 Super Sam, 7-9	C. Cooper	J.F. Watts	P. Robinson	16	5-1
1966 Le Cordonnier, 9-2	Mrs S. Jacobson	S. Ingham	G. Lewis	19	100-7
1967 Sucaryl, 8-8	Lady Sassoon	N. Murless	G. Moore	12	5-6
1968 Principal Boy, 8-1	Lady Hothfield	J. Clayton	E. Eldin	12	4-1
1969 Irish Mail II, 8-0	A. Macdonald-Buchanan	H.A. Waugh	E. Eldin	8	7-1
1970 Sol Argent, 7-7	Mrs G. Harris	T. Gosling	D. Cullen	13	20-1
1971 Spoiled Lad, 9-3	Sir J. Thorn	B. van Cutsem	B. Taylor	8	7-2
1972 Warpath, 8-4	G. Reed	S. Hall	A.J. Russell	15	11-1
1973 Cupid, 7-7	Sir M. Sobell	W. Hern	D. Cullen	12	10-1
1974 Take A Reef, 9-11	A. Villar	B. Hobbs	J. Gorton	18	13-1
1975 Duboff, 8-0	Mrs C. Radclyffe	B. Hills	W. Carson	12	7-1
1976 Il Padrone, 8-1	M. Davis	J. Sutcliffe	R. Fox	13	12-1
1977 Ad Lib Ra, 9-0	Mrs J. Rodgers	R.J. Houghton	L. Piggott	14	4-1
1978 Crimson Beau, 8-2	H. Spearing	P. Cole	G. Baxter	7	4-1
1979 Lindoro, 9-0	Sir M. Sobell	W. Hern	W. Carson	8	6-4
1980 Karamita, 7-7	Aga Khan	M. Stoute	P. Robinson	10	5-1

	OWNER	TRAINER	JOCKEY	RAN	SP
1981 Indian Trail, 8-3	R. Sangster	B. Hills	S. Cauthen	9	3-1
1982 Busaco, 9-1	R. McCreery	W. Hern	W. Carson	10	7-1
1983 Millfontaine, 8-13	S. Niarchos	G. Harwood	G. Starkey	12	6-1
1984 Free Guest, 8-6	M. Boffa	L. Cumani	D. McHargue	15	4-1
1985 Fish 'N' Chips, 8-3	M. Boffa	L. Cumani	P. Eddery	13	9-4

Vodafone Nassau Stakes 1¼m

Three-year-olds and upwards fillies. 3-y-o 8st 5lb, 4-y-o & upwards 9st 3lb (plus penalties). First run 1840. For three-year-olds only before 1975. No race 1940-45. Run as Nassau Stakes before 1985. Group Two.

	OWNER	TRAINER	JOCKEY	RAN	SP
1930 Quinine, 8-10	Lord Ellesmere	F. Darling	F. Fox	8	100-30
1931 Suze, 8-10	R.S. Clark	A. Molony	R.A. Jones	6	100-8
1932 Ada Dear, 9-1	Lord Glanely	T. Hogg	R. Perryman	4	9-4
1933 Solfatara, 8-5	Miss J. Courtauld	B. Jarvis	G. Richards	6	6-4
1934 Zelina, 9-1	Z. Michalinos	H. Powney	S. Donoghue	3	4-5
1935 Coppelia, 9-1	Lord Hirst	F. Templeman	G. Richards	11	9-2
1936 Barrowby Gem, 8-10	Sir F. Eley	F. Templeman	G. Richards	9	6-5
1937 First Flight, 9-1	Lord Londonderry	O. Bell	H. Wragg	7	11-2
1938 Valedeh, 8-5	Aga Khan	Frank Butters	D. Smith	10	100-8
1939 Olein, 9-8	Lord Glanely	B. Jarvis	T. Lowrey	12	13-2
1946 Wayward Belle, 9-1	Lord Milford	J. Jarvis	E. Smith	7	11-8
1947 Wild Child, 8-10	Mrs S. Joel	R. Perryman	T. Lowrey	8	11-2
1948 Goblet, 9-8	F. Darling	N. Murless	G. Richards	7	13-2
1949 Jet Plane, 9-8	Lord Astor	R.J. Colling	G. Richards	6	8-1
1950 Flying Slipper, 9-1	Mrs W. Wyatt	C. Boyd-Rochfort	W.H. Carr	8	8-1
1951 Sea Parrot, 8-5	G. Loder	N. Murless	G. Richards	7	7-4
1952 Hortentia, 8-10	Lord Derby	G. Colling	D. Smith	7	11-2
1953 Happy Laughter, 9-8	H. Wills	J. Jarvis	W. Rickaby	3	5-6
1954 Key, 9-5	Mrs D. Fitzpatrick	N. Murless	W. Snaith	10	4-1
1955 Reel In, 8-10	G. Fairlie	N. Cannon	A. Breasley	6	13-8
1956 Dilettante, 8-10	Lord Derby	J.F. Watts	D. Smith	9	6-1
1957 Swallowswift, 8-10	F. Robinson	G. Colling	E. Mercer	8	100-9
1958 Darlene, 8-10	Miss D. Paget	G. Richards	A. Breasley	6	100-30
1959 Crystal Palace, 9-5	H.J. Joel	T. Waugh	E. Smith	6	3-1
1960 Desert Beauty, 9-1	R. Evans	G. Richards	A. Breasley	5	2-1
1961 Rachel, 8-10	E. Covell	J. Gosden	J. Lindley	6	7-2
1962 Nortia, 9-3	L. Holliday	W. Hern	J. Mercer	7	100-30
1963 Spree, 8-5	J. Morrison	J. Tree	J. Lindley	4	15-8
1964 Cracker, 8-5	L. Holliday	W. Wharton	J. Mercer	6	10-1
1965 Aunt Edith, 8-5	J. Hornung	N. Murless	L. Piggott	6	7-4
1966 Haymaking, 9-3	C. Nicholson	R.J. Houghton	L. Piggott	9	13-2
1967 Fair Winter, 8-10	W. Barnett	D. Candy	J. Mercer	5	7-2
1968 Hill Shade, 8-10	G. Pope Jnr	N. Murless	A. Barclay	7	5-6
1969 Lucyrowe, 8-9	L. Freedman	P. Walwyn	F. Durr	5	1-2
1970 Pulchra, 8-4	B. Hager	J. Sirett	G. Lewis	5	20-1
1971 Catherine Wheel, 8-4	T. Blackwell	B. Hobbs	G. Lewis	5	4-1
1972 Crespinall, 8-8	Mrs B. Davis	R. Hannon	R. Hutchinson	4	25-1
1973 Cheveley Princess, 8-8	R. Moller	H. Wragg	L. Piggott	9	15-2
1974 Mil's Bomb, 8-8	L. Freedman	N. Murless	G. Lewis	4	10-11
1975 Roussalka, 3-8-8	N. Phillips	H. Cecil	L. Piggott	6	9-4
1976 Roussalka, 4-9-6	N. Phillips	H. Cecil	L. Piggott	10	15-8
1977 Triple First, 3-8-5	R. Clifford-Turner	M. Stoute	G. Starkey	8	13-2
1978 Cistus, 3-8-5	Sir M. Sobell	W. Hern	W. Carson	7	4-7
1979 Connaught Bridge, 3-8-5	H. Barker	H. Cecil	J. Mercer	10	5-1
1980 Vielle, 3-8-5	T. Blackwell	B. Hobbs	G. Baxter	7	8-15
1981 Go Leasing, 3-8-8	W. Norton	G. Harwood	G. Starkey	11	15-2
1982 Dancing Rocks, 3-8-5	Sir P. Oppenheimer	H. Wragg	P. Eddery	11	12-1
1983 Acclimatise, 3-8-5	J. Hambro	B. Hobbs	G. Baxter	6	4-1
1984 Optimistic Lass, 3-8-8	Sheikh Mohammed	M. Stoute	W.R. Swinburn	5	5-2
1985 Free Guest, 4-9-8	Fittocks Stud Ltd	L. Cumani	P. Eddery	11	11-2

Waterford Crystal Mile   1m

Three-year-olds and upwards. 3-y-o 8st 6lb, 4-y-o & upwards 9st, fillies allowed 3lb (plus penalties). First run 1967. Run as Wills Mile 1967-70, Goodwood Mile 1971-74. Run at Ascot 1979 (rebuilding). No race 1985 (waterlogged). Group Two.

		OWNER	TRAINER	JOCKEY	RAN	SP
1967	St Chad, 3-8-3	Mrs N. Murless	N. Murless	G. Moore	7	9-4
1968	Jimmy Reppin, 3-7-13	Mrs S. Bates	J. Sutcliffe	G. Lewis	6	5-1
1969	Habitat, 3-8-6	C. Engelhard	R.J. Houghton	L. Piggott	6	9-2
1970	Humble Duty, 3-8-1	Jean, Lady Ashcombe	P. Walwyn	D. Keith	5	4-6
1971	Brigadier Gerard, 3-8-6	Mrs J. Hislop	W. Hern	J. Mercer	3	1-6
1972	Sallust, 3-8-13	Sir M. Sobell	W. Hern	J. Mercer	3	1-2
1973	Jacinth, 3-8-10	Lady Butt	B. Hobbs	J. Gorton	5	2-5
1974	Pitcairn, 3-8-8	A. Struthers	J. Dunlop	R. Hutchinson	3	4-9
1975	Gay Fandango, 3-8-8	A. Clore	V. O'Brien	P. Eddery	8	5-1
1976	Free State, 3-8-3	Mrs D. McCalmont	P. Walwyn	P. Eddery	6	13-8
1977	Be My Guest, 3-8-7	Mrs A. Manning	V. O'Brien	L. Piggott	6	6-4
1978	Captain James, 4-8-13	S. McGrath	S. McGrath	J. Mercer	5	25-1
1979	Kris, 3-8-12	Ld Howard de Walden	H. Cecil	J. Mercer	8	30-100
1980	Known Fact, 3-8-12	K. Abdulla	J. Tree	W. Carson	6	5-2
1981	To-Agori-Mou, 3-8-12	Mrs A. Muinos	G. Harwood	G. Starkey	6	5-4
1982	Sandhurst Prince, 3-8-4	J. Thompson	G. Harwood	G. Starkey	8	7-4
1983	Montekin, 4-8-13	P. Winfield	J. Dunlop	B. Rouse	6	8-1
1984	Rousillon, 3-8-6	K. Abdullah	G. Harwood	G. Starkey	5	8-13

HAMILTON PARK

Penrose Hill, Moffat, Dumfriesshire, Scotland. DG10 9BX. (0683-20131)
Clerk of the Course: David McHarg

Right-handed loop course.
EFFECT OF DRAW: High numbers slightly favoured.

Best Times

DISTANCE	TIME	AGE	WEIGHT	GOING	HORSE	DATE	
5f	58	5	8 6	Firm	Golden Sleigh	Sept. 6,	1972
5f	58	2	7 8	Firm	Fair Dandy	Sept. 25,	1972
6f	1.9·3	4	8 7	Firm	Marcus Game	July 11,	1974
6f	1.10·1	2	7 5	Hard	Yoohoo	Sept. 8,	1976
8f 40y	1.42·7	6	7 7	Firm	Cranley	Sept. 25,	1972
8f 40y	1.45·8	2	8 11	Firm	Hopeful Subject	Sept. 24,	1973
9f 10y	1.54·2	3	8 2	Hard	Fairman	Aug. 20,	1976
11f	2.20.5	3	9 3	Firm	Wang Feihoong	July 21,	1983
12f	2.32	4	7 4	Firm	Fine Point	Aug. 24,	1981
		4	10 0	Firm	Hold Tight	Aug. 22,	1983
13f	2.46·9	5	8 4	Firm	Point North	July 21,	1983

HAYDOCK PARK

The Racecourse, Newton-le-Willows, Merseyside. WA12 0HQ. (0942-727345)
Clerk of the Course: Major Philip Arkwright

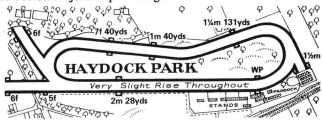

Left-handed course with electrical timing apparatus.

EFFECT OF DRAW: High numbers slightly favoured over 5f when stalls on stands side;
high numbers slightly favoured on round 6f.

Best Times

DISTANCE	TIME	AGE	WEIGHT	GOING	HORSE	DATE	
5f	58·9	3	7 5	Firm	Fish and Chips	June 6,	1970
5f	59·2	2	9 4	Firm	Money For Nothing	Aug. 12,	1964
6f	1.11·8	4	7 5	Firm	Kellac	June 6,	1970
6f	1.12.3	2	8 7	Hard	I Believe	June 5,	1970
7f 40y	1.27.21	4	9 4	Firm	Indian King	June 5,	1982
7f 40y	1.30·57	2	8 11	Hard	Go Grandly	Sept. 30,	1972
8f 40y	1.40.9	3	9 6	Firm	Spanish Pool	May 29,	1982
8f 40y	1.43·44	2	9 1	Firm	The Noble Player	Sept. 3,	1982
10f 131y	2.11·14	3	8 2	Hard	Hill Top	Sept. 29,	1972
12f	2.26·4	5	8 2	Firm	New Member	July 4,	1970
14f	2.58.17	3	8 1	Firm	Red Duster	Aug. 5,	1983
16f 28y	3.27.09	4	8 13	Firm	Prince of Peace	May 26,	1984

Race Results

Harp Lager Lancashire Oaks   1½m

*Three-year-old fillies. 8st 11lb. First run 1939. Run at Manchester over 1m 3f before
1963; run as Duchy Stakes 1946, otherwise as Lancashire Oaks before 1986. No race
1940-45, 1964. Group Three.*

	OWNER	TRAINER	JOCKEY	RAN	SP
1939 Cestria, 8-5	Sir R. Brooke	W. Jarvis	H. Wragg	8	2-1
1946 Live Letters, 8-7	J. Rank	N. Cannon	T. Weston	4	11-10
1947 Smoke Screen, 8-7	Lord Derby	W. Earl	D. Smith	7	5-2
1948 Young Entry, 8-7	King George VI	C. Boyd-Rochfort	W. Nevett	6	5-4
1949 Eyewash, 8-7	M. Wickham-Boynton	P. Beasley	J. Caldwell	7	11-8
1950 Dutch Clover, 8-11	G. Plummer	P. Beasley	E. Smith	9	evens
1951 Dollarina, 8-4	L. Holliday	G. Brooke	P. Evans	6	8-1
1952 Stream of Light, 8-7	The Queen	C. Boyd-Rochfort	W.H. Carr	4	evens
1953 Harvest Festival, 8-4	J. Paine	R Poole	W. Nevett	8	12½-1
1954 Blue Prelude, 8-7	Mrs S. Glover	W. Bellerby	G. Littlewood	5	15-2
1955 Jenny Lind, 8-7	H.J. Joel	C. Elsey	E. Britt	8	11-2
1956 Hustle, 8-4	H.J. Joel	T. Leader	E. Smith	10	11-2
1957 Lobelia, 8-4	A. Plesch	H. Leader	E. Smith	8	7-4
1958 St Lucia, 8-4	Lord Sefton	P. Hastings-Bass	G. Lewis	7	11-10
1959 Noble Lassie, 8-4	L. Holliday	W. Hern	D. Smith	5	20-1
1960 Chota Hazri, 8-13	Sir P. Loraine	H. Wragg	D. Smith	8	3-1
1961 Irristable, 8-7	R. Dennis	G. Brooke	D. Smith	9	2-1
1962 French Cream, 8-4	R. Dennis	G. Brooke	D. Smith	7	10-1

		OWNER	TRAINER	JOCKEY	RAN	SP
1963	Red Chorus, 8-5	J. Hindley	N. Murless	L. Piggott	6	9-4
1965	Without Reproach, 8-12	E. Hall	W. Elsey	W. Hide	6	9-4
1966	Royal Flirt, 8-12	W. Lovejoy Jnr	G. Brooke	D. Smith	7	9-2
1967	The Nun, 8-12	J. Astor	W. Hern	J. Mercer	6	9-2
1968	Bringley, 8-12	R. Midwood	H. Leader	B. Taylor	8	9-4
1969	Gambola, 8-12	Lady Z. Wernher	G. Smyth	W. Williamson	2	4-9
1970	Amphora, 8-12	J. Weston-Evans	B. Hobbs	J. Gorton	5	11-10
1971	Maina, 8-12	H.J. Joel	N. Murless	L. Piggott	6	1-2
1972	Star Ship, 9-0	C. St George	H.R. Price	A. Murray	7	4-6
1973	Istiea, 8-6	R. More O'Ferrall	H. Wragg	P. Eddery	4	6-1
1974	Mil's Bomb, 8-6	L. Freedman	N. Murless	G. Lewis	8	85-40
1975	One Over Parr, 8-11	L. Freedman	P. Walwyn	P. Eddery	5	3-1
1976	Centrocon, 8-11	W. Barnett	H. Candy	P. Waldron	9	5-1
1977	Busaca, 8-11	Countess M. Esterhazy	P. Walwyn	P. Eddery	5	1-2
1978	Princess Eboli, 9-1	T. Blackwell	B. Hobbs	G. Lewis	9	13-2
1979	Reprocolor, 9-1	Helena Springfield Ltd	M. Stoute	G. Starkey	5	9-2
1980	Vielle, 8-11	T. Blackwell	B. Hobbs	P. Cook	6	4-5
1981	Rhein Bridge, 8-11	R. Sangster	J.W. Watts	E. Hide	7	10-1
1982	Sing Softly, 8-11	Mrs P. Harris	H. Cecil	L. Piggott	8	5-4
1983	Give Thanks, 9-1	Mrs O. White	J. Bolger	D. Gillespie	13	4-1
1984	Sandy Island, 8-11	Ld Howard de Walden	H. Cecil	L. Piggott	9	5-6
1985	Graecia Magna, 8-11	A. Christodoulou	G. Harwood	G. Starkey	8	5-4

Vernons Sprint Cup   6f

Three-year-olds and upwards. 3-y-o 8st 12lb, 4-y-o & upwards 9st 3lb, fillies allowed 3lb. First run 1966. Run as Vernons November Sprint Cup 1966-67. No race 1968 (fog). Group Two.

		OWNER	TRAINER	JOCKEY	RAN	SP
1966	Be Friendly, 2-8-0	P. O'Sullevan	C. Mitchell	C. Williams	15	15-2
1967	Be Friendly, 3-9-4	P. O'Sullevan	C. Mitchell	A. Breasley	9	2-1
1969	Tudor Music, 3-9-4	D. Robinson	M. Jarvis	F. Durr	11	11-4
1970	Golden Orange, 4-9-10	Lady Clifden	K. Cundell	J. Lindley	5	10-1
1971	Green God, 3-9-6	D. Robinson	M. Jarvis	L. Piggott	7	7-4
1972	Abergwaun, 4-9-7	C. St George	V. O'Brien	L. Piggott	10	11-10
1973	The Blues, 2-8-0	G. van der Ploeg	W. Marshall	R. Marshall	8	10-1
1974	Princely Son, 5-9-10	W. Sherman	K. Cundell	J. Seagrave	9	8-1
1975	Lianga, 4-9-7	D. Wildenstein	A. Penna	Y. Saint-Martin	7	2-1
1976	Record Token, 4-9-8	Sir H. Ingram	P. Walwyn	P. Eddery	8	3-1
1977	Boldboy, 7-9-8	Lady Beaverbrook	W. Hern	W. Carson	7	evens
1978	Absalom, 3-9-6	Mrs C. Alington	R. Jarvis	M.L. Thomas	14	20-1
1979	Double Form, 4-9-8	Baroness H. Thyssen	R.J. Houghton	G. Lewis	8	11-4
1980	Moorestyle, 3-8-12	Moores Furnishings Ltd	R. Armstrong	L. Piggott	8	8-13
1981	Runnett, 4-9-3	Miss V. Evans	J. Dunlop	B. Raymond	6	6-1
1982	Indian King, 4-9-3	J. Levy	G. Harwood	G. Starkey	9	3-1
1983	Habibti, 3-8-9	M. Mutawa	J. Dunlop	W. Carson	6	8-13
1984	Petong, 4-9-3	T. Warner	M. Jarvis	B. Raymond	9	11-1
1985	Orojoya, 3-8-12	R. Sangster	J. Hindley	B. Thomson	8	11-1

KEMPTON PARK

United Racecourses Ltd., Kempton Park Racecourse, Sunbury-on-Thames,
    Middlesex. TW16 5AG. (09327-82292)
Clerk of the Course: Major Michael Webster

Right-handed course with electrical timing apparatus.

EFFECT OF DRAW: High numbers favoured when stalls on far side on sprint course, low numbers favoured when on stands side.

Best Times

DISTANCE	TIME	AGE	WEIGHT	GOING	HORSE	DATE	
5f	58·2	3	7 6	Firm	Hen Pecked	June 2,	1966
5f	58·3	2	9 7	Firm	Schweppeshire Lad	June 3,	1978
6f	1.10·06	4	7 7	Firm	Gusty's Gift	June 3,	1978
6f	1.10·8	2	8 10	Good	Zabara	Sept. 22,	1951
7f Jubilee	1.23·79	3	8 11	Firm	Swiss Maid	Aug. 19,	1978
7f Jubilee	1.24·92	2	8 11	Firm	Silver Hawk	Sept. 5,	1981
7f (rnd)	1.25·7	4	7 11	Firm	Gaykart	July 14,	1971
		3	7 9	Good	Glen Na Smole	May 7,	1984
7f (rnd)	1.27·52	2	8 6	Good	Duke of Ragusa	Sept. 1,	1972
8f (rnd)	1.35·81	4	9 1	Firm	County Broker	May 23,	1984
8f (rnd)	1.43.4	2	7 0	Good	Fascinating	Nov. 3	1956
8f Jubilee	1.35·93	3	8 5	Firm	Soprano	June 1,	1985
		3	9 4	Firm	Diaglyphard	June 1,	1985
8f Jubilee	1.42·5	2	7 4	Good	Bantanollus	Oct. 19,	1962
9f	1.51·19	5	9 1	Firm	Welsh Rarebit	July 12,	1972
10f Jubilee	2.0·14	4	9 5	Firm	Lord Helpus	May 21,	1977
11f 30y	2.16·20	4	9 2	Firm	Shernazar	Sept. 6,	1985
12f	2.30·18	6	8 5	Firm	Going Going	Sept. 7,	1985
16f	3.23·8	4	7 6	Firm	Incredule	July 26,	1956

Race Results

British Car Auctions 'Jubilee' Handicap   1m

First run 1887. Run as Great Jubilee Handicap 1887-1968; Mark Lane Jubilee Handicap 1969-71; William Hill Jubilee Handicap 1972; Jubilee Handicap 1973-74, 1979, 1981-83; Silver Jubilee Handicap 1977; Ultramar Jubilee Handicap 1975-76, 1978, 1980. Run over 1¼m before 1979. No race 1940-45.

	OWNER	TRAINER	JOCKEY	RAN	SP
1930 Lucky Tor, 5-7-8	W. Singer	J. Lawson	F. Fox	15	8-1
1931 Racedale, 5-8-1	Lady Nunburnholme	C. Boyd-Rochfort	A. Wragg	14	9-4
1932 Venturer, 4-7-9	H. Eves	G. Clancy	K. Gethin	15	100-9
1933 Colorado Kid, 4-7-12	Lieut-Col G. Loder	V. Gilpin	C. Buckham	16	100-9
1934 Cotoneaster, 4-7-11	E. T-Smith	F. Templeman	G. Nicoll	14	10-1

	OWNER	TRAINER	JOCKEY	RAN	SP
1935 Wychwood Abbot, 4-9-2	O. Watney	T. Leader	H. Wragg	11	7-1
British Quota, 4-7-6	A. Saville	J. Beary	T. Weston	–	11-2
1936 Inflation, 4-8-0	C. Winn	C. Boyd-Rochfort	C. Richards	16	20-1
1937 Commander III, 7-8-9	N. Christie	C. Elsey	H. Wragg	16	100-7
1938 Monument, 5-8-13	Duke of Marlborough	C. Boyd-Rochfort	P. Beasley	14	10-1
1939 Antonym, 4-9-2	M. Holdert	H. Count	A. Tucker	13	10-1
1946 Paper Weight, 4-8-9	Sir A. Butt	Frank Butters	H. Wragg	10	4-1
1947 Royal Tara, 4-7-12	D. Morris	J. Beary	T. Gosling	18	100-8
1948 Royal Tara, 5-8-11	D. Morris	J. Beary	K. Gethin	12	20-1
1949 Fil d'Or II, 5-8-3	Aga Khan	Frank Butters	G. Richards	7	6-1
1950 Peter Flower, 4-8-4	Lord Rosebery	J. Jarvis	W. Rickaby	12	10-1
1951 Roman Way, 6-8-1	Mrs J. Bryce	C. Boyd-Rochfort	D. Savage	11	100-8
1952 Durante, 4-7-7	Maj D. McCalmont	H. Persse	J. Sirett	12	10-1
1953 Durante, 5-7-11	Maj D. McCalmont	H. Persse	P. Evans	13	100-9
1954 Chatsworth, 4-8-10	Maj L. Holliday	H. Cottrill	F. Barlow	11	9-2
1955 Swept, 4-7-0	Maj T. Bardwell	W. Stephenson	D. Ryan	12	100-9
1956 Tudor Jinks, 4-7-7	A. Tompsett	M. Feakes	D. Forte	15	7-1
1957 Orinthia, 4-6-13	P. Bull	C. Elsey	G. Starkey	14	4-1
1958 Alcimedes, 4-8-3	Lord Astor	J. Colling	J. Mercer	15	100-8
1959 Alcimedes, 5-8-3	Lord Astor	J. Colling	J. Mercer	12	10-1
1960 Rocky Royale, 4-7-9	J. Norris	D. Whelan	D. Smith	13	3-1
1961 Chalk Stream, 6-7-5	Mrs R. Sangster	E. Cousins	B. Lee	16	8-1
1962 Water Skier, 5-7-10	D. Murray	E. Cousins	P. Robinson	14	100-7
1963 Water Skier, 6-7-11	D. Murray	E. Cousins	D. Yates	22	8-1
1964 Commander in Chief, 5-8-7	H. Whitehouse	E. Cousins	F. Durr	16	100-7
1965 Antiquarian, 4-7-9	H. Blagrave	H. Blagrave	J. Sharman	12	10-1
1966 Antiquarian, 5-7-11	H. Blagrave	H. Blagrave	P. Cook	13	6-1
1967 Red Bar, 5-8-2	C. Clore	H.R. Price	R.P. Elliott	17	20-1
1968 Pally's Double, 4-6-11	G. Cooper	J.F. Watts	J. Lowe	15	33-1
1969 Sovereign Ruler, 4-7-0	H. Blagrave	H. Blagrave	D. East	12	6-1
1970 Blue Yonder, 4-8-2	J. Whitney	J. Tree	A. Murray	12	15-2
1971 Welsh Rarebit, 4-7-11	Lord Rosebery	D. Smith	B. Jago	11	15-1
1972 Grandrew, 6-8-8	S. Lay	J. Sutcliffe	W. Carson	14	12-1
1973 Brigade Major, 4-8-5	Mrs J. Hislop	W. Hern	P. Tulk	12	9-1
1974 Jumpabout, 4-7-12	W. Maskell	J. Sutcliffe	R. Hutchinson	11	11-4
1975 Jumpabout, 5-8-5	W. Maskell	J. Sutcliffe	B. Rouse	14	7-1
1976 Royal Match, 5-9-0	Mrs F. Allen	R. Jarvis	M.L. Thomas	11	7-4
1977 Lord Helpus, 4-9-5	M. Standen	B. Hills	L. Piggott	16	11-2
1978 Sunday Guest, 4-8-12	Sir C. Clore	M. Stoute	P. Cook	14	5-1
1979 Smartset, 4-7-0	G. Ward	J. Winter	P. Robinson	12	20-1
1980 Blue Refrain, 4-9-5	Mrs L. Wood	C. Benstead	B. Rouse	8	3-1
1981 Greenwood Star, 4-9-2	D. Young	G. Hunter	G. Starkey	10	11-2
1982 Tugoflove, 6-8-3	Electrogrange Ltd	R. Laing	P. Eddery	12	8-1
1983 Elmar, 4-8-10	R. Smith	J. Dunlop	B. Rouse	12	15-2
1984 Larionov, 4-9-11	Mrs P. Rossdale	J. Winter	P. Eddery	11	10-1
1985 Portogon, 7-7-11	T. Marshall	M. Usher	A. McGlone	11	14-1

BonusPrint September Stakes   1m 3f 30yds

*Three-year-olds and upwards. 3-y-o 8st 4lb, 4-y-o & upwards 9st, fillies allowed 3lb
(plus penalties). First run 1979. Run as September Stakes before 1986. Group Three.*

	OWNER	TRAINER	JOCKEY	RAN	SP
1979 Cracaval, 3-8-10	A. Shead	B. Hills	S. Cauthen	9	20-1
1980 More Light, 4-9-2	R. Budgett	W. Hern	W. Carson	7	7-4
1981 Kind of Hush, 3-8-4	A. Shead	B. Hills	S. Cauthen	11	9-2
1982 Critique, 4-9-2	G. Vanian	H. Cecil	L. Piggott	7	8-11
1983 Lyphard's Special, 3-8-4	Lady Harrison	G. Harwood	B. Rouse	6	12-1
1984 Bedtime, 4-9-0	Lord Halifax	W. Hern	W. Carson	8	13-8
1985 Shernazar, 4-9-2	Aga Khan	M. Stoute	W.R. Swinburn	5	4-1

LEICESTER

The Racecourse, Leicester. LE2 4AL. (0533-716515)
Clerk of the Course: David Henson

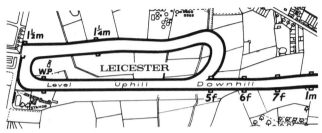

Right-handed course.

EFFECT OF DRAW: Low numbers favoured up to 1m when stalls on far side, especially on soft going.

Best Times

DISTANCE	TIME	AGE	WEIGHT	GOING	HORSE	DATE	
5f	58·6	3	9 2	Firm	Rapid River	Sept. 24,	1973
5f	59	2	8 10	Firm	Whimsical Walker	Sept. 21,	1953
6f	1.10	3	8 6	Firm	Preparation	Sept. 20,	1982
6f	1.10·7	{ 2	7 13	Firm	Gentilhombre	Sept. 22,	1975
		{ 2	8 11	Firm	Full Of Life	Nov. 4,	1985
7f	1.22·7	5	7 13	Firm	Can Run	Nov. 7,	1978
7f	1.23·4	2	7 10	Firm	Astara	Sept. 20,	1982
8f	1.34.4	3	8 3	Hard	Mariapolis	Sept. 19,	1961
8f	1.36·6	2	9 0	Firm	Ambler	Nov. 7,	1978
10f	2.7·2	2	8 13	Firm	Hardly Fair	Oct. 21,	1985
10f	2.9·4	2	8 8	Firm	Vestal King	Oct. 17,	1977
12f	2.28·5	{ 4	7 11	Hard	Gyroscope	Sept. 21,	1964
		{ 3	9 3	Firm	Summer Ridge	Oct. 21,	1985

LINGFIELD PARK

The Racecourse, Lingfield, Surrey. RH7 6PQ. (0342-83 4966)
Clerk of the Course: Major David Cameron

Left-handed course with electrical timing apparatus.

EFFECT OF DRAW: High numbers favoured when stalls on stands side on straight course, low numbers favoured when on far side.

Best Times

DISTANCE	TIME	AGE	WEIGHT	GOING	HORSE	DATE	
5f	56·8	3	8 9	Firm	Marguerite	Oct. 7,	1964
5f	57·36	2	8 12	Firm	Rough Love	June 24,	1977
6f	1.8·4	4	7 4	Firm	Royal Yacht	June 11,	1965
6f	1.8·6	2	9 3	Firm	The Ritz	June 11,	1965
7f	1.20·2	8	7 10	Hard	Polar Jest	Aug. 19,	1955
7f	1.21·34	2	7 6	Firm	Manday	Oct. 3,	1980
7f 140y	1.27·41	5	8 4	Hard	Nearly New	June 26,	1976
7f 140y	1.29·93	2	8 12	Firm	Rather Warm	Nov. 7,	1978
9f	1.53·6	8	9 9	Firm	Traquair	July 8,	1977
10f	2.5·9	3	6 13	Firm	Picture Palace	Oct. 8,	1964
12f	2.33·28	6	9 0	Hard	Palei	Sept. 26,	1978
16f	3.24·7	4	7 7	Firm	Frontin	Oct. 7,	1969

NEWBURY

The Racecourse, Newbury, Berkshire. RG14 7NZ. (0635-40015)
Clerk of the Course: Captain Charles Toller

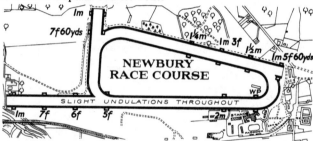

Left-handed course with electrical timing apparatus.

EFFECT OF DRAW: High numbers slightly favoured when stalls on stands side on straight course; low numbers favoured up to 1m on round course.

Best Times

DISTANCE	TIME	AGE	WEIGHT	GOING	HORSE	DATE	
5f	59·8	3	8 12	Good	Minstrels Gallery	June 18,	1955
5f	1.0·6	2	8 7	Firm	Zuccherene	June 25,	1959
6f	1.11·2	4	8 1	Good	Rolled Gold	Oct. 3,	1959
6f	1.11.61	2	8 6	Firm	Bright Crocus	June 10,	1982
7f (str)	1.24·4	3	9 7	Firm	Firestreak	May 29,	1959
7f (str)	1.25·93	2	9 0	Good	Zoffany	Aug. 14,	1982
7f 60yd (rnd)	1.26·8	4	7 1	Firm	Bucktail	June 25,	1959
7f 60yd (rnd)	1.29·12	2	9 7	Firm	Kalaglow	Sept. 19,	1980
8f (rnd)	1.36·41	4	9 7	Firm	Dominion	June 9,	1976
8f (rnd)	1.37·29	2	8 11	Firm	Master Willie	Oct. 1,	1979
8f (str)	1.36·21	4	9 7	Firm	Kris	May 17,	1980
8f (str)	1.39·71	2	8 11	Good	Shergar	Sept. 19,	1980
10f	2.5·22	3	8 6	Firm	Raft	July 21,	1984
11f	2.18·54	5	9 8	Firm	Shady Nook	May 17,	1980
12f	2.29·2	4	8 9	Hard	Vidi Vici	June 21,	1951
13f 60y	2.47·5	5	8 1	Firm	Poaching	May 4,	1957
16f	3.26·41	3	7 13	Firm	Sunyboy	Sept. 8,	1973

Race Results

Lanes End John Porter Stakes   1½m

Four-year-olds and upwards. 8st 8lb, fillies allowed 3lb (plus penalties). First run 1928. For three-year-olds 1928; for three and four-year-olds 1936-38; for three-year-olds as handicap 1941. Run over 1m 5f 1928-35, 1941; run over 1¼m as John Porter Plate 1936-38, otherwise as John Porter Stakes before 1986. No race 1939-40, 1942-48, 1951 (waterlogged), 1966 (snow). Group Three.

		OWNER	TRAINER	JOCKEY	RAN	SP
1930	Wedding Favour, 3-7-11	Ld Howard de Walden	D. Waugh	F. Fox	3	8-13
1931	Birthday Book, 3-9-0	Lord Astor	J. Lawson	R. Dick	8	25-1
1932	Corn Belt, 4-8-10	M. Field	C. Boyd-Rochfort	J. Childs	4	9-2
1933	Sarum, 4-8-7	Sir C. Hyde	N. Scobie	B. Carslake	4	8-1
1934	Felicitation, 4-9-10	Aga Khan	Frank Butters	G. Richards	6	5-6
1935	Night Owl, 3-7-9	J. Whitney	C. Boyd-Rochfort	C. Richards	6	7-2
1936	St Botolph, 4-8-1	F. Dennis	G. Digby	G. Richards	6	20-1
1937	Haulfryn, 4-9-7	F. Minoprio	R. Metcalfe	G. Richards	3	7-4
1938	Fair Copy, 4-9-10	Lord Derby	C. Leader	R. Perryman	4	2-9
1941	Ruscus, 3-8-13	Lord Londonderry	O. Bell	H. Wragg	13	8-1
1949	Solar Slipper, 4-9-1	J. McGrath	W. Stephenson	E. Smith	9	4-6
1950	Native Heath, 5-9-5	Sir M. McAlpine	V. Smyth	A. Breasley	12	3-1
1952	Neron, 4-9-1	Begum Aga Khan	H. Wragg	G. Richards	4	7-2
1953	Wilwyn, 5-9-5	R. Boucher	G. Colling	E. Mercer	7	7-4
1954	Harwin, 4-9-1	T. Robinson	J. Dines	W.H. Carr	9	11-8
1955	Entente Cordiale, 4-8-5	Lord Derby	G. Colling	D. Smith	9	5-4
1956	Acropolis, 4-9-1	Alice, Lady Derby	G. Colling	D. Smith	6	2-7
1957	China Rock, 4-9-1	H. Blagrave	H. Blagrave	F. Durr	10	100-6
1958	Doutelle, 4-9-1	The Queen	C. Boyd-Rochfort	W.H. Carr	4	5-6
1959	Cutter, 4-8-12	R. Hollingsworth	J. Oxley	J. Lindley	3	11-8
1960	Aggressor, 5-9-5	Sir H. Wernher	J. Gosden	J. Lindley	12	11-8
1961	High Perch, 5-9-5	H. Allen	J. Gosden	J. Lindley	8	6-4
1962	Hot Brandy, 4-9-1	A. Kennedy	W. Nightingall	D. Keith	9	4-1
1963	Peter Jones, 4-8-5	P. Wright	A. Budgett	E. Smith	11	4-1
1964	Royal Avenue, 6-9-5	C. St George	N. Murless	L. Piggott	12	100-8
1965	Soderini, 4-9-1	L. Lawrence	S. Ingham	G. Lewis	7	4-1
1967	Charlottown, 4-9-1	Lady Z. Wernher	G. Smyth	J. Lindley	8	4-6
1968	Fortissimo, 4-8-5	V. McCalmont	R. Fetherstonhaugh	G. Lewis	9	3-1
1969	Crozier, 6-9-5	A. Oldrey	P. Walwyn	D. Keith	7	15-8
1970	Torpid, 5-9-5	R. Hollingsworth	J. Oxley	B. Taylor	8	6-1
1971	Meadowville, 4-9-1	D. Robinson	M. Jarvis	F. Durr	12	11-8
1972	Rock Roi, 5-9-5	F. Hue-Williams	P. Walwyn	D. Keith	5	6-4
1973	Rheingold, 4-9-1	H. Zeisel	B. Hills	Y. Saint-Martin	15	10-11
1974	Freefoot, 4-8-6	R. Moller	H. Wragg	L. Piggott	12	13-2
1975	Saldo, 4-8-10	Mrs P. Isaacs	P. Mitchell	W. Carson	9	33-1
1976	Quiet Fling, 4-9-0	J. Whitney	J. Tree	L. Piggott	11	5-1
1977	Decent Fellow, 4-8-9	W. Gilbride	G. Balding	L. Piggott	11	4-1
1978	Orchestra, 4-9-0	Lord Donoughmore	J. Oxx	R. Carroll	10	6-1
1979	Icelandic, 4-8-11	P. Prendergast	P. Prendergast	C. Roche	12	11-4
1980	Niniski, 4-9-0	Lady Beaverbrook	W. Hern	W. Carson	16	2-1
1981	Pelerin, 4-8-8	Sir P. Oppenheimer	H. Wragg	B. Taylor	9	16-1
1982	Glint of Gold, 4-9-0	P. Mellon	I. Balding	J. Matthias	11	2-1
1983	Diamond Shoal, 4-8-8	P. Mellon	I. Balding	S. Cauthen	8	7-2
1984	Gay Lemur, 4-8-8	Eva, Lady Rosebery	B. Hobbs	G. Baxter	13	20-1
1985	Jupiter Island, 6-8-8	S. Threadwell	C. Brittain	G. Starkey	14	11-2

Juddmonte Lockinge Stakes   1m

Three-year-olds and upwards. 3-y-o 7st 13lb, 4-y-o & upwards 9st 1lb, fillies allowed 3lb (plus penalties). First run 1958. Run as Lockinge Stakes before 1984. No race 1975 (waterlogged). Group Two.

		OWNER	TRAINER	JOCKEY	RAN	SP
1958	Pall Mall, 3-8-6	The Queen	C. Boyd-Rochfort	W.H. Carr	4	4-6
1959	Pall Mall, 4-9-7	The Queen	C. Boyd-Rochfort	W.H. Carr	5	1-2
1960	Sovereign Path, 4-9-7	R. Mason	R. Mason	L. Piggott	5	7-4
1961	Prince Midge, 3-7-11	J. Astor	R.J. Colling	D. Keith	8	11-2
1962	Superstition, 3-7-4	Mrs C. Iselin	C. Boyd-Rochfort	D.W. Morris	10	100-30
1963	Queen's Hussar, 3-8-3	Lord Carnarvon	T. Corbett	A. Breasley	10	9-2
1964	The Creditor, 4-9-4	Lady Sassoon	N. Murless	L. Piggott	6	10-11
1965	Young Christopher, 4-9-3	J. McShane	F. Maxwell	W. Williamson	10	6-1
1966	Silly Season, 4-9-5	P. Mellon	I. Balding	G. Lewis	13	7-1
1967	Bluerullah, 4-8-12	S. McGrath	S. McGrath	W. Williamson	5	4-1
1968	Supreme Sovereign, 4-8-12	Mrs R. Hodges	H. Wragg	R. Hutchinson	5	5-6
1969	Habitat, 3-7-11	C. Engelhard	R.J. Houghton	R. Hutchinson	6	10-1
1970	Welsh Pageant, 4-8-12	H.J. Joel	N. Murless	A. Barclay	6	8-13
1971	Welsh Pageant, 5-9-2	H.J. Joel	N. Murless	G. Lewis	6	evens
1972	Brigadier Gerard, 4-9-5	Mrs J. Hislop	W. Hern	J. Mercer	5	1-4
1973	Sparkler, 5-8-12	Mrs M. Mehl-Mulhens	R. Armstrong	L. Piggott	12	7-2
1974	Boldboy, 4-8-12	Lady Beaverbrook	W. Hern	J. Mercer	8	15-8
1976	El Rastro, 6-9-0	D. Wildenstein	A. Penna	W. Pyers	8	9-2
1977	Relkino, 4-9-0	Lady Beaverbrook	W. Hern	W. Carson	9	4-1
1978	Don, 4-9-4	E. Ryan	W. Elsey	B. Rouse	10	5-1
1979	Young Generation, 3-8-4	A. Ward	G. Harwood	G. Starkey	10	4-1
1980	Kris, 4-9-7	Ld Howard de Walden	H. Cecil	J. Mercer	7	4-9
1981	Belmont Bay, 4-9-0	D. Wildenstein	H. Cecil	L. Piggott	6	11-10
1982	Motovato, 4-9-0	R. Sangster	B. Hills	S. Cauthen	7	7-4
1983	Noalcoholic, 6-9-4	W. du Pont III	G. Pritchard-Gordon	G. Duffield	10	7-2
1984	Cormorant Wood, 4-9-5	R.J. McAlpine	B. Hills	S. Cauthen	6	7-1
	Wassl, 4-9-8	A. Al-Maktoum	J. Dunlop	W. Carson	—	9-2
1985	Prismatic, 3-7-13	Ld Howard de Walden	H. Cecil	Paul Eddery	11	10-1

NEWCASTLE

High Gosforth Park, Newcastle Upon Tyne. NE3 5HP. (0632-362020)
Clerk of the Course: John Smith

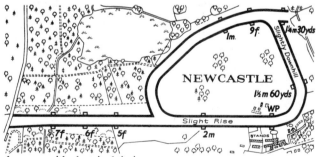

Left-handed course with electrical timing apparatus.
EFFECT OF DRAW: Low numbers usually favoured, especially on soft.

Best Times

DISTANCE	TIME	AGE	WEIGHT	GOING	HORSE	DATE	
5f	58·6	4	9 0	Hard	Weensland	June 21,	1951
5f	59·2	2	8 2	Good	Dunce Cap	Aug. 6,	1962
6f	1.11·6	3	9 3	Hard	Comobeau	June 23,	1960
6f	1.13·31	2	9 3	Firm	Kayus	Aug. 9,	1983
7f (str)	1.23·53	3	8 5	Firm	Beaudelaire	July 23,	1983
7f (str)	1.26·82	2	8 8	Firm	Nice Balance	Aug. 10,	1976
7f (rnd)	1.38·4	5	8 1	Soft	Christmas Cottage	April 2,	1983
8f (rnd)	1.39·8	4	6 12	Hard	Brink	Oct. 4,	1947
8f (rnd)	1.43·05	2	9 0	Fast	Caro's Gift	Oct. 4,	1983
9f	1.52	3	6 3	Good	Ferniehurst	June 23,	1936
10f	2.6·61	4	7 8	Firm	Doogali	July 24,	1978
10f 30y	2.10·6	8	7 5	Firm	Heckley	Oct. 14,	1959
12f 60y	2.38·4	4	8 13	Firm	Kesrullah	June 25,	1953
16f	3.22	4	7 12	Good	Nectar II	June 23,	1937

Race Result

Newcastle 'Brown Ale' Northumberland Plate   2m

Handicap. First run 1833. Run as Northumberland Plate 1833-1971; as Coral Northumberland Plate 1972-81; Miner's Northumberland Plate 1982-84. Run at Liverpool 1946. No race 1940-45, 1982 (waterlogged).

	OWNER	TRAINER	JOCKEY	RAN	SP
1930 Show Girl, 4-8-4	Lady Ludlow	J. Watts	E.C. Elliott	12	100-8
1931 Blue Vision, 4-7-4	M. Evans	I. Anthony	K. Gethin	8	11-4
1932 Pomarrel, 5-7-5	J. Thompson	M. Peacock	J. Dines	10	8-1
1933 Leonard, 7-7-9	H. Clayton	C. Elsey	W. Bullock	10	100-7
1934 Whiteplains, 4-7-11	Sir W. Burbidge	J. Jarvis	E. Smith	15	25-1
1935 Doreen Jane, 5-7-8	Sir A. Bailey	H. Cottrill	D. Smith	8	15-8
1936 Coup de Roi, 4-7-13	Sir P. Loraine	R. Dawson	E. Smith	7	5-2
1937 Nectar II, 4-7-12	Sir E. Bushby	F. Armstrong	P. Maher	11	100-8
1938 Union Jack, 4-8-0	N. Christey	C. Elsey	W. Nevett	12	10-1
1939 Oracion, 4-8-0	Maj D. McCalmont	G. Lambton	T. Weston	13	9-1
1946 Gusty, 4-9-2	Lord Allendale	C. Elsey	H. Wragg	5	7-4
1947 Culrain, 6-7-2	G. Cullington	T. Hall	D. Smith	9	9-2
1948 Pappatea, 5-9-5	R. Simpson	G. Boyd	H. Blackshaw	15	20-1
1949 Fol Ami, 4-7-1	Maharaja of Baroda	F. Armstrong	W. Snaith	13	9-2
1950 Light Cavalry, 4-7-6	A. McLeod	M. Everitt	J. Sime	8	10-1
1951 Sycomore II, 4-8-3	Maharaja of Morvi	F. Armstrong	E. Britt	15	9-4
1952 Souepi, 4-7-6	G. Digby	G. Digby	H. Packham	6	5-4
1953 Nick la Rocca, 4-8-11	F. Williams	J. Colling	J. Mercer	14	9-4
1954 Friseur, 4-8-2	Mrs R. Ryan	N. Murless	G. Richards	20	7-1
1955 Little Cloud, 4-8-4	Sir V. Sassoon	N. Murless	L. Piggott	16	13-2
1956 Jardiniere, 4-8-0	T. Lilley	N. Murless	D. Smith	12	2-1
1957 Great Rock, 4-7-8	Mrs A. Straker	W. Dutton	E. Hide	17	10-1
1958 Master of Arts, 5-8-4	J. Astor	R.J. Colling	J. Mercer	21	7-2
1959 Cannebiere, 6-7-9	E. Walker	A. Barclay	Don Morris	17	100-7
1960 New Brig, 4-8-8	J. Kennedy	G. Boyd	N. Stirk	13	10-1
1961 Utrillo, 4-7-1	J. Gerber	W. O'Gorman	D. Cullen	20	100-7
1962 Bordone, 4-8-5	A. Grant	G. Fenningworth	G. Littlewood	13	100-7
1963 Horse Radish, 4-7-8	N. Wachman	F. Maxwell	P. Robinson	14	8-1
1964 Peter Piper, 4-7-9	Mrs V. Phillips	R. Mason	J. Wilson	18	28-1
1965 Cagirama, 6-7-5	Mrs S. Carson	G. Boyd	N. McIntosh	16	9-1
1966 Sweet Story, 4-8-4	Duke of Roxburghe	R. Peacock	J. Etherington	15	100-7
1967 Piaco, 4-9-1	Mrs O.V. Watney	G. Barling	M.L. Thomas	13	100-30
1968 Amateur, 4-7-9	Lord Derby	B. van Cutsem	W. Carson	14	100-9
1969 Even Say, 4-7-11	S. Terry	R. Jarvis	F. Durr	16	6-1
1970 Philoctetes, 6-7-12	P. Bull	S. Ingham	P. Eddery	16	20-1
1971 Tartar Prince, 4-7-8	J. Parker	T. Waugh	J. Higgins	18	5-1
1972 Scoria, 6-7-6	J. Lang	C. Crossley	R. Smyth	13	17-2

	OWNER	TRAINER	JOCKEY	RAN	SP
1973 Tom Cribb, 4-8-4	Lord Rosebery	B. Hobbs	B. Jago	11	11-1
1974 Attivo, 4-7-8	P. O'Sullevan	C. Mitchell	R. Wernham	11	7-4
1975 Grey God, 4-8-9	D. Robinson	M. Jarvis	B. Raymond	12	8-1
1976 Philominsky, 5-8-0	S. Hallam	W. Marshall	R. Marshall	11	20-1
1977 Tug of War, 4-8-7	Mrs Y. Perry	D. Whelan	B. Rouse	15	16-1
1978 Tug of War, 5-9-2	Mrs Y. Perry	D. Whelan	B. Rouse	10	11-2
1979 Totowah, 5-8-2	Lady Beaverbrook	M. Jarvis	B. Raymond	11	5-1
1980 Mon's Beau, 5-7-7	M. Vine	E. Beeson	S. Salmon	15	40-1
1981 Dawn Johnny, 4-8-6	Sir G. White	M. Stoute	M. Birch	18	5-1
1983 Weavers Pin, 6-8-8	Mrs M. Francis	M. Francis	Paul Eddery	14	20-1
1984 Karadar, 6-9-10	Aga Khan	M. Stoute	A. Kimberley	19	10-1
1985 Trade Line, 4-7-10	M. Scott	R. Sheather	T. Williams	13	17-2

NEWMARKET

Jockey Club Office, Newmarket, Suffolk. CB8 8JC. (0638-664151)
Clerk of the Course: Captain Nick Lees

Rowley Mile Course

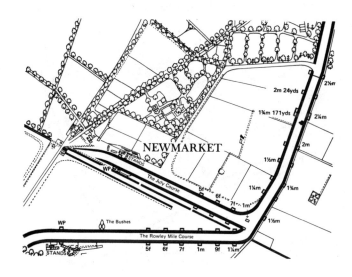

Right-handed course with electrical timing apparatus.
EFFECT OF DRAW: High numbers slightly favoured up to 1m.

Best Times

ROWLEY MILE COURSE

COURSE	DIST.	TIME	AGE	WGHT.		GOING	HORSE	DATE	
Rous	5f	57·4	5	8	9	Firm	Knight's Armour	April 6,	1938
Rous	5f	58·99	2	7	5	Firm	Katysue	Oct. 2.	1980
Bretby Stakes	6f	1.10·66	5	7	12	Firm	Welsh Blossom	Oct. 1,	1980
Bretby Stakes	6f	1.11·04	2	9	10	Firm	Junius	Oct. 5,	1978
Dewhurst Stakes	7f	1.24·14	3	8	6	Firm	Chalon	May 1,	1982
Dewhurst Stakes	7f	1.23·63	2	9	0	Firm	Goblin	Oct. 1,	1977
Rowley Mile	8f	1.35·8	3	9	0	Hard	My Babu	April 28,	1948
Rowley Mile	8f	1.37·43	2	8	7	Firm	Demetrius	Sept. 28,	1977
Cambridgeshire	9f	1.47·45	3	8	3	Firm	Sin Timon	Oct. 1,	1977
A.F.	10f	2.1·04	3	8	10	Good	Palace Music	Oct. 20,	1985
A.F.	10f	2.4·65	2	9	4	Good	Highland Chieftain	Nov. 2,	1985
Casarewitch	12f	2.29·8	6	9	3	Hard	High Stakes	April 28,	1948
Casarewitch	14f	2.56·19	4	8	11	Firm	Buckhound	Oct. 1,	1953
Casarewitch	16f	3.22·48	3	8	2	Firm	Misalliance	Oct. 1,	1977
Cesarewitch	18f	3.47·5	3	7	12	Hard	Whiteway	Oct. 15,	1947
Cesarewitch	20f	4.26·8	8	9	4	Fast	Mayotte	Oct. 28,	1983

July Course

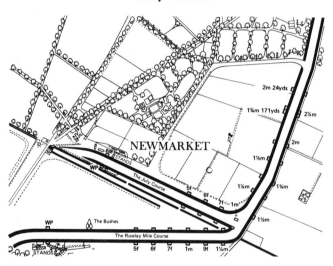

EFFECT OF DRAW: No advantage.

Best Times

JULY COURSE

COURSE	DIST.	TIME	AGE	WGHT.		GOING	HORSE	DATE	
Chesterfield	5f	58·68	3	8	6	Firm	Light Grey	July 3,	1962
Chesterfield	5f	58·8	2	9	0	Hard	Dante	June 17,	1944

COURSE	DIST.	TIME	AGE	WGHT.	GOING	HORSE	DATE	
Bunbury Mile	6f	1.11.22	3	7 1	Firm	Questa Notte	July 20,	1974
Bunbury Mile	6f	1.11·74	2	8 6	Good	Fatah Flare	June 30,	1984
Bunbury Mile	7f	1.23·6	5	7 8	Hard	Ti-Chin	June 17,	1944
Bunbury Mile	7f	1.24·93	2	8 7	Firm	Sexton Blake	July 30,	1977
Bunbury Mile	8f	1.36·8	4	9 7	Hard	Pink Flower	June 6,	1944
Bunbury Mile	8f	1.40·28	2	9 4	Fast	Lear Fan	Aug. 27,	1983
Suffolk Stakes	10f	2.28	3	9 7	Firm	Borealis	May 2,	1944
Suffolk Stakes	12f	2.29·31	3	7 11	Firm	Height of Fashion	July 6,	1962
Summer	14f 171y	3.8·76	4	9 3	Good	Trapeze Artist	Aug. 23,	1985
Summer	16f 24y	3.18	4	8 0	Good	Luncheon Hour	Nov. 21,	1940

Race Results

Ladbroke European Free Handicap   7f

Three-year-olds. First run 1929. Run as Free Handicap 1929-41, 1945-68; as Newmarket Free Handicap 1944; as Totalisator Free Handicap 1969-73; as Tote Free Handicap 1974-80; as Tote European Free Handicap 1981-82. No race 1942-43.

	OWNER	TRAINER	JOCKEY	RAN	SP
1930 Quothquan, 7-4	Ld Hamilton of Dalzell	M. Peacock	W. Nevett	32	100-8
1931 Zanoff, 7-5	Z. Michalinos	A. Molony	J. Sirett	26	7-1
1932 Rolling Rock, 9-0	Mrs L. Rihll	V. Gilpin	P. Beasley	19	100-7
1933 Cotoneaster, 6-13	E. Thornton-Smith	F. Templeman	W. Rickaby	30	25-1
1934 Phaleron Bay, 7-7	Sir L. Philipps	J. Jarvis	E. Smith	19	7-1
1935 Knighted, 8-12	C. Jarvis	P. Allden	A. Wragg	25	100-8
1936 Pay Up, 8-2	Lord Astor	J. Lawson	J. Sirett	19	6-1
1937 Mid-day Sun, 7-2	Mrs G. Miller	Fred Butters	K. Robertson	19	100-9
1938 Lapel, 7-0	D. McCalmont	E. Lambton	W. Wells	13	4-1
1939 Solar Cloud, 7-6	Mrs R. M-Buchanan	F. Darling	C. Richards	29	6-1
1940 Salt Spring, 8-12	H. Lester	V. Hobbs	C. Miles	20	100-7
1941 Orthodox, 8-3	J. Rank	N. Cannon	D. Smith	19	20-1
1944 Roadhouse, 7-12	Lord Rosebery	J. Jarvis	E. Smith	12	11-2
1945 Grandmaster, 8-13	M. Freedman	W. Nightingall	T. Carey	21	10-1
1946 Cama, 8-5	Aga Khan	Frank Butters	G. Richards	17	100-7
1947 Benedictine, 8-7	G. Marsden	H. Leach	M. Beary	15	11-2
1948 Rear Admiral, 8-11	C. Wade	H. Smyth	H. Packham	18	6-1
1949 Spy Legend, 8-0	H. Leggat	P. Beasley	P. Evans	19	10-1
1950 The Moke, 7-2	Mrs N. Cheatle	W. Stephenson	T. Mahon	17	100-7
1951 Wilwyn, 7-12	R. Boucher	G. Colling	E. Mercer	19	5-1
1952 Caerlaverock, 7-12	Duke of Norfolk	W. Smyth	F. Durr	21	12½-1
1953 Good Brandy, 8-5	R.S. Clark	H. Peacock	D. Smith	12	6-1
1954 Sun Festival, 8-2	T. Lilley	N. Murless	G. Richards	21	20-1
1955 Counsel, 8-11	Lord Astor	R.J. Colling	J. Mercer	19	7-1
1956 Honeylight, 8-7	Sir V. Sassoon	C. Elsey	E. Britt	18	100-8
1957 Quorum, 8-7	T. Farr	W. Lyde	A.J. Russell	13	15-2
1958 Faultless Speech, 8-4	H. Wallington	H. Wallington	A. Breasley	14	10-1
1959 Petite Etoile, 9-0	Prince Aly Khan	N. Murless	G. Moore	10	9-1
1960 Running Blue, 8-4	J. Philipps	J. Jarvis	J. Limb	20	100-7
1961 Erudite, 8-6	Duke of Roxburghe	R.D. Peacock	J. Etherington	19	100-6
1962 Privy Councillor, 8-4	G. Glover	T. Waugh	J. Sime	18	100-7
1963 Ros Rock, 8-1	C. Engelhard	J. Tree	P. Tulk	16	25-1
1964 Port Merion, 8-9	R. Macdonald-Buchanan	G. Richards	A. Breasley	23	100-8
1965 Short Commons, 8-4	J. Mitchell	P. Rohan	R. Maddock	11	100-8
1966 Kibenka, 8-4	B. Attenborough	T. Corbett	R. Hutchinson	16	10-1
1967 Supreme Sovereign, 8-1	Mrs R. Hodges	A. Vasey	P. Robinson	15	7-1
1968 Panpiper, 7-13	Lord Blakenham	R. Smyth	E. Johnson	13	100-7
1969 Welsh Pageant, 8-10	H.J. Joel	N. Murless	A. Barclay	15	5-2
1970 Shiny Tenth, 8-3	A. Holland	T. Corbett	G. Lewis	12	4-1
1971 No Mercy, 8-5	C. Vittadini	H. Leader	B. Taylor	16	10-1
1972 Panama Canal, 7-11	R. Chinn	W. Marshall	R. Marshall	16	20-1

	OWNER	TRAINER	JOCKEY	RAN	SP
1973 Pitskelly, 8-5	D. Robinson	M. Jarvis	W. Williamson	16	2-1
1974 Charlie Bubbles, 8-3	L. Sainer	P. Walwyn	P. Eddery	14	4-1
1975 Green Belt, 8-9	Sir P. Oppenheimer	H. Wragg	E. Eldin	15	5-1
1976 Man of Harlech, 8-4	Duchess of Norfolk	J. Dunlop	R. Hutchinson	19	14-1
1977 Mrs McArdy, 8-0	Mrs E. Kettlewell	M.W. Easterby	M.L. Thomas	19	8-1
1978 Remainder Man, 7-10	Mrs D. Jardine	R. Hollinshead	M. Wigham	12	15-2
1979 Lyric Dance, 8-10	Mrs E. Longton	J. Tree	P. Eddery	14	3-1
1980 Moorestyle, 8-10	Moores Furnishing Ltd	R. Armstrong	L. Piggott	13	6-1
1981 Motavato, 8-13	R. Sangster	B. Hills	S. Cauthen	13	13-2
1982 Match Winner, 9-4	D. Wildenstein	H. Cecil	L. Piggott	13	9-4
1983 Boom Town Charlie, 8-11	Mrs P. Yong	W.O'Gorman	T. Ives	8	13-2
1984 Cutting Wind, 8-8	Mrs P. Meynet	M. Hinchliffe	W.R. Swinburn	17	20-1
1985 Over The Ocean, 8-11	M. Fustok	O. Douieb	A. Lequeux	11	85-40

General Accident 1,000 Guineas Stakes   1m

Three-year-old fillies. 9st. First run 1814. Run as New 1,000 Guineas on July Course 1940-45. Run as 1,000 Guineas Stakes before 1984. Group One.

	OWNER	TRAINER	JOCKEY	RAN	SP
1900 Winifreda	L. Brassey	T. Jennings	S. Loates	10	11-2
1901 Aida	Sir J. Miller	G. Blackwell	D. Maher	15	13-8
1902 Sceptre	R. Sievier	R. Sievier	H. Randall	15	1-2
1903 Quintessence	Lord Falmouth	J. Chandler	H. Randall	12	4-1
1904 Pretty Polly	Maj E. Loder	P. Gilpin	W. Lane	7	1-4
1905 Cherry Lass	W.H. Walker	W. Robinson	G. McCall	19	5-4
1906 Flair	Sir D. Cooper	P. Gilpin	B. Dillon	12	10-11
1907 Witch Elm	W.H. Walker	W. Robinson	B. Lynham	17	4-1
1908 Rhodora	R. Crocker	G. Allen	L. Lyne	19	100-8
1909 Electra	L. Neumann	P. Gilpin	B. Dillon	10	9-1
1910 Winkipop	W. Astor	W. Waugh	B. Lynham	13	5-2
1911 Atmah	J. de Rothschild	F. Pratt	F. Fox	16	7-1
1912 Tagalie	W. Raphael	D. Waugh	L. Hewitt	13	20-1
1913 Jest	J. Joel	C. Morton	F. Rickaby	22	9-1
1914 Princess Dorrie	J. Joel	C. Morton	W. Huxley	13	9-1
1915 Vaucluse	Lord Rosebery	F. Hartigan	F. Rickaby	15	5-2
1916 Canyon	Lord Derby	G. Lambton	F. Rickaby	14	9-4
1917 Diadem	Lord d'Abernon	G. Lambton	F. Rickaby	14	6-4
1918 Ferry	Lord Derby	G. Lambton	B. Carslake	8	50-1
1919 Roseway	Sir E. Hulton	F. Hartigan	A. Whalley	15	2-1
1920 Cinna	Sir R. Jardine	T. Waugh	W. Griggs	21	4-1
1921 Bettina	W. Raphael	P. Linton	G. Bellhouse	24	33-1
1922 Silver Urn	B. Parr	H. Persse	B. Carslake	20	10-1
1923 Tranquil	Lord Derby	G. Lambton	E. Gardner	16	5-2
1924 Plack	Lord Rosebery	J. Jarvis	E.C. Elliott	16	8-1
1925 Saucy Sue	Lord Astor	A. Taylor	F. Bullock	11	1-4
1926 Pillion	A. de Rothschild	J. Watson	R. Perryman	29	25-1
1927 Cresta Run	Lieut-Col G. Loder	P. Gilpin	A. Balding	28	10-1
1928 Scuttle	King George V	W. Jarvis	J. Childs	14	15-8
1929 Taj Mah	S. Guthmann	J. Torterolo	W. Sibbritt	19	33-1
1930 Fair Isle	Lord Derby	Frank Butters	T. Weston	19	7-4
1931 Four Course	Lord Ellesmere	F. Darling	E.C. Elliott	20	100-9
1932 Kandy	M. de St. Alary	V. Gilpin	E.C. Elliott	19	33-1
1933 Brown Betty	W. Woodward	C. Boyd-Rochfort	J. Childs	22	8-1
1934 Campanula	Sir G. Bullough	J. Jarvis	H. Wragg	10	2-5
1935 Mesa	P. Wertheimer	M.P. Corbiere	W. Johnstone	22	8-1
1936 Tide-way	Lord Derby	C. Leader	R. Perryman	22	100-30
1937 Exhibitionnist	Sir V. Sassoon	J. Lawson	S. Donoghue	20	10-1
1938 Rockfel	Sir H. C-Owen	O. Bell	S. Wragg	20	8-1
1939 Galatea II	R. Clark	J. Lawson	R. Jones	18	6-1
1940 Godiva	Lord Rothermere	W. Jarvis	D. Marks	11	10-1
1941 Dancing Time	Lord Glanely	J. Lawson	R. Perryman	13	100-8
1942 Sun Chariot	King George VI	F. Darling	G. Richards	18	evens
1943 Herringbone	Lord Derby	W. Earl	H. Wragg	12	15-2
1944 Picture Play	H.J. Joel	J. Watts	E.C. Elliott	11	15-2
1945 Sun Stream	Lord Derby	W. Earl	H. Wragg	14	5-2
1946 Hypericum	King George VI	C. Boyd-Rochfort	D. Smith	13	100-6

	OWNER	TRAINER	JOCKEY	RAN	SP
1947 Imprudence	Mme P. Corbiere	J. Lieux	W. Johnstone	20	4-1
1948 Queenpot	Sir P. Loraine	N. Murless	G. Richards	22	6-1
1949 Musidora	N. Donaldson	C. Elsey	E. Britt	18	100-8
1950 Camaree	J. Ternynck	A. Lieux	W. Johnstone	17	10-1
1951 Belle of All	H. Tufton	N. Bertie	G. Richards	18	4-1
1952 Zabara	Sir M. McAlpine	V. Smyth	K. Gethin	20	7-1
1953 Happy Laughter	H. Wills	J. Jarvis	E. Mercer	14	10-1
1954 Festoon	J. Dewar	N. Cannon	A. Breasley	12	9-2
1955 Meld	Lady Z. Wernher	C. Boyd-Rochfort	W.H. Carr	12	11-2
1956 Honeylight	Sir V. Sassoon	C. Elsey	E. Britt	19	100-6
1957 Rose Royale II	Aga Khan	A. Head	C. Smirke	20	6-1
1958 Bella Paola	F. Dupré	F. Mathet	S. Boullenger	11	8-11
1959 Petite Etoile	Aly Khan	N. Murless	D. Smith	14	8-1
1960 Never Too Late II	Mrs H. Jackson	E. Pollet	R. Poincelet	14	8-11
1961 Sweet Solera	Mrs S. Costello	R. Day	W. Rickaby	14	4-1
1962 Abermaid	R.M. O'Ferrall	H. Wragg	W. Williamson	14	100-6
1963 Hula Dancer	Mrs P. Widener	E. Pollet	J. Deforge	12	1-2
1964 Pourparler	Lady Granard	P. Prendergast	G. Bougoure	18	11-2
1965 Night Off	Maj L. Holliday	W. Wharton	W. Williamson	16	9-2
1966 Glad Rags	Mrs J.P. Mills	V. O'Brien	P. Cook	21	100-6
1967 Fleet	R. Boucher	N. Murless	G. Moore	16	11-2
1968 Caergwrle	Mrs N. Murless	N. Murless	A. Barclay	14	4-1
1969 Full Dress II	R. Moller	H. Wragg	R. Hutchinson	13	7-1
1970 Humble Duty	Jean, Lady Ashcombe	P. Walwyn	L. Piggott	12	7-2
1971 Altesse Royale	Col F. Hue-Williams	N. Murless	Y. Saint-Martin	10	25-1
1972 Waterloo	Mrs R. Stanley	J.W. Watts	E. Hide	18	8-1
1973 Mysterious	G. Pope Jnr	N. Murless	G. Lewis	14	11-1
1974 Highclere	The Queen	W. Hern	J. Mercer	15	12-1
1975 Nocturnal Spree	Mrs D. O'Kelly	S. Murless	J. Roe	14	14-1
1976 Flying Water	D. Wildenstein	A. Penna	Y. Saint-Martin	25	2-1
1977 Mrs McArdy	Mrs E. Kettlewell	M.W. Easterby	E. Hide	18	16-1
1978 Enstone Spark	R. Bonnycastle	B. Hills	E. Johnson	16	35-1
1979 One In A Million	Helena Springfield Ltd	H. Cecil	J. Mercer	17	evens
1980 Quick As Lightning	O.M. Phipps	J. Dunlop	B. Rouse	23	12-1
1981 Fairy Footsteps	H.J. Joel	H. Cecil	L. Piggott	14	6-4
1982 On The House	Sir P. Oppenheimer	H. Wragg	J. Reid	15	33-1
1983 Ma Biche	M. Al-Maktoum	Mme C. Head	F. Head	18	5-2
1984 Pebbles	M. Lemos	C. Brittain	P. Robinson	15	8-1
1985 Oh So Sharp	Sheikh Mohammed	H. Cecil	S. Cauthen	17	2-1

Jockey Club Stakes   1½m

Four-year-olds and upwards. 8st 7lb, fillies allowed 3lb (plus penalties). First run 1894. Run over 1¾m before 1963. No race 1939-44. Group Two.

	OWNER	TRAINER	JOCKEY	RAN	SP
1930 Pyramid, 3-7-6	Lord Derby	Frank Butters	T. Weston	7	7-1
1931 Shell Transport, 3-8-12	W. Cazalet	J. Lawson	R. Dick	11	8-1
1932 Firdaussi, 3-8-12	Aga Khan	Frank Butters	M. Beary	7	4-1
1933 Tai-Yang, 3-7-9	H. Morriss	F. Darling	G. Richards	7	4-1
1934 Umidwar, 3-8-9	Aga Khan	Frank Butters	F. Fox	11	13-2
1935 Plassy, 3-8-6	Lord Derby	C. Leader	R. Perryman	7	8-1
1936 Precipitation, 3-8-9	Lady Z. Wernher	C. Boyd-Rochfort	R. Perryman	7	9-2
1937 Solfo, 3-8-9	J. Courtauld	B. Jarvis	T. Lowrey	6	9-1
1938 Challenge, 3-8-1	Sir L. Philipps	J. Jarvis	E. Smith	8	6-4
1945 Black Peter, 3-7-10	Mrs M. Harvey	J.C. Waugh	S. Wragg	4	7-2
1946 Rising Light, 4-8-11	King George VI	C. Boyd-Rochfort	D. Smith	7	6-1
1947 Esprit de France, 3-8-1	Aga Khan	H. Hartigan	D. Smith	5	9-4
1948 Alycidon, 3-8-4	Lord Derby	W. Earl	D. Smith	5	8-11
1959 Dust Devil, 3-7-9	Aga Khan	Frank Butters	D. Smith	4	1-3
1950 Holmbush, 3-7-9	Sir D. Bailey	A. Budgett	L. Piggott	6	5-1
1951 Pardal, 4-9-0	M. Boussac	C. Semblat	W.R. Johnstone	4	4-6
1952 Mister Cube, 3-8-1	Sir A. Jarvis	J. Jarvis	E. Mercer	5	100-30
1953 Buckhound, 4-8-11	B. Hornung	N. Murless	G. Richards	7	7-2
1954 Brilliant Green, 3-7-12	J. de Rothschild	D. Watson	E. Smith	5	3-1
1955 Nucleus, 3-8-8	Miss D. Paget	C. Jerdein	L. Piggott	5	evens
1956 Kurun, 4-9-0	M. Boussac	E.C. Elliott	C. Smirke	7	5-2

	OWNER	TRAINER	JOCKEY	RAN	SP
1957 Court Harwell, 3-8-1	J. Mullion	G. Richards	A. Breasley	6	8-11
1958 All Serene, 3-7-9	Princess Royal	N. Bertie	D. Smith	5	10-1
1959 Court Prince, 3-8-5	T. Lilley	N. Murless	L. Piggott	5	100-30
1960 Prolific, 3-8-4	Mrs C. Evans	W. Nightingall	D. Keith	2	10-11
1961 St Paddy, 4-9-6	Lady Sassoon	N. Murless	L. Piggott	5	4-6
1962 Gaul, 3-8-6	Lord Sefton	P. Hastings-Bass	G. Lewis	11	100-8
1963 Darling Boy, 5-9-7	J. Astor	W. Hern	J. Mercer	7	11-2
1964 Fighting Ship, 4-9-6	Lord Rosebery	J. Jarvis	P. Robinson	6	5-1
1965 Bal Masque, 5-9-1	Mrs H. Jackson	E. Fellows	W. Pyers	3	5-1
1966 Alcalde, 4-9-0	Lord Derby	B. van Cutsem	D. Smith	13	7-2
1967 Acrania, 4-9-0	R. Zelker	G. Harwood	J. Lindley	3	100-8
1968 Crozier, 5-9-10	A. Oldrey	P. Walwyn	D. Keith	7	7-1
1969 Torpid, 4-9-6	R. Hollingsworth	J. Oxley	G. Starkey	9	5-1
1970 Queen of Twilight, 4-8-11	Mrs L. Smith	H. Leader	B. Taylor	9	20-1
1971 Meadowville, 4-9-6	D. Robinson	M. Jarvis	F. Durr	3	4-6
1972 Knockroe, 4-8-13	V. McCalmont	P. Nelson	L. Piggott	5	4-5
1973 Our Mirage, 4-9-3	Mrs S. Enfield	B. Hills	F. Durr	9	15-8
1974 Relay Race, 4-8-9	Sir R. Macdonald-Buchanan	H. Cecil	L. Piggott	5	4-5
1975 Shebeen, 4-8-10	Sir K. Butt	B. Hobbs	G. Baxter	6	5-1
1976 Orange Bay, 4-9-8	C. Vittadini	P. Walwyn	P. Eddery	8	3-1
1977 Oats, 4-9-1	A. Oldrey	P. Walwyn	P. Eddery	11	9-4
1978 Classic Example, 4-9-5	F. Hue-Williams	P. Walwyn	P. Eddery	7	11-4
1979 Obraztsovy, 4-8-11	H. Demetriou	H.R. Price	B. Taylor	9	5-1
1980 More Light, 4-8-11	R. Budgett	W. Hern	W. Carson	8	4-1
1981 Master Willie, 4-8-12	R. Barnett	H. Candy	P. Waldron	6	2-1
1982 Ardross, 6-8-12	C. St George	H. Cecil	L. Piggott	6	evens
1983 Electric, 4-8-10	R. Clifford-Turner	M. Stoute	W.R. Swinburn	11	12-1
1984 Gay Lemur, 4-8-7	Eva Lady Rosebery	B. Hobbs	G. Baxter	6	8-1
1985 Kirmann, 4-8-7	Aga Khan	R.J. Houghton	S. Cauthen	8	11-1

General Accident 2,000 Guineas Stakes 1m

Three-year-old colts and fillies. 9st, fillies allowed 5lb. First run 1809. Run as New 2,000 Guineas on July Course 1940-45. Run as 2,000 Guineas Stakes before 1984. Group One.

	OWNER	TRAINER	JOCKEY	RAN	SP
1900 Diamond Jubilee	Prince of Wales	R Marsh	H. Jones	10	11-4
1901 Handicapper	Sir E. Cassel	F. Day	W. Halsey	17	33-1
1902 Sceptre	R. Sievier	R. Sievier	H. Randall	14	4-1
1903 Rock Sand	Sir J. Miller	G. Blackwell	J. Martin	11	6-4
1904 St. Amant	L. de Rothschild	A. Hayhoe	K. Cannon	14	11-4
1905 Vedas	W. de W-Fenton	W. Robinson	H. Jones	13	11-2
1906 Gorgos	A. James	R. Marsh	H. Jones	12	20-1
1907 Slieve Gallion	Capt J. Greer	S. Darling	W. Higgs	10	4-11
1908 Norman III	A. Belmont	J. Watson	O. Madden	17	25-1
1909 Minoru	King Edward VII	R. Marsh	H. Jones	11	4-1
1910 Neil Gow	Lord Rosebery	P. Peck	D. Maher	13	2-1
1911 Sunstar	J. Joel	C. Morton	G. Stern	14	5-1
1912 Sweeper II	H. Duryea	H. Persse	D. Maher	14	6-1
1913 Louvois	W. Raphael	D. Waugh	J. Reiff	15	25-1
1914 Kennymore	Sir J. Thursby	A. Taylor	G. Stern	18	2-1
1915 Pommern	S. Joel	C. Peck	S. Donoghue	16	2-1
1916 Clarissimus	Lord Falmouth	W. Waugh	J. Clark	17	100-7
1917 Gay Crusader	'Mr Fairie'	A. Taylor	S. Donoghue	14	9-4
1918 Gainsborough	Lady J. Douglas	A. Taylor	J. Childs	13	4-1
1919 The Panther	Sir A. Black	G. Manser	R. Cooper	12	10-1
1920 Tetratema	Maj D. McCalmont	H. Persse	B. Carslake	17	2-1
1921 Craig an Eran	Lord Astor	A. Taylor	J. Brennan	26	100-6
1922 St Louis	Lord Queensborough	P. Gilpin	G. Archibald	22	6-1
1923 Ellangowan	Lord Rosebery	J. Jarvis	E.C. Elliott	18	5-1
1924 Diophon	Aga Khan	R. Dawson	G. Hulme	20	11-2
1925 Manna	H. Morriss	F. Darling	S. Donoghue	13	100-8
1926 Colorado	Lord Derby	G. Lambton	T. Weston	19	100-8
1927 Adam's Apple	C. Whitburn	H. Cottrill	J. Leach	23	20-1
1928 Flamingo	Sir L. Philipps	J. Jarvis	E.C. Elliott	17	5-1

		OWNER	TRAINER	JOCKEY	RAN	SP
1929	Mr Jinks	Maj D. McCalmont	H. Persse	H. Beasley	22	5-2
1930	Diolite	Sir H. Hirst	F. Templeman	F. Fox	28	10-1
1931	Cameronian	J. Dewar	F. Darling	J. Childs	24	100-8
1932	Orwell	W. Singer	J. Lawson	R. Jones	11	evens
1933	Rodosto	Princesse de Lucinge	H. Count	R. Brethes	27	9-1
1934	Colombo	Lord Glanely	T. Hogg	W. Johnstone	12	2-7
1935	Bahram	Aga Khan	Frank Butters	F. Fox	16	7-2
1936	Pay Up	Lord Astor	J. Lawson	R. Dick	19	11-2
1937	Le Ksar	E. de St. Alary	F. Carter	C. Semblat	18	20-1
1938	Pasch	H. Morriss	F. Darling	G. Richards	18	5-2
1939	Blue Peter	Lord Rosebery	J. Jarvis	E. Smith	25	5-1
1940	Djébel	M. Boussac	A. Swann	E.C. Elliott	21	9-4
1941	Lambert Simnel	Duke of Westminster	F. Templeman	E.C. Elliott	19	10-1
1942	Big Game	King George VI	F. Darling	G. Richards	14	8-11
1943	Kingsway	A. Saunders	J. Lawson	S. Wragg	19	18-1
1944	Garden Path	Lord Derby	W. Earl	H. Wragg	26	5-1
1945	Court Martial	Lord Astor	J. Lawson	C. Richards	20	13-2
1946	Happy Knight	Sir W. Cooke	H. Jelliss	T. Weston	13	28-1
1947	Tudor Minstrel	J. Dewar	F. Darling	G. Richards	15	11-8
1948	My Babu	Maharaja of Baroda	F. Armstrong	C. Smirke	18	2-1
1949	Nimbus	Mrs M. Glenister	G. Colling	E.C. Elliott	13	10-1
1950	Palestine	Aga Khan	M. Marsh	C. Smirke	19	4-1
1951	Ki Ming	Ley On	M. Beary	A. Breasley	27	100-8
1952	Thunderhead II	E. Constant	E. Pollet	R. Poincelet	26	100-7
1953	Nearula	W. Humble	C. Elsey	E. Britt	16	2-1
1954	Darius	Sir P. Loraine	H. Wragg	E. Mercer	19	8-1
1955	Our Babu	D. Robinson	G. Brooke	D. Smith	23	13-2
1956	Gilles de Retz	A. Samuel	C. Jerdein	F. Barlow	19	50-1
1957	Crepello	Sir V. Sassoon	N. Murless	L. Piggott	15	7-2
1958	Pall Mall	The Queen	C. Boyd-Rochfort	D. Smith	14	20-1
1959	Taboun	Aly Khan	A. Head	G. Moore	13	5-2
1960	Martial	R. Webster	P. Prendergast	R. Hutchinson	17	18-1
1961	Rockavon	T. Yuill	G. Boyd	N. Stirk	22	66-1
1962	Privy Councillor	G. Glover	T. Waugh	W. Rickaby	19	100-6
1963	Only For Life	Miss M. Sheriffe	J. Tree	J. Lindley	21	33-1
1964	Baldric II	Miss H. Jackson	E. Fellows	W. Pyers	27	20-1
1965	Niksar	W. Harvey	W. Nightingall	D. Keith	22	100-8
1966	Kashmir II	P. Butler	C. Bartholomew	J. Lindley	25	7-1
1967	Royal Palace	H.J. Joel	N. Murless	G. Moore	18	100-30
1968	Sir Ivor	R. Guest	V. O'Brien	L. Piggott	10	11-8
1969	Right Tack	J. Brown	J. Sutcliffe	G. Lewis	13	15-2
1970	Nijinsky	C. Engelhard	V. O'Brien	L. Piggott	14	4-7
1971	Brigadier Gerard	Mrs J. Hislop	W. Hern	J. Mercer	6	11-2
1972	High Top	Sir J. Thorn	B. van Cutsem	W. Carson	12	85-40
1973	Mon Fils	Mrs B. Davis	R. Hannon	F. Durr	18	50-1
1974	Nonoalco	Mme M.-F. Berger	F. Boutin	Y. Saint-Martin	12	19-2
1975	Bolkonski	C. d'Alessio	H. Cecil	G. Dettori	24	33-1
1976	Wollow	C. d'Alessio	H. Cecil	G. Dettori	17	evens
1977	Nebbiolo	N. Schibbye	K. Prendergast	G. Curran	18	20-1
1978	Roland Gardens	J. Hayter	D. Sasse	F. Durr	19	28-1
1979	Tap On Wood	A. Shead	B. Hills	S. Cauthen	20	20-1
1980	Known Fact	K. Abdullah	J. Tree	W. Carson	14	14-1
1981	To-Agori-Mou	Mrs A. Muinos	G. Harwood	G. Starkey	19	5-2
1982	Zino	G. Oldham	F. Boutin	F. Head	26	8-1
1983	Lomond	R. Sangster	V. O'Brien	P. Eddery	16	9-1
1984	El Gran Senor	R. Sangster	V. O'Brien	P. Eddery	9	15-8
1985	Shadeed	M. Al-Maktoum	M. Stoute	L. Piggott	14	4-5

Princess of Wales's Stakes   1½m

Three-year-olds and upwards. 3-y-o 8st, 4-y-o & upwards 9st, fillies allowed 3lb (plus penalties). First run 1894. No race 1940-44. Group Two.

		OWNER	TRAINER	JOCKEY	RAN	SP
1930	Press Gang, 3-8-5	Lord Woolavington	F. Darling	F. Fox	4	15-8
1931	The Recorder, 4-9-3	J. Dewar	F. Darling	F. Fox	7	10-11
	Shell Transport, 3-8-5	W. Cazalet	J. Lawson	R. Dick	—	6-1
1932	Jacopo, 4-9-3	M. Field	C. Boyd-Rochfort	J. Childs	8	4-1
1933	Raymond, 3-7-8	Sir A. Bailey	J. Lawson	G. Richards	11	7-1
1934	Bright Bird, 3-7-7	Lord Astor	J. Lawson	F. Fox	7	7-4
1935	Fairbairn, 3-7-8	G. Loder	V. Gilpin	G. Richards	9	5-2
1936	Taj Akbar, 3-8-8	Aga Khan	Frank Butters	C. Smirke	6	4-1
1937	Flares, 4-9-6	W. Woodward	C. Boyd-Rochfort	R.A. Jones	6	11-2
1938	Pound Foolish, 3-8-5	Lord Astor	J. Lawson	G. Richards	9	3-1
1939	Heliopolis, 3-8-8	Lord Derby	W. Earl	R. Perryman	8	4-6
1945	Stirling Castle, 3-8-0	A. Saunders	J. Lawson	E. Smith	7	9-2
1946	Airborne, 3-8-10	J. Ferguson	R. Perryman	T. Lowrey	4	9-4
1947	Nirgal, 4-9-6	M. Boussac	C. Semblat	E.C. Elliott	9	13-8
1948	Alycidon, 3-8-5	Lord Derby	W. Earl	T. Lowrey	5	12½-1
1949	Dogger Bank, 3-7-10	Lord Derby	W. Earl	D. Smith	6	100-9
1950	Double Eclipse, 3-8-8	Lady Z. Wernher	C. Boyd-Rochfort	W.H. Carr	6	6-5
1951	Pardal, 4-8-12	M. Boussac	C. Semblat	W.R. Johnstone	5	evens
1952	Zucchero, 4-9-6	G. Rolls	W. Payne	L. Piggott	7	20-1
1953	Rawson, 4-9-6	S. Wootton	S. Wootton	K. Gethin	4	3-1
1954	Woodcut, 3-7-10	R. Sharples	C. Boyd-Rochfort	E. Smith	5	5-1
1955	Cobetto, 3-7-13	Prince Aly Khan	C. Semblat	J. Massard	8	9-1
1956	Cash and Courage, 3-8-0	T. West	S. Hall	E. Smith	8	9-4
1957	Wake Up!, 3-7-11	Lord Derby	J.F. Watts	D. Smith	7	9-4
1958	Miner's Lamp, 3-8-12	The Queen	C. Boyd-Rochfort	W.H. Carr	7	3-1
1959	Primera, 5-9-6	C. Dracoulis	N. Murless	L. Piggott	4	4-5
1960	Primera, 6-9-6	S. Joel	N. Murless	L. Piggott	6	9-4
1961	Apostle, 4-9-5	Mrs D. Montagu	S. Ingham	L. Piggott	6	4-6
1962	Silver Cloud, 3-8-2	T. Blackwell	J. Jarvis	E. Smith	4	5-1
1963	Trafalgar, 3-8-2	R. Watson	G. Richards	A. Breasley	6	15-2
1964	Carrack, 3-7-7	R. Hollingsworth	J. Oxley	D. Cullen	8	5-1
1965	Lomond, 5-9-2	W. Ruane	R. Jarvis	E. Eldin	7	10-1
1966	Lomond, 6-9-5	W. Ruane	R. Jarvis	E. Eldin	5	3-1
1967	Hopeful Venture, 3-8-2	The Queen	N. Murless	G. Moore	7	13-8
1968	Mount Athos, 3-8-2	A. Struthers	J. Dunlop	R. Hutchinson	10	3-1
1969	Harmony Hall, 3-7-11	Sir H. Wernher	G. Smyth	W. Carson	2	1-3
1970	Prince Consort, 4-9-2	H.J. Joel	N. Murless	A. Barclay	6	2-1
1971	Lupe, 4-9-6	Mrs S. Joel	N. Murless	G. Lewis	4	8-13
1972	Falkland, 4-9-5	Ld Howard de Walden	H. Cecil	G. Starkey	8	5-2
1973	Our Mirage, 4-9-9	Mrs S. Enfield	B. Hills	F. Durr	7	15-8
1974	Buoy, 4-9-9	R. Hollingsworth	W. Hern	J. Mercer	9	2-1
1975	Libra's Rib, 3-7-11	Mrs J. Rogers	R.J. Houghton	W. Carson	10	8-1
1976	Smuggler, 3-7-11	Lord Porchester	W. Hern	E. Johnson	6	11-4
1977	Lord Helpus, 4-9-2	M. Standen	B. Hills	L. Piggott	8	5-1
1978	Pollerton, 4-9-2	Mrs R. Vereker	H.T. Jones	L. Piggott	4	7-1
1979	Milford, 3-8-2	The Queen	W. Hern	W. Carson	6	11-8
1980	Nicholas Bill, 5-9-2	W. Barnett	H. Candy	P. Waldron	9	12-1
1981	Light Cavalry, 4-9-9	H.J. Joel	H. Cecil	L. Piggott	8	11-4
1982	Height of Fashion, 3-7-11	The Queen	W. Hern	W. Carson	4	4-1
1983	Quilted, 3-8-0	J. Fluor	M. O'Toole	W. Newnes	11	7-2
1984	Head For Heights, 3-8-6	Sheikh Mohammed	W. Hern	L. Piggott	9	100-30
1985	Petoski, 3-8-0	Marcia, Lady Beaverbrook	W. Hern	W. Carson	5	8-1

Norcros July Cup   6f

Three-year-olds and upwards. 3-y-o 8st 11lb, 4-y-o & up 9st 6lb, fillies allowed 5lb.
First run 1876. Run as William Hill July Cup 1978-83. No race 1940, 1942-44. Group
One.

		OWNER	TRAINER	JOCKEY	RAN	SP
1930	Sir Cosmo, 4-10-1	Sir R. Garton	W. Walters	G. Swann	10	20-1
1931	Xandover, 4-10-8	J. Schwob	B. Jarvis	E.C. Elliott	4	7-2
1932	Concerto, 4-10-1	Sir H. Cunliffe-Owen	O. Bell	H. Wragg	6	11-2
1933	Myrobella, 3-9-7	Lord Lonsdale	F. Darling	G. Richards	4	4-6
1934	Coroado, 4-10-1	F. Lundgren	W. Easterby	H. Gunn	7	5-2
1935	Bellacose, 3-9-10	P. Dunne	R.J. Colling	P. Beasley	11	6-1
1936	Bellacose, 4.10-8	P. Dunne	R.J. Colling	P. Beasley	6	evens
1937	Mickey the Greek, 3-8-10	N. Frieze	H. Leach	H. Wragg	6	9-2
1938	Shalfleet, 7-8-5	J. Walker	H. Leader	R. Perryman	5	8-11
1939	Portobello, 3-8-7	P. Dunne	R.J. Colling	T. Lowrey	10	10-1
1941	Comatas, 4-8-8	Miss K. Farrar	O. Bell	W. Nevett	8	13-2
1945	Honeyway, 4-9-6	Lord Milford	J. Jarvis	E. Smith	4	8-11
1946	The Bug, 3-8-3	N. Wachman	H. Wellesley	C. Smirke	3	8-11
1947	Falls of Clyde, 3-8-3	Miss P. Vaughan	E. Williams	S. Wragg	5	100-30
1948	Palm Vista, 3-7-10	E. Broadbelt	P. Beasley	E. Smith	9	13-8
1949	Abernant, 3-8-10	R. Macdonald-Buchanan	N. Murless	G. Richards	3	2-11
1950	Abernant, 4-9-8	R. Macdonald-Buchanan	N. Murless	G. Richards	6	8-13
1951	Hard Sauce, 3-8-10	Sir V. Sassoon	N. Bertie	G. Richards	6	8-1
1952	Set Fair, 3-8-2	C. Bell	W. Nightingall	E. Smith	4	15-8
1953	Devon Vintage, 3-8-7	R. Boucher	R.J. Colling	G. Richards	5	11-4
1954	Vilmoray, 4-8-8	A. Green	B. Bullock	W. Snaith	4	6-4
1955	Pappa Fourway, 3-8-10	Mrs E. Goldson	W. Dutton	W.H. Carr	3	1-6
1956	Matador, 3-8-10	Mrs J. Ferguson	J.A. Waugh	W. Rickaby	5	11-2
1957	Vigo, 4-9-8	T. Farr	W. Dutton	L. Piggott	4	7-2
1958	Right Boy, 4-9-8	G. Gilbert	W. Dutton	L. Piggott	4	4-5
1959	Right Boy, 5-9-8	G. Gilbert	P. Rohan	L. Piggott	6	11-10
1960	Tin Whistle, 3-8-10	B. Grainger	P. Rohan	L. Piggott		walked over
1961	Galivanter, 5-9-8	L. Holliday	W. Hern	W.H. Carr	3	9-2
1962	Marsolve, 4-9-1	Sir M. McAlpine	R. Day	W. Rickaby	4	5-1
1963	Secret Step, 4-8-11	P. Mellon	P. Hastings-Bass	G. Lewis	8	2-1
1964	Daylight Robbery, 3-8-2	R. Budgett	A. Budgett	A. Breasley	7	100-9
1965	Merry Madcap, 3-7-13	Mrs H. Frelinghuysen	F. Maxwell	R. Hutchinson	14	100-8
1966	Lucasland, 4-8-11	J. Baillie	J.A. Waugh	E. Eldin	18	100-6
1967	Forlorn River, 5-9-0	Mrs W. Richardson	W.A. Stephenson	B. Raymond	9	8-1
1968	So Blessed, 3-8-2	D. Robinson	M. Jarvis	F. Durr	7	7-2
1969	Tudor Music, 3-8-6	D. Robinson	M. Jarvis	F. Durr	3	4-5
1970	Huntercombe, 3-8-6	H. Renshaw	A. Budgett	A. Barclay	4	8-13
1971	Realm, 4-9-3	R. Boucher	J. Winter	B. Taylor	8	11-2
1972	Parsimony, 3-8-7	E. Holland-Martin	R.J. Houghton	R. Hutchinson	5	16-1
1973	Thatch, 3-8-10	J. Mulcahy	V. O'Brien	L. Piggott	6	4-5
1974	Saritamer, 3-8-10	C. St George	V. O'Brien	L. Piggott	9	11-4
1975	Lianga, 4-9-4	D. Wildenstein	A. Penna	Y. Saint-Martin	13	10-1
1976	Lochnager, 4-9-6	C. Spence	M.W. Easterby	E. Hide	10	3-1
1977	Gentilhombre, 4-9-6	J. Murrell	N. Adam	P. Cook	8	10-1
1978	Solinus, 3-8-11	D. Schwartz	V. O'Brien	L. Piggott	14	4-7
1979	Thatching, 4-9-6	R. Sangster	V. O'Brien	L. Piggott	11	2-1
1980	Moorestyle, 3-8-11	Moores Furnishings Ltd	R. Armstrong	L. Piggott	14	3-1
1981	Marwell, 3-8-8	E. Loder	M. Stoute	W.R. Swinburn	14	13-8
1982	Sharpo, 5-9-6	Miss M. Sheriffe	J. Tree	P. Eddery	16	13-2
1983	Habibti, 3-8-8	M. Mutawa	J. Dunlop	W. Carson	15	8-1
1984	Chief Singer, 3-8-11	J. Smith	R. Sheather	R. Cochrane	9	15-8
1985	Never So Bold, 5-9-6	E. Kessly	R. Armstrong	S. Cauthen	9	5-4

Tattersalls Cheveley Park Stakes 6f

Two-year-old fillies. 8st 11lb. First run 1870. Run at Nottingham 1940. Run as Cheveley Park Stakes 1870-1972; William Hill Cheveley Park Stakes 1973-83. No race 1939. Group One.

	OWNER	TRAINER	JOCKEY	RAN	SP
1930 The Leopard, 8-7	Sir C. Hyde	N. Scobie	B. Carslake	16	15-8
1931 Concordia, 8-7	A. Cox	J. Lawson	R. Jones	10	evens
1932 Brown Betty, 9-7	W. Woodward	C. Boyd-Rochfort	J. Childs	10	2-1
1933 Light Brocade, 9-7	Lord Durham	Frank Butters	B. Carslake	8	11-8
1934 Lady Gabriel, 8-7	D. Sullivan	H. Persse	B. Carslake	12	13-8
1935 Ferrybridge, 8-7	R. Watson	M. Hartigan	M. Beary	17	5-1
1936 Celestial Way, 8-7	H. Cecil	G. Lambton	B. Carslake	12	3-1
1937 Stafaralla, 8-12	Aly Khan	Frank Butters	H. Wragg	9	4-9
1938 Seaway, 8-12	Maj J. Courtauld	B. Jarvis	T. Lowrey	13	20-1
1940 Keystone, 8-12	P. Beatty	F. Darling	G. Richards	5	8-13
1941 Perfect Peace, 8-12	Lord Glanely	J. Lawson	H. Wragg	5	2-1
1942 Lady Sybil, 8-12	M. Benson	W. Pratt	G. Richards	11	11-10
1943 Fair Fame, 8-12	Mrs B. Lavington	H. Leader	F. Lane	9	5-4
1944 Sweet Cygnet, 8-12	H. Leven	T. Rimell	E.C. Elliott	8	100-6
1945 Neolight, 8-12	J. Dewar	F. Darling	G. Richards	3	13-8
1946 Djerba, 8-12	M. Boussac	C. Semblat	E.C. Elliott	6	9-2
1947 Ash Blonde, 8-12	Lord Astor	R.J. Colling	P. Evans	7	100-8
1948 Pambidian, 8-12	C. Harper	W. Nightingall	G. Richards	7	100-6
1949 Corejada, 8-12	M. Boussac	C. Semblat	E.C. Elliott	3	9-4
1950 Belle of All, 8-12	H. Tufton	N. Bertie	G. Richards	8	5-4
1951 Zabara, 8-12	Sir M. McAlpine	V. Smyth	G. Richards	8	10-11
1952 Bebe Grande, 8-12	J. Gerber	F. Armstrong	G. Richards	6	1-2
1953 Sixpence, 8-12	A. Hawkins	P. Prendergast	G. Richards	6	4-1
1954 Gloria Nicky, 8-12	Mrs R. Digby	N. Bertie	A. Breasley	10	10-1
1955 Midget II, 8-12	P. Wertheimer	A. Head	R. Poincelet	8	evens
1956 Sarcelle, 8-12	K. Mason	N. Cannon	A. Breasley	7	4-6
1957 Rich and Rare, 8-12	T. Blackwell	J. Jarvis	E. Mercer	8	5-1
1958 Lindsay, 8-12	F. Ellison	R. Peacock	E. Mercer	15	100-8
1959 Queensberry, 8-12	Col. B. Hornung	J.A. Waugh	E. Smith	6	2-5
1960 Opaline II, 8-12	Aly Khan	A. Head	G. Moore	6	11-10
1961 Display, 8-11	Lady Granard	P. Prendergast	R. Hutchinson	10	8-11
1962 My Goodness Me	D. Robinson	G. Brooke	E. Smith	10	100-8
1963 Crimea II	Mrs J. Hanes	C. Boyd-Rochfort	W.H. Carr	12	9-1
1964 Night Off	Maj L. Holiday	W. Wharton	J. Mercer	6	20-1
1965 Berkeley Springs	P. Mellon	I. Balding	G. Lewis	11	100-8
1966 Fleet	R. Boucher	N. Murless	L. Piggott	8	5-2
1967 Lalibela	J.P. Philipps	V. O'Brien	L. Piggott	5	5-1
1968 Mige	Mme P. Wertheimer	A. Head	J. Taillard	18	5-2
1969 Humble Duty	Jean, Lady Ashcombe	P. Walwyn	D. Keith	8	11-4
1970 Magic Flute	Ld Howard de Walden	N. Murless	A. Barclay	11	13-8
1971 Waterloo	Mrs R. Stanley	J.W. Watts	E. Hide	17	100-30
1972 Jacinth	Lady Butt	B. Hobbs	J. Gorton	13	9-2
1973 Gentle Thoughts	N.B. Hunt	T. Curtin	W. Pyers	14	9-1
1974 Cry of Truth	Miss P. Johnston	B. Hobbs	J. Gorton	15	4-1
1975 Pasty	G. Williams	P. Walwyn	P. Eddery	14	9-1
1976 Durtal	R. Sangster	B. Hills	L. Piggott	15	5-1
1977 Sookera	R. Sangster	D. Weld	W. Swinburn	10	3-1
1978 Devon Ditty	Sir E. McAlpine	H.T. Jones	G. Starkey	7	11-8
1979 Mrs Penny	E. Kronfeld	I. Balding	J. Matthias	12	7-1
1980 Marwell	E. Loder	M. Stoute	L. Piggott	8	4-9
1981 Woodstream	R. Sangster	V. O'Brien	P. Eddery	13	5-2
1982 Ma Biche	Mme A. Head	Mme C. Head	F. Head	9	11-4
1983 Desirable	Mrs J. Corbett	B. Hills	S. Cauthen	12	12-1
1984 Park Appeal	P. Burns	J. Bolger	D. Gillespie	13	4-1
1985 Embla	C. St George	L. Cumani	A. Cordero	14	20-1

Jockey Club Cup   2m

Three-year-olds and upwards. 3-y-o 8st 4lb, 4-y-o & upwards 9st, fillies allowed 3lb (plus penalties). First run 1873. Run over $2\frac{1}{4}$m before 1959, $1\frac{1}{2}$m 1959-62. Run at Nottingham 1940. No race 1939, 1941. Group Three.

		OWNER	TRAINER	JOCKEY	RAN	SP
1930	Brumeux, 5-9-0	A. Macomber	S. Darling	G. Richards	3	21-20
1931	Noble Star, 4-9-0	F. Cundell	L. Cundell	F. Fox	3	evens
1932	Brulette, 4-8-11	Lord Woolavington	F. Darling	G. Richards		walked over
1933	Nitsichin, 5-8-11	D. Kennedy	P. Thrale	G. Richards	3	11-8
1934	Felicitation, 4-9-0	Aga Khan	Frank Butters	G. Richards	3	1-4
1935	Quashed, 3-7-11	Lord Stanley	C. Leader	T. Weston	3	5-4
1936	Quashed, 4-8-11	Lord Stanley	C. Leader	R. Perryman	2	2-5
1937	Buckleigh, 5-9-2	Lord Glanely	T. Hogg	B. Carslake	4	13-2
1938	Foxglove II, 3-8-4	P. Beatty	F. Darling	G. Richards	5	6-5
1940	Atout Maitre, 4-9-3	H. Blagrave	H. Blagrave	E.C. Elliott	7	5-2
1942	Afterthought, 3-8-0	Lord Rosebery	J. Jarvis	E. Smith	12	11-4
1943	Shahpoor, 4-9-2	A. Allnatt	J. Lawson	G. Richards	6	7-2
1944	Ocean Swell, 3-8-3	Lord Rosebery	J. Jarvis	E. Smith	7	evens
1945	Amber Flash, 3-8-2	Lord Astor	R.J. Colling	C. Richards	4	2-1
1946	Felix II, 3-8-4	G. de Waldner	P. Carter	P. Evans	4	100-7
1947	Laurentis, 4-9-2	H. Frost	G.J. Houghton	E. Britt	5	15-2
1948	Vic Day, 3-8-4	H. Blagrave	H. Blagrave	G. Richards		walked over
1949	Vic Day, 4-9-2	H. Blagrave	H. Blagrave	G. Richards	4	5-2
1950	Colonist II, 4-9-2	W. Churchill	W. Nightingall	T. Gosling	3	8-11
1951	Eastern Emperor, 3-8-4	Lord Milford	J. Jarvis	W. Rickaby	4	7-4
1952	Blarney Stone, 3-8-4	M. McAlpine	V. Smyth	W. Rickaby	4	25-1
1953	Ambiguity, 3-8-1	Lord Astor	R.J. Colling	J. Mercer	4	9-4
1954	Yorick II, 3-8-4	G. de Rothschild	G. Watson	P. Blanc	8	9-4
1955	Romany Air, 4-9-3	G. Chesterman	R. Day	W. Rickaby	5	8-1
1956	Donald, 3-8-4	Lord Rosebery	J. Jarvis	W. Rickaby	5	evens
1957	Flying Flag II, 4-9-3	H. Baranez	J. Laumain	F. Palmer	3	11-4
1958	French Beige, 5-9-3	R. Dennis	H. Peacock	G. Littlewood	5	3-1
1959	Vacarme, 5-9-4	M. Goudchaux	N. Bertie	A. Breasley	6	7-2
1960	Parthia, 4-9-0	Sir H. de Trafford	C. Boyd-Rochfort	W.H. Carr	4	10-11
1961	Apostle, 4-9-0	Mrs D. Montagu	S. Ingham	E. Hide	8	13-2
1962	Pardao, 4-9-0	Mrs C. Iselin	C. Boyd-Rochfort	W.H. Carr	7	2-1
1963	Gaul, 4-9-6	Lord Sefton	P. Hastings-Bass	G. Lewis	3	2-1
1964	Oncidium, 3-8-7	Ld Howard de Walden	G. Todd	A. Breasley	7	7-2
1965	Goupi, 3-8-7	H. Wingate	S. Ingham	G. Lewis	4	10-11
1966	Hermes, 3-8-7	R. Hollingsworth	J. Oxley	G. Starkey	10	7-1
1967	Dancing Moss, 3-8-1	D. Drewery	R. Fetherstonhaugh	G. Lewis	11	6-1
1968	Riboccare, 3-8-7	C. Engelhard	J. Tree	L. Piggott	8	100-7
1969	High Line, 3-8-4	W. Barnett	D. Candy	J. Mercer	3	5-2
1970	High Line, 4-9-6	W. Barnett	D. Candy	J. Mercer	5	100-30
1971	High Line, 5-9-6	W. Barnett	D. Candy	J. Mercer	5	8-11
1972	Irvine, 4-9-3	C. St George	H. Cecil	L. Piggott	5	3-1
1973	Parnell, 5-9-6	R. More O'Ferrall	B. van Cutsem	W. Carson	5	4-6
1974	Petty Officer, 7-9-3	Mrs J. Benskin	A. Budgett	E. Hide	6	7-2
1975	Blood Royal, 4-9-6	Mrs G. Getty	V. O'Brien	L. Piggott	6	11-10
1976	Bright Finish, 3-8-6	J. Whitney	M. Stoute	L. Piggott	6	2-1
1977	Grey Baron, 4-9-3	P. Parnell	B. Hobbs	G. Baxter	5	6-4
1978	Buckskin, 5-9-7	D. Wildenstein	H. Cecil	J. Mercer	6	2-1
1979	Nicholas Bill, 4-8-11	W. Barnett	H. Candy	P. Waldron	8	5-1
1980	Ardross, 4-9-5	Exors P. Prendergast	K. Prendergast	L. Piggott	5	5-6
1981	Centroline, 3-8-4	R. Barnett	H. Candy	P. Waldron	9	6-4
1982	Little Wolf, 4-9-5	Lord Porchester	W. Hern	W. Carson	8	9-4
1983	Karadar, 5-9-3	Aga Khan	M. Stoute	W.R. Swinburn	5	evens
1984	Old Country, 5-9-7	Mrs O. Abegg	L. Cumani	D. McHargue	4	5-2
1985	Tale Quale, 3-8-4	R. Barnett	H. Candy	T. Ives	10	25-1

Tattersalls Middle Park Stakes   6f

Two-year-old colts and fillies. 9st, fillies allowed 3lb. First run 1866. Run as Middle Park Stakes before 1973; William Hill Middle Park Stakes 1973-83; Middle Park Stakes 1984. Run at Nottingham 1940. Group One.

	OWNER	TRAINER	JOCKEY	RAN	SP
1930 Portlaw, 9-3	Sir A. Bailey	H. Persse	H. Beasley	8	evens
1931 Orwell, 9-3	W. Singer	J. Lawson	R. Jones	5	4-11
1932 Felicitation, 9-0	Aga Khan	Frank Butters	M. Beary	6	3-1
1933 Medieval Knight, 9-0	J. Dewar	F. Darling	G. Richards	11	100-30
1934 Bahram, 9-0	Aga Khan	Frank Butters	F. Fox	6	2-7
1935 Abjer, 9-0	M. Boussac	G. Lambton	E.C. Elliott	13	8-1
1936 Fair Copy, 9-0	Lord Derby	C. Leader	R. Perryman	7	13-8
1937 Scottish Union	J. Rank	N. Cannon	G. Richards	5	10-1
1938 Foxbrough II	W. Woodward	C. Boyd-Rochfort	P. Beasley	10	13-8
1939 Djebel	M. Boussac	C. Semblat	E.C. Elliott	20	9-1
1940 Hyacinthus	A. Bassett	H. Persse	P. Beasley	7	10-1
1941 Sun Chariot, 8-11	King George VI	F. Darling	H. Wragg	4	11-4
1942 Ribbon, 8-11	Lord Rosebery	J. Jarvis	E. Smith	8	9-2
1943 Orestes	Miss D. Paget	W. Nightingall	T. Carey	9	7-4
1944 Dante	Sir E. Ohlson	M. Peacock	W. Nevett	4	2-5
1945 Khaled	Aga Khan	Frank Butters	G. Richards	6	2-5
1946 Saravan	Prince Aly Khan	Frank Butters	E.C. Elliott	8	100-8
1947 The Cobbler	Lieut-Col G. Loder	F. Darling	G. Richards	4	8-11
1948 Abernant	Maj R. M-Buchanan	N. Murless	G. Richards	3	1-7
1949 Masked Light	E. Wanless	N. Scobie	D. Smith	5	7-2
1950 Big Dipper	Mrs J. Bryce	C. Boyd-Rochfort	W. Carr	5	2-5
1951 King's Bench	A. Tompsett	M. Feakes	E.C. Elliott	8	7-2
1952 Nearula	W. Humble	C. Elsey	E. Britt	9	13-2
1953 Royal Challenger	A. Gordon	P. Beasley	G. Richards	5	4-1
1954 Our Babu	D. Robinson	G. Brooke	D. Smith	10	6-1
1955 Buisson Ardent	Aga Khan	A. Head	D. Smith	6	9-2
1956 Pipe of Peace	S. Niarchos	Sir G. Richards	A. Breasley	8	8-1
1957 Major Portion	H.J. Joel	T. Leader	E. Smith	7	11-2
1958 Masham	A. Ellis	G. Brooke	D. Smith	5	2-1
1959 Venture VII	Aly Khan	A. Head	G. Moore	5	1-4
1960 Skymaster	Duke of Norfolk	W. Smyth	A. Breasley	4	100-30
1961 Gustav	J. Whitney	J. Tree	J. Lindley	7	100-6
1962 Crocket	D. van Clief	G. Brooke	E. Smith	4	5-4
1963 Showdown	Mrs D. Prenn	F. Winter	D. Smith	11	100-30
1964 Spanish Express	Mrs G. Marcow	L. Hall	J. Mercer	4	9-1
1965 Track Spare	R. Mason	R. Mason	J. Lindley	9	10-1
1966 Bold Lad	Lady Granard	P. Prendergast	D. Lake	5	2-7
1967 Petingo	M. Lemos	F. Armstrong	L. Piggott	3	1-4
1968 Right Track	J. Brown	J. Sutcliffe	G. Lewis	7	11-2
1969 Huntercombe	H. Renshaw	A. Budgett	E. Johnson	7	3-1
1970 Brigadier Gerard	Mrs J. Hislop	W. Hern	J. Mercer	5	9-2
1971 Sharpen Up	Mrs B. van Cutsem	B. van Cutsem	W. Carson	5	5-6
1972 Tudenham	L.B. Holliday	Denys Smith	J. Lindley	7	4-1
1973 Habat	C. Vittadini	P. Walwyn	P. Eddery	7	4-6
1974 Steel Heart	R. Tikkoo	D. Weld	L. Piggott	8	10-11
1975 Hittite Glory	R. Tikkoo	A. Breasley	F. Durr	8	9-2
1976 Tachypous	G. Cambanis	B. Hobbs	G. Lewis	11	5-1
1977 Formidable	P. Goulandris	P. Walwyn	P. Eddery	7	15-8
1978 Junius	S. Fraser	V. O'Brien	L. Piggott	10	7-1
1979 Known Fact	K. Abdullah	J. Tree	W. Carson	7	10-1
1980 Mattaboy	R. Tikkoo	R. Armstrong	L. Piggott	9	7-1
1981 Cajun	J. Stone	H. Cecil	L. Piggott	13	20-1
1982 Diesis	Ld Howard de Walden	H. Cecil	L. Piggott	5	10-11
1983 Creag-an-Sgor	Mrs W. Tulloch	C. Nelson	S. Cauthen	9	50-1
1984 Bassenthwaite	S. Niarchos	J. Tree	P. Eddery	8	7-2
1985 Stalker	P. Fetherston-Godley	P. Walwyn	J. Mercer	6	9-2

William Hill Cambridgeshire Handicap   1m

First run 1839. Run on Summer Course 1939, 1941; run at Nottingham 1940. Run as Cambridgeshire Handicap before 1971; Irish Sweeps Cambridgeshire Handicap 1971-77. No race 1942-44.

	OWNER	TRAINER	JOCKEY	RAN	SP
1930 The Pen, 3-7-4	Mrs M. Hartigan	M. Hartigan	C. Richards	31	50-1
1931 Disarmament, 3-7-11	H. Clayton	C. Elsey	W. Nevett	24	18-1
1932 Pullover, 3-6-11	Mrs C. Robinson	M. Peacock	A. Richardson	33	100-1
1933 Raymond, 3-8-4	Sir A. Bailey	J. Lawson	G. Nicoll	26	33-1
1934 Wychwood Abbot, 3-8-6	O. Watney	T. Leader	R. Perryman	33	9-1
1935 Commander III, 5-7-11	G. Foster	A.B. Briscoe	T. Hawcroft	40	28-1
1936 Dan Bulger, 3-7-13	Sir A. Bailey	H. Cottrill	T. Weston	22	7-1
1937 Artist's Prince, 4-6-12	Maj R. Glover	J. Dines	A. Richardson	26	13-1
1938 Helleniqua, 5-6-12	J. Meller	W. Webb	B. Guimard	29	50-1
1939 Class I: Gyroscope, 3-7-7	Mrs H. Leader	H. Leader	R. Lacey	27	100-6
Class II: Orichalque, 6-8-10	Lord Dufferin	W. Beatty	J. Simpson	27	25-1
1940 Caxton, 4-7-9	Maj T. Rigg	F. Armstrong	P. Evans	15	100-7
1941 Rue de la Paix, 5-8-13	L. Abelson	G. Beeby	T. Carey	19	18-1
1945 Esquire, 3-6-3	J. Bueno	R. Colling	G. Packer	28	40-1
1946 Sayani, 3-9-4	Mme J. Lieux	J. Lieux	W. Johnstone	34	25-1
1947 Fairey Fulmar, 4-8-12	G. Tachmindji	O. Bell	T. Gosling	39	28-1
1948 Sterope, 3-7-4	J. Townley	P. Beasley	D. Schofield	32	25-1
1949 Sterope, 4-9-4	J. Townley	P. Beasley	E.C. Elliott	39	25-1
1950 Kelling, 3-7-10	C. Jarvis	A. Waugh	D. Smith	31	100-7
1951 Fleeting Moment, 5-7-13	Mrs M. Johnson	T. Bartlam	A. Breasley	45	28-1
1952 Richer, 3-8-0	G. Baylis	S. Ingham	K. Gethin	42	100-6
1953 Jupiter, 3-8-3	Lord Lambton	P. Beasley	G. Richards	29	100-6
1954 Minstrel, 3-7-0	Lord Rosebery	J. Jarvis	C. Gaston	36	66-1
1955 Retrial, 3-7-1	Lady Z. Wernher	C. Boyd-Rochfort	P. Robinson	40	18-1
1956 Loppylugs, 4-7-8	J. Beary	J. Beary	E. Smith	34	100-7
1957 Stephanotis, 4-8-5	A. Plesch	J. Rogers	W.H. Carr	38	100-6
1958 London Cry, 4-9-5	M. Sobell	G. Richards	A. Breasley	33	22-1
1959 Rexequus, 3-8-7	J. Adam	G. Boyd	N. Stirk	36	25-1
1960 Midsummer Night II, 3-7-12	P. Mellon	P. Hastings-Bass	D. Keith	40	40-1
1961 Violetta III, 3-7-8	R. Moller	H. Wragg	L.C. Parkes	27	33-1
Henry the Seventh, 3-8-4	H.J. Joel	W. Elsey	E. Hide	—	100-8
1962 Hidden Meaning, 3-9-0	Cmdr K. Grant	H. Leader	A. Breasley	46	7-1
1963 Commander-in-Chief, 4-8-0	H. Whitehouse	E. Cousins	F. Durr	23	100-7
1964 Hasty Cloud, 6-7-10	G. Walters	H. Wallington	J. Wilson	43	100-8
1965 Tarqogan, 5-9-3	J. McGrath	S. McGrath	W. Williamson	30	100-8
1966 Dites, 4-7-4	R. Midwood	H. Leader	D. Maitland	34	33-1
1967 Lacquer, 3-8-6	R. Moller	H. Wragg	R. Hutchinson	34	20-1
1968 Emerilo, 4-7-9	D. Green	P. Allden	M.L. Thomas	35	20-1
1969 Prince de Galles, 3-7-12	A. Swift	P. Robinson	F. Durr	26	5-2
1970 Prince de Galles, 4-9-7	A. Swift	P. Robinson	F. Durr	27	6-1
1971 King Midas, 3-7-9	Exors late Maj H. Holt	D. Candy	D. Cullen	29	10-1
1972 Negus, 5-9-0	R. Watson	D. Candy	P. Waldron	35	16-1
1973 Siliciana, 4-8-5	D. Back	I. Balding	G. Lewis	37	14-1
1974 Flying Nelly, 4-7-7	S. Digby	W. Wightman	D. Maitland	39	22-1
1975 Lottogift, 4-8-2	A. Richards	D. Hanley	R. Wernham	36	33-1
1976 Intermission, 3-8-6	J. Whitney	M. Stoute	G. Starkey	29	14-1
1977 Sin Timon, 3-8-3	Lady Ness	J. Hindley	A. Kimberley	27	18-1
1978 Baronet, 6-9-0	F. Harris	C. Benstead	B. Rouse	18	12-1
1979 Smartset, 4-8-8	G. Ward	R.J. Houghton	J. Reid	24	33-1
1980 Baronet, 8-9-3	F. Harris	C. Benstead	B. Rouse	19	22-1
1981 Braughing, 4-8-4	W. Gredley	C. Brittain	S. Cauthen	28	50-1
1982 Century City, 3-9-6	I. Allan	L. Cumani	J. Mercer	29	20-1
1983 Sagamore, 4-7-8	E. Naughton	F. Durr	M.L. Thomas	30	35-1
1984 Leysh, 3-8-7	Prince Y. Saud	S. Norton	J. Lowe	34	33-1
1985 Tremblant, 4-9-8	K. Abdullah	R. Smyth	P. Eddery	31	16-1

William Hill Dewhurst Stakes   7f

Two-year-old colts and fillies 9st, fillies allowed 3lb. First run 1875. Run on Summer Course 1940-44. Run as Dewhurst Stakes before 1972. No race 1939. Group One.

	OWNER	TRAINER	JOCKEY	RAN	SP
1930 Sangre, 8-9	W. Chanler	H. Persse	H. Beasley	8	11-10
1931 Firdaussi, 8-13	Aga Khan	F. Butters	M. Beary	6	11-10
1932 Hyperion, 9-5	G. Lambton	G. Lambton	T. Weston	6	100-7
1933 Mrs Rustom, 9-3	Aga Khan	F. Butters	M. Beary	9	5-4
1934 Hairan, 9-5	Aga Khan	F. Butters	F. Fox	5	8-13
1935 Bala Hissar, 8-9	Aga Khan	F. Butters	C. Smirke	12	5-2
1936 Sultan Mohamed, 8-9	Aga Khan	F. Butters	G. Richards	6	20-1
1937 Manorite, 8-9	D. Kennedy	P. Thrale	E. Smith	7	20-1
1938 Casanova, 8-9	Lady Z. Wernher	C. Boyd-Rochfort	P. Beasley	4	8-11
1940 Fettes, 8-9	Mrs R. M-Buchanan	F. Darling	G. Richards	9	3-1
1941 Canyonero, 9-2	F. Bezner	W. Nightingall	T. Carey	5	13-8
1942 Umiddad, 8-9	Aga Khan	F. Butters	D. Smith	8	6-4
1943 Effervescence, 9-2	Mrs M. Hartigan	R.J. Colling	G. Richards	10	6-1
1944 Paper Weight, 9-2	Sir A. Butt	F. Butters	A. Wragg	5	11-8
1945 Hypericum, 8-11	King George VI	C. Boyd-Rochfort	D. Smith	10	4-7
1946 Migoli, 9-0	Aga Khan	F. Butters	G. Richards	8	5-1
1947 Pride of India, 8-13	H.J. Joel	J. Watts	J. Sime	11	5-2
1948 Royal Forest, 9-3	Mrs R. M-Buchanan	N. Murless	G. Richards	11	5-4
1949 Emperor II, 8-13	M. Boussac	C. Semblat	E.C. Elliott	7	7-2
1950 Turco II, 8-13	W. Woodward	C. Boyd-Rochfort	W.H. Carr	6	11-8
1951 Marsyad, 8-9	M. Boussac	C. Semblat	W. Johnstone	11	7-1
1952 Pinza, 8-13	Sir V. Sassoon	N. Bertie	G. Richards	9	evens
1953 Infatuation, 9-3	Sir M. McAlpine	V. Smyth	K. Gethin	5	11-8
1954 My Smokey, 8-9	Mrs D. Robinson	J.F. Watts	D. Smith	9	7-2
1955 Dacian, 8-9	Maj L. Holliday	H. Cottrill	W. Snaith	10	7-1
1956 Crepello, 8-9	Sir V. Sassoon	N. Murless	L. Piggott	4	1-2
1957 Torbella III, 8-6	Comte de Chambure	W. Clout	A. Breasley	7	9-4
1958 Billum, 8-13	W. Humble	C. Elsey	E. Hide	8	6-1
1959 Ancient Lights, 8-9	H.J. Joel	T. Leader	E. Smith	12	100-7
1960 Bounteous, 8-13	Mrs H. Leggatt	P. Beasley	J. Sime	7	2-1
1961 River Chanter, 9-2	R. Sigtia	G. Todd	J. Mercer	8	100-30
1962 Follow Suit, 8-12	Lieut-Col G. Loder	N. Murless	L. Piggott	10	10-1
1963 Kings Lane, 8-12	L. Chamberlain	S. Hall	J. Sime	9	10-1
1964 Silly Season, 9-2	P. Mellon	I. Balding	G. Lewis	11	13-2
1965 Pretendre, 8-12	J. Lilley	J. Jarvis	R. Hutchinson	11	11-2
1966 Dart Board, 8-12	M. Sobell	Sir G. Richards	D. Smith	13	10-1
1967 Hametus, 8-12	Lady Beaverbrook	W. Nightingall	F. Durr	7	100-9
1968 Ribofilio, 8-12	C. Engelhard	R.J. Houghton	L. Piggott	11	8-11
1969 Nijinsky, 8-12	C. Engelhard	V. O'Brien	L. Piggott	6	1-3
1970 Mill Reef, 8-12	P. Mellon	I. Balding	G. Lewis	3	4-7
1971 Crowned Prince, 8-11	F. McMahon	B. van Cutsem	L. Piggott	11	4-9
1972 Lunchtime, 9-0	Col R. Poole	P. Walwyn	P. Eddery	8	11-8
1973 Cellini, 9-0	C. St George	V. O'Brien	L. Piggott	7	40-85
1974 Grundy, 9-0	C. Vittadini	P. Walwyn	P. Eddery	8	6-5
1975 Wollow, 9-0	C. d'Alessio	H. Cecil	G. Dettori	7	6-4
1976 The Minstrel, 9-0	R. Sangster	V. O'Brien	L. Piggott	11	6-5
1977 Try My Best, 9-0	R. Sangster	V. O'Brien	L. Piggott	7	4-6
1978 Tromos, 9-0	G. Cambanis	B. Hobbs	J. Lynch	6	11-4
1979 Monteverdi, 9-0	R. Sangster	V. O'Brien	L. Piggott	6	15-8
1980 Storm Bird, 9-0	R. Sangster	V. O'Brien	P. Eddery	5	4-5
1981 Wind and Wuthering, 9-0	R. Cyzer	H. Candy	P. Waldron	9	11-1
1982 Diesis, 9-0	Ld Howard de Walden	H. Cecil	L. Piggott	4	2-1
1983 El Gran Senor, 9-0	R. Sangster	V. O'Brien	P. Eddery	10	7-4
1984 Kala Dancer, 9-0	R. Tikkoo	B. Hanbury	G. Baxter	11	20-1
1985 Huntingdale, 9-0	Mrs P. Threlfall	J. Hindley	M. Hills	8	12-1

Dubai Champion Stakes $1\frac{1}{4}$ m

Three-year-olds and upwards. 3-y-o 8st 10lb, 4-y-o & upwards 9st 3lb, fillies allowed 3lb. First run 1877. Run on Summer Course 1940-44. Run as Champion Stakes before 1982. No race 1939. Group One.

		OWNER	TRAINER	JOCKEY	RAN	SP
1930	Rustom Pasha, 3-8-7	Aga Khan	R. Dawson	H. Wragg	9	6-1
1931	Goyescas, 3-8-7	M. Boussac	B. Jarvis	E.C. Elliott	5	5-1
1932	Cameronian, 4-9-0	J. Dewar	F. Darling	G. Richards	6	11-10
1933	Dastur, 4-9-0	Aga Khan	F. Butters	M. Beary	3	2-5
	Chatelaine, 3-8-4	E. Thornton-Smith	F. Templeman	G. Richards	–	9-2
1934	Umidwar, 3-8-7	Aga Khan	F. Butters	F. Fox	9	5-4
1935	Wychwood Abbot, 4-9-0	O. Watney	T. Leader	R. Perryman	7	4-6
1936	Wychwood Abbot, 5-9-0	O. Watney	T. Leader	P. Perryman	4	10-11
1937	Flares, 4-9-0	W. Woodward	C. Boyd-Rochfort	P. Beasley	4	evens
1938	Rockfel, 3-8-5	Sir H. C-Owen	O. Bell	H. Wragg	5	2-1
1940	Hippius, 3-8-8	Lord Rosebery	J. Jarvis	E. Smith	8	100-8
1941	Hippius, 4-9-0	Lord Rosebery	J. Jarvis	E. Smith	5	6-4
1942	Big Game, 3-8-3	King George VI	F. Darling	G. Richards	5	11-10
1943	Nasrullah, 3-8-6	Aga Khan	F. Butters	G. Richards	6	100-30
1944	Hycilla, 3-8-2	W. Woodward	C. Boyd-Rochfort	W. Nevett	17	10-1
1945	Court Martial, 3-8-7	Lord Astor	J. Lawson	C. Richards	4	4-11
1946	Honeyway, 5-9-0	Lord Milford	J. Jarvis	E. Smith	8	8-1
1947	Migoli, 3-8-8	Aga Khan	F. Butters	G. Richards	4	evens
1948	Solar Slipper, 3-8-8	J. McGrath	H. Smyth	E. Smith	7	6-1
1949	Djeddah, 4-9-0	M. Boussac	C. Semblat	E.C. Elliott	5	4-6
1950	Peter Flower, 4-9-0	Lord Rosebery	J. Jarvis	W. Rickaby	7	3-1
1951	Dynamiter, 3-8-7	M. Boussac	C. Semblat	E.C. Elliott	19	100-8
1952	Dynamiter, 4-9-0	M. Boussac	J. Glynn	E.C. Elliott	5	4-5
1953	Nearula, 3-8-7	W. Humble	C. Elsey	E. Britt	7	4-1
1954	Narrator, 3-8-7	Maj L. Holliday	H. Cottrill	F. Barlow	6	20-1
1955	Hafiz, II, 3-8-7	Aga Khan	A. Head	R. Poincelet	5	100-30
1956	Hugh Lupus, 4-9-0	Lady S. Vernon	N. Murless	W. Johnstone	11	3-1
1957	Rose Royale II, 3-8-4	Aly Khan	A. Head	J. Massard	7	5-2
1958	Bella Paola, 3-8-4	F. Dupré	F. Mathet	G. Lequeux	7	4-1
1959	Petite Etoile, 3-8-5	Aly Khan	N. Murless	L. Piggott	3	2-11
1960	Marguerite Vernaut, 3-8-7	Marchese della Rochetta	U. Penco	E. Camici	4	9-4
1961	Bobar II, 3-8-7	Mme G. Courtois	R. Corme	M. Garcia	8	100-8
1962	Arctic Storm, 3-8-7	Mrs E. Carroll	J. Oxx	W. Williamson	7	6-1
1963	Hula Dancer, 3-8-4	Mrs P. Widener	E. Pollet	J. Deforge	11	9-2
1964	Baldric II, 3-8-7	Mrs H. Jackson	E. Fellows	W. Pyers	9	7-2
1965	Silly Season, 3-8-7	P. Mellon	I. Balding	G. Lewis	13	100-8
1966	Pieces of Eight, 3-8-7	Contesse de la Valdene	V. O'Brien	L. Piggott	8	5-4
1967	Reform, 3-8-7	M. Sobell	Sir G. Richards	A. Breasley	7	100-30
1968	Sir Ivor, 3-8-7	R. Guest	V. O'Brien	L. Piggott	6	8-1
1969	Flossy, 3-8-4	H. Berlin	F. Boutin	J. Deforge	9	100-7
1970	Connaught, 5-9-5	H.J. Joel	N. Murless	A. Barclay	8	5-4
1971	Brigadier Gerard, 3-8-7	Mrs J. Hislop	W. Hern	J. Mercer	10	1-2
1972	Brigadier Gerard, 4-9-3	Mrs J. Hislop	W. Hern	J. Mercer	9	1-3
1973	Hurry Harriet, 3-8-7	M. Thorp	P. Mullins	J. Cruguet	16	33-1
1974	Giacometti, 3-8-10	C. St George	H.R. Price	L. Piggott	14	4-1
1975	Rose Bowl, 3-8-7	Mrs C. Engelhard	R.J. Houghton	W. Carson	9	11-2
1976	Vitiges, 3-8-11	Mme M. Laloum	P. Walwyn	P. Eddery	19	22-1
1977	Flying Water, 4-9-0	D. Wildenstein	A. Penna	Y. Saint-Martin	8	9-1
1978	Swiss Maid, 3-8-7	M. Fine	P. Kelleway	G. Starkey	10	9-1
1979	Northern Baby, 3-8-10	Mme A d'Estainville	F. Boutin	P. Paquet	14	9-1
1980	Cairn Rouge, 3-8-7	D. Brady	M. Cunningham	A. Murray	3	6-1
1981	Vayrann, 3-8-10	Aga Khan	F. Mathet	Y. Saint-Martin	16	15-2
1982	Time Charter, 3-8-7	R. Barnett	H. Candy	W. Newnes	14	9-2
1983	Cormorant Wood, 3-8-7	R. McAlpine	B. Hills	S. Cauthen	19	18-1
1984	Palace Music, 3-8-10	N.B. Hunt	P. Biancone	Y. Saint-Martin	15	18-1
1985	Pebbles, 4-9-0	Sheikh Mohammed	C. Brittain	P. Eddery	10	9-2

Tote Cesarewitch Handicap   2¼m

*First run 1839. Run over 2m 24yds on Summer Course 1939-41. Run as Cesarewitch
Handicap before 1971; SKF Cesarewitch Handicap 1971-77. No race 1942-44.*

	OWNER	TRAINER	JOCKEY	RAN	SP
1930 Ut Majeur, 3-8-3	Aga Khan	R. Dawson	M. Beary	28	100-8
1931 Noble Star, 4-8-12	F. Cundell	L. Cundell	F. Fox	26	100-6
1932 Nitsichin, 4-8-9	D. Kennedy	P. Thrale	M. Beary	26	10-1
1933 Seminole, 4-8-0	J. Widener	C. Boyd-Rochfort	F. Fox	33	100-6
1934 Enfield, 3-7-10	M. Field	C. Boyd-Rochfort	J. Sirett	27	7-1
1935 Near Relation, 3-7-9	Sir A. Butt	Frank Butters	E. Smith	29	22-1
1936 Fet, 5-6-12	S. Freeman	H. Hedges	A. Richardson	24	10-1
1937 Punch, 4-7-11	T. Westhead	C. Tabor	S. Wragg	31	17-1
1938 Contrevent, 3-6-10	Princess de F. Lucinge	H. Count	A. Tucker	28	100-7
1939 Cantatrice II, 4-7-5	Sir A. Butt	Frank Butters	D. Smith	36	7-2
1940 Hunter's Moon IV, 4-9-5	E. Esmond	F. Darling	G. Richards	14	100-8
1941 Filator, 3-7-12	Lady Cunliffe-Owen	O. Bell	S. Wragg	21	100-9
1945 Kerry Piper, 4-8-1	Sir H. Bruce	F. Armstrong	E. Britt	26	25-1
1946 Monsieur l'Amiral, 5-8-5	H. Barnard-Hankey	E. Charlier	H. Wragg	27	33-1
1947 Whiteway, 3-7-12	Capt D. FitzGerald	W. Pratt	W. Evans	22	100-8
1948 Woodburn, 3-7-13	Lord Allendale	C. Elsey	E. Britt	32	100-9
1949 Strathspey, 4-7-11	J. Rank	N. Cannon	E. Smith	37	25-1
1950 Above Board, 3-7-10	King George VI	C. Boyd-Rochfort	E. Smith	38	18-1
1951 Three Cheers, 3-7-8	C. Crofts	P. Thrale	E. Mercer	30	17-2
1952 Flush Royal, 7-8-13	G. MacLean	J. Fawcus	W. Nevett	36	33-1
1953 Chantry, 4-8-4	S. Ingham	S. Ingham	K. Gethin	25	4-1
1954 French Design, 7-8-3	S. Banks	G. Todd	D. Smith	31	100-6
1955 Curry, 4-7-6	F. Honour	F. Armstrong	P. Tulk	21	100-6
1956 Prelone, 3-7-3	A. Allen	W. Hide	E. Hide	19	20-1
1957 Sandiacre, 5-7-8	T. Farr	W. Dutton	D. Smith	24	100-8
1958 Morecambe, 5-9-1	J. Bullock	S. Hall	J. Sime	30	15-2
1959 Come to Daddy, 4-7-8	T. Farr	W. Lyde	D. Smith	17	6-1
1960 Alcove, 3-7-8	Lord Derby	J.F. Watts	D. Smith	20	100-30
1961 Avon's Pride, 4-7-11	Maj L. Holliday	W. Hern	E. Smith	27	100-8
1962 Golden Fire, 4-7-11	G. Ridley	D. Marks	D. Yates	25	25-1
1963 Utrillo, 6-8-0	J. Gerber	H.P. Price	J. Sime	25	100-8
1964 Grey of Falloden, 5-9-6	Lord Astor	W. Hern	J. Mercer	26	20-1
1965 Mintmaster, 4-7-9	E. Collington	A. Cooper	J. Sime	18	13-2
1966 Persian Lancer, 8-7-8	Lord Belper	H.R. Price	D. Smith	24	100-7
1967 Boismoss, 3-7-1	J. Spriggs	M.W. Easterby	E. Johnson	23	100-9
1968 Major Rose, 5-9-4	R. Heaton	H.R. Price	L. Piggott	33	9-1
1969 Floridian, 5-7-4	A. Patchett	L. Shedden	D. McKay	23	20-1
1970 Scoria, 4-7-0	J. Lang	C. Crossley	D. McKay	21	33-1
1971 Orosio, 4-8-2	C. St George	H. Cecil	G. Lewis	18	5-1
1972 Cider With Rosie, 4-7-11	A. Mullings	S. Ingham	M.L. Thomas	21	14-1
1973 Flash Imp, 4-7-8	Mrs O. Negus-Fancy	R. Smyth	T. Cain	29	25-1
1974 Ocean King, 8-7-7	V. Lawson	A. Pitt	T. Carter	27	25-1
1975 Shantallah, 3-8-10	R. More O'Ferrall	H. Wragg	B. Taylor	17	7-1
1976 John Cherry, 5-9-13	J. Whitney	J. Tree	L. Piggott	14	13-2
1977 Assured, 4-8-4	Mrs G. Kent	H. Candy	P. Waldron	11	10-1
1978 Centurion, 3-9-8	Col J. Berry	I. Balding	J. Matthias	17	9-2
1979 Sir Michael, 3-7-8	Cheveley Park Stud	G. Huffer	M. Rimmer	11	10-1
1980 Popsi's Joy, 5-8-6	V. Lawson	M. Haynes	L. Piggott	27	10-1
1981 Halsbury, 3-8-4	A. Oldrey	P. Walwyn	J. Mercer	30	14-1
1982 Mountain Lodge, 3-7-10	Lord Halifax	J. Dunlop	W. Carson	28	9-1
1983 Bajan Sunshine, 4-8-8	P. Green	R. Simpson	B. Rouse	28	7-1
1984 Tom Sharp, 4-7-5	M. Yarrow	W. Wharton	S. Dawson	26	40-1
1985 Kayudee, 5-8-2	Kenton Utilities & Dev. Ltd	J. FitzGerald	A. Murray	21	7-1

NOTTINGHAM

The Racecourse, Colwick Park, Nottingham. (0602-580620)
Clerk of the Course: David Henson

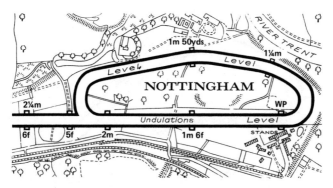

Left-handed course.

EFFECT OF DRAW: High numbers favoured when stalls on stand side on straight course, especially on soft.

Best Times

DISTANCE	TIME	AGE	WEIGHT		GOING	HORSE	DATE	
5f	58·4	4	7	7	Firm	Vilgora	Apr. 12,	1976
		6	8	8	Good	Minstrel King	Mar. 29,	1960
5f	58·6	2	8	11	Firm	Al Sylah	May 1,	1984
		3	8	2	Good	Janeat	July 10,	1962
6f	1.10·8	3	9	0	Firm	Fahdi	July 21,	1984
		4	8	0	Firm	Out of Hand	Aug. 8,	1983
6f	1.11·4	2	8	11	Firm	Jameelapi (USA)	Aug. 8,	1983
8f 50y	1.39.9	5	7	3	Firm	Sterlonia	July 4,	1981
8f 50y	1.41	2	9	7	Firm	Mashhur	Oct. 1,	1985
10f	2.2·3	3	8	8	Firm	Ayaabi	July 21,	1984
10f	2.5·6	2	9	0	Firm	Al Salite	Oct. 38,	1985
11f	2.20	3	9	0	Hard	Hurry de Savoie	July 5,	1937
13f	2.44·8	3	7	11	Good	Alignment	Aug. 12,	1968
14f	2.57·8	3	8	10	Firm	Buster Jo	Oct. 1,	1985
16f	3.24	5	7	7	Firm	Fez	Oct. 5,	1936
18f	3.59·6	3	9	7	Firm	Sneak Preview	Oct. 25,	1983

PONTEFRACT

33 Ropergate, Pontefract, West Yorkshire. WF8 1LE. (0977-702210, race days only; 0977-703224, admin)
Clerk of the Course: Norman Gundill

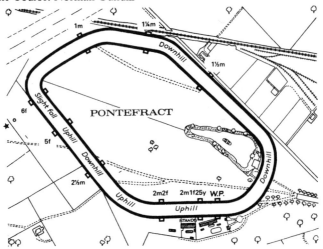

Left-handed course.
EFFECT OF DRAW: Low numbers slightly favoured up to $1\frac{1}{4}$m.

Best Times

DISTANCE	TIME	AGE	WEIGHT		GOING	HORSE	DATE	
5f	1.1·1	5	7	7	Hard	Regal Bingo	Sept. 29,	1971
5f	1.2	2	9	0	Hard	Bonderite Boy	July 23,	1979
6f	1.12·6	3	7	13	Firm	Merry One	Aug. 29,	1970
6f	1.14	2	9	3	Firm	Fawzi	Sept. 6,	1983
8f	1.41·4	4	7	12	Firm	Paddy's Amour	June 29,	1970
8f	1.42·8	2	9	13	Firm	Star Spray	Sept. 6,	1983
10f	2.8·2	3	7	13	Hard	Tom Noddy	Aug. 21,	1972
		4	7	8	Hard	Happy Hector	July 9,	1979
10f	2.15·5	2	8	3	Firm	One-Cal	Oct. 10,	1977
12f	2.34·3	4	8	9	Hard	Ezra	June 23,	1975
16f 24y	4.0·6	4	9	7	Soft	Crusader Castle	April 6,	1983
18f	3.51·7	5	7	8	Firm	The Irish Rhine	June 21,	1983
21f 133y	4.47·8	4	8	4	Firm	Physical	May 14,	1984

REDCAR

The Racecourse, Redcar, Cleveland. TS10 2BY. (0642-484068/484254)
Clerk of the Course: John Cleverly

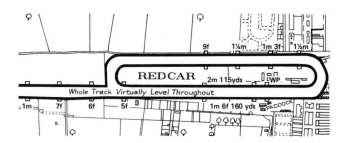

Left-handed course.

EFFECT OF DRAW: High numbers slightly favoured up to 1m; low numbers slightly favoured on round course.

Best Times

DISTANCE	TIME	AGE	WEIGHT	GOING	HORSE	DATE	
5f	56·7	4	7 10	Firm	Mels Choice	Sept. 25,	1982
5f	57·2	{ 2	9 2	Firm	Captain Nick	July 27,	1978
		{ 2	7 8	Firm	English Star	Sept. 24,	1982
6f	1.9	6	8 4	Firm	Flying William	May 2,	1958
6f	1.11·5	2	9 0	Fast	Mr Meeka	Sept. 23,	1983
7f	1.22·1	3	8 2	Firm	Marston	July 25,	1978
7f	1.21·9	2	8 11	Firm	Nagwa	Sept. 27,	1975
8f	1.35·3	4	9 2	Firm	Aliante	Aug. 6,	1977
8f	1.38·4	2	8 5	Fast	Tophams Taverns	Sept. 13,	1983
9f	1.51·1	3	9 7	Firm	Fish N' Chips	June 21,	1985
9f	1.54·7	2	8 11	Firm	Cri De Coeur	Oct. 20,	1983
10f	2.2·4	5	7 8	Firm	Tale of Two Cities	May 21,	1956
11f	2.18·3	6	8 5	Firm	Eagle Island	Sept. 15,	1981
12f	2.30·1	3	9 0	Firm	High Tension	June 22,	1985
14f 160y	3.9	8	9 1	Good	Petty Officer	May 28,	1973
16f 115y	3.33·3	4	9 8	Firm	Special Vintage	Aug. 10,	1984

RIPON

Ripon Race Co. Ltd., Boroughbridge Road, Ripon, North Yorkshire.
  (0765-3696/2156)
Clerk of the Course: Freddie Newton

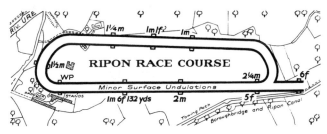

Right-handed course.

EFFECT OF DRAW: Low numbers slightly favoured when stalls on stands side in straight; high numbers favoured on round course.

Best Times

DISTANCE	TIME	AGE	WEIGHT	GOING	HORSE	DATE	
5f	58	4	7 2	Firm	Castle Mona	July 22,	1966
5f	58·3	2	8 11	Firm	Jonacris	June 2,	1982
6f	1.9·8	5	7 0	Firm	Quoit	July 23,	1966
6f	1.11·2	2	9 3	Firm	Domynsky	June 2,	1982
8f	1.37	4	7 10	Firm	Crown Witness	Aug. 25,	1980
8f	1.41·2	2	7 2	Good	Roanstreak	Sept. 5,	1970
9f	1.49·9	3	6 12	Firm	Countly Lad	May 24,	1972
10f	2.3·5	3	8 11	Firm	Leysh	July 21,	1984
12f	2.32·2	6	8 7	Firm	Cholo	Sept. 27,	1941
14f 134y	3·8	5	9 13	Good	Grey of Falloden	July 25,	1964
16f	3.24·4	4	8 2	Girm	Betto	May 16,	1970
18f	3.51·3	3	7 8	Firm	Beechwood Seeker	Sept. 1,	1981

SALISBURY

The Racecourse, Netherhampton, Salisbury, Wiltshire. SP2 8PN.
  (0722-26461/27327)
Clerk of the Course: Michael Meredith

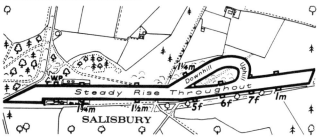

Right-handed loop course with electrical timing apparatus.

EFFECT OF DRAW: Low numbers strongly favoured up to 1m when stalls on stands side.

Best Times

DISTANCE	TIME	AGE	WEIGHT	GOING	HORSE	DATE	
5f	59·88	3	9 10	Good	Imperial Jade	Sept. 11,	1985
5f	1.0·38	2	8 8	Firm	Miss Anagram	Sept. 9,	1982
6f	1.12·47	5	9 9	Firm	Al Trui	July 13,	1985
6f	1.13·06	2	8 11	Firm	Jakomima	Sept. 9,	1971
7f	1.26·07	4	8 7	Firm	The Godson	May 8,	1975
7f	1.26·78	2	9 2	Fast	Raft	Aug. 11	1983
8f	1.40·38	3	8 4	Firm	Pictograph	July 13,	1985
8f	1.43·86	2	9 3	Fast	Carocrest	Sept. 1,	1983
10f	2.5·16	4	8 7	Firm	Wephen	June 23,	1976
12f	2.32·9	6	9 8	Firm	Crested Lark	July 10,	1982
14f	2.58·01	4	10 0	Fast	Dancing Affair	Aug. 16,	1984

SANDOWN PARK

Sandown Park Ltd., Esher, Surrey (0372-63072/64348)
Clerk of the Course: Mark Kershaw

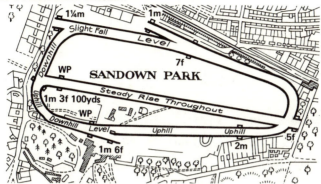

Right-handed course with electrical timing apparatus.

EFFECT OF DRAW: High draw essential, especially on soft ground, when stalls on far side on sprint course.

Best Times

DISTANCE	TIME	AGE	WEIGHT	GOING	HORSE	DATE	
5f	59·31	5	9 2	Fast	Alev	April 27,	1984
5f	59·48	2	9 3	Firm	Times Time	July 22,	1982
7f	1.26·69	5	8 10	Firm	Young Daniel	July 2,	1983
7f	1.28·15	2	9 1	Firm	Attempt	Aug. 19	1983
8f	1.39·08	3	8 8	Firm	Linda's Fantasy	Aug. 19,	1983
8f	1.41·2	2	9 7	Firm	Untold	Aug. 30,	1985
10f	2.2·14	4	8 11	Firm	Kalaglow	May 31,	1982
11f 100y	2.21·61	4	8 3	Fast	Aylesfield	July 7,	1984
14f	2.53·82	3	9 3	Firm	Verdance	Sept. 25,	1985
16f	3.31·16	3	9 3	Firm	Ardross	June 1,	1982

Race Results

Trusthouse-Forte Mile   1m

Four-year-olds and upwards. 9st, fillies allowed 3lb (plus penalties). First run 1985. Group Two.

	OWNER	TRAINER	JOCKEY	RAN	SP
1985 Pebbles, 4-9-4	Sheikh Mohammed	C. Brittain	S. Cauthen	7	11-8

Guardian Classic Trial   1¼m

Three-year-old colts and geldings. 8st 7lb (plus penalties). Run as Royal Stakes before 1971, Ladbroke Classic Trial 1971-73, Classic Trial 1974-80. Group Three.

	OWNER	TRAINER	JOCKEY	RAN	SP
1971 L'Apache, 8-7	S. Threadwell	T. Gosling	A. Murray	10	33-1
1972 Pentland Firth, 8-12	V. Hardy	G. Barling	P. Eddery	13	5-2

	OWNER	TRAINER	JOCKEY	RAN	SP
1973 Ksar, 8-12	Lady Rotherwick	B. van Cutsem	W. Carson	6	8-15
1974 Bustino, 8-9	Lady Beaverbrook	W. Hern	J. Mercer	9	5-2
1975 Consol, 9-0	A. Oldrey	P. Walwyn	P. Eddery	9	10-11
1976 Riboboy, 9-0	Lady Beaverbrook	W. Hern	J. Mercer	7	9-2
1977 Artaius, 8-9	Mrs G. Getty	V. O'Brien	L. Piggott	5	evens
1978 Whitstead, 8-11	H. Demetriou	H.R. Price	B. Taylor	8	9-2
1979 Troy, 8-7	Sir M. Sobell	W. Hern	W. Carson	5	4-7
1980 Henbit, 8-7	Mrs A. Plesch	W. Hern	W. Carson	6	9-4
1981 Shergar, 8-7	Aga Khan	M. Stoute	W.R. Swinburn	8	evens
1982 Peacetime, 8-7	Beckhampton Ltd	J. Tree	P. Eddery	11	9-2
1983 Gordian, 8-7	S. Niarchos	G. Harwood	G. Starkey	7	10-1
1984 Alphabatim, 9-0	K. Abdullah	G. Harwood	B. Rouse	8	4-1
1985 Damister, 8-7	K. Abdullah	J. Tree	S. Cauthen	4	10-11

Coral Eclipse Stakes   1¼m

Three-year-olds and upwards. 3-y-o 8st 8lb, 4-y-o & upwards 9st 7lb, fillies allowed 3lb. First run 1886. Run at Ascot 1945; at Kempton 1973. Run as Eclipse Stakes 1886-1973; Benson & Hedges Eclipse Stakes 1974-75. No race 1940-45. Group One.

	OWNER	TRAINER	JOCKEY	RAN	SP
1930 Rustom Pasha, 3-8-9	Aga Khan	R. Dawson	H. Wragg	11	4-1
1931 Caerleon, 4-9-4	Lord Derby	G. Lambton	T. Weston	11	25-1
1932 Miracle, 3-8-9	Lord Rosebery	J. Jarvis	H. Wragg	13	10-1
1933 Loaningdale, 4-9-7	Col G. Wilson	C. Boyd-Rochfort	J. Childs	10	9-2
1934 King Salmon, 4-9-7	Sir R. Brooke	O. Bell	H. Wragg	10	4-1
1935 Windsor Lad, 4-9-10	M. Benson	M. Marsh	C. Smirke	5	4-7
1936 Rhodes Scholar, 3-8-9	Lord Astor	J. Lawson	R. Dick	9	11-8
1937 Boswell, 4-9-10	W. Woodward	C. Boyd-Rochfort	P. Beasley	6	20-1
1938 Pasch, 3-8-12	H. Morriss	F. Darling	G. Richards	6	13-8
1939 Blue Peter, 3-8-12	Lord Rosebery	J. Jarvis	E. Smith	8	2-7
1946 Gulf Stream, 3-8-6	Lord Derby	W. Earl	H. Wragg	5	8-13
1947 Migoli, 3-8-9	Aga Khan	Frank Butters	C. Smirke	5	7-2
1948 Petition, 4-9-7	Sir A. Butt	Frank Butters	K. Gethin	8	8-1
1949 Djeddah, 4-9-4	M. Boussac	C. Semblat	E.C. Elliott	7	6-4
1950 Flocon, 4-9-4	Baron de Waldner	P. Carter	F. Palmer	6	100-9
1951 Mystery IX, 3-8-2	Mrs E. Esmond	P. Carter	L. Piggott	8	100-8
1952 Tulyar, 3-8-2	Aga Khan	M. Marsh	C. Smirke	7	1-3
1953 Argur, 4-9-0	M. Boussac	J. Glynn	E.C. Elliott	7	100-9
1954 King of the Tudors, 4-9-7	F. Dennis	W. Stephenson	K. Gethin	6	9-2
1955 Darius, 4-9-7	Sir P. Loraine	H. Wragg	L. Piggott	7	11-10
1956 Tropique, 4-9-7	Baron de Rothschild	G. Watson	P. Blanc	8	3-1
1957 Arctic Explorer, 3-8-9	Lieut-Col G. Loder	N. Murless	L. Piggott	5	100-30
1958 Ballymoss, 4-9-7	J. McShain	V. O'Brien	A. Breasley	7	8-11
1959 Saint Crespin III, 3-8-9	Aly Khan	A. Head	G. Moore	9	5-2
1960 Javelot, 4-9-0	Baron de Waldner	P. Carter	F. Palmer	9	4-1
1961 St Paddy, 4-9-7	Sir V. Sassoon	N. Murless	L. Piggott	7	2-13
1962 Henry the Seventh, 4-9-0	H.J. Joel	W. Elsey	E. Hide	7	8-11
1963 Khalkis, 3-8-2	Lord Elveden	P. Prendergast	G. Bougoure	9	7-4
1964 Ragusa, 4-9-0	J. Mullion	P. Prendergast	G. Bougoure	11	4-6
1965 Canisbay, 4-9-5	The Queen	C. Boyd-Rochfort	S. Clayton	8	20-1
1966 Pieces of Eight, 3-8-7	Contesse de la Valdene	V. O'Brien	L. Piggott	10	11-10
1967 Busted, 4-9-5	S. Joel	N. Murless	W. Rickaby	9	8-1
1968 Royal Palace, 4-9-5	H.J. Joel	N. Murless	A. Barclay	5	9-4
1969 Wolver Hollow, 5-9-5	Mrs C. Iselin	H. Cecil	L. Piggott	7	8-1
1970 Connaught, 5-9-5	H.J. Joel	N. Murless	A. Barclay	3	5-4
1971 Mill Reef, 3-8-7	P. Mellon	I. Balding	G. Lewis	6	5-4
1972 Brigadier Gerard, 4-9-5	Mrs J. Hislop	W. Hern	J. Mercer	6	4-11
1973 Scottish Rifle, 4-9-5	A. Struthers	J. Dunlop	R. Hutchinson	6	15-8
1974 Coup de Feu, 5-9-5	F. Sasse	D. Sasse	P. Eddery	12	33-1
1975 Star Appeal, 5-9-7	W. Zeitelhack	T. Grieβer	G. Starkey	16	20-1
1976 Wollow, 3-8-8	C. d'Alessio	H. Cecil	G. Dettori	9	9-4
1977 Artaius, 3-8-8	Mrs G. Getty	V. O'Brien	L. Piggott	10	9-2
1978 Gunner B, 5-9-7	Mrs P. Barratt	H. Cecil	J. Mercer	9	7-4

	OWNER	TRAINER	JOCKEY	RAN	SP
1979 Dickens Hill, 3-8-8	Mme J. Binet	M. O'Toole	A. Murray	7	7-4
1980 Ela-Mana-Mou, 4-9-7	S. Weinstock	W. Hern	W. Carson	6	85-40
1981 Master Willie, 4-9-7	R. Barnett	H. Candy	P. Waldron	7	6-4
1982 Kalaglow, 4-9-7	A. Ward	G. Harwood	G. Starkey	9	11-10
1983 Solford, 3-8-8	R. Sangster	V. O'Brien	P. Eddery	9	3-1
1984 Sadler's Wells, 3-8-8	R. Sangster	V. O'Brien	P. Eddery	9	11-4
1985 Pebbles, 4-9-4	Sheikh Mohammed	C. Brittain	S. Cauthen	4	7-2

THIRSK

Thirsk Racecourse Ltd., Station Road, Thirsk, North Yorkshire. YO7 1QL.
  (0845-22276)
Clerk of the Course: John Cleverly

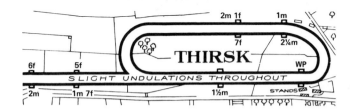

Left-handed course.
EFFECT OF DRAW: High numbers favoured when stalls on stands side on straight
course, but low numbers favoured on soft going.

Best Times

DISTANCE	TIME	AGE	WEIGHT	GOING	HORSE	DATE	
5f	57	3	8 8	Firm	Bold and Free	June 3,	1972
5f	57·8	3	8 11	Firm	Fearless Lad	Sept. 5,	1981
6f	1.9·6	3	8 10	Firm	Cedar Grange	Sept. 3,	1977
6f	1.10·8	2	8 2	Good	Spritely Star	Oct. 2,	1936
7f	1.22·6	5	6 11	Firm	Tuanwan	May 29,	1970
7f	1.24·6	2	8 12	Firm	Man of Harlech	Aug. 2,	1975
8f	1.36·2	5	9 0	Firm	Teamwork	May 8,	1982
8f	1.39·5	2	8 7	Firm	High Port	Sept. 5,	1981
12f	2.30	4	8 2	Firm	Casting Vote	Aug. 1,	1964
16f	3.22·3	3	8 11	Firm	Tomaschek	July 17,	1981

WARWICK

The Racecourse, Hampton Street, Warwick. (0926-491553, race days only;
  0242-513014, admin)
Clerk of the Course: Edward Gillespie

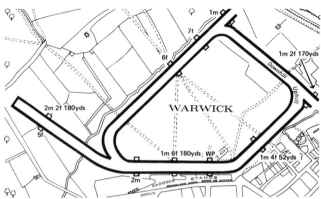

Left-handed course.

EFFECT OF DRAW: High numbers slightly favoured over 5f when stalls on far side.

Best Times

DISTANCE	TIME	AGE	WEIGHT	GOING	HORSE	DATE	
5f	57·7	3	9 6	Firm	Truth Will Out	June 21,	1980
5f	58·6	2	9 0	Firm	Tircelyn	June 8,	1957
6f	1.11·8	4	9 5	Firm	Pride of Kilmalloch	July 1,	1960
6f	1.12·9	2	8 11	Firm	Burbridge Dancer	June 18,	1983
7f	1.23·8	6	7 12	Hard	Blackshore	May 19,	1956
7f	1.24·8	2	9 4	Firm	Nocino	July 28,	1979
8f	1.36	3	9 0	Firm	Academic World	Aug. 25,	1975
8f	1.37·7	2	9 7	Fast	Frisky Wharf	Aug. 29,	1983
10f 170y	2.13·8	3	8 13	Firm	Castellita	July 28,	1984
12f 52y	2.37·2	5	8 12	Hard	Noirmont Buoy	June 19,	1967
16f	3.26·8	4	8 11	Hard	Flighty Eyes	Aug. 15,	1955
18f 180y	4.3·9	5	9 10	Fast	Fitzpatrick	Aug. 27,	1984

WINDSOR

The Racecourse, Windsor, Berkshire. (0753-865234/864726)
Clerk of the Course: Hugo Bevan

Figure of eight course.

EFFECT OF DRAW: High numbers slightly favoured at 1m 70yds.

Best Times

DISTANCE	TIME	AGE	WEIGHT		GOING	HORSE	DATE	
5f	59·2	3	9	7	Fast	La Tuerta	July 15,	1985
5f	58·9	2	9	0	Firm	Strictly Private	July 22,	1974
		2	7	0	Firm	Miss Merlin (disq)	Sept. 11,	1978
6f	1.10·1	3	8	12	Firm	Free Style	June 27,	1964
		3	8	4	Firm	Sweet Relief	Sept. 11,	1978
6f	1.10·1	2	9	3	Firm	Rosier	Aug. 17,	1981
8f 70y	1.41·5	4	7	2	Firm	Blowing Bubbles	July 16,	1984
10f 22y	2.3	3	9	1	Firm	Moomba Masquerade	May 19,	1980
11f 150y	2.21·5	3	9	2	Firm	Double Florin	May 19,	1980

WOLVERHAMPTON

The Racecourse, Gorsebrook Road, Wolverhampton. WV6 0PE
   (0902-24481/772038)
Clerk of the Course: Lt-Comm John Ford

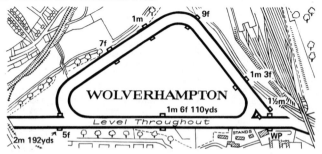

Left-handed course.
EFFECT OF DRAW: Low numbers strongly favoured over 5f on soft going when stalls on
stands side, and slightly favoured up to 1m 1f.

Best Times

DISTANCE	TIME	AGE	WEIGHT		GOING	HORSE	DATE	
5f	56·6	3	7	13	Firm	Balvima	Sept. 17,	1979
5f	57·1	2	9	0	Good	Soverena	July 3,	1967
7f	1.25·4	3	7	7	Firm	Steady Hand	June 25,	1979
7f	1.26·6	2	8	11	Firm	Nepula	July 4,	1983
8f	1.37·3	3	8	8	Firm	Tender Sovereign	July 4,	1983
8f	1.40·6	2	8	4	Firm	Cinderwench	Sept. 15,	1980
9f	1.47·4	3	8	8	Firm	Mailman	May 18,	1982
9f	1.51·8	2	8	12	Firm	Connaught Bridge	Oct. 9,	1978
11f 25y	2.17·5	3	7	12	Firm	Wrong Page	Aug. 15,	1981
12f	2.30·9	3	9	0	Firm	Salient	July 8,	1985
16f 192y	3.36·9	5	7	10	Firm	The Griggle	Aug. 3,	1976
17f	3.36·3	4	9	0	Firm	Dark Proposal	May 17,	1982

YARMOUTH

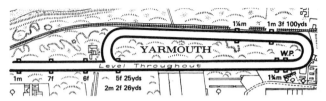

Left-handed course.
EFFECT OF DRAW: High numbers slightly favoured up to 1m when stalls on stands side.

Best Times

DISTANCE	TIME	AGE	WEIGHT		GOING	HORSE	DATE	
5f 25y	1.0·8	3	8	8	Firm	King Silver	June 14,	1972
		3	8	12	Firm	Hunters Isle	June 13,	1978
5f 25y	1.0·9	2	8	8	Firm	Aberbevine	June 14,	1967
		2	8	10	Fast	Sam's Wood	July 13,	1983
6f	1.10·4	4	8	4	Good	Denikin	July 4,	1951
		3	7	7	Firm	Gold Prospector	Sept. 19,	1978
6f	1.10·8	2	8	7	Firm	Smart Sam	June 9,	1970
7f	1.22·4	5	7	7	Hard	Brother Victor	July 9,	1959
7f	1.23·7	2	9	2	Firm	Contralto	Sept. 19,	1978
8f	1.35	6	9	5	Firm	Laureat II	Sept. 14,	1936
8f	1.37·2	2	7	12	Firm	Clashing	Sept. 14,	1972
10f	2.4·2	3	8	1	Firm	On The Foan	Aug. 17,	1983
11f 100y	2.23·8	3	9	0	Firm	Laken Heath	June 10,	1981
		3	9	0	Firm	His Turn	June 9,	1981
14f	2.58·3	4	8	10	Firm	Top Straight	July 1,	1976
18f 26y	3.56	6	9	2	Firm	Dolben Lad	Sept. 21,	1978

YORK

The Racecourse, York. YO2 1EX. (0904-20911)
Clerk of the Course: John Sanderson

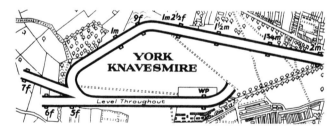

Left-handed course with electrical timing apparatus.
EFFECT OF DRAW: Low numbers slightly favoured when stalls on stands on straight course.

Best Times

DISTANCE	TIME	AGE	WEIGHT		GOING	HORSE	DATE	
5f	57·24	4	8	11	Good	Committed	Aug. 23,	1984
5f	58·6	2	9	0	Firm	Easy Going	Aug. 24,	1938
6f	1.9·9	3	7	8	Firm	Alphadamus	June 16,	1973
6f	1.10·82	2	8	11	Firm	Al Bahathri	Aug. 22,	1984
7f	1.22·72	3	9	0	Firm	Luck of the Draw	Sept. 4,	1980
7f	1.23·73	2	8	11	Good	Gorytus	Aug. 17,	1982
8f	1.36·02	4	9	9	Fast	Teleprompter	May 16,	1984
8f	1.39·12	2	9	1	Good	Shotgun	Sept. 3,	1980
9f	1.50·07	4	8	10	Firm	Music Lover	July 8,	1983
10f 110y	2.7·1	3	8	10	Good	Roberto	Aug. 15,	1972
12f	2.28	4	7	11	Firm	Firefright	May 15,	1973
14f	2.54·5	4	8	6	Good	Crazy Rhythm	Aug. 16,	1972
16f	3.21·6	4	7	6	Hard	Blue Pennant	May 23,	1946

Race Results

Mecca-Dante Stakes   1m 2½f

Three-year-olds. 9st, fillies allowed 3lb. First run 1958. Run as Dante Stakes before 1976. Group Two.

	OWNER	TRAINER	JOCKEY	RAN	SP
1958 Bald Eagle, 9-0	H. Guggenheim	C. Boyd-Rochfort	W.H. Carr	7	11-10
1959 Dickens, 9-0	Lady Z. Wernher	C. Boyd-Rochfort	W.H. Carr	9	100-8
1960 St Paddy, 9-0	Sir V. Sassoon	N. Murless	L. Piggott	10	8-11
1961 Gallant Knight, 9-0	H.J. Joel	T. Leader	E. Smith	5	3-1
1962 Lucky Brief, 9-0	W. Cockerline	W. Gray	B. Connorton	5	9-2
1963 Merchant Venturer, 9-0	Sir F. Robinson	J. Oxley	G. Starkey	6	9-2
1964 Sweet Moss, 9-0	Lady Sassoon	N. Murless	L. Piggott	9	3-1
1965 Ballymarais, 9-0	W. Stoker	W. Gray	W. Pyers	11	10-1
1966 Hermes, 9-0	R. Hollingsworth	J. Oxley	G. Starkey	9	3-1
1967 Gay Garland, 9-0	A. Askew	H. Wragg	R. Hutchinson	5	100-7
1968 Lucky Finish, 9-0	C. Nathhorst	H. Leader	B. Taylor	10	10-1
1969 Activator, 9-0	Duke of Sutherland	G. Barling	M.L. Thomas	15	6-1
1970 Approval, 9-0	Sir H. de Trafford	H. Cecil	G. Starkey	8	9-4
1971 Fair World, 9-0	J. Dellal	G. Todd	J. Lindley	8	6-1
1972 Rheingold, 9-0	H. Zeisel	B. Hills	E. Johnson	9	4-1
1973 Owen Dudley, 9-0	L. Freedman	N. Murless	G. Lewis	10	5-4
1974 Honoured Guest, 9-0	H.J. Joel	N. Murless	G. Lewis	6	7-1
1975 Hobnob, 9-0	R. Moller	H. Wragg	W. Carson	9	15-2
1976 Trasi's Son, 9-0	J. Hickman	M. Tate	E. Hide	15	50-1
1977 Lucky Sovereign, 9-0	R. Moller	H. Wragg	M.L. Thomas	15	20-1
1978 Shirley Heights, 9-0	Lord Halifax	J. Dunlop	G. Starkey	9	10-1
1979 Lyphard's Wish, 9-0	C. d'Alessio	H. Cecil	J. Mercer	14	100-30
1980 Hello Gorgeous, 9-0	D. Wildenstein	H. Cecil	J. Mercer	8	4-1
1981 Beldale Flutter, 9-0	A. Kelly	M. Jarvis	P. Eddery	6	11-1
1982 Simply Great, 9-0	D. Wildenstein	H. Cecil	L. Piggott	6	11-10
1983 Hot Touch, 9-0	E. Moller	G. Wragg	P. Eddery	9	11-1
1984 Claude Monet, 9-0	D. Wildenstein	H. Cecil	S. Cauthen	15	2-1
1985 Damister, 9-0	K. Abdullah	J. Tree	P. Eddery	5	5-1

John Smith's Magnet Cup   1m 2½f

Handicap. Three-year-olds and upwards. First run 1960. Run as Magnet Cup 1960-69.

	OWNER	TRAINER	JOCKEY	RAN	SP
1960 Fougalle, 3-7-0	R. Booth	P. Beasley	N. McIntosh	14	9-1
1961 Proud Chieftain, 4-8-10	Maj L. Holliday	W. Hern	W.H. Carr	17	5-2
1962 Nortia, 3-8-4	Maj L. Holliday	W. Hern	F. Durr	16	100-7
1963 Raccolto, 6-8-3	L. Lazarus	S. Hall	J. Sime	19	6-1

	OWNER	TRAINER	JOCKEY	RAN	SP
1964 Space King, 5-8-9	J. Crow	W. Hide	E. Hide	15	25-1
1965 Dark Court, 4-8-6	M. Sobell	Sir G. Richards	A. Breasley	12	5-2
1966 David Jack, 3-7-6	J. Fisher	E. Lambton	P. Robinson	14	4-1
1967 Copsale, 4-7-13	H. Hartley	R. Smyth	L.G. Brown	11	8-1
1968 Farm Walk, 6-8-13	W. Barker	P. Beasley	J. Seagrave	10	8-1
1969 My Swanee, 6-9-7	A. Stevens	W. Marshall	L. Piggott	6	5-2
1970 Timon, 4-7-4	Lord Rosebery	D. Smith	G. Welsh	15	10-1
1971 Prominent, 4-8-8	Col P. Wright	A. Budgett	G. Baxter	12	10-1
1972 Prominent, 5-9-4	Col P. Wright	A. Budgett	G. Baxter	8	4-1
1973 Peleid, 3-7-9	Col W. Behrens	W. Elsey	M.L. Thomas	8	6-1
1974 Take A Reef, 3-8-12	A. Villar	B. Hobbs	G. Baxter	13	11-1
1975 Jolly Good, 3-7-8	Mrs J. Bricken	B. Hobbs	W. Carson	15	9-2
1976 Bold Pirate, 4-9-3	Sir M. Sobell	W. Hern	J. Mercer	9	15-2
1977 Air Trooper, 4-9-6	S. Digby	W. Wightman	M.L. Thomas	8	9-2
1978 Town and Country, 4-8-13	Lord Porchester	W. Hern	W. Carson	9	5-1
1979 Tesoro Mio, 4-8-3	Mrs P. Yong	J. Etherington	E. Hide	9	8-1
1980 Fine Sun, 3-7-8	W. Hobson	Miss S. Hall	N. Howe	12	10-1
1981 Amyndas, 3-8-5	G. Cambanis	B. Hobbs	T. Lucas	11	7-1
1982 Buzzards Bay, 4-9-8	Mrs V. McKinney	H. Collingridge	M. Birch	6	7-1
1983 Bedtime, 3-7-9	Lord Halifax	W. Hern	W. Carson	9	7-2
1984 Straight Man, 3-8-11	Sir M. Sobell	W. Hern	S. Cauthen	9	2-1
1985 Chaumiere, 4-9-7	C. Booth	R. Williams	T. Ives	12	14-1

Benson & Hedges Gold Cup   1m 2½f

Three-year-olds and upwards. 3-y-o 8st 10lb, 4-y-o & up 9st 6lb, fillies allowed 3lb. First run 1972. Sponsorship discontinued after 1985. Group One.

	OWNER	TRAINER	JOCKEY	RAN	SP
1972 Roberto, 3-8-10	J. Galbreath	V. O'Brien	B. Baeza	5	12-1
1973 Moulton, 4-9-7	R. Moller	H. Wragg	G. Lewis	8	14-1
1974 Dahlia, 4-9-4	N.B. Hunt	M. Zilber	L. Piggott	9	8-15
1975 Dahlia, 5-9-4	N.B. Hunt	M. Zilber	L. Piggott	6	7-2
1976 Wollow, 3-8-10	C. d'Alessio	H. Cecil	G. Dettori	7	9-4
1977 Relkino, 4-9-6	Lady Beaverbrook	W. Hern	W. Carson	8	33-1
1978 Hawaiian Sound, 3-8-10	R. Sangster	B. Hills	L. Piggott	10	2-1
1979 Troy, 3-8-10	Sir M. Sobell	W. Hern	W. Carson	10	1-2
1980 Master Willie, 3-8-10	W. Barnett	H. Candy	P. Waldron	12	13-2
1981 Beldale Flutter, 3-8-10	A. Kelly	M. Jarvis	P. Eddery	9	9-1
1982 Assert, 3-8-10	R. Sangster	D. O'Brien	P. Eddery	7	4-5
1983 Caerleon, 3-8-10	R. Sangster	V. O'Brien	P. Eddery	9	100-30
1984 Cormorant Wood, 4-9-3	R.J. McAlpine	B. Hills	S. Cauthen	9	15-1
1985 Commanche Run, 4-9-6	I. Allan	L. Cumani	L. Piggott	6	5-1

Yorkshire Oaks   1½m

Three-year-old fillies. 9st. First run 1849. No race 1940-45. Group One.

	OWNER	TRAINER	JOCKEY	RAN	SP
1930 Glorious Devon, 7-12	Lord Glanely	T. Hogg	G. Richards	12	9-4
1931 Rackety Lassie, 7-12	S. Vlasto	C. Boyd-Rochfort	J. Dines	9	100-6
1932 Will o' the Wisp, 8-5	Lord Woolavington	F. Darling	G. Richards	6	13-8
Nash Light, 8-5	Lord Glanely	T. Hogg	F. Rickaby	—	6-1
1933 Star of England, 7-12	Lord Glanely	T. Hogg	G. Nicholl	7	10-1
1934 Dalmary, 7-12	Maj H. Cayzer	C. Boyd-Rochfort	F. Fox	5	11-8
1935 Trigo Verde, 7-12	J. Rank	N. Cannon	G. Richards	9	11-10
1936 Silversol, 9-1	M. Peacock	M. Peacock	W. Nevett	14	8-1
1937 Sculpture, 7-12	Lord Astor	J. Lawson	G. Richards	10	6-1
1938 Joyce W., 7-12	Sir V. Sassoon	J. Lawson	W. Nevett	12	11-2
1939 Night Shift, 7-12	Lord Derby	W. Earl	A. Richardson	6	20-1
1946 Live Letters, 8-10	J. Rank	N. Cannon	T. Weston	11	8-1
1947 Ladycross, 8-5	Sir R. Sykes	C. Boyd-Rochfort	W.H. Carr	6	2-1
1948 Angelola, 8-10	King George VI	C. Boyd-Rochfort	E. Britt	9	4-1
1949 Unknown Quantity, 8-5	H. Wills	J. Jarvis	W. Rickaby	6	3-1

	OWNER	TRAINER	JOCKEY	RAN	SP
1950 Above Board, 8-0	King George VI	C. Boyd-Rochfort	E. Smith	5	100-30
1951 Sea Parrot, 8-10	Lieut-Col G. Loder	N. Murless	G. Richards	8	13-2
1952 Frieze, 9-3	Capt A. Keith	C. Elsey	E. Britt	4	5-4
1953 Kerkeb, 8-5	Aga Khan	M. Marsh	G. Richards	8	7-4
1954 Feevagh, 8-5	J. McGrath	W. Stephenson	K. Gethin	10	20-1
1955 Ark Royal, 9-3	R. Hollingsworth	G. Colling	E. Mercer	5	evens
1956 Indian Twilight, 8-5	J. Astor	R.J. Colling	J. Mercer	9	13-2
1957 Almeria, 9-0	The Queen	C. Boyd-Rochfort	W.H. Carr	7	11-10
1958 None Nicer, 9-0	Maj L. Holliday	W. Hern	S. Clayton	8	4-1
1959 Petite Etoile, 9-0	Aly Khan	N. Murless	L. Piggott	3	2-15
1960 Lynchris, 9-0	Mrs E. Fawcett	J. Oxx	W. Williamson	7	5-4
1961 Tenacity, 9-0	Mrs W. Riley-Smith	Sir G. Richards	A. Breasley	7	7-1
1962 West Side Story, 9-0	H.J. Joel	T. Leader	E. Smith	5	2-1
1963 Outcrop, 9-0	Maj J. Priestman	G. Barling	E. Smith	11	9-1
1964 Homeward Bound, 9-0	Sir F. Robinson	J. Oxley	G. Starkey	7	2-1
1965 Mabel, 9-0	G. Williams	P. Walwyn	J. Mercer	5	7-4
1966 Parthian Glance, 9-0	Mrs W. Riley-Smith	G. Todd	L. Piggott	8	3-1
1967 Palatch, 9-0	C. Vittadini	H. Leader	B. Taylor	6	7-1
1968 Exchange, 9-0	Mrs R. Midwood	H. Leader	B. Taylor	8	7-2
1969 Frontier Goddess, 9-0	C. Spence	P. Walwyn	D. Keith	4	3-1
1970 Lupe	Mrs S. Joel	N. Murless	A. Barclay	3	4-6
1971 Fleet Wahine	R. Ohrstrom	H.T. Jones	G. Lewis	6	9-4
1972 Attica Meli	L. Freedman	N. Murless	G. Lewis	6	13-2
1973 Mysterious	G. Pope Jnr	N. Murless	G. Lewis	5	4-6
1974 Dibidale	N. Robinson	B. Hills	W. Carson	3	1-3
1975 May Hill	G. Williams	P. Walwyn	P. Eddery	5	4-1
1976 Sarah Siddons	Mrs J. Mullion	P. Prendergast	C. Roche	13	100-30
1977 Busaca	Countess M. Esterhazy	P. Walwyn	P. Eddery	8	5-1
1978 Fair Salinia	S. Hanson	M. Stoute	G. Starkey	10	5-1
1979 Connaught Bridge	H. Barker	H. Cecil	J. Mercer	5	9-2
1980 Shoot a Line	R. Budgett	W. Hern	L. Piggott	7	13-8
1981 Condessa	P. Barrett	J. Bolger	D. Gillespie	11	5-1
1982 Awaasif	Sheikh Mohammed	J. Dunlop	L. Piggott	7	11-4
1983 Sun Princess	Sir M. Sobell	W. Hern	W. Carson	6	6-5
1984 Circus Plume	Sir R. McAlpine	J. Dunlop	W. Carson	5	5-6
1985 Sally Brown	R. Cowell	M. Stoute	W.R. Swinburn	7	6-1

Tote-Ebor Handicap   1¾m

First run 1843. Run as Ebor Handicap before 1967; Johnnie Walker Ebor Handicap 1967-73; Terry's All Gold Ebor Handicap 1974-75. Run at Pontefract 1943-44. No race 1940-42.

	OWNER	TRAINER	JOCKEY	RAN	SP
1930 Gentlemen's Relish, 4-7-5	J. Arkwright	H. Persse	J. Dines	13	20-1
Coaster, 4-8-0	Sir H. Hirst	F. Templeman	F. Fox	—	100-8
1931 Brown Jack, 7-9-5	Sir H. Wernher	I. Anthony	S. Donoghue	19	10-1
1932 Cat o' Nine Tails, 5-7-8	Mrs J. Carruthers	J. Colling	G. Richards	19	9-1
1933 Dictum, 5-7-4	Lady B. Smith	T. Rimell	J. Dines	11	8-1
1934 Alcazar, 3-8-5	W. Woodward	C. Boyd-Rochfort	J. Childs	14	10-1
1935 Museum, 3-7-13	Sir V. Sassoon	J. Rogers	S. Donoghue	12	100-8
1936 Penny Royal, 3-7-9	E. Thornton-Smith	F. Templeman	G. Richards	14	100-8
1937 Weathervane, 4-7-10	Sir A. Bailey	J. Lawson	T. Weston	17	100-6
1938 Foxglove II, 3-8-1	P. Beatty	F. Darling	G. Richards	12	8-1
1939 Owenstown, 5-8-8	Sir T. Dixon	M. Peacock	J. Taylor	12	11-2
1943 Yorkshire Hussar, 4-8-7	J. Hetherton	C. Elsey	G. Littlewood	19	100-6
1944 The Kernel, 4-8-7	G. Oxtoby	G. Oxtoby	P. Evans	14	100-8
1945 Wayside Inn, 3-8-6	Lord Derby	W. Earl	H. Wragg	14	20-1
1946 Foxtrot, 3-7-13	H. Morriss	E. Lambton	E. Britt	13	3-1
1947 Procne, 4-8-4	H.J. Joel	C. Elsey	J. Sime	11	8-1
1948 Donino, 4-8-12	W. Cockerline	A. Cooper	J. Sime	20	100-7
1949 Miraculous Atom, 5-8-11	H. Halmshaw	S. Hall	W. Nevett	16	100-7
1950 Cadzow Oak, 4-7-12	Maj G. Renwick	J. Thwaites	J. Thompson	21	100-8
1951 Bob, 4-6-12	J. Hetherton	C. Elsey	E. Carter	25	8-1
1952 Signification, 3-7-12	A. Bird	J. Pearce	H. Jones	15	10-1

	OWNER	TRAINER	JOCKEY	RAN	SP
1953 Norooz, 4-8-4	Aga Khan	M. Marsh	R. Fawdon	21	100-9
1954 By Thunder!, 3-6-12	J. Gerber	F. Armstrong	W. Swinburn	22	7-1
1955 Hyperion Kid, 3-7-2	Miss R. Olivier	H. Wragg	P. Robinson	25	100-8
1956 Donald, 3-7-10	Lord Rosebery	J. Jarvis	D. Smith	17	5-1
1957 Morecambe, 4-7-9	J. Bullock	S. Hall	J. Sime	30	100-8
1958 Gladness, 5-9-7	J. McShain	V. O'Brien	L. Piggott	25	5-1
1959 Primera, 5-9-0	S. Joel	N. Murless	L. Piggott	21	6-1
1960 Persian Road, 5-8-4	J. Whitney	J. Tree	G. Moore	21	18-1
1961 Die Hard, 4-8-9	Maj L. Gardner	V. O'Brien	L. Piggott	21	11-2
1962 Sostenuto, 4-8-10	P. Bull	W. Elsey	Don Morris	18	9-1
1963 Partholon, 3-7-8	Mrs A. Biddle	T. Shaw	J. Sime	22	100-6
1964 Proper Pride, 5-7-11	Maj L. Holliday	W. Wharton	D. Smith	20	28-1
1965 Twelfth Man, 4-7-5	R. Moller	H. Wragg	P. Cook	25	6-1
1966 Lomond, 6-9-2	W. Ruane	R. Jarvis	E. Eldin	23	100-8
1967 Ovaltine, 3-6-11	G. Cooper	J.F. Watts	E. Johnson	22	100-8
1968 Alignment, 3-7-8	Lord Allendale	W. Elsey	E. Johnson	20	9-1
1969 Big Hat, 4-7-3	Mrs M. Tennant	D. Hanley	R. Still	19	40-1
1970 Tintagel II, 5-8-5	Mrs R. Sturdy	R. Sturdy	L. Piggott	21	6-1
1971 Knotty Pine, 5-8-7	D. Robinson	M. Jarvis	F. Durr	21	9-2
1972 Crazy Rhythm, 4-8-6	K. Dodson	S. Ingham	F. Durr	21	19-2
1973 Bonne Noel, 4-9-2	Mrs Parker Poe	P. Prendergast	C. Roche	20	4-1
1974 Anji, 5-7-8	G. Coleman	J. Sutcliffe	T. McKeown	18	20-1
1975 Dakota, 4-9-4	G. Reed	S. Hall	A. Barclay	18	7-1
1976 Sir Montagu, 3-8-0	Mrs S. Enfield	H.R. Price	W. Carson	15	11-4
1977 Move Off, 4-8-1	W. Barker	J. Calvert	J. Bleasdale	14	9-1
1978 Totowah, 4-8-1	Lady Beaverbrook	M. Jarvis	P. Cook	22	20-1
1979 Sea Pigeon, 9-10-0	P. Muldoon	M.H. Easterby	J. O'Neill	17	18-1
1980 Shaftesbury, 4-8-5	J. McCaughey	M. Stoute	G. Starkey	16	12-1
1981 Protection Racket, 3-8-1	S. Fradkoff	J. Hindley	M. Birch	22	15-2
1982 Another Sam, 5-9-2	J. Norman	R. Hannon	B. Rouse	15	16-1
1983 Jupiter Island, 4-9-0	S. Threadwell	C. Brittain	L. Piggott	16	9-1
1984 Crazy, 3-8-13	Marshall Racing	G. Harwood	W.R. Swinburn	14	10-1
1985 Western Dancer, 4-8-6	Mrs G. Stone	C. Horgan	P. Cook	19	20-1

Scottish Equitable Gimcrack Stakes   6f

Two-year-olds. 9st, fillies allowed 3lb (plus penalties). First run 1846. Run as C & G Gimcrack 1975-76, and as Scottish Equitable Gimcrack from 1985. No race 1940-44. Group Two.

	OWNER	TRAINER	JOCKEY	RAN	SP
1930 Four Course, 8-9	Lord Ellesmere	F. Darling	F. Fox	13	8-15
1931 Miracle, 8-7	Lord Rosebery	J. Jarvis	H. Wragg	7	4-7
1932 Young Lover, 8-7	Sir A. Butt	Frank Butters	R. Perryman	7	100-8
1933 Mrs Rustom, 8-9	Aga Khan	Frank Butters	M. Beary	10	4-7
1934 Bahram, 8-12	Aga Khan	Frank Butters	R. Perryman	5	2-7
1935 Paul Beg, 8-7	Lord Milton	W. Easterby	H. Gunn	8	20-1
1936 Goya II, 8-7	M. Boussac	G. Lambton	C. Elliott	15	6-1
1937 Golden Sovereign, 8-7	Sir A. Bailey	H. Cottrill	T. Weston	6	6-1
1938 Cockpit, 8-12	Lord Derby	C. Leader	R. Perryman	11	7-4
1939 Tant Mieux, 8-12	Aly Khan	F. Darling	G. Richards	14	6-1
1945 Gulf Stream, 9-0	Lord Derby	W. Earl	H. Wragg	4	7-2
1946 Petition, 9-0	Sir A. Butt	Frank Butters	H. Wragg	5	13-8
1947 Black Tarquin, 9-0	W. Woodward	C. Boyd-Rochfort	W.H. Carr	7	3-1
1948 Star King, 9-0	W. Harvey	J.C. Waugh	S. Wragg	12	15-2
1949 Palestine, 9-0	Aga Khan	Frank Butters	G. Richards	2	1-25
1950 cortil, 8-7	M. Boussac	C. Semblat	W. Johnstone	10	11-2
1951 Windy City, 9-0	R. Bell	P. Prendergast	G. Richards	10	5-4
1952 Bebe Grande, 8-11	J. Gerber	F. Armstrong	W. Snaith	10	7-2
1953 The Pie King, 9-0	R. Bell	P. Prendergast	G. Richards	9	1-3
1954 Precast, 9-0	F. Ellison	R. Peacock	W. Nevett	11	25-1
1955 Idle Rocks, 9-0	D. Robinson	G. Brooke	D. Smith	5	8-1
1956 eudaemon, 9-0	Mrs E. Foster	C. Elsey	E. Brit	7	8-1
1957 Pheidippides, 9-0	P. Bull	C. Elsey	D. Smith	9	100-8
1958 Be Careful, 8-11	W. Hill	C. Elsey	E. Hide	12	10-1
1959 Paddy's Sister, 8-11	Mrs J. Mullion	P. Prendergast	G. Moore	10	4-11
1960 Test Case, 9-0	Sir A. Jarvis	J. Jarvis	E. Larkin	7	100-7

	OWNER	TRAINER	JOCKEY	RAN	SP
1961 Sovereign Lord, 9-0	Duke of Norfolk	G. Smyth	A. Breasley	11	10-1
1962 Crocket, 9-0	D. van Clief	G. Brooke	D. Smith	5	2-5
1963 Talahasse, 9-0	H. Loebstein	T. Corbett	L. Piggott	7	11-8
1964 Double Jump, 9-0	C. Engelhard	J. Tree	J. Lindley	7	evens
1965 Young Emperor, 9-0	Mrs P. Poe	P. Prendergast	L. Piggott	8	5-1
1966 Golden Horus, 9-0	Mrs D. Solomon	W. O'Gorman	J. Mercer	9	7-1
1967 Petingo, 9-0	M. Lemos	F. Armstrong	L. Piggott	9	1-6
1968 Tudor Music, 9-0	D. Robinson	M. Jarvis	F. Durr	7	10-1
1969 Yellow God, 9-0	D. Robinson	P. Davey	F. Durr	11	7-2
1970 Mill Reef, 9-0	P. Mellon	I. Balding	G. Lewis	8	4-5
1971 Wishing Star, 8-11	D. Robinson	P. Davey	F. Durr	12	12-1
1972 Rapid River, 9-0	Mrs W. Richardson	W.A. Stephenson	T. Kelsey	9	8-1
1973 Giacometti, 9-0	C. St George	H.R. Price	A. Murray	11	11-10
1974 Steel Heart, 9-0	R. Tikkoo	D. Weld	L. Piggott	10	17-2
1975 Music Boy, 9-0	K. Mackey	S. Wainwright	J. Seagrave	14	14-1
1976 Nebbiolo, 9-0	N. Schibbye	K. Prendergast	G. Curran	7	2-1
1977 Tumbledownwind, 9-0	J. Wilson	B. Hobbs	G. Lewis	5	6-5
1978 Stanford, 9-0	D. Cock	N. Callaghan	P. Eddery	11	15-2
1979 Sonnen Gold, 9-0	P. Muldoon	M.H. Easterby	M. Birch	7	5-1
1980 Bel Bolide, 9-0	K. Abdulla	J. Tree	P. Eddery	9	11-2
1981 Full Extent, 9-0	M. Korn	S. Norton	J. Lowe	8	13-2
1982 Horage, 9-0	A. Rachid	M. McCormack	A. Murray	7	8-13
1983 Precocious, 9-0	Lord Tavistock	H. Cecil	L. Piggott	6	8-11
1984 Doulab, 9-0	H. al-Maktoum	H.T. Jones	A. Murray	8	10-1
1985 Stalker, 9-0	P. Fetherston-Godley	P. Walwyn	J. Mercer	6	17-2

Great Voltigeur Stakes   1½m

Three-year-old colts & geldings. 8st 7lb (plus penalties). First run 1950. Run as Voltigeur Stakes 1950-56. Group Two.

	OWNER	TRAINER	JOCKEY	RAN	SP
1950 Castle Rock, 9-7	Lord Rosebery	J. Jarvis	W. Rickaby	5	5-6
1951 Border Legend, 9-0	Duke of Northumberland	R. Peacock	W. Nevett	13	4-1
1952 Childe Harold, 9-3	T. Farr	W. Dutton	J. Brace	7	7-4
1953 Premonition, 9-7	Brig W. Wyatt	C. Boyd-Rochfort	W.H. Carr	6	4-5
1954 Blue Sail, 9-0	G. Bell	P. Prendergast	W. Rickaby	9	3-1
1955 Acropolis, 9-7	Lady Derby	G. Colling	D. Smith	5	2-7
1956 Hornbeam, 9-3	Lord Astor	J. Colling	J. Mercer	4	6-4
1957 Brioche, 9-0	W. Humble	C. Elsey	E. Britt	7	100-6
1958 Alcide, 9-0	Sir H. de Trafford	C. Boyd-Rochfort	W.H. Carr	5	3-1
1959 Pindari, 9-0	The Queen	N. Murless	L. Piggott	4	11-10
1960 St Paddy, 9-0	Sir V. Sassoon	N. Murless	L. Piggott	4	4-11
1961 Just Great, 9-0	Mrs J. Allen	S. Ingham	A. Breasley	8	3-1
1962 Hethersett, 9-0	Maj L. Holliday	W. Hern	F. Durr	11	15-2
1963 Ragusa, 9-0	J. Mullion	P. Prendergast	G. Bougoure	5	2-5
1964 Indiana, 9-0	C. Engelhard	J.F. Watts	J. Lindley	6	4-7
1965 Ragazzo, 9-0	E.M. O'Ferrall	P. Prendergast	L. Piggott	6	13-8
1966 Hermes, 9-0	R. Hollingsworth	J. Oxley	G. Starkey	8	15-2
1967 Great Host, 9-0	L. Gelb	P. Prendergast	W. Williamson	6	3-1
1968 Connaught, 9-0	H.J. Joel	N. Murless	A. Barclay	4	1-3
1969 Harmony Hall, 9-0	Sir H. Wernher	G. Smyth	W. Williamson	6	4-6
1970 Meadowville, 9-0	D. Robinson	M. Jarvis	L. Piggott	4	8-13
1971 Athens Wood, 9-0	Mrs J. Rogerson	H.T. Jones	L. Piggott	5	13-8
1972 Our Mirage, 9-0	N. Cohen	B. Hills	L. Piggott	7	11-4
1973 Buoy, 9-0	R. Hollingsworth	W. Hern	J. Mercer	5	11-10
1974 Bustino, 9-0	Lady Beaverbrook	W. Hern	J. Mercer	3	15-8
1975 Patch, 9-0	C. Vittadini	P. Walwyn	P. Eddery	4	6-4
1976 Hawkberry, 8-7	L. Gelb	P. Prendergast	C. Roche	7	4-1
1977 Alleged, 8-11	J. Fluor	V. O'Brien	L. Piggott	7	5-2
1978 Whitstead, 8-7	H. Demetriou	H.R. Price	B. Taylor	8	3-1
1979 Noble Saint, 8-7	R. Guest	R. Armstrong	L. Piggott	5	12-1
1980 Prince Bee, 8-7	Sir M. Sobell	W. Hern	L. Piggott	5	4-6
1981 Glint of Gold, 9-0	P. Mellon	I. Balding	J. Matthias	6	evens
1982 Electric, 8-7	R. Clifford-Turner	M. Stoute	W.R. Swinburn	7	7-4
1983 Seymour Hicks, 8-7	P. Brant	J. Dunlop	W. Carson	5	11-2
1984 Rainbow Quest, 8-7	K. Abdullah	J. Tree	P. Eddery	7	evens
1985 Damister, 8-11	K. Abdullah	J. Tree	P. Eddery	4	7-4

William Hill Sprint Championship   5f

Two-year-olds and upwards. 2-y-o 7st 10lb, 3-y-o 9st 2lb, 4-y-o & upwards 9st 6lb, fillies allowed 3lb. First run 1903. Run at Newmarket 1943-44. Run as Nunthorpe Selling Stakes 1903-21; Nunthorpe Stakes 1922-75. No race 1940-42. Group One.

	OWNER	TRAINER	JOCKEY	RAN	SP
1930 Tag End, 6-8-9	J. Joel	C. Peck	B. Carslake	5	11-4
1931 Portlaw, 3-8-7	Sir A. Bailey	H. Persse	H. Beasley	5	5-1
1932 Greenore, 3-8-4	Lady Ludlow	O. Bell	H. Wragg	6	8-1
1933 Concerto, 5-8-12	Sir H. C-Owen	O. Bell	B. Carslake	3	6-1
1934 Gold Bridge, 5-8-12	Lord Beatty	W. Beatty	E.C. Elliot	6	6-5
1935 Shalfleet, 4-8-9	H. Leader	H. Leader	H. Jelliss	6	9-4
1936 Bellacose, 4-8-12	P. Dunne	J. Colling	P. Beasley	9	evens
1937 Ipsden, 4-8-9	Lady Ludlow	O. Bell	S. Wragg	8	7-1
1938 Mickey the Greek, 4-8-12	H. Leach	H. Leach	H. Wragg	4	5-1
1939 Portobello, 3-8-11	P. Dunne	J. Colling	G. Richards	4	15-8
1943 Linklater, 7-9-0	A. Saunders	W. Smyth	E. Smith	8	9-2
1944 Sugar Plum, 6-9-0	Maj A. Bonsor	F. Hartigan	E.C. Elliott	11	8-1
1945 Golden Cloud, 4-9-5	Mrs G. Lambton	E. Lambton	M. Beary	7	100-8
1946 The Bug, 3-9-0	N. Wachman	M. Marsh	C. Smirke	4	4-6
1947 Como, 5-9-5	Capt J. Fielden	G. Armstrong	W.H. Carr	6	3-1
1948 Careless Nora, 3-8-11	G. Frampton	J. Dines	E.C. Elliott	6	6-4
1949 Abernant, 3-9-0	Maj R. M-Buchanan	N. Murless	G. Richards	4	2-11
1950 Abernant, 4-9-5	Maj R. M-Buchanan	N. Murless	G. Richards	3	7-100
1951 Royal Serenade, 3-9-0	Mrs G. Kohn	H. Wragg	E.C. Elliott	6	4-1
1952 Royal Serenade, 4-9-5	G. Bell	H. Wragg	G. Richards	5	4-6
1953 High Treason, 2-7-3	H.J. Joel	T. Leader	D. Greening	8	9-4
1954 My Beau, 2-7-3	A. Wimbush	P. Prendergast	T. Carter	11	7-1
1955 Royal Palm, 3-9-0	J. Gerber	F. Armstrong	W. Snaith	4	11-10
1956 Ennis, 2-7-3	C. Harper	W. Nightingall	P. Tulk	5	11-2
1957 Gratitude, 4-9-5	Maj L. Holliday	H. Cottrill	W. Snaith	5	7-2
1958 Right Boy, 4-9-5	G. Gilbert	W. Dutton	L. Piggott	3	8-100
1959 Right Boy, 5-9-5	H. Wills	H. Rohan	L. Piggott	6	4-9
1960 Bleep-Bleep, 4-9-5	Mrs M. Turner	H. Cottrill	W.H. Carr	7	9-2
1961 Floribunda, 3-9-0	Mrs J. Mullion	P. Prendergast	R. Hutchinson	6	4-1
1962 Gay Mairi, 3-8-11	A. Macdonald	H. Whiteman	A. Breasley	9	100-8
1963 Matatina, 3-8-11	Mrs R. Wilson	F. Armstrong	L. Piggott	6	7-2
1964 Althrey Don, 3-9-0	J. Done	P. Rohan	R. Maddock	10	3-1
1965 Polyfoto, 3-9-0	Mrs C. Reavey	E. Reavey	J. Wilson	8	20-1
1966 Caterina, 3-8-11	R. Scully	F. Armstrong	L. Piggott	11	13-2
1967 Forlorn River, 5-9-5	Mrs W. Richardson	W.A. Stephenson	B. Raymond	12	6-1
1968 So Blessed, 3-9-2	D. Robinson	M. Jarvis	F. Durr	5	4-6
1969 Tower Walk, 3-9-2	V. Hardy	G. Barling	L. Piggott	6	7-1
1970 Huntercombe, 3-9-2	H. Renshaw	A. Budgett	A. Barclay	3	5-4
1971 Swing Easy, 3-9-2	J. Whitney	J. Tree	L. Piggott	9	2-1
1972 Deep Diver, 3-9-2	D. Robinson	P. Davey	W. Williamson	7	100-30
1973 Sandford Lad, 3-9-2	C. Olley	H.R. Price	A. Murray	8	4-1
1974 Blue Cashmere, 4-9-7	R. Clifford-Turner	M. Stoute	E. Hide	12	18-1
1975 Bay Express, 4-9-7	P. Cooper	P. Nelson	W. Carson	10	100-30
1976 Lochnager, 4-9-6	C. Spence	M.W. Easterby	E. Hide	11	4-5
1977 Haveroid, 3-9-2	T. Newton	N. Adam	E. Hide	8	10-1
1978 Solinus, 3-9-2	D. Schwartz	V. O'Brien	L. Piggott	9	1-2
1979 Ahonoora, 4-9-6	E. Alkhalifa	F. Durr	G. Starkey	9	3-1
1980 Sharpo, 3-9-2	Miss M. Sheriffe	J. Tree	P. Eddery	11	3-1
1981 Sharpo, 4-9-0	Miss M. Sheriffe	J. Tree	P. Eddery	9	14-1
1982 Sharpo, 5-9-0	Miss M. Sheriffe	J. Tree	S. Cauthen	11	13-1
1983 Habibti, 3-8-7	M. Mutawa	J. Dunlop	W. Carson	10	13-8
1984 Committed, 4-8-11	R. Sangster	D. Weld	B. Thomson	8	5-1
1985 Never So Bold, 5-9-0	E. Kessly	R. Armstrong	S. Cauthen	7	4-6

APPENDIX II

Leading amateur riders (male)

1946	J. Hislop	13
1947	J. Hislop	12
1948	J. Hislop	15
1949	J. Hislop	8
1950	J. Hislop	9
1951	J. Hislop	7
1952	J. Hislop	4
1953	P. Bennett	3
	J. Hislop	3
1954	J. Hislop	5
	A. Moralee	5
1955	J. Hislop	7
1956	J. Hislop	4
1957	H. Wallington	3
1958	J. Lawrence	3
1959	J. Lawrence	3
1960	A. Biddlecombe	3
1961	J. Lawrence	2
	Sir W. Pigott-Brown	2
1962	J. Lawrence	2
	R. McCreery	2
	Sir W. Pigott-Brown	2
1963	G. Price	2
1964	N. Gaselee	2
	R. McCreery	2
	D. Ward	2
1965	N. Gaselee	3
	R. McCreery	3
1966	W. O'Gorman	4
1967	P. Mitchell	7
1968	P. Mitchell	4
1969	P. Mitchell	7
1970	P. Mitchell	11
1971	N. Gaselee	4
1972	P. Mitchell	6
1973	N. Richards	5
1974	C. Platts	4
1975	R. Linley	3
1976	C. Platts	8
1977	R. Hutchinson	6
1978	T. Easterby	5
	R. Hutchinson	5
1979	R. Hutchinson	8
1980	R. Hutchinson	8
1981	R. Hutchinson	8
1982	T. Thomson Jones	7
1983	A.J. Wilson	4
1984	R. Hutchinson	5
1985	A.J. Wilson	6

Leading amateur riders (female)

1972	Meriel Tufnell	3
1973	Linda Goodwill	4
1974	Brooke Sanders	6
1975	Joy Gibson	4
	Elain Mellor	4
1976	Diana Bissill	5
1977	Elain Mellor	8
1978	Marie Tinkler	6
1979	Gaie Johnson Houghton	4
	Elain Mellor	4
1980	Franca Vittadini	7
1981	Elain Mellor	6
1982	Gay Kelleway	6
1983	Elain Mellor	8
1984	Julie Cecil	5
	Elain Mellor	5
1985	Sandy Brook	6

Leading apprentices:

1946	J. Sime	40
1947	D. Buckle	20
1948	D. Buckle	25
1949	W. Snaith	31
1950	L. Piggott	52
1951	L. Piggott	51
1952	J. Mercer	26
1953	J. Mercer	61
1954	E. Hide	53
1955	P. Robinson	46
1956	E. Hide	75
1957	G. Starkey	45
1958	P. Boothman	37
1959	R.P. Elliott	27
1960	R.P. Elliott	39
1961	B. Lee	52
1962	B. Raymond	13
1963	D. Yates	24
1964	P. Cook	46
1965	P. Cook	62
1966	A. Barclay	71
1967	E. Johnson	39
1968	D. Coates	40
	R. Dicey	40
1969	C. Eccleston	41
1970	P. Waldron	59
1971	P. Eddery	71
1972	R. Edmondson	45
1973	S. Perks	41

1974	A. Bond	40
1975	A. Bond	66
1976	D. Dineley	54
1977	J. Bleasdale	67
1978	K. Darley	70
1979	P. Robinson	51
1980	P. Robinson	59
1981	B. Crossley	45
1982	W. Newnes	57
1983	M. Hills	39
1984	T. Quinn	62
1985	G. Carter	37
	W. Ryan	37

Leading breeders:

		£
1946	Lt-Col. H. Boyd-Rochfort	23,059
1947	Aga Khan	41,165
1948	Aga Khan	38,509
1949	Aga Khan	69,976
1950	M. Boussac	59,859
1951	M. Boussac	44,444
1952	Aga Khan	93,058
1953	F. Darling	48,099
1954	Major L.B. Holliday	45,651
1955	Someries Stud	50,125
1956	Major L.B. Holliday	37,333
1957	Eve Stud	53,823
1958	R. Ball	46,653
1959	Prince Aly Khan and late Aga Khan	100,668
1960	Eve Stud	96,689
1961	Eve Stud	39,653
1962	Major L.B. Holliday	72,617
1963	H.F. Guggenheim	66,012
1964	Bull Run Stud	98,270
1965	J. Ternynck	65,301
1966	Someries Stud	80,154
1967	H.J. Joel	109,882
1968	Mill Ridge Farm	97,075
1969	Lord Rosebery	65,491
1970	E.P. Taylor	161,302
1971	P. Mellon	133,902
1972	J.L. Hislop	155,571
1973	Claiborne Farm	88,250
1974	N.B. Hunt	123,702
1975	Overbury Stud	194,480
1976	Dayton Ltd	232,599
1977	E.P. Taylor	241,120
1978	Cragwood Estates	136,012
1979	Ballymacoll Stud	346,981

		£
1980	P. Clarke	237,435
1981	Aga Khan	445,368
1982	Someries Stud	265,525
1983	White Lodge Stud	282,223
1984	E.P. Taylor	348,693
1985	Dalham Stud	324,214

Leading Weights in Free Handicap (2yo)

1928	Tiffin (filly)
1929	Diolite
1930	Jacopo
1931	Orwell
1932	Myrobella (filly)
1933	Colombo
1934	Bahram
1935	Bala Hissar
1936	Foray
1937	Portmarnock
1938	Foxbrough II
1939	Tant Mieux
1940	Poise (gelding)
1941	Sun Chariot (filly)
1942	Lady Sybil (filly)
1943	Orestes
1944	Dante
1945	Gulf Stream
1946	Tudor Minstrel
1947	My Babu
1948	Abernant
1949	Masked Light
1950	Big Dipper
1951	Windy City
1952	Nearula
1953	The Pie King
1954	Our Babu
1955	Star of India (filly)
1956	Sarcelle (filly)
1957	Major Portion
1958	Tudor Melody
1959	Sing Sing
1960	Opaline II (filly)
1961	La Tendresse (filly)
1962	Crocket
1963	Talahasse
1964	Double Jump
1965	Young Emperor
1966	Bold Lad
1967	Petingo
1968	Ribofilio
1969	Nijinsky
1970	My Swallow

1971	Crowned Prince
1972	Jacinth (filly)
1973	Apalachee
1974	Grundy
1975	Wollow
1976	J.O. Tobin
1977	Try My Best
1978	Tromos (91)
1979	Monteverdi (83)
1980	Storm Bird (88)
1981	Green Forest (88)
1982	Diesis (87)
1983	El Gran Señor (88)
1984	Kala Dancer (84)
1985	Bakharoff (83)

Top weight 9st 7lb, except 1929 when 9st 3lb, and 1964 and 1965 when 10st. Rating against a norm of 100 introduced in 1978; qualification extended to rest of European Pattern countries in 1980; concept of norm discontinued in 1985.

Free Handicap first run for horses as three-year-olds in 1929. Free Handicap for four-year-olds run from 1946 to 1958 at Newmarket; over 1¼m in 1946 and '47, and over 1½m for rest.

Leading Jockeys

1850	E. Flatman	88
1851	E. Flatman	78
1852	E. Flatman	92
1853	J. Wells	86
1854	J. Wells	82
1855	G. Fordham	70
1856	G. Fordham	108
1857	G. Fordham	84
1858	G. Fordham	91
1859	G. Fordham	118
1860	G. Fordham	146
1861	G. Fordham	106
1862	G. Fordham	166
1863	G. Fordham	103
1864	J. Grimshaw	164
1865	G. Fordham	142
1866	S. Kenyon	123
1867	G. Fordham	143
1868	G. Fordham	110
1869	G. Fordham	95
1870	W. Gray & C. Maidment	76
1871	G. Fordham & C. Maidment	86

1872	T. Cannon	87
1873	H. Constable	110
1874	F. Archer	147
1875	F. Archer	172
1876	F. Archer	207
1877	F. Archer	218
1878	F. Archer	229
1879	F. Archer	197
1880	F. Archer	120
1881	F. Archer	220
1882	F. Archer	210
1883	F. Archer	232
1884	F. Archer	241
1885	F. Archer	246
1886	F. Archer	170
1887	C. Wood	151
1888	F. Barrett	108
1889	T. Loates	167
1890	T. Loates	147
1891	M. Cannon	137
1892	M. Cannon	182
1893	T. Loates	222
1894	M. Cannon	167
1895	M. Cannon	184
1896	M. Cannon	164
1897	M. Cannon	145
1898	O. Madden	161
1899	S. Loates	160
1900	L. Reiff	143
1901	O. Madden	130
1902	W. Lane	170
1903	O. Madden	154
1904	O. Madden	161
1905	E. Wheatley	124
1906	W. Higgs	149
1907	W. Higgs	146
1908	D. Maher	139
1909	F. Wootton	165
1910	F. Wootton	137
1911	F. Wootton	187
1912	F. Wootton	118
1913	D. Maher	115
1914	S. Donoghue	129
1915	S. Donoghue	62
1916	S. Donoghue	43
1917	S. Donoghue	42
1918	S. Donoghue	66
1919	S. Donoghue	129
1920	S. Donoghue	143
1921	S. Donoghue	141
1922	S. Donoghue	102
1923	S. Donoghue & E.C. Elliott	89
1924	E.C. Elliott	106
1925	G. Richards	118

1926	T. Weston	95	1956	D. Smith	155
1927	G. Richards	164	1957	A. Breasley	173
1928	G. Richards	148	1958	D. Smith	165
1929	G. Richards	135	1959	D. Smith	157
1930	F. Fox	129	1960	L. Piggott	170
1931	G. Richards	145	1961	A. Breasley	171
1932	G. Richards	190	1962	A. Breasley	179
1933	G. Richards	259	1963	A. Breasley	176
1934	G. Richards	212	1964	L. Piggott	140
1935	G. Richards	210	1965	L. Piggott	160
1936	G. Richards	177	1966	L. Piggott	191
1937	G. Richards	214	1967	L. Piggott	117
1938	G. Richards	206	1968	L. Piggott	139
1939	G. Richards	155	1969	L. Piggott	163
1940	G. Richards	68	1970	L. Piggott	162
1941	H. Wragg	71	1971	L. Piggott	162
1942	G. Richards	67	1972	W. Carson	132
1943	G. Richards	65	1973	W. Carson	164
1944	G. Richards	88	1974	P. Eddery	148
1945	G. Richards	104	1975	P. Eddery	164
1946	G. Richards	212	1976	P. Eddery	162
1947	G. Richards	269	1977	P. Eddery	176
1948	G. Richards	224	1978	W. Carson	182
1949	G. Richards	261	1979	J. Mercer	164
1950	G. Richards	201	1980	W. Carson	166
1951	G. Richards	227	1981	L. Piggott	179
1952	G. Richards	231	1982	L. Piggott	188
1953	G. Richards	191	1983	W. Carson	159
1954	D. Smith	129	1984	S. Cauthen	130
1955	D. Smith	168	1985	S. Cauthen	195

Leading horses on the International Classification
(irrespective of distance groups)

	2-Y-O	3-Y-O	4-Y-O & UPWARDS
1977	—	98 Alleged 95 The Minstrel Blushing Groom	94 Balmerino Orange Bay 93 Buckskin Sagaro Gentilhombre
1978	91 Tromos 89 Irish River Sigy	95 Ile de Bourbon 92 Acamas Shirley Heights	91 Buckskin Sanedtki 89 Crow
1979	83 Dragon Monteverdi 82 Nice Havrais Nureyev Super Asset	96 Troy 91 Kris 88 Dickens Hill	95 Ile de Bourbon 92 Thatching 91 Gay Mecene

	2-Y-O	3-Y-O	4-Y-O & UPWARDS
1980	88 Storm Bird 87 To-Agori-Mou 83 Robellino	91 Moorestyle 90 Argument 89 Known Fact Nureyev	90 Ela-Mana-Mou 89 Le Marmot Kris Le Moss
1981	88 Green Forest 85 Wind and Wuthering 84 Count Pahlen	100 Shergar 91 Bikala 90 Cut Above Marwell	92 Northjet 91 Moorestyle 90 Ardross Gold River Sharpo
1982	87 Diesis 86 Saint Cyrien 85 Danzatore Gorytus	94 Golden Fleece 93 Assert Green Forest	93 Kalaglow 91 Ardross 88 April Run Bikala Sharpo
1983	88 El Gran Senor 87 Rainbow Quest 84 Lear Fan	93 Shareef Dancer 91 Habibti 90 Caerleon	92 All Along 89 Diamond Shoal 88 Time Charter
1984	84 Kala Dancer 83 Law Society 82 Gold Crest Local Suitor Triptych	98 El Gran Senor 92 Chief Singer 91 Darshaan	95 Teenoso 93 Sagace 88 Cormorant Wood Morcon
1985	83 Bakharoff 82 Huntingdale 80 Baiser Vole Bold Arrangement Nomination Sure Blade	95 Slip Anchor 94 Petoski 91 Shadeed	93 Rainbow Quest Sagace 92 Pebbles

Leading owners

		£			£
1900	Prince of Wales	29,585	1916	Mr E. Hulton	13,764
1901	Sir G. Blundell Maple	21,370	1917	Mr Fairie*	11,751
1902	Mr R.S. Sievier	23,686	1918	Lady James Douglas	14,735
1903	Sir James Miller	24,768	1919	Lord Glanely	30,514
1904	Sir James Miller	28,923	1920	Sir Robert Jardine	19,385
1905	Col. W. Hall Walker	23,687	1921	Mr S.B. Joel	33,048
1906	Lord Derby	32,926	1922	Lord Woolavington	32,090
1907	Col. W. Hall Walker	17,910	1923	Lord Derby	40,388
1908	Mr J.B. Joel	26,246	1924	HH Aga Khan	44,367
1909	Mr Fairie*	37,719	1925	Lord Astor	35,723
1910	Mr Fairie*	35,352	1926	Lord Woolavington	47,256
1911	Lord Derby	42,781	1927	Lord Derby	40,355
1912	Mr T. Pilkington	20,822	1928	Lord Derby	65,603
1913	Mr J.B. Joel	25,430			
1914	Mr J.B. Joel	30,724			
1915	Mr L. Neumann	13,546			

* 'Mr Fairie' was the *nom de course* of Mr A.W. Cox.

		£			£
1929	HH Aga Khan	39,886	1983	Mr R. Sangster	461,488
1930	HH Aga Khan	46,259	1984	Mr R. Sangster	395,901
1931	Mr J.A. Dewar	39,034	1985	Sheikh Mohammed	1,082,668
1932	HH Aga Khan	57,778			
1933	Lord Derby	27,559			
1934	HH Aga Khan	64,898			
1935	HH Aga Khan	49,201			
1936	Lord Astor	38,131			
1937	HH Aga Khan	30,655			
1938	Lord Derby	34,434			
1939	Lord Rosebery	38,465			
1940	Lord Rothermere	6,869			
1941	Lord Glanely	8,762			
1942	King George VI	10,536			
1943	Miss D. Paget	13,146			
1944	HH Aga Khan	13,985			
1945	Lord Derby	25,067			
1946	HH Aga Khan	24,118			
1947	HH Aga Khan	44,020			
1948	HH Aga Khan	46,393			
1949	HH Aga Khan	68,916			
1950	M. Boussac	57,044			
1951	M. Boussac	39,340			
1952	HH Aga Khan	92,519			
1953	Sir Victor Sassoon	58,579			
1954	The Queen	40,994			
1955	Lady Zia Wernher	46,345			
1956	Maj. L.B. Holliday	39,327			
1957	The Queen	62,211			
1958	Mr J. McShain	63,264			
1959	Prince Aly Khan	100,668			
1960	Sir Victor Sassoon	90,069			
1961	Maj. L.B. Holliday	39,227			
1962	Maj. L.B. Holliday	70,206			
1963	Mr. J.R. Mullion	68,882			
1964	Mrs H.E. Jackson	98,270			
1965	M.J. Ternynck	65,301			
1966	Lady Zia Wernher	78,075			
1967	Mr H.J. Joel	120,925			
1968	Mr R. Guest	97,075			
1969	Mr D. Robinson	92,553			
1970	Mr C. Engelhard	182,059			
1971	Mr P. Mellon	128,786			
1972	Mrs J. Hislop	155,191			
1973	Mr N.B. Hunt	124,771			
1974	Mr N.B. Hunt	147,217			
1975	Dr C. Vittadini	209,493			
1976	Mr D. Wildenstein	244,501			
1977	Mr R. Sangster	348,023			
1978	Mr R. Sangster	160,406			
1979	Sir Michael Sobell	339,751			
1980	Mr S. Weinstock	236,332			
1981	HH Aga Khan	441,654			
1982	Mr R. Sangster	397,749			

Racehorse of the Year

In 1965 the Racecourse Association introduced a Racehorse of the Year award, judged by a panel of journalists. In 1978 it came under the auspices of the Racegoers Club, whose members are invited to take part in a separate poll. The award has regularly gone to a middle-distance runner, usually the winner of the Derby or King George VI and Queen Elizabeth Diamond Stakes, but in the 1980s there has been a change of emphasis, with wins for two sprinters (Moorestyle and Habibti), a stayer (Ardross) and the only two-year-old (Provideo).

1965	Sea Bird II (3yo colt)
1966	Charlottown (3yo colt)
1967	Busted (4yo colt)
1968	Sir Ivor (3yo colt)
1969	Park Top (5yo mare)
1970	Nijinsky (3yo colt)
1971	Mill Reef (3yo colt)
1972	Brigadier Gerard (4yo colt)
1973	Dahlia (3yo filly)
1974	Dahlia (4yo filly)
1975	Grundy (3yo colt)
1976	Pawneese (3yo filly)
1977	The Minstrel (3yo colt)
1978	Shirley Heights (3yo colt)
1979	Troy (3yo colt)
1980	Moorestyle (3yo colt)
1981	Shergar (3yo colt)
1982	Ardross (6yo horse)
1983	Habibti (3yo filly)
1984	Provideo (2yo colt)
1985	Pebbles (4yo filly)

Leading Sires

		£
1900	St Simon	58,625
1901	St Simon	28,964
1902	Persimmon	36,868
1903	St Frusquin	26,526
1904	Gallinule	30,925

		£			£
1905	Gallinule	25,229	1959	Petition	75,955
1906	Persimmon	21,737	1960	Aureole	90,088
1907	St Frusquin	25,355	1961	Aureole	90,898
1908	Persimmon	28,484	1962	Never Say Die	65,902
1909	Cyllene	35,550	1963	Ribot	121,290
1910	Cyllene	42,518	1964	Chamossaire	136,507
1911	Sundridge	33,284	1965	Court HGarwell	114,268
1912	Persimmon	21,993	1966	Psidium	101,378
1913	Desmond	30,973	1967	Ribot	128,530
1914	Polymelus	29,607	1968	Ribot	119,355
1915	Polymelus	17,738	1969	Crepello	88,538
1916	Polymelus	16,031	1970	Northern Dancer	247,450
1917	Bayardo	12,337	1971	Never Bend	133,160
1918	Bayardo	15,650	1972	Queen's Hussar	185,337
1919	The Tetrarch	27,376	1973	Vaguely Noble	127,908
1920	Polymelus	40,447	1974	Vaguely Noble	151,885
1921	Polymelus	34,307	1975	Great Nephew	313,284
1922	Lemberg	32,888	1976	Wolver Hollow	210,765
1923	Swynford	37,897	1977	Northern Dancer	380,982
1924	Son-in-Law	32,008	1978	Mill Reef	312,922
1925	Phalaris	41,471	1979	Petingo	471,574
1926	Hurry On	59,109	1980	Pitcairn	463,693
1927	Buchan	45,918	1981	Great Nephew	559,999
1928	Phalaris	46,393	1982	Be My Guest	469,421
1929	Tetratema	53,025	1983	Northern Dancer	442,206
1930	Son-in-Law	44,588	1984	Northern Dancer	1,041,346
1931	Pharos	43,922	1985	Kris	588,701
1932	Gainsborough	34,789			
1933	Gainsborough	38,138			
1934	Blandford	75,707			
1935	Blandford	57,538			
1936	Fairway	57,931			
1937	Solario	52,888			
1938	Blandford	31,840			
1939	Fairway	53,481			
1940	Hyperion	13,407			
1941	Hyperion	25,837			
1942	Hyperion	13,801			
1943	Fairway	12,133			
1944	Fairway	15,704			
1945	Hyperion	39,727			
1946	Hyperion	54,021			
1947	Nearco	45,087			
1948	Nearco	41,541			
1949	Bois Roussel	57,161			

Leading Trainers

Before 1967 win totals only; from 1967 win and place totals.

1950	Fair Trial	38,323			Races	£
1951	Nasrullah	47,055	1900	R. Marsh	31	43,321
1952	Tehran	86,072	1901	J. Huggins	42	29,142
1953	Chanteur II	57,929	1902	R.S. Sievier	10	23,686
1954	Hyperion	46,894	1903	G. Blackwell	24	34,135
1955	Alycidon	54,954	1904	P.P. Gilpin	44	35,694
1956	Court Martial	49,237	1905	W.T. Robinson	52	34,466
1957	Court Martial	58,307	1906	Hon G. Lambton	46	34,069
1958	Mossborough	66,471	1907	A. Taylor	31	24,708
			1908	C. Morton	20	26,431
			1909	A. Taylor	49	47,825
			1910	A. Taylor	47	52,364
			1911	Hon G. Lambton	48	49,769
			1912	Hon G. Lambton	55	22,884
			1913	R. Wootton	66	28,284
			1914	A. Taylor	39	52,052
			1915	P.P. Gilpin	12	15,324

		Races	£
1916	R.C. Dawson	32	16,386
1917	A. Taylor	25	17,924
1918	A. Taylor	33	36,629
1919	A. Taylor	41	33,208
1920	A. Taylor	47	35,907
1921	A. Taylor	51	48,280
1922	A. Taylor	55	52,059
1923	A. Taylor	46	49,190
1924	R.C. Dawson	26	48,857
1925	A. Taylor	51	56,570
1926	F. Darling	48	63,408
1927	F. Butters	54	57,468
1928	F. Butters	50	67,539
1929	R.C. Dawson	58	74,754
1930	H.S. Persse	46	49,487
1931	J. Lawson	69	93,899
1932	F. Butters	62	72,436
1933	F. Darling	64	44,277
1934	F. Butters	79	88,844
1935	F. Butters	48	59,688
1936	J. Lawson	49	61,773
1937	C. Boyd-Rochfort	43	61,213
1938	C. Boyd-Rochfort	44	51,350
1939	J.L. Jarvis	34	56,219
1940	F. Darling	25	16,166
1941	F. Darling	37	19,206
1942	F. Darling	20	12,843
1943	W. Nightingall	29	13,383
1944	F. Butters	34	17,585
1945	W. Earl	41	29,557
1946	F. Butters	60	56,140
1947	F. Darling	56	65,313
1948	N. Murless	63	66,542
1949	F. Butters	42	71,721
1950	C.H. Semblat (France)	11	57,044
1951	J.L. Jarvis	62	56,397
1952	M. Marsh	30	92,093
1953	J.L. Jarvis	60	71,546
1954	C. Boyd-Rochfort	39	65,326
1955	C. Boyd-Rochfort	38	74,424
1956	C.F. Elsey	83	61,621
1957	N. Murless	48	116,898
1958	C. Boyd-Rochfort	37	84,186
1959	N. Murless	63	145,727
1960	N. Murless	42	118,327
1961	N. Murless	36	95,972
1962	W.R. Hern	39	70,206
1963	P. Prendergast (Ireland)	19	125,294
1964	P. Prendergast (Ireland)	17	128,102
1965	P. Prendergast (Ireland)	11	75,323

		Races	£
1966	M.V. O'Brien (Ire)	8	123,848
1967	N. Murless	60	256,899
1968	N. Murless	47	141,509
1969	A. Budgett	35	105,349
1970	N. Murless	53	199,524
1971	I. Balding	45	157,488
1972	W.R. Hern	42	206,767
1973	N. Murless	34	132,985
1974	P. Walwyn	96	206,784
1975	P. Walwyn	121	382,527
1976	H. Cecil	52	261,301
1977	M.V. O'Brien (Ire)	18	439,125
1978	H. Cecil	109	382,301
1979	H. Cecil	128	683,971
1980	W. Hern	65	831,964
1981	M. Stoute	95	723,786
1982	H. Cecil	111	872,614
1983	W. Hern	57	549,598
1984	H. Cecil	108	551,939
1985	H. Cecil	132	1,148,189

Trainers of Derby and Grand National winners

James Jewitt – Derby: dead heat 1884, Harvester; 1893, Isinglass. Grand National: 1882, Seaman.

Richard Dawson – Derby: 1916, Fifinella; 1929, Trigo; 1930, Blenheim. Grand National: 1898, Drogheda.

George Blackwell – Derby: 1903, Rock Sand; Grand National: 1923, Sergeant Murphy.

Willie Stephenson – Derby: 1951, Arctic Prince. Grand National: 1959, Oxo.

Vincent O'Brien – Derby: 1962, Larkspur; 1968, Sir Ivor; 1970, Nijinsky; 1972, Roberto; 1977, The Minstrel; 1982, Golden Fleece. Grand National: 1953, Early Mist; 1954, Royal Tan; 1955, Quare Times.

Trainers of 100 winners in a season since 1945:

1975 – P. Walwyn, 121
1976 – P. Walwyn, 110
1977 – P. Walwyn, 110
1978 – H. Cecil, 109
1979 – H. Cecil, 128
1980 – M. Stoute, 101

1981 – H. Cecil, 107
1982 – G. Harwood, 120; H. Cecil, 111,
M. Stoute, 103
1983 – G. Harwood, 104
1984 – H. Cecil, 108
1985 – H. Cecil, 132; M. Stoute, 120

Trainers of Classic winners 1945-84

19 – N. Murless: 2,000 Guineas (1957,
1967), 1,000 Guineas (1948, 1959,
1967, 1968, 1971, 1973), Derby
(1957, 1960, 1967), Oaks (1957,
1959, 1970, 1971, 1973), St Leger
(1949, 1960, 1961).
16 – V. O'Brien: 2,000 Guineas (1968,
1970, 1983, 1984), 1,000 Guineas
(1966), Derby (1962, 1968, 1970,
1972, 1977, 1982), Oaks (1965,
1966), St Leger (1957, 1970,
1972).
13 – W. Hern: 2,000 Guineas (1971),
1,000 Guineas (1974), Derby
(1979, 1980), Oaks (1977, 1980,
1983), St Leger (1962, 1965, 1974,
1977, 1981, 1983).
9 – C. Boyd-Rochfort: 2,000 Guineas
(1958), 1,000 Guineas (1955),
Derby (1959), Oaks (1955), St
Leger (1948, 1953, 1955, 1958).
9 – H. Cecil: 2,000 Guineas (1975,
1976), 1,000 Guineas (1979, 1981,

1985), Derby (1985), Oaks (1985),
St Leger (1980, 1985)
6 – C. Elsey: 2,000 Guineas (1953),
1,000 Guineas (1949, 1956), Oaks
(1949, 1952), St Leger (1959).
– H. Wragg: 2,000 Guineas (1954),
1,000 Guineas (1962, 1969, 1982),
Derby (1961), St Leger (1969).
5 – F. Mathet: 1,000 Guineas (1958),
Derby (1955, 1963), Oaks (1956,
1958).
– E. Pollet: 2,000 Guineas (1952),
1,000 Guineas (1960, 1963),
Derby (1965), Oaks (1960).

Trainers of three or four Classic winners in a season since 1945

1950 – C. Semblat (Derby, Oaks, St
Leger)
1955 – C. Boyd-Rochfort (1,000
Guineas, Oaks, St Leger)
1957 – N. Murless (2,000 Guineas,
Derby, Oaks)
1967 – N. Murless (2,000 Guineas, 1,000
Guineas, Derby)
1970 – V. O'Brien (2,000 Guineas,
Derby, St Leger)
1976 – A. Penna (1,000 Guineas, Oaks,
St Leger)
1985 – H. Cecil (1,000 Guineas, Derby,
Oaks, St Leger)

APPENDIX III

TELEVISED RACING ... Number of days covered

	1973	1974	1975	1976	1977	1978	1979	1980	1981	1982	1983	1984
BBC												
Flat	183	176	152	175	157	173	164	186	190	191	151	185
Jumping	104	122	104	90	129	112	101	143	128	137	129	150
Total	287	298	256	265	286	285	265	329	318	328	280	335
ITV												
Flat	374	375	372	371	375	393	192	328	315	316	279	310
Jumping	150	153	135	148	125	117	79	145	104	117	87	84
Total	524	528	507	519	500	510	271	437	419	433	366	394
Combined												
Flat	557	551	524	546	532	566	356	514	505	507	430	495
Jumping	254	275	239	238	254	229	180	288	232	254	216	234
Total	811	826	763	784	786	795	536	802	737	761	646	729